The Informed Argument

EIGHTH EDITION 8

The Informed Argument

ROBERT P. YAGELSKI
State University of New York at Albany

ROBERT K. MILLER
University of St. Thomas

WITH AMY J. CROUSE-POWERS
SUNY College at Oneonta

WADSWORTH
CENGAGE Learning

Australia • Brazil • Japan • Korea • Mexico • Singapore • Spain • United Kingdom • United States

WADSWORTH
CENGAGE Learning

The Informed Argument: Eighth Edition
Robert P. Yagelski, Robert K. Miller

Sr. Publisher: Lyn Uhl

Executive Editor: Monica Eckman

Acquisitions Editor: Margaret Leslie

Senior Development Editor: Kathy Sands-Boehmer

Assistant Editor: Amy Haines

Editorial Assistant: Elizabeth Ramsey

Associate Media Editor: Janine Tangney

Marketing Director: Jason Sakos

Marketing Coordinator: Ryan Ahern

Senior Marketing Communications Manager: Stacey
    Purviance

Content Project Manager: Corinna Dibble

Senior Art Director: Jill Ort

Print Buyer: Susan Spencer

Senior Rights Acquisition Specialist, Image:
    Jen Meyer-Dare

Senior Rights Acquisition Specialist, Text: Katie Huha

Production Service: Elm Street Publishing Services

Text Designer: Elm Street Publishing Services

Cover image: istockphoto.com © parkhomenko

Compositor: Integra Software Services Pvt. Ltd.

For product information and technology assistance, contact us at
Cengage Learning Customer & Sales Support, 1-800-354-9706

For permission to use material from this text or product,
submit all requests online at **www.cengage.com/permissions.**
Further permissions questions can be e-mailed to
permissionrequest@cengage.com.

Library of Congress Control Number: 2010929507

ISBN-13: 978-1-4282-6230-0

ISBN-10: 1-4282-6230-X

Wadsworth
20 Channel Center Street
Belmont, MA 02210
USA

Cengage Learning is a leading provider of customized learning solutions with office locations around the globe, including Singapore, the United Kingdom, Australia, Mexico, Brazil and Japan. Locate your local office at **international.cengage.com/region.**

Cengage Learning products are represented in Canada by Nelson Education, Ltd.

For your course and learning solutions, visit
www.cengage.com.

Purchase any of our products at your local college store or at our preferred online store **www.cengagebrain.com.**

Printed in the United States of America
1 2 3 4 5 6 7 14 13 12 11 10

Contents

Preface

Like the previous editions, *The Informed Argument*, Eighth Edition, grows out of the belief that argumentation can be a powerful vehicle for individual learning and for social transformation. The book is designed to help students see that arguments involve much more than trying to win a debate. They can be a way to discover truth and to solve problems. In this regard, learning to write and to analyze arguments effectively can contribute to the development of students as informed, literate citizens in a complex and changing society.

This book encourages students to read, to analyze, to reflect, and to write by drawing upon the strategies and conventions of effective argumentation in different media—media ranging from editorials and scholarly articles to advertisements, web pages, and blogs. Our hope is that as students inquire into argumentation, develop an understanding of its complexities, and gain the competence to engage effectively in argumentation, they will also acquire a sense of the possibilities for argument to serve social and ethical purposes. In other words, we hope students will come to appreciate argument not just as a useful set of writing, reading, and thinking skills but also as a means of negotiating their way in a complicated world. Accordingly, this edition emphasizes that argumentation should be a means of negotiating differences to address the problems we face as consumers, citizens, and members of various communities.

The book is organized so that students can explore argumentation and gain competence as writers and readers of arguments by addressing important issues in popular culture, public policy, education, and social life. The early chapters present an overview of argument, emphasizing an understanding of the rhetorical nature of argumentation and the crucial role of context in constructing effective arguments. These chapters help students gain a sophisticated understanding of argumentation as a foundation for writing their own arguments to accomplish their purposes in a variety of contexts.

This edition of *The Informed Argument* incorporates recent scholarly thinking about the nature of argument—including significant attention to the importance of visual rhetoric and digital media—into a framework based on such principles of classical rhetoric as *ethos*, *logos*, and *pathos* and the importance of arrangement, or organization. In addition, our approach to argument draws on recent theories of language and discourse to provide students with a sophisticated lens through which to view the arguments they read and to help them develop their own written arguments. By bringing a contemporary understanding of the way cultural context shapes arguments to the application of classical rhetoric, the book provides students with a sophisticated yet accessible perspective through which to view the arguments they see, read, and write.

A Contemporary Perspective on Traditional Argumentation

Throughout the book, argument is presented as an activity that occurs within specific contexts and is intended to serve a wide range of social and political purposes. The four chapters of Part I, "Understanding Arguments," introduce students to concepts that can help them to evaluate arguments composed by others and to compose arguments of their own. Chapter 1, "The Purposes of Argument," will help students appreciate how argumentation occurs for a variety of ends and how purpose shapes many of the rhetorical choices writers need to make. Chapter 2, "The Contexts of Argument," explores how the different aspects of context, including cultural diversity, influence argumentation. Chapter 3, "The Media for Argument," examines how various media, including important new digital media, shape argumentation and can be powerful tools for argument in their own right; this chapter pays special attention to visual rhetoric, an increasingly important concern for understanding and composing effective arguments. Chapter 4, "The Strategies for Argument," introduces students to various approaches to argumentation, including classical and contemporary strategies for organizing an argument; this chapter includes an extended treatment of logic and logical fallacies—areas that are often poorly understood but can be powerful tools for students to negotiate the challenges of argumentation as both writers and readers.

In Part II, "Composing Arguments," students learn to explore their subject matter through various means of research, organize their arguments effectively, and manage source material appropriately. Chapter 5, "Constructing Arguments," presents the process of writing as an integral part of inquiry and of successfully communicating the results of that inquiry; it also helps students analyze their audiences to emphasize the rhetorical nature of argument, and it includes discussion of the crucial task of structuring an argument in a way that reinforces the treatment of logic in Part I. As in previous editions, student essays illustrate the importance of revision and organization.

Research as an Integral Part of Argument

Like all previous editions, the eighth edition includes substantial treatment of research—from exploring a topic to finding and documenting sources. Because effective argumentation is informed argumentation, research is an integral part of the process of writing a good argument. Chapters 6 ("Doing Research") and 7 ("Documenting Your Sources") guide students through the process of identifying, evaluating, using, and citing various kinds of source material. In these chapters students will find useful advice for discovering relevant sources and incorporating material from these sources into their own writing. Both MLA and APA style documentation are discussed in detail in Chapter 7, and arguments that model documented research can be found throughout the book.

Diverse Readings

The reading selections in this edition reflect the book's focus on argumentation as a way to negotiate differences and solve problems. The readings are organized around six main themes, each of which is further divided into three subthemes, or "clusters," that respond to questions that cannot be answered simply—for example, "Who owns words and ideas?" and "Should there be limits on free speech?" This organizing scheme grows out of the view that anthologies that cast arguments in a familiar pro–con pattern tend to oversimplify important issues, deepen divisions, and thus work against problem solving. Accordingly, while the readings represent diverse points of view, they cannot be easily classified as pro or con advocacy. Although each cluster of readings can stand on its own, the three clusters in each chapter are closely related. This pattern of organization allows students to reflect upon a range of different issues while nevertheless seeing how many of these issues intersect. At the same time, the four readings in each cluster present various perspectives on an issue and thus reinforce the view that arguments about complex and important issues should not be reduced to pro–con patterns. Moreover, the number of readings included in this edition provides instructors with many options for selecting the pieces that are best suited for their own courses.

The themes of these six chapters are also diverse. In response to both reviewers and students, this edition retains the focus of previous editions on issues from popular culture while at the same time addressing traditional issues, such as education, and including familiar essays that represent classic arguments and argumentative strategies. Even the more traditional chapters offer fresh perspectives. For example, the chapter on communication includes a new cluster that addresses the question, How should we talk to each other in the digital age? And the chapter on the environment includes a new cluster focusing on what and how we should eat, an issue that has become increasingly important in the past few years and one that students must now confront in their lives.

The writers included in this book represent a range of interests, professions, perspectives, and cultural backgrounds. They also differ in the proficiency with which they present their ideas. Students using this edition will learn that some arguments are more persuasive than others—a useful development in critical thinking—but all of the readings are treated respectfully in the apparatus. Most of the readings are recent, reflecting contemporary points of view. They also reflect a diversity of media: There are selections from traditional print publications such as the *New York Times,* newer publications such as *Z Magazine,* online journals, as well as blogs. Some classic arguments, such as Martin Luther King, Jr.'s "Letter from a Birmingham Jail" and an excerpt from Rachel Carson's *Silent Spring,* have been retained from previous editions to help students better understand that arguments occur in a historical context.

All the readings will not only help students gain insight into the issues at hand and become more informed about these issues, but they will also provide a variety of models, perspectives, and argumentative strategies for students to consider.

Innovative Pedagogical Features

- Historically significant excerpts that help establish how the readings in each chapter are part of important ongoing cultural, political, and philosophical discussions.
- Accessible introductions to each cluster of readings and to individual reading selections that place readings in context and orient students to the arguments they will encounter in the readings.

- Three kinds of supplementary boxes for each reading selection that are color-coded to the text to help students better understand the nuances of the contexts with which each piece was written:

  - *Gloss:* Information on specific people, events, or concepts in the reading. Glosses are linked to the text with green coloring.
  - *Context:* Background on issues, ideas, events, or persons in the reading as well as excerpts from texts that are referred to in the readings. Context boxes are linked to the text with green coloring.
  - *Complication:* Information that complicates the argument made in the reading. Complication boxes are linked to the text with green coloring.

- Questions for Discussion for each reading that include four main kinds of questions:

  - Questions to help students understand the selection.
  - Questions that focus attention on argumentative strategies and context.
  - Questions that engage students in analysis and evaluation of the text to deepen their understanding of the concepts introduced in Chapters 1 through 5.
  - Questions that encourage students to be self-reflective about their views.

- Negotiating Differences assignments at the end of each cluster that engage students in argumentation as a way to solve a problem related to the cluster topic.

New to This Edition

- Changes in organization of the first five chapters that make the principles of argument easier for students to grasp
- A new chapter of readings on "Communication"
- Twenty-nine new reading selections
- Expanded and updated discussion of media in Chapter 3, including greater attention to online and digital media
- Updated treatment of visual rhetoric, including advertisements, cartoons, graphs, icons, paintings, photographs, posters, and websites
- Expanded and updated discussion of the uses of evidence in argumentation
- Updated discussion of MLA and APA styles of documentation
- Expanded discussion of using sources to help students effectively incorporate source material and avoid plagiarism

Resources for Instructors and Students

Online Instructor's Manual Available for download on the book companion website, the password-protected Instructor's Manual is designed with the needs of first- to second-year college students in mind. To help you plan the logistics of your course, features include: highlights of each chapter for your quick reference, graphic representations of key points from the text, suggested class activities for groups and individuals, and two sample syllabi.

Book Companion Website   Visit the book companion website to access valuable course resources. Students will find an extensive library of interactive exercises and animations that cover grammar, diction, mechanics, punctuation, research, and writing concepts, as well as a complete library of student papers and a section on avoiding plagiarism. The site also offers a downloadable Instructor's Manual.

Enhanced Insite™ for Argument   Easily create, assign, and grade writing assignments with Enhanced Insite™. Instructors can manage the flow of papers, check for originality, access electronic grademarking tools, and conduct peer reviews—all online. Students can access a multimedia eBook, private tutoring options, anti-plagiarism tutorials, and a suite of resources specifically for Argument. These resources include:

- Sample visual arguments
- Video clips of argument in popular culture
- Sample Student Papers
- Debate topics and writing prompts

Acknowledgments

A new edition of a textbook is an extensive collaboration among many different people, many of whom it is impossible to thank sufficiently here. I am deeply grateful to Lyn Uhl for having the confidence in me to rejoin the team for this title and write this new edition. Margaret Leslie, the editor in charge of this project, always provided insight, guidance, and gentle encouragement. Development editor Kathy Sands-Boehmer shouldered the challenge of keeping this project on schedule. I owe her a great debt for her dedication to the project, her encouragement, and her patience. I also wish to acknowledge my debt to Robert Miller for inviting me to be part of this project.

Special thanks to Amy Crouse-Powers, of the State University of New York at Oneonta, who served as research assistant and sometime writer for this project. As my research assistant on this and other projects, Amy is ever reliable and efficient, and the quality of this edition owes much to her skill as a researcher.

I am ever so grateful to Carol Forman-Pemberton, co-director of the Capital District Writing Project (CDWP), for her never-ending support for my work and for her wisdom and advice, and to my other wonderful CDWP colleagues, especially Alicia Wein, Aaron Thiell, Molly Fanning, and Liza Schofield, for keeping me grounded in the realities of the classroom and showing me what it means to be a dedicated teacher.

Thanks also to Corinna Dibble, Content Project Manager; Katie Huha, Permissions Acquisitions Manager; Jennifer Meyer-Dare, Image Permission Manager; Lauren Traut, Production Editor, of Elm Street Publishing Services; and Jill Ort, Art Director.

In addition, I am grateful to the following reviewers who offered useful suggestions as I undertook this edition: Jill M. Adams, Jefferson Community and Technical College; James Allen, College of DuPage; Jason Denmar, Utica College; Rick Gianni, Westwood

College; Anna Maheshwari, Schoolcraft College; and Anne Wilson Twite, Eastern New Mexico University, Ruidoso.

I also wish to acknowledge my great debt to my two sons, Adam and Aaron, my best buddies, who have taught me more about argumentation—and solving problems—than they know.

Most important, I am blessed to have as my partner, Cheryl Hafich Yagelski, my wife of 28 years, whose tireless support, love, confidence, and especially patience helped me complete this book under a tight deadline. She always provides me safe harbor.

—*R.P.Y.*

Understanding Arguments

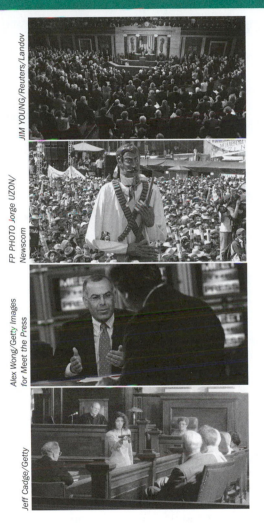

JIM YOUNG/Reuters/Landov

FP PHOTO Jorge UZON/Newscom

Alex Wong/Getty Images for Meet the Press

Jeff Cadge/Getty

1

The Purposes of Argument

JIM YOUNG/Reuters/Landov

What Is an Argument?

Argument is a means of discovering truth, negotiating differences, and solving problems. When you ask your teacher to extend the deadline for an assignment, apply for a job, request a raise, petition for an extension of health insurance benefits, or seek admission to a study-abroad program or a graduate school, you are putting yourself in a position that requires effective argumentation. Such situations require you to organize, articulate, and support your beliefs so that others will take them seriously.

One of the most common misconceptions about argument is that it is only about winning. Look again at the examples in the preceding paragraph: Each case involves people trying to address a complicated situation and solve a problem satisfactorily. The need to ask a teacher for a deadline extension, for example, may have arisen from circumstances involving, say, an illness, which may include many factors that complicate an apparently simple situation. For one thing, the assignment deadline itself is part of your teacher's effort to organize the course, anticipate the time it takes for grading, and accommodate the school calendar. For another thing, you probably have other responsibilities to fulfill—a work schedule, assignments for other classes, maybe meetings for a club you belong to—all of which are also affected by your illness. All these factors complicate the problem created by your illness. In asking for a deadline extension, you are attempting to solve that problem. So you make an argument to justify an extension.

But the matter doesn't end there, because extending your deadline may create further problems for your teacher. She may, for instance, have a tight deadline of her own for reading her students' essays, and she may also worry about being fair to other students. So your argument is not just a matter of convincing your teacher that you need an extension; it is also an attempt to solve your problem in a way that takes into account the potential problems your teacher faces. Ideally, a successful argument in this case would mean that both you and your teacher "win." In this sense, you might think of argumentation as an intellectual effort intended to solve a problem by drawing people together.

As this example suggests, argument requires you to look beyond the surface. When you address a difficult or controversial issue, argument may also involve moral or ethical choices. Imagine a situation in which you are trying to decide on medical treatment for a family member who is comatose. You may feel strongly that your relative would not want to remain on artificial life support, and you may even have ethical misgivings about such medical treatment. You might argue, too, that the financial and emotional costs of such life support outweigh the potential benefits. Of course, you would want to listen carefully to what other members of your family have to say and consider what doctors and nurses advise. In such a situation, it would be irresponsible to try only to "win" the argument. Rather, you would want to use argument to build consensus so that your family will be content with its decision.

Fortunately, most argumentation does not involve such weighty matters. But if you consider the many different kinds of arguments you may encounter or make in your daily life, you quickly begin to see that argument is not just an important skill that will serve you well as a college student or an employee; argument is also an important part of how you live your life with others. It is a central feature of the way our communities, social networks, and institutions function.

Written argumentation, in particular, which can take many forms, is a way for you to work out your own position on an issue. Constructing an effective written argument requires you to think clearly about an issue or problem without letting your feelings dominate what you say. It encourages careful inquiry that can lead to a deeper understanding of the issue or problem. It can also be satisfying to succeed in helping other people understand what you mean and to engage with them in a genuine effort to address a problem. You may not always convert others to your point of view, but you can earn their respect and perhaps enhance understanding of an important issue on all sides. This, in the end, is what argument is all about: engaging with others to address problems.

Effective argumentation requires an ability to understand differences, for you cannot solve a problem or resolve a conflict that you do not understand. When writing an argument, you must often give consideration to beliefs that may differ from your own, recognizing what makes those beliefs appealing in a given situation. Indeed, the fact that many arguments involve deeply held beliefs is one reason that argumentation can be so challenging. Becoming familiar with diverse points of view will help you write arguments that address the concerns of people who may disagree with you. In the process, you may learn more about your own beliefs. Ideally, such learning will not only enable you to develop your own thinking and be more persuasive in your arguments, but it may also enable you to negotiate differences with others and thus solve problems to everyone's advantage.

As you can see, in our view argument is more than persuasion. Genuine argument seeks to clarify thought, not obscure it; it relies on evidence or widely accepted truths and does not necessarily dictate any particular course of action. The truly effective argument would have well-supported claims that ultimately lead to a satisfactory resolution of the problem at hand. While such a goal may not be realistic in every situation that calls for argumentation, it is the ideal toward which we hope you will strive when you write an informed argument.

Given the adversarial nature of so much public debate today, especially with the proliferation of radio and television talk shows, blogging, and online social media, it is easy to mistake quarreling for argument. Often, in popular media, the primary purpose is to entertain, criticize, or promote a specific point of view—not to inform, address a problem, or resolve a conflict. Not surprisingly, discussions in popular media rarely move beyond staking out a position or criticizing others. Such discussions are not very different from a quarrel between two roommates about what kind of music to play on the stereo.

Some scholars believe that genuine argument is not a conflict between adversaries but an effort to find truth (see sidebar). This idea can help us distinguish argument from other kinds of discourse in which participants seek to win or promote their point of view without concern for the truth of their claims or positions. Let's return to our earlier example of a student asking a teacher to extend an assignment deadline. In that case, the ideal goal was to solve the problem created by the student's illness to the satisfaction of both student and teacher. That goal assumes good intentions on all sides. But if the student cares only about getting the extension to solve *his* problem, he may ignore the teacher's concerns and make claims without concern for their truth-value. By our definition, he would be engaged in something other than genuine argumentation, no matter how persuasive he might be. Genuine argumentation should be an ethical endeavor.

If argument were only about getting your way—about winning—then it would not be an effective tool for living our complicated lives with each other. In fact, it is precisely because our lives are complicated—and because we must live among others with their own complicated needs and opinions—that a view of argument as an ethical way to solve problems and negotiate differences is so important.

Understanding the Purposes of Argument

Almost anything can be argued, but not everything should be argued. The decision about what to argue and how to make an argument not only is a practical one (*What topic should I choose for my next assignment in my writing class?*) but also can be an ethical one (*What position should I take on stem-cell research? What are the potential consequences of opposing an increase in tuition at my school?*). To make an argument is to engage in a social activity that can have consequences for you and others, and it's part of your responsibility as a writer to consider those consequences as you decide what to argue and how to do so. To make such a decision, it is helpful to consider *why* people engage in argument.

We engage in argumentation in many different situations to achieve various goals. Consider the following situations:

Example 1. A controversial radio personality recently spoke on your campus at the invitation of a student group affiliated with one of the national political parties. The event was not sponsored by the university and the university contributed no funds to it; however, university facilities were used, and the student group that extended the invitation used university resources (such as a systemwide message delivered by e-mail) to publicize the event. The student group raised the money to fund part of the speaker's fee; the balance was contributed by private donors who chose to be anonymous. The event drew a large crowd. Many students present were shocked by the speaker's views, which seemed extreme to them, and by crude language used to describe members of the government whose opinions differed from those of the speaker. Some students were especially upset because they felt that the speaker twisted and ridiculed their questions during the question-and-answer period that followed the speech. Imagine that you were one of those students. As you followed discussions of the event as well as news coverage of it during the following week, you received a message sent to all students, faculty, and staff by your university's president, who had not been present at the event. He expressed "deep regret" about the controversy and emphasized that the event had not been sponsored by the university. Unsatisfied by this official response, you decide to write a letter to the school newspaper. In your letter you assert that you are not paying tuition so that you can be insulted when you ask a reasonable question. You also argue that the university should not have allowed its facilities to be used for a speaker who has a history of being so controversial and incendiary.

> **ARGUMENT TO ASSERT**
>
> Your letter would be an **argument to assert**, which means to make a claim or to state an opinion. Asserting your opinion in this case cannot undo what has already happened. You are simply explaining and justifying the nature of your concerns so that they can be understood by others. It is possible, however, that your assertion will influence the selection of future speakers or the guidelines made available to them when an invitation to speak is extended.

Example 2. A state legislator delivers a stinging speech after the legislature has voted against the reform of the state's laws regarding criminal penalties for drug offenses. He criticizes his colleagues who voted against the reforms, charging that they care more about their political careers than about the lives of people who have been treated unfairly under the state's drug laws. Although those laws were implemented in the 1980s to combat large-scale drug dealers, the laws have been used to imprison thousands of individual drug users for relatively minor offenses. As a result, legal experts consider the laws too harsh, unfair, and ineffective, and opinion polls show that a majority of the state's voters believe that the laws should be changed. A proposal to reform the laws to ensure that they target drug dealers rather than users moved through the legislature but was opposed by the governor, who feared they would make the state appear soft on drug-related crimes. At the last minute, the governor's party mustered enough votes to defeat the reform bill. The legislator knows his speech cannot change the outcome of the vote, but he delivers an angry attack on his colleagues nevertheless, arguing that they have voted in a way that undermines the principles of fairness and justice on which the legal system rests. Although the vote on the drug reform bill is now finished, he knows that his speech will be carried on television and reported in newspapers around the state and will therefore be heard by many voters.

Example 3. You and your two roommates are considering buying a share in a local farm that is part of the growing movement called community-supported agriculture (CSA). All three of you enjoy buying locally grown fresh produce, which you regularly do at nearby farmers markets, and you have read that buying local produce is one way to reduce your contribution to greenhouse gases. Also, buying a farm share in a CSA would help support a local business. But one of your roommates is worried that the CSA farm share would cost more than buying produce at the farmers market or local supermarket. Your other roommate points out that it is also less convenient, because you can only pick up your farm share vegetables once each week at the farm itself, which is a 15-minute drive from your apartment; the farmers market, on the other hand, is only a few blocks away, and the supermarket is also in your neighborhood. You still think that the CSA might be a good idea, but you're not sure. So you decide to look more closely at the issue. You search the Internet to learn more about the CSA movement, and you contact the local farm for information about their farm shares, including costs. You also talk to some friends who have purchased a share at the farm about their experience, and you do an analysis of how much you and your roommates spend on fresh produce at the farmers market and supermarket. You read some arguments against buying exclusively local produce, and you consider how having a farm share might affect your diet. After examining all this information, you conclude that although there are some trade-offs, especially in terms of convenience, buying a farm share will not only provide you and your roommates with better produce but also encourage you to learn to use different kinds of produce and cook your meals according to when various kinds of produce are harvested, which means you wouldn't be buying vegetables at the supermarket trucked from hundreds of miles away. At about the same time that you are making your case to your roommates in favor of buying a farm share, you see an article in the local newspaper about the pros and cons of CSAs, and you decide to write a letter to the editor in which you argue in favor of the CSA movement.

Example 4. You are a member of the school board that makes decisions for a large district. Both of your children are attending public schools in this district, which has the reputation of being one of the best in the state. During this school year, the board must approve the use of a new textbook for American history for high school seniors. Administrative policy calls for reconsideration of authorized textbooks every five years. The current textbook has been used for more than four years, and the selection of a new text will be difficult. Some parents have formed a group called Citizens for American Education and have launched a campaign against the current text, a new edition of which will be out within a year. They complain that this text is "un-American" because it gives extensive coverage to issues such as slavery, the treatment of Native Americans, and the imprisonment of Japanese Americans during the Second World War. Arguing that emphasis on issues such as these demoralizes students and turns them against their own country, this group of parents has endorsed an alternative textbook—one that emphasizes the nation's positive achievements. This alternative textbook has received poor reviews from historians, and many teachers argue that the adoption of this text would contribute to "dumbing down" of the curriculum and would leave students with a distorted vision of the past. Moreover, some teachers and parents are concerned about the rising price of textbooks and point out that the proposed textbook, with its colorful illustrations and cutting-edge design, is more expensive than other available textbooks. Some educators insist that a visually appealing design in a textbook is essential for holding students' attention; others argue that attention can be gained in other ways. In the midst of this controversy, the school board convenes a special committee of parents, teachers, and other community members to examine the issues and make a recommendation about which textbook to purchase. You are a member of that committee. Obviously, the committee's task is complicated. In the first place, it must somehow address serious ideological differences among many parents and teachers about what students should be taught in history classes. At the same time, it must address differences of opinion about the cost and style of a textbook. With these concerns in mind, the committee meets with various people representing the differ-

ARGUMENT TO NEGOTIATE DIFFERENCES

The committee report that you helped write is an example of an **argument to negotiate differences**, which means reconciling people engaged in some kind of conflict. Your committee did not begin with a fixed position (as in arguing to assert or to prevail). Instead, it listened carefully to what others had to say and facilitated a productive exchange of views. You and your colleagues then worked with the ideas and information that were generated through discussion and research to reconcile differences with a multilayered solution. Had you simply "compromised" by pushing for a middle-of-the-road text that split the difference between those who wanted a more conservative text and those who wanted a more progressive one, you might have achieved a short-term solution, but in such a case no one really gets what he or she wants. By proposing to launch an educational website and a new program for parents, you and your colleagues provided conflicting parties with the sense that they are part of the solution. Ultimately, you all have the same goal—a sound history curriculum for the students—and your report is an effort to reconcile opposing positions in a way that will achieve that goal.

ent perspectives involved in the debate to hear their concerns in a respectful setting. It invites history and education professors from local colleges to offer their views on these issues. It also arranges for publishers to provide sample copies of current and forthcoming texts for American history for the twelfth grade and invites parents and teachers to assess the clarity, accuracy, and balance of the books and to look into what education research indicates about the relationship between visual presentation and learning. After several weeks of meeting and public discussions, the committee writes a report to make its recommendations to the school board. The report examines the major issues in this controversy and presents the viewpoints of parents and teachers in the district; it also includes the viewpoints of experts in history and education. It recommends the use of a textbook that is considered less controversial than the current one and not as expensive as the proposed alternative, but it also recommends several measures to be taken to supplement the textbook that allow for various other voices to be heard on the subject of American history. These measures include a district-sponsored website on which parents, teachers, and students can post links to additional documents about topics addressed in the school's history classes; in addition, the committee proposed establishing a special program to invite parents and others to share their views about such topics.

As these four examples show, people engage in argument for many reasons. But in order to understand argumentation better, we can identify at least four broad purposes for argument:

- to assert
- to prevail
- to inquire
- to negotiate differences

These purposes may overlap. For example, in an argument to prevail it may be necessary to assert a position, and it is often necessary to inquire before you can negotiate differences. Moreover, all arguments contain certain essential elements, such as an identifiable position on a subject, specific claims, and supporting evidence, and many arguments address several purposes at once. You will examine arguments that illustrate these points later in this book. You will also consider other issues, such as how to organize and to support an argument. But before you do so, let's look more closely at these four main purposes of argument. Doing so will help you analyze arguments written by others and compose effective arguments of your own.

Arguments to Assert

In the first example (on page 5), when you complained about the behavior of an on-campus speaker, you saw the need to publicize your view. You wished to assert your position so that others would understand how you felt, and you saw this as part of a wider discussion at your school. Your letter may influence others and have unexpected consequences in the future if it made a memorable impression, but your primary purpose was simply to assert—not to argue for a specific reform and provide evidence that such a reform would be helpful.

You can probably imagine many situations in which your primary goal is to assert a position on which there may be disagreement or controversy:

- in a class discussion about gay marriage
- in a meeting of a student organization that is considering whether to call for a boycott of local stores that sell goods produced in sweatshops
- in your place of employment as your coworkers decide how to respond to a new overtime policy

In such situations, many voices may be heard, and each one asserts a position on the issue. To assert your position effectively can not only contribute to resolution of an issue, but it can also help you gain credibility as a thoughtful participant in the discussion of the issue.

In some ways, all arguments are arguments to assert. Even advertisements whose primary purpose is to persuade people to purchase a product often assert a position or perspective (see Figure 1-1).

Courtesy of Advertising Archives

FIGURE 1-1

Advertising as Arguing to Assert

This advertisement for Toyota, one of the world's leading automobile manufacturers, might be seen as an argument to assert a particular point of view about cars and the environment. Although we can assume that its primary purpose is to persuade consumers to buy Toyota cars, the ad also makes an argument that automobiles can be part of a green economy and sustainable future.

Arguments to Prevail

When most people think of formal arguments, they likely think of arguments whose primary purpose is to prevail. The most common example is an argument made in a legal case. A lawyer might be arguing before a judge to grant bail to her client—say, a young man accused of stealing a credit card—so that the client will not have to remain in jail while waiting for the trial to begin. In such a case, the lawyer has one main goal: to win. She wishes only to convince the judge that the client should be free on bail. Her opponent, the prosecutor, will try to counter the defense lawyer's argument so that the young man remains imprisoned. In most such cases, the arguments tend to be adversarial and the opponents easily identified; the writer of the argument usually will try to muster any available evidence and employ any appropriate strategy to win. We might encounter other such arguments to prevail—for example, protests against a particular law or corporation or activity (see Figure 1-2).

But legal cases are not always so clear-cut. Consider a different example of a young man pulled over for drunk driving:

> A man in his twenties with no criminal record and a clean driving record is driving home late at night from a party celebrating his company's recent increase in sales. On the way home he realizes that he has had too much to drink and that it is dangerous for him to be driving. So he pulls onto the shoulder of the road, puts the car in park, and then falls asleep with the car still idling. Later, a police officer stops to investigate and, realizing that the young man has been drinking, arrests him for drunk driving.

According to the laws in that state, the young man is guilty of driving while intoxicated, because he was seated behind the wheel of the car while the car was still running. In the eyes of the law, it doesn't matter that the car was parked and not moving at the time the officer found the man. In his summary argument to the jury, the defense lawyer pointed out that his client is indeed technically guilty but that convicting him would punish him for making the safe and responsible decision to stop his car and wait until he sobered up before continuing to drive home. In other words, the lawyer argued that his client did the right thing, even though he was legally guilty of driving while intoxicated. Why, he asked, should this young man, with no prior offenses, be punished for making the right decision?

In this case, the lawyer's purpose was to win—to prevail over his opponent, the prosecutor—by convincing the jury that they should find the defendant not guilty. And his argument that his client did the "right" thing—if not the legal thing—can be

D. Falconer/PhotoLink/Getty Images

FIGURE 1-2

A Poster Opposing Drunk Driving

Drawing upon the simplicity of a road sign, the designer of this poster makes an argument to prevail: Driving after drinking alcohol must be stopped. MADD stands for "Mothers Against Drunk Driving," and those initials contribute to the argument by suggesting that drunk driving is "mad" (insane) as well as indicating that mothers and those who support them are "mad" (angry) about drunk driving.

seen as a strategy to win the jury's sympathy and appeal to their sense of justice. But if you consider the argument in the larger context of the state's efforts to impose laws that will reduce drunk driving accidents, then the lawyer argued in a way that contributes to that larger purpose. He tried to persuade the jury that what his client did—pulling over his car so that he would avoid an accident—was really what the drunk driving laws are all about. Punishing the young man for his decision therefore would make no sense. In short, the social and ethical considerations of the case go beyond the immediate goal of winning the argument and the case.

As Example 2 above suggests, you can make an argument whose purpose is to prevail even when winning is not likely. In that instance, winning the argument wasn't necessarily the goal. A closer look reveals that the legislator might "lose" the immediate argument to reform the state drug laws, but his speech might win the larger battle for public opinion about those laws. In other words, he can use his defeat in the vote on the reform bill as part of his effort to change the public's attitude about drug laws—and perhaps win a later vote to change the drug laws.

You can also make an argument to prevail for personal and professional reasons, such as when trying to convince a potential employer to hire you. Moreover, arguing to prevail does not necessarily mean putting yourself in an adversarial position. Someone who comes on too strong when applying for a job is unlikely to get it. If you were to claim that you alone were capable of filling the position and were to ignore what could be seen as weaknesses in your background, you probably would not be taken seriously. Instead, by demonstrating good credibility (what is called *ethos* in classical rhetoric), you would claim no more than you can support, present yourself as respectful and professional, and frankly acknowledge areas in which you need to gain more experience. And even if you lose the immediate argument—by failing to get the job you are seeking—you can achieve a larger purpose: understanding what kind of rhetoric works in the job market so that you approach your next application with more experience and, in time, expertly assess the people you interview when you are in a position of authority.

You can probably think of many occasions during which you might need to use argument to prevail. For example:

- getting admitted to a school to which you want to transfer
- winning a required debate in a course in political science or communications
- retaining your ability to drive after having been ticketed for speeding

At some point you will likely find yourself in a situation in which winning an argument is extremely important to you. Understanding arguments to prevail can help you construct an effective argument in that situation.

Arguments to Inquire

In the third example provided earlier (on page 6), the letter to the editor does argue in favor of a position—that consumers should support community-supported agriculture (CSA)—and the argument might be seen as an effort to convince others to do the same.

But its primary purpose is to explore the complexities of the decision to buy a farm share and examine its environmental and economic implications. This exploration—which involves both research and debate—helps you make a good decision. Instead of emphasizing an assertion as the foundation for the decision (as in arguing to assert or to prevail), you have reached an assertion (that supporting CSAs makes sense) as a result of your inquiry into the question (see Figure 1-3).

You probably engage in similar kinds of arguments. Perhaps the best example is class discussion. In a sociology class, for instance, you might find yourself discussing health care reform. As a student in the class, you are not considered an expert on health care reform, nor do your arguments or your classmates' arguments have consequences outside your class (unlike, say, a doctor's arguments to an insurance company that his patient's medical treatment should be covered). Most important, your arguments in this situation are not necessarily intended to convince your classmates to support or oppose a particular position about health care reform; rather, in making your arguments and listening to those of your classmates, you are engaged in a collective inquiry into the sociological issues surrounding health care reform. You are arguing to learn and to understand.

FIGURE 1-3

Local Harvest Web Page

Local Harvest is an organization that promotes community-supported agriculture (CSA). On its website it asks, "Thinking about signing up for a CSA but want to learn more about the idea before you commit?" The rest of the article might be seen as an argument to inquire into that question. (http://www.localharvest.org/csa/)

Courtesy of Local Harvest

As a college student, you will probably find that much academic writing can be characterized as arguments to inquire. Arguments in the natural and social sciences, for example, often cite previous studies and reach tentative conclusions that recognize the need for additional research. Such arguments are exploratory and informative, implicitly inviting readers to join the inquiry at hand. Consider the following excerpt from the opening chapter of *Writing Space,* a book by Jay David Bolter about how new computer technologies are changing the nature of writing. As this excerpt suggests, Bolter believes that computers are fostering dramatic changes in how and what people write. His position is not universally shared, however. Bolter knows this. He isn't concerned about convincing other scholars that he's right and they're wrong; rather, he wishes to examine a complex issue that other scholars want to understand better:

In Victor Hugo's novel *Notre-Dame de Paris, 1482,* the priest remarked "Ceci tuera cela": this book will destroy that building. He meant not only that printing and literacy would undermine the authority of the church but also that "human thought...would change its mode of expression, that the principal idea of each generation would no longer write itself with the same material and in the same way, that the book of stone, so solid and durable, would give place to the book made of paper, yet more solid and durable" (p. 199). The medieval cathedral crowded with statues and stained glass was both a symbol of Christian authority and a repository of medieval knowledge (moral knowledge about the world and the human condition). The cathedral was a library to be read by the religious, who walked through its aisles looking up at the scenes of the Bible, the images of saints, allegorical figures of virtue and vice, visions of heaven and hell....Of course, the printed book did not eradicate the encyclopedia in stone; it did not even eradicate the medieval art of writing by hand. People continued to contemplate their religious tradition in cathedrals, and they continued to communicate with pen and paper for many purposes. But printing did displace handwriting: the printed book became the most valued form of handwriting. And printing certainly helped to displace the medieval organization and expression of knowledge. As Elizabeth Eisenstein has shown, the modern printing press has been perhaps the most important tool of the modern scientist. (See *The Printing Press as an Agent of Change* by Elizabeth Eisenstein, 1979, especially vol. 2, pp. 520ff.)

Hugo himself lived in the heyday of printing, when the technology had just developed to allow mass publication of novels, newspapers, and journals. Hugo's own popularity in France (like Dickens' in England) was evidence that printed books were reaching and defining a new mass audience. Today we are living in the late age of print. The evidence of senescence, if not senility, is all around us. And as we look up from our computer keyboards to the books on our shelves, we must ask ourselves whether "this will destroy that." Computer technology (in the form of word processing, databases, electronic bulletin boards and mail) is beginning to displace the printed book....

The printed book, therefore, seems destined to move to the margin of our literate culture....The shift to the computer will make writing more flexible, but it will also threaten the definitions of good writing and careful reading that have been fostered by the technique of printing. The printing press encouraged us to think of a written text as an unchanging artifact, a monument to its author and its age....Electronic writing emphasizes the impermanence and changeability of text, and it tends to reduce the distance between author and reader by turning the reader into an author. It is changing the cultural status of writing as well as the method of producing books. It is changing the relationship of the author to the text and of both the author and text to the reader.

To write an effective argument of inquiry requires researching the topic and examining the issues surrounding it. It might require using evidence, but the evidence might be used to *illustrate* a point rather than to support it. For example, in the preceding excerpt, Bolter refers to historian Elizabeth Eisenstein to help him develop his point about the important effect of the printing press. He does this not as a way to say, "I'm right," but as a way to lend credibility to his main point about writing and technology.

What is especially noteworthy about an argument to inquire is that your own position might change or evolve as you examine the topic and go through the process of planning, writing, and revising your argument. In fact, you might begin the process of writing this kind of argument without a clear position on the topic. Your position will emerge through the process of writing. These arguments, then, are exploratory in two ways: (1) They encourage the writer to explore a topic in order to arrive at a reasonable position, and (2) they invite other writers to engage in exploring that topic.

As noted earlier, arguing to inquire is common in academic writing as well as in other situations:

- discovering the right major for you
- deciding what kind of car to buy
- determining your position on an important issue in your community

Arguments to Negotiate and Reconcile

Glance through your morning newspaper, and you will quickly find examples of situations in which people have seemingly irreconcilable or even intractable differences about an issue, or they may occupy such divergent perspectives that no option seems to exist except for one side defeating or silencing the other. At the same time, communications technologies have brought people into more frequent contact with one another, so we now routinely confront all kinds of differences—social, cultural, religious, political, ethnic, regional, and so on. Such diversity enriches our lives, but it also challenges us to learn how to live together peacefully. In this sense, one of the main purposes of argument is to confront the complexity that arises from diversity in order to negotiate and, ideally, to reconcile differences. This might be the most difficult kind of argument.

The problem facing the school board's textbook committee in Example 4 (on page 7) reveals how the need to negotiate and reconcile is especially important in situations involving multiple parties with multiple points of view—all of which need to be respected. The solution in this case required a lengthy process of research, discussion, and negotiation in which many different considerations were taken into account. However, the committee pursued a larger goal—providing a good education to the community's children—that most of the people involved in the controversy shared. Working toward that goal enabled the committee to construct an argument that was intended to provide a solution rather than defeat an opponent.

Such an outcome might sound idealistic, but many situations are argued in this way. For example, lawyers representing different sides in a legal case do not always argue to prevail. It is quite common for defense lawyers and prosecutors to negotiate a plea bargain, which amounts to a compromise in which each side gains something and neither side loses everything. In such a situation, both sides would argue in front of a judge in a way intended to work out an agreement that is fair and appropriate. That agreement usually involves the defendant pleading guilty to a lesser charge, and it would appeal to prosecutors who are uncertain about prevailing in court when arguing for a more serious charge. It would also appeal to prosecutors who believe they can resolve other cases through information provided by the defendant as part of the plea bargain—thus advancing the common good, even if a specific individual may be getting off lightly.

Arguing to negotiate differences is sometimes called *Rogerian argument,* after the influential psychotherapist Carl Rogers, who emphasized the importance of communication to resolve conflicts. Rogers believed that most people are so ready "to judge, to evaluate, to approve or disapprove" that they fail to understand what others think. He urged people to "listen with understanding" and recommended a model for communication in which listeners are required to restate what others have said before offering their own views. This restatement should be done fairly and accurately, without either praise or blame, so that the original speaker is able to confirm, "Yes, that is what I said."

Although this model might seem simple, Rogers cautioned that it takes courage to listen carefully to views that are contrary to one's own, especially in volatile situations or on charged and difficult issues (such as abortion or capital punishment). It is extremely hard to listen when feelings are strong. The greater the conflict, the greater the chance of misinterpreting what others have said. Moreover, it's easy to think of situations in which any kind of listening seems impossible because the people involved are engaged in such deep conflict. Rogers envisioned situations in which individuals are engaged in dialogue, and his commitment to the importance of restating others' ideas (without evaluating them) rests on the assumption that language can be neutral—an idea that has been seriously questioned by modern linguists and philosophers. And Rogers's emphasis on the importance of listening may be more helpful to people who are used to speaking than to those who have been silenced. Feminists, for instance, have argued that because public discourse has long been dominated by men, women need to learn how to assert themselves and men need help in learning to listen. For these reasons, many scholars questioned the extent to which Rogers's ideas can be applied to written arguments.

Nevertheless, if you think carefully about the role of argument in resolving conflict and achieving social cooperation, Rogers's perspective on communication can be useful in helping you formulate effective arguments. And the examples cited here underscore the advantages of approaching argument in this way when a situation is characterized by a difficult conflict. Indeed, given the scale of the conflicts we face today within our communities, in our cultures, and in the world, a Rogerian perspective might be the most ethical way to approach an argument and might offer the only viable alternative available in certain situations. Think, for example, of the situation faced by Nelson

FIGURE 1-4

Nelson Mandela

In helping to reconstruct his country after apartheid was dismantled in 1991, former president of South Africa Nelson Mandela made many speeches that can be considered Rogerian argument.

Mandela as the new president of South Africa after the previous apartheid government was dismantled (see Figure 1-4). The long history of oppression and conflict that characterized South Africa and the terrible struggle that Mandela and his supporters endured to defeat apartheid and achieve equality would have made it easy for Mandela to argue for his new government's policies with only the goals of domination and victory in mind. Instead, Mandela recognized that even supporters of the defeated apartheid government were citizens of his country and that it was in everyone's interest to confront and negotiate their differences. As a result, he often argued with the goal of resolution in mind.

The usefulness of an approach to argument that emphasizes negotiating differences extends to more common situations. For example, neighbors in conflict over a drainage problem on the boundary between their properties might be better served by arguing to their town supervisor for a resolution that fairly addresses the problem on both sides of the boundary rather than by one neighbor trying to force the other to fix the problem by winning the case in court. Or you might find yourself working with classmates as part of a group project for one of your college courses; if a conflict arises between group members, it's possible that a "victory" by one group member over another could result in a project that is less effective and therefore earns a lower grade for all group members. In short, arguing to negotiate differences rather than to defeat an opponent might best serve your interests and those of the other people involved, and it may be the best way to avoid further conflict.

There is no question that some differences may be irreconcilable. The news headlines about bombings in the Middle East or religious conflict in Asia and Europe or deep divisions about abortion in the United States remind us that no matter how genuinely we engage with one another in arguments, negotiation and resolution might not always be possible. And there are times when winning an argument, rather than negotiating differences, may be ethical. Still, in all but the most extreme situations, genuine engagement in argument as a way to solve a problem, negotiate serious differences, and work toward resolution can offer the best alternative for all concerned. As a writer, you also benefit from writing arguments in this way, in the sense that your engagement in such argumentation may lead to a greater understanding of the situation, which can enrich your perspective on conflict and enhance your ability to engage in future arguments.

2

The Contexts of Argument

FP PHOTO Jorge UZON/Newscom

Whenever we engage in argumentation, we must do more than examine the topic carefully and construct a sound argument in support of our position. We must also take into account our audience, the specific situation we and they are in, the cultural factors that might affect how an audience responds to a particular argument, even the historical moment we are in as we argue. In short, we always argue within a context— actually, within several contexts simultaneously—and we must consider context if we expect to argue effectively.

Imagine that you have been given an assignment to take a position on the federal government's right to access personal e-mail for reasons of national security and to write an argument justifying your position. Assume further that your essay will be read to your class, which includes students who differ in terms of gender, religion, and political beliefs. The electronic surveillance of personal mail is a controversial issue in part because with such measures genuine concerns about "national security" seem to conflict with citizens' right to privacy. After reading a number of articles and essays, you decide that despite your concerns about electronic surveillance, you believe it can be an important tool for fighting terrorism. You write an argument in which you acknowledge serious problems that can result from the use of electronic surveillance by law enforcement agencies, but you justify its use on the grounds of security and public safety. In your argument you try to address your teacher and your classmates, some of whom have voiced strenuous opposition to electronic surveillance. You wish to make an effective argument that your classmates, even those opposed to electronic surveillance, will take seriously, though you are mindful that some of them might reject what you have to say because of their own passionate engagement with the issue. You also know that your teacher will be assessing your argument and that your classmates' reactions might influence her assessment. So you gather evidence that surveillance has prevented violence, and you identify what you consider to be good arguments in support of policies that can protect citizens' privacy and civil rights. But you also know that the charged nature of the topic will make some of these arguments seem less than convincing to some of your classmates. What will you write?

The answer to this question requires that you consider the context of your argument. No matter what kind of argument you wish to make, no matter what your purpose, there are at least three main contexts you should consider as you construct an argument:

- the rhetorical situation
- the cultural context
- the moment in which you are arguing, which we will call the *historical context*

The Rhetorical Situation

Rhetoricians have long used the metaphor of a triangle to help define the rhetorical situation (see Figure 2-1). The classical rhetorical triangle reminds us that when we write an argument, we are engaged in an interaction with a particular audience about a particular subject. Both audience and writer have a connection to the subject matter in the form of knowledge about the subject, opinions about it, experience with it, and so on. But the writer and the audience will never have identical connections to that subject. A big part of the challenge, then, is to try to understand your audience and its connection to your subject so that you can address your audience effectively in your argument.

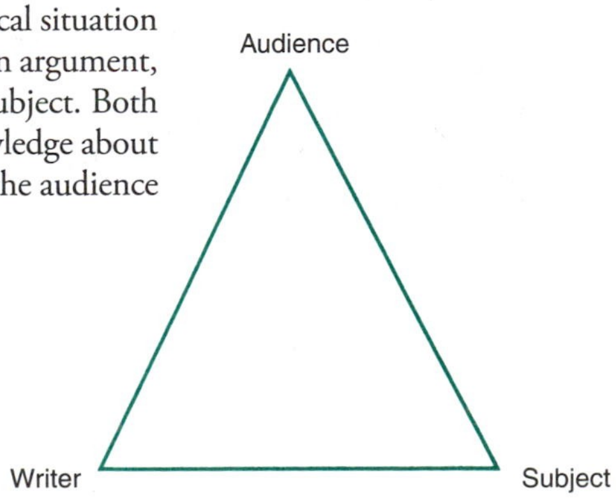

Analyzing Your Audience

The audience for an argument can vary dramatically from one situation to another, and as we will explain in more detail later in this chapter, the specific characteristics of the rhetorical situation (when and where someone is making an argument, for example) can profoundly affect how a writer addresses an audience and how an audience

FIGURE 2-1
The Rhetorical Situation

might respond to an argument. But because an argument is often an attempt to communicate with an audience about a conflict or a problem, and because ideally an argument will effectively address that conflict or resolve the problem, it is essential for writers to try to understand their audience to the extent that they can. There are some general guidelines for doing so.

First, try to determine what you already know about your intended audience. In some cases, the audience for an argument will be specific. In the hypothetical example above, you would be familiar with your audience (your teacher and your classmates), and you would have some sense of their knowledge and opinions about your subject (electronic surveillance). Moreover, because you would have engaged in class discussion about this topic, you might even know how some of your classmates (and perhaps your teacher) might react to specific arguments in favor of or against electronic surveillance. You can imagine other situations in which you might know your audience well. For instance, if you were writing a letter to your school newspaper in support of a proposal for a new fitness center, you would know something about the people who might read your letter. You would have a good sense of who the readers would be because you see and hear them whenever you are on campus. A writer can draw on such knowledge to identify arguments that might be effective for those specific readers. In some ways this is almost an ideal situation for a writer, because there would be little of the uncertainty about the audience that writers usually face in writing an argument. If the goal is to try to solve a problem, then knowing the audience can lead to a better understanding of their positions and a more genuine engagement with them about the issue.

It is important to remember, however, that there is much that you may not know about an audience with which you are familiar. Obvious characteristics such as gender or race do not mean that readers will have similar views and experiences. So it's important not to make broad assumptions about people who seem similar. Not all women, for example, embrace feminist views. When addressing a familiar audience, therefore, draw upon what you know but do not make assumptions about what you do not know for certain.

In many cases, writers are likely to have only limited knowledge about their audience. Imagine the difference between writing a letter to the editor of a newspaper, which is read by a few hundred people who live in the same town, and writing a letter to the editor of a national publication such as *USA Today,* which is read by millions of people from all over the country. The assumptions that you can reasonably make about these audiences can differ dramatically. It isn't feasible to analyze a general audience, such as the readership of *USA Today,* in depth because that audience is far too diverse for you to know anything about it in detail. Nevertheless, you can approach such an audience in a way that is likely to engage a majority of readers and address them effectively. In other words, even though there is a limit to what you can know about an audience (after all, even a close friend can surprise you), you can make some general assumptions about your audience that will help you argue effectively.

You can begin by assuming an intelligent and fair-minded audience. Assume as well that intelligent and fair-minded people tend to be skeptical about sweeping generalizations and unsupported claims. In some cases you might be able to expect your audience to agree with you. For example, chances are that most people at a political convention will share the viewpoint of the keynote speaker. But if you are attempting to reconcile differences or solve a conflict through argument, you should probably assume that your audience might disagree with you. Some members of your audience might be neutral about the issue you're addressing, but imagining a skeptical audience will enable you to anticipate and respond to opposing views or objections to your position, thus building a stronger case.

Imagining Your Audience

In some ways, imagining an audience is a creative act. The twentieth-century scholar Walter Ong once wrote that "the writer's audience is always a fiction," because writers must always create a sense of an audience that doesn't necessarily correspond directly to a "real" audience. This act of "fiction," Ong maintained, is necessary because rarely do writers know in detail just whom they are writing to or for. But this imagined audience is always based on a general sense of who might read what you are writing, your experiences with people in general, your experiences as readers of other people's writing, and your knowledge of the conventions of writing. All these figure into the imagined audience. In other words, the imagined audience is based on real experiences with writing and with other people. When it comes to argument, this act of imagining an audience influences the specific arguments you will make in support of your position on an issue.

Even when imagining a general audience, writers often make specific assumptions about their readers, beyond assuming that they are intelligent but skeptical. Consider, for example, the following letter, which was written to the editors of *Newsweek* in response to an essay by columnist Allan Sloan criticizing greed and unethical behavior by large corporations:

> Right on, Allan Sloan! I have long thought that no economic system, certainly not capitalism, can function successfully without the moderating effects of virtuous, ethical behavior on the part of the key players. That said, I'm afraid that we have yet to widely acknowledge that such behavior can never be reliably coerced by endless rounds of civil regulation. In a free society there will always be loopholes to be identified and exploited by those with selfish, greedy attitudes.

Notice that this writer implicitly assumes that his readers are not necessarily those with "selfish, greedy attitudes"; nor are they likely to be the "key players" in the capitalist system. In other words, he assumes that his readers are "average" people who share his basic values regarding ethical behavior. He can further assume that his readers have read Allan Sloan's essay and that they probably have a basic understanding of the principles of capitalism that Sloan discussed. The point is that even a "general" audience can be specific in certain respects. Narrowing an audience in this way can help a writer determine how to cast an argument so that it effectively addresses that general audience.

Sometimes, a writer can define a general audience more directly by explicitly excluding specific kinds of readers. In the following letter, which was also written to the editors of *Newsweek,* the writer is responding to an article about electroshock therapy:

> I was surprised to find no mention of neurofeedback in your article "Healthy Shocks to the Head." Noninvasive, relatively inexpensive and proving to be effective with a long list of central nervous-system disorders, this procedure should be given an opportunity to demonstrate its effectiveness before more invasive procedures are tried. It's too bad the medical community is so enamored with drugs and surgery.

Notice that this writer refers to "the medical community" in a way that excludes members of that community from his audience. In effect, he is addressing everyone outside the medical community. This writer probably knows that members of that community are likely to read his letter, too, so indirectly he is addressing them—as well as criticizing them—and perhaps inspiring an Ong-like fiction: "You're a *good* doctor or nurse, not one of those types I am referring to here." But by referring to them as he does, he defines his intended audience as those readers who are not members of that community, thus narrowing his "general" audience and assuming that they might share his concerns.

It is worth noting that the writer's purpose in this example is to assert a position on the issue of electroshock therapy. If the writer hoped to try to negotiate the apparent conflict that exists between those who advocate noninvasive techniques for treating disorders of the central nervous system, as he does, and those in the medical community who might have a different view, then he would need to address the medical community directly. In other words, a sense of purpose for an argument will shape the writer's sense of audience.

The audience for an argument is also influenced by the specific circumstances in which the argument is being made. In the previous example, the writer is addressing a general audience made up of readers of *Newsweek,* and he is doing so in response to a specific article that appeared in that magazine. If he were making the same argument—in favor of noninvasive techniques for treating disorders of the central nervous system—in a letter written to the *Journal of Mental Health*, his audience would be composed primarily of mental health professionals who read that journal—that is, members of the medical community that he criticized in his original letter. Although his basic argument might not change, this writer would now be able to use more technical language and would likely have to address his readers differently if he wished them to take him seriously. He would also likely make different claims that might be effective for an audience of medical professionals but not necessarily with a general audience. For one thing, he could assume that his audience knows more about the treatments in question than a general audience, such as the readers of *Newsweek*, are likely to know, which would affect what information he might include in his argument and how he might present it. The circumstances for his argument would therefore affect several important aspects of his argument even if his basic position is the same.

As these examples suggest, the circumstances within which an audience is being addressed can have a big effect on how that audience will respond to a specific argument. It is impossible for a writer to know about everything that is part of a rhetorical situation, just as it is impossible for a writer to be able to anticipate how every member of the audience will react to a specific word, phrase, tone, fact, or line of argumentation. Human beings are simply too complex. But arguments are usually effective only within a specific rhetorical situation. What works in one situation might not work in another. So it is crucial for writers of arguments to examine the rhetorical situation they are in and make their best judgments about how to address their audience in that situation.

Cultural Context

When writers engage a particular audience in argumentation, they never address generic readers, even when they are addressing the kind of general audience described in the previous section. Instead, they address individuals, each of whom brings a different set of experiences, knowledge, beliefs, and background to the interaction. In other words, who we are as individuals shapes how we will react to an argument. And who we are is a complex matter that encompasses race, gender, and other aspects of our identity. In this regard, culture will always be part of any rhetorical situation and thus shape any argument.

Understanding Culture

Culture can be understood in several ways when it comes to argumentation. As suggested in the preceding paragraph, culture is your sense of identity as it relates to your racial and ethnic backgrounds, your religious upbringing (if any), your membership in a particular social class (working class, for example), and the region where you live (for example, rural West Virginia versus urban Los Angeles). These aspects of identity affect how individuals understand themselves in relation to others and as members of various communities. Culture in this sense will shape how you view the world, what you believe and value, and how you experience various aspects of life. Culture can also be envisioned as the nation in which you live and interact with others, as in the culture of the United States or the culture of Japan. These ways of understanding culture overlap, but they provide a sense of the powerful influence that culture will have on individual writers and readers as they engage in argumentation.

Consider how classmates with different cultural backgrounds might react to an argument in favor of racial profiling (the police practice of stopping and searching people because of their race or ethnicity rather than because of evidence of criminal behavior). An African American student might be highly sensitive to the subject—and perhaps passionate about it— because the controversy about the subject has directly involved African Americans. In addition, if that student grew up in an urban neighborhood where relations between residents and police are strained, geography is also likely to shape his or her views on the subject. Compare that student to, say, an exchange student from Japan, where racial issues have a very different history. A Japanese student might also have a different sense of authority and of the relationship between individuals and the government than American students have. To invoke a somewhat different example, what if one of your white classmates was raised in a Quaker household that emphasized a lifestyle based on nonviolence? How might that person react to an argument in favor of racial profiling? All of these hypothetical examples indicate the various ways in which culture can influence both the writing and the reading of an argument.

These examples tell us something else: that culture is complex. The student who was raised as a Quaker, for example, is white but can legitimately claim a different cultural identity from other white students in your class, even though all of them can claim to be part of American culture. The same can be said of two different black students: one who might have grown up in a middle-class suburb and another whose parents might be working-class immigrants from the Caribbean. In other words, even if two people have similar cultural backgrounds, they will not have *identical* cultural backgrounds and will not have identical experiences as members of that culture. As a writer of arguments you can't be expected to sort out all of these subtle complexities, but you should always be sensitive to culture and assume that culture will play an important role in argumentation. Brian Fay, a philosopher of social science, describes the influence of culture in this way:

> My experience has been deeply shaped by the fact that I am male, a (former) Catholic, American, and middle class. Because of these characteristics I look at the world in a certain way, and people treat me in a particular manner. My Catholic upbringing, for example, gave me a view of myself as fallen and as needing to be redeemed by something other than myself or the natural world; it made me think that certain desires and behaviors are bad, and led me to (try to) repress them; even my body was shaped by certain typical Catholic disciplines (kneeling, for instance). Even when in later life I reacted against this upbringing, I was still reacting against my particular Catholic heritage, and in this way this heritage continues to shape me; it will do so until I die.

It seems obviously true that I am in part who and what I am in strong measure because of the groups to which I belong (to which in many cases I had no choice but to belong). If I had been born and raised in New Guinea then I would be quite other than what I am: I would not only describe the world differently, I would experience it differently.

Fay does not use the term *culture* in this passage, but he is referring to aspects of one's background—such as religious upbringing, social class, gender, and national origin—usually associated with culture and considered part of one's cultural identity. Think of how these aspects of Fay's cultural identity might affect his reaction to an argument about racial profiling.

Considering Culture in Argument

The role of culture in argument is clearly illustrated in the following editorial by sports columnist Harvey Araton about two tennis players—one an Israeli and the other a Pakistani—who played together successfully at the Wimbledon tennis championship in 2002 at a time when the conflict in the Middle East between Arabs and Jews was becoming especially bloody. (See Figure 2-2.)

They played together, then sat together, Pakistani and Israeli, Muslim and Jew, and wanted everyone to know it was no big deal. There was no statement made, no cause advanced, other than the bid to go as far as they could in the Wimbledon draw. Pragmatism, not peacemaking, made doubles partners of Aisam ul-Haq Qureshi and Amir Hadad.

"We are not here to change anything," said Qureshi, 22, of Lahore, Pakistan. "I don't like to interfere religion or politics into sport."

Hadad, 24, of Ramala, Israel, near Tel Aviv, said: "I know Aisam is very good on grass, one serve, good volley, and also I like him as a person. When he asked me to play, we didn't even think it's going to get so big."

Then they survived the qualifying tournament and won two rounds in the main draw last week. No Pakistani had lasted past this round at Wimbledon, or in any Grand Slam event. What would have been a feel-good story in Pakistan became an inflamed issue when Qureshi, the country's No. 1 player, from a family with a rich tennis history, made a bit of his own history with Hadad—until they were dispatched by the Czechs Martin Damm and Cyril Suk yesterday, 6–1, 7–6 (5), 6–4.

It was, for them, a productive pairing, one they said they might reprise at the United States Open next month, no matter the ominous reports from Pakistan that Qureshi has read on the Internet.

His family, stationed by Court 5 yesterday in the shadow of Center Court, was only interested in what was happening here, saying they had received support from Pakistanis all over London. His mother, Nosheen, formerly No. 1 in Pakistan and still an active player at 41, kissed the Israeli, Hadad, on the cheek and called him a good boy. The father, Ihtsham, a 50-year-old businessman, videotaped the third round match, right down to the volley his son misplayed on match point. An uncle, Khalid Rashid, dismissed the protests, calling them the work of "Al Qaeda and extremists in the north."

The reports, without subtlety, said otherwise. A former Pakistani champion, Saeed Haid, was quoted in *The Times* of London saying, "The bloodshed in the Middle East means his pairing with an Israeli is wrong." A director of the country's official Sports Board, Brig.

Saulat Abbas, told Agence France-Presse: "Although he is playing in his private capacity, we officially condemn his playing with an Israeli player and an explanation has been sought from him. Since we have no links with Israel, Qureshi may face a ban."

In the heart of aristocratic-mandated civility, the lawns neatly manicured and the sportswear lily white, this sounded like hardened geopolitical zealotry bordering on lunacy. A cautious Ihtsham Qureshi said it was his understanding that the Pakistani news media were supporting his son, and many positive e-mail messages had been received. His wife, whose father was the best player in India before partition in 1947, said "People with the right perspective don't think like that."

Within this insular sport, which rears wandering citizens of the world, the players sounded mature and wise as they spoke of a friendship formed along the endless road of small-time events for those on the far periphery of fame. They joked about how their greatest faith must be in their ability to stay fit and focused in the pursuit of almighty computer points.

"I don't pray at all, but I practice a lot," Hadad said.

Araton's essay was published in the *New York Times,* whose readership includes Arabs and Jews, both in the United States and abroad. But that readership is composed primarily of people living in the United States, most of whom are American citizens. American readers who are neither Jewish nor Muslim are likely to react differently to Araton's argument than Jews or Muslims will. Araton quotes former Pakistani tennis champion Saeed Haid as criticizing Aisam ul-Haq Qureshi, the current Pakistani tennis player, for playing with a Jewish partner in view of the bloodshed between Arabs and Jews; Araton also quotes the Pakistani sports director as condemning Qureshi. Araton suggests that these criticisms amount to zealotry and lunacy, but his argument grows

FIGURE 2-2

Professional tennis players Aisam ul-Haq Qureshi (left) and Amir Hadad

Ezra Shaw/Getty Images

out of a cultural context (that of the United States) in which pluralism and tolerance for religious diversity are deeply held values. The former Pakistani tennis champion and sports director are arguing out of a different cultural context (that is, an Arab and Muslim nation) that does not necessarily share those values. In such a context, the criticisms of Qureshi would not sound like zealotry at all. As is often the case in situations in which different cultures come into conflict, this situation is not simply a matter of differing opinions or a disagreement about whether Qureshi was right to take Amir Hadad as his doubles partner; rather, the different cultural contexts complicate the matter. Araton brings to his argument a different worldview, which grows out of his American cultural identity, from that of the Pakistani tennis champion or the sports director. These cultural differences profoundly shape not only how these individuals view the situation with Qureshi and Hadad but also what kinds of claims or assertions are likely to be persuasive to each.

Culture not only influences how individual readers or writers might react to an argument but also can affect how people engage in argumentation. Different cultures might have different values, as you saw in the example of the Pakistani tennis player Qureshi, and they might have different ways of engaging in argument. For example, in some cultures it is considered impolite or even disrespectful to question another's statements, claims, or credibility. In such cultures, people follow certain implicit protocols that govern what they can say to each other. In Japan, for example, if it is raining and you are without an umbrella, it would be impolite to directly ask a person who has an umbrella if you may borrow it. Instead, you would be expected to make a statement such as "It's raining very hard" or "We are likely to get wet," which the other person would know to interpret as a request to borrow the umbrella. Such cultural protocols govern how a writer might structure an argument and support a position on an issue. A Japanese writer arguing in favor of, say, having American troops leave Okinawa, which is a Japanese-controlled island, might focus his argument on the capabilities of the Japanese security forces to protect Okinawa rather than asserting that Americans have no business occupying that island.

Considering Gender

We can also think of culture as encompassing important aspects of our identity such as gender, sexual orientation, and age. It is risky to generalize about such things, and many arguments are directed toward audiences without regard to such factors. But it is important to be sensitive to how these factors can influence the way an audience might react to an argument. Moreover, there are times when it is appropriate to take these factors into account in making an argument. Sometimes an argument is intended specifically for an audience of, say, young women or retired men. Sometimes the topic might be one that has different implications for different audiences. An argument in favor of a woman's right to choose an abortion will mean something different to women than it will to men, and it will mean something different to young women than it will to older women—no matter whether men and women of any age agree with the argument. In such cases, writers will make certain assumptions based on these important aspects of their readers' identities and will adjust their claims and appeals accordingly.

Consider the following two arguments about differences in how men and women are treated. The first is a letter written to the editor of *Health* magazine, which is devoted to health-related and lifestyle issues for women. The writer was responding to an article about changing ideas of beauty:

Dorothy Foltz-Gray's article "The Changing Face of Beauty" [July/August] is a stunning example of a woman co-opted by our patriarchal society's focus on skin-deep appearance.

She writes that the power of beauty gets you "more than just admiration." And that "it was exhilarating to think I had a little of that power, too."

After 15 years in the corporate world, I have had my fill of women getting ahead because of their looks. Foltz-Gray was careful to assert that she got the "homely" woman's job based upon her own merits, even though she does acknowledge that her looks played a part. She did "feel uncomfortable" with that but accepted the job.

I would have liked to see the article point the finger at the real culprit (men in power) and advocate for change, rather than continuing to accept the status quo. I believe that the media has an obligation to expose abuses of power, especially a magazine devoted to women's total wellness.

This writer is addressing the magazine's editors directly, but she makes it clear that she assumes *Health* to be a magazine for and about women. She also makes an assertion that might be acceptable to most readers of *Health* magazine (most of whom are women) but would be controversial for other audiences: that "men in power" are the reason for women's struggles to advance in the workplace. Given the audience for *Health,* she perhaps doesn't need to worry about alienating male readers. She seems to be saying to her female readers, "C'mon, let's call this problem what it is!" If she were writing for a different audience—say, a more general audience that would include as many men as women or readers of a business-oriented publication such as the *Wall Street Journal*—she would have to assume that her assertion would not be accepted by many in her audience, and she would probably have to defend it.

The second example also addresses the issue of differences in how men and women are treated, but it does so in a less strident way and for a less specific audience. Nevertheless, although the writer, Susan Brownmiller, is addressing a broader audience than the readers of *Health* magazine, she seems to address male and female readers differently. This excerpt is taken from her book *Femininity* :

We are talking, admittedly, about an exquisite esthetic. Enormous pleasure can be extracted from feminine pursuits as a creative outlet or purely as relaxation; indeed, indulgence for the sake of fun, or art, or attention, is among femininity's great joys. But the chief attraction (and the central paradox, as well) is the competitive edge that femininity seems to promise in the unending struggle to survive, and perhaps to triumph. The world smiles favorably on the feminine woman: it extends little courtesies and minor privilege. Yet the nature of this competitive edge is ironic, at best, for one works at femininity by accepting restrictions, by limiting one's sights, by choosing an indirect route, by scattering concentration and not giving one's all as a man would to his own, certifiably masculine, interests. It does not require a great leap of imagination for a woman to understand the feminine principle as a grand collection of compromises, large and small, that she simply must make in order to render herself a successful woman. If she has difficulty in satisfying femininity's demands, if its illusions go against her grain, or if she is criticized for her shortcomings and imperfections, the more she will see femininity as a desperate strategy of appeasement, a strategy she may not have the wish or the courage to abandon, for failure looms in either direction.

Brownmiller is addressing the same basic issue as the previous writer: the potential effect of being a woman on success in life. Brownmiller knows that her readers will be both men and women. Yet there seems to be a subtle difference in the way she addresses readers who are men compared with readers who are women. For one thing, she is writing as a woman, and in doing so, she refers to experiences that only women readers will be able to relate to. For example, she describes the "enormous pleasure" of "feminine pursuits." Although she always uses the third person and never speaks of women as "we," these references to the female experience might help create a bond between her and women readers that cannot exist with male readers because women readers will be able to share these experiences with her. But she makes these references without referring to men in a way that might alienate them (as the previous writer seems to do). No doubt Brownmiller understands that men and women might react differently to her argument, but she takes advantage of those different reactions in presenting her argument—assuming, it seems, that women will know what she is talking about and perhaps inviting men to try to understand the experience of femininity that she is describing.

Considering Age

Look again at the passage written by Susan Brownmiller and imagine that she is writing for an audience composed mostly of older readers—for example, the readers of *AARP The Magazine,* published by the American Association of Retired Persons. She might wish to handle the issue of femininity somewhat differently, because many of those readers would probably experience gender in different ways than younger readers would. (See Figure 2-3.) In this sense the age of an intended audience can influence how a writer makes an argument.

In some cases an argument is intended for readers of a specific age, and the writer's language, strategies, and even topics will be shaped accordingly. An argument in favor of a particular kind of retirement fund might play well with readers of *AARP The Magazine,* but it wouldn't appear in *Seventeen* magazine or in a flyer from a college career development service. Consider how writer Shari Lifland takes the age of her audience into account in the following excerpt from an essay titled "Old People Need 'Friends,' Too: Using Social Media," which appeared on the website of the American Society of Mechanical Engineers (ASME):

□ wrinkled?
□ wonderful?

Will society ever accept old can be beautiful?

Image courtesy of The Advertising Archives

FIGURE 2-3

This image originally appeared as part of an advertising campaign by Dove that was designed to challenge conventional representations of how women appear in advertisements for products such as shampoo. Note how this woman does not regret being "old" and is beautiful in her own way.

When I recently set up my new Facebook account, it didn't take long—only about 10 minutes—before my cell phone rang. It was my son Logan, a college freshman, and he wasn't pleased. "What are you doing on Facebook?" he scowled. "Are you doing it just to stay close to me?" (Heaven forbid!)

"No," I patiently explained. "I'm doing it for business networking purposes. It has absolutely nothing to do with you. If you don't want to accept me as an online friend, that's fine."

My response seemed to satisfy him, but an hour later I found the following posted on my Facebook "wall": "Why do all these old people have Facebooks?" My response, which I posted on his wall: "Old people need friends, too."

For those of you who don't know about Facebook, it is, according to the website's fact sheet, "a social utility that helps people communicate more efficiently with their friends, family and coworkers." Founded in 2004, it is the #1 social networking site in the world and the fourth most-trafficked website in the world.

Those of you who *do* know about Facebook, perhaps through your teenage children, may view it as a secret online society that no one over 21 can infiltrate. Yet here's the truth: more than half of Facebook's 90 million active users are older than college age and its fastest growing demographic is people 25 years and older. When I set up my Facebook account, my son and teenage nieces became part of my network—but so did many of the working adults I know, in my own workplace and others. People from my current and former home town reached out to me, along with coworkers, professional colleagues, and former classmates.

In making her argument that older professionals (such as those who belong to ASME) should take advantage of new social media in their businesses, Lifland does not assume that her readers are familiar with social media like *Facebook*. Instead, she assumes that many of them associate such media with young people, and she uses that assumption to help make her argument that these media can be useful for people of *all* ages. Notice that she introduces her topic with an anecdote about her son with which many older readers are likely to identify. In this way, she tries to connect with her readers on the basis of age. To appreciate her strategy, imagine how much younger, tech-savvy readers—for example, readers of *Wired* magazine—might react to her opening paragraphs.

In short, age matters, and sometimes the rhetorical situation requires the writer to account for age in very specific ways that shape his or her argument.

Considering Sexual Orientation

To turn to another kind of cultural context, consider the implications of the simple question "Do you have a family?" In the United States, when one adult asks another whether he or she has a family, the question usually means "Are you married with children?" So how is a single gay man to respond? He might cut the conversation short by interpreting it to be a query about marriage and children and simply respond, "No." Or he might take the question literally (or subversively) by saying, "Yes, I have two brothers and several nieces."

What might happen, then, if you use an expression such as "family values" or "our children" in an argument? Strictly speaking, no one is excluded from these words on the basis of sexual orientation. Anyone can create a family, and increasing numbers of same-gender couples are adopting children. Nevertheless, someone who is gay, lesbian, bisexual, or transgendered might associate expressions such as "family values" and "our children" with a heterosexual majority to which he or she does not belong. The phrase "family values" is especially problematic because it has often been used in rhetoric designed to limit the rights of minorities—as in the campaign against state laws allowing same-sex marriage.

If it can be problematic for writers to assume that all members of their audience are heterosexual, it can be challenging to write about sexual orientation. Words such as *gay* and *queer* are emotionally charged, and occasions for stereotyping abound. For example, a reference to the "gay community" implies that all gay individuals (regardless of religion, race, or social class) socialize together. It might not be clear whether the "gay community" includes women, because there are women who describe themselves as gay and others who insist on the use of *lesbian* on the grounds that *gay* was taken over by men. Thus, it may be more appropriate to write about "gay and lesbian communities" rather than placing so many different people into a single group about which a generalization is going to be made.

In the introduction to *A Queer Geography,* Frank Browning writes,

> As an American, as a white man, as a creature of the late twentieth century, as a male who grew up when the *New York Times, Time, Life, Newsweek,* and all of television and radio regarded homosexuality as either criminal or diseased, I am incapable of experiencing my desires as either a young Neapolitan in Italy or a Sambia tribesman in New Guinea—two places where homosexuality has a rich and ancient history and few make much effort to disguise. The strategies of social and psychological survival I have employed set me apart radically from middle-class Brazilians or Filipinos and even from most of the young men I write about in this book.

In other words, Browning sees his cultural context as being defined by nationality (American), race (white), gender (male), and age (being no longer young in the late twentieth century) in addition to sexual orientation (homosexual). As Browning suggests, sexual orientation is an element of culture that does not exist separately from other aspects of cultural context. For writers of argument, it can thus be risky to assume that anyone could be either completely defined by sexual orientation or completely understood without some consideration of it.

Historical Context

The earlier example of Harvey Araton's essay about Qureshi, the Pakistani tennis player (see pages 24–25), points to another crucial kind of context for argumentation: the moment at which an argument is being made. Araton's essay might have had a certain effect because it was published in the midst of intense, terrible fighting between Israelis and Palestinians in the Middle East in 2002. It was also published during the Wimbledon tennis championship, the world's most prestigious tennis tournament. If Araton had written his essay a year earlier (assuming that Qureshi and Hadad were playing as doubles partners at that time), when the conflict in the Middle East was not as intense and when international attention was not focused on that part of the world, his argument might have been less provocative or persuasive for many readers. It might even have had an entirely different significance. Araton's main argument, which focused on achieving a peaceful solution to a long-standing and bloody conflict, was really not about tennis, but he used the decision by Qureshi and his tennis partner Hadad—and the controversy surrounding their decision—to give his argument a timeliness and force it might not otherwise have had. In other words, *when* an argument is made can be as important as *how* it is made.

The ancient Greek rhetoricians used the term *kairos* to describe an opportune moment for making a specific argument or trying to persuade an audience to act in a specific situation. We might think of *kairos* as making the right argument at the right time. Araton's essay is a good example of an author taking advantage of a particular moment to make an argument. Historical context, then, can refer to understanding when to make a particular argument and how to take that moment into account in constructing an argument. A particular appeal might be persuasive at one time but not at another. Circumstances change, and that change can affect what a writer chooses to write in an argument, as well as how readers respond to that argument. After the horrible events of September 11, 2001, for example, many people thought that certain kinds of statements and criticisms were inappropriate. Comedians refrained from skewering politicians, especially President George W. Bush; editorialists and political commentators did likewise. In such a climate, arguments that relied on criticisms of the President would widely be considered not only ineffective but also inappropriate and even disrespectful. Indeed, filmmaker and political essayist Michael Moore found himself in this situation when his publisher hesitated to release Moore's book *Stupid White Men* after the events of September 11. Given the sudden change in the American political climate as a result of September 11, the publisher asked Moore to rewrite the book, which was a humorous but irreverent attack on the Bush presidency. In effect, Moore was asked to change his argument about the Bush administration because the times had changed. Although Moore refused to do so, it took many months before his book was made available for sale to the public. Three years later, however, Moore was able to release *Fahrenheit 9/11*, a widely distributed film highly critical of President Bush and the policies that led to the invasion of Iraq. The context had changed. The sense of national unity felt immediately after the terrorist attacks of September 11 had given way to increasing controversy as the 2004 presidential election approached. Moore's experience is a dramatic but revealing example of how events can profoundly affect what audiences will accept as appropriate in argumentation.

Historical context encompasses more than just making the right argument at the right time. The time in which an argument is made can profoundly affect not only how an audience reacts to it but also its meaning and import (see sidebar "Argument in Historical Context"). Think of the connotations of the phrase "support our troops," which became common during the wars in Iraq and Afghanistan after September 11, 2001. In times of peace, these words may enjoy wide appeal. In time of war, however, these same words can inspire significantly different responses. For example, some people might interpret the phrase as a simple belief that American troops should be well equipped and receive reassuring messages from home; on the other hand, critics of these wars may interpret the phrase as code for "support the political decisions that sent

ARGUMENT IN HISTORICAL CONTEXT

The opening paragraph of the Declaration of Independence introduces one of the most famous arguments ever written:

> When in the Course of human events, it becomes necessary for one people to dissolve the political bands which have connected them with another, and to assume among the powers of the earth, the separate and equal station to which the Laws of Nature and Nature's God entitle them, a decent respect to the opinions of mankind requires that they should declare the causes which impel them to the separation.

These well-known words are general, although we know that they refer to a specific situation and to specific events that occurred in 1776 and before. But some of the abstract ideas in this passage carried different meanings in 1776 than they do today. For example, the idea of a colony or state separating from a monarchy such as ruled Great Britain at that time was radical and even unthinkable to many people. Today, such a notion does not seem so radical. The most famous lines from the Declaration of Independence make an argument that most Americans probably accept as universal but which Thomas Jefferson, author of the Declaration, knew to be extremely radical in his day:

> We hold these truths to be self-evident, that all men are created equal, that they are endowed by their Creator with certain unalienable Rights, that among these are Life, Liberty and the pursuit of Happiness.

Such "truths" were not widely considered "self-evident," as Jefferson surely knew, which gave his argument a kind of shock value it would not have today. Perhaps an even more revealing illustration of how the historical context can affect the meaning of an assertion is contained in the famous statement that "all men are created equal." Today such a statement might carry a sexist message that it would not have had for readers in 1776. Indeed, today this statement might be interpreted as a negative one because of what we now consider to be sexist language.

the troops into battle." Writers should be mindful of these nuances when constructing their arguments.

Even in cases that are not quite as dramatic as these, historical context is part of any argument and affects how that argument works and what it means. Good writers attend to historical context, and careful readers are attuned to it.

In composing an argument, you can never address every possible contextual factor. But you will always be making your argument about a specific issue at a specific moment in a specific rhetorical situation. The more carefully you consider those factors, the more effective your argument is likely to be.

3

The Media for Argument

Alex Wong/Getty Images for Meet the Press

David Brooks from PBS
NewsHour

David Brooks is a well-known commentator who is a regular guest on television shows devoted to political affairs as well as on National Public Radio's *All Things Considered* news program. Brooks also writes a syndicated column for newspapers. His arguments about political and social issues are moderately conservative; his basic message regarding the limits of government in American social and economic life is constant. But do his arguments change in any way when he is making them on a political affairs television show or a radio news program as compared to his columns or essays? Here is a passage from a column Brooks wrote in 2009 about President Barack Obama's style of governing:

> The advantage of the Obama governing style is that his argument-based organization is a learning organization. Amid the torrent of memos and evidence and dispute, the Obama administration is able to adjust and respond more quickly than, say, the Bush administration ever did.
>
> The disadvantage is the tendency to bureaucratize the war. Armed conflict is about morale, motivation, honor, fear and breaking the enemy's will. The danger is that Obama's

analytic mode will neglect the intangibles that are the essence of the fight. It will fail to inspire and comfort. Soldiers and Marines don't have the luxury of adopting President Obama's calibrated stance since they are being asked to potentially sacrifice everything.

Brooks's essay is a careful analysis of President Obama's style of political leadership and a tightly reasoned argument that Obama's analytical approach is good for the United States. Even in this short passage, you can see that both Brooks's reasoning and his writing style are sophisticated. Do you think Brooks would use the same kind of language and carefully crafted sentences to make this point if he were speaking on a television or radio news show? Would he structure his argument differently if he were writing on a blog? In other words, what role does the medium play in his arguments—or anyone's arguments?

In this chapter, we examine the role of the medium in argumentation. As you will see, many elements of argumentation, such as addressing an audience appropriately and using evidence effectively, apply to all media. But although print remains an important medium for making arguments, other media, including digital media such as blogs, Twitter, and Internet discussion groups, have become increasingly significant as forums for public discourse. To argue effectively in these media requires an understanding of how a specific medium might influence or change the way you construct and present an argument.

Analyzing Arguments in Print

We live in a culture defined by print—so much so that we take it for granted. We tend to see print as a natural medium for literacy and for communication. But print isn't natural. It is a technology—or rather, it is a set of technologies that transform human speech into visual form. These technologies have evolved—from the printing press in the fifteenth century, to the typewriter in the nineteenth, to word-processing programs in the twentieth, to the digital media we now use for texting and blogging. Nevertheless, print continues to permeate our lives.

In this section, we examine how arguments tend to be made in print so that you can become a more careful reader of written arguments and apply the lessons of argument in print to the other media that have now become important contexts for argumentation.

Reading Arguments Critically in Print Form

Reading is not a passive activity. When you read a newspaper editorial, for example, you are not simply trying to understand the writer's point. You are also engaged in a sophisticated intellectual and social activity in which you analyze, evaluate, and react to the argument. The more carefully you do so, the more substantive will be your engagement with the argument and the better your understanding of the issue at hand. Ideally, reading an argument should be as careful and sophisticated an act as writing an argument. The more you know about the strategies writers use in constructing their arguments, the better able you will be to analyze and evaluate those arguments (see Chapter 4).

Print is often considered the traditional medium for formal argument (even though formal arguments have always been made orally as well, for example, in a courtroom, government hearing, or political rally). And print can influence arguments in other media.

For example, arguments delivered as speeches are usually written out first; similarly, radio or television essays are crafted in written form first. But print is not a monolithic medium for arguments. There are countless varieties of print forums within which people can argue:

- magazines and newspapers of all kinds
- flyers and circulars
- memos, letters, and pamphlets
- financial reports
- essays written for college classes
- books

Reading an argument critically means looking carefully at the way a writer tries to address a specific audience for a specific publication. It means being aware of how your perspective, beliefs, and values might influence your reaction to particular arguments. It requires you to take into account the specific forum in which that argument appears, because different forums lend themselves to different kinds of arguments. For example, an editorial in the conservative business newspaper the *Wall Street Journal* will usually differ in tone, style, and content from an essay in the left-leaning magazine *Mother Jones.* Each of these publications has a different purpose and addresses a somewhat different audience. To understand an argument published in each of these print forums, you must have some sense of those differences.

Let's look at arguments in two very different publications to see how the nature of the publication affects the way each writer approaches his argument. The first example is taken from an essay in *USA Today* by its founder and publisher Al Neuharth. In the opening paragraphs of his essay, Neuharth introduces the issue of the early starting dates for the school year:

"Back to School." The three most wonderful words for the ears of most parents.

This year, more classrooms in grades K–12 are opening sooner than ever. August has become back-to-school month. Some will open as early as next week. Many on August 12. Most by August 19.

The audience for *USA Today* is a general one, and Neuharth knows that. The style of writing on the Opinion page of *USA Today,* where this essay appeared, tends to be somewhat informal, and the topics tend to be current events. Notice that although Neuharth implicitly addresses the broad audience of all readers of his newspaper, he also narrows the audience somewhat by referring to parents of school-age children. By attempting to establish this connection with a specific audience, Neuharth may strengthen his argument with those many readers who share his experience of preparing children for school in August. As a reader, you may want to evaluate the extent to which sharing that experience affects your own response to his argument, which rests on the assumption, as he writes, that "most kids get a little bored with fun and games by August." While that may be true—and it may resonate with parents who must deal with their own bored children—it may not address more complex implications associated with starting school earlier in August. For example, businesspeople who rely on summer tourism for their livelihood might point out that income would be lost as a result of families not vacationing in August; for such readers, Neuharth's appeal may ring hollow. However, given the nature of *USA Today's* Opinion page and its broad audience, Neuharth probably doesn't need to address such specific aspects of the issue. In short, his general argument—and his strategy of trying to establish a connection with his readers as parents—is appropriate for this publication.

Compare Neuharth's approach to the following essay from *Climbing* magazine, in which editor Duane Raleigh addresses a very specialized topic for a much narrower audience:

> You've seen the ads in this magazine and you've visited the websites. Euro dot.coms selling top-brand merchandise for as much as half what you'd pay for the same gear at your local shop. High-end shoes for $60, ropes for $70, ice tools for less than retailers pay at wholesale. Crazy! These are the prices I used to pay for much, much lower-tech gear back in the 1970s. Something screwy must be going on—what's the catch?
>
> The catch is not simple, and takes a tangled, often convoluted and contradictory path. Mostly, foreign dot.coms, because they typically buy directly from the manufacturer (usually also European) and sell directly to you, bypass the usual distribution (the importers here in the U.S.) and sales channels (your retail climbing shops). Cutting out these two channels eliminates two U.S.-based markups, which largely explains why their prices are so low.

In this instance, Raleigh's audience is obviously composed of people who climb and would therefore be interested in the prices of climbing gear. His magazine has a very narrow focus on climbing-related issues, which would perhaps seem esoteric to a more general audience. If you are not a climber, Raleigh's appeal may not have much impact on you—and indeed, if you are not a climber, he may not care, since it is unlikely that you buy climbing gear or are concerned about the effect of Internet sales on American climbing retailers. Moreover, nonclimbers would probably not understand the importance of the prices Raleigh quotes in his first paragraph. (In 2002, when this essay was published, climbing shoes typically sold in the United States for between $100 and $160, ropes for $120 to $180; you need to know this to understand his argument.)

Raleigh's argument is shaped by the nature of the magazine he writes for in other ways. For one thing, his conversational writing style is typical of *Climbing* magazine. An assertion like "Crazy!" fits here, whereas it might be inappropriate for other publications. In addition, Raleigh refers to the 1970s in a way that establishes his authority as someone who understands the markets for climbing gear as a result of his many years of experience as a climber. That strategy is likely to be persuasive to his readers, since climbers often associate credibility with climbing experience. In these ways, Raleigh's argument is very specifically tuned to his magazine.

In these examples, the writers tailor their strategies to the audiences that read the publications in which their arguments are published. In a sense, they write in a way that assumes a community of readers, defined by the specific publication as a medium. But writers can also intentionally provoke an audience in making their argument. For example, a person who is opposed to teaching evolution in schools and is responding to an editorial in favor of teaching evolution might intentionally criticize advocates of evolution on moral grounds, knowing that such readers would object to such a criticism. Those readers would very likely not be persuaded by an anti-evolution argument in any case. So the writer's criticisms would play well with supporters of his or her stance. Such a strategy is common in some kinds of publications, such as letters to newspaper editors, but it may be inappropriate for others, especially for academic papers of the kind you are assigned in your college courses.

In reading an argument critically, you should try to account for these strategies and be aware of how an argument can be shaped by the specific print publication it is written for. Some teachers may advise you always to read skeptically, and that can be good advice, because it can help you guard against subtle but powerful appeals that may shape your reaction to an argument. The reading selections provided in Chapters 8–13 come from many kinds of publications—ranging from popular magazines to academic journals. When you read them, consider how the nature of different print forums influences the nature of the argument.

Analyzing Arguments in Visual Media

Images have power. Think about the impact of the image of an American flag, for example (see Figure 3-1). It is no coincidence that in the months following the terrible events of September 11, 2001, the American flag and the colors red, white, and blue began to appear everywhere: in television and print advertisements, on flyers and posters, on book and magazine covers, on the windows of cars and trucks. Because of its deep associations with patriotism, the flag could be used effectively to send various messages, as in Figure 3-1.

We take for granted that images are used in this way. Living in an age of multimedia communications, we are surrounded by images on television, in print, and on the World Wide Web; on signs and billboards; on flyers and pamphlets; from the logos on race cars to the Nike swoosh on the uniforms of professional and amateur athletes. Not only advertisers, but also politicians, advocates for all kinds of causes, institutions like schools and hospitals, and even individuals all use visual elements to communicate an idea or position and to influence a particular audience. They all use *visual rhetoric* to make arguments. And although images have always had power, they have become increasingly powerful as more people are exposed to them on a regular basis in this digital age.

Photographs as Argument

To appreciate the power of images to convey ideas, look at the photograph of President George W. Bush in Figure 3-3, which appeared in magazines and newspapers in August 2002, when the President was trying to generate support for his proposed new Department of Homeland Security. This photo was taken by an Associated Press photographer, but it was almost certainly set up by the President's staff, who would have determined where photographers could stand during the news conference; in that way, they set the angle from which photographs of the President could be taken. Those photographs would thus produce a desired effect: to show the President dramatically in front of the famous faces of past American presidents carved into Mount Rushmore.

What does such a photograph communicate about President Bush? How might it have influenced readers' opinions about him and about his proposal for a Department of Homeland Security? In answering those questions, consider the cultural significance of the Mount Rushmore national monument to Americans. It not only invokes the idea of patriotism for many Americans but also suggests greatness with its gigantic figures of four revered American presidents. The photograph associates President Bush—and, by extension, his proposal—with those ideas of patriotism and greatness. Now consider how

http://www.sunsetauction.com/PatrioticStuff.html

We will never forget

FIGURE 3-1 AND FIGURE 3-2

Using Images to Send a Message

Both these images rely on the American flag to convey their messages, but each uses the flag in a different way. The first image shows a poster. The second shows the cover of a book about American foreign policy. Consider how the familiar image of the flag helps send a very different message in each case.

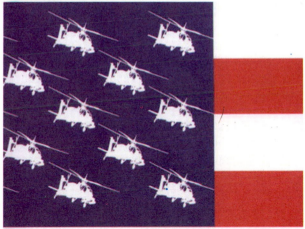

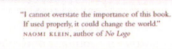

"I cannot overstate the importance of this book. If used properly, it could change the world."
NAOMI KLEIN, author of *No Logo*

THE AMERICAN EMPIRE AND THE FOURTH WORLD

ANTHONY J. HALL

Montreal: McGill-Queen's University Press, 2003.

Ken Lambert/AP Wide World Photos

FIGURE 3-3

Photograph of President George W. Bush at Mount Rushmore

What does this photograph communicate about President Bush? What argument does it seem to make?

different the impact of a photograph of the President might be if the background at his press conference had been a wall at an airport or a dark blue curtain in a hotel conference room rather than the deeply symbolic stone visages of Mount Rushmore.

Obviously, the setting in which President Bush was photographed (the Mount Rushmore national monument) is an essential component of this image and its message. But consider as well how the historical context can shape the message of an image. When it was first published in 2002, not too long after the terrorist attacks of September 11, 2001, this photograph might have conveyed a powerful positive message about President Bush's leadership at a time of national crisis. What message might it convey today, many years later, when the impact of the terrorist attacks is not so fresh? Is its meaning changed by the fact that George W. Bush is no longer the president? These questions underscore how an image can derive its meaning and impact depending upon when it is viewed.

Figures 3-4 and 3-5 provide additional examples of how context influences the meaning of an image. Figure 3-4 is a famous photograph, taken in 1936 by Dorothea Lange, a photographer commissioned by the U.S. government to document the effects of the Great Depression on the rural poor. Lange took the photo in a camp for migrant farm workers in California. Consider how your own reaction to the photo might be influenced by that historical context. The photo seems intended to evoke our compassion (see the discussion of pathos in Chapter 4, pages 73–78), but is your emotional response to it changed by the knowledge that it was taken in a camp for poverty-stricken Americans whose lives were disrupted by the Great Depression? Given that historical context, we might interpret this photo as an argument to assert (see pages 8–9): The image can be seen as asserting that the American economy was having a devastating impact on a family whose mother remained central to holding the family together. Or we might read the photo as an argument to negotiate differences (see pages 14–17), in which case the image

United States Postal Service

FIGURE 3-5

"Migrant Mother" Postage Stamp

Courtesy of the Dorothea Lange Collection, Oakland Museum of California

FIGURE 3-4

"Migrant Mother"

By Dorothea Lange.

could be seen as arguing for providing government relief to families who were displaced by the Depression.

But what happens when the context of such an image changes? In 1998, Lange's photograph was used on a U.S. postage stamp (see Figure 3-5). Does this format change the way you react to or interpret this image? Is its emotional impact weakened because it is now on a postage stamp? Does the caption on the stamp ("America Survives the Depression") change the image's meaning or the argument it might be making? And what if you knew that one of the people shown in the photograph disapproved of its use on the postage stamp? Would that change its meaning in any way? In 1998, Katherine McIntosh, the woman who was once the little girl hiding behind the mother's right shoulder in the photo, testified that she was about five years old when Lange snapped her famous photograph and that the image was an accurate portrayal of her mother's strength. But she said,

Last September the U.S. Post Office issued a stamp with the picture on it. But they did not even invite us to the launching. In October a copy of the picture with Lange's writing on it was sold at Sotheby's in New York for $244,500. What upsets us is that people are making money out of our mother's pain. But we are proud that she has become a part of history. (From An Interview of Katherine McIntosh by Peter Lennon Published In *The Guardian*, a well-respected British newspaper)

PHOTOGRAPHY AS ARGUMENT

This photograph was taken in 2002 several months after U.S. armed forces defeated the Taliban, a group that had previously imposed a strict Islamic government on Afghanistan. What argument do you think this photograph makes? In answering that question, consider the contrast between the traditional dress of the girls in the photograph, which is intended to hide a woman's physical appearance, and the Western beauty items on the shelf, which are intended to enhance physical beauty. Consider, too, the uncovered face of the girl, placed at the center of the photo, just in front of her companion, whose face remains obscured by the traditional dress. How do these elements help make a statement?

Tyler Hicks/The New York Times

Kabul, Afghanistan. September 13, 2002. Manizha, 13 (center), and Mina, 16, in front of an array of beauty products that were not openly available under Taliban rule.

Lange's well-known photograph helps illustrate the important role of context in the impact of an image and the argument it might be used to make. (See "Photography as Argument" on this page for another example of how context can shape the meaning of a photograph.)

Advertisements as Argument

Print and video advertisements use images to promote products or services, announce events, and advocate certain behaviors. A close look at advertising can help us appreciate the power of images to convey a point or influence our thinking and behavior, and help us understand the subtlety and complexity of visual elements in argument. Figures 3-6 and 3-7 illustrate two important considerations in visual rhetoric: the role of **design** and **the interaction between written text and imagery**.

First, consider the design of the ads shown in Figures 3-6 and 3-7. Both ads illustrate the roles of **color** and **arrangement** in the design of advertisement. The colors in each case were selected to achieve a specific effect on an audience. For example, both ads use red, white, and blue, but in Figure 3-7 the colors are clearly those of the American flag (in addition to being the colors of the Tommy Hilfiger logo), which has a special significance, especially to an American audience. In Figure 3-6 the background color blue suggests the sky, which is both pleasant and consistent with the ad's message. Also, both ads are characterized by careful arrangement of visual elements and text. In Figure 3-6, the container of cream cheese is shown slightly above the center of the advertisement and appears to be lifted up or supported by a feather. This arrangement reinforces the idea that the cream cheese is light; it also gives prominence to the product in a way that attracts your eye to it. Similarly, the arrangement of visual elements in the ad in Figure 3-7 emphasizes the product—in this case, a bottle of "tommy girl" cologne. Although the bottle is placed toward the bottom of the advertisement, it occupies the foreground in a way that makes it appear tall. Moreover, the red stripes of the flag in the background are slightly out of focus, which draws a viewer's eye to the in-focus cologne bottle, making it appear even more prominent. In these ways, both ads use design elements carefully to achieve specific effects.

ARGUMENT VS. PERSUASION IN ADVERTISING

Like any argument, visual elements used in advertising can appeal to our emotions (*pathos*), make logical arguments (*logos*), or address character (*ethos*). However, it is important to distinguish between argument and persuasion. We can describe an advertisement like the "tommy girl" ad in Figure 3-7 as an argument (for example, in favor of using cologne, or in support of a certain kind of lifestyle, or even to assert that cologne is an important part of who you are), but the primary purpose of such ads is to persuade you to purchase a product. Genuine argumentation, by contrast, seeks to clarify thought in an effort to address an issue or solve a problem; ideally, it aspires to truth. Persuasion of the kind generally used in advertising has no such goal. The appeal to patriotism in advertising like the "tommy girl" ad is intended to persuade you to buy that company's products; if that appeal is successful, it is not likely to have been the result of careful, critical evaluation on your part, but rather on the strength of your emotional response to that patriotic appeal.

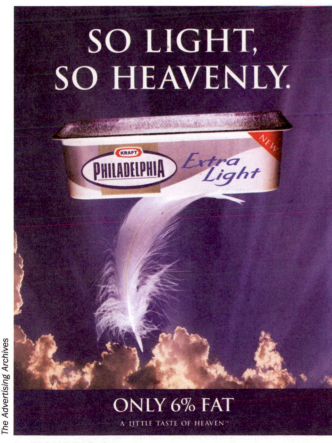

The Advertising Archives

▌ FIGURE 3-6

▌ FIGURE 3-7

Second, both ads use carefully chosen language in combination with the visual elements. In Figure 3-6, the word "light" clearly relates to the images of the feather and the clouds, and "heavenly" is connected to the image of the clouds as well; the images and words thus reinforce each other. Note, however, that the ad relies on several meanings of each word. "Light" means "not heavy" (referring to the physical weight of an object) but it also means "low in calories." Similarly, "heavenly" relates to the religious idea of heaven, but is also used in an informal way to mean "delicious," as reinforced by the tagline at the bottom of the ad ("a little taste of heaven"). Notice, too, that the images of the clouds and the feather together with the word "light" implicitly remind a viewer of the cliché about something being "light as a feather." The combination of text and image helps convey the message that Philadelphia Extra Light cream cheese is a good product to buy not only because it is delicious but also because it is good for you (in the sense of being a low-calorie food).

In a similar way, the ad in Figure 3-7 uses familiar language and images to convey the idea that using tommy girl cologne is an expression of independence, an idea that would likely resonate with many Americans. The tagline ("a declaration of independence") obviously evokes the famous Declaration of Independence, an association that is reinforced by the colors of the American flag. The text at the bottom of the ad reads, "introducing tommy girl—the new fragrance for women from the American designer Tommy Hilfiger. tommy girl is refreshing, energetic, spirited, and designed for today's woman." These adjectives, which differ from words like *romantic, sensual,* or *sexy* that often appear in perfume ads, support the claim that women purchasing this product are making "a declaration of independence." Advertisements often make patriotic appeals in this way—appeals that suggest that buying a product (or supporting a political policy) is good for our country (see also Figure 3-1).

Both these ads reveal how complex an advertisement can be in trying to persuade its intended audience. Being aware of how these various elements can be used in visual communication can help you read advertisements more critically and understand—and perhaps even resist—their attempts to persuade you. Moreover, authors who understand these design principles can

MANIPULATING AN IMAGE TO MAKE A POINT

This ad by a group called Adbusters (http://adbusters.org) makes a statement by altering an image from an advertisement for a popular vodka. The ad uses the same layout and color scheme as the original ad, the same image of the vodka bottle, and even the name of the vodka itself. But here the image of a sagging bottle and the advertising tag line ("Absolut impotence"), which parodies the original tag line, create an association between vodka and sexual dysfunction. Consider how effectively this ad employs visual elements to make its argument. Would a print advertisement explaining the connection between alcohol and impotence work in the same way?

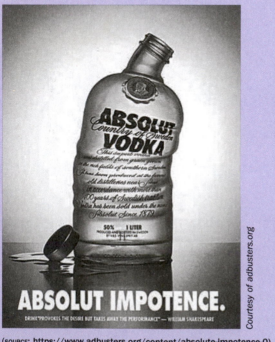

Courtesy of adbusters.org

(SOURCE: https://www.adbusters.org/content/absolute-impotence-0)

employ them to enhance the effectiveness of their own arguments.

Art as Argument

You might not associate art with argument, but the design principles discussed in the previous sections apply to paintings and other kinds of art. You can think of any painting as an argument for the artist's vision. Consider, for example, the painting shown in Figure 3-8 by Francisco José de Goya, one of the great European painters of the nineteenth century. Completed in 1814, the painting, which Goya titled *The Third of May, 1808*, depicts the execution of Spanish citizens by French troops, which were occupying Spain. On May 2, 1808, Spaniards in Madrid rebelled against the occupying French troops after the French announced that they planned to take the Spanish royal family to France. There was fierce fighting in Madrid. On the following day, French troops sought revenge, and Goya's painting dramatically conveys the horror of the French reprisals. Note how Goya uses color to help convey his perspective on the scene. Most of the painting is dark, symbolizing the darkness of the event. Bright color is reserved for the man who is about to be shot. He is wearing a white shirt, which implies purity, and gold trousers, a warm color that contributes to the sense that he is someone worthy of sympathy. Light has positive connotations, especially when surrounded by darkness. So the man in white and gold is shown in the light created by the white and yellow lantern.

Goya uses other design elements to direct attention to this man. The man's arms are raised in what could be seen as either a gesture of surrender or an embrace that encompasses the soldiers. The guns are not only aimed at him; they also direct the viewers' eyes to him. Furthermore, the man in the white shirt is one of the few figures with eyes you can see. (The other two are also victims.) The expression in his eyes seems tender

USING ICONS TO MAKE AN ARGUMENT

This poster, which appeared after the scandal at the Abu Graib prison in Iraq was made public in 2004, relies on a familiar corporate logo to help convey its message. In the poster, Iraq is presented as iRaq, mimicking the iPod logo. The familiar apple icon associated with iPod has been changed to a bomb, yet the bright pink background ironically suggests pop art of the kind often used in iPod advertisements. The creators of this poster have carefully brought together different forms of visual rhetoric to make a powerful antiwar statement. How would you interpret that statement? Critic Sarah Boxer points out that several iconic images combine to make the poster an instantly recognizable statement against the war in Iraq: "The triangle of the hood suggests Christ on the cross.... As a symbolic shape, the hood is almost as strong as a cross. The difference is that the hood has generally been the sign of the persecutor, not of the victim. It is the uniform of the executioner, the sheet of the Klansman, the mask of Death. Until now. In these images, you can see the hood's meaning begin to change and take root."

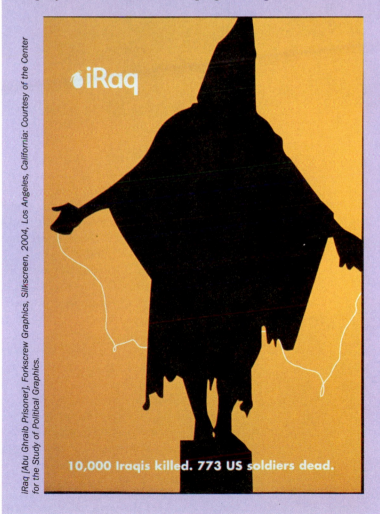

iRaq [Abu Ghraib Prisoner], Forkscrew Graphics, Silkscreen, 2004, Los Angeles, California: Courtesy of the Center for the Study of Political Graphics.

FIGURE 3-8

Painting as Subversive Argument

Francisco José de Goya's famous painting, *The Third of May, 1808,* which depicts the execution of Spanish citizens by French soldiers, might be seen as an argument against government oppression.

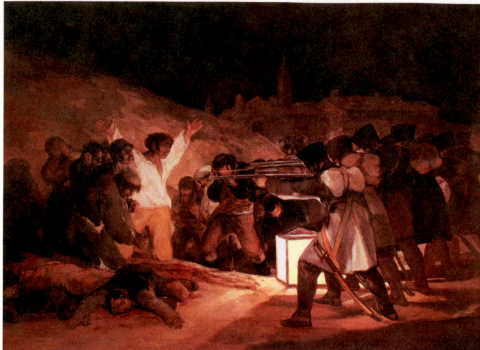

Archivo Icongrafico, S.A./Corbis

rather than fierce, contributing to the sympathy Goya creates for him. Significantly, you cannot see the eyes of any of the French soldiers; they are presented as part of a faceless mass.

What claim does Goya's painting make? Interpretations vary. But the painting seems to convey sympathy for the victim. Some critics interpret it as a stark statement about the brutality of war and the injustice of government power. It might also suggest that governments do wicked things under the cover of night, or perhaps that the repression of a people cannot last forever.

Sometimes art is enlisted directly in an effort to persuade or to put forth a particular position on an issue. During World War II, for example, the U.S. government used paintings and sketches to encourage enlistment in the armed forces, sell war bonds, publicize efforts to conserve items such as gasoline and butter, and generally exhort citizens to support the war effort. You might think of these images in the same way that you think of contemporary print or television advertisements: as propaganda whose purpose was to persuade rather than to engage viewers in serious argumentation. However, if you understand World War II as a moral endeavor to combat the evils of totalitarianism and ethnic extermination, then you might view these posters as part of a larger attempt to engage U.S. citizens in a collective effort to oppose evil. From such a perspective, individual posters can be seen as making an argument for a particular kind of activity associated with the war effort. Each poster might be posing a version of the question, "Won't this particular activity help in the war effort?"

For example, the message in the poster in Figure 3-9 seems clear: Buy war bonds to help the U.S. airmen. In a sense the claim made in this poster is that war bonds will help the war effort by keeping U.S. airmen flying; the warrant, or fundamental assumption

PAINTING AN ENVIRONMENTAL ARGUMENT

The landscape paintings of the famous Hudson Valley School in the nineteenth century are sometimes described as making a case for environmental conservation. They presented an idealized version of nature as beautiful and sublime, worthy of admiration and protection, at a time when many people were concerned about the destructive effects of industrialization. Consider what claim Thomas Cole might be making in this painting of a well-known mountain along the Hudson River. How does his depiction of Storm King Mountain make a case for a particular view of nature?

© Ball State University Museum of Art, Muncie, Indiana. Used with permission. Frank C. Ball Collection, gift of the Ball Brothers Foundation.

Thomas Cole, *Storm King of the Hudson*, circa 1825–1827.

on which a statement of belief can be made (see pages 87–91), is that sustaining the war effort is desirable. The image of the airman in the poster, with his eyes looking skyward, his hands holding his combat equipment, a determined expression on his face, is noble and inspiring. The phrase at the top of the poster seems to be a statement this airman would make, and the large, bright words at the bottom of the poster drive the argument home. But notice that this airman is African American. At a point in history (the 1940s) before the civil rights movement and before the landmark U.S. Supreme Court rulings that helped guarantee rights to African Americans, this image would have struck many citizens as unusual and even disturbing, because this airman was fighting for a country that did not extend full rights to people of his racial background. Indeed, at that time the U.S. armed forces were still segregated. Yet the poster seems to suggest that *all* Americans are part of the war effort. And it might have spoken especially powerfully to Black Americans, whose experience of racism might have made them hesitant to support the U.S. government's efforts. The airman in this poster might suggest to those citizens that their support is needed and appropriate.

The poster in Figure 3-10 can also be seen as presenting an argument rather than simply trying to persuade. This poster was used in General Motors automobile factories in 1942, when that company was producing vehicles for the war effort. However, even during the war, companies and workers faced many of the same challenges that they face in peacetime, and labor relations were always a potentially difficult matter. Strikes by auto workers in the 1930s had a serious economic and social impact on the country. But a labor conflict—especially a strike—during war time could have been disastrous. In such a context you might see this poster as making an argument about the need for good relations between workers and their employers. The claim might be stated as follows: Avoiding labor conflict will aid the U.S. war effort because it will enable the company to continue production of military vehicles. Again, the warrant is that aiding the war effort is desirable for all Americans.

The design of the poster is intended to present its claim effectively. The most noticeable item is the word *together*, which appears in large red letters at the top of the page. The images of the two fists—both clenched, both exuding strength, both exposed by

FIGURE 3-9 AND FIGURE 3-10

Art in Support of a War Effort

These posters were distributed by the U.S. government during World War II. Their message of support for the U.S. war effort is obvious, but what specific appeals do these posters make?

rolled-up sleeves as if to suggest getting down to work—reinforce the idea of working together. Both are identical in every respect except for the color of their shirt sleeves, which are used to reinforce their respective positions: blue for the blue-collar workers, white for management. The light yellow background not only highlights the arms by bringing them into relief but also conveys a sense of possibility: Yellow is associated with the sun, with the idea of a new day. Notice, too, that aside from that background color and the green tank and fighter aircraft, everything else on the poster is red, white, or blue, colors associated with patriotism. Every element of the design thus supports the poster's claim.

Integrating Visual Elements and Text

The examples included in this chapter reveal that combining text and visual elements can be extremely effective in argumentation. When you encounter textual arguments that incorporate visual elements, it is important to be aware of the effect that the combination of text and image can have on you as a reader or viewer. Consider, for example, the open letter in Figure 3-11, which was distributed as a newspaper advertisement by St. Lawrence Cement, a company that found itself in an environmental controversy in 2002 when it sought to build

CARTOONS AS ARGUMENT

One of the most common and effective kinds of argument employing visual elements is the political cartoon. In this cartoon the artist plays off the familiar image of a light bulb to indicate an idea or brainstorm; however, in an age when many people are concerned about global climate change and living a "carbon-neutral" lifestyle, a traditional light bulb, which some would consider energy-inefficient, might not be so appealing, as the words of the woman in the cartoon suggest. Note that the artist combines a familiar image and carefully selected words to convey a point. What argument might this cartoon be making about our collective reaction to growing worries about global warming?

a cement plant in upstate New York. The letter includes an extended written argument in which the company presents its claim that its proposed plant will not harm the environment. You might see this argument as an example of an argument to negotiate differences (see pages 14–17): It addresses its audience in a way that is respectful and direct, acknowledging the validity of its opponents' concerns; it presents evidence that supports its central claim that its plant will not cause environmental damage; and it rests this claim on a warrant that seems acceptable to its intended audience (that all residents want and will benefit from a healthy environment).

But the text of the letter in this advertisement is only part of the argument. The ad also includes a photograph, along with several graphs that reinforce the claim. Those graphs ostensibly present factual evidence that the company's new plan will significantly reduce its impact on the environment. Note that the visual form of the graphs highlights facts that might otherwise be difficult for readers to pick out of the lengthy text.

FIGURE 3-11

Enhancing an Argument with Graphic Elements

In this "open letter to the community," the St. Lawrence Cement Company uses graphs and a photograph to help make its argument in favor of a new plant.

An Open Letter to the Community:

The community plays an important role in shaping the quality of life for the individuals and families who live there. Communities, and all the people who make them up, are concerned with whether a new facility, such as the St. Lawrence Cement Greenport replacement plant, will be good for the environment. They want to know if the project will stimulate the local economy and create new jobs, and whether the company will operate as a responsible community member. Overall, the community wants to be assured that any proposed facility is safe and that it upholds the high environmental standards that many have worked hard to establish.

At St. Lawrence Cement, we believe that this is all as it should be. We regard ourselves as part of this community, both Hudson and Greenport locally as well as New York State. We believe that we should be open with the community and share our plans for the new Greenport facility and its benefits. We also feel compelled to correct misinformation, misleading statements and untruths about the plant. This is especially important when issues begin to drive a wedge between community members. Finally, we are convinced that our proposed project to replace the existing Catskill plant with the new Greenport facility will provide an overall net benefit to the communities and regions in which we operate.

St. Lawrence Cement has been a community member for nearly two decades, operating a cement facility at Catskill since 1984. We are proud of our track record in Catskill, and we hold it up to the community as an indicator of the commitment we have to meet and exceed the most rigorous environmental standards in the country.

Environmental Benefits

While the current Catskill plant is safe and emissions are well under the allowable standards, the Catskill plant is also older and unable to accommodate new environmental control technologies that are now available. Economically, it is not feasible to try to retro-fit the existing plant. This is why St. Lawrence Cement has proposed to build a replacement facility at Greenport—a new plant for a new age.

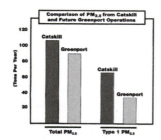

Our proposed Greenport replacement facility will incorporate a unique combination of environmental control technologies, making it one of the most environmentally friendly cement plants in the world. The replacement of Catskill with the new state-of-the-art Greenport plant will allow us to substantially lower those emissions that the public tends to be most concerned about.

Emissions of fine particulates (most commonly referred to as PM 2.5) will be cut by 14%, with the most troublesome combustion-related particulate matter dropping by 40%. Emissions of mercury will be reduced by 95% and lead emissions by 94%. Similarly, the emissions that cause acid rain—

sulfur dioxide and nitrogen oxides emissions—will be reduced by 45%. Studies by the EPA and NYSDEC corroborate these figures, providing credible and expert third-party validation that the environmental benefits we promise are real.

St. Lawrence also recognizes the community's concerns about the impact of plant emissions on historic structures and facades. Emissions from our Catskill plant are already well below allowable limits, and do not accelerate the deterioration of historic buildings and facades. The even lower emissions at Greenport should re-assure the community that St. Lawrence Cement is committed to the community and the preservation of our historic buildings—valuable community assets that enrich our area and attract tourists.

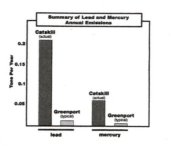

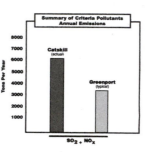

Economic Benefits

The history of this region is grounded in the cement industry. The community recognizes the importance of industry to create a diverse economy, one that takes advantage of tourism while also providing meaningful jobs for the families who live here. The Greenport replacement plant respects this need for balance, and promises to bring economic improvements to the area while preserving and enhancing the community's overall appeal.

The replacement plant, for example, will use a different process for cement production than the Catskill facility. Instead of the current 'wet' process utilized at Catskill, the Greenport plant will employ a dry process. The net benefit here it that the replacement facility will use 99% less Hudson River water and discharge absolutely nothing back into the River. Add to this St. Lawrence's restoration of 3.0 acres of former inter-tidal wetland in South Bay, an area filled over a half-century ago (long before St. Lawrence bought the property) that has been deemed extremely well-suited, if restored, for fish and wildlife habitation.

Of course, the Greenport replacement plant also holds enormous economic promise for the community, Columbia County and upstate New York. In addition to the costs of constructing the new facility (much of which will be spent right here in Greenport), jobs will be both preserved and created, a host of products and services will be required, and local, county and state taxes will be paid. St. Lawrence Cement is committed to the local community, its economy and its future, and we've proposed a project that promises multiple benefits for all of us.

St. Lawrence Cement welcomes this opportunity to provide our community with important facts and information that will help the community better understand the environmental and economic impact of our proposed replacement plant in Greenport. For certain, we want to see a successful conclusion to the process, but we also want our fellow members of the local and regional community to know the facts, recognize the benefits and support the plant.

ST. LAWRENCE CEMENT

The photograph doesn't present evidence in the way the graphs do, but it reinforces the company's message that it is staffed by concerned and competent professionals. Notice that the four people in the photograph represent racial and gender diversity as well, sending another positive message about the company to readers. The layout of the ad also contributes to the argument. Because the photo is placed before the first paragraph, readers are likely to view it before reading the text. If they have a positive reaction to that image, they might be more agreeable to the company's argument. In addition, the letter discusses environmental issues before economic ones, which seems to reinforce the company's claim that it is concerned about the environment. The subheadings ("Environmental Benefits," "Economic Benefits") highlight these concerns and make them easier for readers to access. In short, the combination of these visual elements with the text of the letter contributes subtly to the effectiveness of this argument.

This example illustrates both the importance and the potential risks of using visual elements in genuine argumentation about controversial issues. If you engage in argument with an honest intent to address difficult problems, then it makes sense to employ whatever strategies and resources are available, including visual elements, to make the argument as effectively as possible. In the case of the St. Lawrence Cement company, it is easy to suspect the company's motives and accuse it of trying to manipulate public opinion. (Of course, the same can be true of the company's opponents.) From such a perspective, you might see the use of visual elements as part of an effort to win at any cost, and you might be right. One element in analyzing the argument in a case like this is the company's track record in such disputes. Has the company been forthcoming about the environmental effect of its plants in the past? Has it engaged in underhanded tactics to manipulate public opinion? If so, you would have reason to be skeptical of the company's motives and you should assess its argument accordingly. You might, for example, view the photograph negatively because you may suspect that the company is trying to soften its image and divert attention from its environmental record.

But it might also be true that many long-time residents of the town work for the company and therefore have a sincere interest in ensuring that the new plant will not harm the local environment. Because those workers live in the community where the plant will be built, their interests will be similar to those of opponents of the plant who hope to preserve the health of the local environment. From this perspective, the argument made by the company—and arguments made by other parties in the conflict—can be seen as negotiating differences among the participants. Visual elements become tools that all participants employ as they seek to resolve the problems created by the company's plans to build the new plant. If it turned out that the company or other parties in the controversy did not have honorable motives, you could still evaluate their arguments thoughtfully and decide on their merits accordingly. Your attention to the visual elements is an important part of that evaluation.

Analyzing Arguments in Electronic Media

Because they offer capabilities that are not available in print forms, electronic media provide a rich context for argumentation that can differ significantly from print media. For example, radio allows speech, music, and other sound effects to be used in arguments in ways that cannot be reproduced in print. Television enables the use of sound in addition to moving images, graphics, and text. And the digital media used on the Internet offer previously unseen configurations of text, image, and sound that can be more interactive than other media.

Because of the rapid development of new technologies, the characteristics of electronic media are changing constantly. No one can anticipate how these media will influence the ways you engage in argumentation about important issues. Who could have predicted twenty years ago that e-mail would become as commonplace as the telephone or that texting would become an important means of communication? But what you can do is examine some of the important features of these media and begin to explore how they can be used to make effective arguments.

The Internet

Because the Internet has become so important in how people interact and communicate with each other, it is inevitably influencing how arguments are made. The multimedia capabilities of Internet technologies allow users to make arguments in ways that are not possible in conventional print forms. With these technologies, it is possible to create an online experience to promote a perspective or make a point. For example, consider Figure 3-12, which shows the home page for the U.S. Army website. Like Figures 3-9 and 3-10, this website is designed to encourage support for the military and to attract recruits as well. Like most home pages, this one includes numerous links to other pages in the U.S. Army website, each of which has additional images and links. Frozen in print, as it is here, and viewed only as an example of a static graphic design, Figure 3-12 seems more cluttered than the posters in Figures 3-9 and 3-10. But the U.S. Army home page was not designed to appear as it is here. When accessed on the Internet, it is accompanied by music and moving pictures—features that convey messages and invite the visitor

FIGURE 3-12

U.S. Army Home Page

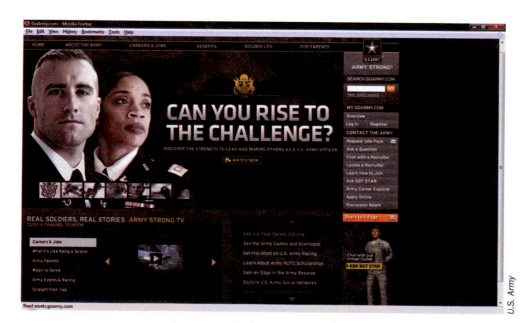

U.S. Army

to explore the site in ways that are not possible in print. The links on the home page allow a visitor to wander through the website gathering information about the Army and perhaps developing a certain positive perspective on what it would be like to be in the military. Some links launch brief videos about army life; others take the visitor to pages with various kinds of information about the Army. In these ways, websites can be dynamic rather than static; they can also be interactive, allowing a visitor to control part of the experience of visiting that website. These capabilities allow arguments to be made in an interactive medium in which image, sound, video, and text can be combined in sophisticated ways. Using the Internet in this way can change how we think about making an argument.

The emergence of the Internet as a means of communication and as a forum for public discussion has been touted by some observers as a watershed development for democratic societies, which—in theory, at least—are built around the idea that citizens make collective decisions about how they should be governed. Some believe that Internet technologies like e-mail and social media like Facebook will eventually enable many more people to participate directly in the political process than could without these technologies. Indeed, the U.S. presidential elections in 2004 and 2008 revealed some of the possibilities for using these media to mobilize political support and carry on political campaigns (see Figure 3-13). Today, e-mail discussion lists, social media such as Facebook, blogs, and web-based discussion forums enable millions of people to participate in conversations about important issues that directly affect their lives. With access to these online forums, you can debate a recent congressional decision or

barackobama.org

FIGURE 3-13

Political Participation on the Web

During the 2008 U.S. presidential election, political parties used the Internet to promote their candidates, recruit volunteers, solicit contributions, and seek ideas from voters. President Barack Obama's website, shown here in 2010, seems to invite the viewer to get involved. Some critics believe that such uses of the Internet create possibilities for greater political participation.

political election with someone from across the country almost as easily as—perhaps *more* easily than—you can debate your neighbors or roommate. Moreover, the Internet enables people with similar interests or concerns to form "virtual communities," in which they can share ideas quickly and easily without having to be in the same place at the same time. Online forums now exist for every imaginable kind of group, from anthropologists to zoologists, from sales to sailing. These forums allow participants to engage in conversations about issues important to them, and many professional organizations use online forums for conducting meetings, circulating petitions, voting, and similar activities. In these ways, Internet technologies help people form and maintain communities by providing a ready medium for communication, discussion, debate, and argumentation.

Chances are that you have participated in an online forum or used social media or even maintained a blog. If so, you might share the enthusiasm expressed by many commentators for these technologies. You might also have experienced the "flame wars" that frequently occur in online forums and social media. Visit the discussion board on a blog, for instance, and you quickly see that much of the discussion that occurs in some of these forums is not argumentation but more like the quarreling you see on television talk shows. This is true even in online forums devoted to serious issues and maintained by professionals such as lawyers or academics. As a result, many critics have expressed skepticism about the possibilities of these forums to enhance public debate about serious issues. They worry about the overwhelming volume of online discussion and of information on the Internet, and they raise questions about the usefulness of online discussion. Here, for example, is Mark Slouka, a well-known writer specializing in issues related to these new technologies:

> Clearly, there's something very powerful (and potentially very positive) about a technology that allows millions of people to share ideas and allows them to side-step the occasionally ignorant or biased "filters" like magazine Op-Ed editors. My concern (a viable one, to judge from the mass of stuff online) is that the Net will privilege "venting" over debate and knee jerk speed over reflection. There's a very real chance that what the Net will produce is not "tons of useful information," but virtual mountains of babble among which the occasionally useful tidbit of information (the kind not available in the local library) will be as easy to find as a nickel in a landfill.

Slouka expresses two of the main concerns that skeptics often cite in their criticism of online forums for public discourse: the questionable nature of much of the discussion that occurs online and the sheer volume of online discussions. A single web-based discussion forum can generate hundreds of messages in one day, far too many for any person to sort through carefully. In addition, as Slouka notes, many online discussions are characterized by superficial exchanges of opinions instead of careful, considered debate. Genuine argumentation is often as hard to find online as it is on talk radio.

What does all this mean for those interested in argument? No one can be sure, but the Internet and the digital technologies associated with it are not likely to disappear. To the contrary, they will continue to evolve, and they will very likely become more important for communication and argumentation in our society. The capabilities of these technologies seem to promise new ways of engaging in argument for the purpose of solving problems and negotiating differences. But it is also true that these technologies will complicate argumentation in ways that we cannot anticipate.

In the meantime you will almost certainly encounter arguments in online forums, and you might present your own arguments in such forums. For the most part, the principles of effective argumentation apply to arguments in any forum, online or otherwise. But there are some characteristics of online technologies that can shape argumentation, and you should be aware of how these characteristics might affect arguments online.

Not all online forums are alike, and online forums used primarily for discussion— including e-mail mailing lists, blogs, and web-based discussion boards—should be distinguished from websites, which can advance arguments but do not necessarily involve discussion and which have multimedia capabilities that discussion forums often lack.

Websites

The World Wide Web offers intriguing possibilities for structuring and presenting arguments. This section reviews some of the characteristics of the websites and their implications for argument.

Online Versions of Print Arguments

To begin, it is important to point out that there are different kinds of websites. Some websites essentially offer online versions of print documents. For example, many newspapers and magazines are available on the Web in more or less the same format as their print versions. If you visit a site such as the *Los Angeles Times* online, you will find the same articles that appear in the printed newspaper. Although the online versions of these articles might have links to other websites and might include graphics that do not appear in the print versions, their content and format are essentially the same as the printed versions. In terms of structure, content, and related matters, therefore, arguments on such websites are not very different from arguments in a print medium. An editorial essay in the *Los Angeles Times* is the same essay online and in print (see Figure 3-14).

However, the Web offers hypertextual capabilities that many writers exploit. **Hypertext** refers to the capacity to link documents through **hyperlinks,** which enable a user to move directly from one document to another. Writers now routinely embed hyperlinks in their essays to link to related documents. For example, here is the opening paragraph of an essay by Glenn Greenwald that was published in the online magazine *Salon.com*. Greenwald begins his essay with a reference to an essay by *New York Times* columnist David Brooks; the underlined text is a hyperlink that takes the reader directly to Brooks's essay on the *New York Times* website:

> I never thought I'd hear myself say this, but David Brooks actually had *an excellent column* in yesterday's *New York Times* that makes several insightful and important points. Brooks documents how "childish, contemptuous and hysterical" the national reaction has been to this latest terrorist episode, egged on—as usual—by the always-hysterical American media. The citizenry has been trained to expect that our Powerful Daddies and Mommies in government will—in that most cringe-inducing, child-like formulation—Keep Us Safe. Whenever the Government fails to do so, the reaction—just as we saw this week—is an

FIGURE 3-14

Print Publications on the Web

This screenshot shows part of an editorial essay from the *Los Angeles Times* website. Aside from the links and graphics on the screen, the editorial is identical to the one that appeared in the print version of the newspaper that day.

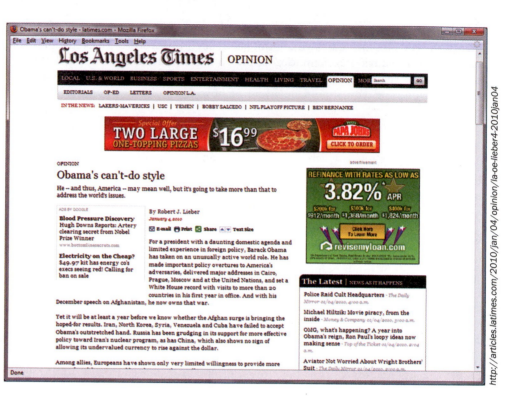

http://articles.latimes.com/2010/jan/04/opinion/la-oe-lieber4-2010jan04

ugly combination of petulant, adolescent rage and increasingly unhinged cries that More Be Done to ensure that nothing bad in the world ever happens. Demands that genuinely inept government officials be held accountable are necessary and wise, but demands that political leaders ensure that we can live in womb-like Absolute Safety are delusional and destructive. Yet this is what the citizenry screams out every time something threatening happens: *please, take more of our privacy away; monitor more of our communications; ban more of us from flying; engage in rituals to create the illusion of Strength; imprison more people without charges; take more and more control and power so you can Keep Us Safe.*

Greenwald provides a brief summary of Brooks's essay, but the ability to include a hyperlink to the original essay itself means that Greenwald probably does not have to summarize as much of Brooks's essay as he would if he were writing for a print publication. Later in his essay, Greenwald includes many additional hyperlinks, like those underlined in the excerpt:

These are the calculations that are now virtually impossible to find in our political discourse. It is fear, and only fear, that predominates. No other competing values are recognized. We have Chris Matthews <u>running around shrieking</u> that he's scared of kung-fu-wielding Terrorists. <u>Michael Chertoff is demanding</u> that we stop listening to "privacy ideologues"—*i.e.*, that there should be no limits on Government's power to invade and monitor and scrutinize. <u>Republican leaders</u> have spent the decade preaching that only Government-provided Safety, <u>not the Constitution, matters</u>. All in response to this week's single failed terrorist attack, there are—as always—hysterical calls that we <u>start more wars</u>, <u>initiate racial profiling</u>, <u>imprison innocent people indefinitely</u>, and <u>torture even more indiscriminately</u>. These are the by-products of the weakness and panic and paralyzing fear that Americans have been fed in the name of Terrorism, continuously for a full decade now.

In this passage each underlined phrase includes a hyperlink to a different website. For example, if you were to click on the phrase "start more wars," you would be taken to an article on the website of a political publication called *The Hill*; the article reports on the comments of a U.S. congressman about the possibility of a new front in the war against terrorism in the Middle East. Clicking "torture even more indiscriminately" would take you to a report on a news website called *The Sphere* about an opinion poll showing that a majority of Americans support the waterboarding (which many people consider a form of torture) of terrorist suspects. Notice that Greenwald can use these hyperlinks for various purposes: to direct his readers to websites that provide evidence to support his claims; to link to sites that provide additional information about an event or an issue he discusses; or to take readers directly to original texts that he refers to (as in the case of the link to the essay by David Brooks in Greenwald's opening paragraph). This enables Greenwald to draw easily on various resources, including multimedia resources such as videos, without having to develop them himself or include them entirely in his document. No doubt this capability influences the way a writer like Greenwald structures an argument; it also can change the way you read an argument.

Hyperlinks used in this way resemble traditional footnotes in a print text. But hyperlinks are faster, easier, and less cumbersome to read than footnotes, and they enable a writer to link to a wealth of online documents in a way that would be much too expensive and inconvenient in a printed text. Imagine, for example, if a print magazine published Greenwald's essay and included in its pages each of the documents to which Greenwald hyperlinked in his essay; doing so would dramatically increase the number of pages in the magazine and make the reader's task of wading through those pages somewhat tedious. On the other hand, numerous hyperlinks can make it more challenging for a reader to work through an argument. If you follow each of the links in Greenwald's essay, it could take you quite a while to finish reading it, and you might lose your train of thought or become sidetracked as you try to follow his argument. Writers using hyperlinks in their arguments should be mindful of such potential pitfalls as they structure their arguments and decide which links to include. At the same time, this example suggests some of the intriguing new possibilities that the Web offers for people to address complex issues and try to solve problems through argumentation.

Websites as Arguments

We have been discussing arguments that are published on websites. But websites themselves can also be seen as making arguments. Today, advocacy groups, political organizations, government and nongovernmental agencies, institutions, and community groups of all kinds maintain websites on which they present themselves to the public and take advantage of the Web's capabilities to make arguments.

For example, visit the homepage of your college or university, and you are likely to encounter a website that makes an implicit argument about the quality and character of that institution. The home page of the University at Albany, also called UAlbany, which is part of the State University of New York (Figure 3-15), is typical of university and college websites

in several respects. It projects a positive image of the institution and an appealing sense of the experience of being a student there. The images, colors, and overall design are intended to feel inviting. The large photograph that appears in the center of the page, for instance, shows the main campus entrance on a pleasant summer day with a fountain shooting dramatically toward the blue sky. At the same time, the site makes several explicit and implicit claims about the institution. The university's tagline promises "the world within reach." The white text on the large photograph in the center of the page proclaims "excellence at a great value" and further promises "a strong foundation for those seeking to learn, succeed, and create lasting connections." These claims seem to be aimed at prospective students as much as at the general public. Less obvious are claims made about the quality of the education that is offered on that campus and the other work that is done there. For instance, below the main photograph appear headlines about campus events and about honors earned by the university's students and faculty; those headlines and the accompanying photographs include links to stories with more information. Taken together, these headlines seem to imply that this university is a place where good things happen and where accomplished individuals work and learn together.

The website for the Food Project, a nonprofit organization that promotes a sustainable food system, takes similar advantage of the capabilities of the Web, but it conveys its vision somewhat more directly. Its mission, according to its website, is "to grow a thoughtful and productive community of youth and adults from diverse backgrounds who work together to build a sustainable food system" and "to inspire and support others to create change in their own communities." Its website is designed not only to describe its work but also to make a case for the value of that work. The photographs on the left side of the organization's homepage (Figure 3-16), which show positive images of young people at work growing and harvesting locally produced foods, reflect the organization's mission. Notice, too, that

FIGURE 3-16

Advocacy on the Web

The Food Project, a nonprofit organization, uses its websites to promote its views about the value of locally produced foods and community-supported agriculture.

the logo at the top left of the page, which depicts three human figures holding up a large vegetable, and the accompanying phrase ("Youth. Food. Community.") also reflect the organization's mission. The large photograph of tomatoes in the center of the home page presents an unmistakeable image of a familiar kind of food that the organization produces. The ripe, glistening tomatoes look appetizing and healthy and are clearly meant to be appealing, but this photograph also seems intended to reflect the organization's values. Many Americans associate tomatoes with summer cookouts, backyard gardens, and local markets, so tomatoes are likely to have positive connotations about healthy foods and communities—more so than less familiar or popular vegetables. Moreover, all the images on the home page reinforce the assertions made in the accompanying text: "Local food tastes better! Local food is better for the environment! Local food supports your community's economy!" In short, this simple website design, which uses common design features such as appealing images and carefully chosen text, makes a clear statement about the way humans should produce their food.

Social Media

Perhaps the most dramatic development in online technologies in recent years is the rapid emergence of "social media" such as Facebook, Twitter, and blogs. These new forums for communication extend the capabilities of older online forums, such as e-mail discussion lists and web-based discussion boards. Today these various media have become familiar components of many college classes, and classes that meet exclusively online through web-based technologies are becoming increasingly common. In short, students today often go online to engage in argumentation about course-related issues.

One advantage that an online forum has over a more traditional print medium (such as a newspaper editorial page) is that it opens the possibility for more voices to enter the conversation. You can post a comment on a blog in which you defend a position on an issue, and within a few hours or even minutes many people might respond to your post. Their responses are immediately visible to other readers, who might then post their own responses. In such a medium, many more people can join the conversation than could possibly do so in a face-to-face group discussion or in the letters-to-the-editor section of a magazine. In addition, these online forums can supplement or even replace traditional face-to-face discussions. They allow for class discussions to take place at any time, not just during the class meeting itself. In online forums, students can sort through messages and analyze them before posting a response. In this respect, these forums give participants time to consider their responses before posting them, which is not always possible in face-to-face classroom discussions.

Outside college campuses, online discussion forums, blogs, and other social media have become increasingly lively and important forums for argument. It's worth examining how the features of such media can shape the way participants engage in argumentation. Consider the following blog post that appeared in early 2010 on *The Daily Kos*, one of the most popular political blogs. In this post, a regular blogger on *The Daily Kos* whose screen name is "mcjoan" takes a position on a specific provision of a health care reform bill that was being debated in the U.S. Senate at the time:

Buy More, Get Less, Die Sooner?
    by mcjoan
    Via Nate, here are two pretty striking representations of the same data on the costs of health care, versus one measure of effectiveness of a system—life expectancy.

Health care spending and life expectancy: a parallel coordinates plot

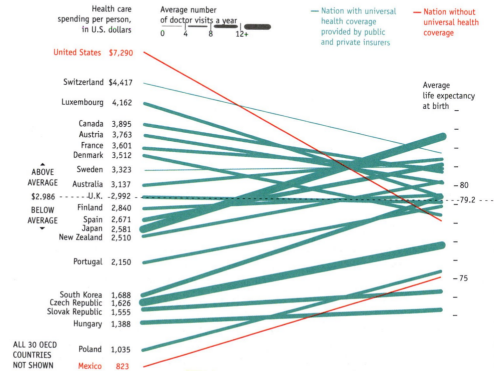

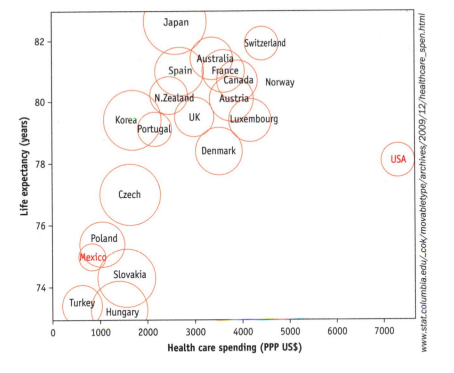

www.stat.columbia.edu/~cok/movabletype/archives/2009/12/healthcare_spen.html

Health care spending and life expectancy: a scatterplot

The first one, originally from *National Geographic*'s NGM Blog Central demonstrates perhaps even more graphically how much of an outlier the U.S. is when it comes to spending per person on health care. The width of each of the lines, representing various countries, shows utilization of care, in terms of average doctor visits per year. That same statistic is represented by the size of the bubble for each country.

So we spend more, use less, and have worse outcomes. The low life expectancy in the U.S. is also a factor of the huge number of uninsured we have in this country, accounting for as many as 45,000 deaths annually. What these graphs ultimately show is that the existing system is severely out of whack, and the dollars being poured in are largely misdirected.

Gearing a "reformed" system toward reinforcing low utilization, as the Senate bill does with its high deductibles and out-of-pocket expenses, might not be the silver bullet to reducing costs in the overall system after all.

This blog post illustrates some features that are typical of arguments on blogs. First, it is brief. Not all blog posts are brief, but in general they tend to be shorter than essays published in many newspapers or magazines. Both readers and writers expect blog entries to be relatively short so that they can be read quickly. Second, the writer gets quickly to the main point—in this case, that a specific provision of the Senate bill intended to reduce health care costs will not necessarily accomplish that goal. Third, the post begins with a direct reference to another blog that was pointed out by a reader named "Nate." The name "Nate" is a hyperlink to that other blog, which is a political affairs blog called "FiveThiryEight" and which included a comment about the second graph shown here. In effect, "mcjoan" is picking up on a point made by another blogger to make an argument about the Senate health care bill. In this sense, blogs are "in conversation" with one another. (This ongoing "conversation" is sometimes referred to as the *blogosphere*.) Finally, this blog post includes graphics as well as links to other websites.

All these features represent tools that offer both possibilities and limitations to the writer. The typically brief length of blog entries means that writers usually focus narrowly on a specific point and get to the heart of the argument quickly. The debate about health care reform in the United States in 2009 and 2010 was extremely complicated, and the question of health care costs encompassed many other factors than "mcjoan" included in this post. But "mcjoan" focuses on a single point that the U.S. health care system is inefficient: Despite very high spending on health care in the United States, health "outcomes" are not better than in many other developed nations. The graphs included in the post provide evidence that "the system is out of whack," and the reasoning leads to the conclusion that the Senate bill, which is intended to reduce the use of expensive visits to the doctor's office or the hospital, won't likely reduce costs or necessarily lead to greater "life expectancy." There is much more to say about the matter, but on a blog the writer usually sticks to a single point. Moreover, as we saw in other web-based arguments, bloggers can rely on links to other websites that provide additional information or related discussion. These features, in addition to the conversational writing style that many bloggers adopt, can give blogs a feeling of the immediacy of a conversation that invites response and participation.

Indeed, response and participation are hallmarks of blogs and other Internet discussion forums. Some bloggers point out that the possibility of quick responses from many readers makes writing a blog very different from writing an essay for a more traditional print publication, such as a newspaper; they also note that this sense of immediacy makes the writer feel more accountable to his or her readers. At the same time, the readers use the blog as a forum to participate directly in the argument itself to hold the writer and each other accountable for their arguments. In the case of the blog post by "mcjoan" about health care costs, 302 readers posted responses within 24 hours of the publication of "mcjoan's" post on *The Daily Kos* website. Here are several of the first few responses ("Sanders" in some of these responses refers to Senator Bernie Sanders, who sponsored an amendment to the Senate health care bill; "CBO" refers to the Congressional Budget Office, which provides costs estimates for congressional bills):

It's distressing that we (the nation, as well as the netroots) could go through such an extensive discussion about health care reform, and what a great step forward the Senate bill was, without pausing to look at this graph, which the supposed "reform" does nothing to address. **By alan in sf**

what do you mean? it does nothing to address? Removal of pre-existing conditions will lead to people visiting the doctor more. So will Sanders' enhancements.
Cost controls are designed to slow the rate of health care spending overall. Both will move the data points in the right directions over time. **by tunesmith**

But it will also increase our per capita spending by exactly......a lot. And for those with the cadillac plans, they will utilize less as those plans get replaced with high deductible ones to avoid the tax. **by Nailbanger** it will increase temporarily. there's a startup cost, but then it lowers the curve over time compared to the status quo—within a few years, we will be at lower per capita spending than we would be if we did nothing. **by tunesmith**

meaningless. "within a few years, we will be at lower per capita spending than we would be if we did nothing."

your argument means absolutely nothing without even an estimate as to how much people would pay if we did nothing. Seems to me that most people could very easily be screwed either way—going bankrupt because they can't afford to pay a quarter of their disposable income on health care as opposed to a third.

when people are going to go broke regardless, all your vague bullshit about "bending the curve" isn't too comforting. **by Red Rabbit**

It's cheaper to catch and treat heart disease now than it is to perform open heart surgery on someone tomorrow. The typical family doctor's visit is under $50, not counting lab work (which brings it closer to $100.) With insurance, that can drop as low as $25. That blood work can detect diseases such as high cholesterol. The patient, now aware of that condition, can treat the cholesterol for as low as $10 a month, even without insurance, through a county health department or CHC. $120 a year, for how many years, compared to a $20,000 open heart surgery if it is left untreated? **by catwho**

it sounds like you agree with me. sanders health clinics...expanded medicaid...20,000 new primary care physicians...end of pre-existing conditions. lots more preventative medicine will be practiced. **by tunesmith**

CBO estimates that U.S. health care costs will grow 71 percent in the next decade if Senate bill passes—or if it doesn't. In other words, it's expected to have virtually no impact.

Bending the curve means slightly slowing the growth rate. Since we're starting from a base more than twice what other countries spend per capita. So we'll be heading off a cliff at a slightly reduced speed.

Questionable whether pre-existing conditions regs will help much on costs. sanders community health clinics are definitely the best thing in the bill; it'd be better to scrap everything else and just put the money into community clinics. **by alan in sf**

Reading through these responses, you can see how readers quickly become engaged in discussion and debate about the issue raised by the original blog post. You can also see how readers bring in evidence to support their points or positions. In a sense, the blog post is just the beginning of the argument, and the writer ("mcjoan"), an experienced blogger, surely knows that. Because blog posts can generate discussion in this way, the writer doesn't necessarily have to go into detailed explanations about some of the more complicated points of the issue at hand. "Mcjoan" knows that readers of this blog are likely to go into some of those issues on their own, as they do in these comments. The writer also knows that these readers know a great deal about health care issues and have a sophisticated understanding of the issues to their reading of the blog post, as their comments suggest. "Mcjoan" can rely on their knowledge when deciding what to include in an argument.

This example illustrates how argumentation can occur in online forums like blogs and web-based discussion boards. Notice that the participants seem genuinely concerned about health care reform, and it is likely that they follow this blog precisely because they are interested in such issues. The blogger crafts his or her arguments accordingly. The blogger also knows that the readers who post comments will engage each other as well as the blog post itself. Here the readers respond directly to one another's arguments. Notice that the participants follow some of the conventions of traditional argument. For example, they present claims (for example, prevention can lower health care costs), support their claims (in many cases, with facts and statistics), and imply warrants (for example, health care should be provided for everyone). In addition, participants seem to make certain assumptions about their audience and about the larger context of the discussion. For example, the readers who post comments on this blog all seem familiar with American health care issues and the ongoing debate about health care reform in the United States. These are all features of effective argumentation—in any medium.

The matter of credibility can also be complicated in online forums. Generally, there is no way of knowing who the participants really are, whether they have any legitimate knowledge or experience related to the topic at hand, and whether they are being honest about what they say. Participants in online forums can establish their own credibility over time through the messages they post, but you often have no way to verify what others say in their messages. To an extent, one's credibility is always constructed, even in a respected print medium. But writers whose essays appear in a magazine such as *Time* or a newspaper such as the *Wall Street Journal* must work with editors and generally have well-established credentials. Just being published in a respected magazine gives them a measure of credibility. By contrast, anyone can log onto a website and post a message. And a participant can claim to be an expert without having to provide proof. If you know that people are who they claim to be, you are more likely to take their arguments seriously. But without a way to verify their claims, you should always view their messages with at least a small measure of skepticism. It goes without saying that, as a participant in an online discussion, you are likely to be more effective in making your arguments if you can establish credibility, just as you would in a print medium.

Although the advice offered here applies generally to any kind of online discussion forum, all online forums are not the same. Public blogs such *The Daily Kos* tend to be much more freewheeling and informal than specialized newsgroups for professionals, which are often moderated (that is, a moderator reviews messages and decides whether they are appropriate for the forum; the moderator is the equivalent of a newspaper or magazine editor). The protocols governing online behavior can vary widely from one forum to another. Sarcasm and ad hominem attacks that are common on many public newsgroups might result in your removal from a moderated academic mailing list. The audiences for online forums can differ dramatically as well, and the nature of the audience will affect the kinds of topics discussed in a forum and the ways in which participants engage with each other. Flame wars, for example, are much less common in specialized professional forums than in discussion boards about movies, for instance. The expectations for claims and evidence are likely to be more rigorous in a professional forum as well. Even the length of messages and the conventions for how people identify themselves can be different in these different forums. Because of these differences, to engage effectively in argumentation in any online forum, you need to become familiar with the forum and its protocols. It makes sense to read a newsgroup or mailing list for several days or even weeks before jumping into the discussion. If you do so, you will probably find that online discussions can be fruitful and interesting and can be part of your effort to solve problems and negotiate difference through argument.

The well-known critic Marshall McLuhan once famously asserted that the medium *is* the message. This chapter has examined some ways in which McLuhan may have been right. But we have also pointed out that in many ways, argument is argument is argument. In other words, the principles of sound argumentation apply in any medium. Moreover, our motives for argument will determine much of what we say and how we make use of a particular medium. If we are genuinely committed to engaging in argumentation in order to solve problems, then our uses of media can enhance our arguments and contribute powerfully to our efforts to negotiate differences as we address the many complex issues that affect us as we live and work together.

The Strategies for Argument

Jeff Cadge/The Image Bank/Getty Images

When you write an argument, you might feel confident about what you want to say or about the position you wish to take on an issue. In such a case your primary challenge is to examine the issue carefully so that you can develop the most effective argument. In other situations you might be faced with the prospect of arguing about an issue about which you are unsure or have mixed emotions. In that case writing your argument will involve exploring the issue more fully and perhaps even discovering your position as you write. In both cases, however, you are engaged in what classical rhetoricians termed **invention,** that is, exploring and developing ideas about a specific topic to make an effective argument about it. Aristotle, whose treatise on rhetoric is still an important work for rhetoricians today, defined rhetoric as "the faculty of observing in any given case the available means of persuasion." In other words, **rhetoric** is finding an effective way to persuade other people to believe or do something. You can usefully think of argumentation in similar terms.

In his *Rhetoric,* Aristotle identified three primary modes of persuasion:

- Ethical, or arguments based on the speaker's character
- Emotional, or arguments that appeal to the emotions
- Logical, or arguments based on reason and evidence

Scholars continue to refer to these modes by their names in Greek: *ethos* (from which *ethical* derives), *pathos* (from which *pathetic* derives), and *logos* (from which *logic* derives). In practice, most arguments use all three modes of persuasion in some way. Logic alone can be persuasive, and an illogical argument is unlikely to be convincing. But because humans have values and feelings, an argument that appeals only to the mind may not be as effective as an argument that speaks to the heart. Moreover, no matter how clever an argument may be, it is unlikely to endure if it is unethical. Misrepresentation and manipulation can sometimes secure a short-term victory, but as we noted in Chapter 1, genuine argument is ultimately about truth.

So we believe that the ethical dimension of an argument is of primary importance. But an ethically based argument implies that claims can be supported by evidence and that clear thinking has led to reasonable conclusions. *Ethos* and *logos* are thus closely related. This chapter will describe the principles of logical reasoning (as well as the use of emotional appeals) after beginning with an explanation of how writers convey ethos to readers.

Understanding Ethos: Appeals to Character

"You can count on her."

"I wouldn't trust a word he says."

How many times have you heard—or spoken—some version of those two statements? Very likely you have done so often, perhaps without realizing that you were engaging in one of the most basic and long-standing strategies for argument: invoking character. Aristotle identified character, or *ethos,* as one of the most powerful components of persuasion available to a speaker: "We believe good men [and women] more fully and more readily than others," he wrote, adding that a speaker's character "may almost be called the most effective means of persuasion he [or she] possesses" (*Rhetoric*). But character is not just a strategy; it is also a quality. Like Aristotle, the famous Roman rhetorician Quintillian believed that the most effective orator is a "good" person. Above all, Quintillian wrote, the effective orator "must possess the quality which…is in the very nature of things the greatest and most important, that is, he [or she] must be a good man [or woman]" (*Institutio Oratoria,* Book XII). In short, the best way to sound or appear ethical in an argument is to *be* ethical.

We often rely on our sense of someone's character when making decisions in our daily lives. For example, you might seek advice about attending graduate school from a relative or a teacher you trust and whom you know to be careful with advice about such matters. In some cases character might grow out of authority and expertise: Your professor's knowledge of universities and education can lead to useful advice about graduate school. You wouldn't necessarily have the same confidence about such advice from, say, a friend who is a chef. From her you might seek suggestions for a good restaurant or recipe. Authority or expertise is not the same thing as character (a professor can be unethical and untrustworthy, for instance), but it is usually part of character and can be a powerful source of appeals in argument.

This kind of appeal is common in advertising. Corporations select celebrities to represent them or their products—for example, former basketball star Michael Jordan for Nike shoes. The implicit argument is that if someone like Jordan endorses this product, it must be good. And when a celebrity who endorses a product in this way gets into trouble, companies sometimes decide to discontinue advertisements that feature that celebrity—as occurred with professional golfer Tiger Woods when his personal troubles became widely publicized. In such a case the implication is that the person can no longer be trusted and the company can no longer base its argument for using its product on that person's character.

Character is especially important in the arenas of law and politics. In court, for instance, lawyers will try to establish or undermine the credibility of witnesses as they try to convince a judge or jury about a person's guilt or innocence. Defense lawyers sometimes call "character witnesses" to establish that the defendant was a particular kind of person (usually a good person). Similarly, when it comes to politics, character often looms large. Consider how often candidates for elected office try to establish their credibility as trustworthy and dependable. Advertisements showing a candidate's family, for example, are standard fare in U.S. elections. Such advertisements intend to convey the idea that politicians who are married and have children are more reputable than candidates who are single—an old-fashioned idea that has been strangely enduring even though most people these days recognize that there's nothing necessarily odd about being single and that families who smile together are not necessarily happy. Just as common are advertisements attacking an opponent's credibility. Often such "attack ads" will suggest that a candidate is not concerned with issues affecting voters and therefore isn't to be trusted.

A writer can raise questions about someone's credibility to support a particular point or position on an issue. Consider, for instance, the following excerpt from an editorial by *Chicago Tribune* columnist Clarence Page. Page is arguing in favor of a controversial policy at the University of North Carolina requiring all incoming first-year students in 2002 to read a book about the Koran. The purpose was to encourage students to learn and think carefully about an important book that they might not be familiar with. Page is reacting specifically to an appearance by a University of North Carolina professor on *The O'Reilly Factor,* a popular television news talk show hosted by journalist Bill O'Reilly:

The important thing, as Robert Kirkpatrick, the professor who chose the book, explained on "The O'Reilly Factor" TV show is this: First-year students need to know that "as a member of an academic community they have to learn to think and to read and to write and to defend their opinions."

That's right. Start pushing a book on college freshmen and, who knows? They might try reading another one.

That's what college is supposed to be about. It is not just a time for learning but a time to arouse curiosity in preparation for a lifetime of learning.

That process begins when you learn not only to have opinions but also how to express and defend them.

"And defending the right not to read the book is something that will be very interesting to read," the professor said.

Indeed, it should be at least as interesting as listening to showman-journalist O'Reilly explain why he will not read the book. According to a Fox transcript, he called UNC's assignment "unbelievable," compared it to assigning "Mein Kampf" during World War II and asked why should freshmen be required to study "our enemy's religion."

Yes, there is a lot more to Islam than Osama bin Laden and his violent brethren, but apparently not in O'Reilly's mind.

"I mean, I wouldn't give people a book during World War II on [how] the emperor is God in Japan. Would you?"

"Sure," Kirkpatrick said. "Why not? Wouldn't that have explained kamikaze pilots?"

That's a sensible answer, not that sensibleness gets you anywhere on high energy cable TV news-talk shows these days or, for that matter, in politics—especially religious politics.

Here, Page supports his own position in favor of the reading requirement by questioning O'Reilly's credibility (and even his common sense) on the issue. He suggests that O'Reilly's interest as a TV talk-show host is not in arriving at a "sensible" answer to the question raised by the University of North Carolina requirement but rather in being a "showman." Such a strategy can be effective when a person advocating a certain position is well known and likely to be considered credible by many people. Because of his television show, O'Reilly was widely known in the United States, and it is likely that many of his viewers saw him as an important voice on issues such as public education. By calling O'Reilly's credibility on the issue into question, Page could weaken O'Reilly's position and strengthen his own argument that the reading requirement is justified and sound.

A writer can take the opposite approach in making a character-based argument: that is, he or she can invoke certain positive aspects of someone's character in order to advance an argument. In the following essay syndicated columnist Nicholas Kristoff makes an argument for a certain strategy for fighting terrorism in Afghanistan and Pakistan, which were both suffering through war and ongoing ethnic and religious conflict when Kristoff's essay was published in 2008. Kristoff rests his argument in large part on the work of an American named Greg Mortenson, who succeeded in establishing dozens of schools in remote villages in both Afghanistan and Pakistan, despite the ongoing conflicts in those regions. But notice that Kristoff does not simply point to the success of Mortenson's efforts to build schools as a way to combat terrorism; he also emphasizes Mortenson's character as a key to his success. In this sense, Kristoff is making an ethical argument in favor of Mortenson's approach to achieving peace in that region of the world.

Since 9/11, Westerners have tried two approaches to fight terrorism in Pakistan, President Bush's and Greg Mortenson's.

Mr. Bush has focused on military force and provided more than $10 billion—an extraordinary sum in the foreign-aid world—to the highly unpopular government of President Pervez Musharraf. This approach has failed: the backlash has radicalized Pakistan's tribal areas so that they now nurture terrorists in ways that they never did before 9/11.

Mr. Mortenson, a frumpy, genial man from Montana, takes a diametrically opposite approach, and he has spent less than one-ten-thousandth as much as the Bush administration. He builds schools in isolated parts of Pakistan and Afghanistan, working closely with Muslim clerics and even praying with them at times.

The only thing that Mr. Mortenson blows up are boulders that fall onto remote roads and block access to his schools.

Mr. Mortenson has become a legend in the region, his picture sometimes dangling like a talisman from rearview mirrors, and his work has struck a chord in America as well. His superb book about his schools, "Three Cups of Tea," came out in 2006 and initially wasn't reviewed by most major newspapers. Yet propelled by word of mouth, the book became a publishing sensation: it has spent the last 74 weeks on the paperback best-seller list, regularly in the No. 1 spot.

Now Mr. Mortenson is fending off several dozen film offers. "My concern is that a movie might endanger the well-being of our students," he explains.

Mr. Mortenson found his calling in 1993 after he failed in an attempt to climb K2, a Himalayan peak, and stumbled weakly into a poor Muslim village. The peasants nursed him back to health, and he promised to repay them by building the village a school.

Scrounging the money was a nightmare—his 580 fund-raising letters to prominent people generated one check, from Tom Brokaw—and Mr. Mortenson ended up selling his beloved climbing equipment and car. But when the school was built, he kept going. Now his aid group, the Central Asia Institute, has 74 schools in operation. His focus is educating girls.

Note how Kristoff establishes Mortenson as a man of great character and dedication. He seems to suggest that this is a man we should pay attention to. And he quotes Mortenson to support his own position that the United States should shift its focus away from military means to humanitarian efforts:

"Schools are a much more effective bang for the buck than missiles or chasing some Taliban around the country," says Mr. Mortenson, who is an Army veteran.

Kristoff adds to Mortenson's credibility here by noting that Mortenson is an Army veteran. Later in his essay, Kristoff quotes a U.S. Army colonel, who agrees with Mortenson that education, rather than military might, is the best long-term strategy for peace.

Without establishing Mortenson's integrity and commitment in this way, Kristoff's argument would lose some of its impact. Kristoff suggests that it is precisely the kind of character possessed by Mortenson that can help overcome hatred and religious conflict. In this regard, Kristoff is employing a character-based argument as a way to try to address a horrible conflict; his essay is an example of an argument whose ultimate purpose is to negotiate deep differences that seem intractable and that have led to great suffering.

The character of the writer himself or herself can also play a powerful role in an argument. In the previous example, readers who don't know anything about Nicholas Kristoff can still find his argument, based in part on Greg Mortenson's character, effective. But sometimes the writer's character becomes an important basis for an argument. Consider the following letter to the editor of the *Cleveland Plain Dealer*, written in response to an editorial about the promise of medical technology:

The *Plain Dealer's* Aug. 13 editorial "Miracles on demand" was right that emerging medical breakthroughs hold incredible promise in overcoming serious diseases like cancer and heart failure. And it was right that, in our imperfect world, it is impossible to provide an absolute guarantee of the safety of medical technology. But it missed the fact that manufacturers and the Food and Drug Administration are doing an excellent job making sure new tests and treatments are as safe as possible....

FDA data on product recalls show that the agency's system of pre-market and post-market regulations is working well. Even as the number and complexity of medical technologies has increased, the total number of recalls has remained steady over the last 10 years. The vast majority of recalls are not considered a serious public-health issue and are due to issues like labeling errors that can be easily corrected. Are medical technologies always perfect? Unfortunately, no. But manufacturers and the FDA have maintained an impressive safety record as a result of their mutual commitment to the safest possible products.

The agency itself concludes: "The public's confidence in FDA is well justified." After examining the facts, we wholeheartedly agree.

The letter was signed as follows:

Pamela G. Bailey.

Bailey is president of the Advanced Medical Technology Association, which represents more than 1,100 innovators and manufacturers of medical devices, diagnostic products and medical information systems.

Bailey is making a logical argument about the safety of medical technologies. But her argument might have greater impact on readers who notice that she is president of an organization of medical technology professionals. You might consider whether you assign greater credibility to this argument on the basis of your knowledge of Bailey's position. (Your reaction will depend in part on your opinion of large companies that manufacture medical technologies. For some readers, knowing who Bailey is will undermine her argument.)

The public prominence of a person can work in much the same way in an argument. In the summer of 2002, the *New York Times* published an essay in favor of school vouchers by the famed economist Milton Friedman. After the Supreme Court decision in June 2002 upholding the voucher program in Cleveland, Ohio, city schools, many editorialists wrote arguments supporting or opposing the court's ruling. Many of those writers had no authority as either legal experts or educators. In that regard, their character probably did not figure prominently into their arguments—or in readers' reactions to their arguments. Friedman, by contrast, is an internationally known figure who is one of the most influential economists of the twentieth century. Consider how this blurb, which was included at the end of his essay, might influence your reaction to his argument:

Milton Friedman, the 1976 recipient of the Nobel Prize in economics, is a senior research fellow at the Hoover Institution.

Writers of arguments need not have such impressive reputations as Friedman's to employ character effectively. Establishing credibility is an important strategy in argumentation that all writers can use. When you refer to your experiences, for example, as a way to indicate to your readers that you know something about a situation or an issue, you are establishing credibility that can give your argument greater weight. Here is writer Joshua Wolf Shenk, addressing the issue of legalizing drugs:

There's no breeze, only bare, stifling heat, but Kevin can scarcely support his wispy frame. He bobs forward, his eyes slowly closing until he drifts asleep, in a 45-degree hunch. "Kevin?" I say softly. He jerks awake and slowly rubs a hand over his spindly chest. "It's so hot in here I can hardly think," he says. . . .

This July I spent a long, hot day talking to junkies in New York City, in a run-down hotel near Columbia University. Some, like Kevin, were reticent. Others spoke freely about their lives and addictions. I sat with Melissa for 20 minutes as she patiently hunted her needle-scarred legs for a vein to take a spike. She had just fixed after a long dry spell. "I was sick," she told me. "I could hardly move. And Pap"—she gestures toward a friend sitting across from her—"he helped me out. He gave me something to make me better. . . ."

Making drugs legally available, with tight regulatory controls, would end the black market, and with it much of the violence, crime, and social pathology we have come to understand as "drug-related." And yet, history shows clearly that lifting prohibition would allow for more drug use, and more abuse and addiction.

I spent that day in New York to face this excruciating dilemma. It's easy to call for an end to prohibition from an office in Washington, D.C. What about when looking into Kevin's dim eyes, or confronting the images of crack babies, shriveled and wincing?

Joshua Wolf Shenk, *The Washington Monthly*, October 1995. phone: 202-393-5155; www.washingtonmonthly.com., 733 15th St., NW, Ste. 520, Washington, DC 20005

Shenk uses his own experience not only to make his point about the horrors of drug addiction but also to establish himself as someone who knows about this problem from direct experience. Notice, too, that Shenk's gentle, sympathetic descriptions of the addicts he met help convey a sense of him as caring and deeply concerned, which might add to his credibility for many readers. (Obviously, there is an emotional appeal here, too.)

If writers of arguments try to connect with readers by establishing credibility, readers have the option of resisting that connection. In other words, they might not identify with the writer—or with the audience he or she directly addresses—or they might not *wish* to identify with the writer. There can be many reasons to resist such a connection, but one important reason has to do with how readers perceive the writer's credibility. As a reader, you are not likely to be persuaded by a writer whose credibility you question, no matter how inclined you might be to agree with his or her argument. For example, consider the following letter to the editor of *USA Today*, which was written in response to an article about actor Mike Myers:

The sheer stupidity of what many Americans find entertaining never ceases to amaze me. Another tired, hackneyed sequel to the foolish *Austin Powers* series is dragged out for the people who wouldn't get a joke if it didn't include obvious "you're-supposed-to-laugh-now" cuts.

The debate still rages as to who is less funny: Jim Carrey or *Austin Powers'* Mike Myers. Both couldn't act their way out of a wet paper bag, so instead they pump out inane movies with a grade-school humor level. It's as if IQ is unwelcome in movie production these days.

Honestly, who couldn't star in *Austin Powers*? The only difference between Myers' embarrassing himself and any number of fools we've all had to tolerate is that Myers has cultivated an entire career by being gratingly unfunny.

I gave in this past weekend and managed to suffer through about 15 minutes of *The Spy Who Shagged Me*, playing on cable. I want my 15 minutes back, Mr. Myers.

This writer's opening sentence immediately creates a distinction between him and the "many Americans" who find Myers's movies entertaining. That distinction might serve the writer's purpose, because he obviously excludes himself from that category of readers. But consider how the writer's tone might affect his *ethos* among other readers, who might even agree with his assessment of Myers. This writer offers no evidence to support his main contention that Myers's acting ability is poor; instead, he offers simple assertions to that effect. Although readers who share the writer's opinion might nod in agreement, it is worth considering how other readers, who might have no strong opinion about Myers, might react to this argument. For such readers this writer might sound arrogant or unreasonable, and his credibility therefore suffers. In this case, then, the writer's *ethos* might undermine his argument for some readers but enhance it for others.

Establishing an honest, straightforward voice as a writer can help convince readers that you are credible and believable and that they can take you seriously. Indeed, the quality of your writing can help establish your credibility by demonstrating your competence to readers. Acknowledging your own limitations can be an effective strategy for establishing credibility, too. For example, imagine that you wish to contribute to a discussion of standardized testing in your community, an important educational issue that affects all students (including you). In writing a letter to your local school board, for instance, you might concede at the outset that you are not an expert in educational testing but that your experiences as a student give you insight into the problems associated with testing. Such a statement can gain you credibility by showing that you are not trying to claim expertise that you don't have, yet you are genuinely concerned about the issue at hand. In this sense you are being honest with your readers and thereby communicating to them that they can trust you. You are, in other words, establishing your character as the writer of an argument.

The examples in this section reveal that ethical appeals can be extremely powerful in argumentation, and as a writer you do well to explore the use of such appeals as you construct an argument. At the same time, like all appeals, the appeal to character can be complicated and should always be assessed in terms of the specific situation at hand.

Understanding *Pathos*: Appeals to Emotion

There is perhaps no more powerful way to construct an argument than to appeal to readers' emotions. You see emotional appeals in all contexts: newspaper editorials, political blogs, commercials, public service announcements (see "The Crying Indian"). No argument is devoid of emotional appeal, but some arguments rely on emotions more than others do. And because emotional appeals can be so powerful, they carry risk for both writer and reader.

One reason that emotional arguments don't work in all circumstances is that emotion is so complex and often poorly understood. Think for a moment about the range

THE CRYING INDIAN

In this famous public service ad from the 1970s, a Native American is shown crying because of the environmental destruction that pollution was causing. It was part of an anti-pollution advertising campaign sponsored by an organization called Keep America Beautiful. Television versions of the ad depicted the man, dressed in clothes considered to be traditional Indian garb, standing on a roadside in a wide open prairie as trash was thrown at his feet from a passing car. The ad illustrates how a powerful emotional appeal can be employed to advocate a position or urge a specific action (in this case, resisting pollution of the nation's land, air, and water).

Keep America Beautiful www.kab.org

of emotions that might figure into an argument about, say, capital punishment: anger, pity, worry, fear, sadness, relief. Trying to anticipate how readers might react emotionally to a specific point about such a charged issue can be daunting. You might try to inspire sympathy among your readers by, for instance, invoking a call to patriotism in an argument about measures to be taken against terrorism but find that your argument sparked anger among some readers instead. It is impossible to know with certainty what emotional responses you might elicit with a particular line of argument; you can only try to anticipate responses on the basis of your experience, your knowledge of your readers, and your understanding of the rhetorical context.

Because of this uncertainty and because emotions will very likely be involved in any argument, it is a good idea to think of the use of emotion in argument as an ethical matter. You might suspect that a line of argument may evoke strong emotions in some readers and, as a result, make those readers more susceptible to that line of argument. In other words, you might be able to "push the buttons" of your readers intentionally to elicit strong emotions. Doing so might enable you to win the argument, but will it truly solve the problem about which you are arguing? Is it the right way to address the issue at hand?

Used carefully and ethically, emotional appeals can be effective. Consider how one writer employs emotion in an argument about the long-standing controversy over gun control. In this case the writer, Jeanne Shields, argues in favor of restricting the sale and ownership of handguns. But she writes from an especially wrenching position: Her own son was murdered by someone using a handgun. Here is her argument, first published in 1978 when many Americans were concerned about increasing rates of violent crime.

Why Nick?

If the telephone rings late at night, I always mentally check off where each child is, and at the same time get an awful sinking feeling in the pit of my stomach.

Four years ago, April 16, we had a telephone call very late. As my husband answered, I checked off Pam in Long Beach (California), Nick in San Francisco, David in New Brunswick (New Jersey) and Leslie outside Boston. The less my husband spoke, the tighter the knot got in my stomach. Instinctively, I knew it was bad news, but I wasn't prepared for what he had to tell me. Our eldest son, Nick, 23, had been shot dead on a street in San Francisco.

Nick was murdered at about 9:30 p.m. He and a friend, Jon, had come from lacrosse practice and were on their way home. They stopped to pick up a rug at the home of a friend. While Jon went in to get the rug, Nick rearranged the lacrosse gear in the back of their borrowed Vega. He was shot three times in the back of the head and died instantly, holding a lacrosse stick.

Nick was the fourteenth victim of what came to be called the "Zebra killers." Between the fall of 1973 and April 16, 1974, they had randomly killed fourteen people and wounded seven others—crippling one for life. Four men were subsequently convicted of murder in a trial that lasted thirteen months.

My son was tall, dark and handsome, and a good athlete. He was particularly good at lacrosse and an expert skier. Nick was an ardent photographer and wrote some lovely poetry. He was a gentle and sensitive man with an infectious grin and the capacity to make friends easily. It was hard for me to believe he was gone.

The generous support and love of our friends gave us the strength to go on during those days. The calls and letters that poured in from those who knew Nick were overwhelming. In his short life, Nick had touched so many people in so many ways. It was both heartwarming and very humbling.

But always, running through those blurred days was the question. Why? Why Nick? My deep faith in God was really put to the test. Yet, nothing that I could do or think of, or pray for, was ever going to bring Nick back.

Because Nick was shot two days after Easter, the funeral service was filled with Easter prayers and hymns. Spring flowers came from the gardens of friends. The day was mild, clear and beautiful, and a kind of peace and understanding seeped into my aching heart.

No matter how many children you have, the death of one leaves a void that cannot be filled. Life seems to include a new awareness, and one's philosophy and values come under sharper scrutiny. Were we just to pick up the pieces and continue as before? That choice became impossible, because a meaning had to be given to this vicious, senseless death.

That summer of 1974, the newspapers, magazines and television were full of Watergate. But I couldn't concentrate on it or anything else. Instead I dug hard in the garden for short periods of time, or smashed at tennis balls.

On the other hand, my husband, Pete, immersed himself in a study of the gun-control issue. Very near to where Nick had died, in a vacant lot, two small children found a gun—*the gun*. It was a .32-caliber Beretta. Police, in tracing it, found that initially it had been bought legally, but then went through the hands of seven different owners—most of whom had police records. Its final bullets, fired at close range, had killed my son—and then it was thrown carelessly away.

Pete's readings of Presidential commission recommendations, FBI crime statistics and books on the handgun issue showed him that our Federal laws were indeed weak and ineffective. He went to Washington to talk to politicians and to see what, if anything, was being done about it. I watched him wrestle with his thoughts and spend long hours writing them down on paper—the pros and cons of handgun control and what could logically be done about the proliferation of handguns in this nation.

Through friends, Pete had been introduced in Washington to the National Council to Control Handguns, a citizens' lobby seeking stricter Federal controls over handguns. As Pete became more closely associated with the NCCH as a volunteer, it became increasingly obvious that he was leaning toward a greater involvement.

Consequently, with strong encouragement from me and the children, Pete took a year's leave of absence from his job as a marketing executive so that he could join NCCH full time. A full year and a half later, he finally resigned and became the NCCH chairman.

The main adversaries of handgun control are members of the powerful and financially entrenched National Rifle Association, macho men who don't understand the definition of a civilized society. They are aided by an apathetic government which in reality is us, because we citizens don't make ourselves heard loud and clear enough. How many people are in the silent majority, who want to see something done about unregulated sale and possession of handguns? Why do we register cars and license drivers, and not do the same for handguns? Why are the production and sale of firecrackers severely restricted—and not handguns?

I now work in the NCCH office as a volunteer. One of my jobs is to read and make appropriate card files each day from a flood of clippings describing handgun incidents. The daily newspapers across the country recount the grim litany of shootings, killings, rapes, and robberies at gun point. Some of it's tough going, because I am poignantly aware of what a family is going through. Some of it's so appalling it makes me literally sick.

Some people can no longer absorb this kind of news. They have almost become immune to it, because there is so much violence. To others, it is too impersonal; it's always something that happens to somebody else—not to you.

But anybody can be shot. We are all in a lottery, where the likelihood of your facing handgun violence grows every day. Today there are 50 million handguns in civilian hands. By the year 2000, there will be more than 100 million.

So many families have given up so much to the deadly handgun. It will take the women of this country—the mothers, wives, sisters and daughters—to do something about it. But when will they stand up to be counted and to be heard? Or will they wait only to hear the telephone ringing late at night?

—Jeanne Shields

In setting up her argument, Shields describes a situation that she knows is likely to evoke strong emotions among her readers. Readers who are parents will almost surely identify with Shields and her husband, and other readers are likely to feel empathy for them. Those feelings can make readers more open to Shields's support for tougher gun laws, even if those readers are not in favor of gun control in principle. Notice how the opening paragraphs of her essay describe two vivid scenes: two parents receiving a dreaded late-night phone call and an innocent young man shot in cold blood while doing an everyday task. Such a strategy is likely to give many readers pause, because the emotions surrounding these scenes can be deep and powerful.

Notice that Shields does not rely on an emotional appeal alone in making her argument. Later in her piece, despite her own unequivocal support for stronger gun laws, she discusses both the pros and cons of gun control and she refers to well-funded lobbies that oppose such laws. In this way, she employs logic as well as emotion. In short, her emotional appeal becomes an integral part of the argument she makes regarding gun control.

Shields's essay illustrates some of the pitfalls of relying too heavily on emotional appeals in an argument. A close look at her essay reveals weaknesses in her logical reasoning and gaps in her use of evidence. For example, she advocates "stricter Federal controls over handguns," but she also reports that the gun used to kill her son had been initially purchased legally and she does not explain how "stricter" gun controls would prevent a legally purchased weapon from falling into the hands of criminals. She also makes the unsupported claim that it will take the "women of this country" to control handguns immediately after emphasizing that her husband had resigned from a well-paying job to lobby for stricter gun laws (while she gardened and played tennis). And in describing the members of the National Rifle Association as "macho men who don't understand the definition of a civilized society" she makes a sexist claim (because women also belong to the NRA) that is also an *ad hominem* argument (see page 75).

Shields also leaves out some important information about the "Zebra killings." There were seventy-one "Zebra killings," and these murders were racially motivated. The killers were black, and the victims were white. Shields reports that her son was the fourteenth victim of this killing spree, but she does not explain the larger situation, which might have shifted the readers' attention from the death of an individual (her son). By choosing to say nothing about the racial factors involved in her son's murder, Shields ignores the social complexity of the killings. The individual victims were chosen at random, but those random killings were the result of a specific ideology espoused by a racially motivated extremist group. In trying to make a persuasive emotional appeal, Shields constructs a weak logical argument that can even be considered misleading.

This example illustrates that emotional appeals must be used judiciously and ethically. It is easy to imagine some readers rejecting Shields's argument in favor of gun control and turning her appeal to the opposite position. The same emotions she invokes in favor of gun control can be used in an argument opposing it. For example, a parent whose child was murdered might take the position that arming oneself with a handgun can help prevent violent crime and might have saved his or her child. Moreover, the logical weaknesses in her argument might disturb some readers who might interpret her emotional appeal as unfair. In evaluating positions like these, it is important to sort out the emotional appeals, as well as the specific logical arguments, each person is making.

Arguments about controversial issues such as gun control are fertile ground for emotional appeals, but emotion can be used in any argument. Here's an excerpt from an essay by Filip Bondy published the day after Brazil's soccer team won the 2002 World Cup:

> He cried, he laughed, he scored. Ronaldo put his mark on this special World Cup Sunday with a redemptive samba—two second-half goals in the 2-0 championship victory by Brazil over Germany, and eight goals in seven matches.
>
> Ronaldo's tale is now one for the ages, from the streets of Rio to the Yokohama stadium where he trotted about the field in triumph, hugging everyone, with a Brazil flag draped from his broad shoulders.
>
> The son of a drug-addicted father and a rock-steady mother, Ronaldo had blown off school as a youngster to play street soccer, to become that odd athletic combination of bull and gazelle that made him such a unique talent.
>
> He wouldn't listen to his mother, who wanted him to study hard and to become a doctor. Instead, he aimed for something even more impossible—a career in soccer—and somehow succeeded. The trail, however, was not always as direct as his style.

In this argument celebrating Ronaldo, Bondy appeals not only to his readers' admiration for Ronaldo's achievement but also to the joy that sports fans so often feel when they witness a victory by a great champion. In addition, in referring to the story of Ronaldo's difficult childhood, Bondy is also likely to stir up positive feelings about family, hard work, and the pursuit of individual dreams. Although he is not writing about something as controversial as gun control, Bondy's appeal to these emotions may help make his argument about Ronaldo's achievement more convincing to his readers, whether they are fans of Brazil's soccer team or not.

This example illustrates that emotional appeals can work on several levels. Notice, for example, that the idea of a world championship in sports can be used to evoke pride or admiration in readers, emotions that become integral to the entire argument. By contrast, the brief descriptions of Ronaldo's childhood can elicit different emotions, which the writer uses for different purposes—in this case, to help support his

Ronaldo celebrating Brazil's
World Cup win

http://news.bbc.co.uk/media/images/38107000/jpg/_38107505_roanldo_ap300.jpg

point that Ronaldo's achievement is a special one and perhaps to create additional admiration for Ronaldo as an individual. Visual details and individual words or phrases can have the same effect. For example, think about your own reaction to the description of Ronaldo "hugging everyone, with a Brazil flag draped from his broad shoulders" or of Ronaldo's father as "drug-addicted." Certain words have powerful associations; in this case "drug-addicted" might create greater sympathy for Ronaldo. Terms such as *family values, environmentally friendly, freedom of choice,* and *American* are often used precisely because of the emotions they evoke. As a writer, you can employ such carefully chosen words as you build your argument. But be mindful of the potential risks of doing so. A single word, such as *drugs,* can elicit different responses in different readers, and it is important to try to understand the associations that a particular word or phrase might carry for readers. It is equally important to recognize how such words might influence you when you encounter them in someone else's argument.

How you use the power of emotion in an argument depends not only on your ability to assess the impact of a line of reasoning or an emotional appeal on your audience but also on what you hope to accomplish with an argument. If your purpose is to address a problem or to negotiate differences regarding a difficult or complex issue, then you must take care to employ emotional appeals appropriately and ethically. The challenge, when drawing upon *pathos,* is to make sure that the feelings being expressed or evoked contribute to the argument rather than distract from it.

Understanding *Logos*: Appeals to Reason

Because *logos* sounds so much like logic, it is easy to assume that the two are synonymous. They are certainly similar. Classical rhetoricians such as Aristotle devoted much attention to how to reason logically and how to use logic to persuade an audience. But in addition to logic, *logos* involves having good command of information and language. It is impossible to argue logically, after all, if you use words imprecisely or cannot support your claims with evidence.

Logic is often associated with objectivity. We tend to think of a logical argument as one that is made objectively on the basis of facts or reason rather than emotion. Consider the following letter written in 2002 by Gerald Gordon to the *New York Times* editor in response to an editorial by David Plotz. In his editorial, Plotz criticized the government of Fairfax County in Virginia for its policies concerning growth and development and argued that the county was in crisis. Gordon who was president of the Fairfax County Economic Development Authority at the time, challenged Plotz's position:

> I disagree that the county is in crisis. In 2001, my agency helped 164 companies that said they would create more than 11,500 jobs here. Compare that with tech centers like San Jose, California, and Atlanta, which have been shedding jobs by the tens of thousands.
>
> Also, Mr. Plotz says there is only enough "greenery left for a side salad." Funny line, but the county has more than 30,000 acres of dedicated parkland, including a national wildlife refuge established to protect bald eagles and one of the largest urban marshes on the east coast.

Gordon makes his main argument—that Fairfax County is not in crisis—by claiming that the county has plentiful jobs as well as substantial open green spaces. He cites specific figures (the potential creation of 11,500 jobs by 164 companies; 30,000 acres of parks) to support his claim. His argument relies on the following logic: Jobs and open spaces are indicators of a healthy county, and Fairfax County has both; therefore, it is a healthy county (it is not in crisis). Gordon's major assumption is that jobs and open spaces are good for a county. If you share that assumption, his argument will probably be persuasive to you; if not, then the support he offers becomes meaningless. For example, you might assume that a truly healthy county is one in which the majority of residents are home owners and have median incomes above the national average. If so, then the existence of jobs alone would not indicate a healthy county, nor would the existence of green space. In other words, the effectiveness of a logical argument depends in large part on whether or not the main assumption—usually called the *main premise* in formal logic—is valid or acceptable.

Arguments rarely rely on logic alone, but the use of logic in an argument can be extremely effective, in part because we tend to think of reason as superior to emotion when it comes to argumentation. Objective, rational arguments are often considered more valid than openly emotional ones. Of course, the very idea of objectivity has been questioned, and because we often engage in argument over complex and important issues that matter deeply to us, avoiding emotion is rarely possible and not necessarily even desirable. Nevertheless, logic can be a powerful component of a writer's effort to engage in argumentation, and even when we make arguments that appeal to emotion or character, we will probably incorporate some elements of logic and reason.

Patterns of Logic

Logical arguments can take several forms. The most common, which are derived from classical rhetoric, are *inductive reasoning* and *deductive reasoning*. In the late twentieth century, however, communication specialists became interested in a pattern of reasoning called the Toulmin method. This chapter introduces all three of these approaches.

Reasoning Inductively   When you use induction, you are drawing a conclusion based on specific evidence. Your argument rests on a foundation of details accumulated for its support. This is the type of reasoning used most frequently in daily life. In the morning you look at the sky outside the window, check the outdoor temperature, and perhaps listen to a weather forecast before dressing for the day. If the sun is shining, the temperature is high, and the forecast is favorable, you are drawing a reasonable conclusion if you decide to dress lightly and leave the umbrella at home. You haven't *proved* that the day will be warm and pleasant; you have only *concluded* that it will be. This is all you can usually do in an inductive argument: arrive at a conclusion that seems likely to be true on the basis of available evidence. Ultimate and positive proof is usually beyond reach. In this sense, induction can be seen as a way for a writer of an argument to deal with probability.

Listen, for example, to literary critic Sven Birkerts as he considers the technological changes he saw taking place in the 1990s. Birkerts is concerned that new electronic media, especially those driven by computers, are adversely affecting our lives, in particular how we read and write, without our being aware of it. "A change is upon us," he asserts, "away from the patterns and habits of the printed page and toward a new world distinguished by its reliance on electronic communication":

> The evidence of the change is all around us, though possibly in the manner of the forest that we cannot see for the trees. The electronic media, while conspicuous in gadgetry, are very nearly invisible in their functioning. They have slipped deeply and irrevocably into our midst, creating sluices and circulating through them. I'm not referring to any one product or function in isolation, such as television or fax machines or the networks that make them possible. I mean the interdependent totality that has arisen from the conjoining of parts—the disk drives hooked to modems, transmissions linked to technologies of reception, duplication, and storage. Numbers and codes and frequencies. Buttons and signals. And this is no longer "the future," except for the poor or the self-consciously atavistic—it is now. Next to the new technologies, the scheme of things represented by print and the snailpaced linearity of the reading act looks stodgy and dull. Many educators say that our students are less and less able to read, or analyze, or write with clarity and purpose. Who can blame the students? Everything they meet with in the world around them gives them the signal: That was then, and electronic communications are now.

Notice that Birkerts offers a series of observations about the effect of the technological changes he sees in our lives. He cites examples to illustrate the effects that these changes seem to be having on how we communicate. He then concludes that students no longer learn to read and write as they did before the advent of these new technologies. He cannot be certain of this result; no one can. But the evidence around him suggests that such a result is not only possible but perhaps even likely. He is reasoning inductively from available evidence.

This kind of reasoning is common in scientific research. Scientists may have a theory that explains some phenomenon, but they must carry out many experiments to prove the theory is valid. These experiments will enable the scientists to eliminate certain variables and gather enough data to justify a generally applicable conclusion. Ideally, a well-researched scientific conclusion will reach a point at which it seems uncontestable. One such example is the warning on cigarette packages. Over the years so much evidence has accumulated to link cigarette smoking to cancer that the warning has evolved from a probability to a veritable certainty. Most writers of arguments cannot hope to reach such certain conclusions through induction. Instead, like Birkerts, they try to draw reasonable conclusions based on their observations and the evidence they present. If writers are careful and thorough and have gathered sufficient evidence, their conclusions will usually seem valid to readers.

In making an inductive argument, you will reach a point at which you will decide that you have offered enough evidence to support your conclusion. When you are writing a college paper, you will probably decide that you have reached this point sooner than a scientist might. But whether you are writing a short argument or conducting a major investigation, the reasoning process is essentially the same. When you stop citing evidence and move on to your conclusion, you have made what is known as an *inductive leap*. In an inductive argument, you offer interpretation or analysis of the evidence you have introduced; however, there will always be a slight gap between your evidence and your conclusion. So your evidence must be in proportion to their conclusion.

If you listen closely to the conversations of people around you, chances are good that you'll hear examples of weak inductive reasoning. For instance, if someone who has never eaten Mexican food other than tacos from a fast-food chain says, "I don't like Mexican food," that person is drawing a sweeping conclusion inductively from minimal evidence. As a result, you cannot take this judgment seriously. Sound inductive reasoning, by contrast, is like the work of a good police detective, who draws conclusions carefully from sufficient evidence. The detective does not arrive at the scene of a crime already certain about what happened. Although he may already have a suspicion about who is responsible, he will study every piece of evidence that can be gathered and keep searching for clues that will solve the case and lead to a just and successful prosecution. He analyzes the evidence carefully and arrives at a logical conclusion about what happened. Writers who make effective arguments from inductive reasoning work in the same way.

Reasoning Deductively   When an argument rests on a fundamental truth, right, or value, rather than on available evidence, it employs deductive reasoning. Whereas in inductive reasoning a writer begins with observations or evidence and draws conclusions from those, in deductive reasoning the writer begins with a basic truth or belief and proceeds from there. Evidence is still cited in support of the argument, but evidence is of secondary importance. The writer's first concern is to define a commonly accepted value or belief that will prepare the way for the argument she or he wants to make.

One of the most famous examples of an argument based on deductive reasoning is the Declaration of Independence, written by Thomas Jefferson. (To read the Declaration of Independence, go to page 567.) Jefferson rested his argument on the belief that "all men are created equal" and that they have "certain unalienable Rights," and he cited numerous grievances to provide evidence that King George III had violated those rights. This was a revolutionary idea in the eighteenth century, and even today there are people who question it. But if you accept the idea that all people are created equal and have an inherent right to "Life, Liberty, and the pursuit of Happiness," as Jefferson asserted, then certain conclusions follow. The writer's task is to work logically toward those conclusions. Accordingly, Jefferson argued for a specific action—the separation of the colonies from England—based on the principle of equality. In other words, having established the fundamental truth of the equality of all people, he reasoned that the king's actions were unacceptable and concluded that the colonies must become independent.

The truth, right, or belief from which a writer deduces an argument is called the **premise.** Often, the main premise of a deductive argument is not immediately obvious, but even when you don't recognize it, it is the crucial element holding together the argument. Look at a more current example of an argument based on deductive reasoning, a *New York Times* editorial written in 2002 in response to a controversial court ruling that declared the Pledge of Allegiance unconstitutional:

> Half a century ago, at the height of anti-Communist fervor, Congress added the words "under God" to the Pledge of Allegiance. It was a petty attempt to link patriotism with religious piety, to distinguish us from the godless Soviets. But after millions of repetitions over the years, the phrase has become part of the backdrop of American life, just like the words "In God We Trust" on our coins and "God bless America" uttered by presidents at the end of important speeches.
>
> Yesterday, the United States Court of Appeals for the Ninth Circuit in California ruled 2 to 1 that those words in the pledge violate the First Amendment, which says that "Congress shall make no law respecting an establishment of religion." The majority sided with Michael Newdow, who had complained that his daughter is injured when forced to listen to public school teachers lead students daily in a pledge that includes the assertion that there is a God.
>
> This is a well-meaning ruling, but it lacks common sense. A generic two-word reference to God tucked inside a rote civic exercise is not a prayer. Mr. Newdow's daughter is not required to say either the words "under God" or even the pledge itself, as the Supreme Court made clear in a 1943 case involving Jehovah's Witnesses. In the pantheon of real First Amendment concerns, this one is off the radar screen.
>
> The practical impact of the ruling is inviting a political backlash for a matter that does not rise to a constitutional violation. We wish the words had not been added back in 1954. But just the way removing a well-lodged foreign body from an organism may sometimes be more damaging than letting it stay put, removing those words would cause more harm than leaving them in. By late afternoon yesterday, virtually every politician in Washington was rallying loudly behind the pledge in its current form.
>
> Most important, the ruling trivializes the critical constitutional issue of separation of church and state. There are important battles to be fought virtually every year over issues of prayer in school and use of government funds to support religious activities. Yesterday's decision is almost certain to be overturned on appeal. But the sort of rigid overreaction that characterized it will not make genuine defense of the First Amendment any easier.

Obviously, the editors of the *New York Times* disagree with the court's ruling. They support the idea of the separation of church and state, which is a fundamental principle contained in the U.S. Constitution. Notice that they are not arguing for or against this principle; they accept it as true and good. Their argument proceeds from that principle. They criticize the ruling not because it violates this principle but because they see no genuine threat to this principle that would justify the court's decision. According to the editors, the ruling is intended to help maintain the constitutional separation of church and state, which they believe is admirable. But in their view, common sense indicates that the words "under God" in the Pledge of Allegiance do not represent a significant threat to that constitutional principle. So you might articulate the editors' main premise as follows:

Premise: Serious threats to the constitutional separation of church and state should be opposed.

In this instance no serious threat exists in the editors' view; therefore, the ruling makes no sense. They develop their argument by examining what they consider to be some of the negative consequences of the ruling.

This kind of argumentation is quite common. Glance at an editorial page of any newspaper, and you're likely to see one or more examples of an argument based on deductive reasoning. But as the preceding example shows, formulating—or identifying—a good premise can be a challenge. A good premise should satisfy at least two basic requirements:

- It should be general enough that an audience is likely to accept it, thus establishing a common ground between writer and audience.
- It should be specific enough to prepare the way for the argument that will follow.

In this example, the editors can be confident that most of their readers will understand the idea of the separation of church and state. Certainly, not all of their readers will agree that this principle is a good one that should be maintained, but most American readers very likely will agree. So the editors' task is to build an argument that might convince those readers that no threat to that principle exists in this case.

What makes formulating a good premise difficult is that a premise usually refers to or invokes fundamental values or beliefs that we don't often examine consciously. In the case of the Declaration of Independence, Jefferson clearly articulated a fundamental belief in equality, which most of us today understand and accept. The *New York Times* editors invoke a constitutional principle that, while controversial, is nevertheless well known and easily identified. In some cases the premise will be harder to identify. But being able to identify the basic premise of an argument is an important skill that will help you more effectively evaluate arguments you encounter; it will also help you write effective arguments.

The Syllogism   Deductive reasoning often follows a pattern of what is called a **syllogism,** a three-part argument in which the conclusion rests on two premises, the first of which is the **major premise,** because it is the main assumption on which the argument rests. Here's a simple example of a syllogism:

Major Premise: All people have hearts.
Minor Premise: John is a person.
Conclusion: Therefore, John has a heart.

If both premises are true—as they are in this case—then the conclusion should also be true. Note that the major and minor premises have a term in common (in this example, *people* or *person*). In a written argument the minor premise usually involves a specific case that relates to the more general statement with which the essay began. For instance, you might set up a syllogism based on the *New York Times* editorial on page 82 like this:

Major Premise:	Serious threats to the constitutional separation of church and state should be opposed.
Minor Premise:	The phrase "under God" in the Pledge of Allegiance does not constitute a serious threat to the constitutional separation of church and state.
Conclusion:	Therefore, the Pledge of Allegiance should not be opposed. (That is, the appeals court ruling that the Pledge is unconstitutional is incorrect.)

Notice that the minor premise cites a specific threat, whereas the major premise refers to a more general principle or belief. You can see from this example, however, how quickly syllogistic reasoning can become complicated. You can also see that the major and minor premises are not universally held to be true or valid; many people may disagree with either or both of them. The writers of this editorial surely knew that, and they probably calculated that most of their readers would accept their major premise as true.

The Enthymeme

Because it can be difficult to follow the rules of logic, faulty reasoning is common. Consider another simple example:

Major Premise:	All women like to cook.
Minor Premise:	Elizabeth is a woman.
Conclusion:	Therefore, Elizabeth likes to cook.

Technically, the form here is correct. The two premises have a term in common, and if you accept both premises as true, then you also have to accept the conclusion. But the major premise is faulty. Elizabeth, like many women (and men), might hate to cook, preferring to go out bowling at night or to read the latest issue of the *Journal of Organic Chemistry.* A syllogism may be valid in terms of its organization, but it can be untrue if it rests on a major premise that is false or can easily be disputed. Usually, the major premise is a generalization, as in this example, but some generalizations make sense and will be widely accepted whereas others will not. And it is easy to confuse generally accepted truths with privately held beliefs. In this case some people might believe that all women like to cook, but many people will not hold that belief. You can argue in favor of a private belief, but you cannot expect an audience to accept an easily debatable opinion as the foundation for an argument on behalf of yet another opinion. In other words, the validity of the logic of your argument depends on the validity of your premises.

It is also important to realize that in many arguments a premise might be implied but not stated. You might overhear a conversation like this one:

"I hear you and Elizabeth are getting married."

"Yes, that's true."

"Well, now that you've got a woman to cook for you, maybe you could invite me over for dinner sometime."

"Why do you think that Elizabeth will be doing the cooking?"

"Because she's a woman."

The first speaker has made a number of possible assumptions. He or she might believe that all women like to cook or perhaps that all women are required to cook whether they like it or not. But these assumptions were not stated. If they were, it would be easy for the other speaker to point out the flaw in the first speaker's reasoning.

This example suggests why many people see formal logic as too rigid for everyday arguments. Although formal logic can help us understand arguments and identify the assumptions used in argument, rarely do writers of arguments consciously try to follow its rules. However, we routinely use logic in our day-to-day discussions and arguments, though more informally. We regularly make and support claims, make and evaluate assumptions, and draw or oppose conclusions, and our doing so according to the rules of formal logic would be cumbersome and perhaps even silly. Consider the following statement:

"I'd better close the windows, because the sky is getting darker."

If you examined this statement carefully, you could devise a syllogism to reveal the logic inherent in the statement:

Major Premise:	A dark sky indicates rain.
Minor Premise:	The sky is getting darker.
Conclusion:	Therefore, it will probably rain (and I should close the windows).

You'll notice that in the original statement the major premise is implicit. Yet the statement is a form of logic nonetheless. Indeed, it would sound silly if we spoke in formal syllogisms in such situations. The point is that we need to make claims and provide reasons as we conduct our day-to-day affairs, but we need to do so efficiently. And we can usually assume certain beliefs or knowledge on the part of our listeners without having to state them explicitly.

For centuries theorists have been exploring the uses of such informal logic in arguments. Aristotle called this kind of informal logic a rhetorical syllogism, or an **enthymeme.** You might think of an enthymeme as a syllogism that consists of only two parts: In the preceding example, the major premise is missing. Or think of an enthymeme in terms of practical logic. In other words, rather than trying to follow the rigid rules of formal logic when making an argument, you are applying logic where it is most useful to you. Aristotle understood that in most situations such informal uses of logic are not only efficient and practical but effective as well.

There are two important ways in which understanding logic and employing informal logic, such as enthymemes, can be helpful to you: (1) as a reader (or listener) who is trying to make sense of and evaluate an argument and (2) as a writer who is trying to construct an effective argument. As a reader, you are often confronted with arguments—on a newspaper editorial page, in a reading assignment for a college course, in a political flyer you received in the mail, in advertising (see "Logical Arguments in Advertising"). Being able to identify the premises on which an argument is based, especially when they are implicit, enables you to evaluate the argument and perhaps to uncover problems or flaws in the argument. For writers, logic can be a powerful way not only to make a persuasive case for a position but also to organize an argument. (See pages 119–144 for a discussion of organizing an argument.)

LOGICAL ARGUMENTS IN ADVERTISING

Advertising regularly employs informal logical, relying on readers or viewers to understand the implicit premises of the argument made by an ad. For example, this advertisement for the popular soft drink Coca-Cola seems to make an argument that you should buy the soft drink because the company is concerned about the environment. As concerns about global climate change grew in the past decade, many companies began to draw on those concerns in their advertising. In this image, the familiar red color of the Coca-Cola can is replaced with green, the color associated with environmental awareness. The ad's major premise might be stated as follows: We should all be concerned about the environment. The green color of the Coca-Cola can seems to suggest that the company is concerned about the environment. Therefore, the ad seems to conclude, buying Coca-Cola can be seen as good for the environment.

Marc Simon Photography

Cultural Differences in Logical Arguments

It is important to keep in mind that people from different cultural backgrounds might make different assumptions that they take for granted their audience shares. For example, in making an argument against sweatshops in which U.S. corporations employ young workers in Asian countries, an American writer might assume that his or her readers share a belief that child labor is a bad thing. That would probably be a safe assumption with an American audience: Child labor has long been illegal in the United States (except under certain circumstances), and Americans generally seem to agree that it should be illegal. However, a reader from a rural community in Bangladesh, for instance, where children routinely work on local farms to help their families earn a living, might not share that assumption. In such a case the writer's argument would likely have different effects on these different readers. You can easily think of more dramatic examples of such cultural differences and how they might affect logical argument. The suicide bombings that have taken place in the midst of religious and ethnic conflicts in the Middle East and elsewhere in the world have been the subject of intense debate, which has revealed deep differences in how people can view violence, suicide, national identity, and religious belief. In such a charged and difficult context a writer cannot safely assume, for instance, that his or her readers will accept the view that suicide is inherently wrong. Even when engaging in argumentation about less controversial issues, you will almost certainly encounter the need to understand how cultural differences might influence the way readers will react to your assumptions (see "Cultural Differences in the Informal Logic of Advertising" on page 87).

CULTURAL DIFFERENCES IN THE INFORMAL LOGIC OF ADVERTISING

Advertisements can be seen as arguments to buy a certain product or patronize a specific business. Often, ads rely on implicit assumptions that are culturally specific. For example, this image is from an advertisement for EA Sports, a company that produces popular sports video games. The implicit argument seems to be that EA Sports video games are desirable because they embrace the idea of challenge. The implicit assumption is that to "challenge everything" is desirable. EA Sports video games embrace this idea; therefore, they are desirable. It is probably safe for the advertiser to assume that audiences in the United States will find the tagline "challenge everything" appealing, because such an idea is strong in American culture. But in some cultures, openly challenging others is considered disrespectful; the tagline "challenge everything," therefore, is unlikely to be appealing to audiences in those cultures.

AP Images/Eckehard Schulz

The Toulmin Model of Argumentation

Formal logic, although it is a powerful framework for argumentation, has its limitations. Most people prefer not to be bound by a predetermined method of structuring an argument and regard the syllogism, in particular, as unnecessarily rigid. Many writers therefore combine inductive and deductive reasoning in making an argument and often make arguments without the use of formal logic. Partly for these reasons scholars have long explored alternative ways of employing logic so that it becomes more practical and effective in arguments. One of the best-known systems for doing so was developed by a British philosopher named Stephen Toulmin in the 1950s. Emphasizing that logic is concerned with probability more often than with certainty, Toulmin provided a new way of analyzing arguments that focused on the nature of claims.

Toulmin's model includes three main components: the claim, the data or reasons, and the warrant. According to Toulmin, the basis of all arguments is the **claim,** which is the writer's (or speaker's) statement of belief—the conclusion or point he or she wishes to prove. The **data** or reasons are the evidence or information a writer or speaker offers to support the claim. The **warrant** is a general statement that establishes a trustworthy relationship between the data and the claim; it is a fundamental assumption (similar to the major premise in formal logic) on which a claim can be made and supported. In an argument, the claim and data will be explicit, but the warrant is often implied, especially if the person making the argument assumes that the audience accepts the warrant. In that case the task is simply to present sufficient evidence to support the claim. However, if the audience disagrees with the warrant or finds it unacceptable, then the writer must defend it to make the claim.

ELEMENTS OF THE TOULMIN SYSTEM OF ARGUMENT

Claim: The conclusion or the main point being argued.

Data: The evidence supporting the claim. Also called the reasons.

Warrant: Basic principle or assumption that connects the data and the claim.

To better understand these terms, consider an example adapted from one of Toulmin's examples:

Claim:	Raymond is an American citizen.
Data:	Raymond was born in Puerto Rico.
Warrant:	Anyone born in Puerto Rico is an American citizen.

These three statements might remind you of the three elements in a deductive argument. If arranged as a syllogism, they might look like this:

Major Premise:	Anyone born in Puerto Rico is an American citizen.
Minor Premise:	Raymond was born in Puerto Rico.
Conclusion:	Raymond is an American citizen.

In this example, the conclusion can be true *only if* the major premise is true. The advantage of Toulmin's model becomes apparent when you realize that the major premise here might not be true. For example, Raymond might have been born to French parents who were vacationing in Puerto Rico. Because the rigid logic of the syllogism is designed to lead to a conclusion that is *necessarily* true, Toulmin argued that it is ill suited for working toward a conclusion that is *probably* true, as in this example. Believing that the syllogism was over-emphasized in the study of logic, Toulmin saw a need for a "working logic" that would be easier to apply in the rhetorical situations in which most people find themselves—a kind of logic that would function in the kinds of arguments that people engage in every day. His model therefore easily incorporates **qualifiers** such as "probably," "presumably," and "generally." Here is a revision of the first example, employing Toulmin's model:

Claim:	Raymond is probably an American citizen.
Data:	Raymond was born in Puerto Rico.
Warrant:	Anyone born in Puerto Rico is entitled to American citizenship.

Both the claim and the warrant have been modified. Toulmin's model does not dictate any specific pattern in which these elements must be arranged, which is a great advantage for writers. The claim can be made at the beginning of an argument, or it can just as easily be placed after a discussion of the data and the warrant. Similarly, the warrant may precede the data, it may follow it, or it may be implied, as we already noted.

It is easy to see that claims and warrants can be extremely complicated and controversial, and one advantage of Toulmin's system is that it not only offers writers flexibility in constructing effective arguments but also provides readers with a way to evaluate arguments carefully. Chapter 5 discusses how Toulmin's model can help you structure your own arguments. For now it's important to examine some of the complexities of claims and warrants.

Understanding Claims and Warrants

There are different kinds of claims supported by different kinds of data: claims supported by facts, claims supported by expert opinion, claims supported by values. For example, if you wanted to argue that the stock market should be subject to greater regulation, you could base your claim primarily on facts: You could define current regulations, report on laws governing markets, cite specific abuses and scandals involving insider trading, and include figures for the money lost to investors as a result of unethical trading practices. You would present these various facts to support your claim that greater regulation is needed. By contrast, another writer might argue in favor of regulating the stock market on the basis of the values of honesty and fair play. Of course, when we argue, we often use several different kinds of claims. For example, if you wanted to argue against capital punishment, your data might consist of facts (such as the numbers of executions performed annually, differences in these figures by state or by race, and the number of death row inmates), the views of criminologists or legal experts regarding the death penalty, and an appeal to a moral value (such as the sanctity of human life) that you believe your audience might share. In short, you would present different types of data depending on the nature of the claim you are making.

Warrants (the basic principle that connects your data with your claim) are also complex, and the nature of a warrant will differ from one argument to another. Some warrants may be relatively straightforward. For example, law often constitutes a warrant. A lawyer arguing on behalf of someone claiming American citizenship might invoke the Jones Act of 1917, which guarantees U.S. citizenship to citizens of Puerto Rico. That law would become the lawyer's warrant for the claim that a person born in Puerto Rico should be considered a U.S. citizen. But because warrants sometimes reflect assumptions or beliefs, they can be disputable and controversial. For example, in arguing that capital punishment should be banned in the United States, your warrant might be that the taking of any human life is wrong. That warrant is not shared by everyone, so you should be prepared to defend it. In such a case you would strengthen your argument against capital punishment, if you explained and defended your view about the wrongness of taking human life. Simply stating or implying such a controversial warrant would likely result in some readers dismissing your argument altogether.

These examples reflect the challenges that writers—and readers—can face when they engage in argumentation about difficult or charged issues, and they are reminders that no model, including Toulmin's, will always lead to convincing arguments. But if the goal is to understand the issues adequately in order to address a problem or negotiate differences that create conflict or discord, then Toulmin's model can be a useful framework for both writers and readers.

Evaluating Claims and Warrants

Being able to make strong claims and support them adequately is a crucial part of making an effective argument. It is also a challenge, largely because most claims deal with probability rather than certainty. If you engage in serious argumentation out of a desire to address an important issue or solve a problem, you need to understand how claims function and how to evaluate claims effectively. Toulmin's ideas about claims, data, and warrants can be useful tools in helping you make and evaluate claims.

Let's look at an example of an argument about an issue that became deeply important to Americans after the terrorist attacks on the United States on September 11, 2001: national security. In response to those attacks, the U.S. government began removing information that had previously been available on many of its websites. Among the kinds of information removed were environmental statistics, emergency plans, and data on health and safety risks to Americans. A year after the attacks and several months after the government began censoring its websites, writer Mary Graham argued in the *Atlantic Monthly* that keeping such information secret in the interest of national security is not only wrong but also dangerous. She asserted that "the wholesale censorship of information on Web sites carries insidious costs." To support this central claim, Graham described how this censorship policy can undermine, rather than increase, national security. She also asserted that this kind of censorship is unfair, and she questioned whether secrecy will actually accomplish the goal of enhancing security: "National security is everyone's concern, and the idea that openness can be more effective than secrecy in reducing risks has received too little attention."

Evaluating Graham's argument requires us to examine how these assertions relate to her central claim. You might restate her claim as follows:

> Claim: The censorship of information on U.S. government websites should end because it is unfair to Americans and does not necessarily increase Americans' security.

Graham's claim is straightforward, but her claim rests on a basic assumption—her warrant—that isn't as obvious. You might state her warrant as follows:

> Warrant: Americans have a right to information related to their security.

Notice that this warrant invokes a legal principle (a specific legal right that Americans have to information); it also invokes more general ethical values (openness and fairness). Because such a warrant is likely to be acceptable to most readers of a magazine like the *Atlantic Monthly*, Graham need not defend it and can therefore concentrate on supporting her claim by offering reasons that the government's censorship policy won't achieve its goal of enhancing security. In short, her claim is clear, supported with various data, and strengthened by a warrant that is generally acceptable to her intended audience. As a reader, you can disagree with her claim, and no doubt some readers will also disagree with her warrant (believing, for example, that only government officials should have access to the kinds of information that has been censored from government websites). But if you accept her warrant, you can evaluate her argument against censorship on the basis of the evidence (data) she presents.

If a claim is based on a warrant that isn't necessarily acceptable to an audience, the writer might have to defend that warrant. Otherwise, the argument for the claim might be less persuasive to the audience. Let's examine an example in which the writer might have misjudged his audience and relied on a warrant that might be questionable for that audience. The following passage was taken from an essay in which the writer, Gary Foreman, argued against a national boycott of gasoline in 2000, when gas prices were rising quickly in the United States. At the time, some consumer advocates and environmental groups proposed a boycott—called a "gas out"—in response to rising prices. Foreman disagreed with this proposal. Because gas prices have climbed even higher since then, his argument is still relevant. He made this claim against the boycott:

> I can pretty much tell you that "Gas Out 2000" won't work. It might draw some media attention. But it won't change the price you pay at the pump by one penny. And if you'll consider the facts you'll understand why.

We might restate Foreman's claim as follows:

> Claim: A "Gas Out" won't reduce the price of gas.

Most of Foreman's essay is devoted to an explanation of the economics of gasoline production and distribution, which he uses to support his claim. In other words, the data he uses to support his claim are facts about the economics of the gasoline market that demonstrate why a boycott cannot reduce prices. But what is his warrant?

Foreman begins his essay by stating that "I'm sure tired of rising gas prices. And based on my mail many of you feel the same way." Later in his essay he writes,

> So if a "Gas Out" won't help, what can you do? One very practical thing. Use less gas. Carpool, take public transportation, combine trips or get your car tuned up. Anything you can do to save gas will put more money in your pocket. And that's the one "statement" that oil producers will notice. More importantly, you'll notice it in your wallet, too.

In these statements he implicitly conveys his warrant, which we might restate as follows:

Warrant: Paying less money for gas is desirable.

Notice that this warrant is likely to be acceptable to many people. But this essay was published in a newsletter called *Simple Living*, which promotes an environmentally sound lifestyle. The readers of that newsletter are likely to be as concerned about the environmental effects of gasoline combustion as they are about gasoline prices. In other words, for such an audience, Foreman could safely use a more environmentally conscious warrant; he could have made an argument that focused on the environmental impact of using less gas. Such an argument would likely have resonated with the readers of *Simple Living*. In fact, it is likely that many of those readers would find Foreman's argument *less* persuasive precisely because he focuses on reducing gas prices and ignores the ethical and environmental concerns that those readers probably share. In this case, readers of *Simple Living* might accept Foreman's claim that a boycott may not be a good idea but resist his warrant.

This last example highlights that claims and warrants, like other aspects of argument such as style or tone, must be understood in rhetorical context. No claim is universally valid; no warrant is universally acceptable. The audience, the cultural context, and the rhetorical situation all influence the effect of an argument. It's worth noting here, too, that because *Simple Living* was published both in print and on the World Wide Web, the writer might have assumed his audience to be much larger than just the subscribers to the printed newsletter. If so, you can see how the medium can influence an argument's warrant. (See Chapter 3 for a discussion of how media can affect argument.)

Appraising Evidence

No matter what kind of argument you are making, identifying and using appropriate evidence is crucial; it is also challenging. Consider the following examples. The first is a letter to the editors of *Consumer Reports* magazine in which the writer challenges a recommendation made in a report on how to save money:

> I disagree with your money-saving recommendation to stick with regular gasoline. I own a 2001 Chrysler Sebring and a 1996 Ford Taurus GL, both of which are supposed to use regular. But I've found that using midgrade 89-octane fuel increases highway mileage by 2 to 5 mpg.

Here's the editors' response:

> It's good to hear that something yields better fuel economy, but we wouldn't credit the fuel. We have found that temperature and climate conditions affect mileage more than octane.

Who is right? Or, to rephrase the question, whose evidence is more convincing? The writer of the letter provides evidence from his own experience that using a higher-octane fuel improves fuel economy; the magazine editors refer to their own tests as evidence suggesting otherwise. How do you judge the evidence in such a case?

As these examples suggest, almost anything can be used as evidence: statistics, opinions, observations, theories, anecdotes. It is not always easy to decide whether a particular kind of evidence might be appropriate for a specific claim. Moreover, what counts as appropriate and persuasive evidence always depends upon context. Personal experience might be acceptable to readers of a popular consumer magazine but not necessarily for a technical report on fuel economy for a government agency. The rhetorical situation in which an argument is made will help determine not only what kinds of evidence are most appropriate for that argument but also whether that evidence is likely to be persuasive.

With that in mind, let's examine four commonly used kinds of evidence:

- Facts or statistics
- Personal experience
- Authority
- Values

Facts as Evidence

In the following excerpt from an essay published in the online public interest journal *TomPaine.com,* writer Joan Wile argues against a tax refund that President George W. Bush sponsored in 2001. Wile contends that opposition to the Bush tax policies is important, even a year after the policy was adopted. Writing in 2002, she asserts,

> However, the tax abatement issue is still, if not more, critical today than a year ago. Our needs are even greater but with less revenue to address them—our receding economy; our health care crisis; our worsening environment; our failing education system; the reestablished deficit; our increasing numbers of poor with the concomitant smaller numbers of rich controlling greater amounts of wealth, as well as the necessity for greater defense (but sane and non-threatening to our civil liberties) measures against terrorism.

Wile tries to establish the importance of the tax abatement issue by presenting evidence that the nation's ongoing "needs" continue to be great. Her evidence consists of references to the problems facing the United States: "our receding economy; our health care crisis; our worsening environment; our failing education system; the reestablished deficit; our increasing numbers of poor." Notice that Wile refers to these problems as facts without necessarily establishing them as such. For example, she refers to the "receding economy" without providing, say, statistics on economic activity or stock market performance to demonstrate that the economy is indeed in recession. She can do so because in September 2002, when her essay was published, the U.S. economy was in recession. So simply referring to the economic situation suffices as evidence in this instance. Similarly, she cites "our worsening environment" and "failing education system" without specific information about them. Given the audience for *TomPaine.com,* Wile can assume that most of her readers will accept these references as adequate evidence, because she knows that those readers are likely to view both the environment and the education system as being in crisis; they will not demand further information to support her assertions. But what if she were writing for a politically conservative journal? In that case she would most likely have to supply additional evidence—perhaps in the form of figures indicating increased air and water pollution or declining scores on standardized educational tests—to persuade readers that such crises do exist. In short, what counts as a fact and what is considered ample evidence depend in part on context and audience.

Whatever the writer's intended audience, a reader must decide whether the evidence presented in support of a claim is adequate. In this example, Wile's argument that the tax refund was a bad idea rests on her claim that the nation has pressing problems that require tax dollars. She supports that claim by listing those problems. If you agree that the problems she lists are real and pressing, then you will likely accept her claim and find her argument persuasive. If you don't agree that such problems exist, her evidence will not be adequate to persuade you that the tax refund should be opposed. Sometimes, simply referring to something won't suffice. More specific evidence is required. Here is part of an essay by a college president who believes that the problems in U.S. schools will not be solved unless teachers are adequately supported in their work:

> We often marginalize our teachers rather than celebrate and reward their contributions. Recent national data reveal that the average annual earnings of young teachers between the ages of 22 and 28 was 30 percent less than similarly aged professionals in other fields. By the time these teachers reach 50, the salary gap almost doubles—a little more than $45,000 for veteran teachers versus almost $80,000 for non-teachers. Of course, many of these new teachers don't stay in the profession to age 50. We lose 30 percent of our new teachers in their first five years of teaching and more than 40 percent in large metropolitan areas like New York City.

This writer, R. Mark Sullivan, provides statistical data to support his claim that teachers are not celebrated and rewarded for their contributions. His audience is a general one: the readers of a regional newspaper. He can assume that they will be familiar with some of the problems facing schools, but he probably cannot assume that all his readers will accept his claim that teachers are not supported adequately. To establish that point, he cites evidence showing income disparities between teachers and other professionals. For many readers such figures can be compelling, because income is such an important factor in most people's lives. As a result, many readers will likely see figures demonstrating lower incomes for teachers as good evidence that teachers are not well supported.

But look carefully at the second set of statistics Sullivan offers: the percentage of new teachers who quit teaching within five years. Does this evidence really support his claim that teachers are not well supported? On the surface it might seem so. One explanation for the seemingly high number of teachers leaving the profession might be their low salaries (which is what Sullivan suggests). Another explanation (which Sullivan does not suggest) might be that teachers' working conditions are difficult. These figures might also suggest that not everyone can be a good teacher, and perhaps those teachers who quit shouldn't be teaching anyway. If it is true that young teachers quit because they simply have not been effective teachers, then the figures Sullivan cites might work against his claim: His statistics could suggest that the best teachers remain in the classroom and the ineffective ones leave. Moreover, Sullivan never gives the attrition rates for other professions. How many accountants or engineers quit their jobs within five years, for example? That information could change the significance of the figures that Sullivan cites. If 25 percent of accountants or engineers quit in their first five years, then 30 percent of teachers might not seem so high a number—in which case it would not be persuasive evidence for Sullivan's claim.

This example suggests the importance of examining evidence carefully to determine whether it supports a claim. As a reader, you should pay close attention to *how* a writer is using evidence, as well as to *what* evidence is presented. In this example Sullivan uses statistical evidence, which is usually considered valid and can be persuasive for many audiences. But as noted, it is important to examine just what the statistics might indicate. Even if statistical evidence is accepted as true, it may be open to interpretation. Think about the ongoing debates about global warming. In these debates participants often point to statistics showing the rising average temperature of the earth. Most scientists seem to agree that the average global temperature has increased in the past century, but they do not agree about what that means. Do rising global temperatures *prove* that humans have caused global warming? Or do they reflect natural cycles of warming and cooling? A statistical fact by itself has no inherent significance. How it is used and in what context it is used make all the difference.

Personal Experience as Evidence

In the previous example, writer R. Mark Sullivan's use of statistics can be seen as a savvy strategy because many readers are likely to accept statistical evidence as valid. But Sullivan might have used other kinds of evidence to support his claim that teachers are not adequately rewarded for their work. For example, he might have included statements from people who have left teaching because they didn't feel supported. Or he might have referred to his own experience as a teacher (assuming that he had such experience) or perhaps to the experience of someone he knows well—say, a colleague or neighbor—who left teaching for that reason. The readers of a regional newspaper might find that kind of evidence as compelling as statistical evidence.

Consider how the writer of the following passage uses his own experience as evidence. The passage is taken from an essay that argues against the designation of New York's Adirondack Mountains as "wilderness":

> The irony is that one actually has a truer "wilderness experience" in Adirondack lands designated "wild forest" than in those designated "wilderness." How can this be? The answer is in the numbers—of people, that is. Without the "status" of wilderness, the lowly wild forest just grows on, with little to no human molestation. While there may be a road or two, it is the road less traveled. There may not be a High Peak to bag, but chances are you'll see real wildlife… and some lower elevation vistas that fewer eyes have seen. And amazingly enough, you will probably not see another human. I can say this because I have experienced it.

This writer supports his claim about the wilderness experience in "wild forest" areas by stating that he himself has had that experience. It can be hard to deny the validity of such experience. Think of the weight often given to eyewitness testimony in legal cases: If a person saw something, it must be true. But the extent to which readers will find such first-hand evidence compelling will vary. And readers can question this kind of evidence, just as they can question statistical data. For one thing, where exactly did this writer go in the Adirondacks? It's possible that he visited a few unusual locations that are not representative of most "wild forest" areas. Also, when did he go? He would almost certainly encounter fewer (or no) other hikers on some trails in February than he would in July. And how often did he visit these places? If he visited them only once or twice, then his experience might not be typical for those areas. If so, that experience becomes much less forceful as evidence for his claim than it would be if he regularly visited these areas throughout the year. Raising questions like these will help you evaluate personal experience used as evidence.

Authority as Evidence

Citing experts or authorities as evidence is common in all kinds of arguments, but it is especially important in many academic disciplines. Here is an excerpt from *Ecological Literacy,* in which scholar David Orr argues that perpetual economic growth cannot be sustained without irreparable damage to the earth's ecosystems:

> In a notable book in 1977, economist Fred Hirsch described other limits to growth that were inherently social. As the economy grows, the goods and services available to everyone theoretically increase.... After basic biological and physical needs are met, an increasing portion of consumption is valued because it raises one's status in society. But, "If everyone in a crowd stands on tiptoe," as Hirsch puts it, "no one sees better." Rising levels of consumption do not necessarily increase one's status.

In this passage, Orr draws on the work of a respected economist to support his claim about the dangers of constant economic growth. Notice that Orr underscores the authority of Hirsch's work by describing his book as "notable." Then he presents Hirsch's views about economic growth. Following this passage, Orr summarizes what Hirsch describes as the effects of the desire for more consumption, including such unhappy consequences as "a decline in friendliness, the loss of altruism and mutual obligation, increased time pressures," and so on. Then Orr concludes, "In short, after basic biological needs are met, further growth both 'fails to deliver its full promise' and 'undermines its social foundations.'"

In this case Orr does not offer factual evidence; rather, he cites Hirsch's theories to make the claim that unchecked economic growth is undesirable. In effect, Orr is deferring to Hirsch's expertise as an economist to support this claim. Although what Hirsch offers is essentially an interpretation of economic data and social and economic developments, rather than the data themselves, his status as an expert gives his interpretation weight. Orr relies on that status in using Hirsch's ideas as evidence.

In evaluating an argument like Orr's, you must decide how credible the authority or expert really is. If you know nothing about the work of Hirsch, you have to take Orr's word for it or find Hirsch's book and examine it for yourself. Notice that Orr summarizes Hirsch's key ideas in this passage. He probably assumed that many of his readers would not be familiar with Hirsch's theories. So telling us that Hirsch is an economist who authored a "notable" book helps establish Hirsch's authority on the subject. Orr's claim depends largely on whether his readers accept that authority as credible.

Using a well-known authority or expert to support has obvious advantages. Not only will readers be familiar with the authority, but a widely accepted authority might have an established credibility that a writer can rely on. Consider how Martin Luther King, Jr., in this passage from his famous "Letter From a Birmingham Jail," draws on biblical and historical figures to support his claim that being an extremist for freedom is just and right:

> But though I was initially disappointed at being categorized as an extremist, as I continued to think about the matter I gradually gained a measure of satisfaction from the label. Was not Jesus an extremist for love: "Love your enemies, bless them that curse you, do good to them that hate you, and pray for them which despitefully use you, and persecute you." Was not Amos an extremist for justice: "Let justice roll down like waters and righteousness like an overflowing stream." Was not Paul an extremist for the Christian gospel: "I bear in my body the marks of the Lord Jesus." Was not Martin Luther an extremist: "Here I stand; I cannot do otherwise, so help

me God." And John Bunyan: "I will stay in jail to the end of my days before I make a butchery of my conscience." And Abraham Lincoln: "This nation cannot survive half slave and half free." And Thomas Jefferson: "We hold these truths to be self-evident, that all men are created equal."

Clearly, King expects these names to have credibility with his readers. The moral weight of the names he cites will give force to the quotations he uses as evidence in this passage.

Values as Evidence

The passage from King's "Letter From a Birmingham Jail" points to a final kind of evidence: values or beliefs. (You can read King's "Letter From a Birmingham Jail" on pages 576–587.) Although King uses the authority of the names he cites in this passage, he is also invoking deeply held moral values. Elsewhere in his "Letter" he uses these values directly as evidence to support specific claims. For example, in arguing that he and his followers were justified in breaking laws that prohibited Blacks from visiting public places, King cites a moral principle:

> One has not only a legal but a moral responsibility to obey just laws. Conversely, one has a moral responsibility to disobey unjust laws. I would agree with St. Augustine that "an unjust law is no law at all."

In effect, King uses the value of justice as evidence that his disobedience was justified and even necessary. Using values or beliefs as evidence in this way can be tricky. If you invoke a principle or value that your readers do not share, your evidence will not be persuasive to them and your argument may be weakened. In addition, values and beliefs can be open to interpretation, just like factual evidence or personal experience. Consider, for example, the ongoing controversies about capital punishment. Both opponents and supporters of capital punishment cite moral values to support their arguments—sometimes, the same value or principle (for example, "Thou shalt not kill"). In assessing such evidence, be aware of how it might be received by your intended readers.

Presenting Evidence in Visual Form

Evidence, especially factual or statistical evidence, is sometimes presented in visual formats within a written argument. In some cases presenting evidence graphically can be more effective than simply incorporating it into the text.

For example, imagine that you are making a claim that the decrease in housing prices that occurred in the United States between 2004 and 2008 was the worst such drop in two decades. In support of this claim, you can cite statistics showing that housing prices dropped by approximately 40 percent during that period; in addition, you might note that in the previous two decades, the largest drop in housing prices that occurred was less than 20 percent (between 1989 and 1991). Such figures would provide strong support for your claim. But they might work much more effectively if presented in a chart, such as in Figure 4-1, which graphically illustrates the dramatic drop in housing values that occurred after 2004.

Word processing and desktop publishing computer software, along with the rise of the World Wide Web as a medium with multimedia capabilities, make it easy for writers to incorporate visual elements into their arguments in this way. At the same time, these technologies make it even more important for readers to develop the ability to evaluate evidence carefully. Evidence presented visually, as in Figure 4-1, can be appealing and persuasive, but it should be subjected to the same careful scrutiny that you would use to assess any evidence.

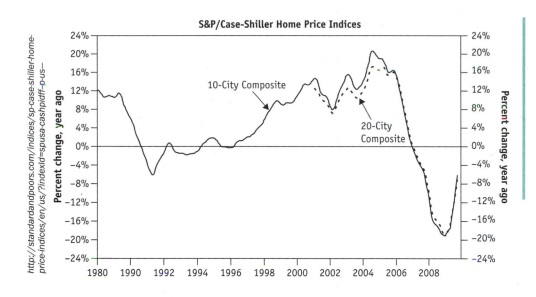

http://standardandpoors.com/indices/sp-case-shiller-home-price-indices/en/us/?indexId=spusa-cashpidff-p-us—

FIGURE 4-1

Presenting Evidence Visually

A chart such as this one, which shows the dramatic drop in housing prices in the United States after 2004, can be used to present evidence effectively in support of a claim.

SOURCE: Standard & Poor's & FiServ

Recognizing Logical Fallacies

If you look closely at any apparently logical argument, you can often find serious flaws. Here is an excerpt from a letter written by a person opposed to a federal appeals court decision in 2002 ruling that the phrase "under God" in the Pledge of Allegiance is unconstitutional:

> In light of the events of this past September (9/11/01), I think it would be hypocrisy to omit an acknowledgement of a divine being under which the ideals and beliefs of this nation were created. And if you don't think so, ask everyone how many of them prayed to God that day.

This writer suggests that a large number of people praying is evidence of the existence of God. Whether or not you agree with him that there is a God, you can easily see that the number of people who pray does not necessarily prove God's existence. This flaw in the writer's reasoning is called a **logical fallacy** (specifically **attributing false causes,** which is discussed on page 99). Fallacies are often unintentional. You might think that you are making a strong argument but have actually used flawed reasoning without realizing it, as is likely to have been the case with the writer in this example. Sometimes, however, writers know that their reasoning may be suspect but deliberately use it to win an argument. Some fallacies can be powerful strategies for writers of arguments. But if you are concerned about truth—about addressing a problem or negotiating a conflict—then it makes sense to guard against fallacies so that you do not undermine your efforts to come to a reasonable resolution. And it is important to be able to identify fallacies in the arguments of others. In this section we discuss some common fallacies.

Appealing to Pity

Writers are often justified in appealing to the pity of their readers when the need to inspire this emotion is closely related to whatever they are arguing for and when the entire argument does not rest on this appeal alone. For example, someone who is attempting to convince you to donate one of your kidneys for a medical transplant would probably assure you that you could live with only one kidney and that there is a serious need for the kidney you are being asked to donate. In addition to making these crucial points, the arguer might move you to pity by indicating that unless you agree to donate your organ, the person who needs the transplant will suffer and probably die.

When the appeal to pity stands alone, even in charitable appeals in which its use is fundamental, the result is often questionable. Imagine a large billboard advertisement for the American Red Cross. It features a close-up photograph of a distraught man and this caption: PLEASE, MY LITTLE GIRL NEEDS BLOOD. Although we might already believe in the importance of donating blood, we should question the implications of this ad. Can we donate blood and ask that it be reserved for the exclusive use of children? Are the lives of children more valuable than the lives of adults? Few people would donate blood unless they sympathized with those who need transfusions, and it might be unrealistic to expect logic in advertising. But consider how weak an argument becomes when the appeal to pity has little to do with the issue in question. A student who often skipped class and has failed all his examinations but then tries to argue, "I deserve to pass this course because I've had a lot of problems at home," is making a fallacious appeal to pity. The "argument" asks the instructor to feel sorry for the student for reasons that have little to do with the class; moreover, it asks the instructor to overlook relevant evidence that undermines the student's position. You should be skeptical of any appeal to pity that is irrelevant to the conclusion or that seems designed to distract attention from the other factors you should be considering.

Appealing to Prejudice

Writers of argument can benefit from appealing to their readers' values. Such appeals become fallacious, however, when they distract attention from whether the case at hand is reasonable and well informed or when they are couched in inflammatory language. Racist, sexist, classist, and homophobic language can be used to incite a crowd to support a position or take an action that isn't justified. Appeals to prejudice can also take more subtle forms. For example, think about those common political advertisements in which politicians state that they were born and raised in "this great state" and that they love their children and admire their spouses. Such factors might appeal to the average voter, who might be a proud resident of the state and supports "family values," but these factors are unlikely to affect the candidate's performance in office. Such ads are good examples of appeals to prejudice.

Appealing to Tradition

Although you can learn from the past and often benefit from honoring tradition, you can seldom make decisions based on tradition alone. Appealing to tradition is fallacious when tradition becomes the only reason for justifying a position. "We cannot let women join our club because we've never let women join in the past" is no less problematic than arguing, "We shouldn't buy computers for our schools because we didn't have computers in the past." What people have done in the past is not necessarily appropriate for the future. If you believe that a traditional practice can guide people in the future, you need to show why this is the case.

Arguing by Analogy

An analogy is a comparison that works on more than one level. They are commonly used to make a point, and it is possible to use analogy effectively when reasoning inductively. But to do so you must be sure that the things you are comparing have several characteristics in common and that these similarities are relevant to the conclusion you intend to draw. For example, you might use analogy to argue that competition is good for schools: Because competition is considered good for businesses, it will improve schools. In this case, you would be comparing schools to businesses and arguing that what's good for business is also good for schools. But the strength of this argument would depend on the degree to which schools are analogous to businesses, so you would need to demonstrate that there are important similarities between the two. Your argument would be stronger if you can show that schools have more similarities to businesses than differences.

Unfortunately, analogies are often misused. For example, if a political candidate asks people to vote for him because of his outstanding record as a football player, he might claim that politics, like football, involves teamwork. But because a successful politician needs many skills and will probably never need to run across a field or knock someone down, this analogy is questionable. The differences between football and politics outweigh the similarities, and it would be fallacious to pretend otherwise. Moreover, similarities can be deceptive. In the previous example of an argument that competition will improve schools, what appears similar between schools and businesses may in fact not be similar. For example, teachers may seem to be employees in the same sense that someone who works for a large corporation is an employee, but the jobs and their responsibilities might be decidedly different. So comparing teachers to such employees might be misleading—and fallacious.

Attacking the Character of Opponents

If you make personal attacks on opponents but ignore what they have to say or distract attention from it, you are using what is often called an *ad hominem* argument (Latin for "to or against the man"). Although an audience often considers the character of a writer or speaker in deciding whether to trust what he or she has to say (as we noted earlier in this chapter), most of us realize that good people can make bad arguments and even a liar can sometimes tell the truth. It is always better to give a thoughtful response to an opponent's arguments than to ignore those arguments and indulge in personal attacks. If you criticize your opponent for being untrustworthy or having broken a law in the past, you have not undermined or addressed his or her argument, which may be valid and effective, no matter how untrustworthy you claim he or she is. Despite the fallacious nature of such attacks on an opponent's character, they are all too common in much popular media and political debate, so it is a good idea to be alert for them as you consider an argument.

Attributing False Causes

If you assume that an event is the result of something that merely occurred before it, you have committed the fallacy of false causation. Assumptions of this sort are sometimes called *post hoc* reasoning, from the Latin phrase *post hoc, ergo propter hoc,* which means "after this, therefore because of this." Superstitious people offer many examples of this type of fallacious thinking. They might tell you, "Everything was going fine until the lunar eclipse last month; *that's* why the economy is in trouble." Some professional baseball play-ers believe that a hitting streak results from a certain ritual, such as taking batting practice at exactly the same time every day or wearing a certain batting glove.

Such fallacy can be seen in more serious contexts. For example, in criminal cases, sus-pects are sometimes identified simply because they were observed near the scene of the crime. This suspicion might lead to the discovery of evidence, but it could just as easily lead to the false arrest of someone who just happened to be near the crime scene at a cer-tain time. Being observed near the scene of a crime proves nothing by itself. A prosecuting attorney who would be foolish enough to base a case on such a flimsy piece of evidence would be guilty of *post hoc* reasoning. It is important to recognize the distinction between *causes* and what might simply be *coincidences.* Sequence is not a cause because every event is preceded by an infinite number of other events, not all of which can be held responsible for whatever happens today.

This fallacy can be found in more subtle forms in essays on abstract social problems. For example, a writer might argue that an increase in violent crime among young people is caused by the popularity of violent video games. Although an increase in crime might occur at the same time that violent video games became more popular among young people, the one cannot be said to have caused the other without much more evidence to demonstrate such a cause. Similarly, the popular complaint that students' weak writing skills result from the use of text messaging is a good example of an argument attributing something to false causes. Such arguments are common, and it is important to be careful not to imply a cause-and-effect relationship where one may not exist.

Attributing Guilt by Association

When a writer or speaker tries to discredit an idea or a position because it is supported by or associated with someone disreputable, he or she is implying guilt by association. It is the equivalent of saying, "If a bad person supports this idea, it must be a bad idea." By such reasoning, you would reject an idea or position simply because it is supported by someone you dislike or distrust—not because the idea or position itself is flawed. Such faulty reasoning is common in political campaigns, during which candidates some-times criticize their opponents because they are associated with someone who might be unpopular at the time, such as the president. Similarly, candidates will argue against a proposed law because it was proposed by an unpopular politician. In such cases, the rea-soning follows the faulty logic of guilt by association: "Senator Smith is an untrustworthy (or unpopular) politician. He proposed this law; therefore, this law is a bad idea and should not be supported." The flaws in such reasoning are easy to see. It is clear that no proposed law is a bad idea simply because it was proposed by someone you might dislike or mistrust. In such cases, nothing specific has been argued, but a negative association has been either created or suggested through hints and innuendo. An argument based on guilt by association can be appealing in a charged atmosphere when political controversies are being debated, but such an argument is fallacious.

Begging the Question

In the fallacy known as begging the question, a writer begins with a premise that is acceptable only to anyone who will agree with the conclusion subsequently reached—a conclusion often similar to the premise. Thus, the argument goes around in a circle (and is sometimes referred to as **circular reasoning**). For instance, someone might begin an essay by claiming, "Required courses like first-year composition are a waste of time" and end with the conclusion that "first-year composition should not be a required course." It might indeed be arguable that first-year composition should not be required, but the author who begins with the premise that first-year composition is a waste of time has assumed what the argument should be devoted to proving; in effect, he or she begins with the conclusion. Because it is much easier to *claim* something is true than to *prove* it is true, it is tempting to beg the question you set out to answer. But it is a weak strategy for argument.

Equivocating

Someone who equivocates uses vague or ambiguous language to mislead an audience. In argumentation, equivocation often takes the form of using one word in two (or more) senses without acknowledging the change in meaning. It is especially easy to equivocate when using abstract language. In particular, terms such as *right, society, freedom, law, justice,* and *real* are often used in this way.

A common example of equivocation occurs in debates about the teaching of evolution in schools. Sometimes, those who oppose the teaching of evolution argue that because it is a *theory*, it should not be presented to students as fact. The flaw in this logic arises from the multiple meanings of the term *theory*. In informal usage, *theory* typically means a conjecture, a belief, or an assumption based on limited knowledge—as in "I have a theory about why my favorite football team always seems to lose its playoff games." But *theory* also has a more technical meaning: a coherent set of propositions or principles that are used to explain certain phenomena. In scientific terms, a theory that has been tested and can explain the phenomena that it was developed to explain is considered true—that is, it becomes a statement of fact because it has been proven to explain certain phenomena accurately. In the example of the argument against teaching evolution in schools, *theory* is being used in the informal sense (as a conjecture); thus, the argument seems valid: something that is a conjecture should not be taught as fact. But evolution (or more accurately, natural selection) is a theory in the scientific sense, so technically it is a fact.

This example reveals that subtle differences in the meanings of words can have an important impact on how reasoning is used in argument. In this case, it can be easy to miss the difference in the meanings of *theory* and thus overlook the faulty logic in the argument. As both a writer and reader of arguments, you should be alert to such flaws in reasoning.

Ignoring the Question

When someone says, "I'm glad you asked that question!" and then promptly begins to talk about something else, that person is guilty of ignoring the question. Politicians are famous for exploiting this technique when they don't want to be pinned down on a subject. Students (and teachers) sometimes use it when asked a question that they want to avoid. Ignoring the question is also likely to occur when friends or partners have a fight. In the midst of a quarrel, you might hear remarks like "What about you?" or "Never mind the budget! I'm sick of worrying about money! We need to talk about what's happening to our relationship!"

Jumping to Conclusions

This fallacy is so common that it has become a cliché. In fact, the old cliché, "Where there's smoke, there's fire," is a good example of jumping to a conclusion. The source of the smoke in a given instance could be fire, but it could also be something else, such as a chemical reaction that results in smoke without a fire. As this example suggests, jumping to conclusions means that the conclusion in question has not been supported by an adequate amount of evidence. Because one green apple is sour, it does not follow that all green apples are sour. Failing one test does not mean that you will necessarily fail the next. An instructor who seems disorganized on the first day of class might eventually prove to be the best teacher you ever had. These examples demonstrate that it is risky—and often illogical—to draw a conclusion from a single example or piece of evidence. You should always try to support an argument with more than one example—and be wary of conclusions that seem hasty or rest on insufficient evidence.

Opposing a Straw Man

Because it is easier to demolish a man of straw than to address a live opponent fairly, arguers are sometimes tempted to pretend that they are responding to the views of their opponents when they are only setting up a type of artificial opposition that they can easily refute. The most common form of this fallacy is to exaggerate the views of others or to respond only to an extreme view that does not adequately represent the arguments of opponents. For example, during debates about reforming health care insurance in the United States in 2009, opponents sometimes argued that proposed reforms would result in a government takeover of health care in which government "death panels" would decide whether or not a gravely ill patient should receive a potentially life-saving medical treatment. These opponents would argue that since the reforms would create such "death panels," they should be opposed. It is easy to see the appeal of such an argument, since few people would support such "death panels." It is also easier to argue against something so outrageous rather than focusing on the more complicated details of a comprehensive health reform bill. In this case, the argument rested on an exaggeration about the nature of the proposed reform—on a "straw man." Such arguments can be appealing, which is one reason to be vigilant about them as both a writer and a reader.

Presenting a False Dilemma

A false dilemma is a fallacy in which a speaker or writer poses a choice between two alternatives but overlooks other possibilities or implies that no other possibilities exist. A college freshman who receives low grades at the end of the first semester and then claims, "What's wrong with low grades? Is cheating any better?" is pretending that there is no possibility other than cheating or earning a low grade—such as that of earning higher grades by studying harder, a possibility recognized by most students and teachers.

Presenting a false dilemma is extremely common and occurs regularly in intense public debates about controversial or emotional issues. For example, after the terrorist attacks of September 11, 2001, debates arose about measures that the U.S. government took to protect national security that also seemed to violate the right to privacy of American citizens. Participants in these debates often made their arguments on the basis of a false dilemma: "If we preserve our right to privacy, we become ever more vulnerable to terrorist attack because we make it easy for terrorists to hide." "Implementing security measures that violate our privacy will only mean that the terrorists have won because we are undermining our own most cherished rights, the very rights that define us as Americans." In both cases, the argument rests on a false dilemma: We can have security that violates our right to privacy, or we can preserve our right to privacy by making ourselves less secure and thus more vulnerable to terrorism.

Because such flawed reasoning is so common in debates about important issues such as security and privacy, it is important to be able to recognize and avoid this fallacy.

Reasoning That Does Not Follow ("Non Sequitur")

Although almost any faulty argument is likely to have gaps in reasoning, this fallacy, sometimes called the *non sequitur* (Latin for "it does not follow"), describes a conclusion that does not follow logically from the explanation given for it. We often see logical gaps of this sort within specific sentences. An example of this type of *non sequitur* would be "Because the teacher likes Joe, Joe passed the quiz in calculus." It does not logically follow that Joe passed his test simply because his teacher likes him. In this case, a cause-and-effect relationship has been claimed but not explained. It might well be that Joe studied harder for his quiz because he believes that his teacher likes him, and that in turn resulted in Joe passing the quiz. But someone reading the sentence as written could not be expected to know this.

Non sequiturs sometimes form the basis for an entire argument. A common example in recent years arose in the debates about global climate change. A point of controversy was the question of whether or not rising global temperatures in the latter half of the twentieth century were caused by human activity. Sometimes it was argued that because scientists have shown that fluctuations in global temperatures have occurred naturally over many thousands of years, humans did not cause the recent rise in global temperatures. Whether or not human activity has caused climate change, this argument is a *non sequitur*: It does not follow that because past fluctuations occurred naturally, the current temperature rise is also natural and therefore not caused by humans.

Non sequiturs are often subtle and easy to miss, which is a good reason to be alert for them in any argument.

Sliding Down a Slippery Slope

According to this fallacy, one step will inevitably lead to an undesirable end—that it will result in our slipping down the slope toward something bad. An example would be claiming that censoring pornography will lead to the end of freedom of the press. Although it is important to consider the probable effects of any step that is being debated, it is fallacious to claim that a specific set of happenings will necessarily result from any one action. Censoring pornography is unlikely to lead to an end to freedom of the press by itself; in fact, it is not difficult to imagine that restricting the publication of some kinds of pornography could result in greater freedom of expression (for example, if such restrictions created a widespread backlash that in turn led to even fewer restrictions on the press). Being able to recognize these logical fallacies can help you read arguments more critically. It can also help you construct more effective arguments, a topic we will take up in Chapter 5.

II

Composing Arguments

© Hill Street Studios/Blend Images/Corbis 42-22579159

Yellow Dog Productions/Getty Images

John Coletti Photography

5

Constructing Arguments

© Hill Street Studios/Blend Images/Corbis 42-22579159

- An assignment for your cultural anthropology course requires you to write an essay examining the ethical issues faced by Western anthropologists who study nonindustrialized societies in places such as the Amazon basin. In your essay you are to take a position on the ethical guidelines for such research that have been proposed by a professional organization for anthropologists.

- You have been asked by other residents of your college dormitory to write a letter to the campus director of residential life to urge him not to implement new security measures that the college is considering. These measures include a new policy that would prohibit students from having visitors in their dorms except during specified hours in the early evening. You and your dormmates oppose these measures. Your letter to the director of residential life will try to convince him that the proposed measures would significantly restrict students' social activities without enhancing campus security.

■ A local organization that you belong to advocates sustainable community development. A national retail business has requested a permit to build a large store on farmland near a residential neighborhood in your community. Many residents are pleased because they believe that the new store will improve the community's economic status. Others worry about the impact of the new store on surrounding land, especially regarding water runoff into a nearby marsh that is part of a community park and natural area. Your organization has decided to oppose the building of the new store on the proposed site unless certain measures to protect the marsh are required. You are part of a team that will create a new website devoted to presenting your organization's perspective on the new store.

How do you proceed?

The answer to that question is the same for each of these situations. It is also different for each of them.

In each of these cases you would try to present and support your claims to your intended audience in a way that is persuasive. To make an effective argument, you must examine the issue carefully so that you understand it well, which might require some research. You must also gather and present evidence to support the claims you will make in your argument. You will want to consider how your intended audience is likely to respond to your claims and warrants in each case. And you must adopt a style—and, in the case of the website, a design—that most effectively presents your case.

But each of these situations is different, and arguing effectively means understanding the specific factors involved in each case.

1. *The rhetorical situation.* The audience and circumstances for each of these writing tasks are different. Your anthropology teacher, for instance, will have different expectations for your paper than the director of residential life will have for your letter. And the audience for the website would be an entire community, with complex and perhaps divergent expectations for a persuasive argument.

2. *The goals for argument.* Although you can see each of these arguments as part of an effort to solve a problem, the problems in each instance represent different challenges to you as writer. In your anthropology course you hope to understand the ethical issues of anthropology research sufficiently to make an effective argument to earn you a good grade. Your letter to the residential life director is intended to convince him not to implement new security rules that would have a direct impact on your living situation. And your organization hopes that its website will generate support among community residents for environmental restrictions on a large construction project.

3. *The medium.* The anthropology paper will have to adhere to the conventions of academic writing in the field of anthropology. The letter to the residential life director is also a print document, but one that follows different conventions for writing. And the website is an entirely different medium that requires you to consider such matters as layout, color, and hyperlinks.

Adapting to different situations like these is part of making effective arguments. Everything included in the first four chapters of this book is intended to help you understand argumentation in order to construct effective arguments in any situation. The principles examined apply to all kinds of arguments. But this chapter offers a more focused discussion of how to construct arguments, whatever the situation.

Managing the Composing Process

Understanding Composing as Inquiry

In some ways composing an argument, whatever the medium, is like any other kind of writing: You must define your topic, develop your ideas, gather sufficient information, organize your material, revise accordingly, and edit so that your writing is accurate, effective, and correct. In other words, you must move through the composing process. Composing arguments can make that process both easier and harder. It can make the process easier in the sense that some of the conventions of argumentation will help you determine what you will say and how you will say it. For example, in an argument you will generally be expected to make your claims clearly and support them with adequate evidence. Knowing that can help you generate ideas and organize the information more easily. But argumentation involves confronting the complexities of human beliefs and opinions. Part of your challenge in composing your argument is managing that complexity and showing that you are knowledgeable and fair-minded. For example, the essay for your anthropology course will probably address issues of racial diversity, and you will have to consider how the controversial nature of race relations might figure into your argument. In addition, if your goal is to address a serious issue and try to solve a problem through argumentation, you will always be concerned about arguing ethically and honestly. In other words, your goal is to engage with others in order to work through a difficult problem. That goal requires you to consider the implications of your argument and the potential effects of your claims on your audience.

Of course, you can't hope to do everything at once. Think of the process of composing an argument as an ongoing process of inquiry. By composing an argument, you are carefully exploring an issue and learning about that issue as well as about yourself and others. That learning might require you to rethink your claims or your position on the issue at hand. For instance, you might begin your essay for your anthropology course believing that strict ethical guidelines for anthropology research are not necessary, but you might find as you compose your essay that the issue is more complicated than you initially thought. That process of inquiry might therefore lead you to revise your original position.

If you approach the writing of an argument in this way, you are more likely to construct effective arguments; moreover, you might gain a deeper understanding of the issue at hand and perhaps address the problem more effectively.

Defining Your Topic

In the scenarios at the beginning of this chapter, the topic for argument in each case may seem clear. But it is important to distinguish between a *subject* and a *topic*. That distinction is even more important if you are faced with a situation in which you are asked to write an argument about anything you want (which is not uncommon in a college writing class). In the case of the anthropology essay, for example, the subject is anthropology, or more specifically, anthropology research; you might define the topic as the ethical problems facing anthropologists who study other cultures. You can narrow that topic even further: the specific ethical problem of the relationship between the anthropologist and the people he or she is studying. Because issues like this are so complex, narrowing the topic will enable you to address it adequately in your essay. It would be impossible to write anything but a superficial five-page essay about an issue as big as the ethics of anthropological research. Entire books have been written about that issue. But you can feasibly write a five-page essay arguing for specific ethical guidelines relating to the personal relationship between an anthropologist and the people being studied in a specific situation.

If you are given the flexibility to write an argument on any topic, part of your challenge is to select a suitable topic worth arguing about. The best topics are complex: They are about issues that matter to people; they generate controversy; and usually there is a variety of views about them. The topics in the scenarios at the beginning of this chapter are good topics for those reasons.

ARGUMENTS AND OPINIONS

Almost all intelligent arguments involve *opinions,* but not all opinions lead to good arguments. Simply having an opinion about something is not the same thing as taking a position on an issue and being able to make a considered argument about it. And some opinions are just not worth arguing. What would be the point of making an argument that golden retrievers are more handsome dogs than poodles? You might love golden retrievers, but will such a topic generate much interest among your classmates? Is such an issue really worth exploring through argument? Probably not. It would be better to choose a topic that has some genuine consequence for you and will matter to others.

Darrell Lecorre/Masterfile

But it is important that the topic you choose matters to *you.* Composing an effective argument is an intellectually rigorous process. There is no point in carefully examining an issue that you're not interested in or concerned about.

It is also important to distinguish between opinions that are a matter of taste and those that are a question of judgment. Some things—whether broccoli tastes good, for example—are a matter of personal preference. You might be able to write an amusing essay about broccoli, but no matter how hard you try, you will not convince someone who hates green vegetables to rush to the produce department of the nearest supermarket. And why would you want to? Questions of judgment, on the other hand, are more substantial. Judgments are determined by beliefs, which in turn grow out of basic principles to which people try to remain consistent. These principles lead people to decide that some judgments are correct and others are not. Should a university require first-year students to live in dormitories? Should it restrict their social activities? Does the state have a right to execute criminals? Should couples live together before getting married? All of these are questions of judgment that are worthy of serious argument.

Questions like these provide rich topics for argumentation because they are complex and offer many avenues to explore. But the very richness of these topics can be challenging when you are composing an argument. Arguments written about these topics can take many directions. Trying to explore too many directions at once can lead to confusing and

---

DEFINING YOUR TOPIC

The following questions can help you define the topic for your argument and begin to explore it:

- Do I know what my specific topic is? If so, can I summarize it in a few sentences?
- Is the topic suitable for the assignment or situation for which I am writing? Is it a topic that matters to me and to my intended audience? Why is it important to me or potentially to my audience?
- Is my topic manageable for the kind of argument I will write? Is it too broad? If so, how might I narrow it sufficiently?
- Do I have an opinion about this topic? What is that opinion based on?
- On what grounds might anyone disagree with my opinion? How can I address possible objections to my opinion?
- What evidence do I have to support my opinion? Is my evidence sufficient?

---

ineffective arguments. For this reason defining your topic is only one step in the process of composing an argument. As noted earlier, composing an argument includes exploring your topic fully and perhaps changing it along the way. In some cases you might have a clearly defined topic even before you begin to write. The letter to the director of residential life in the example at the beginning of this chapter is one such instance. But often you will find that your specific topic will change as you explore the issue you are writing about.

Considering Audience

The questions in the previous section (see "Defining Your Topic") are reminders that an argument is always made with an audience in mind. That audience will shape an argument from the beginning of the composing process. So carefully considering your audience is an important part of the process of exploring your topic and developing your argument. In Chapter 2 we examined the rhetorical context of argument and discussed the role of audience in argumentation. As you prepare to compose an argument of your own, you might find it useful to review that chapter. In this chapter we will focus on how audience considerations will affect how you compose your argument.

Identifying Your Audience

In some situations your audience is already well defined. Look again at the scenarios at the beginning of this chapter. That letter in which you argue against new dormitory restrictions has a specific audience: the director of residential life. Your essay about the ethical problems facing anthropologists also has a specific audience: your teacher, though your teacher will probably expect you to assume a larger audience (for example, people interested in anthropology). The website about the new store proposed for your town has a more general audience, though even this audience is relatively specific (residents of your community). In each case, as you work through the process of composing your argument, you should try to identify what you know about your audience's interests, views, and knowledge of the topic you are addressing. Your sense of what your audience knows or believes can help you define your topic in a way that will connect with that audience; it can also help you explore your topic so that you can develop ideas for making your argument.

For example, in writing the letter to the director of residential life at your college, you can make several reasonable assumptions about what your audience (the director) knows about the issue at hand and its importance to him:

- He understands the problems associated with security in campus housing.
- He most likely feels a great sense of responsibility for the security of students living on campus.
- He probably wants students not only to feel secure on campus but to enjoy their living arrangements as well.

As you develop your argument against new restrictions on dormitory visitors, you can use these assumptions to identify claims and warrants that are likely to be acceptable to the director, and you can more easily identify common ground. For example, you might point out that you and the other students in your dorm share his concerns about safety in the dorms. You can research problems with security on your campus and use that information to support your contention that the new visitor restrictions will not likely enhance security. In short, your understanding of your audience can help you generate specific ideas for your argument and formulate those ideas in ways that might resonate with that audience.

If you approach argumentation as problem solving, you will tend to see your audience not as an opponent but as a partner in your effort to address the issue at hand. In this example, you and your dormmates might have different priorities than the residential life director, and your responsibilities are different. But all of you care about safety, and all of you hope for a pleasant and enjoyable campus lifestyle. Understanding that shared ground can lead you to formulate an argument that works toward a solution rather than a victory. The same can be true even when your audience is more general.

At times, you and your audience might hold different views on an issue, and your respective positions can seem irreconcilable. Because arguments are so often made about controversial matters, it is quite likely that you will find yourself constructing an argument for an audience that might be passionately opposed to your point of view. Just skim the newspaper on any morning, and you'll quickly find such issues: abortion, capital punishment, tax increases, religious freedom, stem-cell research. Because such issues are so important to people, they can make the process of considering your audience more complicated, and they require that you take greater care in understanding your audience.

Imagine, for instance, that you are making an argument to a general audience—say, in an article for your local newspaper—about an issue as emotional and complicated as capital punishment. You can be certain that some members of that audience will hold views opposed to your own. As you develop your argument, assume that such readers will be skeptical. But don't dismiss their views; rather, consider their reasons for opposing your viewpoint and try to address their concerns as you build your case. Doing so not only will help you make a more convincing argument but also might enable you to find common ground with those readers.

A METHOD FOR EXPLORING YOUR IDEAS AND YOUR AUDIENCE IN AN ARGUMENT

Whenever you are making any argument, it can be useful to make a list of the reasons you believe as you do about the issue. You will probably not be able to discuss, in a short essay, all points you have listed about the issue, and it is likely that as you compose and revise your argument, you will generate even more ideas—ideas that might prove to be even more important than those on your list. But you can benefit from identifying the reasons for your position and considering the impact they might have on your intended audience. To do so, follow these steps:

1. List the reasons for your own position on the issue about which you are writing your argument.
2. Rank those reasons in order of importance (first the most important, then the next-most important, and so on).
3. List any reasons you can think of why people might disagree with your position on the issue.
4. Write a brief response to each of these reasons.

Following these steps enables you to explore your own position on your issue and begin to identify possible claims and warrants for your argument. It can also help you anticipate objections to your position and generate ideas for presenting and supporting your claims effectively. You are likely to discover that those who hold views opposed to yours have at least one good argument that you cannot answer.

Making Concessions

Sometimes in argumentation about complex and controversial issues such as capital punishment, you can find yourself believing that your position is right and those who believe otherwise are simply ignorant or harbor dubious motives. But life is seldom so simple that one side is unequivocally right and the other wrong. Serious controversies almost always continue because each side of the issue has valid concerns that cannot be dismissed. Identifying these concerns enables you to understand the issue better and to construct an argument that might be more convincing as well as more useful. This might mean conceding a point or two to those who oppose your position. If you have no rebuttal to a particular point and recognize that your opponents' case has some merit, be honest and generous enough to say so. Making such a concession should not be considered simply a strategic move on your part. It also signals your willingness to take the members of your audience seriously, even when they disagree with you, and it reflects your genuine interest in addressing the problem at hand effectively and ethically. In this way you might bridge the gap between you and members of your audience who oppose your position, making it easier to reach a more substantial agreement. Insisting in a belligerent way that your opponents are completely wrong will hardly convince them to take you seriously.

Having a good sense of your audience will help you decide what concessions to make. Different audiences will have different expectations. Some might want to hear concessions before listening to opposing views. Some might expect lengthy discussions of conceded points; others might not. When making concessions, address what you think are your audience's most pressing concerns. Doing so can help you develop important points in your argument and organize them more effectively.

Understanding Audience Expectations

Having a good sense of audience can also help you decide on the examples and evidence that will best illustrate and support your claims (see "A Method for Exploring Your Ideas and Your Audience in an Argument" on page 112). You will want to use examples that your audience will understand, and you will want evidence that will be convincing to them. Examples of actual cases in an argument opposing capital punishment can be persuasive for a general audience, such as readers of your local newspaper. For a college course in legal theory, however, you will probably need to use a court's formal opinion or statistical data if you wish to be persuasive.

There is a great difference, however, between responding to the interests of your audience by discussing what it wants to know and twisting what you say to please an audience with what it wants to hear. A writer should try to tell the truth as he or she sees it. "Truth" can have many dimensions. When limited space forces you to be selective, it is wise to focus on the facets of a topic that will be most effective with the audience you are hoping to convince. But it is one thing to focus and another to mislead. Never present anything to one audience that you would be compelled to deny to another. Doing so not only damages your credibility but also undermines any legitimate effort to solve problems through argumentation.

Remember that advice about considering audience can be profoundly influenced by culture (see "Considering Culture in Argument" on page 24). The idea of truth, for example, can vary from one culture to another or between two people who follow different religious practices. Different cultures can have different fundamental values. Even the idea of "factual evidence" can be shaped by cultural background. Western societies such as the United States place a high value on scientific evidence, but some cultures do not share that faith in science. Indeed, even in the United States there are communities that, because of religious beliefs or ideological leanings, harbor a deep mistrust of science. You might never have to address such audiences in an argument, but it is always important to remember that whenever you make an argument to an audience, you do so in a cultural context.

MAKING CONCESSIONS VERSUS PANDERING

Politicians are often accused of pandering to different audiences in order to win their support—that is, changing their positions on important issues so that they seem to agree with a specific audience. During the 2008 U.S. presidential election, Senator Barack Obama, the Democratic candidate, was criticized for not wearing a U.S. flag lapel pin, as many politicians do. Subsequently, he was sometimes seen wearing one and sometimes not. His critics claimed that he wore the lapel pin when speaking to certain audiences, such as U.S. military groups, who were believed to be very patriotic, but not for other audiences. Whether or not you believe Obama was pandering to certain audiences, the controversy over his lapel pin illustrates the potential risks of changing your positions or claims merely to tell an audience what you believe it wants to hear in an argument.

How One Student Addresses Her Audience

The following essay, which was originally published as an editorial in a college newspaper, illustrates the importance of taking audience into account in argumentation.

In this essay Karen chose a topic that would certainly interest many college students, the audience for whom she saw herself writing. Her thesis is clear: Class attendance should not be required of college students. And her writing is lively enough to hold the attention of many readers. All this is good.

But Karen's argument also has some weaknesses. In her sixth paragraph she presents a logical fallacy called a *false dilemma:* offering a choice between only two alternatives when others exist (see page 102). By asking, "So who's the better student—the one who makes a meaningless appearance or the one who is busy with something else?" she has ignored at least two other possibilities. Appearance in class is likely to be meaningful to at least some students, and cutting class may be meaningless if the "something else" occupying a student's attention is a waste of time. The comparison in the tenth paragraph between reserving the right to lower grades because of poor attendance and "calling the front seat" is confusing. In point 1 of her summary, Karen claims, "Roughly the same number of students will either skip or attend, regardless of what a piece of paper says," but she offers no evidence to support this claim. And because Karen admits that many students skip class despite mandatory attendance policies, her claim in point 5 that required attendance "abolishes free choice" does not hold up.

To Skip or Not to Skip: A Student Dilemma

This is college, right? The four-year deal offering growth, maturity, experience, and knowledge? A place to be truly independent?

Because sometimes I can't tell. Sometimes this place downright reeks of paternal instincts. Just ask the freshmen and sophomores, who are by class rank alone guaranteed two full years of twenty-four-hour supervision, orchestrated activities, and group showers.

But the forced dorm migration of underclassmen has been bitched about before, to no avail. University policy is, it seems, set in stone. It ranks right up there with ingrown toe nails for sheer evasion and longevity.

But there's another university policy that has no merit as a policy and no place in a university. Mandatory Attendance Policy: wherein faculty members attempt the high school hall monitor–college instructor maneuver. It's a difficult trick to justify as professors place the attendance percentage of their choice above a student's proven abilities on graded material.

Profs rationalize out a lot of arguments to support the policy. Participation is a popular one. I had a professor whose methods for lowering grades so irritated me I used to skip on purpose. He said, "Classroom participation is a very important part of this introductory course. Obviously, if you are not present, you cannot be participating."

Equally obvious, though not stated by the prof, is the fact that one can be perpetually present but participate as little as one who is absent. So who's the better student—the one who makes a meaningless appearance or the one who is busy with something else? And who gets the points docked?

The rest of his policy was characteristically vague, mentioning that absences "could" result in a lower grade. Constant ambiguity is the second big problem with formal policies. It's tough for teachers to figure out just how much to let attendance affect grade point. So they doubletalk.

According to the UWSP catalog, faculty are to provide "clear explanation" of attendance policy. Right. Based on the language actually used, ninety-five percent of UWSP faculty are functionally incapable of uttering a single binding statement. In an effort to offend no one while retaining all power of action, profs write things like (these are actual policies): "I trust students to make their own judgments and choices about coming, or not coming, to class." But then continues: "Habitual and excessive absence is grounds for failure." What happened to trust? What good are the choices?

Or this: "More than three absences may negatively affect your grade." Then again, they may not. Who knows? And this one: "I consider every one of you in here to be mature adults. However, I reserve the right to alter grades based on attendance."

You reserve the right? By virtue of your saying so? Is that like calling the front seat? Another argument that profs cling to goes something like, "Future employers, by God, aren't going to put up with absenteeism." Well, let's take a reality pill. I think most students can grasp the difference between cutting an occasional class, which they paid for, and cutting at work, when they're the ones on salary. See, college students are capable of bi-level thought control, nowadays. (It's all those computers.)

In summary, mandatory attendance should be abolished because:

1. It is irrelevant. Roughly the same number of students will either skip or attend, regardless of what a piece of paper says. If the course is worth anything.

2. It is ineffective. It automatically measures neither participation, ability, or gained knowledge. That's what tests are for. Grades are what you end up knowing, not how many times you sat there to figure it out.

3. It is insulting. A college student is capable of determining a personal schedule, one that may or may not always meet with faculty wishes. An institution committed to the fostering of personal growth cannot operate under rules that patronize or minimize the role an adult should claim for himself.

4. It is arbitrary. A prof has no right and no ability to factor in an unrealistic measure of performance. A student should be penalized no more than what the natural consequence of an absence is—the missing of one day's direct delivery of material.

5. It abolishes free choice. By the addition of a factor that cannot be fought. We are not at a university to learn conformity. As adults, we reserve the right to choose as we see fit, even if we choose badly.

Finally, I would ask the faculty to consider this: We have for some time upheld in this nation the sacred principle of separation of church and state; i.e., You are not God.

Karen Rivedal

Editor

But the major problem with Karen's argument is that she seems to have misjudged her audience. Her argument seems aimed at students, but she seems to have ignored professors, who also read the school newspaper. Students cannot change the policies of their professors, but the professors themselves usually can, so she has overlooked the very audience that she most needs to reach. Moreover, she has actually insulted professors, describing most of them as "functionally incapable of uttering a single binding statement" (paragraph 8). Although such a criticism of professors will strike some students as funny, it is unlikely to persuade professors to change their attendance policies. Karen does address the faculty in her final paragraph, but only to make a final insult.

Despite the problems with her argument, Karen does boldly call attention to attendance policies that might indeed be wrong. Recognizing that her original argument could be stronger but still firmly believing that mandatory class attendance is inappropriate for college students, Karen decided to rewrite her editorial as an essay. Here is her revision:

Absent at What Price?

by Karen Rivedal

This is college, right? A place to break old ties, solve problems, and make decisions? Higher education is, I always thought, the pursuit of knowledge in a way that's a step beyond the paternal hand-holding of high school. It's the act of learning performed in a more dynamic atmosphere, rich with individual freedom, discourse, and debate.

But sometimes I can't tell. Some university traditions cloud the full intent of higher education. Take mandatory attendance policies, wherein faculty members attempt the high school hall monitor–college instructor maneuver. It's a difficult trick to justify as professors place the attendance percentage of their choice above a student's proven abilities on graded material.

This isn't to say that the idea of attendance itself is unsound. Clearly, personal interaction between teacher and students is preferable to textbook teaching alone. It's the *mandatory* attendance policy, within an academic community committed to the higher education of adults, that worries me.

Professors offer several arguments to support the practice. Participation is a popular one. I had a professor whose methods for lowering grades so irritated me that I used to skip class out of spite. He said, "Classroom participation is a very important part of this introductory course. Obviously, if you are not present, you cannot be participating."

Equally obvious, though, is the fact that one can be perpetually present, but participate as little as one who is absent. Participation lacks an adequate definition. There's no way of knowing, on the face of it, if a silent student is necessarily a learning student. Similarly, an instructor has no way of knowing for what purpose or advantage a student may miss a class and therefore no ability to determine its relative validity.

As a learning indicator, then, the mandatory attendance policy is flawed. It automatically measures neither participation nor ability. That's what tests are for. A final grade should reflect what a student ends up knowing rather than the artificial consequences of demerit points.

Some faculty recognize the shortcomings of a no-exceptions mandatory attendance policy and respond with partial policies. Constant ambiguity is characteristic of this approach and troublesome for the student who wants to know just where he or she stands. It's tough for teachers to figure out just how much to let attendance affect grade point. So they double-talk.

This, for example, is taken from an actual policy: "I trust students to make their own judgments and choices about coming, or not coming, to class." It then continues: "Habitual and excessive absence is grounds for failure." What happened to trust? What good are the choices?

Or this: "More than three absences may negatively affect your grade." Then again, they may not. Who knows? And this one: "I consider every one of you in here to be mature adults. However, I reserve the right to alter grades based on attendance."

This seems to say, what you can prove you have learned from this class takes a back seat to how much I think you should know based on your attendance. What the teacher says goes—just like in high school.

Professors who set up attendance policies like these believe, with good reason, that they are helping students to learn by ensuring their attendance. But the securing of this end by requirement eliminates an important element of learning. Removing the freedom to make the decision is removing the need to think. An institution committed to fostering personal growth cannot operate under rules that patronize or minimize the role an adult should claim for himself or herself.

A grading policy that relies on the student's proven abilities certainly takes the guess work out of grade assigning for teachers. This take-no-prisoners method, however, also demands a high, some say unfairly high, level of personal student maturity. Younger students especially may need, they say, the extra structuring that a policy provides.

But forfeiting an attendance policy doesn't mean that a teacher has to resign his humanity, too. Teachers who care to can still take five minutes to warn an often-absent student about the possible consequences, or let the first test score tell the story. As much as dedicated teachers want students to learn, learning is still a personal choice. Students must want to.

A "real-world" argument that professors often use goes something like "Future employers aren't going to put up with absenteeism, so get used to it now." Well, let's take a reality pill. I think most students can differentiate between cutting an occasional class, which they paid for, and missing work, when they're the ones on salary.

Students who intelligently protest an institution's policies, such as mandatory attendance requirements, are proof-in-action that college is working. These students are thinking; and learning to think and question is the underlying goal of all education. College is more than its rules, more than memorized facts. Rightly, college is knowledge, the testing of limits. To be valid, learning must include choice and the freedom to make mistakes. To rely on mandatory attendance for learning is to subvert the fullest aims of that education.

In revising her essay, Karen has retained both her thesis and her own distinctive voice. Such phrases as "the high school hall monitor–college instructor maneuver," the "take-no-prisoners method," and "let's take a reality pill" are still recognizably her own. But her argument is now more compelling. In addition to eliminating the fallacies in her original version, Karen included new material that strengthens her case. For example, the third paragraph offers a clarification to reassure readers that an argument against a mandatory attendance policy is not the same as an argument against attending class. In addition, the conclusion of this essay is much improved. It successfully links the question of mandatory attendance policies with the purpose of higher education as defined in the opening paragraph.

Even more noticeable, however, are the revisions Karen made to address her varied audiences more effectively. For example, the seventh paragraph begins with a fairly sympathetic reference to professors, and the eleventh paragraph opens with a clear attempt to anticipate opposition. The twelfth paragraph includes another attempt to anticipate opposition, and the thirteenth paragraph, with its reference to "dedicated teachers," is much more likely to appeal to the professors in Karen's audience than her original version did. She still makes a forceful argument, but she doesn't lapse into insults. In her revised essay, she has more effectively managed the complicated task of addressing the different (and even conflicting) concerns of her intended audience.

You might think that Karen's revision has suppressed the strong, critical voice of her original version. As a result, you might feel that her revised essay will not resonate as well with students. However, consider this: If Karen's essay is an effort to address a legitimate concern for both students *and* faculty, is her revised version a more effective attempt to solve the problem of cutting classes?

Defining Your Terms

To make sure that your ideas are understandable in an argument, it is important to clarify any terms essential to your argument. Unfortunately, many writers of argument fail to define the words they use. It is not unusual, for example, to find writers advocating

USING A DICTIONARY

If you consult a dictionary to help you define a term, remember that dictionaries are not all the same. For daily use, most writers usually refer to a good desk dictionary such as *The American Heritage Dictionary, The Random House Dictionary,* or *Merriam-Webster's Collegiate Dictionary.* A good general dictionary of this sort will usually provide you with an adequate working definition. You might also want to consider consulting the multivolume *Oxford English Dictionary,* which is available in most college libraries and is especially useful in showing how the usage of a word has changed over the years. Your audience might also appreciate the detailed information that specialized dictionaries in various subject areas can provide. Many such dictionaries are likely to be available in your college library. For example, if you are working on an English literature paper, you might consult *A Concise Dictionary of Literary Terms* or *The Princeton Handbook of Poetic Terms.* For a paper in psychology, you might turn to *The Encyclopedic Dictionary of Psychology,* or for a paper on a musical topic, you could consult *The New Grove's Dictionary of Music and Musicians.* There are also dictionaries for medical, legal, philosophical, and theoretical terms as well as for each of the natural sciences.

You will also find dictionaries online, including http://www.merriam-webster.com, http://dictionary.reference.com, http://www.askoxford.com/, and http://www.websters-online-dictionary.com/definition/fallacy. Although these online dictionaries are handy and useful, some are much better than others in providing detailed information about words. Many online dictionaries do not include multiple definitions or explanations of the differences in word usage. If you use online dictionaries, be aware of these limitations and be prepared to consult other sources.

(or opposing) gun control without defining exactly what they mean by *gun control.* Sometimes words such as *censorship, society, legitimate,* and *moral* are used so loosely that it is impossible to decide exactly what the writer means. When this happens, the entire argument can break down.

You don't need to define every word you use, but you should define any important term that your audience might misunderstand. Avoid defining a word by using the same term or another term that is equally complex. For example, if you are opposed to the sale of pornography, you should be prepared to define what you mean by *pornography.* It would not be helpful to tell your audience that pornography is "printed or visual material that is obscene" because this only raises the question: What is obscene? In an important ruling, the U.S. Supreme Court defined *obscene* as material that "the average person, applying community standards, would find ... as a whole, appeals to the prurient interest," but even if you happened to have this definition at hand, you might wonder whether "the average person" understands what *prurient* means—not to mention what the court might have meant by *community standards.* So define your terms carefully, and avoid unnecessarily abstract language.

Dictionaries can be helpful when you're defining your terms (see "Using a Dictionary"). But often the important terms in an argument cannot be satisfactorily defined with a dictionary. Consider the term *sustainability,* which is sometimes used in arguments about environmental issues. Such a term has specific and specialized meanings in environmental debates, so a dictionary definition might be inadequate. Instead of relying exclusively on dictionaries, try to define such key terms in your own words using the following strategies:

- Give synonyms.
- Compare the term with other words with which it is likely to be confused, and show how your term differs.
- Define a word by showing what it is *not.*
- Provide examples.

When writing an argument, you will usually need to define your terms within a paragraph or two. In addition to achieving clarity, definition helps control an argument by eliminating misunderstandings that can cause an audience to be inappropriately hostile or to jump to a conclusion different from your own. By carefully defining your terms, you limit a discussion to what you want to discuss. This increases the likelihood that you will gain a fair hearing for your views.

Structuring an Argument

One of the biggest challenges in composing an argument is structuring it. Once you have explored your topic and developed your ideas, you will need to consider the following questions:

- How should I begin my argument?
- In what order should I arrange the points I want to make?
- How can I most effectively respond to opposing arguments?
- How should I conclude?

The answers to these questions will vary from one essay to another and from one kind of argument (such as a newspaper editorial) to another (a web page). Even if no single plan will work for all arguments, you can benefit from being familiar with some basic principles of argumentation that may help you organize your argument effectively. This chapter explains three traditional ways of structuring an argument:

- Classical arrangement
- Rogerian argument
- Logical arrangements

USING AN OUTLINE

Using an outline can save you time and help you write a more effective argument. It can help you keep track of your main ideas and make sure that the important parts of your argument fit together effectively. It can also help you identify areas in which you may need to do more research.

You can use a standard formal outline:

I. Major idea
   A. Supporting idea
      1. Minor idea
         a. Supporting detail
         b. Supporting detail
      2. Minor idea
         a. Supporting detail
         b. Supporting detail
   B. Supporting idea
II. Major idea

And so forth. Or you can follow the patterns for classical arrangement and Rogerian argument (pages 120 and 126.), which can be adopted for papers of almost any length. Many writers prefer to work with less formal outlines, such as listing and mapping. To organize a paper by **listing,** simply create a list of the various points you want to make without worrying about Roman numerals or indentation; then number the points on the list in the order in which you plan to discuss them. When **mapping,** you can create circles or blocks on a page, starting with a main idea. Each different idea is noted in a separate circle or block, and then lines are drawn to connect related ideas.

No single method works equally well for all writers. Unless you are specifically instructed to complete a certain type of outline, practice whatever kind of outlining works best for you. And keep in mind that an outline is not an end in itself; it is only a tool to help you write a good paper. You can rewrite an outline more easily than you can rewrite a paper, so be prepared to rework any outline that does not help you write better.

Classical Arrangement

Because classical theories of rhetoric developed when most arguments were oral, the great works of classical rhetoric recommended strategies that could be easily understood by listeners. If speakers adhered to the same basic plan, listeners were able to follow long, complex arguments because the main components were easily recognizable and the order in which they appeared signaled what was likely to follow.

The common plan for organizing an argument along classical lines included six main components: introduction, statement of background, proposition, proof, refutation, and conclusion, as follows:

Introduction (*Exordium*)	In the introduction you urge your audience to consider the case that you are about to present. This is where you capture your readers' attention and introduce your issue.
Statement of Background (*Narratio*)	In the statement of background you narrate, or tell, the key events in the story behind your case. This is where you provide information so that your audience will understand the nature of the facts in the case.
Proposition (*Partitio*)	This component divides (or partitions) the part of the argument focused on information from the part focused on reasoning, and it outlines the major points that will follow. You must state the position you are taking, based on the information you have presented, and then indicate the lines the rest of your argument will follow.
Proof (*Confirmatio*)	Adhering carefully to your outline, you now present the heart of your argument: You make (or confirm) your case. You must discuss the reasons you have taken your position and cite evidence to support each of those reasons.
Refutation (*Refutatio*)	In this key section you anticipate and refute opposing views. By showing what is wrong with the reasoning of your opponents, you demonstrate that you have studied the issue thoroughly and have reached the only acceptable conclusion in this case.
Conclusion (*Peroratio*)	The concluding paragraph(s) should summarize your most important points. In addition, you can make a final appeal to values and feelings that are likely to leave your audience favorably disposed toward your case.

Classical rhetoricians allowed variations on this plan, depending on, as the great Roman orator and scholar Cicero wrote, "the weight of the matter and the judgment of the speaker." For example, a speaker was encouraged to begin with refutation when an audience was already strongly committed to an opposing point of view. But because this basic plan remains strong and clear, it can still help writers organize their thoughts.

One advantage of this method of arrangement is that it helps writers generate ideas for their arguments. If you follow the common classical plan for organizing your argument, you will have to generate ideas for each of the main parts. For example, you will have to provide background information about the issue at hand and include arguments to refute opposing points. As a result, your argument will tend to be thorough.

Much of classical rhetoric focused on political discourse, in which speakers publicly debated issues that required action by elected officials or legislatures. Because of this, classical arrangement can be especially useful when you feel strongly about an issue and you are trying to convince an audience to undertake a proposed course of action. Because classical rhetoric tends to assume that an audience can be persuaded when it is presented with solid evidence and a clear explanation of the flaws in opponents' reasoning, this plan for arranging an argument might be most effective when you are writing for people who share your basic values.

The following essay by Tyler Sunderman provides an example of an argument constructed according to classical arrangement. It advocates snowmobiling in Yellowstone National Park and was composed for an audience that included people who care about enjoying the outdoors and protecting the environment. As you read this complex and well-documented argument, notice where Tyler moves from providing background to introducing his proposition; also notice how he responds to views other than his own. He advances a clear proposition yet conveys respect for both the environment and the people who have opposed the stand he is taking.

Snowmobiles in Yellowstone: The Case for Fair Access

by Tyler Sunderman

In 1872, Congress set aside the Northwestern corner of the Wyoming Territory as our first National Park. Yellowstone was to be administered by the Department of the Interior for the purpose of being "a public park or pleasuring-ground for the benefit and enjoyment of the people" (Our Mission). With the designation of these 2.2 million acres, Congress created a vast public property that has become part of the culture of our nation (History Page). Comprised of geysers, old-growth forests, rivers and gorges, Yellowstone has become the destination of generations of American travelers. Setting out in wagons, then automobiles, and then mini-vans and motor homes, Americans have taken to the road to experience the ruggedness of the American West in Yellowstone National Park.

Many Americans, when thinking about Yellowstone remember the family road trips of their childhood, singing the "Fifty, Nifty, United States," and waiting for the next Wall Drug sign as they headed toward the land of Old Faithful and the bubbling mud pots. For the inn keepers and restauranteurs of West Yellowstone, Montana, this is only a part of the tourist season. As the vanloads of families from all corners of America begin to wane in the fall of each year, the locals prepare for the arrival of the snowmobilers.

Since 1968, when the snowmobile was in its infancy, enthusiasts have been permitted to ride on the snow atop the blacktop roads that traverse the park, allowing many Americans to experience the wildlife and scenery of Yellowstone in the winter (Yellowstone Snowmobile). For many years, the economy in the gateway community of West Yellowstone survived by the steady flow of year round tourists, who allowed the local motels and restaurants and filling stations to remain open throughout the year. Generations of Americans have traveled to Yellowstone to see the steam rising from the geysers, the Bison plowing through the snow, and the moose wading in the steaming geyser-fed rivers.

Today, this tradition is under attack. Seven years ago, the Fund for Animals filed suit against the National Park Service, seeking to stop all motorized winter recreation in Yellowstone National Park. The group claimed that the snowmobiles, even though only allowed on the roadways, were harmful to the environment and the wildlife that inhabit the park. In the aftermath of the lawsuit, the National Park Service (NPS) announced in 2000 that it would begin the process of eliminating snowmobile travel within the park. Under this plan, there was to be no further winter travel in Yellowstone by the winter of 2003–2004. The snowmobile industry took action in response, however, and the U.S. District Court for Wyoming found that the NPS had not properly conducted its environmental impact studies. After further examination, the court found limited winter travel to be acceptable, creating provisions to make sure that snowmobiles were operating in the most environmentally friendly way (Yellowstone Snowmobile). Despite the declaration by the NPS in November of 2003 that snowmobiling was to be allowed in the park, litigation has continued, and the future of motorized winter recreation in Yellowstone National Park is still in doubt.

On one side of the argument are environmental advocacy groups that have been attempting to stop motorized travel in Yellowstone in the winter, allowing only snowshoes and cross-country skiing. In direct opposition are the snowmobilers and local businesses, who are trying to keep the park open to motorized recreation. The NPS has attempted to forge a compromise that allows motorized winter recreation, while protecting the environment from as much disruption as possible. Under the most recent proposal, the NPS plans to allow up to 720 snowmobiles into the park each day, led by professional guides who will assure that all park policies are followed. In addition, the NPS will only allow snowmobiles that employ state-of-the-art emissions control technology (Bohrer).

Despite the fact that environmental groups such as the Sierra Club have continued to protest the presence of snowmobiles, I believe that we must continue to allow snowmobiles in Yellowstone National Park. The proposal that has been put forward by the NPS has taken significant steps to meet the needs of both the environment and the local businesses that rely on the park for their livelihood. To lose the right to visit the park on snowmobiles would be to deny the purposes for which Yellowstone was established. The national park system was created for the recreation and enjoyment of the American people. We must work to find ways to co-exist with nature, not to seal ourselves away from it. With modern technological advances, it is possible to limit our impact on the environment, while retaining our rights as citizens to have access to our national treasures.

When Yellowstone National Park was first created, the horse was the primary mode of transportation, and it is unlikely that any member of Congress who voted to establish Yellowstone could have foreseen such an invention as the snowmobile. However, the presence of the snowmobile is in keeping with the original intentions of the park's creation. Yellowstone National Park was created for the purpose of recreation. It was created as a place where nature could be preserved, and the American people would be able to experience it first hand. This experience has always taken on many different forms, from hiking, to boat tours, camping, and yes, even snowmobiles.

Under the policies that have been in place since snowmobiles entered the park in 1968, snowmobiles have been restricted to the paved road surfaces. The NPS does not plow the roads in the winter, allowing snow to accumulate, providing an excellent place for snowmobiles to ride. The 185 miles of roads within the park provide an excellent way for snowmobilers to experience the park. This is not altogether different from the experiences of motorists in the summer months, who are restricted to paved road surfaces. The snowmobile essentially provides an opportunity for visitors to experience the park with personal freedom and ease.

Snowmobiling tourists are key to the survival of the local economy. The money that is spent on motel rooms, fuel, and food helps to ensure the survival of many small businesses in the city of West Yellowstone. The effect that a park closure would have on the local economy would be significant. Many of the snowmobilers that enter the park are new to the sport, and it is necessary for them to rent the necessary equipment for the trip, which generates a great deal of local business. The closing of the park to snowmobiles would remove one of the largest tourist attractions from the community and leave it reeling. In addition, the states of Wyoming and Idaho generate a great deal of their state revenue from the sales taxes collected in the region. As states that rely on tourism for their economic wellbeing, the restriction of motorized recreation would have a negative impact on the states' economic wellbeing.

The environmental groups that oppose motorized winter recreation in Yellowstone have several primary justifications. The number one issue cited by the Sierra Club is the issue of air pollution as a result of snowmobiles in Yellowstone. They point out the fact that snowmobiles emit 68% of all carbon monoxide emissions within the park (Libkind). Furthermore, they claim that snowmobiles account for an even larger share of the hydrocarbon emissions. This data, however, is based on old technology in the snowmobile industry.

For years, snowmobiles employed two cycle engines that are less fuel efficient and more polluting. In recent years, there have been giant leaps in emissions control technology and the development of four cycle engines that will minimize the amount of air pollution, while maximizing fuel efficiency. For example, the manufacturer Arctic Cat recently announced that three of its models have been approved for use in National Parks by the U.S. Department of the Interior. The Arctic Cat T660 model, which is equipped with a four cycle engine, reduces carbon monoxide emissions by over 70%, and hydrocarbons by a factor of 90% (Arctic Cat). These new stringent requirements are assuring that the environmental impact of snowmobiles is minimal. Though older models were responsible for significant emissions, the problem has been mitigated by technological advancement.

When speaking about the Yellowstone snowmobiling issue, Marcus Libkind, President of the Snowlands Network, claimed that snowmobiles "harm soils, vegetation, and wildlife. Their use with insufficient snow-cover leads to compaction of the soil, damage to vegetation, and stresses on sub-nivean animals" (Libkind). While this may be the case, it is not an applicable argument in Yellowstone, where snowmobiles ride atop hard packed snow covering the paved road that cars use in the summer months. The damage that is posed to soil and vegetation is negligible given the fact that snowmobiles are not allowed to ride in meadows or wooded areas where such habitats exist. This is enforced by constant patrols by park rangers. Furthermore, under new National Park Service guidelines, all snowmobilers allowed in Yellowstone are under the supervision of professional guides. This will assure that all policies are followed.

Yellowstone is the home to many animal species, which range from moose and bison, to the newly re-introduced wolves. Many groups have claimed that snowmobiles disrupt and harass wildlife within the park. From my own personal experience as a wintertime visitor to the park, I have seen that this is not the case. While traveling through Yellowstone several years ago on my snowmobile, my uncle and I came along a herd of bison that were walking slowly down the road. Along the side of the trail, all of the snowmobilers shut off their machines and waited, allowing the herd to pass. When we entered the park, we were told that if we encountered a herd of wildlife, we should be respectful of their space, and allow them to pass. This was the case with the approximately 50 snowmobiles stopped on the side of the trail. Though it would be ridiculous to argue that wildlife is never bothered by snowmobilers, it should be noted that there are many instances each year when wildlife is antagonized by summer visitors. It is therefore unfair to blame snowmobiles en-masse for the disruption of the park's wildlife.

As the debate continues over whether the National Park Service should allow snowmobiles in Yellowstone National Park, it is important to be informed about the ways in which the environment is impacted. Though older snowmobiles have caused pollution, new technology has emerged that makes snowmobiles much more environmentally friendly. Therefore, it would make no sense to ban motorized winter recreation based on outdated information. Claims that have been made with regard to the effect that snowmobiles have on native flora and fauna are based on a misunderstanding of the actual rules in the park. All motorized travel is restricted to the paved roadways, thus avoiding increased erosion and damage to native species. In addition, only 720 snowmobiles are to be allowed within the park each day, which is infinitesimal compared with the invasion of cars, motor homes and SUVs in the summer months.

The National Park System was created for the use of the American people. It was created as a place where the citizens of our country could experience a piece of wild America. The ability of snowmobilers to traverse the roads of the park is crucial to keeping with this tradition. Modern technological advances are allowing cleaner, more fuel efficient snowmobiles to be produced. The National Park Service has worked to develop a proposal that limits the number of snowmobiles and mandates emissions control technology, while requiring guided tours of the park. This proposal should be reasonable for all parties, because it retains the rights of the snowmobilers to access the park, while addressing the concerns of environmental groups. This is the best option for Yellowstone and its local economy, and the best option for America.

WORKS CITED

"Arctic Cat 4-Stroke Snowmobiles Certified by U.S. Department of the Interior." Press Release. Arctic Cat Inc. 5 Sept. 2003. Web. 18 Nov. 2004.

Bohrer, Becky. "Park Service Proposes Allowing Snowmobiles in Yellowstone." *Billings Gazette and Associated Press* 9 August 2004. Print.

Libkind, Marcus. "Defending Winter from the Roar and Stench of Snowmobiles." *San Francisco Sierra Club Yodeler* November 2003. Print.

"The National Park Service—Our Mission." U.S. National Park Service, n.d. Web. 10 Nov. 2004.

"Yellowstone National Park History." Yellowstone Net, 10 Nov. 2004. Web. 10 Nov. 2004.

"Yellowstone Snowmobile History." *Yellowstone Park Winter Guide*, n.d. Web. 10 Nov. 2004.

Tyler's essay generally follows a classical arrangement:

- His first two paragraphs serve as his Introduction. (They also include background information.)
- Paragraphs 3–5 provide the background for the issue.
- In paragraph 6, Tyler states his proposition ("We must work to find ways to co-exist with nature, not to seal ourselves away from it. With modern technological advances, it is possible to limit our impact on the environment, while retaining our rights as citizens to have access to our national treasures.")
- Paragraphs 7–9 present Tyler's Proof—his main reasons in support of his proposition.
- In paragraphs 10–13 Tyler refutes the views of environmentalists opposed to the use of snowmobiles in Yellowstone National Park.
- Paragraphs 14 and 15 represent Tyler's conclusion, in which he restates his position and makes a final appeal in support of his proposition.

Notice that Tyler carefully selects background information that is unlikely to alienate the readers he needs to persuade, but it is nevertheless useful for the case he is making. For example, the first quotation in the paper establishes that Yellowstone was intended to give people pleasure when they visit the park, which is a different mission from what would inspire the creation of a wildlife sanctuary. And by establishing early on that snowmobiling has been practiced in Yellowstone since 1968, Tyler shows that he is arguing to preserve a tradition rather than to violate one. This background becomes important to his proposition that snowmobiling in the park is consistent with environmental preservation. In support of that proposition he provides evidence and reasoning. For example, he argues that snowmobiling is a reasonable means of enjoying the park that is consistent with the park's original purpose, and he emphasizes that snowmobilers generate winter revenue for the owners of small businesses near the park. He also argues that snowmobiles now benefit from improved technology, so they produce less pollution than they once did. And he draws upon relevant personal experience to show how snowmobilers can treat wildlife with respect. Tyler is respectful of contrary viewpoints, but he relies on evidence from various sources as well as his personal experience to refute opposing arguments.

In short, classical arrangement enables Tyler to manage a very complex argument very effectively.

Rogerian Argument

In Chapter 1 we discussed how the ideas of psychotherapist Carl Rogers have influenced scholars interested in argumentation. Rogers focused on listening with understanding to avoid miscommunication that can too often accompany serious conflicts. For Rogers the key to resolving conflict is to try honestly to understand what others mean.

Despite questions raised by some scholars about the extent to which Rogers's ideas can be applied to written arguments, you can benefit from viewing argument as a means to resolve conflict and achieve social cooperation instead of thinking that the point of an argument is to defeat your opponents. Accordingly, planning a Rogerian argument means emphasizing concessions rather than refutations and placing concessions early in your essay. Like classically arranged arguments, Rogerian arguments have six identifiable parts, as follows:

Introduction	State the problem that you hope to resolve. By presenting your issue as a problem in need of a solution, you raise the possibility of positive change. This strategy can interest readers who would not be drawn to an argument that seems devoted to tearing something down.
Summary of Opposing Views	As accurately and neutrally as possible, state the views of people with whom you disagree. By doing so, you show that you are capable of listening without judging and that you have given a fair hearing to people who think differently from you—the people you most need to reach.
Statement of Understanding	Having summarized views different from your own, you now show that you understand that there are situations in which these views are valid. In other words, you are offering a kind of concession. You are not conceding that these views are always right, but you are recognizing that there are conditions under which you would share the views of your opponents.
Statement of Your Position	Having won the attention of both your opponents as well as those readers who do not have a position on your issue, you can state your own position. Now that your readers know that you've given fair consideration to views other than your own, they should be prepared to listen fairly to your views.
Statement of Contexts	Similar to the statement of understanding, in which you have described situations where you would be inclined to share the views of your opponents, the statement of contexts describes situations in which you hope your views would be honored. By showing that your position has merit in a specific context or contexts, you establish that you don't expect everyone to agree with you all the time. The limitations you recognize increase the likelihood that your opponents will agree with you at least in part.
Statement of Benefits	You conclude your argument by appealing to the self-interest of people who do not already share your views but are beginning to respect them because of your presentation. When you conclude by showing how such readers would benefit from accepting your position, your essay's ending is positive and hopeful.

(Adapted from Richard Coe, *Form and Substance.* New York: Wiley, 1981.)

Depending on the complexity of the issue, the extent to which people are divided about it, and the points you want to argue, any part of a Rogerian argument can be expanded. It is not necessary to devote precisely the same amount of space to each part. You should try to make your case as balanced as possible, however. If you seem to give only superficial consideration to the views of others and then linger at length on your own, you are defeating the purpose of a Rogerian argument.

Any style of arrangement—classical, Rogerian, or otherwise—can strive toward the goal of solving problems through argumentation. But a Rogerian argument might be most effective in situations in which people are deeply divided as a result of different values or perceptions. It is especially useful when you are trying to reconcile conflicting parties and achieve a compromise. However, there will be situations in which such an approach might not be the most effective one. If you hold strong views about a particular issue, for instance, you might find that it is better to consider other ways of organizing your argument. In some situations presenting a strong argument for a specific course of action or viewpoint might be the most ethical way to proceed, even if the goal is to resolve a conflict. The point is that planning and organizing your argument should be thought of in the larger context of your purposes for engaging in argument.

Here is a student essay about a complicated and controversial issue: gay adoption. As you'll see, Rachel uses the principles of Rogerian argument to make her case in favor of a national policy for adoption by same-sex couples.

A Reasonable Approach to Gay Adoption

by Rachel Guetter

Adoption by gay parents recently became an open topic with the help of talk show host Rosie O'Donnell. O'Donnell, who went public with her sexuality in 2001, has adopted several children and is a foster mother (Huff and Gest 2). She is currently taking on a Florida law that bans homosexuals from adopting. In doing so, she is prompting everyone to address a situation that is likely to become more common: gay couples seeking to adopt children.

Currently, there is no national policy regarding gay adoptions, and state laws offer a mixed bag of approaches and restriction. For example, Florida is the only state that has enacted a law explicitly banning gay adoptions. In the states that do not have prohibitory laws, gays and lesbians can file for adoption in court (Maxwell, et al.). It is then up to each court to decide whether a petition for adoption meets the state's adoption policies. Many homosexuals have children from previous marriages, or they become parents by donating their own sperm or egg. Only California, Connecticut, and Vermont have legislation that would allow gays and lesbians to adopt their partner's child (Berman). The forty-six other states must rely on their individual judges to consider the petition. One would hope that a judge would not let personal preference get in the way of a fair ruling, but unfortunately this does not always happen.

The many different state laws may reflect the resistance of many Americans to the idea of gay adoption. Those who feel that children should not be brought up in homosexual households state that their concerns are not the product of homophobia, but are the product of what they find to be in the best interest of the children. These people believe that the best way for a child to be raised is in a family with married mother and father. Also, some opponents of gay adoption argue that children who grow up with same-sex parents are not provided with the same legal benefits and securities as those who are raised in heterosexual, married households.

One reason for this resistance is that America is still dealing with the lack of acceptance for and recognition of homosexuals. Until homosexuality is more widely received, children with gay and lesbian parents will have to deal with the fact that their family is viewed as pejoratively different. Glenn Stanton, senior research analyst for Focus on the Family, says, "While there may be very nice people who are raising kids in homosexual situations, the best model for kids is to grow up with mom and dad" (Stanton). It seems reasonable to believe that having both a mother and father benefits children. Women and men have different parenting traits that give a strong balance for the development of a child. Stanton also states, "Fathers encourage children to take chances … mothers protect and are more cautious." There exist in parents different disciplining, communication, and playing styles that can be advantages in raising a child. Sandy Rios, president of Concerned Women for America, agrees, "As the single mother of a son, I can see quite clearly that having a mother and father together would be far better for my son" ("Pediatrics").

Another problem is that children who have gay and lesbian parents are not necessarily given the same benefits as children from two-parent, heterosexual families. Often, one person in a same-sex relationship is the biological parent and the other will help raise the child as his or her own. According to the American Academy of Pediatrics (AAP), children in this situation lose "survivor benefits if a parent dies and legal rights if the parents break up" (Berman 1). Both situations leave a dramatic impact on the child, who then is caught in the middle of legal battles. Another benefit that the child would not be given is health insurance from both parents. In all of these cases, the child is not given the same economic stability as one who has a married mother and father.

Many gays and lesbians are like any other people who dream of one day having a family. But they face great obstacles. Often, one parent in a same-sex family is not given the same rights as the other when one partner has a biological child. Sometimes neither partner in a same-sex family is able to obtain a child through adoption. Despite such obstacles, it cannot be denied that homosexual families exist. Depending on which study you consult, there are anywhere from 1.5 to 5 million children being raised in gay and lesbian families (Maxwell, et al.). The children, however, are the ones who are being hurt by the lack of legality of the situation that they are in. We owe it to these children—and to the same-sex couples who are committed to raising them—to address this problem in a way that is satisfactory for all concerned.

This issue needs to be examined from a national point of view for two reasons. First of all, people who wish to adopt a child are not restricted to adopting within their own states. Often, the demand for certain children requires couples to look in another state. Secondly, people tend to move from state to state. A couple may adopt a child in one state and later decide to move to another with different laws governing parenthood. The adoption needs to be legally recognized in all states, so if a couple adopts in one state, they can move to another and still be protected by law as legal parents. Instead of allowing each state to make its own decision concerning this matter, federal legislation needs to be enacted that would not only permit homosexuals to adopt their partner's child, but also allow gay couples to adopt children together. Obviously, such legislation would make it easier for same-sex families to raise their children in safe and happy homes. But it might also address the problem of children who need to be adopted. If homosexuals are legally permitted to adopt, more children waiting to be adopted can be given homes and the homosexual families that currently exist will become legally recognized.

There are children who are constantly being shifted from one foster home to another and deservingly need to be placed in a permanent and stable environment. There are currently not enough homes that children can be adopted into. In 1999, about 581,000 children were a part of the U.S. foster care system. Of those, 22 percent were available for adoption ("Foster Care Facts"). A report by the Vera Institute of Justice states that children raised without a permanent home are more likely to exhibit emotional and behavioral problems and be involved with the juvenile justice system ("Safe and Smart"). This is not to say that the foster care system is bad, but it suggests how important a permanent home and family are for children. Same-sex couples could provide such a home for many of these children.

Florida, the state that bans homosexuals from adopting, nevertheless allows homosexuals to become foster parents (Pertman). It is interesting to think that someone could be allowed to clothe, feed, discipline, and love a child yet not be allowed to call that child their own. By allowing a couple to be foster parents, the state has made a statement about what kind of people those foster parents are: responsible and caring and able to provide a good home and family environment. Why should they not be allowed to become legal parents of their own adopted children?

Both sides agree that children need to be raised in loving and caring families. It is wrong to think that a gay couple cannot provide that. A study in Minnesota shows that "in general, gay lesbian families tended to score the most consistently as the healthiest and strongest of the family structures" (Maxwell, et al.). Married couples placed a strong second, and unmarried heterosexual couples were found to be the least healthy and least strong, especially when children were a part of the family (Maxwell, et al.). The study done by the courts discloses that homosexual couples deliberately plan to have children and arrange their lives so that both parents are significantly involved with raising the child (Maxwell, et al.). Opponents say that it takes more than just a loving environment; it takes both a mom and dad. As the Minnesota study proved, though, perhaps mother–father households are not as stable as once thought. Gays and lesbians have to make extensive plans in order to obtain or even conceive a child, so the likelihood that a child was an "accident" or unwanted is rare.

In February 2002, AAP issued a new statement titled, "Coparent or Second-Parent Adoption by Same-Sex Parents." It explains the AAP's stance on what is in the best interest of children being raised in same-sex families. Dr. Steven Berman offers a summary: "The AAP concluded that legalizing second-parent adoptions is in the best interest of the children" (Berman). Also in this statement is the reassurance that children are not more inclined to become homosexual or to possess homosexual tendencies from being raised by homosexual parents. Although the AAP does not endorse or condemn homosexuality, they, like the rest of the U.S., cannot ignore the growing number of same-sex families and must deal with what truly would be in the best interest of the children who are caught in the middle.

Whether the stance is for or against gay and lesbian adoption, both sides base their reasoning on what is in the best interest for the children. It would be safe to say that most would agree that having a child brought up in a loving, same-sex family is better than having a child moved from foster home to foster home or raised in an abusive home. Being homosexual does not mean that one loses the right to raise a child. Being an unwanted child does not mean that one loses the right to find a loving home, whether that home is single parent, married, heterosexual or even homosexual.

WORKS CITED

Berman, Steven. "Homosexuals and Adoption." *Rocky Mountain News* 23 Feb 2002:1, final ed.: 1W. Print.

"Foster Care Facts." The Evan B. Donaldson Adoption Institute, 2002. Web. 10 Apr. 2002.

Huff, Richard, and Emily Gest. "Rosie Takes on Prez About Gay Adoption." *New York Daily News* 14 Mar. 2002, final ed.: 2. Print.

Maxwell, Nancy G., Astrid A.M. Mattijssen, and Charlene Smith. "Legal Protection for All the Children: Dutch-American Comparison of Lesbian and Gay Parent Adoptions." *Electronic Journal of Comparative Law* 3.1 (August 1999): n. pag. Web. 20 Sept. 2002.

"Pediatrics Academy's Endorsement of Homosexual Adoption." *US Newswire* 04 Feb. 2002. Print.

Pertman, Adam. "Break Down Barriers to Homosexual Adoption." *The Baltimore Sun* 20 Mar. 2002, final ed.: A23. Print.

"Safe and Smart." Vera Institute of Justice, n.d. Web. 10 Apr. 2002.

Stanton, Glenn T. "Why Children Need a Male and Female Parent." Focus on the Family, n.d. Web. 13 May 2002.

Notice that Rachel follows the Rogerian structure described on page 127. After her introduction she presents the views of those who oppose gay adoptions, and she does so without criticism. She offers a statement of understanding, conceding that the concerns of opponents are valid. But she also offers her own concerns, which are based on the same basic goal of protecting children that opponents of gay adoptions hold. This is the common ground that enables her to present her proposal for national legislation regarding gay adoptions—legislation that she believes will protect children in such situations as well as foster children waiting to be adopted. She clearly lays out the benefits of such legislation.

Although you do not need to follow the Rogerian structure, you can see that it might help you organize your argument in a way that is likely to connect with your opponents—which is one of the goals of Rogerian argument. As in the case of Rachel's essay, an argument structured according to a Rogerian approach places your opponents' concerns first. Notice, too, that Rachel's tone is measured, respectful, and concerned throughout her essay, another indication of her desire to seek common ground and find a solution to the problem she is writing about.

Logical Arrangements

Arguments can also be shaped by the kind of reasoning a writer employs. In Chapter 4 we discussed the two basic kinds of logic: **inductive reasoning** and **deductive reasoning.** We also discussed informal logic, in particular the Toulmin model. These kinds of logic can be the basis for strategies you can use to make your arguments, and like the classical and Rogerian approaches, they can be helpful in deciding how to structure an argument.

Inductive Reasoning

When you base an argument on inductive reasoning, you are drawing a conclusion based on evidence that you present. For example, imagine that you are making an argument for more stringent enforcement of driving laws in your state. In doing so, you might present a variety of relevant information:

- Experiences you've had with speeding drivers.
- Anecdotes about friends or family members who have been in accidents that resulted from reckless driving.
- Statistics from the U.S. Department of Transportation about automobile accidents and their relationship to speed limits.
- Information about the costs of automobile accidents in terms of medical expenses and property damage.
- Quotations from law enforcement officials or experts who advocate lower speed limits but admit that posted speed limits are often not vigorously enforced.

From this evidence you draw the conclusion that higher speed limits are dangerous and that drivers would be safer if laws were enforced more rigorously. Such an argument would be based on inductive reasoning.

In composing an argument based on inductive reasoning, keep the following considerations in mind:

- *Try to arrange your evidence so that it leads your readers to the same conclusion you have reached.* In structuring such an argument, you will need to introduce the issue and demonstrate to your readers that it is a problem worthy of attention. But the primary challenge will be to decide which evidence to present first and in what order the remaining evidence will be presented. In a well-structured inductive argument, your evidence is presented so that it accumulates and leads inevitably to the conclusion you wish to draw.
- *Consider how specific kinds of evidence you have gathered will affect your readers.* Will some kinds of evidence likely be more compelling to them than others? If so, will it be more effective to present such evidence earlier or later in the argument? Answering those questions not only can help you decide how best to organize your essay but also can generate additional ideas for evidence that will make your conclusion as persuasive to your audience as possible.
- *Decide how much evidence is enough.* Eventually, you will reach a point at which you decide that you have offered enough evidence to support your argument. You might reach this point sooner in some contexts than others. For example, in an essay for your college writing class, you are not likely to cite as much evidence as you might be expected to include in a research report for a course in freshwater ecology; an essay in a respected political journal such as *Foreign Affairs* will include more extensive evidence than an editorial in your local newspaper. But whatever the context, the process is essentially the same.
- *Interpret and analyze your evidence for your audience.* In an inductive argument you must not only provide evidence that supports the claims you make but also

explain why the evidence is significant. For example, if you use an anecdote about an accident involving a speeding driver in an essay on the enforcement of driving laws, you will have to explain what that anecdote means for your argument. There will always be a gap between your evidence and your conclusion, and you have to interpret your evidence so that it leads your readers to the conclusion you wish to draw.

Organizing an argument inductively gives you a great deal of flexibility. But as the advice given here suggests, you will structure the argument primarily around your evidence. As always, the decisions you make about how to present and explain that evidence will reflect your purpose and your sense of how best to address your audience.

> **A METHOD FOR IDENTIFYING YOUR PREMISE IN A DEDUCTIVE ARGUMENT**
>
> Because it can be difficult to formulate a good premise, it is often useful to work backward when you are planning a deductive argument. Follow these steps:
>
> 1. If you know the conclusion you want to reach, write it down, and number it as statement 3.
> 2. Now ask yourself why you believe statement 3. That question should prompt a number of reasons; write them down and group them together as statement 2.
> 3. Now that you can see your conclusion, as well as some reasons that seem to justify it, ask yourself whether you've left anything out—perhaps something basic or obvious that you skipped over because you assumed that your readers would already agree with it. When you can identify this assumption, you have your premise, at least in rough form.

Deductive Reasoning

Deductive reasoning begins with a generalization and works to a conclusion that follows from that generalization. In that respect it can be thought of as the opposite of inductive reasoning, which begins with specific observations and ends with a conclusion that goes beyond those observations. The generalization you start with in a deductively arranged argument is called a **premise** and is the foundation for your argument. As you saw in Chapter 4, it takes careful thought to formulate a good premise. Nevertheless, because so many arguments employ this kind of logic, deductive reasoning can be a powerful way to construct an effective argument.

The process of reasoning deductively might be difficult to grasp in the abstract, but you can follow some general steps that will help you explore your topic and generate an outline for your argument. In effect, you work backward from the conclusion you wish to reach:

1. *Identify your conclusion.* Suppose that because of worries about your own health, you have reconsidered eating meat, and you have begun to adopt a plant-based, or vegetarian, diet. But in exploring a vegetarian diet, you have also learned that meat production has potentially harmful environmental consequences. In particular, you are concerned about the destruction of forests cut down to allow cattle to graze. You believe that if eating meat leads to such environmental damage, it should be stopped.

   Given how prevalent meat consumption is and its prominent place in the American diet, you can't reasonably argue for eating meat to be made illegal or restricted by law in some way. But you can argue that it should be discouraged—perhaps in the same way that smoking is discouraged. Most important, you believe that people should at least eat less meat than they currently do. So your conclusion is clear: People should eat less meat.

2. *Examine your reasons carefully.* Before going any further, you realize that not all of your reasons for opposing meat consumption are equally compelling. For one thing, diet can be a personal choice, and your concerns about your own health are not sufficient grounds to argue against other people eating meat. So you need to make sure that your point about the health risks of eating meat has validity for others. Your own research has shown that eating meat involves a number of health risks. You also know that a vegetarian diet has health benefits. You will want to discuss these risks and benefits in a way that makes them relevant to people in general so that you are not simply discussing your own health choices.

Similarly, it might be difficult to convince people who enjoy eating meat that the loss of forests thousands of miles away from their backyard grill should concern them. So it will be important for you to establish not just that meat production leads to the loss of forest but also that there might be other environmental consequences closer to home. For example, most livestock in the United States are fed grain, and the production of feed grain not only uses up vast amounts of farmland but also contributes to pollution through agricultural runoff. Furthermore, the raising of livestock generates pollution in the form of animal waste, and the chemicals and drugs that are used on livestock can be risky for humans who eat meat. All of these reasons can be compelling to others who might enjoy eating meat but might be unaware of the problems that can be caused by meat production.

In short, think carefully about your reasons for your conclusion, and take your audience into account as you do.

3. *Formulate your premise.* You should now be ready to formulate your premise. Your conclusion is that people should eat less meat, and you will urge others to stop or reduce their meat consumption and adopt an alternative diet. But near the beginning of your argument, you need to establish the principle that supports this conclusion. In this case you believe that it is wrong for people to engage in a practice that harms the environment, especially when there is an alternative to that practice. In effect, you are suggesting that if eating meat has negative consequences for the environment and our health, then it is unethical to continue doing it when we have other options. This is your main premise: People should not engage in practices that have damaging consequences if there are reasonable alternatives.

A premise can be a single sentence, a full paragraph, or more, depending on the length and complexity of the argument. The function of a premise is to establish a widely accepted value that even your opponents should be able to share. You would probably be wise, therefore, to make a fairly general statement early in your argument—something like this:

It is unethical to continue engaging in an activity that is harmful and environmentally destructive.

Such a statement needs to be developed, and you will do so not only by showing how destructive meat production and consumption can be but also by offering better alternatives to eating meat. You will want to suggest that individual choices about things like diet are ethical choices because they can affect others. Now you have the foundation for a logical argument:

If engaging in a practice or activity is harmful to people and their environment, then it should be stopped. Eating meat is such an activity; therefore, we should avoid eating meat and instead adopt an alternative diet.

Now you begin to create a rough outline:

1. We should not engage in practices that can have harmful effects on others and our environment.

2. Consuming meat can be unhealthy, and meat production damages the environment.

3. Americans should consume less meat and eat a diet that emphasizes vegetarian foods.

This example can help you see the utility of structuring an argument deductively. You can see, too, that generating an argument in this way can deepen your engagement with your topic and eventually lead to a more substantive and persuasive essay.

The following student essay by Kristen Montgomery, in which she argues against eating meat, is one example of an argument structured in this way. Notice that Kristen presents her main premise—that doing something harmful and environmentally destructive is unethical—implicitly in her second paragraph, after introducing her topic. In this case, Kristen's question, "Do we have the right to support eating habits that have such negative consequences, especially when these habits are unnecessary?" implies her main premise. Often in a deductive argument, the main premise is explicitly stated at the beginning. Kristen chose a slightly different strategy. But it is clear that she will argue from this basic principle that we have no right to engage in harmful practices when alternatives to those practices exist. Kristen could have stated her premise explicitly in her opening paragraph and then proceeded to her specific evidence. Either approach is acceptable for an argument structured deductively. The important point is to establish the main premise early in the essay and then argue on the basis of that premise, which Kristen does.

Carnivorous Concerns

by Kristen M. Montgomery

Baseball? Apple pie? Shopping? Most Americans love these things, but there is perhaps nothing more American than eating meat. Birthdays, ballgames, and the most American of holidays, the Fourth of July, are all celebrated with barbeques and cookouts featuring burgers, dogs, and steaks. A burger and fries may be the most American meal of all. Each day, Americans eat 46 million pounds. And each year, the average American eats two times his or her weight in meat.

But what if this all-American meal is actually damaging health and home? Is it right to engage in a practice that is not only harmful to our physical health but also destructive to our environment? Do we have the right to support eating habits that have such negative consequences, especially when these habits are unnecessary? Many people oppose eating meat on the grounds that meat production is cruel to animals. And it is. But the consequences for the human population are arguably as bad. And it is simply unethical to engage in a practice that is so damaging to the earth and its inhabitants.

A careful look at meat production shows why eating meat contributes to human illness. The animals we eat are pumped full of chemicals that are often unhealthy to them and to humans; they are also neglected and tortured. Meanwhile, their living conditions are feces-ridden and disease-infested. The animals live in their own excrement next to others who are themselves full of disease. It is only reasonable to expect that these conditions contribute to human illness. In fact, the USDA estimates that salmonella, a dangerous pathogen that can cause serious illness and even death in humans, is present in 35 percent of turkeys, 11 percent of chickens and 6 percent of ground beef. Each year, food-borne pathogens cause 76 million illnesses and 5,000 deaths, according to the Centers for Disease Control. And it is alarming to note that certain bacteria in meat have shown evolutionary changes into more dangerous substances. For example, O157:H7 is a mutant strand of E. coli, which is very hard to treat because of its evasiveness in medical tests. Ultimately, for those who eat meat contaminated with O157:H7, organ failure is the cause of death. It is reasonable to assume that this strand of E. coli is not the only bacterium which may have developed strengths against human antibodies. There are likely more out there and more to come.

Exposing ourselves to such illnesses is unnecessary. We have healthier alternatives to meat as a food source. Although many people view a plant-based diet as unthinkable because of their love of meat, a plant-based diet, with a little bit of research and practice, can have more variety and is much healthier than a meat-based diet. Meat is deficient in carbohydrates and vitamins. Not only is meat lacking important nutrients for proper health, but it is also abundant in harmful substances, such as calories and saturated fat. When cooked, most meats produce a variety of benzenes, among other carcinogenic compounds. Benzene is commonly found in paints, cleaners, and cigarettes, and it is poisonous to humans. In addition, the average American gets five times the amount of needed protein in his or her diet, which strains the kidneys with uric acid and can actually cause nephritis.

By contrast, a plant-based diet enables us to avoid such potentially serious problem. And contrary to popular opinion, there is no nutrient necessary for good health that cannot be obtained from a plant-based diet. That is why mom always made us eat our vegetables. High fruit and vegetable consumption has been associated with a lowered risk for heart disease, several types of cancers, and other chronic illnesses. Also, there is a growing body of medical evidence that eating such things as beans, peanuts, lentils, and peas, which contain a variety of beneficial ingredients, may protect against disease. For example, according to the Journal of American Dietetic Association, soybean consumption is linked with a decreased risk of prostate cancer and increased bone density in post-menopausal women. These facts are just the beginning. If we look at the overall benefits of eating a plant-based diet, it doesn't make sense to risk our health by eating meat.

But if eating meat is unhealthy for our bodies, it may be even worse for our planet. And this alone should make us reconsider our reliance on meat as a food source. Some people worry about big business eating away at rural and suburban land, but urban sprawl is not the leading cause of deforestation. Meat production is to blame: "For every acre of forest land consumed by urban development, seven acres are devoured by the meat industry, for grazing and growing feed. If water used by the meat industry were not subsidized by U.S. taxpayers, a hamburger would cost $35." 125,000 square miles of rain forests are destroyed each year for the purpose of producing meat. For each quarter-pounder fast-food burger made of beef that is raised on land that was once rain forest, fifty five square feet of land is used. Every second, 2.4 acres of forest is turned into grazing land. Moreover, this use of the land is incredibly inefficient. For example, an acre of land can produce approximately 20,000 pounds of potatoes but only 165 pounds of beef. Large amounts of grain are grown to feed the animals that we butcher for food. In fact, 87 percent of all agricultural land in America is used to raise the animals we eat. Instead of feeding the grain to humans, we feed it to cows and chickens. It takes twice the amount of grain to produce beef and four times the amount of grain for poultry production than to feed this grain to humans.

Not only does raising animals for food require a large amount of land, but it also requires a large amount of energy. Consider for a moment that it takes the water from 17 showers to produce a single hamburger. Or instead of driving a small car for 20 miles, consider using the same amount of energy to make that one hamburger patty. That's how much energy is needed to produce the beef for that burger. In the 1980's, one-half of the world's grain harvest was fed not to people, but to livestock. With world starvation rates as they are, this approach to food production doesn't make sense. What's more, it's unethical.

All of this resource depletion also leads to pollution. On the large portion of land on which we raise animals and the grain to feed them, raw waste is produced. Excrement is produced at a rate of 130 times more than what is produced by the entire human population. It must go somewhere, and where it goes is everywhere, sometimes in nearby waterways. According to *Scientific American*, this waste has increased the pathogenic organisms in the water, which has poisoned humans as well as millions of fish, which serve to maintain the delicate balance of the oceanic ecosystem. Not only are the feces poisoning the soil and waterways, but some people living near these areas must actually wear face masks because of the overwhelming stench. In addition to water and land pollution, the EPA estimates that the world's animal population is responsible for 25 percent of anthropogenic emissions of methane gas, which contribute to the greenhouse effect. Therefore, meat production also contributes to air pollution. These facts are compounded by the fact that since the 1950's, the livestock population has increased more rapidly than the human population. So as our consumption of meat increases, so does the damage we are doing to our earth.

Eating meat is enjoyable for many people, but it is an impractical approach to food production that cannot be sustained. We may neglect to see the consequences of depleting our resources and letting our planet become overburdened with animal waste, because the consequences are not immediate and we are a society where immediate is considered best. Few of us see the dramatic effects described above. But we all must seriously consider what our heavy meat consumption means for our future. The slaughtering of animals to satisfy our hunger contributes to the depletion of our world's valuable resources, results in pollution, and causes human disease. The consequences of our murderous appetite may eventually be as deadly for us as for the animals we kill to satisfy this appetite. Perhaps knowing this may curb our appetite for meat. It's time we adopted more sustainable and ethical eating habits, before we eat ourselves—and our world—to death.

Notice that once Kristen establishes her basic premise in her second paragraph, she devotes most of her essay to providing her reasons for her conclusion that eating meat is an unethical activity. By the time she reaches her final paragraph, she has presented a great deal of evidence to support her conclusion. In structuring her essay deductively, Kristen essentially had to decide what order in which to present her reasons. Notice that she presents health-related reasons first and then moves to environmental considerations and finally to ethical issues. This is an effective strategy, especially when addressing ethical and moral issues that involve fundamental beliefs or values that can serve as a sound premise.

Using the Toulmin Model

Even when you are using a logical arrangement to organize your argument, you will rarely follow the rules of logic rigidly. Because most people use logic informally in arguments, the Toulmin model (see pages 87–91) can be extremely useful in helping you construct your argument. The Toulmin model focuses on the claim you want to make—that is, the conclusion you are trying to reach or the assertion you hope to prove. Your task, simply put, is to state your claim clearly and offer persuasive reasons (what Toulmin calls *data*) for that claim. The third element in the Toulmin system is the warrant, which is the assumption that connects the claim and the data. As noted in Chapter 4, the warrant is usually a fundamental value or belief that, ideally, is shared by writer and audience (like the premise in the preceding section on deductive reasoning).

This model dictates no specified pattern for organizing an argument, so the challenge is to determine how best to present your claim to your intended audience and then to offer adequate reasons for your claim. But the value of this model for constructing an argument lies in the way it requires you to articulate your claim precisely and to pay close attention to the adequacy of your reasons and your evidence, without having to follow the rigid rules of formal logic. In this way the Toulmin model can help you refine your claim and develop convincing support for it. This model also encourages you to think through the often unstated assumptions that lie behind your claim: the warrants. Identifying your warrants can lead to a more effective argument because it can help you see points of possible contention between you and your audience.

Imagine that you live in a small town where a businessperson wishes to build a large meat-processing facility. This person has recently applied to the town board for a permit to begin construction of the plant. As a resident who values the quiet lifestyle of your town, as well as its clean and safe environment, you worry about the social and environmental damage the plant might cause. So you decide to write to the town supervisor to express your concerns and urge him to reject the permit for the plant.

Using the Toulmin model for your letter, your first step would be to try to articulate your central claim clearly. You might state your claim as follows:

Claim: We should not allow a meat-processing facility to be built in our town.

Before moving to your reasons for your claim, consider carefully whether that statement accurately represents the position you want to take. Can you be more specific? Can you focus the claim even more narrowly? In thinking about these questions, you might amend your claim as follows:

Claim: Building a meat-packing facility would damage the quality of life and the environment of our town.

Notice that although this version of your claim is related to the first version, it is a bit narrower and more precise. It also points directly to the kinds of data or the reasons you can offer to support the claim. Being clear about your claim is crucial because your reasons must fit that claim closely to be persuasive. Now you can begin exploring your reasons.

At this point it is a good idea to brainstorm, listing the main reasons for your belief that the plant should not be built in your town. You have many reasons: the possible damage to local streams from the waste and runoff from the plant, the increased traffic to and from the plant, the odor, the negative impact of a large plant on the quality of life in a small town. You should examine these reasons and try to identify those that are most compelling. Now you have your claim and main reasons for it:

Claim: Building a meat-packing facility would damage the quality of life and the environment of our town.

Reasons: Meat-packing facilities can cause pollution, endanger the health of local residents, and increase truck traffic on local roads.

Before you begin to develop evidence to support these reasons for your claim, you should think about your warrant—the assumptions that lie behind the claim and connect your reasons to that claim. This is a crucial step in using the Toulmin model because it helps you identify the assumptions behind your claim or the principles on which you base your claim. In Toulmin's model, the warrant is what provides the basis for a claim. Without an acceptable warrant, the claim becomes weak or even invalid. In this case you might state your warrant as follows:

Warrant: We all have a right to live in clean, safe environments.

You can probably be confident that your audience—the town supervisor—would accept this warrant, so you probably don't need to defend it. However, you might decide to state it in your letter, and you might even defend it to drive it home. The point is that you have identified a basic value or belief that you assume others share; without this shared value or belief, your claim has no foundation.

Now you can begin developing specific evidence to support your claim and your reasons. The reasons stated above suggest the kinds of evidence you might gather. For example, to support the assertion that meat-processing facilities damage the environment, you might find reports of increased pollution in streams near existing meat-packing plants. You can perhaps find similar reports about the impact of truck traffic around such plants. Evidence to support the assertion that your town's lifestyle would be adversely affected might be trickier. First, you will want to establish the character of the town as it is. That might mean providing facts about the number of residences compared with businesses, the size and use of roads, and so on. The point is to identify specific and persuasive evidence that fits your reasons for your claim—and to gather evidence that will be acceptable and convincing to your audience.

Here's a letter by a student that takes up this issue. In this letter Kristen Brubaker is writing to the supervisor of her small town in rural Pennsylvania. She expresses concern about a resident's request to build a factory hog farm in the town.

Dear Mr. Smithson:

As township supervisor of Wayne Township, you have had a great impact on our community for the past several years. In the coming months, your service will be needed more than ever. Jack Connolly, a resident of our township, has put forth a plan to build a factory hog farm, called a CAFO. His proposed facility will house 5,600 breeding sows, 100,000 piglets, and will cover nearly five acres of buildings (Weist). I am aware that you support this project, but I think there are some points you may be overlooking. We need to work together to ensure that our basic rights as property owners and citizens are not infringed upon and to protect the quality of life in our community.

I know we share similar values when it comes to the protection of our environment. In fact, you are one of the people who helped to shape my view of the environment. When I was younger, I attended the Dauphin County Conservation Camp that you helped to sponsor. I remember several of our activities, including the stream improvement project we completed and the stocking of trout in Powells Creek. Because of these experiences, I was surprised to find out you did not strongly oppose this project. Were you aware that CAFOs have caused extensive damage to trout streams in many states? I hope we don't have to face the destruction of our creek and surrounding valley before we realize that we made a mistake.

Although the risks to our environment are numerous, the first problem most people associate with CAFOs is the smell. In Powells Valley, we have traditionally been an agricultural community, so we're not afraid of the natural, inevitable odor of farms. Although factory farmers argue that the odor of animal waste is simply part of living in a rural, agricultural area, the air pollution caused by CAFOs is often more than a minor inconvenience. Imagine being unable to hang your clothes out to dry because of a thick, permeating smell that saturates everything it touches. The smell is not harmless either. CAFOs produce dangerous levels of ammonia and methane, gases suspected of causing nausea, flu-like symptoms, and respiratory illness, especially in children or the elderly. These chemicals also return to the ground as rain, polluting our water (Satchell). Another potentially harmful gas produced is hydrogen sulfide. In as small a concentration as 10 parts per million, it causes eye irritation. At 50 parts per million, it causes vomiting, nausea, and diarrhea. At 500 parts per million, hydrogen sulfide causes rapid death (Weist).

Another problem with the proposed location of this facility is its close proximity to houses and the small size of the valley. More than 35 houses are located within a half-mile radius of the proposed operation. Our valley is only a mile wide, so there will be nowhere for the odor to go. It will sit in our valley on hot summer days, saturating the air and everything in it. If this facility must be built, why can't it go somewhere less densely populated or somewhere that would handle odors more effectively?

But the most frightening aspect of having a CAFO in our valley is the strong possibility that we would face severe water pollution. Because of the immense scale of CAFOs, they often produce much more manure than the surrounding land can handle effectively. In cases where overspreading occurs, excess nutrients can run into the streams, disrupting the ecological balance and killing fish. Powells Creek, like most small creeks, sits in a very delicate balance and a small increase of nutrients can seriously alter the habitat of the stream. Nutrients contribute to increased plant and algae life, which can clog waterways and rob them of oxygen. Excess nutrients can also seep into the ground water, creating a problem with illness-causing pathogens such as salmonella (Satchell).

Another cause of water pollution among CAFOs is the waste lagoons used to store manure. Because fields may be spread only certain times of the year, there is a need for immense storage facilities. Most farms use lagoons that can be several acres long, sometimes holding up to 25 million gallons of waste. In North Carolina, waste lagoons are being blamed for the catastrophic fish kills and pollution of the coastal waters that took place in 1996 (Satchell). In the recent flooding in North Carolina due to Hurricane Floyd, over 50 lagoons overflowed, and one burst. Although it is not yet known how these recent spills will affect the environment, more fish kills and contaminated drinking water supplies are virtually guaranteed (Wright).

There are many other problems Powells Valley could face as a result of this facility. The operation that Mr. Connolly is proposing would produce 12 million gallons of waste per year. This waste is going to be spread throughout three townships in our valley. This is a lot of waste for one small stream, yet this is the best-case scenario. Can you imagine what would happen in the case of a leak or spill? Powells Creek is located about 350 feet downhill from these proposed facilities. In the case of an overflow, flood, or leak, the waste would go directly into the creek. To make matters worse, this operation is going to be located in an area that has frequent problems with flooding. In 1996, a small flood destroyed the bridge that crosses Powells Creek just below the proposed operation. If a spill or leak were to occur, the creek's aquatic life would be destroyed. If this facility is approved, we may not have to worry about stocking Powells Creek anymore.

The local increase in traffic is another issue that must be addressed. If this facility goes into operation, there would be approximately 1,750 truck trips per year delivering feed and supplies and transporting the 100,000 piglets to finishing operations. In addition to this, there will be an estimated 3,500 trailer truck trips needed to transport the 12 million gallons of waste (Weist). The roads in our area are not equipped for this kind of traffic. It would put a much greater burden on Wayne Township for the upkeep of its roads. The Carsonville Fire Company, which would be charged with the responsibility of handling any accidents, is dangerously underequipped to handle a large spill. Additionally, the roads entering the area of the proposed operation are small, curvy, and unsafe for large trucks. There are school busses from two school districts traveling these roads. The risk of having a serious accident is simply too high to justify this operation.

One of the key factors that allows these problems to exist largely unchallenged is the lack of regulation for these factory farms. If someone were to build a factory producing the same amount of contaminating waste, they would face numerous regulations. Human waste treatment plants also follow strict environmental controls that ensure that they do not pollute. Because CAFOs are technically agriculture, and not industry, they face virtually no regulations. They are also protected by the "Right to Farm Act," which was originally passed to protect family farms from harassment and lawsuits by developers. This law is making us defenseless because it will back any lawsuit we could make against the owner of the CAFO. Although nutrient management plans are required for a large operation, such a requirement is not enough protection.

As expected, Jack Connolly's plans have not been stifled by the protests of over 100 citizens. His nutrient management plan was recently rejected by the Dauphin County Conservation District, but he continues to build. He realizes that although many people in the community are afraid of his plans, just as many are unwilling to interfere with his right to do what he wants with his property. We don't like being told what we can and cannot do with our land, and when we give up those rights, we feel it starts a dangerous trend. At the same time, we must think of the property rights of those who have inhabited this valley their whole lives. Operations like this can seriously lower property values. People who can't stand the smell would have two choices. They could sell their homes, their sole investments, for a fraction of their worth or live with the smell.

There are some possible benefits to having this operation in our valley. For one, the factory is expected to create between 20 and 30 local jobs. We don't have a problem with unemployment in our valley, though, so it's likely that these jobs will be filled with outsiders. Also, they aren't going to be the high-quality jobs that most of us would want. Another possible benefit, one I'm sure you're aware of, is the possibility of cheap fertilizer. I noticed on the nutrient plan that you were listed among the recipients. Are you aware that if there is an accident with the waste on your land, you are responsible, not Mr. Connolly? If you still decide that this plan is in the best interests of everyone it will affect, do some research of your own to ensure you're not part of the problem by accepting more manure than your land can safely handle. Also, make sure Mr. Connolly hasn't increased your projected amount without your knowledge in order to satisfy his nutrient management plan.

If you agree that his CAFO is not good for our community, there are steps you should take to postpone, or even reject, this proposal. First, you, as township supervisor, can reject his building permits until he gets the necessary approval from the county and state. These agencies will be more likely to approve his plan if he already has a multi-million dollar complex built to house it. You could also pass ordinances to prevent the growth of this "farm." A common scenario is that after the nearby property values are sufficiently lowered due to the offensive smell, a factory farm owner will buy the surrounding land and build more operations. It only makes sense when you consider that the operation Mr. Connolly has proposed is a breeding facility. This means that the piglets will need to be transported to a finishing facility. Wouldn't it be cheaper and more cost effective to build a near-by facility that could house the hogs as they were prepared for slaughter? After that, why not just build a slaughtering facility as well? It's happened before, and it could happen in our valley. Although people tend to be against zoning in rural communities such as ours, sometimes it is imperative to prevent negative changes.

Please think about the possible effects this will have on our valley. As a life-long resident, you must value its beauty. I also assume that you value the right of every person in this community to live in a safe and clean environment. Imagine a day when you couldn't sit on your porch to eat breakfast because of the overwhelming odor that permeates everything it touches. Imagine your grandchildren getting ill because of water-borne bacteria caused by this CAFO. Imagine the day when you can no longer fish in the creek you helped improve. This day could be upon us if we don't take action now.

You're a vital part of this equation, and I trust that we can count on you to help us maintain the land that raised us.

Sincerely,

Kristen Brubaker

REFERENCES

Cauchon, Dennis. "N.C. Farmers, Scientists Begin Taking The Toll." *USA Today* 27 Sept. 1999: 6A. Print.

"Hog Factories vs. Family Farms and Rural Communities." Powells Valley Conservation Association, n.d. Web. 8 Oct. 1999.

Pennsylvania Department of Environmental Protection. n.d. Web. 15 Oct. 1999.

Satchell, Michael. "Hog Heaven—and Hell." *U.S. News and World Report* 22 Jan. 1996: 57. Print.

Weist, Kurt. "Petition to Intervene of the Powells Valley Conservation Association, Inc." Powells Valley Conservation Association, Inc. 1999. Print.

Wright, Andrew G. "A Foul Mess." *Engineering News Record* 4 Oct. 1999: 26. Print.

Notice that Kristen's claim is implicit in her first paragraph, in which she indicates concern about the hog farm, but she doesn't explicitly state that the permit should be denied until the second-to-last paragraph. Notice, too, that she states her warrant in her second paragraph and then reinforces it in her final paragraph. The Toulmin model does not require that the essay be structured in this way—or any particular way. Kristen might just as easily have begun by stating her claim explicitly and proceeded from there; similarly, she might have left her warrant unstated or waited until the final paragraph to state it. Those choices are up to the writer. The value of using the Toulmin model is that it can help identify these elements so that you can work with them in constructing an argument.

Also note that Kristen has chosen to document her evidence with a list of references, an unusual step in a letter. However, that decision can make her letter more persuasive, because it indicates to the town supervisor that Kristen has taken the time to research this issue thoroughly and that her facts and figures have been taken from reputable sources.

In considering these different models for arranging an argument, you should understand that they are not mutually exclusive. In a classically arranged argument, for example, the statement of background can be done in the kind of nonjudgmental language emphasized in Rogerian argument. Similarly, the summary of opposing views in a Rogerian argument requires the kind of understanding that a writer following a classical arrangement would need to have before engaging in refutation. In both cases, the writers need to be well informed and fair-minded. And both classical arrangement and Rogerian argument encourage the use of concessions. The difference between the two is best understood in terms of purpose. Although any argument is designed to be persuasive, the purpose of that persuasion varies from one situation to another (see Chapter 1). You might be writing to assert a position or to inquire into a complex issue. Rogerian arrangement would be less suitable for an argument to prevail or assert than for an argument to negotiate and reconcile. Your plan should fit your purpose.

It is also worth remembering that contemporary arguments rarely follow rigid guidelines, except in certain academic courses or in specialized documents, such as legal briefs, or situations like formal debates. For that reason many teachers today advocate the Toulmin model, emphasizing its flexibility in adapting an argument to a specific situation. Moreover, different media represent different opportunities and challenges for how to present an argument (see Chapter 3). All of this means that you have many options for structuring your argument. The more familiar you are with the principles of organization in argumentation, the more likely it is that you will be able to structure your argument effectively.

Supporting Claims and Presenting Evidence

The arguments by Tyler Sunderman, Rachel Guetter, Kristen Montgomery, and Kristen Brubaker highlight the importance of presenting good evidence to support your argument. Without compelling evidence even the most carefully articulated claim won't be persuasive. But as noted in Chapter 4, what counts as good evidence will vary from one context to another. An important part of generating evidence for your argument is considering your audience and its expectations for evidence, as well as the rhetorical situation in which you are making your argument.

In Kristen Brubaker's case the audience is specific: her town supervisor. She offers evidence that directly addresses a number of issues regarding quality of life that would concern a person in his position. Indeed, one of the strengths of Kristen's argument is that her evidence fits her audience. Another strength is the amount of evidence she provides. She includes statistics and other facts to support her assertions about pollution, road use, odor, and health problems. She also uses values as evidence, appealing to the supervisor's sense of the importance of private property and community well-being (see pages 142–145). Moreover, the amount of evidence suggests that Kristen has done her homework. By presenting so much appropriate evidence so carefully, she helps establish her credibility. And although she is writing specifically to one person, Kristen's evidence would probably resonate with a broader audience—say, readers of the local newspaper— if Kristen were addressing such an audience. Implicitly addressing a broader audience might strengthen her argument as well, because the supervisor will probably be sensitive to the views of other people in the community.

Your audience can affect not just the kind of evidence you use but also whether you need evidence for a particular point. For example, if you are confident that your readers will accept your warrant, then you might decide that you don't need to support it. If it is likely that your audience will

DEVELOPING GOOD EVIDENCE

As you develop your supporting evidence, consider the following questions:

- What specific claims and/or warrants am I making that will need supporting evidence?
- What kinds of evidence are available for those claims or warrants?
- Where can I find such evidence?
- What expectations will my audience have for the evidence I present?
- Have I included sufficient evidence for my audience?
- Does the kind of evidence I have included (factual, firsthand experience, philosophical reasoning, expert testimony) make sense for the claims I am making?

disagree with your warrant, then you will need evidence to back it up. Imagine, for instance, if Kristen were writing for a much broader audience—say she was making an argument against CAFOs for a newspaper like *USA Today*. Some of her readers might be willing to give up some of the characteristics of a small town for greater economic development. For such readers Kristen might want to defend her warrant about a clean environment, perhaps showing that economic development doesn't have to mean damaging the environment. The point is that your sense of audience and its expectations will affect what you decide to present as evidence and even *whether* some kinds of evidence should be included in your essay.

PLANNING AHEAD

When planning a paper, allow ample time for drafting and revising. Ideas often evolve during the writing process. Even if you have extensive notes, you might discover that you lack information to support a claim that occurred to you when you sat down to write. You would then need to do research or modify your claim. The first draft might also include material that, on rereading, you decide does not relate to the focus of your paper and should therefore be removed. Cutting and adding are normal parts of the writing process, so expect to make changes.

Using Language Effectively

In his famous *Rhetoric,* Aristotle wrote that "the way in which a thing is said affects its intelligibility." The way in which something is stated also affects its impact and, potentially, its persuasive force. Style matters. It matters because it is sometimes a reflection of the fact that you have followed the appropriate conventions for a particular argument—for example, you have used the right legal terminology in a letter to your insurance company about a pending lawsuit. And it matters because the way an idea or opinion is presented can profoundly affect how an audience reacts to it. In constructing an effective argument, you should attend to how you employ the power of language—how you use diction, sentence structure, tone, rhythm, and figures of speech. Usually, these are matters you can focus on once you have defined your topic, developed your claims and supporting evidence, and arranged your argument appropriately. But how you use language can be an important consideration in constructing an argument, even from the beginning.

As always, audience is a primary consideration as you decide upon an appropriate style for your argument. Different audiences will have different expectations for what is acceptable—and persuasive—when it comes to your use of language in an argument. You will want to use more formal language in a cover letter to a potential employer (which is a common kind of argument) than you might in a letter to the editor of your school's newspaper. Similarly, an essay advocating a specific research method in a biology class will require a different kind of language than an argument in favor of decriminalizing marijuana laws for the campus newsletter of a student advocacy organization. The specific medium in which you are presenting your argument will also influence your decisions about language. *Wired* magazine publishes writing that is noticeably different in style and tone from those of the essays that appear in public affairs magazines such as *Commentary*. The audiences for each magazine are different, but so is each magazine's sense of purpose. *Wired* sees itself as techy, edgy, and hip, and the language its writers use reflects that sense of itself. By contrast, *Commentary* is a more erudite, staid publication, and the writing style reflects its seriousness. As you work through your argument, think carefully about what kind of language will be most effective for the specific audience, rhetorical situation, and medium you are encountering.

Even within a specific rhetorical situation you have a great deal of latitude in deciding on the style and tone you will adopt for your argument. Consider the following excerpts from an essay that appeared on *Commondreams.org,* a website that publishes essays and news with alternative views about important social and political issues. In the essay from which the following excerpts were taken, the writer, John Borowski, a science teacher from Oregon, harshly criticizes efforts by interest groups to ban school science books that present an environmentalist perspective, and he argues for parents and others to oppose such efforts:

> Remember this phrase: "Texas is clearly one of the most dominant states in setting textbook adoption standards," according to Stephen Driesler, executive director of the American Association of Publisher's school division. And this November the Texas school board inflamed by the anti-environmental science rhetoric by the likes of Texas Citizens for a Sound Economy and Texas Public Policy Foundation (TPPF) may bring Ray Bradbury's "Fahrenheit 451" to life. Recall that "Fahrenheit 451" (the temperature at which paper bursts into flames) depicts a society where independent thought is discouraged, wall-to-wall television and drugs sedate a numb population and "firemen" burn books.
>
> This past fall "book nazis" at the TPPF, led by Republican Senator Phil Gramm's wife (Wendy) and Peggy Venable, director of the 48,000 member Texas Citizens for a Sound Economy, put several environmental textbooks in their "crosshairs." *Environmental Science: Toward a Sustainable Future* published by Massachusetts-based publisher Jones and Bartlett was canned due to political "incorrectness."
>
> We as parents, defenders of the constitution and the vigilant flame-keepers of the light of democracy must rise to meet the challenge.

There is no doubt about how Borowski feels about groups like TPPF. Nor is there any doubt about his goal: to exhort people who share his concerns to action against such efforts to ban books from schools. You might find Borowski's language inflammatory. There is a good chance that he intended it to be so. He certainly knew that the audience for *Commondreams.org* would not likely include many people from organizations such as TPPF. Rather, it would be composed mostly of people who share his political perspective and are likely to be as appalled as he is about these efforts to ban textbooks. Nevertheless, you can ask how those sympathetic readers might react to the strong and critical language Borowski employs. Will such language be more likely to convince those readers that Borowski is right than a more measured style and a less derogatory tone might be? How does it affect his credibility with his readers? Sometimes, provocative language may be warranted. Is this one of those times?

Posing such questions about your own use of language in constructing your argument can lead to a more effective argument. The rhetorical situation and the issue being addressed will help determine your approach to using language from the outset. In this case Borowski might have been angry and concerned enough to have decided, even before he began writing his essay, to adopt a harsh and sarcastic tone.

Sometimes, however, you might not have a clear sense of the most appropriate tone or style until after you have completed a draft. And often you will have much less flexibility in adopting a tone or style. (A science report or legal brief, for example, has strict conventions for such matters.) And bear in mind that at times the choice of a single word can make a great difference in the effect a statement will have on an audience. For example, consider how different this sentence of Borowski's might be if the verb *canned* were replaced by *removed:*

> *Environmental Science: Toward a Sustainable Future* published by Massachusetts-based publisher Jones and Bartlett was canned due to political "incorrectness."

The passage from Borowski's essay illustrates another set of concerns about language in argument: the use of figurative language. At one point Borowski writes that "the vigilant flame-keepers of the light of democracy must rise to meet the challenge." Here he invokes the common metaphors of light and dark to suggest good opposed to evil, right against wrong. Those who share his concerns are "flame-keepers of the light of democracy," a figurative phrase clearly intended not only to address his audience in a positive way but also to stir them to action. Borowski's essay is a rather extreme example of the use of figurative language, and it suggests the power such uses of language can have in efforts to move an audience. But figurative language can also have a more subtle but no less important impact in helping to clarify an important point or emphasizing an idea. Here, for example, is *USA Today* sports columnist Mike Lopresti in an essay about the significance of a loss by an American basketball team to Yugoslavia in the 2002 World Championships:

> But the big issue is the big picture. The years, the Olympiads, and the World Championships ahead. Because American basketball is like an empty soda cup on the field house floor.

Lopresti's use of a simile—in which he compares the international status of American basketball to an empty soda cup—vividly drives home his point with an appropriate image that readers who follow sports will quickly recognize. (Notice, too, the informal style of his writing, which is typical of many sports columnists.)

When deciding how to use language effectively, writers may also use the conventions of argument dramatically. Consider the following excerpt from a review of *The Truth about Hillary: What She Knew, When She Knew It, and How Far She'll Go to Become President,* a book by Edward Klein published in 2005. As you read, note how the first four sentences each begin with "Granted"—an expression that writers frequently use when conceding a point. (This is an example of anaphora, which means using the same word or phrase at the beginning of a series of sentences or clauses to achieve emphasis):

> Granted, it is a very bad book. Granted, it is a lazy, cut-and-paste recycling of other people's work. Granted, it relies too much on nasty personal comments about Senator Clinton provided by anonymous sources. Granted, it sleazily intimates that Hillary Clinton is a lying, scheming, smelly, left-leaning lesbian and a non-maternal parent who consorts with lawyers who defend mobbed-up unions and bears a striking character resemblance to both Richard Nixon and Madonna, and who tacitly approved of her husband's rape of a young woman at a time when Mrs. Clinton may or may not have been bathing, washing her hair or shaving her underarms, while hanging out with short-haired women from the sapphic charnel house Wellesley College. But to suggest, as the talented John Podhoretz did in *The New York Post,* that this is "one of the most sordid volumes I have ever waded through" is to raise serious questions about Podhoretz's sordid wading experiences.
>
> As an expert on sordid non-fiction, I would not put "The Truth About Hillary" anywhere near the top of my list; it pales by comparison with Geraldo Rivera's sublimely vile autobiography, "Exposing Myself," and seems demure, nuanced and levelheaded by comparison with masterpieces of partisan venom like the 60's cold-war classic "None Dare Call It Treason."

No, I am not suggesting that Edward Klein is a fair, balanced, persuasive, scrupulously honest reporter or a gifted writer. Resorting to chilling Rip Van Winklisms like "Bill and Hillary often grooved the night away at Cozy Beach, spinning the latest Jefferson Airplane platters," Klein sometimes sounds like a cryogenically preserved Maynard G. Krebs. Like, dig: the cat is far out.

What I am saying is that if Klein purposely set out to write the sleaziest, most derivative, most despicable political biography ever, he has failed both himself and his readers miserably. "The Truth About Hillary" is only about the 16th sleaziest book I have ever read. Though, in fairness to the author, reading creepy, cut-and-paste books is my hobby.

By describing himself as "an expert in sordid nonfiction," this reviewer, Joe Queenan, is establishing ethos (see pages 67–73). In effect, he is saying, "I have the credentials to say this is a sordid book because I have read lots of such books." Queenan is having fun with language, coining such phrases as "Rip Van Winklisms" (an allusion to a character in a nineteenth-century story who falls asleep for 20 years and cannot adjust to the change that he sees when he wakes up). The extent to which you can experiment with language will depend on your rhetorical situation, but you can always benefit from the strategy Queenan uses in the last two paragraphs reprinted here: clarifying your argument by contrasting what you are saying with what you are not saying. Queenan is using playful language (for example, stating that "reading creepy, cut-and-paste books is my hobby"), but he does so to make a serious point.

As these examples show, a few carefully chosen words can do a great deal of work as you build your argument.

WATCHING YOUR LANGUAGE

The following questions can help you determine whether your style and tone are appropriate for your purpose, your audience, and the situation about which you are arguing:

- Is my overall tone likely to offend my intended audience? If so, what specifically about my tone might be offensive to my audience? What words or phrases might create a negative reaction among my readers? How can I revise to avoid that problem?
- Have I used appropriate words and phrases? Will my audience understand the key terms I have used? Will my audience expect me to use any special language that I have not used?
- Can I use figurative language to enhance my argument? In what way can I do so?

6

Doing Research

Yellow Dog Productions/Getty Images

Writing effective arguments requires being able to locate and use information that will help you develop and support your ideas. Often, you will discover that you must look beyond yourself to gather the necessary information—you must engage in research.

You might think of research as what you do when you are assigned long papers due at the end of a semester, but there are many other occasions when you engage in research. Any time you look for information before making a decision, you are doing research. If you are trying to decide whether to buy a particular car, for example, you might talk to people who already own the same model, read magazine articles about the car, search the Internet for other drivers' opinions about the car, and take a dealer's vehicle for a test drive. In other words, you interview people with expertise on your topic, you conduct a periodical search, you search electronic resources, and you undertake trial testing.

Academic research often requires all of these activities and more. It also requires that you follow specific conventions by using sources responsibly and documenting where your information comes from. But the prospect of doing research shouldn't be intimidating. The key to successful research is simple: Be curious enough about your topic to look in different places until you find what you need.

Traditionally, academic researchers distinguish between primary and secondary research:

1. **Primary research** requires firsthand experimentation or analysis. This is the sort of research conducted in laboratories, in field locations, or in libraries or archives that house original manuscripts. If you interview someone, design and distribute a survey, conduct an experiment, or analyze data that have not been previously published, you are conducting primary research.

2. **Secondary research** involves investigating what other people have already published on a given subject—in other words, finding information about your topic in books, magazine or journal articles, websites, and similar sources. College students are usually expected to be proficient at secondary research.

Writing arguments often requires secondary research, and to do such research efficiently, you must know how to develop a search strategy. Different projects will require different strategies. The strategy outlined in this part of the book assumes that you will be writing arguments using material from Part III of *The Informed Argument* and that you will supplement this material with additional information you find elsewhere. You will probably use different sources for different assignments, but the illustrations in this chapter will provide you with information to help you proceed efficiently when you decide to move beyond the articles gathered in Part III of this book.

Reading Critically

Secondary research requires a kind of reading that might differ from the way you read the morning paper or an article about your favorite musician on a website. The kind of critical reading required for good research is active and engaged; it involves careful thinking about what you are reading. Critical reading means going beyond the obvious meaning of a text to identify key points—such as an author's thesis—and any points that you find difficult to understand. Critical reading also means *evaluating* the material. As a student, you will sometimes be confronted with more information than you can digest with ease. You will also find that different writers may make contradictory statements. Being able to recognize what material deserves the closest reading, and what sources are the most reliable, is essential to coping successfully with the many academic demands made on your time. By learning to read critically, you will acquire a skill that will help you in any college course. And you will be developing an ability that will enable you to write more effective arguments.

You can learn to read critically by engaging in four related activities:

- Previewing
- Annotating
- Summarizing
- Synthesizing

Previewing

Even before you begin to read, you can take steps to help you better understand the reading you are about to undertake and to place it in rhetorical context (see 153). A quick preview or survey of a written text should give you an idea of how long it will take to read, what the reading will probably reveal, and how useful the reading is likely to be. When you scroll through a newspaper website to identify which stories you want to read and which you want to skip, you are practicing a simple type of preview, one usually guided primarily by your level of interest in various issues. But when previewing reading material in college, it is usually wise to ask yourself some questions that go beyond whether you happen to find a topic appealing:

- *How long is this work?* By checking the length of a work before you begin to read, you can estimate how much reading time the material will demand. The length might also be a clue in determining how useful a text may be. Although quantity is no sure guide to quality, a long work might contain more information that is useful for your topic than a short work.
- *What can I learn from the title?* Although some titles are too general to convey adequately the content of an article or book, a title often reveals an author's focus. An article called "Drugs and the Modern Athlete" will differ in focus from one called "Drug Testing in Professional Sports." Moreover, a title can often indicate the author's point of view. For example, an essay titled "Keep the Borders Open" tells you quite clearly what the author's position on immigration will be. Be aware, though, that titles can sometimes be misleading.
- *Do I know anything about the author?* As you do more research, you might begin to recognize the names of established authorities in a field, but many written sources offer information that can help you estimate an author's credibility even when that author is unfamiliar to you. A journal or magazine article might identify the author at the beginning or the end of the piece or on a separate page. A biographical sketch of the author can usually be found on a book jacket, and a list of his or her other published works sometimes appears at the front or the back of the book. Anthologies often include introductory headnotes describing the various writers whose work has been selected. You can also learn more about an author's credibility by using a search engine such as Google to retrieve information from the World Wide Web.
- *What do I know about the publisher?* The publisher's reputation is not an automatic guide to the reliability of a source, but there are a few factors that can help you determine whether a source is likely to be worthwhile. University presses tend to expect a high degree of scholarship, and academic journals usually publish articles only after they have been examined by other experts in that field. If you examine the kinds of articles that a specific magazine or blog tends to publish (such as *Mother Jones* or *The Huffington Post*), you can get a sense of whether the political position of that publication might be characterized as either liberal or conservative. Once you get a sense of the general orientation of such publications, you can usually anticipate what kind of stand will be taken by authors whose articles appear in one of these periodicals. This will help you decide whether an article is likely to be useful to you; it can also alert you to any bias that the author

might hold on the topic at hand. Again, remember that you are only making a preliminary estimate when previewing. The best way to judge a work is to read it carefully.

■ *Is there anything else I can discover by skimming through the material?* A quick examination of the text can reveal a number of other features that can help you orient yourself to what you are about to read:

- *Average paragraph length.* Long paragraphs might indicate a densely written text that you will need to read slowly.

- *Special features.* Tables, figures, or illustrations can provide visual aids for the content.

- *Subtitles.* Subtitles can provide you with a rough outline of the work and the main topics it addresses.

- *Abstracts.* In some cases, a writer will provide you with a summary. Articles from scholarly journals are often preceded by an **abstract** (or summary) that can help you understand the article and determine whether it will be useful to you. Many magazines include brief summaries with each article, usually at the beginning of the text. Often, checking the first few and last few paragraphs can give you a good sense of what the article is about and the stance the writer has taken on the topic.

- *Bibliography.* Check to see whether the work includes a reference list. Scanning a bibliography—noting both how current the research seems and how extensive it is—can help you appraise a writer's scholarship and alert you to other sources that you may want to read on your own.

Annotating

Marking a text with notes, or **annotating** it, can be a great help when you are trying to understand your reading. Annotation can help you remember important points or passages; it can also help you discover points that you might want to question or examine further. Annotating a text is especially useful if you need to summarize that text (see "Summarizing"). One of the advantages of owning a book or having your own photocopy of an article or chapter is that you can mark it as much as you wish. You can also download or scan digital versions of articles or chapters and use a program like *Adobe Acrobat Professional* to annotate them.

Remember that different readers annotate a text in different ways. Some annotations are more thorough and reflective than others, but there is no "correct" way to annotate a text. Simply make the notes that are useful to you as you review the text for your research. Also keep in mind that you might notice different aspects of a text each time you reread it, so your annotations are likely to accumulate in layers. In fact, one benefit of annotating is that you can keep a record of different ideas or points you notice as you reread a text. (Figure 6-1 shows an annotated excerpt from the Declaration of Independence.)

FIGURE 6-1
An Annotated Text

1776

Why should nations have "equal Station" when some are more powerful than others?

Does this include women ???

If the rights to life & liberty are "unalienable" how come we have capital punishment and prisons?

wrongful seizure

impartial

When in the Course of human events, it becomes necessary for one people to dissolve the political bands which have connected them with another, and to assume among the powers of the earth, the separate and equal station to which the Laws of Nature and of Nature's God entitle them, a decent respect to the opinions of mankind requires that they should declare the causes which impel them to the separation.

We hold these truths to be self-evident, that all men are created equal, that they are endowed by their Creator with certain unalienable Rights, that among these are Life, Liberty and the pursuit of Happiness. That to secure these rights, Governments are instituted among Men, deriving their just powers from the consent of the governed. That whenever any Form of Government becomes destructive of these ends it is the Right of the People to alter or to abolish it, and to institute new Government, laying its foundation on such principles and organizing its powers in such form, as to them shall seem most likely to effect their Safety and Happiness. Prudence, indeed, will dictate that Governments long established should not be changed for light and transient causes; and accordingly all experience has shewn, that mankind are more disposed to suffer, while evils are sufferable, than to right themselves by abolishing the forms to which they are accustomed. But when a long train of abuses and usurpations, pursuing invariably the same Object evinces a design to reduce them under absolute Despotism, it is their right, it is their duty, to throw off such Government, and to provide new Guards for their future security. Such has been the patient sufferance of these Colonies; and such is now the necessity which constrains them to alter their former Systems of Government. The history of the present King of Great Britain is a history of repeated injuries and usurpations, all having in direct object the establishment of an absolute Tyranny over these States. To prove this, let Facts be submitted to a candid world.

such as Americans

such as English

Is "Nature's God" different from "God"?

Why "self-evident"?

Couldn't he prove them?

Permanent, "not to be separated"

So the Civil War was ok?

What's the difference between a "right" and a "duty"?

George III (ruled from 1760 to 1820)

Why is the capitalization so weird?

SUGGESTIONS FOR ANNOTATING

When you need to spend more time with a text, and want to be sure that you understand not only its content but also its strengths and weaknesses, consider using the following strategies:

- Use the margins to define new words and identify unfamiliar allusions.
- Write comments that will remind you of what is discussed in various paragraphs.
- Jot down questions that you may subsequently raise in class or explore in a paper.
- Make cross references to remind yourself of how various components of the work fit together and also identify apparent contradictions within the work.
- Make cross references to other works you might be reading for the same assignment.
- Write down your own response to an important point in the text before you lose the thought. (An annotation of this sort can be useful when you are reviewing material before an exam, and it may very well be the seed from which a paper will later grow.)

Summarizing

In argumentation, you will often need to summarize what others have said or written—or even what you have said or written. Being able to summarize effectively is especially important if you are referring to articles or books that have become an important part of your argument. Summary is also important when you are refuting the main arguments of those who oppose your point of view.

The first step in summarizing is distinguishing what is essential from what is not in a source (for example, an article, website, or speech). Begin by identifying what you consider to be the most important ideas or points in that source and build your summary around those. If the material being summarized has a particular bias, your summary should indicate that. The goal is always to convey an accurate sense of the material you are summarizing.

Here's an example of a writer using summary in an argument. In this excerpt from an essay that was published in 2009, former presidential speechwriter Gordon Stewart summarizes a special television speech that President Jimmy Carter made to the American people in 1979. Carter's speech addressed Americans' concerns about severe oil shortages that were causing high gasoline prices and creating long lines at gas stations. In his speech, Carter called on Americans to conserve energy, for which he was later criticized by some politicians, who felt that he made the United States sound weak. In his essay, which was published 30 years after Carter's speech, Gordon Stewart defends the speech and makes an argument that it was an important turning point in American energy policy. Here he summarizes the speech:

> On July 15—30 years ago today—at 10 p.m., President Carter and 100 million people finally faced each other across that familiar Oval Office desk. What they saw and heard was unlike any moment they had experienced from their 39th president. Speaking with rare force, with inflections flowing from meanings he felt deeply, Jimmy Carter called for the "most massive peacetime commitment" in our history to develop alternative fuels.

This summary is brief—only a sentence to summarize a much longer and complicated speech—but it is essential to Stewart's argument. It concisely but clearly conveys the main idea of the speech, using a quotation from the speech itself. Stewart uses this summary to make sure his readers understand Carter's speech, which is necessary if those readers are to

SUMMARY VERSUS PARAPHRASE

The distinction between summary and paraphrase can be subtle and sometimes confusing. A summary is a brief statement, usually no more than a paragraph or two, summing up the main points or ideas of a source. A summary may include direct quotations from the original source. A paraphrase, by contrast, is a restatement or rephrasing in your own words of something you've read. A paraphrase can be as long as (or even longer than) the original material. Summary often contains paraphrase.

Think of it this way: If your doctor gave you a detailed technical explanation of a specific medical procedure that you might need, you would paraphrase that technical explanation—that is, explain it in your own words—to a friend or relative who wants to know what the doctor told you. On the other hand, a medical student who was present during the doctor's explanation might summarize it to another medical student.

So a paraphrase of a text is not a summary of it. In a paraphrase you restate a specific quotation or passage from a source in your own words; you don't necessarily sum up the entire book or article, as you would in a summary.

Summary is important in research in part because it enables you to make the ideas in a long work manageable and accessible in your own essay. Paraphrase is important because it enables you to incorporate ideas and information from other texts into your argument; it also helps you understand what you have read and avoid plagiarizing (see pages 160–162).

understand Stewart's argument in defense of the speech.

Summarizing a source might require you to **paraphrase**—that is, to restate in your own words what is in the source (see "Summary versus Paraphrase"). There are many reasons for paraphrasing, and you've probably paraphrased often—for example, when you describe to someone a tense argument that you witnessed between two friends but you use your own words to convey what was actually said (because the original words are too harsh or rude), you are paraphrasing. Often in writing a summary, you paraphrase to make complex ideas more understandable. For example, you would paraphrase a very technical scientific report if you were referring to that report in an argument for a general audience (as compared to, say, an audience of scientists who would understand the technical language).

When summarizing a source, you should not interject your own opinions about the source. The tone of a summary should be neutral. You might choose to summarize someone's work so that you can criticize it later, but summary is not criticism.

Summaries should be clear, concise, and easy to read, such as the example of Gordon Stewart's summary of President Carter's speech above. Summaries vary in length, depending on the length and complexity of the original material and on how much time or space is available for summarizing it. But you can follow this general rule: Try to do justice to whatever you are summarizing in as few words as possible.

For a good example of how summary can be used effectively in an argument, see "America: Idea or Nation?" by Wilfred M. McClay (pages 541–549). McClay's summary of *Making Patriots*, by Walter Berns, is a key component of his argument.

Synthesizing

Synthesizing ideas from two or more sources is an essential skill in constructing effective arguments. Synthesis requires identifying related material in two or more works and tying them together smoothly. Synthesis is often an extension of summary because writers may need to summarize various sources before they can relate these sources to one another. However, synthesis does not necessarily require you to cover *all* the major points of the individual sources. You might go through an entire article or book and identify only one point that relates to another work you have read. And the relationships involved in your synthesis may be of various kinds. For example, two authors might have made the same claim, or one might provide specific information that supports a generalization made by the other. On the other hand, one author might provide information that makes another author's generalization seem inadequate or even wrong. In either case, synthesis enables you to relate the sources to one another and use their ideas in your own argument.

When you are reading material that you need to synthesize, ask yourself, "How does this material relate to whatever else I have already read on this topic?" Also consider a few more specific questions:

- Does the second of two works offer support for the first, or does it reflect an entirely different thesis?
- If the two sources share a similar position, do they arrive at a similar conclusion by different means or do they overlap at any points?
- Would it be easier to compare the two works or to contrast them?

This process of identifying similarities and differences and then discussing them is essentially what synthesis is all about. When you have determined the points that link your various sources to one another, you are ready to write a synthesis.

One challenge in writing a synthesis is organizing it. For example, suppose you have read four articles on the subject of AIDS written, respectively, by a scientist, a clergyman, a gay activist, and a government official. You were struck by how differently these four writers responded to the rapid spread of AIDS. Although they all agreed that AIDS is a serious problem, each writer advanced a different proposal for fighting the disease. Your synthesis might begin with an introductory paragraph that includes a thesis statement such as "Although there is widespread agreement that AIDS is a serious problem, there is no consensus about how this problem can be solved." Each of the next four paragraphs

A METHOD FOR SUMMARIZING

There is no right way to summarize a text, but here is a straightforward method for summarizing:

1. Identify the topic sentences of the paragraphs you are summarizing, and mark any important supporting details. Limit yourself to marking no more than one or two sentences per paragraph.

2. Copy the material you have noted onto a separate sheet of paper or into a word-processing file. What you now have are notes for your summary: a collection of short quotations that are unlikely to flow smoothly together.

3. Read over the quotations you have compiled, and look for lines that seem too long and ideas that seem unnecessarily complicated. Write a paraphrase of each of these lines. Include any important details that appeared elsewhere in the paragraph from which each line was taken. Keep in mind that you should not have to restate everything. Also, you can include direct quotations, as long as the quotations are relatively short and have a clarity that you cannot surpass.

4. Now put it all together in a draft of your summary. Arrange each paraphrase and quotation in the proper order so that it accurately conveys the meaning of the original text.

5. Reread your draft. Look for gaps between sentences; edit where the writing seems awkward or choppy. Eliminate repetition, and subordinate any ideas that do not need to stand alone as separate sentences.

6. Check to be sure that any direct quotations are placed within quotation marks.

7. Rearrange any sentences that would flow better in a different sequence, and add transitional phrases wherever they can help smooth the way from one idea to the next.

8. Make sure that your sentences follow in a clear and readable sequence, and correct any errors in grammar, spelling, or syntax.

9. Read over your summary one more time, making sure that the content accurately reflects the nature of the text you are summarizing.

could then be devoted to a brief summary of one of the different points of view. A final paragraph might emphasize the relationship that exists among the several sources, either by reviewing the major points of disagreement among them or by emphasizing one or two points about which everyone agreed. Your outline for this type of synthesis would be as follows:

Paragraph 1:   Introduction

Paragraph 2:   Summary of first writer (scientist)

Paragraph 3:   Summary of second writer (clergyman)

Paragraph 4:   Summary of third writer (gay activist)

Paragraph 5:   Summary of fourth writer (government official)

Paragraph 6:   Conclusion

In your concluding paragraph you would refer to your summary of each article and relate them to each other to reinforce your point about the challenge of reaching consensus on a solution to the problem of AIDS. Of course, depending on the source material you are synthesizing and what you want to say, your synthesis might have fewer or more paragraphs. For example, if two of your sources were especially long and complex, you might devote two paragraphs to each of them and summarize your other two sources within single paragraphs.

An alternative method for organizing a synthesis involves linking two or more sources within paragraphs that focus on specific issues or points. This type of organization is especially useful when you have detected important similarities among your sources that you want to emphasize. Suppose that you have read six essays about increasing the minimum age for obtaining a driver's license. Three writers favored increasing the minimum age, at least to 18, for much the same reasons; three writers offered related arguments for opposing such an increase. Your outline for synthesizing this material might be organized like this:

Paragraph 1:   Introduction

Paragraph 2:   One argument in favor of increasing the minimum driving age that was made by several different writers

Paragraph 3:   A second argument in favor of increasing the minimum driving age that was made by several different writers

Paragraph 4:   One argument against increasing the minimum driving age that was made by several different writers

Paragraph 5:   A second argument against increasing the minimum driving age that was made by several different writers

Paragraph 6:   Conclusion

There are other ways of organizing a passage of synthesis in your argument, but however you do so, the key is to present the ideas of the other writers clearly and draw connections among them in a way that will support your argument.

The ability to synthesize arguments is especially useful when writing to reconcile differences (see pages 14–17), constructing a Rogerian argument (see pages 126–131), or using classical arrangement (see pages 120–126), which emphasizes the importance of refutation, to structure an argument.

Integrating Source Material into Your Paper

One of the challenges of writing an argument involving research is integrating source material effectively into a work that remains distinctively your own. The most effective source-based arguments include source material woven smoothly into the paper with well-chosen quotations that are clearly introduced and properly documented. Papers with too many long quotations or quotations that seem arbitrarily placed are weaker because they lack the student's voice and might lead an instructor to be suspicious about how much of the paper is the student's own. You can avoid such problems if you work with your source material to support your own position in an argument and if you follow some basic advice for quoting and citing source material.

First, make sure that any quotations you use fit smoothly into your essay as a whole. Provide transitions that link quotations to whatever has come before them. As a general rule, anything worth quoting at length requires some discussion. After you have quoted someone, you should usually include some analysis or commentary that will make the significance of the quotation clear. Notice how Rachel Guetter, whose essay appears on pages 128–131, follows this advice to weave a quote from one of her sources effectively into her discussion of problems facing gay parents:

> Often, one person in a same-sex relationship is the biological parent and the other will help raise the child as his or her own. According to the American Academy of Pediatrics (AAP), children in this situation lose "survivor benefits if a parent dies and legal rights if the parents break up" (Berman 1). Both situations leave a dramatic impact on the child, who then is caught in the middle of legal battles.

Compare Rachel's passage to a version in which the quotation is not so effectively incorporated into the discussion:

> Often, one person in a same-sex relationship is the biological parent and the other will help raise the child as his or her own. "Children lose survivor benefits if a parent dies and legal rights if the parents break up" (Berman 1). Both situations leave a dramatic impact on the child, who then is caught in the middle of legal battles.

In this version, the quotation seems to be dropped into the middle of the passage without any introduction or transition to help the reader understand why it is there. The passage also sounds choppy as a result. Rachel's version is much better.

Help keep your paper your own, try to avoid using long quotations. Quote only what you need most, and edit long quotations whenever possible. Use the ellipsis (...) to indicate that you have omitted a word or phrase within a sentence, leaving a space before and after each period. (When the ellipsis follows a completed sentence, include the sentence's period before the ellipsis.) When editing quotations in this way, make sure that they remain clear and grammatically correct. If the addition of an extra word or two would help make the quotation more easily understandable, you should enclose the inserted material within square brackets [ ] to let your readers know what had been added to the quotation. Here is another passage from Rachel Guetter's essay illustrating these points:

> Until homosexuality is more widely received, children with gay and lesbian parents will have to deal with the fact that their family is viewed as pejoratively different. Glenn Stanton, senior research analyst for Focus on the Family, says, "While there may be very

nice people who are raising kids in homosexual situations, the best model for kids is to grow up with mom and dad" (Stanton). It seems reasonable to believe that having both a mother and father benefits children. Women and men have different parenting traits that give a strong balance for the development of a child. Stanton also states, "Fathers encourage children to take chances...mothers protect and are more cautious." There exist in parents different disciplining, communication, and playing styles that can be advantages in raising a child.

Notice that Rachel incorporates the quotations from her sources smoothly into this passage so that her own voice is still strong. She also uses ellipses to shorten the second quotation.

Paraphrasing and summarizing are important writing skills (see pages 156 and 155). They can help you avoid writing a paper that sounds like nothing more than one quotation after another or using quotations that are so heavily edited that readers start wondering about what you have cut out. When you put another writer's ideas into your own words (being careful, of course, to provide proper documentation), you are demonstrating that you have control over your material, and by doing so, you can often make your paper more readable.

Above all, remember that you are the writer of your argument. You are using the sources you have found to support your position or to enhance your own ideas.

Avoiding Plagiarism

Plagiarism is a legitimate concern for anyone engaged in research. To plagiarize (from *plagiarius,* the Latin word for *kidnapper*) is to steal—to be guilty of what the Modern Language Association calls "intellectual theft." Plagiarism is also a form of cheating; someone who plagiarizes a paper is losing an opportunity for learning in addition to running

AN EXCERPT FROM THE STATEMENT ON PLAGIARISM FROM THE MODERN LANGUAGE ASSOCIATION

The charge of plagiarism is a serious one for all writers. Students exposed as plagiarists suffer severe penalties, ranging from failure in the assignment or in the course to expulsion from school. They must also live with the distrust that follows an attempt to deceive others for personal gain. When professional writers, like journalists, are exposed as plagiarists, they are likely to lose their jobs, and they are certain to suffer public embarrassment and loss of prestige. For example, a well-known historian charged with plagiarism was asked to resign from prominent public positions even though she admitted responsibility for the theft, compensated the author whose work she took, and announced her intention to issue a corrected edition of her book. Almost always, the course of a professional writer's career is permanently affected by a single act of plagiarism.

The serious consequences of plagiarism reflect the value the public places on trustworthy information. A complex society that depends on well-informed citizens maintains high standards of quality and reliability for documents that are publicly circulated and used in government, business, industry, the professions, higher education, and the media. Because research has the power to affect opinions and actions, responsible writers compose their work with great care. They specify when they refer to another author's ideas, facts, and words, whether they want to agree with, object to, or analyze the source. This kind of documentation not only recognizes the work writers do; it also tends to discourage the circulation of error, by inviting readers to determine for themselves whether a reference to another text presents a reasonable account of what that text says. Plagiarists undermine these important public values.

a serious risk. In the workplace, intellectual theft (of an essay, a song, or a proposal) can lead to lawsuits and heavy financial penalties. In a college or university, plagiarism can result in failing an assignment or a course and can even lead to expulsion from school. They are not the only ones who are hurt, however. In addition to hurting themselves, plagiarists injure the people they steal from; the professors who take the time to read and respond to the work of writers who are not their own students; classmates, whose grades might suffer from comparison if a clever plagiarism goes undetected; and the social fabric of the academic community, which becomes torn when values such as honesty and mutual respect are no longer cherished.

The grossest form of plagiarism involves submitting someone else's paper as your own. If you buy a paper from a service that sells papers or ask a friend to write a paper for you and then submit it to your instructor as your work, you are consciously engaging in plagiarism. On the other hand, it is also possible to plagiarize without meaning to do so. Students sometimes plagiarize by drawing too heavily on their sources. They might forget to put quotation marks around sentences that they have taken word for word from another source, or they might think they don't need to quote if they have changed a few words. The important point to keep in mind when you are using sources is that you must give credit for the *ideas* of others as well as for their *words*. If you take most of the information another writer has provided and repeat it in essentially the same pattern, you are only a half-step away from copying the material, even if you have changed the exact wording.

Here is an example:

Original Source

Hawthorne's political ordeal, the death of his mother—and whatever guilt he may have harbored on either score—afforded him an understanding of the secret psychological springs of guilt. *The Scarlet Letter* is the book of a changed man. Its deeper insights have nothing to do with orthodox morality or religion—or the universal or allegorical applications of a moral. The greatness of the book is related to its sometimes fitful characterizations of human nature and the author's almost uncanny intuitions: his realization of the bond between psychological malaise and physical illness, the nearly perfect, if sinister, outlining of the psychological techniques Chillingworth deployed against his victim.

Plagiarism

Nathaniel Hawthorne understood the psychological sources of guilt. His experience in politics and the death of his mother brought him deep insights that don't have anything to do with formal religion or morality. The greatness of *The Scarlet Letter* comes from its characters and the author's brilliant intuitions: Hawthorne's perception of the link between psychological and physical illness and his almost perfect description of the way Roger Chillingworth persecuted his victim.

This student has simplified the original material, changing some of its wording. But he is still guilty of plagiarism because he is offering someone else's published analysis of *The Scarlet Letter* as his own. This student in fact owes all of his ideas in this passage to another writer, who is not acknowledged. Even the organization of the passage has been copied from the original source. This "paraphrase" would still be considered plagiarism even if it ended with a reference to the original source (page 307 of *Nathaniel Hawthorne in His Times*, by James R. Mellow). A reference or footnote would not reveal the full extent to which this student is indebted to his source.

Here is an acceptable version:

Paraphrase

As James R. Mellow has argued, *The Scarlet Letter* reveals a profound understanding of guilt. It is a great novel because of its insight into human nature—not because of some moral about adultery. The most interesting character is probably Roger Chillingworth because of the way he was able to make Rev. Dimmesdale suffer (307).

This student has not only made a better effort to paraphrase the original material but also introduced it with a reference to the original writer. The introductory reference to Mellow, coupled with the subsequent page reference, clearly shows us that Mellow deserves the credit for the ideas in this passage. Additional bibliographical information about this source is provided by the list of works cited at the end of the paper:

Mellow, James. *Nathaniel Hawthorne in His Times*. Boston: Houghton, 1980.

If you are uncertain about whether you are inappropriately using a source and worried that you might be plagiarizing, be sure to acknowledge the original source of the material you're using. A good rule of thumb is to quote that material if you are not sure whether you might be plagiarizing.

Finding Relevant Material

Up to this point the chapter has focused on how to read and use sources. But you must have relevant sources before you can read them critically and use them effectively. Finding those relevant sources encompasses an important set of research skills.

Getting Started

One of the first goals of any researcher is to decide where to begin. That's easier to do if you already have a specific topic and a good idea of the kind of material you need to find. When you know what you are looking for, you can gauge what you should read and what you can probably afford to ignore—which is a great advantage when you are confronted by the staggering amount of information in a good college library and available on the Internet.

Sometimes you might have no clear topic. In such a situation you can take steps to identify a workable topic for your argument. Sometimes, for example, a specific topic will emerge as you scan information on your subject area by using indexes, online databases, and Internet search engines. By beginning with a general idea of what you plan to write about and then using key words to check different sources, you can refine your topic or even discover topics that have generated recent interest—topics that will interest you as well. You can judge, at this point, which topics would be the most manageable ones to research. As you proceed, keep two general rules in mind:

- If you are overwhelmed by the number of citations you find in your research area, you probably need to *narrow your topic.*
- If you have difficulty finding material, you might need to *broaden your search.*

(For additional information on choosing a topic, see pages 108–110.)

Avoiding Selective Research

One potential risk when doing research is focusing too narrowly on finding only sources that relate directly to your topic or argument. If you look only for sources that support your position on an issue about which you are making an argument, for example, you may overlook potentially important sources that can enrich your understanding of the issue and perhaps enhance the effectiveness of your argument. So it's a good idea not to focus your research too narrowly on a specific topic or position or conclusion that you expect to reach. Instead, think of your search strategy as an attempt to answer a question.

For instance, suppose you are writing an argument about drug-related crime. You can begin seeking and evaluating potential sources as if you are addressing the following question: "What can be done to reduce drug-related crime?" This is different from starting your research with your thesis predetermined. If you begin your research already convinced that the way to reduce drug-related crime is to legalize certain drugs, you might be tempted to take notes only from sources that advocate this position, and you might reject potentially useful sources that discuss problems with legalizing drugs. In this case, your research would not necessarily lead to greater knowledge or understanding. On the contrary, it is being used to reinforce your position on the issue. Even if you feel strongly about the issue, keeping an open mind during your research can often lead to a better understanding of that issue—and a more effective argument.

Almost any topic worth investigating will yield facts and ideas that could support different conclusions. That's because most issues worthy of genuine argumentation are extremely complex, and it is important to remember that fact as you conduct your research. Your own research might ultimately support a belief that you already hold, but if you proceed as if you are genuinely trying to solve a problem or answer a question, your research might deepen your understanding of the issue and lead you to reconsider your opinions about the issue. For this reason, try not to overlook relevant material just because you don't agree with it. Exploring such material can enrich your knowledge and understanding of an issue, and your argument will be stronger if you recognize that disagreement about your topic exists and then demonstrate why you favor one position over another or show how different positions can be reconciled.

With this advice in mind you can more effectively use the many resources now available as you research your topic. In addition to more traditional sources such as books and articles in magazines, journals, and newspapers, you have access to an astonishing amount of information on the Internet. In the remainder of this chapter, we will discuss how best to use these resources.

Using the Internet

LEARNING TO SEARCH THE INTERNET

To learn more about efficiently searching the Internet, check to see whether your library or academic computing office provides workshops or similar services. These workshops can help you learn about various search engines available on the Web and sophisticated strategies for searching the Web. Also, visit your library's website, which is likely to have useful online tutorials and guidelines for online research.

The information that can be found on the Internet is voluminous and incredibly diverse; it includes library catalogs, government documents and data, newspaper and magazine articles, excerpts from books and even entire books, and all kinds of information and material published by government agencies, commercial organizations, and special interest groups. Because of this richness, the Internet has become an invaluable research tool. But the enormous scale of the Internet can also make it difficult to find and evaluate relevant information easily. The very richness of the Internet can be its drawback, and searching for the right information can be time-consuming, confusing, and sometimes frustrating. You can easily find yourself clicking through an endless series of documents or websites and losing sight of your main objective while pursuing an elusive loose end. For this reason it's important to understand some basic principles for searching the Web.

You should also be aware of a key difference between much of the material published on the Internet and material published in print. In most traditional print publications, writers receive professional editorial support; editors decide what material is worth printing and then assist writers in preparing work for publication. This process means that print material has usually been carefully evaluated before it is published. Most of the Internet operates without editors, however. Anyone can publish anything online. In this sense the Internet is wonderfully democratic, giving anyone access to a large audience for their words, images, and ideas. On the other hand, the Internet also carries a great deal of misinformation, hate speech, and deeply biased materials. When searching the Internet, therefore, you must carefully evaluate the material you find and recognize that this material can range from first-rate scholarship to utter trash.

Despite these potential problems, the Internet is an essential resource for research. The challenge is finding your way through the huge amount of material floating around

EVALUATING INTERNET RESOURCES

The advice provided earlier about reading critically (see pages 151–158) applies to Internet resources as well. But because of the great variety of material on the Internet and because anyone can publish anything on a website, you should be especially careful in evaluating the reliability of information you find on the Web. Most libraries have information on their own websites about evaluating Internet resources, so check your school's library website. Here are a few other useful ones:

- *Evaluating Information Found on the Internet*, Sheridan Libraries, Johns Hopkins University: <http://www.library.jhu.edu/researchhelp/general/evaluating>
- *Evaluate*, University Libraries, University at Albany, State University of New York: <http://library.albany.edu/usered/eval/index.html>
- *Evaluating Internet Resources*, Georgetown University Library: <http://www.library.georgetown.edu/tutorials/research-guides/evaluating-internet-content>
- *Judge for Yourself! Do You Really Want to Use That? Evaluating Information*, UCLA College Library: <http://www.sscnet.ucla.edu/library/rtr.php?module=Judge&section=Introduction&page=01>

in cyberspace. **Search engines** are the most obvious tool for doing so. Search engines, such as *Google*, enable you to search for online materials by typing key words or phrases into an entry box. After you have entered your search terms, you will be given a list of websites that match your request. Each of these sites can, in turn, lead you to others. Many search engines also enable you to refine your search by entering more specific information, such as dates or kinds of publications (see Figure 6-2). These advanced search tools can be especially useful when you are searching for materials on a general topic, such as health care or immigration policy, topics for which there will be millions of sites on the Internet. Like other electronic resources, search engines provide help screens with instructions on the best ways to search. It's a good idea to review the information on help screens so that you can learn to make your online searching more efficient.

Remember that the Internet is constantly changing. New sites are launched on the Web literally every minute. And new search systems are always being developed. Although more and more information is being digitized and becoming available online, not every useful resource is available electronically. For example, most books are not yet available in digital form, and many academic journals restrict access to their articles online. So you can sometimes miss important material if you try to do all your research on the Internet.

At the same time, many resources that have traditionally been available only in print form are becoming available on the Internet. Many journals, newspapers, and magazines now offer full-text articles online, which means that you don't always have to go to your

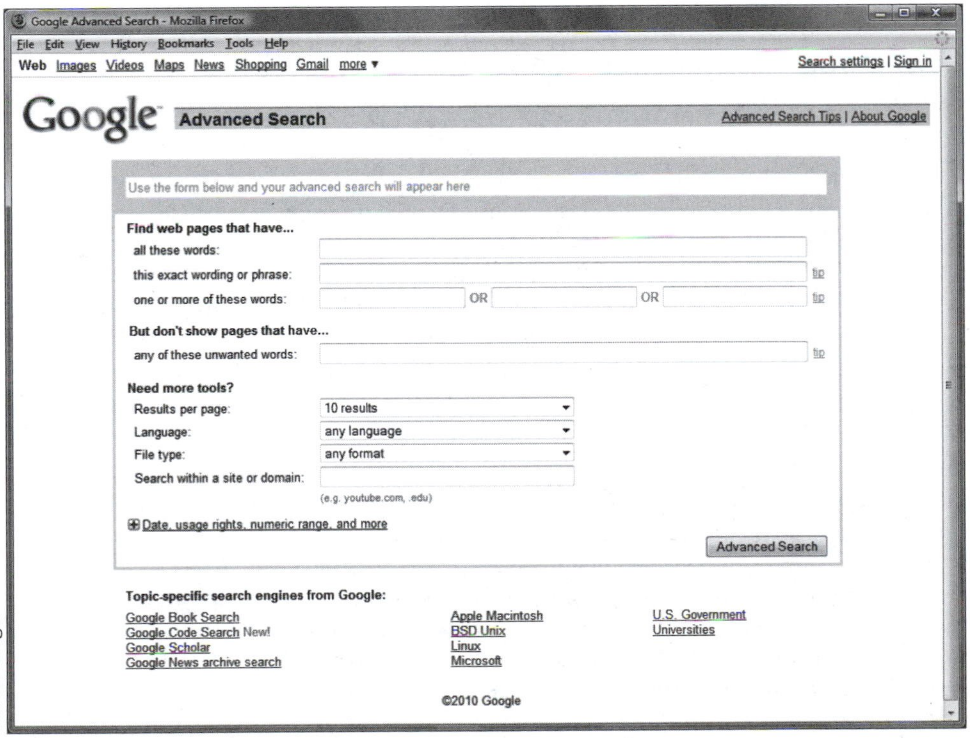

FIGURE 6-2

Google's Advanced Search Page

Source: Google

library to get a copy of an article you might need for your research. In addition, some publications appear only online. For example, *Slate* magazine and *Salon.com* are two respected publications that do not appear in print form; you can access their articles only through the Internet. And organizations of all types sponsor online archives and other sources related to their areas of interest. For example, you can visit the website of the U.S. Department of Health and Human Services to find a great deal of information on a range of topics related to health issues. Thousands of such sites exist on the Web. Learning to navigate the Internet efficiently and to evaluate online sources carefully will enable you to take advantage of the wealth of information available online to enrich your research and help craft effective arguments.

Tips for Efficient Web Searching

Searching for Magazine and Journal Articles

Magazines, bulletins, and scholarly journals are all called **periodicals** (because they are published on a regular schedule: once a week, once a month, etc.). Periodicals often include the most current information about a research area, and they can alert you to other important sources through the citations included in individual articles. In addition, as noted in the previous section, many periodicals are now available on the Internet, which makes them easily accessible to researchers.

To get started searching for periodical literature, visit your school library's website and look for a list of online databases and indexes. (You can also visit your library and talk to a reference librarian.) Typically, college and university libraries subscribe to dozens of general and specialized databases and indexes covering all areas of study, and many schools allow students and faculty to access these resources from personal computers (in addition to the computers provided in the library for searching at the site). Some of the major indexes include *Books in Print, Business Index ASAP, Education Full Text, International Bibliography of the Social Sciences,* and *PAIS.* Some indexes, such as *WebSpirs*, combine several databases, enabling you to search many useful databases simultaneously. If you are writing an argument on a specialized topic in a specific academic subject, such as psychology, you might search an index in that field, such as *PsycInfo.* A specialized index like *PsycInfo* includes references to articles published in academic journals in that field and will enable you to find information that is not likely found in publications intended for general audiences.

Specialized indexes like *PsycInfo* are intended for scholars and researchers in those fields, and you might find that many of the articles you find there are too technical for your purposes. It's a good idea to check with your course instructor for advice about using such databases and indexes. The more you use them, the easier it will become for you to search efficiently to find specialized sources that you need for your assignment.

For many of your assignments, however, you might not need such specialized information, and you will find that using general indexes or databases makes more sense. Among the most familiar indexes are *Gale: Academic OneFile, ArticleFirst, EBSCO: Academic Search Complete, FirstSearch,* and *LexisNexis Academic.* These databases include articles from journals in many different academic fields as well as non-academic sources. *EBSCO,* for example, indexes more than 7,000 periodicals in fields in the humanities, social sciences, sciences, and technology, and as of 2010 *Academic OneFile* included more than 36 million separate articles in its database. Learning to use these resources effectively can enable you to find relevant information quickly.

Let's imagine that you are working on an essay in which you want to make an argument about medical uses of marijuana, a topic of much debate in recent years as some states in the United States have enacted laws allowing people to grow marijuana for their own medicinal uses. You already have some information about the issue from newspapers and magazines that have covered the controversies in states where such laws were proposed or passed. But you need more information about scientific studies of medical uses of marijuana and about some of the legal and political issues associated with this topic. A general database like *Gale: Academic OneFile* is a good place to start your search.

Figure 6-3 shows the opening screen for *Gale: Academic OneFile.* To begin your search, you might use general terms like *marijuana* and *medical.* On the screen in Figure 6-3, "Keyword" is checked (see "Using Boolean Operators" on page 171). In addition, notice that the boxes labeled "to documents with full text" and "to peer-reviewed publications" are checked so that the search will return only references to both academic publications that make the full text of their articles available online. If you wanted to do a broader search that included non-academic publications, you would not check these boxes. You can also use different search terms to refine your search as well—for example, trying more specialized terms such as *therapeutic* or *medicinal.* Your decisions about how broad or narrow to make your search will be determined by your topic, how much you already know about it, what information you think you need, and how early in your research you are. As you do more research on a topic, you will likely need to make your searches more and more specific. Getting familiar with resources like *Gale: Academic OneFile* and trying different search strategies will help make your searches much more productive.

The search in our example in Figure 6-3 yielded 113 articles (see Figure 6-4). Notice that each entry includes important bibliographic information about the article, such as the title of the article and the publication date, as well as a brief summary of the article. These summaries can help you determine whether the article is likely to be relevant to your topic and thus worth reading. If so, you can retrieve the article by clicking the link labeled "Full-text." (If you did not limit your search to full-text articles, you might be unable to obtain some articles online. In that case, you might be able to obtain the article through your library.)

FIGURE 6-3

Opening Screen for *Gale: Academic OneFile*

Cengage Learning

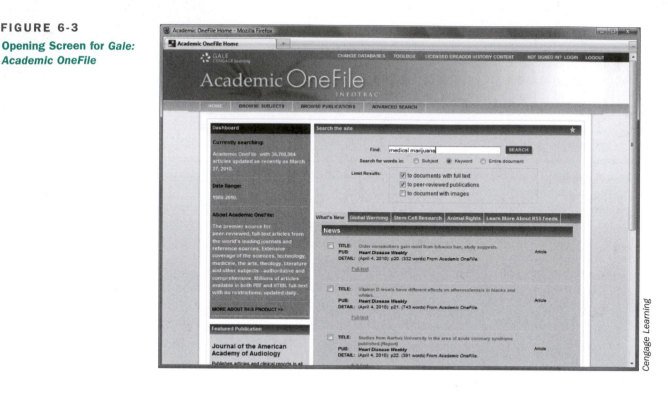

FIGURE 6-4

***Gale: Academic OneFile* Search Results**

Cengage Learning

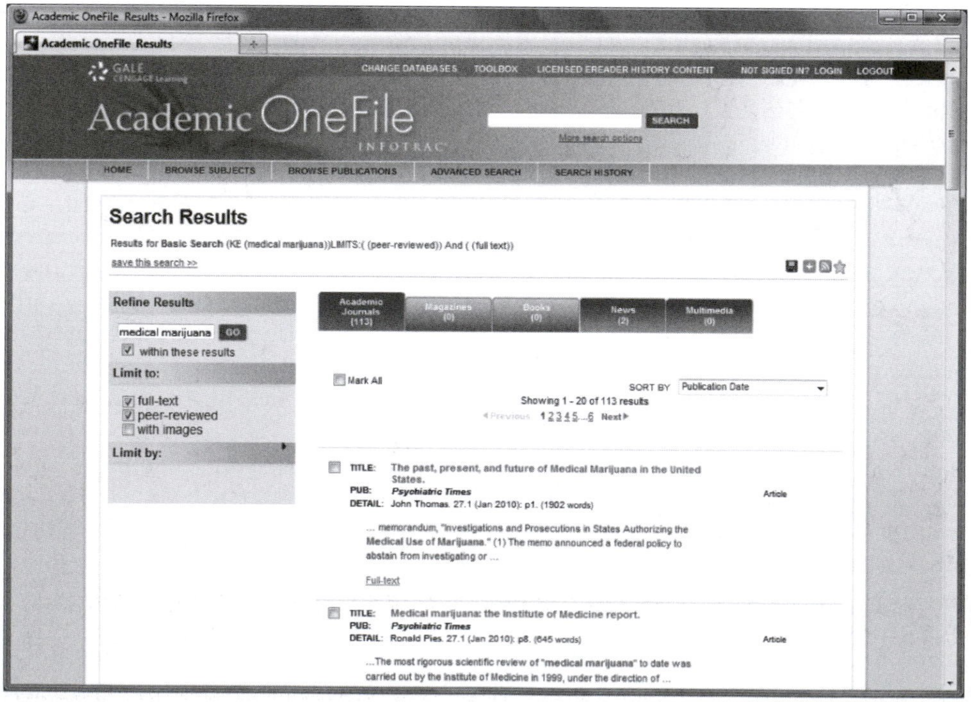

Notice that the left-hand side of the screen in Figure 6-4 includes links that enable you to narrow your search further. Clicking any of these links can yield sources that are potentially more relevant to your topic. If you review the sources listed after a search and don't find the information you need, you can try different search terms or refine your search to focus on specific types of publications. You can also click the link for "Advanced Search" near the top of the page; that will take you to another search screen that will allow you to refine your search according to other criteria, such as publication date and document type.

If you are just beginning your research, you might have to experiment with different search terms and search strategies to yield relevant results. But the more you explore your topic and review different source materials, the more you will become familiar with important ideas and information about your topic, which will help make your searches more efficient.

Although there is some overlapping from one index to another, each index covers different periodicals. The records that you find in one will usually vary from the records that you find in another. This is worth remembering, for two reasons:

1. If you cannot locate any material in the past few years of one index, you can try another index that seems as if it might include records on your subject.

2. Many subjects of general interest will be found in more than one index. If you consult more than one index, you are increasing the likelihood of being exposed to different points of view.

For example, let's use the search terms from our previous example (Figures 6-3 and 6-4) in a different index called *ArticleFirst*. Figure 6-5 shows the main search screen for

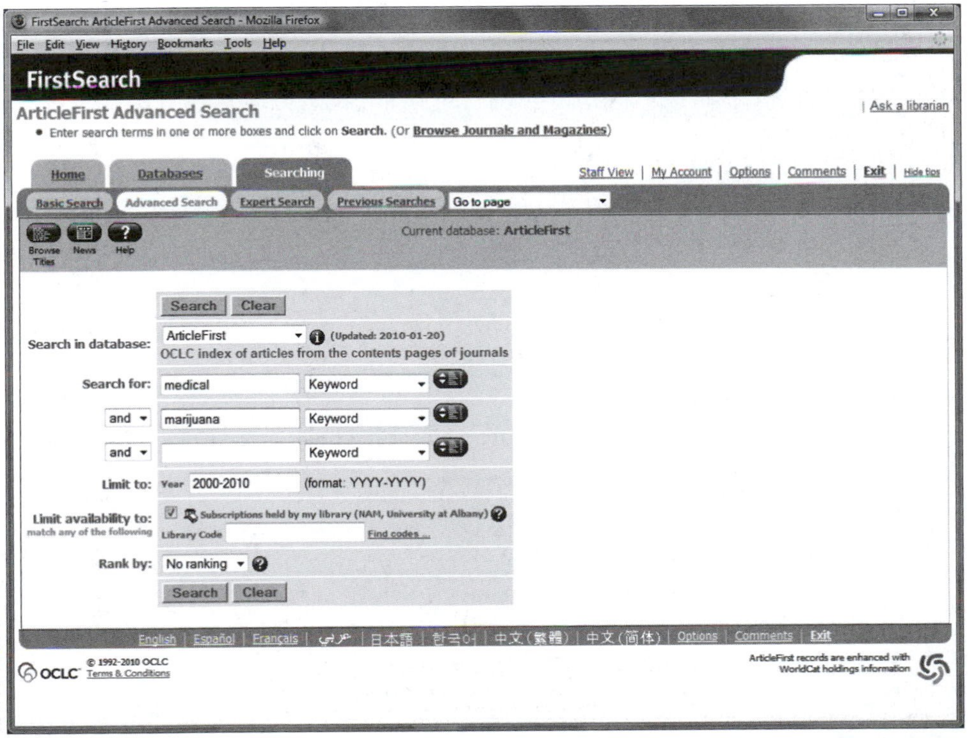

FIGURE 6-5
ArticleFirst **Search Screen**

Source: ArticleFirst

ArticleFirst. The same search terms—*medical* and *marijuana*—have been entered, and the Boolean term *and* appears in the box between those two search terms, which means that only articles with both terms in them will be returned (see "Using Boolean Operators" on page 171). In addition, this search is limited to articles published between 2000 and 2010. Notice, too, that the box labeled "Limit availability to" has been checked; checking that box will return only articles in journals that your library subscribes to, which means that you can easily obtain them without having to use interlibrary loan.

This search returned 86 articles. Figure 6-6 shows the first ten listings (or "records") of the results of this search. If you compare these listings with the results of the search using *Gale: Academic OneFile* in Figure 6-4, which returned 113 articles, you can see that the two indexes located different articles. Although the search of *ArticleFirst* yielded fewer results than the search of *Gale: Academic OneFile*, you might find that the listings in *ArticleFirst* are more relevant for your purposes; in addition, all these articles are available in your school's library. If you experiment in this way with different indexes and databases, you will become more familiar with the ones that will yield the best results for the argument you are working on.

If your assignment requires you to find sources from publications for general audiences, such as newspapers, you can use databases and indexes in the same way. However, specialized academic indexes usually do not include popular publications, so you will need to use a database like *LexisNexis* to find newspaper and magazine articles. Figure 6-7 shows the opening search screen for *LexisNexis Academic*, a powerful database that lists articles from news sources worldwide—often including material only a day or two after its publication. The same search terms—*medical* and *marijuana*—have been used (with the Boolean operator *and* between them), and the same time period (2000–2010). Notice that only the box marked "Major U.S. and World Publications" is checked to limit the

FIGURE 6-6

***ArticleFirst* Search Results**

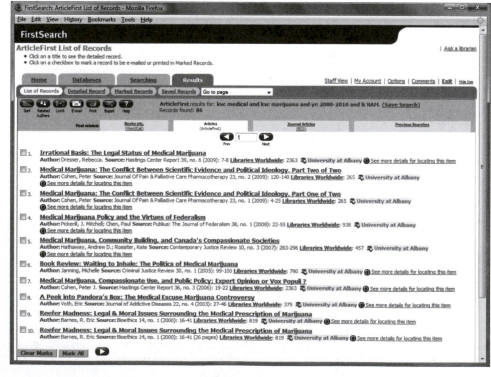

Source: ArticleFirst

USING BOOLEAN OPERATORS

Boolean, or logical, operators are words that command a search engine to define a search in a specific way. The most common Boolean operators are *AND, OR*, and *NOT*. Understanding how they work can help you search the Internet and databases more efficiently:

- *AND* tells the search engine to find only sources that contain both words in your search. For example, if you entered *sports AND steroids*, your search would yield sources that deal with steroids in sports and would not necessarily return sources that deal with steroids or sports in general.
- *OR* broadens a search by telling the search engine to return sources for either term in your search. Entering *sports OR steroids*, for instance, would yield sources on either of those topics.
- *NOT* can narrow a search by telling the search engine to exclude sources containing a specific keyword. For example, entering *steroids NOT sports* would yield sources on steroids but not sources that deal with steroids in sports.

in addition, keep these tips in mind:

- You can use parentheses for complex searches: (*sports AND steroids*) NOT (*medicine OR law*); this entry would narrow the search to specific kinds of sources about sports and steroids that did not include medical or legal matters.
- With most search engines you can use quotation marks to find a specific phrase. For example, "steroid use in sports" would return sources that included that exact phrase.
- Generally, you should capitalize Boolean operators.

search to such news sources. Figure 6-8 shows the results of this search, which returned 1,000 articles. The first three articles listed were published in *USA Today*, the *Washington Post*, and the *New York Times*, all major newspapers.

You can also use a search engine like *Google* to find newspaper and magazine articles. Today many popular publications like the *New York Times* provide their own search functions that enable you to find articles on specific topics.

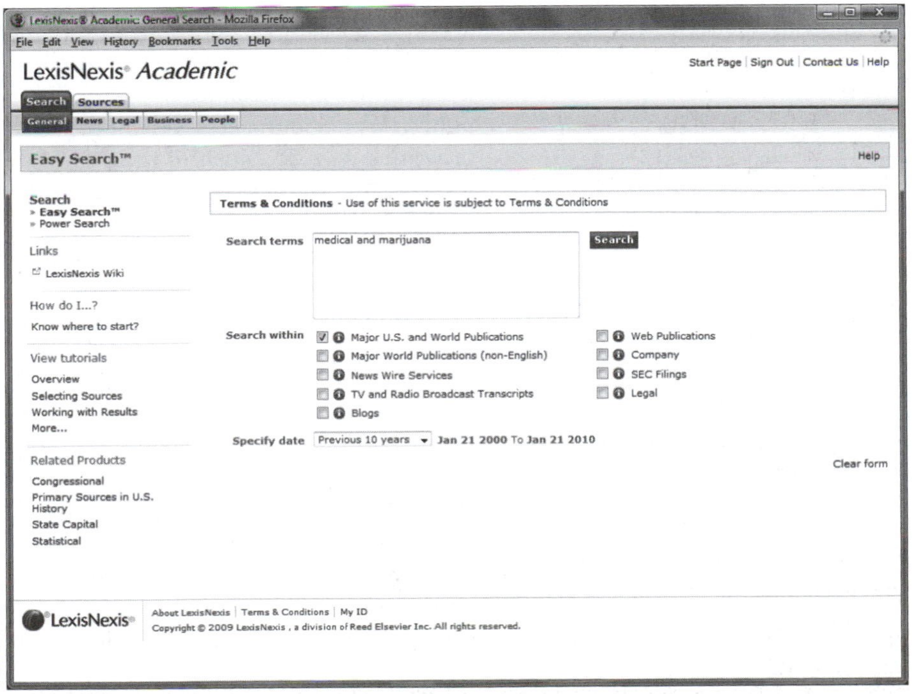

FIGURE 6-7

LexisNexis Academic
Search Screen

Source: LexisNexis

FIGURE 6-8

LexisNexis **Academic Search Results**

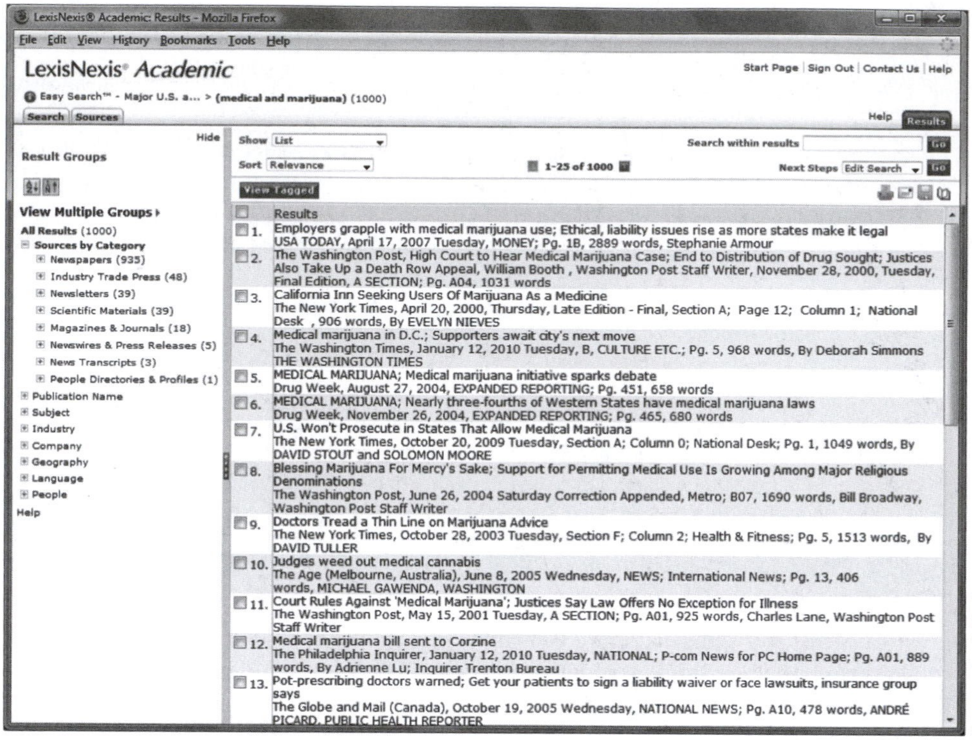

Looking for Books

Despite the convenience of the Internet and online databases, books remain essential to research. They often represent the most prestigious results of someone's research. It is common, for example, for a scholar to publish several journal articles in the process of writing a book. Much of the best information you can find is likely to appear in a book, so you should not assume that your research subject is so new or so specialized that your library will not have books on it.

Most college libraries have electronic catalogs that are accessible both within the library and through the Internet. This accessibility makes it convenient to search the library catalog without having to go to the library itself. Computerized catalogs enable users to search for books by author, title, or subject. Most of these catalogs also permit a search for material using a call number or a **keyword**—a word that is likely to appear somewhere in the title or description. In

---

USING OTHER LIBRARY RESOURCES

Because of the great amount of material being published, libraries save space in several ways, most commonly by using microform, digital technology, and interlibrary loan. In doing research, you might need to use one or more of these resources.

Microform is printed material that has been reduced in size through microphotography. Libraries that use microform provide users with special devices to read the material, whether it is available on microfilm or microfiche (which is a flat sheet of microfilm).

Digital technology, in the form of CD-ROMs or online media, makes articles and other resources available to users electronically rather than in print form. Sometimes, you must read these resources at a computer terminal.

Interlibrary loan enables libraries to give their users access to books held at other libraries. You can usually request articles and books through this service, and today many libraries enable you to make your requests online. Keep in mind, however, that it can take several days or weeks for requested materials to arrive.

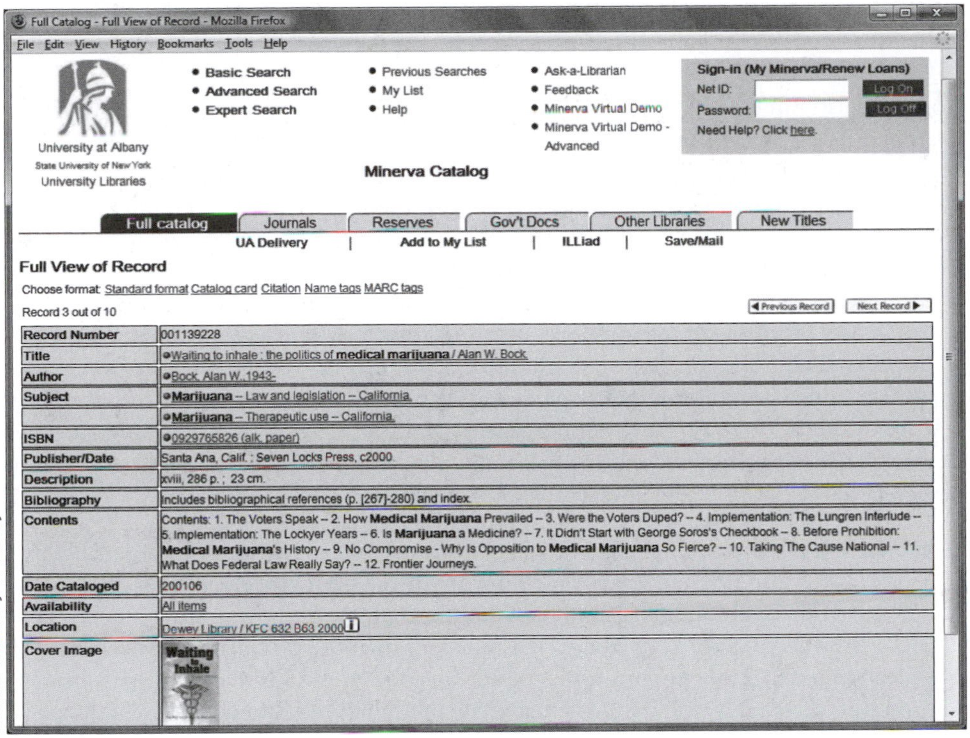

Source: University of Albany

FIGURE 6-9

Online Library Catalog Entry

addition to providing all of the information about a book that could be obtained from a card catalog, computerized catalogs are usually designed to report whether the book is currently available.

Figure 6-9 shows the catalog entry for a book titled *Waiting to Inhale: The Politics of Medical Marijuana*. It contains information about the author, when and where the book was published, and whether it is available in the library. Every library has its own system for displaying information about the books it holds. As you do research, you should expect to find variations on this example. The precise format of a computerized entry depends on the program employed by the library you are using. (If your library still uses index cards in a card catalog, you will find the same basic information displayed on those cards.)

Books take time to read, so you usually need to be strategic about deciding which books might be most useful for your purposes. Here are some things to consider as you decide whether a specific book is likely to be relevant to your argument:

- *The date of publication.* There is no reason to assume that new books are always better than old books, but the date of publication can help you decide whether the material might be out of date.
- *The length of the book.* Longer books aren't necessarily better, but a book's length can help you decide how useful it can be for your assignment and whether it is likely to contain the kind of detailed information you need.
- *The reputation of the publisher.* Academic publishers generally publish books that have gone through rigorous review, which is not always the case with some commercial publishers.

Conducting Interviews and Surveys

For some assignments, you might want to conduct original research on your topic. For example, if you are writing an argument about a campus controversy over new parking fees, you can gather useful information by talking to people on campus (such as the person in charge of parking) or soliciting opinions by students or faculty affected by the new fees. There are many ways to gather information when doing original research, but two of the most common are interviews and surveys.

Interviews might be inappropriate for some kinds of papers (for example, science reports), but they can often be useful sources of information. If you are writing a paper on identity theft, for example, you might interview someone working in law enforcement, such as a police officer or a public defender. You might also interview professionals at a bank or credit card company who deal with identity theft. Whom you interview will depend largely on your topic, but you should always evaluate the credibility of anyone you interview. Here are some other tips for interviewing:

- *Plan ahead for your interviews.* It's a good idea to prepare a list of questions before you go. It also helps to learn something about the person or people you will interview so that you can ask appropriate questions and avoid inappropriate ones.
- *Do your homework.* Your interview is likely to be more productive if you have learned enough about your topic to prepare good questions that will result in useful answers. If you are interviewing a bank official about identity theft, for example, you don't want to waste his or her time (or your own) by asking basic questions like, "What exactly is identity theft?" It is also a good idea to visit the website of the organization or business where the person you are interviewing works. Before interviewing that bank official, for example, visit the bank's website to see what information it has about identity theft.
- *Ask good questions.* Prepare questions that will prompt the person you are interviewing to give detailed answers rather than questions that might be answered with a simple "yes" or "no." If you ask good questions, you will spend more time in the interview listening and less time talking.
- *Be flexible.* Don't necessarily adhere rigidly to the questions you prepare in advance. A good interviewer knows how to ask a follow-up question inspired by a provocative response to an earlier question. However, try not to become so caught up in the interview that you forget to take careful notes.
- *Consider using a tape recorder.* A tape recorder will usually preserve more of the interview than you can capture in your notes, and it will enable you to take notes on important points without having to write everything down. If you want to use a tape recorder, ask permission to do so when you arrange for the interview. Also, make sure that the recorder is working properly before you begin the interview, and check your batteries.
- *Record the date of the interview and the full name and credentials or position of the person you interviewed.* You will need to include this information in your bibliography.

Interviews are appropriate when you want to gather in-depth information or opinions from a few people. If you want information or opinions from many people, you will want to consider conducting a survey. For many undergraduate research projects, a relatively simple survey can produce interesting and useful data. The earlier example of a campus controversy about new parking fees illustrates the usefulness of a survey. If you were writing an argument about that controversy, you could conduct a brief survey to gather information about students' attitudes toward the new fees. Such information can provide potentially persuasive support for your position on the controversy.

Here are some things to consider if you want to use a survey:

- *Carefully compose a list of relevant questions.* Each question should be designed to elicit a clear answer directly related to the purpose of the survey. This is more complicated than it might seem, because the kind of questions you ask will determine what results you get. For example, if you ask students whether they agree with the parking fees, you will get a basic yes-or-no response. However, if you ask students whether they would pay higher fees if they were guaranteed a parking space, you might get different results.

- *Test your questions before conducting your survey.* Because the questions you ask will determine the kind of information you get, it's a good idea to test your survey questions on a few people before conducting your survey. Testing your questions will help you identify any problems with your questions that you didn't notice when you were developing them. It will also allow you to determine whether the questions will result in the kind of information you need.

- *Decide whether you want to administer the survey orally or distribute it in a written form.* One advantage of an oral survey is that you get your results immediately. On the other hand, written surveys give you clear records to work from. A good rule to follow when conducting a written survey is to distribute at least twice as many copies as you need to have returned to you, because people will not always respond to your survey. E-mail is a good way to conduct a survey, but be aware that you may not get all the responses you need. So plan accordingly.

- *Consider conducting your survey online.* E-mail is a good way to conduct a survey if you have access to an e-mail distribution list or the e-mail addresses of the people you hope to survey. More effective survey tools are available online. For example, *Survey Monkey* is a website that enables you to create an online survey and easily collate the responses. If you use a service like *Survey Monkey*, you will need to consider how to invite people you wish to survey to visit the website. For example, if you want to survey students and faculty on your campus about a proposed new parking fee, you might place an announcement in your campus newspaper or post announcements in the campus student center.

- *Decide how many people you will need to survey to have a credible sample of the population that concerns you.* For example, in the case of the campus parking fees, let's say there are 4,000 students at your school but only 1,000 drive to campus. You might want to survey both drivers and nondrivers to see whether you get different results. In that case, if you surveyed 100 students, you might want to make sure that 25 of them are drivers (which would match the 25 percent of student drivers on your campus).

- *Consider whether it would be useful to analyze your results in terms of such differences as gender, race, age, income, or religion.* If so, you must design a questionnaire that will provide this information. In the campus parking controversy it might be that older students are most affected, so you would want to account for the age of your respondents. Therefore, your survey should include questions that allow you to determine the ages of your respondents.

■ *Take steps to protect the privacy of your respondents.* Ask for no more information than you need. Give respondents the option of refusing to answer any question that makes them uncomfortable, and honor any promises you make about how you will use the information you gather.

As this chapter reveals, there are many aspects to doing research and many kinds of resources for the information you need. Which resources you consult and how you search for them will depend on your topic and the specifics of your assignment, such as your deadline and the length of the argument you are writing. But whether you will engage in extensive research or simply look for a few articles about your topic, the general principles guiding research are the same. And the more effective you are as a researcher, the more likely you will be to find the information you need to write an effective argument.

7

Documenting Your Sources

John Coletti Photography

C hapter 6 surveyed many of the strategies that you can use to conduct research for an argument. Doing such research is part of the process of inquiry that you engage in when you make an argument. By researching an issue or controversy carefully, you can gain a better understanding of that issue or controversy and construct a more effective argument that may lead to a satisfactory resolution. That's the goal. But when you draw upon sources for an argument you are composing, you must document those sources properly. In most cases, that means providing both the bibliography that contains all the works you used and the citations within your essay that establish what part of each source you are citing.

Compiling a Preliminary Bibliography

As you use the strategies described in Chapter 6 to begin locating sources for your paper, it is important to record certain essential information about those sources. You will need this information to compile a preliminary bibliography. Here are some things to keep in mind as you work with your sources:

- For books, record the full title, the full name of the author or authors, the city of publication, the publisher, and the date of publication. If you are citing specific pages from that book in your argument, be sure to record those pages.
- For articles in periodicals, record the author(s) of the article, the title of the article, the title of the journal in which it was published, the volume number, the issue number (if there is one), the date of the issue, and the pages of the article.
- If you are using an article or a story from an anthology edited by someone other than the author of the material you are using, make sure to record the author and title of the selection as well as the name of the editor and the title of the volume in which the selection appears.
- For electronic resources, such as websites, be sure to record the Internet address, or URL, accurately and make a note of the date you accessed the site. Note also when the site was posted or last updated.

Today, researchers often use computer programs or online citation services to keep track of sources. You can easily use certain features of a word-processing program such as Microsoft Word to maintain your preliminary bibliography, or you can use specialized software such as *EndNote* that is designed specifically for constructing bibliographies. Online services such as *KnightCite* and *Bibme* (sometimes called "citation generators") also enable you to automatically create bibliographies. However, these programs and online services sometimes result in incorrectly formatted bibliographic citations (see "An Important Word about Automatic Citation Programs and Online Citation Services" on page 179). Whatever method you use, be sure to keep accurate records. It can be frustrating to discover that you neglected to record an important reference, especially if this discovery comes after your paper is written and shortly before it is handed in.

Citing Sources

Anytime you use material from another source, you must cite it properly. Citing your sources simply means revealing the source of any information you report. When you cite your sources, you are providing your readers with information to help them evaluate the

---

AN IMPORTANT WORD ABOUT AUTOMATIC CITATION PROGRAMS AND ONLINE CITATION SERVICES

Software programs, such as *EndNote*, and online citation services (or citation generators), such as *KnightCite* (http://www.calvin.edu/library/knightcite/) and *Bibme* (http://www.bibme. org/), enable you to create bibliographies automatically. In addition, some online indexes and databases, such as *Gale: Academic OneFile* and *EBSCO* (see Tips for Efficient Web Searching on pages 166–172), include citation functions. However, although these programs and services are fast and convenient, online citation functions do not always generate correct citations; in addition, they sometimes produce incompletely formatted citations. For example, *Bibme* does not use a hanging indent for its citations. *EBSCO* sometimes randomly capitalizes things like names and titles, which results in incorrect citations. If you are using these services, it is important to check your bibliographies for errors before submitting your paper.

credibility of your sources, crediting the authors whose work you are citing, and making it possible for readers to find your sources themselves. In general, you must provide documentation for the following:

- Any direct quotation
- Any idea that has come from someone else's work
- Any fact or statistic that is not widely known

There are several styles for documenting your sources; these styles are usually associated with different disciplines or professions. Writers in the humanities usually follow the form of the Modern Language Association (MLA). In the social sciences writers are often expected to follow the format of the American Psychological Association (APA). MLA and APA are the two most widely used systems for documenting sources, and chances are that you will be asked to use one of them for papers you write for your college courses. *The Chicago Manual of Style* (CMS) is another widely used system, though college instructors are less likely to use that system than MLA or APA. When you are writing a source-based paper, check with your instructor to see which system you should use. (If you are writing a source-based argument for publication, check with the editor about that publication's preferred system for documenting sources.)

MLA and APA Sources

Whichever system you use to document your sources, remember that the purpose of all these systems is the same: to provide appropriate information about your sources. And be sure to understand the relationship between the parenthetical, or in-text, citations and the Bibliography, Works Cited, or References page of your essay. When you cite a source in the body of your essay using parenthetical (or in-text) citation format, you are telling your readers where you obtained the quotation or information you are using; your readers can then go to your bibliography for more information about that source.

For example, in this passage from her essay (see page 129), Rachel uses MLA style to cite the source of the quotation she is using:

According to the American Academy of Pediatrics (AAP), children in this situation lose "survivor benefits if a parent dies and legal rights if the parents break up" (Berman 1).

The information in the parentheses includes the author's last name and the page (or pages) on which the quotation appears in that author's work. Readers can then use the author's last name to find the full citation in the bibliography at the end of Rachel's essay, which looks like this:

Berman, Steven. "Homosexuals and Adoption." *Rocky Mountain News* 23 Feb. 2002: 1, final ed.: 1W. Print.

Here's how the same quotation would be documented in Rachel's essay if she were using APA format:

> According to the American Academy of Pediatrics (AAP), children in this situation lose "survivor benefits if a parent dies and legal rights if the parents break up" (Berman, 2002, p. 1).

The citation would appear in her bibliography as follows:

> Berman, S. (2002, February 23). Homosexuals and adoption. *Rocky Mountain News*, p. 1.

Notice that the same basic information is provided, no matter which documentation system is used. But the format for providing that information is different in each system. For example, MLA style requires the use of quotation marks around the title of the article, and the title is capitalized; APA style requires no quotation marks and uses lowercase letters for the title. The remainder of this chapter explains the basic features of the MLA and APA systems of documentation and provides model entries for the most frequently used sources. However, a detailed discussion of these systems is beyond the range of this chapter. If you need more information about either MLA or APA format, consult the official sources for each (see "MLA and APA Sources" on page 180).

For examples of how MLA-style documentation is used in written argument, see pages 183–193. For an example of an APA-style paper, see pages 193–203.

Using Footnotes and Content Notes

Traditionally, footnotes were used to document sources. Strictly speaking, a **footnote** appears at the foot of the page, and an **endnote** appears at the end of the paper. However, both MLA and APA now recommend that writers use parenthetical, or in-text, citations of the kind described here; traditional footnotes are not used for documenting sources. Instead, numbered notes are reserved for additional explanation or discussion that is important but cannot be included within the actual text without a loss of focus. Such notes are called **content notes.** APA discourages the use of such notes unless they are essential to the discussion. If you do use content notes, APA format requires them to be placed on a separate page at the end of the essay (rather than at the bottom of the page as

---

COMMONLY USED STYLE MANUALS

MLA and APA are the two most popular style guides, but there are other manuals that you may need to consult. Here is a list of other commonly used manuals:

> *The Chicago Manual of Style.* 15th ed. (Chicago: University of Chicago Press, 2003).
>
> Council of Science Editors. *Scientific Style and Format: The CBE Manual for Authors, Editors, and Publishers.* 7th ed. New York: Cambridge University Press, 2006. Print.
>
> Coghill, Anne M., and Lorrin R. Garson, eds. *The ACS Style Guide: Effective Communication of Scientific Communication.* 3rd ed. New York: Oxford UP, 2006. Print.
>
> American Institute of Physics. *AIP Style Manual.* 4th ed. New York: Amer. Inst. of Physics, 1990. Print.
>
> JAMA and Archives Journals. *American Medical Association Manual of Style: A Guide for Authors and Editors.* 10th ed. New York: Oxford University Press, 2007. Print.
>
> Harvard Law Review Association. *The Bluebook: A Uniform System of Citation.* 18th ed. Cambridge, MA: Harvard Law Review Assn., 2008. Print.

footnotes). If you are using MLA style, use footnotes or endnotes to provide additional information about sources or topics discussed in your essay.

Using Parenthetical (In-Text) Documentation

As noted earlier in this chapter, the two most common systems for documenting sources, MLA and APA, both recommend the use of parenthetical, or in-text, citations to cite sources. The basic principle for using these parenthetical citations is the same for both MLA and APA styles: You are providing readers with information about a source included in your bibliography. However, there are differences between the two systems. These differences reflect conventions within academic fields regarding which information about a source is most important:

- **MLA style,** which tends to reflect the conventions of the humanities (including the arts, literature, history, and philosophy), emphasizes the author and the author's work and places less emphasis on the date of publication.
- **APA style** emphasizes the author and the date of publication, which are more important in the social science disciplines (for example, psychology, sociology, education, and anthropology).

If you understand these basic differences, you might find it easier to become familiar with the specific differences in the formats used by each documentation system.

Organizing a Bibliography

A bibliography is an essential component of any essay or report that includes references to sources. The bibliography, also called a Works Cited or References page, lists all sources that you have cited in your essay or report. The purpose of a bibliography is to provide information about your sources for your readers.

MLA and APA styles for formatting the entries in your bibliography are described in this chapter. As you'll see, there are some differences between MLA and APA styles. No matter which style you use, your bibliography provides the same basic information about your sources:

- The author's name
- The title of the work
- The date of publication

In addition, entries in your bibliography will provide the name of the magazine, newspaper, or journal for any articles you cite, as well as page numbers (unless you are citing an electronic source without page numbers, such as a web page).

MLA-Style Documentation

This section begins with a discussion of the MLA author/work style used for citations within the text of an argument and then explains how citations should appear in an MLA-style bibliography.

Citing Sources in MLA Style In a parenthetical (or in-text) citation in MLA form, the author's last name is followed by a page reference; in some cases, a brief title should be included after the author's name. It is not necessary to repeat within the parentheses information already provided in the text.

A. WORK BY ONE AUTHOR

If you were citing page 133 of a book called *Ecological Literacy* by David W. Orr, the parenthetical citation would look like this:

> The idea of environmental sustainability can become the centerpiece of a college curriculum (Orr 133).

Alternatively, you could use Orr's name in your sentence, in which case the citation would include only the page reference:

> David Orr has argued persuasively that that the idea of environmental sustainability should be the centerpiece of a college curriculum (133).

There is no punctuation between the author's name and the page reference when both are cited parenthetically. Note also that the abbreviation *p.* or *pp.* is not used before the page reference in MLA style.

B. WORK WITH MORE THAN ONE AUTHOR

If the work you are citing has two or three authors, use the complete names of all of them in your sentence or include their last names in the parentheses:

> Cleanth Brooks and Robert Penn Warren have argued that "indirection is an essential part of the method of poetry" (573).

or

> Although this sonnet may seem obscure, its meaning becomes clearer when we realize that "indirection is an essential part of the method of poetry" (Brooks and Warren 573).

Note that when a sentence ends with a quotation, the parenthetical reference comes *before* the final punctuation mark. Note also that the ampersand (&) is not used in MLA style.

If you are referring to a work by more than three authors, list only the first author's name followed by *et al.* (Latin for "and others"):

> These works "derive from a profound disillusionment with modern life" (Baym et al. 910).

C. WORK WITH A CORPORATE AUTHOR

A "corporate author" is an organization or an agency (rather than an individual or group of individually named authors). When a corporate author has a long name, include it within the text rather than within parentheses. For example, if you were citing a study

---

ITALICS OR UNDERLINES

Traditionally, both APA and MLA recommended underlining titles of books, journals, magazines, and newspapers. However, with the widespread use of word processing, it is now as easy to use italics as it is to underline, and although either is generally acceptable, italics is more common. The MLA now recommends checking with your editor (if you are working with one) before using underlines. According to the MLA, "Although some authors, for the sake of clarity, choose to underline words meant to be italicized in publication, this practice is less common than it once was; check with your editor if you would like to format your manuscript in this way."

by the Council on Environmental Quality called "Ground Water Contamination in the United States," you would do so as follows:

> The Council on Environmental Quality has reported that there is growing evidence of ground water contamination throughout the United States (81).

You could also include the corporate author in the parentheses; omit any initial article:

> There is growing evidence of ground water contamination throughout the United States (Council on Environmental Quality 81).

Although both of these forms are technically correct, the first is preferred because it is easier to read.

D. WORK WITH MORE THAN ONE VOLUME

When you wish to cite a specific part of a multivolume work, include the volume number between the author and the page reference. This example quotes a passage from the second volume of a two-volume book by Jacques Barzun:

> As Jacques Barzun has argued, "The only hope of true culture is to make classifications broad and criticism particular" (2: 340).

Note that the volume number is given an Arabic numeral (in this case, 2) and a space separates the colon and the page reference. The abbreviation *vol.* is not used unless you wish to cite the entire volume: (Barzun, vol. 2).

E. MORE THAN ONE WORK BY THE SAME AUTHOR

If you cite more than one work by the same author, you need to make your references distinct so that readers will know exactly which work you are citing. You can do so by putting a comma after the author's name and then adding a shortened form of the title. For example, if you are discussing two novels by Toni Morrison, *Song of Solomon* and *The Bluest Eye,* your citations might look like this:

> Toni Morrison's work is always concerned with the complexities of racial identity. This theme is perhaps explored most painfully in the character of Pecola Breedlove (Morrison, *Bluest*). But even a crowd of unnamed characters gathered near a hospital, listening to a woman break spontaneously into song and wondering "if one of those things that racial-uplift groups were always organizing was taking place," can become a reminder that race is always part of the picture (Morrison, *Song* 6).

If it is clear from the context that the quotation is from a work by Morrison, there is no need to include her name in the parentheses. If you're not sure, however, include it. This example could have left Morrison's name out of the parentheses because it is clear that it is citing her works.

F. QUOTATION WITHIN A CITED WORK

If you want to use a quotation that you have discovered in another book, your reference must show that you acquired this material secondhand and that you have not consulted the original source. Use the abbreviation *qtd. in* (for "quoted in") to make the distinction between the author of the passage being quoted and the author of the work in which you found this passage.

For example, let's say you were reading a book called *The Abstract Wild* by Jack Turner and you came across a quotation by the naturalist William Kittredge that you wanted to use in your argument. You would cite the Kittredge quotation as follows:

> Many people misquote Henry David Thoreau's famous line about wildness and the preservation of the world. William Kittredge has admitted to making this very mistake: "For years I misread Thoreau. I assumed he was saying wilderness. . . . Maybe I didn't want Thoreau to have said wildness, I couldn't figure out what he meant" (qtd. in Turner 81).

In this case, you are indicating to your readers that you read Kittredge's statement in the book by Jack Turner.

G. WORK WITHOUT AN AUTHOR LISTED

Sometimes a newspaper or magazine article does not include the name of an author. In such a case, include a brief version of the title in parentheses. For example, say you wanted to cite an article from *Consumer Reports* titled "Dry-Cleaning Alternatives" that listed no author:

> Conventional dry-cleaning, which requires the use of dangerous solvents, can result in both air and water pollution. However, if you are concerned about potential environmental damage caused by dry-cleaning your garments, you have several environmentally friendly options, including methods using carbon dioxide and silicone-based techniques ("Dry-Cleaning" 10).

H. ELECTRONIC SOURCES

When citing electronic sources, you should follow the same principles you would use when citing other sources. If you are citing an article from an online journal or newspaper, cite it as you would any print article, using the author's last name or, if you don't know the author, a brief version of the title of the article. However, there are many different kinds of electronic sources, and you might not have access to the same kinds of information that are available for a published book or journal article. For example, websites don't usually have page numbers, and you might not be able to determine the author of an online source. In such cases incorporate sufficient information about the source into your sentence so that readers can easily find the citation in your bibliography:

> On its website, the Conference Board maintains information about global economic developments ("Research Reports").

In this case the author of the web page being cited is unknown, so the title of the web page, "Research Reports," is included in parentheses. Notice that the title of a website is enclosed in quotation marks, just like the titles of articles in periodicals.

In most cases, a citation of an electronic source appears without a page reference because such sources are rarely numbered. You cannot add a page number based on a print-out because readers accessing the same source from a different system may find a different page configuration. But if a page number is included in the source (as in the case of an electronic book) or if paragraphs are numbered, you should provide that information:

> (Dickens 134)

> (Martinez par. 8)

When online sources have page numbers, the parenthetical citation follows the same conventions as those for print sources. If paragraphs are numbered, it is necessary to add the abbreviation *par.* (or *pars.*) so that readers can see that you are not citing page numbers.

Creating a Bibliography or Works Cited Page in MLA Style In an MLA-style bibliography, the works cited are arranged in alphabetical order by the author's last name. Here are the main things to remember when you are creating a bibliography in MLA style:

- Provide the author's first and last name for each entry.
- Capitalize every important word in the titles of books, articles, and journals.
- Italicize the titles of books, journals, and newspapers.
- Place the titles of articles, stories, and poems in quotation marks.
- Indent the second and any subsequent lines one-half inch (or five spaces).

Here's how a typical entry for a single-authored book appears in an MLA-style bibliography:

Abram, David. *The Spell of the Sensuous*. New York: Random House, 1996. Print.

Here are the important parts of the entry:

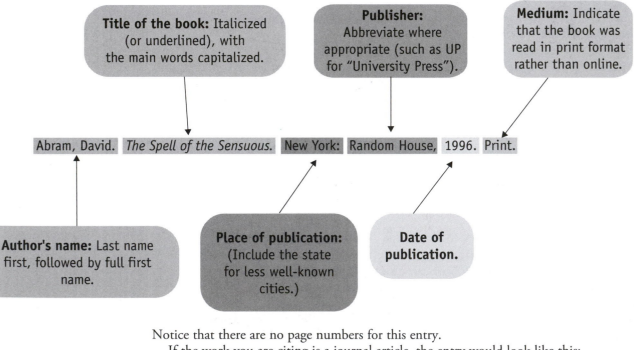

Notice that there are no page numbers for this entry.

If the work you are citing is a journal article, the entry would look like this:

George, Diana. "From Analysis to Design: Visual Communication in the Teaching of Writing." *College Composition and Communication* 54.1 (2002): 11–39. Print.

Here are the parts of this entry:

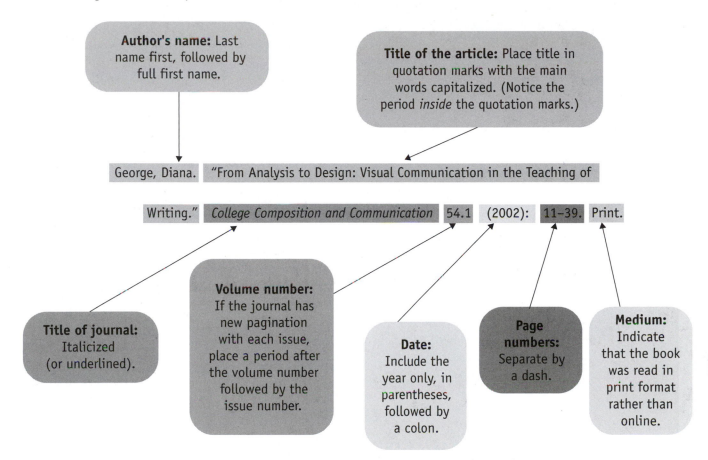

For online sources, include two dates: the publication date (if available) and the date you accessed the site. Also to indicate that the source is a website, place the term "Web" after the date of publication. Here's an entry for an online journal article:

Luebke, Steven R. "Using Linked Courses in the General Education Curriculum." <http://
aw.colostate.edu/articles/luebke_2002.htm>. *Academic Writing* 3 (2002). Web.
16 Dec. 2002.

Notice where the dates are placed in this entry:

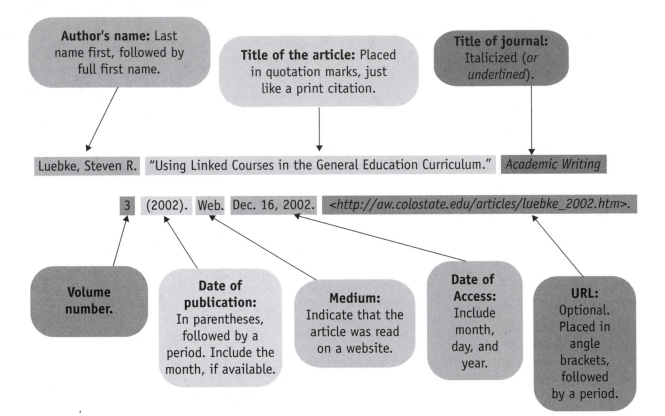

Author's name: Last name first, followed by full first name.

Title of the article: Placed in quotation marks, just like a print citation.

Title of journal: Italicized (*or underlined*).

Luebke, Steven R.   "Using Linked Courses in the General Education Curriculum."   *Academic Writing*

3   (2002).   Web.   Dec. 16, 2002.   *<http://aw.colostate.edu/articles/luebke_2002.htm>.*

Volume number.

Date of publication: In parentheses, followed by a period. Include the month, if available.

Medium: Indicate that the article was read on a website.

Date of Access: Include month, day, and year.

URL: Optional. Placed in angle brackets, followed by a period.

MLA style no longer requires that you include the Internet address, or URL, of the website. However, it is a good idea to include the URL if you think that it would be difficult to locate the source online without it. Also, your instructor may require that you include it. If so, enclose the URL in angle brackets: <http://aw.colostate.edu/articles/luebke_2002.htm>.

All entries in MLA format follow these basic principles, but each entry will contain slightly different information, depending on the kind of source cited. Keep that in mind as you look for the correct format for the sources you are citing in your bibliography.

A. BOOK WITH ONE AUTHOR

Harrison, Kathryn. *Envy*. New York: Random, 2005. Print.

B. BOOK WITH TWO OR THREE AUTHORS

Johnson, Benjamin H., and Andrew R. Graybill. *Bridging National Borders in North America: Transnational and Comparative Histories*. Durham: Duke UP, 2010. Print.

Note that the subtitle is included, set off from the main title by a colon. The second author's name is not inverted, and an abbreviation (UP) is used for *University Press* to shorten the publisher's name. For books with three authors, put commas after the names of the first two authors (invert the name of the first author); separate the second two authors with a comma followed by *and*.

C. EDITED BOOK

Stout, Janis, ed. *Willa Cather and Material Culture*. Tuscaloosa: U of Alabama P, 2005. Print.

D. BOOK WITH MORE THAN THREE AUTHORS OR EDITORS

Black, Laurel, et al., eds. *New Directions in Portfolio Assessment: Practice, Critical Theory, and Large-Scale Scoring*. Portsmouth: Boynton, 1994. Print.

Give the name of the first author or editor only, and add the abbreviation *et al.*

E. SUBSEQUENT EDITIONS OF A BOOK

Tate, Gary, Edward P. J. Corbett, and Nancy Myers, eds. *The Writing Teacher's Sourcebook*. 4th ed. New York: Oxford UP, 1999. Print.

F. WORK IN AN ANTHOLOGY

Owens, Derek. "Sustainable Composition." *Ecocomposition: Theoretical and Pedagogical Approaches*. Eds. Christian R. Weisser and Sidney I. Dobrin. Albany: State U of New York P, 2001. 27–38. Print.

Note that a period comes after the title of the selection but before the second quotation marks. A period is also used to separate the date of publication from the page reference, which is followed by a period.

G. TRANSLATED BOOK

Eco, Umberto. *The Aesthetics of Thomas Aquinas*. Trans. Hugh Bredin. Cambridge: Harvard UP, 1988. Print.

H. WORK IN MORE THAN ONE VOLUME

Leckie, Robert. *The Wars of America*. 2 vols. New York: Harper, 1992. Print.

I. INTRODUCTION, PREFACE, FOREWORD, OR AFTERWORD

Dove, Rita. Foreword. *Jonah's Gourd Vine*. By Zora Neale Hurston. New York: Harper, 1990. vii–xv. Print.

J. ARTICLE IN AN ENCYCLOPEDIA

Daniels, Robert V. "Marxism." *The Encyclopedia Americana*. ed. Print.

In citing material from well-known encyclopedias, give the author's name first, then the article title. If material is arranged alphabetically within the source, which is usually the case, there is no need to include volume and page numbers. You should give the full title of the encyclopedia, the edition (if it is stated), and the year of publication (for example, 11th ed. 1996). When no edition number is stated, identify the edition by the year of publication (for example, 1996 ed.). If the author of the article is identified only by initials, look elsewhere within the encyclopedia for a list identifying the names these initials stand for. If the article is unsigned, give the title first. (Note: This same form can be used for other reference books, such as dictionaries.) For an example of how to cite an electronic encyclopedia, see Sections T and U.

K. GOVERNMENT PUBLICATION

> United States. Federal Bureau of Investigation. *Handbook of Forensic Science.* Washington: GPO, 1994. Print.

For many government publications the author is unknown. When this is the case, the agency that issued the publication should be listed as the author. State the name of the government (for example, United States, Florida, or United Nations) followed by a period. Then give the name of the agency that issued the work, using abbreviations only if you can do so clearly (for example, Bureau of the Census, National Institute on Drug Abuse, or Dept. of Labor) followed by a period. The italicized title of the work comes next, followed by another period. Then give the place of publication, publisher, and date. Most federal publications are printed in Washington by the Government Printing Office (GPO), but there are exceptions. (Note: Treat a government pamphlet just as you would a book.)

L. JOURNAL ARTICLE WITH ONE AUTHOR

> Hesse, Douglas. "The Place of Creative Nonfiction." *College English* 65 (2003): 237–241. Print.

The volume number comes after the journal title without any intervening punctuation. The year of publication is included within parentheses after the volume number. A colon separates the year of publication and the page reference. Leave one space after the volume number and one space after the colon.

M. JOURNAL ARTICLE PAGINATED ANEW IN EACH ISSUE

> Hershon, Joanna. "Crawl." *Virginia Quarterly Review* 81.3 (2005): 63–77. Print.

In this case the issue number (3) is included immediately after the volume number (81), and the two are separated by a period without any intervening space.

N. ARTICLE FROM A MAGAZINE ISSUED MONTHLY

> Gibbons, Ann. "Our Earliest Ancestors." *Smithsonian* Mar. 2010: 34–41. Print.

Instead of citing the volume number, give the month and year of the issue. Abbreviate the month when it has more than four letters. (May, June, and July are spelled out.) For an example of how to list an article from a magazine published monthly that was obtained through a computer database, see Section R.

O. ARTICLE FROM A MAGAZINE ISSUED WEEKLY

> Scherer. Michael. "A Green Seat At the Table." *Time* 15 Mar. 2010: 32–35. Print.

The form is the same as for an article in a magazine issued monthly, but you add the day immediately before the month. A dash between page numbers indicates consecutive pages. When an article is printed on nonconsecutive pages—beginning on page 34, for example, and continuing on page 78—give only the first page number and a plus sign: 34+.

P. ARTICLE FROM A DAILY NEWSPAPER

> Raspberry, William. "Poverty and the Father Factor." *Washington Post* 1 Aug. 2005, District & Maryland ed., A17. Print.

If more than one edition is available on the date in question, specify the edition immediately after the date. If the city of publication is not part of a locally published newspaper's name, identify the city in brackets after the newspaper title. Because newspapers often consist of separate sections, you should cite the section letter if each section has separate pagination. If a newspaper consists of only one section or if the pagination is continuous from one section to the next, then you do not need to include the section letter. If the article is unsigned, begin the entry with the title of the article; alphabetize the article under its title, passing over small words such as "a" and "the." For an example of how to cite a newspaper article accessed through a subscription service such as LexisNexis, see Section U.

Q. EDITORIAL

> Terzian, Philip. "Armed Forces Work Just Fine without Draft." Editorial. *Albany Times Union*
>   14 Jan. 2003: A14. Print.

Editorials are identified as such between the title of the article and the title of the newspaper or magazine.

R. PRINTED MATERIAL ACCESSED FROM A PERIODICALLY PUBLISHED DATABASE ON CD-ROM

Many periodicals and reference works such as bibliographies are now available on CD-ROMs, which are sometimes updated. Here's an example of a print article from a journal called *Managing Office Technology* that was found on a CD-ROM issued by UMI-ProQuest:

> Holtzman, Henry. "Team Management: Its Time Has Come . . . Again." *Managing Office Technology*
>   Feb. 1994: 8. *ABI/Inform*. UMI-ProQuest. Oct. 1994. CD-ROM. 2 Feb. 2010.

Notice that this entry includes the same information that would be provided for a magazine or journal article: author (if known), article title, journal title, date of print publication, and page reference. In addition, cite the database you used (in this case, *ABI/ Inform*) and, if available, the vendor that made this medium available (here, UMI-ProQuest) and the date of electronic publication (in this case, October, 1994). Then indicate the medium (CD-ROM), followed by a period, and conclude with the date on which you accessed the material (in this example, 2 Feb. 2010).

S. EXCLUSIVELY ELECTRONIC MATERIAL ACCESSED FROM A PERIODICALLY PUBLISHED DATABASE

Many reference works today are published exclusively in electronic form on media such as CD-ROM and computer diskettes:

> African Development Bank. "1995 AFDB Indicative Learning Program." *National Trade Data
>   Bank*. U.S. Commercial Service, Mar. 1996. CD-ROM.

Give the author's name (a corporate author in this case), the title of the material in quotation marks, the title of the database (here, *National Trade Data Bank*), the vendor (here, U.S. Commercial Service), the date it was published electronically (March 1996), and the publication medium (in this case, CD-ROM). Note that the title of the database is italicized.

T. NONPERIODICAL PUBLICATION ON CD-ROM

Encyclopedias and similar nonperiodical reference works are now regularly available in digital forms such as CD-ROM. In general, treat these resources as you would a print source. For example, here is an entry for an article from *The Academic American Encyclopedia* on CD-ROM:

> Hogan, Robert. "Abbey Theater." *The Academic American Encyclopedia*. Danbury: Grolier,
>   1995. CD-ROM.

Notice that this entry is identical to a citation for an article from a printed encyclopedia (see Section J) except that the medium is CD-ROM, which is indicated at the end of the entry. If no author is identified, begin with the work's title; if no author or title is available, begin with the title of the product consulted.

If you are citing an article from an encyclopedia available online, use the format for an article accessed through an online database (see Section U).

U. PRINTED PUBLICATION ACCESSED THROUGH AN ONLINE DATABASE

If you are citing a print journal or magazine article that you found through an online database, such as *ArticleFirst* or *LexisNexis*, you have to indicate both the original source of the article and the database. In this example, an article from the print journal *Commentary* was located through a search of the *LexisNexis* database:

> Jeffers, Thomas L. "Plagiarism High and Low." *Commentary* 114.3 (2002): 4–61. *LexisNexis.*
>   Web. 28 Dec. 2009.

In such instances, follow the same pattern you would for the print equivalent (in this case, a journal article), but add the title of the database (in this case, *LexisNexis*), the medium (Web), and the date you accessed the article (28 Dec. 2009). Notice that a period follows each of these items, and the title of the database is italicized.

V. ARTICLE FROM AN ONLINE PERIODICAL

Many periodicals now appear only online (and are not published in print). In general, follow the format for print publications with some additional information. For example, here's an article from an online journal called *Kairos*:

> Sands, Peter. "Pushing and Pulling Toward the Middle." *Kairos* 7.3 (2002): n. pag. Web. 15
>   Oct. 2009.

Cite the article as you would for a print article (see Section L), but add the medium (in this case, Web) and the date you accessed the article (15 Oct. 2009). Notice that there are no page numbers for this article, which is indicated by "n. pag."

For online magazine or newspaper articles, follow the format for print articles (see Sections N, O, and P), but add the sponsor of the website after the name of the magazine or newspaper. Then include the date of publication, the medium, and the date of access. Here's an example from an article from the *New York Time* website:

> Zernike, Kate. "Making College Relevant." *New York Times.* New York Times, 29 Dec. 2009.
>   Web. 22 Jan. 2010.

Notice that in this case the title of the newspaper (*New York Times*) is the same as the sponsor of the website. Also notice that a comma is placed after the name of the sponsor and then the publication date is added followed by the medium (Web) and date of access (22 Jan. 2010). Follow this pattern for articles from any online periodicals as well as for online books.

W. THESIS PUBLISHED ONLINE

Increasingly, authors make their work available on websites. Citing these websites can be tricky because you do not always have access to all publication information. Here's an entry for a thesis that the author published on a website:

> Myers, Rachel. "A critique of Cohen's relational theory of color." MA thesis. 3 April 2007.
>   Web. 18 Jan. 2010.

Notice that this entry follows the same pattern as an online periodical (see Section V): the author's name first, followed by the title of the work, and the date of publication. Then add the medium (Web), followed by a period, and the date on which you accessed the document. If there is no date of publication, use *n.d.* for "no date."

X. ARTICLE ON A WEBSITE

If you are using information from a website, follow the same basic principles for citing the source that you would follow for print sources. Here's an entry for an article found on the website for an advocacy group called the Center for a New American Dream:

> "In the Market? Think Green: The Center for a New American Dream's Guide to Environmentally Preferable Purchasing." *Center for a New American Dream*, n.d. Web. 8 Aug. 2001.

Notice that because there is no author listed on the site, the title of the article is listed first, in quotation marks. The organization hosting the website (Center for a New American Dream) is listed next and is italicized, followed by the date of publication (in this case, "n.d." indicates that there was no date of publication), the medium (Web), and the date of access.

Y. PERSONAL HOME PAGE

> White, Crystal. Home page. 13 Jan. 2003. Web. 22 June 2003.

If the home page has a name, include that in place of "Home page" after the author's name.

Z. INTERVIEW

> Scheurer, Erika. Personal interview. 16 Jan. 2006.

If you include an interview you conducted in your bibliography, indicate whether the interview was a personal (that is, in-person) interview, telephone interview, or e-mail interview.

AA. ONLINE DISCUSSION FORUM POSTING

There are many different kinds of online discussion forums, including e-mail discussion lists and Web-based discussion boards. This example is from a Web-based discussion board:

> SailingDog. "Re: Heavy Weather Sailing." *Sailnet Community*. Sailnet, 22 Oct. 2008. Web. 12 Jan. 2009.

Notice that the author's name (or pseudonym) is first, followed by the subject line, the name of the forum (*Sailnet Community*), the website that sponsors the discussion forum (Sailnet), the date of the posting, the medium (Web), and the date of access (12 Jan. 2009). If you don't know the name of the website that sponsors or publishes the forum, indicate that by including "N.p." after the name of the forum.

For an e-mail discussion list posting, include the name of the mailing list after the date of the posting, as follows:

> Fleischer, Cathy. "Colearn Logins." CoLEARN ResearchTeam Discussion List. N.p. 9 Dec. 2002. Web. 5 Jan. 2003.

Many online discussion forums now maintain archives of their discussions, and it is a good idea to cite the archived version of a posting (which will be easier for a reader to find). If you cannot locate an archived version, however, you should keep a copy of the posting.

BB. WEB LOG (BLOG)

To cite a posting on a web log, or blog, include the author's name, title of the posting, name of the blog, the sponsor or publisher of the blog, date of the posting, medium, and date of access, as follows:

> Kurtz, David. "One Reader's Sob-Story." *TPM Editor's Blog.* Talking Points Memo, 23 Jan. 2010. Web. 24 Jan. 2010.

Notice that a comma follows the sponsor or publisher of the blog (in this case, Talking Points Memo). If the sponsor or publisher is unknown, indicate that by adding "N.p." after the name of the blog. If there is no title for the blog post, write "Web log post" or "Web log comment."

CC. WIKI ARTICLE

Wiki articles do not usually include names of authors, so begin with the title of the article, followed by the name of the wiki, the sponsor or publisher (if known), the date of the most recent update, the medium, and the date of access, as in this example:

> "The Beatles." *Wikipedia.* Wikimedia Foundation, 23 Jan. 2010. Web. 23 Jan. 2010.

Notice that a comma follows the sponsor or publisher.

Many instructors do not allow students to use wiki articles for research-based assignments, so check with your instructor before using a wiki as a source.

As in the preceding discussion of MLA-style documentation, this section begins with how to cite sources parenthetically within the text of an argument and then explains how to cite sources in a bibliography.

APA-Style Documentation

Citing Sources in APA Style The American Psychological Association (APA) requires that in-text documentation identify the author of the work and the year in which the work was published; where appropriate, page numbers are also included, preceded by the abbreviation *p.* or *pp.* This information should be provided parenthetically; it is not necessary to repeat any information already provided directly in the sentence.

A. WORK BY ONE AUTHOR

If you wished to cite a book by Alan Peshkin titled *Places of Memory,* published in 1997, you might do so as follows:

> Native American students face the challenge of trying to maintain their cultural heritage while assimilating into mainstream American culture (Peshkin, 1997).

or

> Peshkin (1997) has argued that the pressures on Native American students to assimilate into mainstream American culture can contribute to poor academic performance.

If the reference is to a specific chapter or page, or if you include a quotation from a specific page, that information should also be included. For example:

> Peshkin's (1997) study focuses on what he calls the "dual-world character of the students' lives" (p. 5).

Note that the date of publication (in parentheses) follows the author's name; the page reference (also in parentheses) is placed at the end of the sentence. If the author's name is not included in the sentence, it should be included in the parentheses:

> The "dual-world character" of the lives of many Native American students can create obstacles to their academic success (Peshkin, 1997, p. 5).

B. WORK WITH TWO OR MORE AUTHORS

If a work has two authors, you should mention the names of both authors every time a reference is made to their work:

> A recent study of industry (Cole & Walker, 1997) argued that...

or

> More recently, Cole and Walker (1997) have argued that...

Note that the ampersand (&) is used only within parentheses.

Scientific papers often have multiple authors because of the amount of research involved. In the first reference to a work with three to five authors, you should identify each of the authors:

> Hodges, McKnew, Cytryn, Stern, and Kline (1982) have shown...

Subsequent references to the same work should use the abbreviated form with the first author's name followed by *et al.*:

> This method was also used in an earlier study (Hodges et al., 1982).

Notice that when you use *et al.*, there is a period after *al* but not after *et*.

If a work has six authors (or more), this abbreviated form should be used even for the first reference. If confusion is possible because you must refer to more than one work by the first author, list as many coauthors as necessary to distinguish between the two works.

C. WORK WITH A CORPORATE AUTHOR

When a work has a corporate author, your first reference should include the full name of the corporation, committee, agency, or institution involved. For example, if you were citing the *Buying Guide 2010*, published by Consumer Reports, you might do so like this:

> There are several strategies you can use to protect yourself when ordering merchandise online (Consumer Reports, 2010, pp. 11–12).

If the corporate name is long, you can abbreviate subsequent references to the same source. If you were citing a report from the Fund for the Improvement of Postsecondary Education (FIPSE), for example, you would use the full name when you first cited it, then use FIPSE for any subsequent references.

D. REFERENCE TO MORE THAN ONE WORK

When the same citation refers to two or more sources, the works should be listed alphabetically, according to the first author's last name, and separated with semicolons:

> Several studies have examined the social nature of literacy (Finders, 1997; Heath, 1983; Street, 1984; Young, 1994).

If you are referring to more than one work by the same author(s), list the works in the order in which they were published:

> The validity of this type of testing is now well established (Collins, 1988, 1994).

If you refer to more than one work by the same author published in the same year, distinguish individual works by identifying them as *a, b, c,* and so on:

These findings have been questioned by Scheiber (1997a, 1997b).

Creating a Bibliography or Works Cited Page in APA Style

In APA style, the bibliography is arranged alphabetically by the author's last name. The date of publication is emphasized by placing it within parentheses immediately after the author's name. The *APA Publication Manual* (6th ed.) recommends a hanging indent style of a half-inch, or five spaces, which is what is shown in the following illustrations.

Here are the main things to keep in mind when preparing a bibliography in APA style:

- Provide the author's last name, followed by an initial for the first name.
- Place the date in parentheses and follow it with a period; the date should always be the second element in an entry.
- Capitalize only the first word and any proper nouns of any title and subtitle (if there is one) in the entry.
- Italicize titles of books, journals, magazines, and newspapers.
- Do *not* place quotation marks around the titles of articles or chapters and do not italicize or underline them.

In APA style, a typical entry for a single-authored book looks like this:

Geertz, C. (2000). *Available light: Anthropological reflections on philosophical topics.* Princeton, NJ: Princeton University Press.

Here are the important parts of the entry:

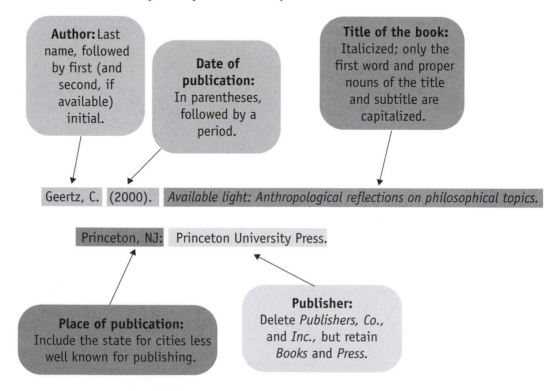

Author: Last name, followed by first (and second, if available) initial.

Date of publication: In parentheses, followed by a period.

Title of the book: Italicized; only the first word and proper nouns of the title and subtitle are capitalized.

Geertz, C. (2000). *Available light: Anthropological reflections on philosophical topics.*

Princeton, NJ: Princeton University Press.

Place of publication: Include the state for cities less well known for publishing.

Publisher: Delete *Publishers, Co.,* and *Inc.,* but retain *Books* and *Press.*

Here is an entry for a journal article:

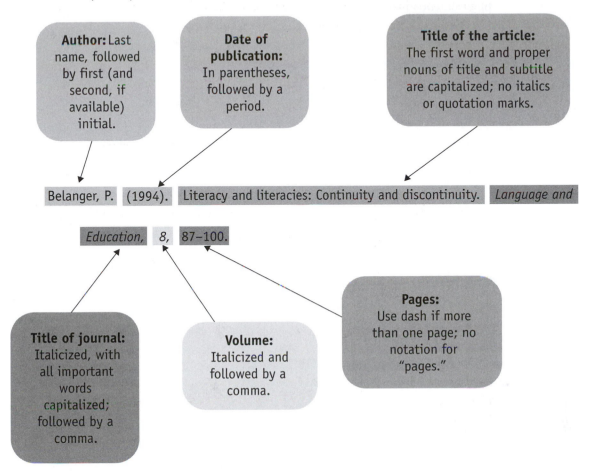

Notice the differences between the entry for a journal article and the following example of an entry for a newspaper article:

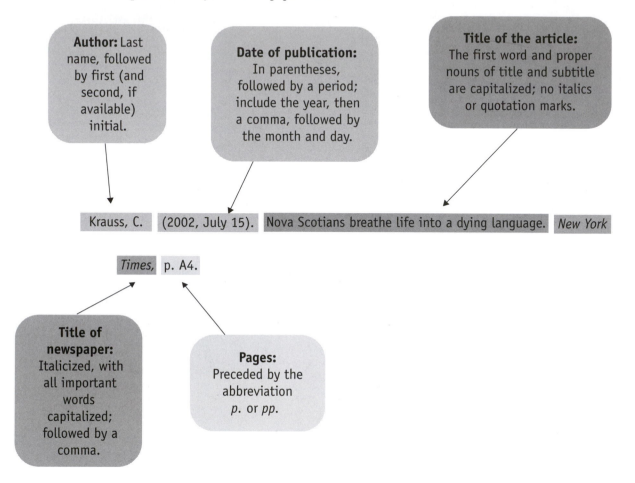

Author: Last name, followed by first (and second, if available) initial.

Date of publication: In parentheses, followed by a period; include the year, then a comma, followed by the month and day.

Title of the article: The first word and proper nouns of title and subtitle are capitalized; no italics or quotation marks.

Krauss, C.   (2002, July 15).   Nova Scotians breathe life into a dying language.   *New York*

Times,   p. A4.

Title of newspaper: Italicized, with all important words capitalized; followed by a comma.

Pages: Preceded by the abbreviation *p.* or *pp.*

For newspaper articles the date includes the month and day, along with the year, in parentheses; for monthly magazines, include only the year and month. Notice, too, that the page numbers are preceded by an abbreviation, unlike the entry for a journal article.

If you were citing a newspaper article that you retrieved from an online database, such as *LexisNexis*, your entry would look like this:

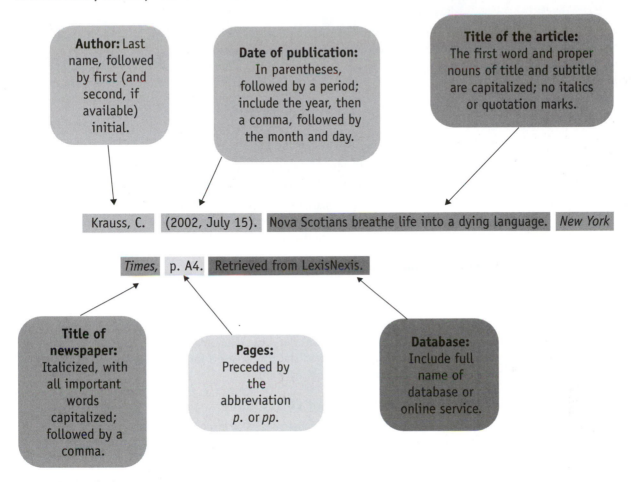

A. BOOK WITH ONE AUTHOR

Fisher, L. (2008). *Rock, paper, scissors: Game theory in everyday life*. New York: Basic Books.

Note that the author's first name is indicated only by an initial. Capital letters are used only for the first word of the title and the first word of the subtitle if there is one. (But when a proper name appears within a title, it retains the capitalization it would normally receive; for example: *A history of ideas in Brazil*.) The name of the publisher, Humanity Books, is given in its entirety. A period comes after the parentheses surrounding the date of publication and after the title and the publisher.

B. BOOK WITH TWO OR MORE AUTHORS

Blitz, M., & Hurlbert, C. M. (1998). *Letters for the living: Teaching writing in a violent age*. Urbana, IL: National Council for Teachers of English.

An ampersand (&) is used to separate the names of two authors. When there are three or more authors, separate their names with commas, keeping each name reversed, and put an ampersand immediately before the last author's name.

C. EDITED BOOK

Street, B. V. (Ed.). (2001). *Literacy and development: Ethnographic perspectives*. New York: Routledge.

The abbreviation for editor is *Ed.;* it should be capitalized and included within parentheses between the name of the editor and the date of publication. Note that a period is placed after the closing parenthesis. The abbreviation for editors is *Eds*. Give the names of all editors, no matter how many there are.

D. ARTICLE OR CHAPTER IN AN EDITED BOOK

Faigley, L. (1999). Beyond imagination: The internet and global digital literacy. In G. E. Hawisher & C. L. Selfe (Eds.), *Passions, pedagogies, and 21st-century technologies* (pp. 129–139). Logan, UT: Utah State University Press.

Notice that the editor's name is not inverted. Notice, too, that the title of the article or chapter is *not* placed in quotation marks. Use a comma to separate the editor from the title of the edited book. The pages of the article are placed in parentheses immediately after the book title. Use *p.* for page and *pp.* for pages.

E. TRANSLATED BOOK

Calasso, R. (1993). *The marriage of Cadmus and Harmony* (T. Parks, Trans.). New York: Random. (Original work published 1988).

Within parentheses immediately after the book title, give the translator's name followed by a comma and the abbreviation *Trans*. If the original work was published earlier, include this information in parentheses at the end of the entry.

F. SUBSEQUENT EDITIONS OF A BOOK

Hopkins, B. R. (1993). *A legal guide to starting and managing a nonprofit organization* (2nd ed.). New York: Wiley.

The edition is identified immediately after the title. Note that edition is abbreviated *ed.*—with a lowercase "e"—and should not be confused with *Ed.* for editor; it is also placed in parentheses, which are followed by a period.

G. BOOK WITH A CORPORATE AUTHOR

American Red Cross. (1993). *Standard first aid*. St. Louis, MO: Mosby.

H. MULTIVOLUME WORK

Eisenstein, E. (1979). *The printing press as an agent of change: Communications and cultural transformations in early-modern Europe* (Vol. 2). Cambridge, England: Cambridge University Press.

The volume number is included within parentheses immediately after the title and followed by a period.

I. JOURNAL ARTICLE WITH ONE AUTHOR

Butler, A. C. (1996). The effect of welfare benefit levels on poverty among single-parent families. *Social Problems, 43,* 94–115.

Do not use quotation marks around the article title. Capitalize and italicize the journal title. Put a comma after the journal title and then give the volume and page numbers. Note that abbreviations are not used for "volume" and "page." The volume number is italicized (but not the page numbers), and a comma is placed between it and the page numbers.

J. JOURNAL ARTICLE WITH MORE THAN ONE AUTHOR

Nugent, J. K., Lester, B. M., Greene, S. M., Wieczorek-Deering, D., & O'Mahoney, P. (1996). The effects of maternal alcohol consumption and cigarette smoking during pregnancy on acoustic cry analysis. *Child Development, 67,* 1806–1815.

Note that all authors' names are listed in the same format: last name followed by a comma and then the first (and second, if available) initial; commas separate all names.

K. JOURNAL ARTICLE PAGINATED ANEW IN EACH ISSUE

Major, B. (1993). Gender, entitlement, and the distribution of family labor. *Journal of Social Issues, 49*(3), 141–159.

When each issue of a journal begins with page 1, include the issue number (in this case, 3) in parentheses immediately after the italicized volume number (49). Do not italicize the issue number.

L. ARTICLE FROM A MAGAZINE ISSUED MONTHLY

Baker, K. (1997, February). Searching the window into nature's soul. *Smithsonian, 745,* 94–104.

Include the month of issue after the year of publication in parentheses immediately after the author's name. Include the volume number after the title of the publication, followed by a comma. Follow the same form for an article in a weekly magazine issued on a specific day, but add the day after the month:

Meacham, J. (2010, January 11). The case for an optimistic stoicism. *Newsweek, 155,* 7.

M. ARTICLE FROM A DAILY NEWSPAPER

Bishop, J. E. (1996, November 13). Heart disease may actually be rising. *The Wall Street Journal,* p. B6.

Place the exact date of issue within parentheses immediately after the author. After the newspaper title, specify the page number(s). Include *The* if it is part of the newspaper title.

N. GOVERNMENT DOCUMENT

U.S. Department of Labor. (1993). *Teaching the scans competencies.* Washington, DC: U.S. Government Printing Office.

List the agency that produced the document as the author if no author is identified. Within parentheses immediately after the document title, give the publication number (which is assigned to the document by the government), if available.

O. ANONYMOUS WORK

A breath of fresh air. (1991, April 29). *Time, 187,* 49.

Alphabetize the work under the first important word in the title (in this case, "breath"), and follow the form for the type of publication in question (in this case, a magazine published weekly).

P. JOURNAL ARTICLE RETRIEVED ONLINE

If you are citing an article from a print journal that you accessed online, cite the article as you would a print article but include the URL where you accessed the article, as follows:

Smith, K. (2001). Critical conversations in difficult times. *English Education, 33*(2), 153–165. Retrieved from http://www.ncte.org/pdfs/subscribers-only/ee/0332-jan01/EE0332Critical.pdf

Notice that there is no period after the URL. You do not need to include the date when you retrieved the article.

Q. ONLINE JOURNAL ARTICLE

For an article from a journal that appears only online (and not in print form), include the date of access and the URL of the site where the article was located:

Lassonde, C. A. (2002). Learning from others: Literacy perspectives of middle-school English teachers. *Networks,* 5(3). Retrieved from http://www.oise.utoronto.ca/~ctd/networks/journal/Vol%205(3).2002dec/Lassonde.html

R. INTERVIEW

Interviews are not considered recoverable data and should not be included in the References. If you are using material from an interview you conducted or an e-mail or personal letter you received, you should indicate that in the body of your paper, including the name of the person you interviewed or who sent you the message in parentheses.

S. PERIODICAL ARTICLE RETRIEVED FROM AN ONLINE DATABASE

If you cite an article from a print journal that you accessed through an online database, such as *EBSCO*, indicate your source as follows:

> Jones, C., & Hathaway, A. D. (2008). Medical marijuana and Canadian physicians: Challenges to meaningful drug policy reform. *Contemporary Justice Review, 11*(2), 165-175. Retrieved from *EBSCO: Academic Search Complete*

However, if the online publication has a Digital Object Identifier, or DOI, which is a number assigned to electronic articles (intended to be more permanent than a URL), you replace the name of the database with the DOI, as follows:

> Jones, C., & Hathaway, A. D. (2008). Medical marijuana and Canadian physicians: Challenges to meaningful drug policy reform. *Contemporary Justice Review, 11*(2), 165-175. doi: 10.1080/10282580802058429

Note that there is no period after the name of the database or the DOI.

T. ARTICLE FROM AN ONLINE REFERENCE WORK

Articles from an online reference such as an encyclopedia are cited in the same way as a print article except that you must indicate the URL where you found the article and the date you found it:

> Flynn, B. (2004). Maurice Merleau-Ponty. *Stanford Encyclopedia of Philosophy*. Retrieved January 22, 2010, from http://plato.stanford.edu

In this example, the date of publication appears in parentheses after the author's name. but the date of access is added after the title of the encyclopedia. There is no period after the URL.

If the article you are citing has no author, begin the entry with the title. If there is no date of publication, indicate that by including "n.d." in the parentheses.

A Checklist for Documentation

1. Remember to document any direct quotation, any idea that has come from someone else's work, and any fact or statistic that is not widely known. **2.** Be sure to enclose all quotations in quotation marks. **3.** Make sure that paraphrases are in your own words but still accurately reflect the content of the original material. **4.** Remember that every source cited in your text should have a corresponding entry in the bibliography. **5.** Try to vary the introductions you use for quotations and paraphrases. **6.** When you mention authorities by name, try to identify who they are so that your audience can evaluate the source (for example, "According to Ira Glasser, Executive Director of the American Civil Liberties Union, recent congressional legislation violates . . ."). However, you need not identify well-known figures. **7.** If in doubt about whether to document a source, you would probably be wise to document it. But be careful not to overdocument your paper.

Preparing Your Final Draft

After investing considerable time in researching, drafting, and revising your paper, be sure to allow sufficient time for editing your final draft. If you rush this stage of the process, the work that you submit for evaluation might not adequately reflect the investment of time you gave to the project as a whole. Unless instructed otherwise, you should be guided by the rules in the following checklist.

A Checklist for Manuscript Form

You should always check with your instructor about the format for submitting assigned papers, but here are some general guidelines to follow:

1. Papers should be typed or word processed. Use nonerasable 8 1/2-by-11-inch white paper. Type on one side of each page. Double-space all lines, leaving a margin of one inch on all sides. **2.** In the upper left corner of page 1 or on a separate title page, include the following information: your name, your instructor's name, the course and section number, and the date the essay is submitted. **3.** Number each page in the upper right corner. If using MLA-style documentation, type your last name immediately before the page number. If using APA-style documentation, type a shortened version of the title (one or two words) before the number. **4.** Make sure that you consistently follow a documentation style that is acceptable to your instructor. **5.** Any quotation of more than four lines in an MLA-style paper or more than forty words in an APA-style paper should be set off from the rest of the text. Begin a new line, indenting one inch (or ten spaces) to form the left margin of the quotation. The indention means that you are quoting, so additional quotation marks are unnecessary in this case (except for quotations within the quotation). **6.** Proofread your paper carefully. If your instructor allows ink corrections, make them as neatly as you can. Redo any page that has numerous or lengthy corrections. **7.** If you have used a word processor for your paper, be sure to separate pages that have been printed on a continuous sheet. Use a paper clip or staple to bind the pages together.

Negotiating Differences

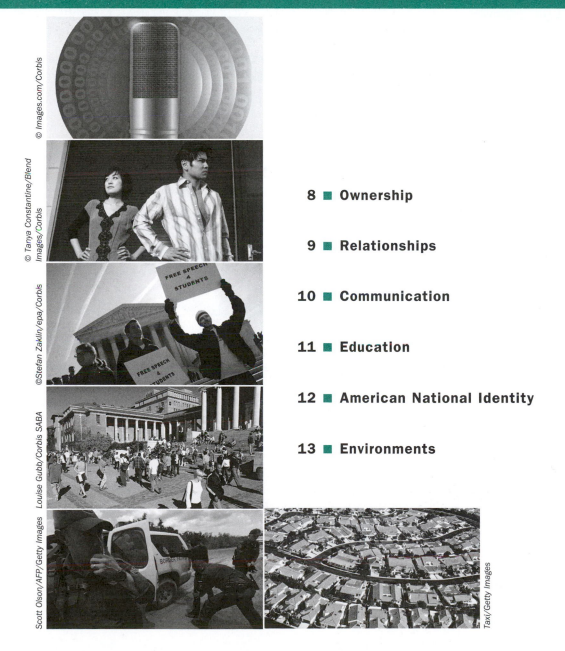

© Images.com/Corbis

© Tanya Constantine/Blend Images/Corbis

©Stefan Zaklin/epa/Corbis

Louise Gubb/Corbis SABA

Scott Olson/AFP/Getty Images

Taxi/Getty Images

8

Ownership

© Images.com/Corbis

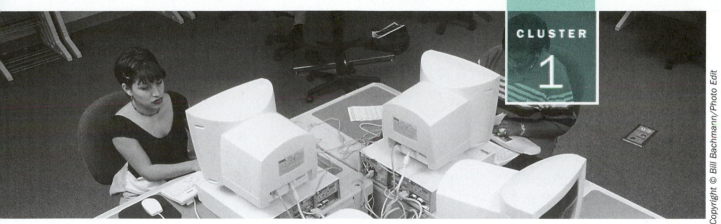

Who Owns Words and Ideas?

For students, plagiarism is usually a straightforward matter: If you present someone else's words or ideas as your own, you have plagiarized. In most schools, if you are caught doing so, the consequences can be severe, including even dismissal from school. The whole matter of plagiarism rests on an assumption that each of us has our own ideas and is responsible for our own words. In this sense, we "own" those words and ideas; we "own" our intellectual work. And we're not allowed to "steal" others' words or ideas. But the ownership of intellectual work—the matter of intellectual property—is not as straightforward as it might seem, especially in this age of digital media. It's easy to see plagiarism when a student hands in a paper written by someone else; in effect, that student is submitting as his or her own someone else's intellectual property. But what if you asked a roommate or a relative for help with an essay you are writing for one of your classes? What if that person suggested a way for you to reword a few sentences or a paragraph? Or maybe that person advised you to reorganize your essay to make it more coherent and effective? If you did so and then submitted your essay to your teacher, is that essay yours? Or does it belong partly to the room-mate or relative who helped you? Who owns the ideas and words in that essay? ■ This example suggests how difficult it can be to determine the source—or "owner"—of an idea or a phrase. It also suggests how little of what we tend to think of as our own intellectual work really is the result of an exclusively individual effort. It's common to ask a friend how a sentence sounds when you are writing an essay or a letter. It's also common for students to work together on projects, problems, or laboratory experiments. And if it's common for students to do so, it's even more common for professionals in many fields. Scientists rarely work alone, and even those who do usually draw on the previous experiments of other scientists. The same is true of professionals in every kind of field or business. Collaboration is the norm in many settings. And when people collaborate, the matter of whose intellectual property results becomes complicated. ■ Moreover, the ideas that are available to us often come from somewhere else altogether. For example, if you are writing a poem about an ill-fated romance, where did the idea for that poem come from? From your experience? From your imagination? From a movie you happened to see? From a story a friend told you? From a post on someone's

Facebook page? Is it wrong to write a poem on the basis of someone else's idea and then present the poem to readers as your work? Are you "stealing" someone else's intellectual property because you have read dozens of love poems written by others? And if you write that poem in an established poetic format, such as a sonnet, are you stealing that format because you didn't create it yourself? ■ Intellectual property is not just an ethical matter; it is a legal and economic matter as well. The U.S. Constitution provides for the establishment of copyright laws to protect the creators of intellectual property. Copyright protection has existed since 1790, when Congress first passed a law decreeing that an author or artist "owned" a work he or she created for fourteen years. But even when intellectual property is defined legally, questions inevitably arise about who owns specific words or ideas and who has the right to use them. The idea of the "fair use" of copyrighted materials, for example, allows scholars to a limited portion of someone else's published work without seeking permission. But even when such a principle is spelled out in the legal code, it can never answer all questions that might arise when determining who owns specific words or a specific idea. ■ Despite these difficulties, the fact that we live in a culture based on private property often means that we have to try to determine the ownership of intellectual property. The authors of the essays in this section all address this need as it emerges in schools and in the commercial culture. They examine questions of the ownership of words and ideas in ways that may help you appreciate the complexity of intellectual property and consider the many interests that people have in trying to determine who owns words and ideas. As a group, these essays also raise a broader question about intellectual property: Is it really possible for anyone to "own" words or ideas?

CON-TEXT

What Is Fair Use?

1 Congress favored nonprofit educational uses over commercial uses. Copies used in education, but made or sold at monetary profit, may not be favored. Courts also favor uses that are "transformative" or that are not mere reproductions. Fair use is more likely when the copyrighted work is "transformed" into something new or of new utility, such as quotations incorporated into a paper, and perhaps pieces of a work mixed into a multimedia product for your own teaching needs or

included in commentary or criticism of the original. For teaching purposes, however, multiple copies of some works are specifically allowed, even if not "transformative." The Supreme Court underscored that conclusion by focusing on these key words in the statute: "including multiple copies for classroom use." . . .

Many characteristics of a work can affect the application of fair use. For example, several recent court decisions have concluded that the unpublished

"nature" of historical correspondence can weigh against fair use. The courts reasoned that copyright owners should have the right to determine the circumstances of "first publication." The authorities are split, however, on whether a published work that is currently out of print should receive special treatment. Courts more readily favor the fair use of nonfiction rather than fiction.

SOURCE: "What is 'Fair Use'?" The Consortium for Educational Technology for University Systems.

① **Standing Up for the Power of Learning**

In the fall of 2001, a student at the Georgia Institute of Technology was accused of cheating because he had discussed an assignment in his computer science course with a friend. By talking about the assignment, the student violated an honor code in that course that prohibits collaboration among students. According to that honor code, "at no time is it acceptable for you to share your solutions to the homework assignments with other students, whether these solutions are complete or partial, nor is it acceptable to compare your solutions with other students." On the surface, such a stipulation might seem reasonable, because students are usually graded on their own ability to do the required work in a course. But as Jay Mathews suggests in the following essay, a closer look at this case raises some tricky questions. For one thing, is it cheating if a student learns by working with a classmate? Do students always learn by themselves? And if a student learns by getting help from someone else, does that mean that the work the student submits to a teacher—such as the solution to a problem in computer science—does not "belong" to that student? In writing about the incident at Georgia Tech, and in praising that university's willingness to change its policy as a result of the incident, Mathews argues for a position on cheating that tries to hold students accountable for doing their own work yet acknowledges the reality that learning is often not an exclusively individual activity. As you read, consider whether Mathews's position on this issue is realistic. Is it possible to distinguish between collaboration and cheating in the way he suggests? Do schools have any choice but to do so? Mathews reports on education for the *Washington Post* and is the author of *Class Struggles: What's Right (and Wrong) with America's Best Public Schools* (1998). This essay appeared in his column in the *Washington Post* in 2002.

JAY MATHEWS, "Standing Up for the Power of Learning"

1 I am barely capable of booting up my office computer in the morning. One of those neighborhood computer consultants just paid a house call because I can't get my new CD burner even to acknowledge my existence. But that did not stop me from telling Georgia Tech in a recent column how to monitor homework in its freshman course, **Computer Science 1321.**

I had help from one of the students in the course, a graduate of one of the Washington area's best high schools, who had the dis- agreeable experience of finding this e-mail addressed to him just before he was to leave on a family skiing vacation last December: "Your name has been turned into the Associate Dean of Students, Karen Boyd, for suspicion of academic misconduct."

Computer Science 1321, Introduction to Computers, is described in the Georgia Tech catalog as follows: "Foundations of computing with an emphasis on the design, construction, and analysis of algorithms. Laboratory-based instruction to computers and software tools."

A computer check designed to catch cheaters had found similarity between his answers and that of a classmate with whom he had discussed a CS 1321 homework assignment. He had worked hard to earn a B in a course that had started disastrously for him. He could have punted the assignment. It was only 2 percent of his grade. But he wanted to get ready for the final exam. He was eager to learn, which was his big mistake.

The CS 1321 honor code said "at no time is it acceptable for you to share your solutions to the homework assignments with other students, whether these solutions are complete or partial, nor is it acceptable to compare your solutions with other students." Students complained of the reign of terror atmosphere the rule encouraged—don't say anything to anybody because if your approach pops up on their homework, you're screwed.

5 My informant thought it made no sense for the course to prohibit students from working together and from consulting outside materials when dealing with difficult homework assignments. He thought his discussion with a classmate was useful discourse that could only make them better students. And now, it turns out, he was right. Acting like the great university it is, Georgia Tech ordered a study of the course. With astonishing speed, it announced Thursday that it was changing the rules in just the way the freshman told me they ought to be changed.

News stories on the university's announcement missed the importance of this. They emphasized that three fourths of the 187 Georgia Tech students accused of cheating on CS 1321 homework last fall were found guilty and punished with everything from a zero on the assignment to suspension. Everybody knew weeks ago that was going to happen. Many freshmen, like my informant, accepted the university's strong recommendation that they swallow their punishment, in his case a C in the course, and move on, even though they felt they had done nothing wrong.

Other universities, such as MIT, do not prohibit students from working together on difficult assignments. They are simply required to mark the places where they collaborated. That makes sense to me. Every successful educational enterprise I know encourages student discussion and cooperation. The anti-collaboration rule was even unusual for Georgia Tech, and only found in that freshman course. I suggested the computerized copying checks be reserved for tests, the proper place to determine what a student has learned. Forcing undergraduates to watch what they say to friends about their homework sounded too much like the rules for discourse in the Chinese universities I used to visit.

The column produced an extraordinary volume of e-mail. That was another sign of my ignorance. I had no idea there were so many people interested in this stuff. (Some messages also discussed my peculiar views on cheating, a separate issue which I will take up in a future column.)

COLLABORATIVE LEARNING

Also referred to as "cooperative learning," collaborative learning has been extensively studied by education researchers. Although there are different kinds of collaborative learning and there is disagreement among scholars on some of the specifics of such learning, most agree that collaborative learning benefits students. Many studies show positive results—including higher academic achievement—when students work together. According to Roger T. Johnson and David Johnson, researchers who have studied cooperative learning, "The fact that working together to achieve a common goal produces higher achievement and greater productivity than does working alone is so well confirmed by so much research that it stands as one of the strongest principles of social and organizational psychology. Cooperative learning is indicated whenever learning goals are highly important, mastery and retention are important, a task is complex or conceptual, problem solving is desired, divergent thinking or creativity is desired, quality of performance is expected, and higher-level reasoning strategies and critical thinking are needed" ("Cooperative Learning: An Overview").

Interestingly, the students, teachers and experts who sent the e-mails were split evenly on the no-collaboration and no-outside-materials rules. Stephen Miller, a senior technical specialist for FleetBoston Financial, said, "Restricting student access to resources in their effort to maximize their learning potential is simply unbelievable. Decreeing that the only valid resources are Georgia Tech staff or course materials is the height of arrogance. To forbid Computer Science students from seeking any help from other students on their homework is to remove one of the prime and fundamental learning tools. Collaboration and cooperation, especially in the computer science field, is one of the tried and true ways of advancement and improvement."

© Monkey Business Images. Used under license from Shutterstock.com

10 But Meredith Skeels, an undergraduate at the University of Washington, said it was vitally important to struggle through your coding assignments on your own, at least while you are learning. "Programming is all about problem solving," she said. "I will be the first to say that it can be very frustrating when you just cannot get the code to work. It drives you crazy. You walk to class thinking about it and you wake up in the morning thinking of some new way to fix it. That is part of the process that makes you a good programmer."

I had expected Georgia Tech to appoint a committee, give it several months to work up some recommendations, and then stick the results in a drawer until the dean in charge pulled them out to read during a vacation as an excuse to limit conversation with his mother-in-law. That is the way such matters would be handled by some of our better known liberal arts universities, the ones thick with Georgian architecture and administrators who used to be lawyers, economists or English professors. I figured it would be a year before any decisions were made, long after most people had forgotten the cheating charges of 2001.

CONTEXT

As of fall 2002, the collaboration policy in Computer Science 1321 at Georgia Tech stated, "Because homework assignments are now not used for assessment, we can now greatly relax the constraints on collaboration with respect to these assignments. Effective this semester, any and all forms of collaboration between students in CS 1321 are permitted, including the sharing of solutions if that is what is needed for a student to learn to develop a working solution to a given homework problem.... As has always been the case, however, plagiarism is not allowed. If you use sources other than those provided for everyone in the course (i.e., instructors, teaching assistants, the textbook, the course website, the course newsgroups, the lectures, or the recitations), you must give appropriate credit to those sources. Note that so long as you give credit where credit is due, your grade will not be affected nor will you be charged with academic misconduct. On the other hand, a failure to give appropriate credit to sources of help (other than course materials or personnel as noted above) will be treated as plagiarism, a violation of Georgia Tech's Student Conduct Code."

Imagine my shock to learn Thursday that Georgia Tech's task force on introductory computer science courses had already made its recommendations, and many had been implemented immediately. It must be nice to have engineers in charge. They seem more interested in getting things done than making certain all the bureaucratic niceties are observed.

In its report, the task force acknowledged that "individual programming skills are the foundation upon which successful group programming projects are based" but "we also know that collaboration supports learning." The nine-member group said "many of us have had the experience of having a 'bug' in our program, explaining the program to another person in hopes that he or she might tell us what is wrong, and in the process of explaining, suddenly understanding why the program does not work!"

The most feasible way to check on student programming skills, the report said, was interactive testing in a computer lab. As for homework in **CS 1321,** it recommended that "any and all kinds of collaboration be allowed . . . including sharing portions of others' programs if that is what is needed for a student to learn to develop a working solution to the assignment." Using such help, as well as outside sources, would be fine "so long as attribution is made."

15 And that, said Bob McMath, a member of the task force and the vice-provost for undergraduate studies, is the way it is going to be, starting right now. "This incident has caused the Georgia Tech community to look closely at the way we teach and the way we hold each other accountable for our actions," he said in a statement. "Because of the serious and thoughtful efforts of many people, I believe that we are coming out of this experience a stronger and better university."

The freshman who told me his story still declines to be identified and is not happy that the university has not wiped clean the records of the many students who, he feels, were punished for doing the best job they could under rules that made no sense.

"I do not like the idea that for the rest of my academic career I will have to explain what happened to me," he said. He is so sour on Georgia Tech that he is transferring to another school, but he said he is "glad that the policy is changed for all of the students that are now going to take the computer science courses."

I think the freshman, and the many parents, students, teachers and alumni who protested the non-collaboration rule, should be proud of standing up for the power of learning from one's peers. And I can think of several other universities who might benefit from studying how Georgia Tech handled this. Its administrators wasted no time in disassembling the trouble-prone course, examining each of its parts, and putting it back together in a way that will help young people come to understand the mysteries of the digital world with a minimum of confusion and trauma.

Questions for Discussion

1. Why do you think Mathews begins this essay by admitting that he hired a consultant to help him with his computer? How does that anecdote relate to his overall argument?

2. Mathews includes quotations from two e-mail messages he received from readers of his column. What purpose do these messages serve in his argument? Assess the effectiveness of these e-mail messages as evidence.

3. Why is Mathews "shocked" when he learns that Georgia Tech quickly addressed the issue of collaboration raised by this incident? What does his reaction suggest about his opinion of universities? Do you agree with him? Why or why not?

4. Consider your own experiences with collaborative learning, either in school or in some other setting where you worked with others. Have those experiences been beneficial to you? Explain. How might those experiences influence the way you respond to Mathews's views about collaboration? What pros and cons can you see in collaborative learning?

5. Do you think the original collaboration policy for Computer Science 1321 at Georgia Tech was a fair and reasonable one? Why or why not? Do you think students should always work individually? Is that possible, in your view? If so, how should that be enforced? If not, how might universities deal with cheating?

② | What's Yours? (Ownership of Intellectual Property)

RALPH CAPLAN

"It isn't always so easy to know what belongs to us." So writes Ralph Caplan in the following essay. Caplan, an expert in architectural design, is referring to ideas. More specifically, he wonders how to determine when someone owns an idea for the design of a building or a mechanical device. In raising this question, Caplan helps demonstrate that arguments about intellectual property are not limited to words, music, or images, which are often the focus of copyright lawsuits. Here, Caplan explores how abstract ideas for something like the design of a building can also be "owned" through copyright and patent laws. As is often the case in disputes about intellectual property, patents for designs involve money. But Caplan asks whether questions about the ownership of such ideas go beyond the matter of who is paid for them. In this sense, his essay, which was published in 1998 in *Print* magazine, suggests that arguments about intellectual property are really about the fundamental value of fairness and about how people wish to share ideas and abilities with one another. Caplan is the author of *By Design: Why There Are No Locks on the Bathroom Doors of the Hotel Louis XIV and Other Object Lessons* (1982) and *Cracking the Whip: Essays on Design and Its Side Effects* (2006).

RALPH CAPLAN, "What's Yours? (Ownership of Intellectual Property)"

Victor Papanek (1926-1998) was a renowned and sometimes controversial expert in architectural design. In his groundbreaking book *Design for the Real World: Human Ecology and Social Change* (1971), he questioned conventional beliefs about industrial and architectural design and argued for an approach to design that focused on making the world a better place. His proposals for design were based on his study of indigenous peoples and their relationship to their environments. His last book, *The Green Imperative: Natural Design for the Real World* (1995), was an ardent call to designers and architects to become more environmentally conscious and for people to live in more ecologically and socially responsible ways.

1 **Victor Papanek** was our most fervent practitioner and preacher of alternative design. By the time of his death earlier this year, he had seen many of his most hotly disputed ideas become accepted design wisdom, if not design practice. One of them, however, remains fiercely controversial. Believing that "there is something basically wrong with the whole concept of patents and copyrights," Papanek declined to patent his designs. His critics scoffed that no one would bother stealing them anyway. Actually, they were ripped off in large numbers, for personal use as well as for profit. "If I design a toy that provides therapeutic exercise for handicapped children, then I think it is unjust to delay the release of the design by a year and a half, going through a patent application," Papanek wrote. "I feel that ideas are plentiful and cheap, and it is wrong to make money off the needs of others."

I don't know how money is ever made except off the needs (real or imagined) of others, but the issue here is not money but the rights to what it can't entirely buy.

The late Dr. Gerald Fagan, a resident psychiatrist at a boys' school, relieved the guilt of students who masturbated by reminding them: "It's yours, isn't it?" But it isn't always so easy to know what belongs to us. The protection, and even the identification, of what's yours has been vastly complicated by technology. As media for distributing ideas are multiplied, amplified, and reduced in price, ownership of so-called intellectual property becomes increasingly ambiguous. Even the ownership of hard goods has been softly defined for generations. In Arthur Miller's *Death of a Salesman,* Willie Loman's refrigerator and car are falling apart at the same time as he is. "Once in my life I would like to own something outright before it's broken!" Willie cries. "They time those things. They time them so when you finally paid for them, they're used up." In the audience we smile and nod in recognition, for we are an audience and a society of renters.

The rights to what we do own are subject to interpretation. When film mavens objected to Ted Turner's colorizing black-and-white movie classics, he replied, "The last time I looked, I owned them"—his way of saying he was entitled to make them all mauve if he wished, or keep anyone else from seeing them.

5 Are there public rights to private property? The nadir of my adolescence was not acne, or being turned down by May Allen for the senior prom, or even being suspended from high school. It was a strike by ASCAP—the American Society of Composers, Authors and Publishers—and until it was settled radio stations were prohibited from broadcasting music or lyrics produced by its members. I don't remember exactly how long it lasted, but for what seemed like forever the only songs we heard were in the public domain, usually by Stephen Foster. We understood dimly that the rights of creators to the material they had created were at stake, but we wanted the music back. If the concept of intellectual property was in legal vogue then, none of us would have thought it applied to "Darn That Dream" or "Flat Foot Floogie with the Floy Floy."

The inheritance of intellectual property is more problematic. The son of a vaudeville comedian, having been given his father's name at birth and taken over his father's act when the old man died, proudly advertised in the trade papers: "This act is not a copy. It is a legacy." Today, Dickensian court battles rage over whether families own in perpetuity the images of their celebrity ancestors. I love a Gershwin tune, but if I can't play one without paying, whom do I pay? Not George and Ira, who have no further use for royalties. The Gershwin Family Trust? Well, why not? If families can inherit money, why shouldn't they inherit cultural resources that can be turned into money?

One reason is that cultural resources not only enrich us but enrich each other through us. Our copyright laws have always acknowledged this by providing only temporary coverage, after which the private holdings become **public domain**. But temporary anything has a way of becoming at least semipermanent. Copyright law has been extended over the years, and there is a good chance it will now be extended for another two decades. (Had that been in effect during the ASCAP revolt of my youth, nothing but Baroque would have been public domain.) A Gershwin trustee warned that without such protection, "someone could turn Porgy and Bess, into rap music." A dreadful prospect, I guess, but folklorist Steve Zeitlin, noting that Gershwin's opera itself drew on African-American musical traditions, asks, "What could be more appropriate?" Zeitlin finds it similarly ironic that Disney, having used "Snow White" and other public domain materials for major productions, anxiously seeks to protect forever the sanctity of Mickey Mouse, which strikes some people as a Mickey Mouse idea.

Designers know the danger of letting work go unprotected—the danger not only of theft by competitors but of erosion through the negligence of managers who can't see, don't care, or have designs (and designers) of their own. The elaborate graphics standards manuals, devised as security systems, have often been ineffective because the people who understood them were not in control of their implementation.

Intellectual property implies the commodification of what cannot be commodified. If we protect it, why not protect emotional property as well? When William Styron wrote about the Nat Turner uprising, blacks challenged his right to write about the slave experience, on the grounds that it belonged to them collectively and exclusively. A comparable possessiveness attaches to the Holocaust as a phenomenon uniquely applicable to Jews but not to the Gypsies and gays who were also sent to Nazi death camps, or to the Armenians and Rwandans slaughtered at other times under other auspices. When David Leavitt based a novel on the homoerotic autobiographical writing of Stephen Spender, the elderly poet sued, telling Leavitt to get his own sex life instead of appropriating someone else's old one.

The term *public domain* refers to the status of a creative work or invention that is not protected by copyright or patent law and is freely available to anyone to use or copy. A work is considered to be "in the public domain" if the creator or inventor does not properly register it for copyright or patent protection or if that protection expires.

American philosopher **Suzanne Langer** (1895–1985) was well known for her ideas about aesthetics and for her writings about language and music. She believed that music was a form of expression of human feelings that cannot adequately be expressed in language.

10 But Leavitt was writing fiction, in which personal experience may be transferable. In Charles Williams's *Descent into Hell*, Pauline tells Peter about a recurring event that terrifies her. He can't do anything about the recurring event, but he offers to carry the fear for her, just as he would carry a parcel or her books. It's still her fear, he explains, but with him as designated schlepper, she won't have to do the fearing.

No one has yet copyrighted an idiosyncrasy or patented a neurosis, but James Thurber has shown us the way: A character in a Thurber story steals another man's dream. Another character in a Thurber cartoon has a friend accompany him to the doctor's office, where he registers the unprecedented medical complaint, "I've got Bright's disease and he's got mine."

"What's mine is yours" is the posture of a saint. "What's yours is mine" is the ideology of a mugger. Frankly, I do not know how to reconcile them. I think I understand rights and privileges in respect to owning things—whether one-of-a-kind or mass produced. If I find a rock, it's mine. If I fashion it into a tool, it is more decisively mine, because my hands shaped it and my imagination told them how. If it is mine, then, because I am no saint, it is not yours. You therefore have been served with a moral injunction not to covet my rock and a criminal code forbidding you to take it if you do covet it. However, if I give it to you or leave it to you, the rock is yours, with all the rights and privileges pertaining thereto.

Thereto is the rub. What rights and privileges pertain to the rocks in your head? And where do they go when your head is gone? Some things that are yours are part of you. No one can take them from you, but it hurts when they try. To be plagiarized is, as Steve Heller indicated recently in *PRINT*, to be "violated." This can be accomplished with dazzling chutzpah, as when someone overseas used a couple of pages from an article of mine without attribution, then quoted an additional paragraph from the same article, as if I had written it, which of course I had. Thus he put me in the curious position of agreeing with myself.

Sometimes what looks like plagiarism is simply coincidence. But not all coincidence is entirely coincidental. After driving to Wesleyan University to hear the brilliant **Suzanne Langer** lecture on signs and symbols, I was disappointed to find that she really had nothing more to say on the subject than I had already said in a lecture of my own. Driving home, I figured out why. My ideas were as good as hers because they were hers to start with! I had absorbed them from reading her books.

Questions for Discussion

1. Caplan argues that music and stage acts are cultural resources that should be available to the public. What support does he offer for this point? How persuasive do you think Caplan is on this point?

2. Caplan writes, "Intellectual property implies the commodification of what cannot be commodified." What does he mean by that statement? In what way is that statement important to his main argument?

3. What examples does Caplan offer as evidence of the ambiguity of determining the ownership of intellectual property? How effective do you think these examples are in illustrating his point?

4. Summarize Caplan's main point in this essay. How does his anecdote of attending a lecture by Suzanne Langer reinforce this main point? Do you agree with Caplan? Why or why not? What counterarguments could you offer in response to his position?

5. Caplan's essay might be seen as an example of an argument to inquire (see pages xx–xx). Evaluate its effectiveness as such an argument. Does his argument help clarify the issues related to intellectual property rights that he addresses? Explain.

③ Copyright Crusaders

DAVID GIBSON

An award-winning writer who focuses on religious issues, David Gibson worked in Rome for Vatican Radio and has produced television documentaries about Catholicism for CNN. "Copyright Crusaders" was originally published by *Fortune* in May 2005, a widely distributed magazine on business. *Fortune* was created by Henry Luce, who also created *Time* magazine and *Sports Illustrated*. Keep this in mind as you read what Gibson has to say about the intersection of faith and business. In his essay, Gibson examines how a religious story of questionable origin has provoked a battle for the revenues generated through the sale of products such as greeting cards and coffee mugs. By doing so, Gibson demonstrates how concerns about "ownership"—in this case an issue of "intellectual property"—are so pervasive today that they occur in unexpected situations. Because of the copyright controversy reported by Gibson, the religious poem in question is not reprinted here. But if you are not already familiar with it, Gibson's opening paragraph will help you understand what it involves. (This opening paragraph is a good example of a writer using summary in his argument. See pages 155–156 for a discussion of summary.)

DAVID GIBSON, "Copyright Crusaders"

1 In the warm and frothy bubble bath that is American spirituality today, it's hard to think of anything quite as familiar and comforting as the mini-homily known as "Footprints in the Sand." For anyone who has somehow managed to avoid the gantlet of Footprints mugs, calendars, greeting cards, and mousepads—to name just a few of its incarnations—the poem is a soft-focus retrospective that imagines life as a walk on the beach with Jesus, a pilgrimage traced by two sets of footprints, the Savior's and the narrator's. The reverie is interrupted by the narrator's shock that at his lowest moments there was just a single set of footprints, indicating that Jesus had bolted when he was needed most. Catharsis comes with the Lord's soothing assurance that he did not abandon his follower during the dark night. Rather, there was only one set of prints because "it was then that I carried you." Or as Jesus put it elsewhere, "O ye of little faith."

The story can be read generously as a haiku of Christian belief vanquishing doubt, or perhaps as proof that there is more unalloyed emotion in religion than in any other field of human expression. But this being America, you can't get something for nothing, and that goes for piety as much as widgets. Hence the rather unseemly legal wrangling over this irenic tale, which is pitting three main contenders (there are apparently dozens of pretenders) for the right to claim authorship of "Footprints"—along with millions of dollars in licensing fees on all those Footprints tchotchkes.

The three claimants are the estate of Mary Stevenson, who died in 1999 at age 76 and said she wrote a version of the poem in 1936 in Chester, Pa.; Margaret Fishback Powers, a poet and co-founder of a children's ministry in Canada, who says she composed "Footprints" in 1964; and Carolyn Carty, a New Jersey woman and self-described "child prodigy" who says she wrote her version in 1963 when she was 6.

Go figure. Each author copyrighted her version (they differ in small details, most significantly in Carty's use of the third person over the first person of the other two), and each has a different tale of the story's genesis. Stevenson told her biographer she was a 14-year-old Philadelphia showgirl during the Depression when she was locked out of her house on a wintry night and was inspired by the sight of a cat leaving paw prints in the snow. Powers cites a stroll on an Ontario beach with her prospective husband during a troubled time in their lives as her inspiration. And Carty's **donnée** was the death of her grandfather; her role models, she says, were Longfellow and John F. Kennedy.

5 Powers has been most successful in marketing "Footprints." She has signed licensing agreements with Hallmark cards and wrote a 1993 book about the poem, along with a series of devotionals. But Carty told Beliefnet. com, which has a lengthy and illuminating column on the competing claims, that she is planning to sue Powers for infringement while at the same time seeking redress from companies that have used her copyrighted version. "I figure they owe me at least $500,000 in back royalties," she told Beliefnet in regard to one calendar maker. Royalties for Stevenson's version were the subject of a six-year legal battle between her son and a friend who for years had sold Footprints products and signed licensing agreements on the late claimant's behalf.

The legal maneuverings and marketing campaigns and megabucks deals are enough to make one yearn for the innocent moralism of "Footprints" itself, yet the story is depressingly familiar. In America today, God is too often turned into **mammon**, and it seems no good deed—or inspirational thought—goes unsold, no profit uncontested.

Even religious teachings are becoming a source of copyright infringement battles rather than universal enlightenment. In an article in *Buffalo Law Review*, a professor at Washington College of Law, Walter Effross, has detailed how many religious groups, especially New Age ones, have sought legal recourse to classify their teachings as "intellectual property" that cannot be used by others without permission. Among the justifications for spiritual secrecy that Effross identifies is the claim that people who use teachings without proper supervision could suffer psychological harm. In other words, "Don't try this at home."

Effross cites the case of the Arica Institute, which created the nine-pointed enneagram personality test based on what it says was ancient wisdom, and has sued Jesuits who often use the enneagram as an evaluation tool for novices. He also describes how a religious group known as Star's Edge has sought to prevent the unauthorized use of its Avatar courses. These groups are even using nondisclosure agreements so that students do not share what they learn.

The problem for many of these religions, Effross says, is that their "teachings" are often so profound or so mundane that they contain "near-universal elements" that cannot be copyrighted. Not surprisingly, there is nothing new under the sun (that's Ecclesiastes, not me) when it comes to spiritual insight, and so piety increasingly becomes a matter of repackaging products in different forms—old wine in new wineskins, to upend another bit of holy writ—and then zealously guarding them to maintain your brand identity and market share.

10 It wasn't always this way. Take the Serenity Prayer: "God, give us grace to accept with serenity the things that cannot be changed, courage to change the things that should be changed, and the wisdom to distinguish the one from the other." Quick: Who wrote it? A common answer is St. Francis, while some trace it back to Cicero or Sanskrit texts. Others attribute

A **donnée** is a set of assumptions or premises on which a literary work is based.

Mammon, a term that appears in the New Testament of the Bible, is often translated as "riches" or "wealth." It is also used to refer to a devil-like entity associated with the pursuit of wealth.

it to an 18th-century German pietist, **Friedrich Oetinger**, which might account for its regular appearance beside Dürer's "Praying Hands" engraving.

The correct answer is Reinhold Niebuhr, the great 20th-century Protestant theologian, although even he conceded his inspiration could have gone back further. Niebuhr said he wrote the prayer in 1943 as a "tag line" to a sermon. He had no interest in copyrighting anything that could be dispersed widely to provide comfort to others, so when Alcoholics Anonymous approached him about using the Serenity Prayer, he quickly agreed. AA has made the prayer a hallmark of its philosophy, while Hallmark cards, and many others, have made the prayer into cash in the form of refrigerator magnets, teddy bears, serving trays, and the like.

Likewise, the ubiquitous WWJD slogan ("What would Jesus do?") never brought any fortune to its author, Charles M. Sheldon, a minister who coined the phrase in an 1896 book, *In His Steps,* in which a fictional pastor uses the phrase to challenge complacent Christians. Sheldon couldn't find a publisher for the book, so he had it serialized in a local newspaper, and it fell into the public domain.

A century later when Janie Tinklenberg, a youth pastor in Michigan, rediscovered Sheldon's book, she hit upon the idea of making WWJD wristbands for the teens in her charge. The idea swept the nation, but like her predecessor, Tinklenberg did not think about merchandising first, and so she watched while retailers raked in millions on WWJD kitsch. Tinklenberg won a victory of sorts in 2000 when the U.S. Patent and Trademark Office awarded her the trademark for "WWJD." But she decided not to invest a small fortune trying to enforce her claim or to set up a manufacturing business because the phrase is already so popular in the marketplace.

And after all, isn't that where religious truths—even spiritual bromides—belong?

CONTEXT

German artist and theorist Albrecht Dürer (1471–1528) is considered one of the great painters of the Renaissance. His sketch, which is widely known today as "The Praying Hands," was a preliminary study that was originally intended to be part of a larger painting called "The Assumption and Coronation of the Virgin" or "The Adoration of the Virgin." But this detailed sketch has become perhaps Dürer's most familiar work and a part of popular culture. It is also the model for many of the kinds of commercial items, such as coffee mugs and calendars, that Gibson criticizes in this essay. This image is in the public domain, which means that anyone can use it without permission for any legal purpose, including marketing and selling religious items. According to a study published in 2010, 96 percent of Americans believe in God and approximately 84 percent are affiliated with an organized religion. Related studies show that the U.S. population is much more religious than the populations of most European nations. These figures suggest that the market for religious goods is potentially very large, which means that copyrights to certain popular religious images or texts, such as the poem that Gibson refers to at the beginning of this essay, can be lucrative.

Lambert/Getty Images

Certainly Christianity is defined by its commitment to spreading the "good news," or evangelion in Greek, the root of today's regnant Evangelicalism. And offering spiritual goods at a price has only gotten Christians in trouble in the past.

15 But historians of religion like to say that Christianity was born in the Middle East as a religion, moved to Greece and became a philosophy, journeyed to Rome and became

Friedrich Oetinger (1702–1782) is the author of numerous works on theology and philosophy. As a "pietist" he argued for the importance of attention to the Bible and individual conscience as opposed to automatic obedience to Church authority.

a legal system, spread through Europe as a culture—and when it migrated to America, Christianity became big business.

The observation is so true today that it probably belongs on a coffee mug or calendar. I just hope it's not under copyright.

Questions for Discussion

1. How would you summarize Gibson's main argument in this essay? Why is he concerned about the marketing of religious or spiritual items and pursuits?

2. Gibson cites many examples of the marketing of religious or spiritual ideas or sayings. Evaluate his use of these examples as evidence to support his main argument. How effectively do you think these examples support his claims? What other evidence does he offer?

3. This essay was originally published in *Fortune* magazine, which focuses on subjects related to business. In what ways do you think Gibson's argument might appeal to readers of this magazine? What strategies does Gibson use to address this audience?

4. Gibson devotes several paragraphs to a summary of an article by Walter Effross, a legal scholar (see par. 7). Why does Gibson spend so much time discussing Effross's article? How effectively do you think this discussion of Effross's ideas supports Gibson's argument?

5. Gibson concludes his argument by claiming that Christianity in the United States has become a "big business." Is this conclusion justified by the evidence he has cited? Explain.

④ | # The Responsible Plagiarist

ABIGAIL LIPSON AND SHEILA M. REINDL

Given how strongly organizations such as the Modern Language Association oppose plagiarism (see page 160), the title of the following argument may seem paradoxical. How could a plagiarist be "responsible"? Isn't any plagiarist irresponsible or worse? But as authors Abigail Lipson and Sheila Reindl demonstrate, students plagiarize for different reasons—and, ironically, some of these reasons are related to the desire to do what they believe is expected of them. This argument was written for an audience of teachers—but it may be useful to hear how teachers discuss students when concerned about improving teaching methods. Abigail Lipson is a clinical psychologist who directs the American University Counseling Center in Washington, D.C. Sheila Reindl is director of the Harvard University Writing Center. "The Responsible Plagiarist" was first published in *About Campus* during the summer of 2003. According to its website, "*About Campus* is a professional magazine designed to serve as a catalyst for educators in colleges and universities to thoughtfully examine a variety of issues, policies, and practices and how they affect the quality of undergraduate education and student learning." As you read, consider how Lipson and Reindl make their case about plagiarism to their intended audience: university and college instructors. As a student, do you find their argument persuasive?

ABIGAIL LIPSON AND SHEILA M. REINDL, "The Responsible Plagiarist"

1 In the academic community, there may be no higher crime or baser act than plagiarism. The word *plagiarist* comes from the Latin word for "kidnapper"—to plagiarize is to steal someone's brainchild. Most universities address the issue of academic integrity by providing students with thorough orientations, required writing courses, and clearly articulated honor codes. Indeed, there is a virtually uniform understanding among college students that plagiarism is wrong. Nevertheless, each year students are brought before their institutions' disciplinary boards on charges that they have misused sources in their schoolwork. We have to wonder, *What were they thinking?*

Universities tend to rely on three explanations for academic conduct violations:

1. *Criminal plagiarism* describes the actions of students who knowingly and intentionally claim others' work as their

CONTEXT

Concerns on the part of college faculty and administrators about plagiarism by students seem to be justified by various studies. One 2007 survey found that 60 percent of college students admit to cheating in school. In recent years, concerns about plagiarism have been intensified by fears that the Internet makes it easier for students to plagiarize. An annual survey of college students called the National Survey of Student Engagement found that 87 percent of students reported knowing classmates who copied material from the Internet for school assignments without citing the source. Students can also purchase papers from many online services and then submit those papers to their instructors as their own work. In view of these developments, many colleges and universities now use online services such as Turnitin.com to help identify plagiarism among their students.

own. Most universities handle incidents of criminal plagiarism on a case-by-case basis, taking care both to preserve the academic standards of the institution and to address the (often dire) circumstances of the student. A student found responsible for criminal plagiarism typically earns a failing grade, a notation on his or her record, and perhaps a required leave or expulsion.

2. *Sloppy scholarship* describes the actions of students who know the rules for proper citation and don't intend to deceive but nevertheless engage in scholarship of inexcusable carelessness (for example, when citations are unintentionally "lost" in a cut-and-paste or notemaking process).The work of these students may look like criminal plagiarism, but they have committed a negligent act of omission rather than an intentional act of commission. Universities tend to treat sloppy scholarship as a serious breach of academic responsibility, despite the lack of criminal intent.

3. *Ignorance of the rules* is considered a weak explanation given the pains taken to ensure students' awareness of the importance and mechanisms of proper citation. Occasionally, though, it becomes clear that a student really is at a loss regarding the basic conventions of source use, perhaps because of poor precollege preparation or widely divergent cultural assumptions about the nature of knowledge or the role of a student. In such instances, students are generally still held accountable for their inappropriate use of sources while their knowledge gaps and cultural adjustments are addressed with remedial instruction or counseling.

In most cases, criminal plagiarism, sloppy scholarship, or ignorance of the rules provides an entirely satisfactory explanation for a student's conduct. Yet there remain students for whom these standard explanations just don't seem to suffice. We hear from these students that their intentions were straightforward and honest: they did not engage in criminal plagiarism. They were fully alert to the basic rules of citation: they did not act out of ignorance. And they were being careful and deliberate: they were not being sloppy. These students

claim, in fact, that as they did their work they were conducting themselves in a most responsible manner.

And we believe them. We believe that their actions made sense to them at the time—not good sense, but their own internal coherent sense. They were taking their academic responsibilities very seriously. It seems that the question to ask about these students is not, "*Were* they behaving responsibly?" but rather, "To *what* were they trying to be responsible?"

MODELS OF RESPONSIBILITY

5 To understand students' private logic, we must listen closely to their descriptions of how they went about their work. Following are outlines of three models of responsibility that stand out especially clearly in our students' self-descriptions. Each model embodies assumptions that students hold about their proper role in the educational process. Each implies a set of responsibilities that students are doing their best to honor. And each results in the unintentional yet sometimes egregious misuse of sources.

The Responsible Apprentice. Sometimes students cast themselves in the role of Responsible Apprentice. Their job is to model their products after those of the masters, so they learn the canon, "lip-synch" the voices of their teachers, and use their readings to reproduce as professional-*looking* a product as they can. They figure that someday they may produce original work of their own, but for now their task is merely to mimic expert examples. One could easily imagine Responsible Apprentices forgetting to sign their names to their essays. They feel no need to sign work that is not their own creation. The notion of academic learning as a form of apprenticeship has been explored by a number of scholars, including Allan Collins, John Brown, and Susan Newman in their work on the craft of teaching.

Responsible Apprentices are particularly susceptible to appropriating language, sans citation, in their written work. They feel that this is an entirely legitimate aspect of their job. So when they are accused of *misusing* sources, they feel tricked: "Wait a minute! I was being responsible! The teacher knows full well where my material came from! All I did was try to do the assignment!"

The Responsible Truth Seeker. Sometimes we hear in our students' voices a joy in searching for the truth and a delight in finding it; they have cast themselves in the noble role of Truth Seeker. In going about their studies, Responsible Truth Seekers are smitten by a particular idea. It rings so true! It is so compellingly right! Responsible Truth Seekers adopt other scholars' material with the certainty that they are simply accepting the Truth—not Author X's truth, which they must attribute to Author X, but Truth itself.

Responsible Truth Seekers are likely to misuse sources in a slightly different way than Responsible Apprentices do. They are more likely to appropriate a whole argument or an entire line of reasoning. They freely use ideas from their reading in their writing, without citation. They assume that even when particular phrases need to be properly cited, the Truth to which the words refer doesn't belong to anybody—it is simply true.

10 When Responsible Truth Seekers find themselves accused of misusing sources, they are likely to react with dismay and disillusionment. They think, "Why should Author X's name be attached to this idea? Author X is just doing the same thing I'm doing—recognizing the Truth and embracing it for what it is." To the Responsible Truth Seeker, quibbling over who is cited as the author of the Truth is irrelevant to the student's primary responsibility: to be passionate and unflagging in the search for Truth itself.

The Responsible Tax Preparer. Sometimes students document a text as though it is a good-faith effort to prepare a tax return. In the role of Responsible Tax Preparer, students are trying to be fair: to credit others with what is rightfully theirs and themselves with what is rightfully their own. They do not claim to be professionals, merely well-meaning laypersons trying to follow the authorities' very complicated code. They get frustrated when there isn't a definitive rule for every possible circumstance, or when different authorities offer inconsistent advice on how to handle the very same citation. They have no basis on which to make judgment calls—they are guided only by their sense of responsibility to dutiful rule-following.

Responsible Tax Preparers' myopic focus on the rules leaves them in danger of *miscitation*, for example, by carefully citing a primary source for material actually found in a secondary source. Their rule-boundness can also result in *overcitation*—not a code violation but nevertheless a poor use of sources. When faced with what feel like risky judgments, Responsible Tax Preparers decide, "When in doubt, footnote!"

When Responsible Tax Preparers find themselves accused of misusing sources, they are likely to feel profoundly unappreciated. "Can't you see I was faithfully following the rules? The rules aren't always so clear, you know! I had, like, thirty footnotes in there—how much more responsible could I have been?!" To be accused of ignorance or neglect or dishonesty, given their extraordinary diligence, feels deeply unjust.

The students' responses to these accusations make some sense. They are all trying to be responsible to some value that they think the academic community holds. In fact, the academic community does share their values, to a degree. A willingness to apprentice oneself to the work of masters, a deep engagement in the quest for truth, a diligent effort to comply with the conventions of text preparation—all of these are indeed important values.

15 So let's grant that the students we have described here are not being entirely irresponsible, nor responsible to entirely unworthy aims. We can still conclude that they are misusing sources. These "responsible" plagiarists have failed to be responsible to a core value that the academic community holds even more dear.

THE COMMUNITY OF THE MIND

The responsibility that these students have failed to meet is the scholar's responsibility to *a set of relationships or connections* between the scholar's own ideas and the ideas of others. As scholars, we have a responsibility to our sources (to acknowledge our indebtedness to them), to our readers (to let them know what our sources were and how they informed us), and to ourselves (to declare our own contributions). Proper documentation traces a family tree of intellectual kinship, in which we place our own ideas and text in *context*. When students misuse sources, they violate not merely a set of rules but a set of relationships.

Richard Marius, a past director of Harvard's writing program, put it this way:

> It is always important to think of the intellectual world as a community of mutual dependence, mutual helpfulness, mutual protectiveness, and common delight. We take ideas from others; we give ideas to others. We are indebted to others, and others are indebted to us. In sharing and acknowledging the community, we define ourselves more certainly as individuals. The ability to describe our sources is also an ability to recognize our own originality and our own selves. All communities depend on generosity, trust, and definition, and the proper use of sources is part of the mortar that holds the community of the mind together.

A scholar's primary responsibility is to this community of the mind to which every one of us belongs—whether student or professor, believer or heretic, expert or novice.

This notion that we all belong to one community of the mind is heartwarming, but problematic. What community? Does a modern-day Brazilian engineering professor belong to the same community of the mind as a Zhou dynasty Chinese poet? Sometimes it's hard enough to imagine that two faculty members in the same department of the same North American university belong to one community of mind, when they subscribe to different journals, attend different conferences, and use different theoretical frameworks and languages.

In actuality, we each belong to many neighboring and nested communities of the mind. On a fairly local level, present-day North American academia is a community defined by some shared values and conventions regarding scholarly conduct. Even more locally, an academic discipline or an academic institution constitutes a community of the mind. On the most global level, the community of the mind consists of the constantly evolving network of relationships among all scholars, across time and place. The human activities of reading and writing, and listening and speaking, continue to hum along, even as the players change and despite sometimes impassable gulfs between languages, ideologies, eras, and cultures. As scholars, our academic integrity depends on honoring our intellectual interconnectedness on all levels, whether reckoning with the nitty-gritty of citation formats or orienting our intellectual constructions in their particular cultural and historical context.

20 The word *integrity* is particularly apt here because of its two equally important meanings. It refers in one sense to personal trustworthiness, good character, moral uprightness. It refers to individual scholars' professional conduct, the soundness of their scholarship, their intellectual honesty. Responsible scholars speak truthfully, fairly represent the work of fellow scholars, and claim their own work, and only their own work, as theirs.

The second meaning of the word *integrity* refers to a wholeness, an entirety. We can apply this meaning to the enterprise of human inquiry itself, the collective process and progress of human understanding. This process has its own intactness, its own enduring and continuing life. It is sustained and defined by its members-of-the moment, but its existence predates the individual scholar and will continue afterward. The integrity of human inquiry in this broad and collective sense refers to the complex interconnectedness of all scholarship.

Integrity on both levels is represented in the efforts of a responsible scholar to document a text in such a way as to ensure the readers' ability to evaluate the scholar's work independently. Readers can reanalyze the writer's sources, see the larger body of data from which the writer selected material, and find in the original sources confirming or discrepant statements. By inviting readers to join in a mutual intellectual discourse, the writer helps preserve and promote the continuity of the conversation in the community of the mind.

Every scholar is, of course, both a reader and a writer. There is a wonderful recursiveness and simultaneity at work here as the human species constructs a collective if multiplistic conversation. The spirit of this conversation springs from the twin desires to learn and to create—to find inspiration in others and to make our own contributions. In practice, there is no choice between these priorities. Both the intellectual effort of the individual and the intellectual evolution of the community rely on the interplay between the two. This is how human knowledge, on the personal and the collective levels, is preserved and advanced: in the intricate dance between what we believe we already know and what we dare to speculate.

VOICELESSNESS

Everyone who has ideas, reactions, beliefs, and musings—in short, everyone—belongs by definition to the community of the mind in its broadest sense. One need not apply for membership and one cannot be thrown out. Every scholar, reader, and student stands *somewhere* in relationship to the texts being read or the words being heard and has *some* response—whether inspiration or outrage, interest or boredom, agreement or disagreement, confusion or conversion. This response is the scholar's voice, the scholar's contribution to the larger conversation.

Some of the students who get into trouble for misusing sources clearly do not experience themselves as members of the community of the mind. It is not simply that they consider themselves to be novice thinkers, or fear that their thinking is different or inadequate. Rather, they do not consider themselves to be thinkers at all; they feel they know only what they are told by others.

Because they experience themselves as voiceless, at least in the domain of their academic work, the voices of these students are missing from the papers they write. As Pat Hoy, at the time a writing teacher at Harvard University, remarked to one of us, it's not just that these students don't know how to *use* a source; it's that they don't know they *are* sources. This may explain in part why some students who have been thoroughly taught the conventions of source use have not learned them. They cannot make clear the relationship between their own ideas and the ideas of others because in their experience they do not have their own ideas, and therefore there is no relationship. They misappropriate their sources' ideas or words because, being voiceless themselves, they default to a master, a truth, or a (poorly understood) rule in performing what they see as their scholarly responsibilities.

One way we can understand the voicelessness of our students is in terms of their intellectual development. Many university educators are familiar with William G. Perry's longitudinal research with Harvard undergraduates, which demonstrated that students' assumptions about the nature of knowledge

CONTEXT

William Perry (1913–1998) was an educational psychologist at Harvard University who became well known for his landmark study of the intellectual and ethical development of undergraduate students at Harvard. In his book *Forms of Intellectual and Ethical Development in the College Years* (1970), Perry described nine stages of development that students progress through as a result of their college experiences. In general, according to Perry, students develop from a relatively simplistic worldview to a complex understanding of the world that leads to a commitment to their own beliefs and values. Although Perry's work was criticized by some scholars because it focused on Harvard students, his theory has been widely accepted and is often cited in discussions of the impact of the college experience on students. Note how the authors of this essay use Perry to help explain plagiarism among college students.

and the locus of authority change as they develop intellectually during the college years. Initially, students tend to see knowledge as discrete and indisputable facts and to see authorities as the possessors of those facts. As they develop, they come to regard knowledge as contextually determined and to regard themselves as constructors and authors of knowledge. Their focus as learners shifts from an effort to amass information to an effort to make meaning. Students in the midst of this developmental process, who have not yet come to regard themselves as makers of meaning, don't experience their own voices as voices of authority.

Another way to understand students' voicelessness is as a function of context and power. For all of us there are some contexts in which we feel confident of our voice and empowered to speak and other contexts in which we feel unsure, unsafe, or unwelcome, and in effect silenced. The less at home we feel in a given context—that is, the more foreign we feel—the more likely it is that we will experience intellectual voicelessness. Of course, *what* is foreign to *whom* is a matter of perspective.

The culture of North American academia can feel foreign to students in various ways. Students who come from a context of origin that does not place a premium on intellectual activity may be unpracticed in declaring their views and opinions on intellectual matters. Students from a culture of origin that values community participation over individual expression may regard such declarations as arrogant or inappropriate. Students might feel that their own culturally based ideas or viewpoints will be discounted or dismissed by the dominant culture. Students whose home culture regards intellectual material as publicly held (belonging to everyone or no one) may be disoriented in an academic community that regards such material as privately owned (and thus requiring attribution). Students might also feel foreign in a linguistic sense, whether the foreign tongue is English, the

language of academic discourse in general, or the jargon of a particular field. Imitation and parroting are essential to learning a new language, but these very activities can leave student writers vulnerable to overrelying on and misappropriating others' voices.

The experience of voicelessness and foreignness can leave students vulnerable to the intense desperation that contributes to sloppy scholarship or criminal plagiarism. Because difficult coursework is even more difficult when it is in a foreign language or context, students adjusting to such circumstances may feel especially overwhelmed and fearful of failing, and thus be at risk for panic and poor judgment regarding source use. Fear and panic are heightened if a student's personal or familial expectations make the prospect of academic failure—or anything short of perfection—intolerable, such as for students who feel trapped in the familial role of trailblazer, redeemer, or shining hope.

TEACHING FOR AUTHORITY AND AUTHORSHIP

Most policy and instruction regarding the use of sources focuses primarily on the legalities of making correct citations and the penalties for failing to do so. In the process, students learn a hidden lesson: the proper use of sources is a matter of avoiding plagiarism (and therefore punishment), which is in turn a matter of complying with specific rules of citation.

When this is the primary lesson we teach our students, we almost guarantee that they will fail to behave as responsible members of the community of the mind. Even if they learn and try to comply with every rule we teach them, they will not necessarily recognize, value, or honor their responsibility to the integrity of human inquiry. They will have learned nothing about their own authority as thinkers and writers and about their own interests in the shared conversation that defines the community of the mind.

For students to behave as truly responsible members of the community of the

WHAT CAN WE DO?

1. **Emphasize the spirit as well as the letter of the law.**

   Teach students to ask spirit-oriented questions about their use of sources (for example, Can my readers tell which ideas belong to whom? Am I clear about how I have used others' ideas in service to my own inquiry?) rather than rule-oriented questions (such as, Are my citations in the right format? Do I have enough footnotes?).

   Help novice writers learn how to specify their sources clearly; for example, have students read one another's papers and respond sentence by sentence only to the question, Whose thoughts or words are these and why do I think so?

2. **Make explicit any assumptions about the various roles that students play as learners and scholars; serve as a guide and informant regarding the culture of scholarship.**

   Help students identify the problematic assumptions they may hold about using sources. Explicitly introduce the concept of academic integrity and the notion that to use sources properly one must also recognize oneself as a source.

   Show students both *by* and *with* examples what responsible documentation means. Review examples of proper and improper attribution, quotation choices, paraphrases, and judgment calls.

   Be alert to the ways in which an assignment may elicit a particular metaphoric approach (for example, an essay assignment based on limited sources may elicit the Truth Seeker approach, or an assignment that calls for recitation of canon may elicit a Responsible Apprentice approach).

3. **Acknowledge the complexity of the task of documentation.**

   Let students know how challenging it is to represent others' work fairly in the context of their own. Summarizing and paraphrasing require translating another's language into one's own with minimal distortion of meaning; even the perfect gem of a quotation must be precisely set into one's own text. These basics are important skills, learned and developed through practice.

   Introduce students to the different conventions employed in different fields and to the personal judgment exercised in every field. While there may be simple answers to hypothetical documentation questions, and uniform agreement about a few documentation decisions, in practice documentation is a complex task.

   Illustrate for students the ways in which all writers struggle with such questions as *What is common knowledge? How do I know what is "enough" documentation? If a classmate or colleague and I have a generative discussion, to whom does our shared conversation belong?* Discuss your own real-world documentation dilemmas with your students.

4. **Treat students as the sources they are; demonstrate that the academic community includes them and values their contributions.**

   Ask students questions that will help them find words for their unvoiced thoughts: What implicit thinking guided their selection of a quotation? What in those words moved them, or inspired them, or bothered them?

   Help students identify instances of their own sense-making. When they point out a problematic assumption, reframe an issue, make an analogy, or note an oversight or counterexample, we need to point this out to them. By doing so we acknowledge their natural efforts at authority, help them recognize their own voices, and teach them how to identify various thinking tools and techniques.

   Let students know that their sense-making contributes to our own. When we learn something new from our students, we need to tell them, so they can know that their voice is effective. When we help students experience their voice as having power, we help them recognize their role in the community of the mind.

mind, they need to experience *themselves* as members of that community. They need to know that that community includes them and values their participation. They need to recognize themselves as contributing thinkers, as makers of meaning. They need to understand that what they violate when they plagiarize is not a rule but a relationship. Only then can they appropriately use others' thinking in the service of, not instead of, their own thinking, and appropriately honor the relationships between their own work and the work of others. Recalling the words of Pat Hoy, we must teach our students not merely how to use sources but how to be sources.

Every time a scholar puts pencil to paper or fingers to keyboard, that scholar has to do the difficult work of documentation. We as teachers shouldn't misrepresent this work as a matter of simply avoiding plagiarism. We must teach our students the hows and whys of expressing their own voices, tracing their intellectual kinships, and honoring their intellectual debts....

We can appreciate the attitude of Martin Price, who in the preface to his book *To the Palace of Wisdom* acknowledges the complexity and ambiguity inherent in documentation. He notes, "I have tried to specify particular sources from which I have drawn. I regret the omissions I have most certainly made, and I would ask in turn the charitable recognition that not all resemblances need represent indebtedness" (p. viii). A sampling of our office bookshelves reveals that many authors, both popular and academic, preface their work with similar statements—not to belittle the importance of proper documentation or to excuse themselves from their responsibilities, but rather to affirm their commitment to the community of the mind while openly acknowledging the difficulties of the task of thorough documentation. We can ask no more and no less of our students.

NOTES

Collins, A., Brown, J. S., and Newman, S. E. "Cognitive Apprenticeship: Teaching the Craft of Reading, Writing, and Mathematics." In L. B. Resnick (ed.), *Knowing, Learning, and Instruction* (pp. 453–494). Hillsdale, N.J.: Erlbaum, 1989.

Hjortshoj, K. *Transition to College Writing*. New York and Boston: Bedford/St. Martin's Press, 2001.

Marius, R. "The Use of Sources for Papers in Expository Writing." Pamphlet. Cambridge, Mass.: Harvard University, 1982.

Morrow, L. "Kidnapping the Brainchildren." *Time*, Dec. 3, 1990, p. 126.

Perry, W. G., Jr. *Forms of Intellectual and Ethical Development in the College Years: A Scheme.* Austin, Tex.: Holt, Rinehart and Winston, 1970.

Price, M. *To the Palace of Wisdom: Studies in Order and Energy from Dryden to Blake.* Garden City, N.Y.: Doubleday, 1964.

Questions for Discussion

1. In their opening paragraph, Lipson and Reindl claim that "academic integrity" is usually explained to students during orientation and that many schools have "clearly articulated honor codes." What is your school's position on academic integrity? How was it made known to you? How might your own experience influence the way you respond to the argument about plagiarism in this essay?

2. The authors identify three main kinds of plagiarism. Why do they believe that these kinds of plagiarism do not adequately explain the reasons that college students plagiarize?

3. Consider the distinction in paragraph 4 "It seems that the question to ask about these students is not, '*Were* they behaving responsibly?' but rather, 'To *what* were they trying to be responsible?' " What is the difference between these two questions? Why is it important for the authors' main argument?

4. The authors focus attention on two meanings of the word *integrity*. Why do they believe this word is important when it comes to the issue of plagiarism? How does this discussion of *integrity* help support the authors' main argument about the reasons that students plagiarize?

5. What do the authors mean by the term "community of the mind"? Why is this term important to their argument about student plagiarism? Why is it problematic to assume that all students (or scholars) "belong to one community of the mind"?

6. In what sense can students be "voiceless," according to the authors? How does this "voicelessness" help create conditions under which students plagiarize? Have you experienced this "voicelessness" as a student? To what extent does the authors' discussion of this problem coincide with your own experience as a student?

7. This essay might be seen as an example of an argument to negotiate differences and solve a problem. Evaluate its effectiveness as such an argument. To what extent do you think the argument in this essay moves toward a resolution of plagiarism, which is a problem for both students and faculty?

DIFFERENCES

NEGOTIATING

The essays in this section indicate that "intellectual property" is a broad and complex category encompassing words, ideas, and symbols, among other things. Moreover, they raise the tricky question of who should own an idea or a phrase. As a student, you must sometimes confront questions about the ownership of words or ideas when you are completing school assignments that require you to draw on sources. And if you have used the Internet to find information, as most of us do today, then you may have encountered additional uncertainties, since much of the information on the Internet is questionable and its origin unknown. If you have ever been tempted to use a sentence or phrase or idea that you found on an obscure web page without acknowledging that source, then you know how easy it can be to violate intellectual property standards.

With this in mind, review the policies of your college or university regarding academic dishonesty and intellectual property. (Most schools post such policies on their websites, but you can usually also find them in the school's library.) Examine these policies to see what standards for the ownership of words and ideas your school applies to student work. Then write an essay in which you either argue in favor of these policies or question them. In your essay, be sure to summarize the main points of your school's policies regarding intellectual property and academic dishonesty, then explain why you agree or disagree with them. Try to identify the principles of fairness and ownership that you hold as a basis for your argument. And try to address the matter of the consequences that students suffer when they are found to have violated your school's policies: What are those consequences? Are they fair? If not, why not? And what alternatives would you provide? Try also to account for new technologies, like those associated with the Internet, and how they might affect intellectual property.

If your teacher allows it, consider working together with several classmates to review your school's policies and collaboratively draft your essay.

Who Owns Music?

In January 2003, in a case known as *Eldred v. Ashcroft*, the U.S. Supreme Court upheld a law that extended the term for copyrights for books, movies, music, and other intellectual property for twenty years beyond the fifty years that previous laws already provided for. The case was considered one of the most important decisions involving intellectual property in recent decades, and the intense debate surrounding it reflects the importance of copyright law in the United States and the deep concerns many citizens have about it—especially when it comes to music.

Although creative works of all kinds are protected under copyright law, music seems to generate particularly intense controversy. Perhaps that's because music is so much a part of the lives of most people; for many people, music is not so much a product as a cultural treasure to which everyone has a right. (See Con-Text on page 238.) It can also be difficult to distinguish among the many different forms of music and the variety of media in which it exists. For example, is a song that is played on the radio subject to the same copyright rules as a song that is played on a personal MP3 player?

Eldred v. Ashcroft highlighted the complexity of questions about who owns music and who controls its distribution. Representatives of media corporations praised the ruling as an important protection for songwriters and musicians, but others complained that the ruling would prevent the public from enjoying the benefits of musical works. Some scholars believe that the framers of the Constitution intended copyright to encourage scientific and creative work and to ensure that such work would eventually benefit the public. But copyright law can also mean profits. It gives songwriters and musicians—and the media companies that produce and distribute their work—the right to earn money from their songs or performances, and it prevents others from profiting unfairly from copyrighted music. And the great popularity of music means that there is a great deal of money at stake.

Recent technological developments have added to the difficulty of sorting through these issues. The capabilities of new computer technologies have made it easier than ever for consumers to reproduce and share music. Like millions of other consumers, you might have visited a website where you can download, free of charge, copies of your favorite songs that someone else has made available on that site. Such capabilities raise questions about when a copy of a song is being used illegally. Is it a violation of copyright law to download a music file that was copied from a CD that another person legally purchased and then made available on a private website? Or is downloading a file the same thing as letting a friend borrow a CD you have purchased so that he or she can record it? The media companies supporting the decision in *Eldred v. Ashcroft* believe that they are losing profits whenever someone downloads a song in this way. Others argue that consumers have the right to share music through the Internet. Although the copyright to a song indicates clearly who "owns" that song, it is less clear how far that copyright extends. Must permission be granted every time that song is played or copied, no matter what the circumstances? Such questions involve legal and economic complexities that will become even more difficult to sort out as new technologies develop.

As the essays in this section indicate, controversies involving the ownership of music are not limited to legal or economic issues. Music can also be considered an expression of cultural identity. But who owns that identity? That question emerged as hip hop and rap music gained popularity in the 1980s and 1990s. These musical forms "borrowed" from other kinds of music in the form of sampling, a practice whereby an artist incorporates or "quotes" from other songs. Some artists believe that sampling requires payment, because parts of songs are protected by copyright law. In turn, rap music, which many consider to be a form of Black cultural expression, influenced other musicians, who then "borrowed" from rap—raising questions about whether such borrowing is simply the influence of one form of music on another or constitutes "stealing" an artist's racial or cultural identity.

Obviously, as such an important and widespread part of culture, music is much more than entertainment. Thus, the questions about the ownership of music raised by the essays in this section reflect important social, legal, economic, and even moral concerns that affect all of us, regardless of our musical tastes. These essays might not provide answers to the kinds of difficult questions regarding intellectual property and music discussed here. But they can help you understand the issues so that you can seek your own answers in a more informed manner.

CON-TEXT

The Importance of Music

Music is a basic function of human existence, arising from the physiological, psychological, and sociological needs of human kind. As such, the value of musical pursuit derives not only from the endeavor to achieve the highest forms of the musical art according to socially accepted norms, but also from the everyday musical encounters of every person. To this end, music is a necessary, life-enhancing experience which should be nurtured in all individuals, not only in those gifted with musical aptitude.

Music is an invariant. It has been present in all cultures, at all times, and throughout the known historical development of the human species, facilitating emotional, physical, and social expression. Music satisfies the human need for aesthetic enjoyment, provides for communication of cultural ideals, integrates, and enculturates.

SOURCE: Kenneth Liske, "Philosophy of Music Education."

① Free Downloads Play Sweet Music

JANIS IAN

In the late 1990s, as digital technologies began to influence the consumer market for music, listeners began to take advantage of the capabilities of the Internet to share music with each other. With powerful new computer technologies, a consumer could purchase a CD by a favorite musician, copy a song from that CD to a computer hard drive, then send that song to a friend—and to many other people—through the Internet. Eventually, websites were established that became clearinghouses for music, usually as MP3 files, a popular digital format for reproducing sound. The best known of these websites was Napster, which at the height of its popularity was visited by hundreds of thousands of users each day, many of whom would download music files using Napster's peer-to-peer software. A lawsuit curtailed much of the file-downloading activity enabled by Napster's software in 2000, but consumers have continued to find ways to share music files digitally, raising concerns among some musicians and among media companies about copyright violations and about lost profits. As media companies seek ways to capture profits from the sale of music file downloads through services like *iTunes*, advocates of free speech and privacy—including some musicians, like Janis Ian—argue that music should be freely available on the Internet, even if that music is protected by copyright. In the following essay, Ian, an accomplished musician and recording artist who has won two Grammy awards, argues that musicians and consumers can benefit from free music downloads; moreover, she suggests that free downloads are good for the art itself by making music more widely available. Although her essay was published before the emergence of services like *iTunes*, it addressed questions about sharing music that are still relevant today. Ian encourages you to consider some of the economic issues involving music downloads, but her argument might also be cause to wonder about who should control the distribution of music once a song has been protected by copyright. This article appeared on ZDNet, an Internet technology network, in 2002. It is a shorter version of the original article, which was published in *Performing Songwriter Magazine* in 2002.

JANIS IAN, "Free Downloads Play Sweet Music"

1 When researching an article, I normally send e-mails to friends and acquaintances, who answer my request with opinions and anecdotes. But when I said I was planning to argue that free Internet downloads are good for the music industry and its artists, I was swamped.

I received over 300 replies—and every single one from someone legitimately in the music business.

Even more interesting than the e-mails were the phone calls. I don't know anyone at the National Academy of Recording Arts & Sciences (NARAS, home of the Grammy

Awards), and I know Hilary Rosen (head of the **Recording Industry Association of America, or RIAA**) only in passing. Yet within 24 hours of sending my original e-mail, I'd received two messages from Rosen and four from NARAS, requesting that I call to "discuss the article."

Huh. Didn't know I was that widely read.

5 Ms. Rosen, to be fair, stressed that she was only interested in presenting RIAA's side of the issue, and was kind enough to send me a fair amount of statistics and documentation, including a number of focus group studies RIAA had run on the matter.

However, the problem with focus groups is the same problem anthropologists have when studying peoples in the field: the moment the anthropologist's presence is known, everything changes. Hundreds of scientific studies have shown that any experimental group *wants to please the examiner*. For focus groups, this is particularly true. Coffee and donuts are the least of the payoffs.

The NARAS people were a bit more pushy. They told me downloads were "destroying

sales," "ruining the music industry," and "costing *you* money."

Costing *me* money? I don't pretend to be an expert on intellectual property law, but I do know one thing. If a music industry executive claims I should agree with their agenda because it will make me more money, I put my hand on my wallet...and check it after they leave, just to make sure nothing's missing.

Am I suspicious of all this hysteria? You bet. Do I think the issue has been badly handled? Absolutely. Am I concerned about losing friends, opportunities, my 10th Grammy nomination, by publishing this article? Yeah. I am. But sometimes things are just wrong, and when they're that wrong, they have to be addressed.

10 The premise of all this ballyhoo is that the industry (and its artists) are being harmed by free downloading.

Nonsense.

Let's take it from my personal experience. My site gets an average of 75,000 hits a year. Not bad for someone whose last hit record

was in 1975. When **Napster** was running full-tilt, we received about 100 hits a month from people who'd downloaded "Society's Child" or "At Seventeen" for free, then decided they wanted more information. Of those 100 people (and these are only the ones who let us know how they'd found the site), 15 bought CDs.

Not huge sales, right? No record company is interested in 180 extra sales a year. But that translates into $2,700, which is a lot of money in my book. And that doesn't include the people who bought the CDs in stores, or came to my shows.

RIAA, NARAS and most of the entrenched music industry argue that free downloads hurt sales. More than hurt—it's destroying the industry.

15 Alas, the music industry needs no outside help to destroy itself. We're doing a very adequate job of that on our own, thank you.

The music industry had exactly the same response to the advent of reel-to-reel home tape recorders, cassettes, DATs, minidiscs, videos, MTV ("Why buy the record when you can tape it?") and a host of other technological advances designed to make the consumer's life easier and better. I know because I was there.

The only reason they didn't react that way publicly to the advent of CDs was because they believed CDs were uncopyable. I was told this personally by a former head of Sony marketing, when they asked me to license *Between the Lines* in CD format at a reduced royalty rate. ("Because it's a brand new technology.")

Realistically, why do most people download music? To hear new music, and to find old, out-of-print music—not to avoid paying $5 at the local used CD store, or taping it off the radio, but to hear music they can't find anywhere else. Face it: Most people can't afford to spend $15.99 to experiment. And an awful lot of records are out of print; I have a few myself!

Everyone is forgetting the main way an artist becomes successful—exposure. Without exposure, no one comes to shows, no one buys CDs, no one enables you to earn a living doing what you love.

20 Again, from personal experience: In 37 years as a recording artist, I've created 25-plus albums for major labels, and I've *never* received a royalty statement that didn't show I owed them money. Label accounting practices are right up there with Enron. I make the bulk of my living from live touring, doing my own show. Live shows are pushed by my website, which is pushed by the live shows, and both are pushed by the availability of my music, for free, online.

Who gets hurt by free downloads? Save a handful of super-successes like Celine Dion, none of us. We only get helped.

Most consumers have no problem paying for entertainment. If the music industry had a shred of sense, they'd have addressed this problem seven years ago, when people like Michael Camp were trying to obtain legitimate licenses for music online. Instead, the industrywide attitude was, "It'll go away." That's the same attitude CBS Records had about rock 'n' roll when Mitch Miller was head of A&R. (And you wondered why they passed on The Beatles and The Rolling Stones.)

NARAS and RIAA are moaning about the little mom-and-pop stores being shoved out of business; no one worked harder to shove them out than our own industry, which greeted every new mega-music store with glee, and offered steep discounts to Target, WalMart, et al., for stocking their CDs. The Internet has zero to do with store closings and lowered sales.

And for those of us with major label contracts who want some of our music available for free downloading...well, the record companies own our masters, our outtakes, even our demos, and they won't allow it. Furthermore, they own our voices for the duration of the contract, so we can't post a live track for downloading even if we want to.

Napster An Internet service for sharing music files (in MP3 format), Napster was founded in 1999 by a college student named Shawn Fanning, who established a website where users could exchange their private music files. Napster quickly became an Internet phenomenon as thousands of users began to use Napster's file-sharing software to share music. As many as 60 million users were visiting the site by early 2001. In 2000, the Recording Industry Association of America (RIAA) filed suit against Napster, alleging copyright infringement, and a drawn-out court battle ensued. A court ruled in favor of the RIAA in 2000 and stopped the free exchange of copyrighted files using Napster's software, but Napster continued to operate in a more limited way until 2002, when additional court rulings finally shut it down. But the issues regarding intellectual property, copyright law, and consumer privacy that the Napster case raised generated intense debate that continued well after Napster ceased its operations.

25 If you think about it, the music industry should be rejoicing at this new technological advance. Here's a foolproof way to deliver music to millions who might otherwise never purchase a CD in a store. The cross-marketing opportunities are unbelievable. Costs are minimal, shipping nonexistent—a staggering vehicle for higher earnings and lower costs. Instead, they're running around like chickens with their heads cut off, bleeding on everyone and making no sense.

There is *zero* evidence that material available for free online downloading is financially harming anyone. In fact, most of the hard evidence is to the contrary.

The RIAA is correct in one thing—these are times of great change in our industry. But at a time when there are arguably only four record labels left in America (Sony, AOL Time Warner, Universal, BMG—and where is the RICO act when we need it?), when entire genres are glorifying the gangster mentality and losing their biggest voices to violence, when executives change positions as often as Zsa Zsa Gabor changed clothes, and "A&R" has become a euphemism for "Absent & Redundant," we have other things to worry about.

We'll turn into Microsoft if we're not careful, folks, insisting that any household wanting an extra copy for the car, the kids, or the portable CD player, has to go out and "license" multiple copies.

As artists, we have the ear of the masses. We have the trust of the masses. By speaking out in our concerts and in the press, we can do a great deal to dampen this hysteria, and put the blame for the sad state of our industry right back where it belongs—in the laps of record companies, radio programmers, and our own apparent inability to organize ourselves in order to better our own lives—and those of our fans.

30 If we don't take the reins, no one will.

COMPLICATION

In "MP3s Great Technology, but Use Must Be Ethical" (2000), Kevin Markham writes: "I admit it, I love technology. Technologically speaking, I think MP3s are a great idea. But I hate music piracy.

"I believe that it is wrong to copy an artist's intellectual property (their music) without their permission. I believe the same about all intellectual property, such as computer software. I think that all intellectual property owners have the absolute right to decide how their creations are distributed.

"Because of the nature of intellectual property, stealing some of that property doesn't physically remove anything. So there's obviously nothing wrong with music piracy, right? To the contrary. Because intellectual property is just an idea or a representation of that idea, distribution rights is the only thing an intellectual property owner actually owns. In other words, downloading music when the artist doesn't give permission robs them of the only thing they actually have—the right to decide who gets to hear their music and how much it costs them."

SOURCE: Kevin Markham, "MP3s Great Technology, but Use Must Be Ethical" (2000).

Questions for Discussion

1. Ian draws heavily on her experience as a musician and a recording artist to support her position on music downloads. Evaluate her use of personal experience as evidence. How effectively do you think it supports her main argument? Do you think she could have used other kinds of evidence to support her argument? Explain. (In answering these questions, you might wish to review the discussion of appraising evidence on pages 91–97).

2. Ian begins her essay by telling an anecdote about the number of messages she received from people who learned that she was writing about free music downloads. Why do you think she begins her essay in this way? Do you think this beginning is an effective way for her to introduce her subject? Explain.

3. Ian writes, "There is *zero* evidence that material available for free online downloading is financially harming anyone. In fact, most of the hard evidence is to the contrary." To what extent do you think Ian provides such "hard evidence" in her essay? Do you think she is persuasive on this point? Why or why not?

4. What sort of persona, or ethos (see pages 67–73) does Ian establish? How might her background and experience as a recording artist contribute to that persona? To what extent do you think her persona contributes to the effectiveness of her argument?

5. Ian devotes a considerable amount of her essay to discussing the positions of music industry people who oppose free music downloads. Why do you think she does so? Do you think she presents their concerns fairly? Explain. How does she characterize the music industry people who oppose her position? In what ways might her argument be strengthened—or weakened—by the way she characterizes these people and their interests?

6. This essay was published in ZDNet, a network of Internet sites that is, according to its website, intended for "IT [information technology] professionals and business influencers" and "provides an invaluable perspective and resources so that users can get the most out of their investments in technology." In what ways do you think Ian addresses this audience? Do you think she does so effectively? Explain.

② | Ringtones: Music to Moguls' Ears

TOM LOWRY

Go to almost any public space today—be it a coffee shop, a mall, a park or a theater—and you are likely to find people using their cell phones. Many people like to customize their cell phones by programming them to play a specific melody or sound called a *ringtone*. The business of producing and selling ringtones has become lucrative, as the following selection by Tom Lowry shows. Since this article was first published in *BusinessWeek* in 2005, ringtones have become an established part of popular culture, and free ringtones are widely available on Internet sites. Lowry examines the potential for profits in the popularity of ringtones and argues that businesses should be wary of the pitfalls of such new media opportunities even as they seek to capitalize on the growth of ringtones. His article underscores the challenges of protecting copyrights in an age when music can take so many different forms in the popular culture. As you read his article, consider how often you think about the source of the ringtones on your phone or the phones of your friends. Tom Lowry is a senior writer for *BusinessWeek* who has also written about media for *USA Today* and the *New York Daily News*.

TOM LOWRY, "Ringtones: Music to Moguls' Ears"

1 Earlier this year, as the rapper 50 Cent was putting the finishing touches on his second album, *The Massacre*, for Interscope Records, the Jamaica (N.Y.) sensation carved out time from his studio schedule for an important task: recording a voice tone and a voice ringback. Those snippets would eventually let cell-phone users paying a one-time fee of $2 to hear him when they received or placed a call. Then a musical ditty from the single, "Candy Shop," was converted into a ringtone, making 50 Cent ubiquitous in wireless—just as *The Massacre* topped the charts in March.

For music executives still stung by Internet piracy and slammed for not moving quickly enough to exploit the Net, the industry is going to great lengths not to blow it with new wireless technologies. They're seeing that cell phones are just as important as CD and MP3 players, radio, and music videos. And ensuring that breakout artists like 50 Cent have content tailored for mobile phones is now a must,

not just for the sake of promotion but as a critical new source of revenue.

Increasingly, selling $13 CDs at retail stores is the old-fashioned way to make money on music. Now there's a host of fresh possibilities, from video game soundtracks to preloaded artist catalogs on hard drives in cars—imagine an Elvis Cadillac or a Britney BMW. Meanwhile, lawyers are working overtime on new publishing, royalty, and licensing agreements for the nascent business models. Cell phones now represent enough promise for all the major music companies to be setting up mobile-business divisions. "With 180 million handsets in the U.S., how could we not be bullish on the mobile market, especially now that downloads to phones are possible?" says Thomas Hesse, president of global digital business at Sony BMG Music Entertainment.

But no matter how many new businesses emerge, music execs still face an uphill battle competing with free. After the first uptick in music sales in years in 2004, the figures dropped again—by 6%—in the first quarter of 2005, to 134.8 million albums, according to Nielsen SoundScan. About 750 million songs are still being swapped unauthorized or free on the Internet every month, according to file-sharing tracker Big Champagne. To understand the magnitude of the threat, consider that the most successful legal download service, Apple Computer Inc.'s iTunes Music Store, has sold less than half of the illegal monthly volume, 300 million songs, since its launch 10 years ago.

Spinning Faster

5 What's more, digital-music sales are still a tiny sliver of the overall pie. Digital music, mostly made up of downloads on the Internet and tones on cell phones, accounts for roughly 2% of the $30 billion global music business. But executives see a quick ramp-up. Alain Levy, CEO of EMI Music, for one, has said that digital sales could be 25% of his company's total in five years, with cell-phone downloads and subscriptions making up a big chunk. In the first six months of its fiscal year ending last November, EMI reported digital sales that doubled year-on-year, to $37.8 million, still just a fraction of its $1.6 billion in total revenues. Much of the digital gain was attributable to online sales in America, mobile revenues in Japan, and ringtone revenues at EMI Publishing.

Ringtones are driving most of the mobile-music business today. The replication of songs into a series of tones costs customers $1 to $3 apiece. As their sound quality improves, so will demand, say executives. If there was any doubt of their importance to the future of music, the industry's stalwart trade magazine, *Billboard*, now compiles a regular chart of the 20 "Hot Ringtones." Thanks to teenagers who sometimes swap out ringtones as many as three to four times a week, they will become a nearly $9.4 billion business in 2008, estimates consultant Strategy Analytics

Inc. "Ringtones are all about personalization. They are self-expression," says Rio Caraeff, vice-president of Universal Mobile Music. "You buy a ringtone for a different reason than you buy a download of a song." How about Joss Stone's "You Had Me" as the ring for an ex-husband, or Sinatra's "New York, New York" for a cousin in Manhattan? Assigning a tune to a caller is an expressive way to make a statement about a person or a relationship.

The fact that the industry is embracing all kinds of new formats for selling music might be the one good thing to come from the nightmare of the past several years, says Mark Harrington, a media analyst at Bear, Stearns & Co. in London. "The music industry is where the movie business was 20 years ago—trying to figure new revenue streams. For Hollywood, it was establishing [staggered] releases to VHS, then DVD, to premium cable, to now [video on demand]." Up until then, film libraries had little value, he says, but now they are being thoroughly mined in a booming DVD market. The message for music and its catalogs is parallel: The new technologies are making it possible to wring even more profit from the industry's vast song libraries. Music execs should no longer care about where revenues come from, says Harrington, especially since operating margins for digital music sales are expected to be 18%, vs. about 12% for CDs. What has music moguls even more upbeat on cell phones is the relative security they offer compared with the Internet, they say. "Cell phones are a closed system," says Sony BMG's Hesse. "And a payment system through credit-card billing is built into the device."

Nobody understands the prospects for digital music better than the publishing side of the business, which collects money for the rights of songwriters from radio plays, live performances, TV commercials, and movies—and now ringtones. Publishing has always been a high-margin part of the business, but it stands to make a killing in this new world because of all the new ways for music to reach fans.

CONTEXT

Sales of ringtones fell far short of the estimate of $9.4 billion quoted here by Lowry. Sales of ringtones in 2008 were $541 million, which was a decrease of 24 percent from 2007. The reason for the decrease, according to one market analysis firm, was that consumers figured out how to create their own ringtones from music they already own, so they didn't have to purchase ringtones for their phones. Like free music downloads, ringtones can be created and shared in ways that circumvent copyright laws, which raises questions about the practicality of "owning" music. (See Janis Ian's essay on page 233.)

"We love additive products, believe me," says Martin Bandier, CEO of EMI Music Publishing, the world's largest music publisher, with a catalog of more than 1 million songs. "It's like we are in the bread-crumb business. Sooner or later, you get a loaf of bread." Bandier says his company collects about 10% of the retail price of ringtones. The songwriter gets paid a royalty from that.

Despite the payoffs, threats still loom. There's new software, Xingtones, costing $20, that converts MP3 files to ringtone formats, pushing once again into the realm of free. Even so, the trick for the music industry will be to learn from the past—that new technologies mean new opportunities. Just ask 50 Cent.

Pennies From Heaven

10 The music industry got burned by the Internet but is now getting a lift from cell phones. Down the road, there's a rosy future in wireless downloads of entire songs. But now, the big bucks are in ringtones.

Questions for Discussion

1. With so many musicians to choose among, why do you think Lowry chose to open his argument by using the rapper 50 Cent as an example? How effective do you think this example is as an introduction to Lowry's article?

2. What evidence does Lowry provide for his claim that the media industry "is going to great lengths not to blow it with new wireless technologies"? How well does his evidence support this claim, in your view?

3. According to Lowry, teenagers change the ringtones on their cell phones as often as three or four times a week. Why is this fact important in Lowry's analysis? What do you think it suggests about copyright law and about who owns and controls music?

4. Consider the quotation in paragraph 6: "Ringtones are all about personalization. They are self-expression." In your opinion, is the sound made by a telephone a genuine form of self-expression? If so, should it be subject to copyright law? Explain.

5. What conclusions does Lowry draw from his analysis of the popularity of ringtones? Do you think his conclusions are supported by the evidence he provides and by his own reasoning? Explain.

③ Hello, Cleveland

JAMES SUROWIECKI

Is it better to hear your favorite band live or on a CD or MP3 file? In the following essay, James Surowiecki suggests that if the popularity of concerts is any indication, most people prefer live music. In an era of declining traditional album and CD sales, Surowiecki points to the healthy music touring businesses as an indication that, when it comes to music, nothing really beats a live performance. Surowiecki's argument adds a twist to the ongoing debates about copyrights and the ownership of intellectual property such as music. Unless you record it, you can't really "own" a live music performance; you can only experience it and remember it. Surowiecki suggests that the experience of a live music performance continues to have great appeal, regardless of the ease with which digital technologies make music so widely available. James Surowiecki was financial editor of online magazine *Slate* before becoming a writer for the *New Yorker*, in which this essay appeared in 2005. His books include *Best Business Crime Writing of the Year* (2002) and *The Wisdom of Crowds*: *Why the Many Are Smarter than the Few and How Collective Wisdom Shapes Business, Societies, and Nations* (2003).

JAMES SUROWIECKI, "Hello, Cleveland"

1 In the summer of 1924, a Kansas City band called **the Coon-Sanders Original Nighthawk Orchestra** did something unusual: it went on tour. Popular as live music was, bands in those days tended to serve as house orchestras or to play long stands in local clubs; there was hardly even a road to go on. But **Jules Stein**, a booking agent from Chicago, convinced the Nighthawk Orchestra that it could make more money by playing a different town every night. The tour, which lasted five weeks, was a smash. Soon, bands all over the country were hitting the road to play ballrooms and dance halls.

Stein's original version hasn't changed much, despite some modifications over the years—parking lots, hair spray, the disposable lighter. Consider Metallica, the Coon-Sanders Original Nighthawk Orchestra of our day. Though Metallica still sells a fair number of CDs from its back catalogue (it has made just one album in the past six years), it makes most of its money from concerts. Two years ago, the band brought in almost fifty million dollars with its Sanitarium tour. Last year, it brought in sixty million with its Madly in Anger with the World tour. God knows what it would take to make Metallica happy.

The music industry may be in crisis, what with illegal file-sharing, stagnant CD sales, and the decline of commercial rock radio, but the touring business is as sturdy as ever. In some ways, it is healthier than some of the mediums (radio, recorded music) that at one point or another were supposed to render it obsolete. Since 1998, annual concert-tour revenue has more than doubled, while CD sales have remained essentially flat. Last year, thirteen different artists grossed more than forty million dollars each at the box office. (Prince made eighty-seven million.) Consumers who seem reluctant to spend nineteen dollars for a CD apparently have few qualms about spending a hundred bucks or more to see a show.

The Coon-Sanders Original Nighthawk Orchestra Led by vocalists Carleton Coon (1894–1932) and Joe Sanders (1896–1965), the Coon-Sanders Original Nighthawk Orchestra was broadcast nationally in the 1920s by NBC radio, which was then a new medium.

Jules Stein (1896–1981) founded the Music Corporation of America, commonly referred to as MCA. By 1941, it was the country's largest agency for booking band concerts. Today, it is one of the largest and most powerful corporations in the entertainment business.

There are still artists who make huge sums of money selling records, but they are the lucky few. A longtime recording-industry rule of thumb holds that just one in ten artists makes money from royalties. Today, it's probably less than that. So the best model, if you're in it for the money, may be the Grateful Dead. Although the Dead didn't sell many records or get much airplay, they worked the big stadiums and arenas long enough and often enough to become one of the most profitable bands out there. As in politics and sales, nothing beats meeting the people face to face.

5 Most musicians, from a business perspective, at least, would wish it otherwise. Selling CDs is, as economists say, scalable: you make one recording, and you can sell it to an unlimited number of people for an unlimited amount of time, at very little cost. A tour, on the other hand, is work. You have to perform nearly every night, before a limited number of people, for hours at a time. You can knock a few seconds off each song, fire a percussionist, or sell more T-shirts, but in the end efficiencies are hard to come by.

The trick is that musicians get a much higher percentage of the money from concerts and merchandise than they do from the sale of their CDs. An artist, if he's lucky, gets twelve percent of the retail price of a CD. But he doesn't get any royalties until everything is paid for—studio time, packaging costs, videos—which means that he can sell a million records and make almost nothing. On tour, though, he often gets more than half of the box-office, so even if he grosses less he can profit more.

Traditionally, tours were a means of promoting a record. Today, the record promotes the tour. The decline in record sales has shrunk the size of the pie for labels and artists to fight over, so they've had to find new ways to make money, and artists have come to see how lucrative touring can be, given what people will pay to see them live. (Ticket prices for the top hundred tours doubled between 1995 and 2003.) And, while high prices may be starting to put a dent in attendance, the dollars keep pouring in. Last summer's concert season was considered a dismal one, yet, according to *Pollstar*, the industry's trade magazine, concert revenues rose for the year.

Inevitably, touring rewards some artists better than others—graying superstars, for example, with their deep-pocketed baby-boomer fans and set lists full of sing-along hits. The economist Alan Krueger has estimated that the top one percent of performers claim more than half of all concert revenues. But even indie rockers are reaping the benefits, with bands like Wilco and Modest Mouse selling out venues like Radio City Music Hall, at decidedly non-indie prices.

The upshot is that the fortunes of musicians and the fortunes of music labels have less and less to do with each other. This may be the first stage of what John Perry Barlow, a former lyricist for the Dead, once called the shift from "the music business" to "the musician business." In the musician-business, the assets that once made the major labels so important—promotion, distribution, shelf space—matter less than the assets that belong to the artists, such as their ability to perform live. As technology has grown more sophisticated, the ways in which artists make money have grown more old-fashioned. The value of songs falls, and the value of seeing an artist sing them rises, because that experience can't really be reproduced. It's funny that, in an era of file-sharing and iPod-stealing, the old troubadour may have the most lucrative gig of all. But then Metallica knew it all along. "Send me money, send me green," the group sang in "Leper Messiah," twenty years ago. "Make a contribution, and you'll get a better seat."

Questions for Discussion

1. What does Surowiecki accomplish by opening his argument with a reference to a band that was popular in the 1920s?

2. According to Surowiecki, "annual concert-tour revenue...more than doubled" between 1998 and 2005. Why is this figure important to Surowiecki's argument?

3. Surowiecki cites a number of examples to support his claim that bands tend to make more money from touring than from royalties. How persuasive do you find his examples? Do you think his examples reveal Surowiecki's assumptions about his readers' musical tastes? Explain.

4. In his final paragraph, Surowiecki writes, "As technology has grown more sophisticated, the ways in which artists make money have grown more old-fashioned." That sentence might serve as a statement of Surowiecki's main argument in this essay. How effectively do you think he supports this argument?

5. Evaluate how Surowiecki structures his argument. To what extent do you think the structure of his argument contributes to its effectiveness? Explain, citing specific passages from the text to support your answer.

6. Why do you think Surowiecki gave his essay the title "Hello, Cleveland"? In what ways does that title relate to his main argument? What do you think the title suggests about his expectations of his audience?

④ | # Collecting Music in the Digital Realm

TOM MCCOURT

People have been collecting music for centuries, but these collections initially took the form of sheet music from which individuals could then play music composed by others. In the late nineteenth century, however, the invention of the gramophone and similar technologies made it possible for people to start collecting cylinders and then vinyl records from which music created by others could be played. Ever since, music lovers have collected recordings in various forms—such as LPs, cassettes, CDs, and MP3 files. But how will music collecting change now that so much music can be stored digitally on devices such as an iPod? This is the question that Tom McCourt sets out to answer in "Collecting Music in the Digital Realm," an argument first published in the academic journal *Popular Music and Society* in May 2005. McCourt, who teaches communication at Fordham University, is the author of *Digital Music Wars: Ownership and Control of the Celestial Jukebox* (2006). (Note: This argument also provides an example of MLA-style documentation. See pages 183–193.)

TOM MCCOURT,   "Collecting Music in the Digital Realm"

1 Musical recordings have a relatively short history, and their evolving physical forms have shaped our interactions with them and our perceptions of their value. For example, the "album" originated with collections of 78 rpm discs that featured elaborate, bulky packaging. These discs were limited to three or four minutes per side, which shaped the contours of the modern pop song. The storage limitations of the 78 disc also explain why the solos of early jazz recordings were compressed, and why these recordings often ended abruptly with cymbal crashes. Each subsequent format has less physical presence while allowing for more storage and greater possibilities for user programming. The LP and cassette allowed for two contiguous halves of up to 24 and 45 minutes per side respectively, each largely self-contained, while CDs accommodate 78 minutes per disc arranged in a long ebb and flow, with a few scraps as bonuses at the end (Strauss 29). An iPod can store up to ten thousand songs in a gleaming white box smaller than a pack of cigarettes.

As recordings shed their mass and/or physicality, their visual and tactile aspects also are reduced. This reduction is particularly pronounced in the transition from LPs to CDs. Vinyl could be shaped, colored, or embedded with pictures; apart from "box sets," specialty packaging has largely been abandoned with CDs. Each format also has reduced the listener's physical interaction with music, which allows music to acquire an increasingly ambient status. A listener would have to rise from their chair to change an LP, turn over a cassette, or load a CD player, but an iPod can be programmed to play until its battery expires. While LPs and CDs allow the user to determine their flow, the work as a whole must initially be engaged on the creator's terms. With an iPod, flow is determined exclusively by the user. Some argue that through digital formats, music may return to an intangible essence altogether, in which it "would stop being something to collect and revert to its age-old transience: something that transforms a moment and then disappears like a troubadour leaving town" (Pareles 22).

CDs have a physical presence of plastic and metal, enhanced by packaging. They retain "aura," although this aura is diminished. Browsing a record collection is emotionally gratifying; it is visual and tactile at the same time. We pore over the jacket art and liner notes. We determine the value of the recording by gauging the wear on the jacket and disc. Browsing a CD collection, on the other hand, is less satisfying. The medium's size limits its visual appeal, and the plastic of the jewel box degrades the tactile sensation. Digital sound files lack potential emotive contexts altogether. They are just data, metadata, and a thumbnail, and therefore emotionally less valuable than a medium you can hold in your hands. Through their immateriality, digital files cannot contain their own history. Unless they are burned onto a CD, they have no physical manifestation. No history is encoded on their surfaces, since they have no surfaces. If a digital product is enshrined in a physical form, like an LP or CD, it is regarded as being valuable. When a product is delivered in a string of bits, rather than presenting itself in a physical form, it appears to have less value. The result is that the world of commodities and the world of things continues to separate and our notions of value become separated from the material purchased. Diminished or nonexistent physical property undermines the notion of intellectual property—hence the widespread illicit copying of software and public support of file sharing.

Paradoxically, the lack of materiality in digital files heightens our sense of "ownership," as well as our desire to sample, collect, and trade music in new ways. Possessing digital files is a more intense and intimate experience than owning physical recordings, based on three things:

CONTEXT

The first record disc was created by Emil Berliner in 1884, and he secured patents for the record and the gramophone in 1887. Because they were easier to store and more economical to produce, these discs—or records, as they came to be called—gradually replaced the cylinders on which the first recordings had been made available by inventors such as Thomas Edison. By 1910, technology allowed records to rotate 78 or 80 times per minute, and the "78" became the industry standard from the late 1920s to the late 1940s, when Columbia Records introduced long-playing (LP) records with up to 30 minutes of playing time per side thanks to the use of very fine grooves. As McCourt notes, LPs eventually became capable of storing 45 minutes per side, but they fell out of favor when the introduction of CDs allowed more music to be stored on a smaller object.

5 ■ The desire for compacting. "Compacting," or compression, is integral to digital media. Codecs pare away a digital signal, in ways that allegedly are imperceptible to listeners or viewers, to facilitate their processing. Similarly, the appeal of digital collecting is predicted in part on the ability to contain huge amounts of data in a small area (witnessed by the popularity of iPods, which heighten the "geek" thrill of massive storage) despite the limited sound quality of MP3s and other file formats.

AP Photo/Jim Cooper

■ The desire for immediacy, in which the ability to sort and regroup files effortlessly transforms the listening experience. A collection of digital files in a hard drive becomes what one writer termed "an ocean of possibility [in which] daily life gets a different kind of soundtrack, endlessly mutable and instantly reconfigurable" (Moon 36). Fluidity becomes more prized than history; speed itself becomes a fetish.

■ The desire to customize, which is heightened by the malleability of digital media. Customization via digital software is expedient, efficient, and accomplished at physical remove (although software nomenclature implies otherwise: we "grab" cuts and personalize collections via "drag and drop" applications). Mix cassettes, on the other hand, are inefficient. They require the precision of starting and stopping, monitoring levels, erasing and re-cuing in real-time.

The popularity of MP3 files and related formats, as well as music in the form of telephone ringtones, indicates that access and convenience are increasingly more important than artifact and sound quality. Greater possibilities for user programming result in music increasingly approached in terms of utility, rather than aesthetics; it is "less about an artist's self-expression than a customer's desire for self-reflection" (Goldberg). Fluidity, rather than integrity, is the defining characteristic of digital technology. While mechanical technology enhances the possibilities for reproducing an original artifact, digital technology increases the possibilities for modifying an original (witness the popularity of "**mashups**" and other recombinant recordings). Digital content is not static or universally commodifiable; instead, we engage in "dialogues" with a work by altering the artifact itself or recontextualizing it through mix CDs or playlists. While most of us lack the talent and abilities required for mixing

and matching vocals and instrumental tracks into mashups, playlists increasingly serve as a form of personal expression. In cyberspace, people collect lists rather than objects. These lists may be geared to a theme, an event, an experience, a relationship. They also serve as a sort of "branding" for the creator, akin to DJ practices.

As aesthetic imagined communities, or "taste tribes," become more formalized and concretized via online tools, playlists may serve the function that CDs serve now. For example, the Rhapsody online music service's playlist function allows users to readily e-mail playlists to other users. If the recipient is a Rhapsody subscriber, he or she can click on an attachment, which will download the playlist. Playlists also reflect a key aspect of the relations of production in cyberspace, which increasingly rely on voluntary and unwaged "free labor" through the creation of web sites and other forms of user-provided content, modifying software packages, and viral marketing (Terranova). Nevertheless, as the historical record reveals, no new technology entirely substitutes for an older technology. Format obsolescence has been crucial to record companies, as it allows them to recycle their catalogs (which is where the industry draws much of its profit). Each new format is marketed as value-added by the record companies: The latest example is the (so far unsuccessful) shift to SACD and DVD-Audio, which are touted as offering improved sound quality as well as visuals, data, and interactivity to create multi-media experiences. The shift to these new formats allows the Big Four record companies to maintain bundled "albums" as a higher price point in the hard goods market, and is intended to counter the evolution of unmoored digital files in peer-to-peer systems. However, these "hardgood" formats have had limited success with consumers to date. Digital files enable heightened utility, power, and control for their users. As one reporter noted, "My records dissolved into the liquid-crystal order of a database.

Mashup describes the product that results from using digital software to place the vocal from one song over the music of another, a process created in 2003 by Jeremy Brown, also known as DJ Reset.

Organizing them was suddenly more than easy. It was a game" (Dibbell).

10 The disappearance of hard goods, in the form of physical recordings, heightens the transition from a world of cultural goods to a world of cultural services. The result is that "value" is not an inherent character of the product, but the manner in which it reaches the consumer. The popularity of song files indicates that digital value is created through mutability and process, rather than the existence of objects; therefore, the necessity to create value for something that has no physical presence accelerates the need for and process of circulation. As Marx reminds us, the status of commodities depends on movement. In cyberspace, the old market-based economy of buyers and sellers is replaced by a new network-based economy of servers and clients. Rifkin claims that "In markets, the parties exchange property. In networks, the parties share access to services and experiences...[it will be] a new kind of economic system based on network relationships, 24/7 contractual arrangements and access rights." This trend is reflected in the growing configuration of online music retailing as a service, rather than a product, in which licensing, rather than sale, provides a direct link between vendor and purchasers, making it easier to enforce limitations on use.

To compensate for their lack of materiality, digital music providers tout greater selectivity, personalization, and community as "value-added" features. In the absence of tangible commodities, the support structure itself, cyberspace, becomes the commodity. In cyberspace, collecting becomes based not on the linkage of people to objects, but of the linkage of individuals to others, realizing Stallabrass's prediction that "Experience will become a substance and a commodity" (63). As goods lose their physicality, they are imbued with greater and greater amounts of constructed value. The digital commodity is refigured continuously, emblematic of the ability of capitalism to endlessly reinvent itself.

CONTEXT

When McCourt refers to philosopher and political theorist Karl Marx (1818–1883), he assumes that his academic audience is familiar with both the man and his economic and political theories. Marx argued that capitalism shaped what he called the relations of production (such as among workers or between workers and managers) through commodities, including labor. In this passage, McCourt is using Marx's theory of commodification to analyze the growing popularity of digital music.

ACKNOWLEDGMENTS

Thanks to Patrick Burkart and Rob Drew for ideas and inspiration.

Vintage Collection/Superstock, Inc.

WORKS CITED

Dibbell, Julian. "Unpacking My Record Collection." *Feed* Mar. 2000. 17 Oct. 2004. http://www.juliandibbell.com/texts/feed_records.html

Goldberg, Michelle. "Mood Radio: Do On-line Make-Your-Own Radio Stations Turn Music Into Muzak?" *San Francisco Bay Guardian* 6 Nov. 2000. 5 July 2001. http://sfbg.com/noise/05/mood.html

Marx, Karl. *Grundrisse.* Harmondsworth: Penguin, 1973. 533–34. (Cited in Stallabrass 62).

Moon, Tom. "Mix Master iPod Opens Up a World of Sound." *Chicago Tribune* 16 Jan. 2003: 36.

Pareles, Jon. "With a Click, a New Era of Music Dawns." *The New York Times* 15 Nov. 1988: 22.

Rifkin, Jeremy. "Where Napster Has Gone, Others Will Follow." *Los Angeles Times* 21 Aug. 2000. 21 Mar. 2001. http://www.latimes.com/news/comment/2000821/t000078663.html

Stallabrass, Julian. *Gargantua: Manufactured Mass Culture.* New York: Verso, 1996.

Strauss, Neil. "The MP3 Revolution: Getting With it." *The New York Times* 18 Jul. 1999. Sec. 2: 29.

Terranova, Tiziana. "Free Labor: Producing Culture for the Digital Economy." *Social Text* 18.2 (2000): 33–58.

Questions for Discussion

1. What does McCourt achieve by opening his argument with a summary of the history of the physical forms of musical recordings? How effectively do you think this summary sets up his main argument?

2. Why is McCourt drawn to the physical appeal of an LP jacket? Why are the size and physical appearance of an LP or CD important, in McCourt's view? What does he mean when he writes that "digital sound files lack potential emotive contexts altogether"? How does this analysis fit into McCourt's main argument?

3. McCourt claims that playlists of music created by individual people "increasingly serve as a form of personal expression" (see par. 8). Why is this development important, in his view? What does it suggest about the role of music in popular culture?

4. How have changes in the way music is recorded and marketed contributed to the theft of intellectual property, according to McCourt? Why is this trend important, in his view? Do you think he's right? Why or why not?

5. What does McCourt mean when he writes that the music business is in "transition from a world of cultural goods to a world of cultural services"? What is the implication of this trend, as he sees it?

6. McCourt ends his essay with the statement, "The digital commodity is refigured continuously, emblematic of the ability of capitalism to endlessly reinvent itself" (see par. 11). Do you think McCourt intends this statement to be a criticism of capitalism? Explain. Do you agree? Why or why not?

7. As noted in the introduction on page 244, this essay was originally published in an academic journal. What characteristics of McCourt's argument identify it as intended for an academic audience? To what extent do you think his main argument would appeal to a more general audience?

DIFFERENCES

NEGOTIATING

The writers in this cluster have addressed how corporations and performers try to profit from music, whereas many individuals seek only to enjoy it—by purchasing it, downloading it for free, hearing it as ringtones, or hearing it live at concerts.

Given these differences, conflicts of interest could easily emerge—as some of the readings collected here indicate. But such conflicts may not be inevitable. Janis Ian, for example, argues that she is not hurt by free downloads of her music. And James Surowiecki argues that concert revenues can be more important for musicians than the royalties they earn by selling CDs.

Because the ways in which people access music are changing so rapidly, it can be difficult to formulate policies that might resolve the problems identified by the essays in this cluster. Yet because so many people enjoy listening to music, it is important to seek solutions that both enable people to enjoy music and reward those who create it. As a way to seek such a solution, this assignment asks you to research how music is most frequently heard and best enjoyed by a representative group of students at your own school and then to propose a policy that you believe will, on one hand, take into account the realities of how students listen to music and, on the other hand, still acknowledge the need to protect copyrights for artists who create music.

To find out how students at your school listen to music, you can talk informally to students, or you can conduct more formal research by conducting interviews or surveys. Consider the following options:

- Following the arguments of Janis Ian and Tom McCourt, you can focus on the procedures and standards used by the people in your survey group when they collect music—especially if they download recordings from the Internet or reproduce recordings for friends. How do they obtain their music? Do they pay for it or not? What do they think about the question, "Who owns the music that they listen to?"
- Drawing on the article by James Surowiecki, you can explore why people enjoy going to concerts even if it means paying for tickets that are priced much more highly than tickets for other events. How often do students at your school attend live music shows? How much are they willing to pay to attend a live performance by one of their favorite groups, as well as what kind of pricing strikes them as fair?
- Consider how technologies influence the way students listen to music and think about copyright. Do they use MP3 players to listen to music that they obtain for free on Internet sites? Do they share music files with friends and thus avoid paying for it that way? Does it matter to them whether music is digital or in other forms when it comes to the question of who owns the music?

Once you have interviewed or surveyed a sufficient number of students, draw on the essays in this cluster as well as on other information or perspectives that you find through your research to formulate what you believe is a fair policy for obtaining music. Your proposal should take into account the habits and perspectives of the students you interviewed or surveyed; it should also consider the needs of musicians and artists, who try to earn a fair price for the music they create. Make a case for your proposed policy on the basis of what you learned through your research.

© Kate Kunz/Corbis

What Should We Own?

Most Americans take it as an article of faith that ownership is a good thing. In fact, ownership seems to be a defining feature of American culture, well established since the days when the first European settlers began to buy and sell the very same land that many Native American communities believed was sacred and could not be owned by anyone. Today, Americans take ownership of the land for granted, and indeed owning land has long been a sign of wealth and power. Owning a home is a fundamental part of the American Dream, and as the readings in the first two clusters of this chapter suggest, ownership extends beyond tangible objects to words and ideas as well.

But the idea of ownership as a fundamental right is not universal. It was foreign to Native American communities when the first Europeans arrived in North America. In many accounts of those early encounters, Europeans often complained that Native Americans were thieves who did not respect private property. In fact, the very idea of private property was absent in many Native American cultures. Often, food, shelter, and other necessities were considered part of the community and shared accordingly, which many Europeans did not understand.

In recent years, as people have become more aware of the damage being done to the earth and its climate by human activity, some Americans have begun to question basic beliefs about ownership. The severe economic downturn in 2008 and 2009 as well as the growing environmental costs of activities such as transportation have caused some people to wonder whether owning a car, which has been an integral part of American culture for a century, is still a good idea for most Americans. And after the crash of the housing market in 2008, others began to question the long-standing belief that owning a home is always a safe long-term investment.

The essays in this cluster take up these questions. When he was running for reelection in 2004, President George W. Bush called the United States an "ownership society" and pledged to implement policies that would make it easier for Americans to buy homes and purchase other consumer items, such as cars. Although such ideas are familiar to most Americans, the authors of the essays in this cluster take a closer look at ownership and its consequences. They ask us to reexamine some of our most basic beliefs not only about what we should own but also about the very idea of ownership.

CON-TEXT

Private Property Ownership

According to the Fifth Amendment to the U.S. Constitution, no person shall be "deprived of life, liberty or property, without due process of law; nor shall private property be taken for public use without just compensation." This clause, known as the eminent domain reservation, gives the state the legal right to take private property for public use without the consent of the owner. But, the owner has a right to his day in court to ensure "just compensation."

The Fourteenth Amendment states that no state shall "deprive any person of life, liberty, or property, without due process of law; nor deny to any person within its jurisdiction the equal protection of the laws." This simply extends legal property protection from all of the amendments in the Bill of Rights down to local government protection of private property ownership.

But just what is private property ownership? *Property* is anything subject to ownership and *private* relates basically to an individual. Ownership relates to a possessory interest in a property. This is the right to exert control over the uses of property to the exclusion of others.

SOURCE: Al Bellerue, *The Freeman* (1995).

① Economy

HENRY DAVID THOREAU

American philosopher Henry David Thoreau (1817–1862) is perhaps best known for his book *Walden*, published in 1854, in which he describes his experiences living alone in an isolated cabin near Walden Pond in Massachusetts. Thoreau's arguments in *Walden* about living frugally and close to the land helped make him a hero to environmentalists who embraced his philosophy more than a century later during the beginning of the modern environmental movement in the 1970s. His ideas remain influential today, but modern readers often seem to forget that *Walden* was more than a description of living in tune with nature; it was also a pointed critique of the American consumer-oriented lifestyle, which Thoreau criticized for its focus on earning money and buying goods. As he notes in a famous quote from *Walden*, "the mass of men lead lives of quiet desperation"—mostly, he believed, because they are slaves to their work and spend their lives trying to earn money rather than enjoying the simple wonders of life. In the following excerpt from *Walden*, Thoreau describes how he built his small cabin in the woods from materials that he re-used from a nearby "shanty." He goes on to criticize the "ornaments" that embellish the homes of many of his fellow citizens, and he even pokes fun at the cost of dormitory rooms at a nearby college. In making such criticisms, Thoreau raises questions about our relationship to one of our most basic necessities: shelter. For many people today, homes are much more than basic shelter.

They are expensive, elaborate reflections of an owner's interests and identity. And they are usually the source of great debt as well. In many ways, when it comes to the homes we live in, things today are not much different from Thoreau's time. As you read his argument about the kind of dwelling that serves us best, consider whether it is relevant to today's ongoing debates about the merits of owning a home.

HENRY DAVID THOREAU, "Economy"

1 Near the end of March, 1845, I borrowed an axe and went down to the woods by Walden Pond, nearest to where I intended to build my house, and began to cut down some tall arrowy white pines, still in their youth, for timber. It is difficult to begin without borrowing, but perhaps it is the most generous course thus to permit your fellow-men to have an interest in your enterprise. The owner of the axe, as he released his hold on it, said that it was the apple of his eye; but I returned it sharper than I received it. It was a pleasant hillside where I worked, covered with pine woods, through which I looked out on the pond, and a small open field in the woods where pines and hickories were springing up. The ice in the pond was not yet dissolved, though there were some open spaces, and it was all dark colored and saturated with water. There were some slight flurries of snow during the days that I worked there; but for the most part when I came out onto the railroad, on my way home, its yellow sand heap stretched away glooming in the hazy atmosphere, and the rails shone in the spring sun, and I heard the lark and pewee and other birds already come to commence another year with us. They were pleasant spring days, in which the winter of man's discontent was thawing as well as the earth, and the life that had lain torpid began to stretch itself. One day, when my axe had come off and I had cut a green hickory for a wedge, driving it with a stone, and had placed the whole to soak in a pond hole in order to swell the wood, I saw a striped snake run into the water, and he lay on the bottom, apparently without inconvenience, as long as I stayed there, for more than a quarter of an hour,

perhaps because he had not yet fairly come out of the torpid state. It appeared to me that for a like reason men remain in their present low and primitive condition; but if they should feel the influence of the spring of springs arousing them, they would of necessity rise to a higher and more ethereal life. I had previously seen the snakes in frosty mornings in my path with portions of their bodies still numb and inflexible, waiting for the sun to thaw them. On the 1st of April it rained and melted the ice, and in the early part of the day, which was very foggy, I heard a stray goose groping about over the pond and cackling as if lost, or like the spirit of the fog.

So I went on for some days cutting and hewing timber, and also studs and rafters, all with my narrow axe, not having many communicable or scholar-like thoughts, singing to myself,

Men say they know many things;
But lo! they have taken wings—
The arts and sciences,
And a thousand appliances;
The wind that blows
Is all that anybody knows.

I hewed the main timbers six inches square, most of the studs on two sides only, and the rafters and floor timbers on one side, leaving the rest of the bark on, so that they were just as straight and much stronger than sawed ones. Each stick was carefully mortised or tenoned by its stump, for I had borrowed other tools by this time. My days in the woods were not very long ones; yet I usually carried my dinner of bread and butter, and read the newspaper in which it was wrapped, at noon, sitting amid the green pine boughs which I had cut off, and to my bread was imparted some of their fragrance, for my hands were covered with a thick coat of pitch. Before I had done I was more the friend than the foe of the pine tree, though I had cut down some of them, having become better acquainted with it. Sometimes a rambler in the wood was attracted by the sound of my axe, and we chatted pleasantly over the chips which I had made.

By the middle of April, for I made no haste in my work, but rather made the most of it, my house was framed and ready for the raising. I had already bought the shanty of James Collins, an Irishman who worked on the Fitchburg Railroad, for boards. James Collins' shanty was considered an uncommonly fine one. When I called to see it he was not at home. I walked about the outside, at first unobserved from within, the window was so deep and high. It was of small dimensions, with a peaked cottage roof, and not much else to be seen, the dirt being raised five feet all around as if it were a compost heap. The roof was the soundest part, though a good deal warped and made brittle by the sun. Doorsill there was none, but a perennial passage for the hens under the door board. Mrs. C. came to the door and asked me to view it from the inside. The hens were driven in by my approach. It was dark, and had a dirt floor for the most part, dank, clammy, and aguish, only here a board and there a board which would not bear removal. She lighted a lamp to show me the inside of the roof and the walls, and also that the board floor extended under the bed, warning me not to step into the cellar, a sort of dust hole two feet deep. In her own words, they were "good boards overhead, good boards all around, and a good window"—of two whole squares originally, only the cat had passed out that way lately. There was a stove, a bed, and a place to sit, an infant in the house where it was born, a silk parasol, gilt-framed looking-glass, and a patent new coffee-mill nailed to an oak sapling, all told. The bargain was soon concluded, for James had in the meanwhile returned. I to pay four dollars and twenty-five cents tonight, he to vacate at five tomorrow morning, selling to nobody else

meanwhile: I to take possession at six. It were well, he said, to be there early, and anticipate certain indistinct but wholly unjust claims on the score of ground rent and fuel. This he assured me was the only encumbrance. At six I passed him and his family on the road. One large bundle held their all—bed, coffee-mill, looking-glass, hens—all but the cat; she took to the woods and became a wild cat and, as I learned afterward, trod in a trap set for woodchucks, and so became a dead cat at last.

I took down this dwelling the same morning, drawing the nails, and removed it to the pond side by small cart loads, spreading the boards on the grass there to bleach and warp back again in the sun. One early thrush gave me a note or two as I drove along the woodland path. I was informed treacherously by a young Patrick that neighbor Seeley, an Irishman, in the intervals of the carting, transferred the still tolerable, straight, and drivable nails, staples, and spikes to his pocket, and then stood when I came back to pass the time of day, and look freshly up, unconcerned, with spring thoughts, at the devastation; there being a dearth of work, as he said. He was there to represent spectatordom, and help make this seemingly insignificant event one with the removal of the gods of Troy.

I dug my cellar in the side of a hill sloping to the south, where a woodchuck had formerly dug his burrow, down through sumach and blackberry roots, and the lowest stain of vegetation, six feet square by seven deep, to a fine sand where potatoes would not freeze in any winter. The sides were left shelving, and not stoned; but the sun having never shone on them, the sand still keeps its place. It was but two hours' work. I took particular pleasure in this breaking of ground, for in almost all latitudes men dig into the earth for an equable temperature. Under the most splendid house in the city is still to be found the cellar where they store their roots as of old, and long after the superstructure had disappeared posterity remark its dent in the earth. The house is still but a sort of porch at the entrance of a burrow.

At length, in the beginning of May, with the help of some of my acquaintances, rather to improve so good an occasion for neighborliness than from any necessity, I set up the frame of my house. No man was ever more honored in the character of his raisers than I. They are destined, I trust, to assist at the raising of loftier structures one day. I began to occupy my house on the 4th of July, as soon as it was boarded and roofed, for the boards were carefully feather-edged and lapped, so that it was perfectly impervious to rain, but before boarding I laid the foundation of a chimney at one end, bringing two cartloads of stones up the hill from the pond in my arms. I built the chimney after my hoeing in the fall, before a fire became necessary for warmth, doing my cooking in the meanwhile out of doors on the ground, early in the morning: which mode I still think is in some respects more convenient and agreeable than the usual one. When it stormed before my bread was baked, I fixed a few boards over the fire, and sat under them to watch my loaf, and passed some pleasant hours in that way. In those days, when my hands were much employed, I read but little, but the least scraps of paper which lay on the ground, my holder, or tablecloth, afforded me as much entertainment, in fact answered the same purpose as the Iliad.

It would be worth the while to build still more deliberately than I did, considering, for instance, what foundation a door, a window, a cellar, a garret, have in the nature of man, and perchance never raising any superstructure until we found a better reason for it than our temporal necessities even. There is some of the same fitness in a man's building his own house that there is in a bird's building its own nest. Who knows but if men constructed their dwellings with their own hands, and provided food for themselves and families simply and honestly enough, the poetic faculty would be universally developed, as birds universally sing when they are so engaged? But alas! we do like cowbirds and cuckoos, which lay their eggs in nests which other birds have built, and cheer no traveler with their chattering and unmusical notes. Shall we forever resign the pleasure of construction to the carpenter? What does architecture amount to in the experience of the mass of men? I never in all my walks came across a man engaged in so simple and natural an occupation as building his house. We belong to the community. It is not the tailor alone who is the ninth part of a man; it is as much the preacher, and the merchant, and the farmer. Where is this division of labor to end? and what object does it finally serve? No doubt another *may* also think for me; but it is not therefore desirable that he should do so to the exclusion of my thinking for myself.

True, there are architects so called in this country, and I have heard of one at least possessed with the idea of making architectural ornaments have a core of truth, a necessity, and hence a beauty, as if it were a revelation to him. All very well perhaps from his point of view, but only a little better than the common **dilettantism**. A sentimental reformer in architecture, he began at the cornice, not at the foundation. It was only now to put a core of truth within the ornaments, that every sugar plum in fact might have an almond or caraway seed in it—though I hold that almonds are most wholesome without the sugar—and not how the inhabitant, the indweller, might build truly within and without, and let the ornaments take care of themselves. What reasonable man ever supposed that ornaments were something outward and in the skin merely, that the tortoise got his spotted shell, or the shellfish its mother-o'-pearl tints, by such a contract

Dilettantism A *dilettante* is someone interested in literature and fine art, but the term is often used as a criticism to describe those whose interest in such art is only superficial.

as the inhabitants of Broadway their Trinity Church? But a man has no more to do with the style of architecture of his house than a tortoise with that of its shell: nor need the soldier be so idle as to try to paint the precise *color* of his virtue on his standard. The enemy will find it out. He may turn pale when the trial comes. This man seemed to me to lean over the cornice, and timidly whisper his half truth to the rude occupants who really knew it better than he. What of architectural beauty I now see, I know has gradually grown from within outward, out of the necessities and character of the indweller, who is the only builder—out of some unconscious truthfulness, and nobleness, without ever a thought for the appearance; and whatever additional beauty of this kind is destined to be produced will be preceded by a like unconscious beauty of life. The most interesting dwellings in this country, as the painter knows, are the most unpretending, humble log huts and cottages of the poor commonly; it is the life of the inhabitants whose shells they are, and not any peculiarity in their surfaces merely, which makes them *picturesque;* and equally interesting will be the citizen's suburban box, when his life shall be as simple and as agreeable to the imagination, and there is as little straining after effect in the style of his dwelling. A great proportion of architectural ornaments are literally hollow, and a September gale would strip them off, like borrowed plumes, without injury to the substantials. They can do without *architecture* who have no olives nor wines in the cellar. What if an equal ado were made about the ornaments of style in literature, and the architects of our bibles spent as much time about their cornices as the architects of our churches do? So are made the **belles-lettres and the beaux-arts** and their professors. Much it concerns a man, forsooth, how a few sticks are slanted over him or under him, and what colors are daubed upon his box. It would signify somewhat, if, in any earnest sense, *he* slanted them and daubed it; but the spirit having departed out of the tenant, it is of a piece with constructing his own coffin—the

CONTEXT

Thoreau's criticisms in this passage of "architectural ornaments" were made at a time when the United States was still a rural society and most Americans lived in small towns or rural areas. As a result, homes were often built for practicality, and "architectural ornaments" were reserved for more elaborate homes in growing cities, such as Boston. Today approximately 80 percent of Americans live in cities of 25,000 residents or more. Moreover, since World War II, the size and complexity of Americans' homes have increased dramatically. In 1950 the average American home had 290 square feet per person living there. By 2003 the average home had 900 square feet per person—about 2,500 square feet in total. In 1970 the National Association of Home Builders did not even keep statistics on the number of homes with three bathrooms because such homes were so rare; by 2005, one out of every four new houses in the United States had three or more bathrooms. To what extent do these developments influence how you respond to Thoreau's argument about the kind of dwelling we should live in?

architecture of the grave, and "carpenter," is but another name for "coffin-maker." One man says, in his despair or indifference to life, take up a handful of the earth at your feet, and paint your house that color. Is he thinking of his last and narrow house? Toss up a copper for it as well. What an abundance of leisure he must have! Why do you take up a handful of dirt? Better paint your house your own complexion; let it turn pale or blush for you. An enterprise to improve the style of cottage architecture! When you have got my ornaments ready I will wear them.

Before winter I built a chimney, and shingled the sides of my house, which were already impervious to rain, with imperfect and sappy shingles made of the first slice of the log, whose edges I was obliged to straighten with a plane.

10 I have thus a tight shingled and plastered house, ten feet wide by fifteen long, and eight-feet posts, with a garret and a closet, a large window on each side, two trap doors, one door at the end, and a brick fireplace opposite. The exact cost of my house, paying the usual price for such materials as I used, but not counting the work, all of which was done by myself, was as follows; and I give the details because very few are able to tell exactly what their houses cost, and fewer still, if any, the

Belles-Lettres and Beaux-Arts
Belles lettres is a French term that refers generally to fine literature or literary art. *Beaux arts*, also a French term, refers in general to the fine arts but also denotes a style of architecture common in France that influenced American architecture in the nineteenth century.

separate cost of the various materials which compose them:

Boards ... $8.03, mostly shanty boards

Refuse shingles for roof
and sides 4.00

Laths. 1.25

Two second-hand windows
with glass 2.43

One thousand old brick 4.00

Two casks of lime . . . 2.40 That was high.

Hair. 0.31

Mantle-tree iron. 0.15

Nails 3.90

Hinges and screws. 0.14

Latch. 0.10

Chalk. 0.01

Transportation . . . 1.40 I carried a good
part on my back

In all $28.12½

These are all the materials excepting the timber, stones, and sand, which I claimed by squatter's right. I have also a small woodshed adjoining, made chiefly of the stuff which was left after building the house.

I intend to build me a house which will surpass any on the main street in Concord in grandeur and luxury as soon as it pleases me as much and will cost me no more than my present one.

I thus found that the student who wishes for a shelter can obtain one for a lifetime at an expense not greater than the rent which he now pays annually. If I seem to boast more than is becoming, my excuse is that I brag for humanity rather than for myself; and my shortcomings and inconsistencies do not affect the truth of my statement. Notwithstanding much cant and hypocrisy— chaff which I find it difficult to separate from my wheat, but for which I am as sorry as any man—I will breathe freely and stretch myself in this respect, it is such a relief to both the moral and physical system; and I am resolved that I will not through humility become the devil's attorney. I will endeavor to speak a good word for the truth. At Cambridge College the mere rent of a student's room, which is only a little larger than my own, is thirty dollars each year, though the corporation had the advantage of building thirty-two side by side and under one roof, and the occupant suffers the inconvenience of many and noisy neighbors, and perhaps a residence in the fourth story. I cannot but think that if we had more true wisdom in these respects, not only less education would be needed, because, forsooth, more would already have been acquired, but the pecuniary expense of getting an education would in a great measure vanish. Those conveniences which the student requires at Cambridge or elsewhere cost him or somebody else ten times as great a sacrifice of life as they would with proper management on both sides. Those things for which the most money is demanded are never the things which the student most wants.

Questions for Discussion

1. Throughout this passage, Thoreau uses metaphor and simile to help make his arguments about what is wrong with the lifestyles of his fellow citizens and about how we should live. In paragraph 1, for example, he compares people to a "torpid" snake that is coming out of hibernation in the spring. Assess Thoreau's use of these metaphors. To what extent do you think they help make his argument more (or less) effective? Are they appropriate to his main argument? Why or why not?

2. Thoreau describes the act of building his cabin in great detail. Why do you think he does so? What purpose does his description of his work on his cabin accomplish? In what ways might it enhance his argument about how we should live?

3. Much of Thoreau's argument about how we should live and the kind of shelter we should have is based on his own experience. How effective is his personal experience as evidence for his main argument? To what extent do you think his arguments would be less effective if he had not lived the way he lived?

4. In paragraph 5, Thoreau describes how he dug the cellar for his cabin, and he discusses the importance of a cellar. He ends the paragraph by stating that "a house is but a sort of porch at the entrance of a burrow." What does he mean by that statement? In what way does that point fit into his larger argument about the kind of shelter we should have?

5. In a sense, much of Thoreau's argument rests on his own character. He criticizes his fellow citizens in part by comparing their lifestyles unfavorably to his own. And he claims, "If I seem to boast more than is becoming, my excuse is that I brag for humanity rather than for myself; and my shortcomings and inconsistencies do not affect the truth of my statement" (par. 13). To what extent does Thoreau's character, as it emerges in this passage, contribute to his argument? (See the discussion of ethos on page 67.) Do you find him appealing? Why or why not? How might your answer to that question influence your reaction to his argument?

6. Why is Thoreau so critical of architecture and what he calls the "ornaments" of houses (see especially par. 8)? What is the basis for his criticism? How does his criticism of "ornament" fit into his larger argument?

7. In the final paragraph of this passage, Thoreau asserts that if "we had more true wisdom," we would need less education and it would cost less. To what extent do you think his criticism of higher education is still valid today?

② | Rethinking Rent

REBECCA TUHUS-DUBROW

As writer Rebecca Tuhus-Dubrow notes in the beginning of the following article, homeownership in the United States is "a central part of the American dream." As of 2010, approximately 67 percent of Americans lived in homes they owned. The apparent benefits of homeownership seem beyond question: more stable neighborhoods, greater civic participation, greater family wealth, among others. All of this seems good for individuals, good for communities, and good for the nation as a whole. So it isn't surprising that for much of the past century, the goal of increasing homeownership in the United States has become so deeply entrenched that it has rarely been seriously questioned. But the severe economic downturn that began in 2008 and serious problems in the U.S. housing market have prompted many people to wonder whether owning a home is really such a good idea; moreover, critics have begun to argue that government policy should not necessarily encourage homeownership. In the following article, which was published in the *Boston Globe* in 2009, Tuhus-Dubrow examines the question of whether it is better to own a home or to rent. In doing so, she raises more fundamental questions about whether the responsibility for basic needs such as shelter should belong to individuals or to government. Tuhus-Dubrow is a contributing writer for the Ideas section of the *Boston Globe*. She has also written about social and political issues for *The Nation*, the *Village Voice*, and other publications.

REBECCA TUHUS-DUBROW, "Rethinking Rent"

1 In the soul-searching sparked by the financial meltdown, Americans have started to look askance at some of the habits and policies that had come to define our country. Excessive consumption and living on credit are no longer seen as acceptable, let alone possible. "Deregulation" is suddenly a dirty word.

Yet despite the housing crisis, one value, more deeply entrenched, remains sacrosanct: homeownership. Irresponsible mortgages have been universally condemned, but it is still widely assumed that we all aspire to own homes—and that we all should aspire to own homes. Homeowners are thought to be more engaged in their communities and to take better care of their houses and neighborhoods. On a nearly subconscious level, buying a home is a central part of the American dream. A picket fence may now be dispensable, but a house of one's own is seen as the proper place to raise an American family—a prerequisite for stability, security, and adult life. And for decades—but increasingly under the Clinton and Bush administrations—federal policies have encouraged citizens to achieve this goal.

But a growing chorus of economists and housing experts say that this mind-set, too, needs fundamental reform. Owning a home is not right for everyone, they say: In some ways it's overrated, and it can even have harmful effects for individuals and society. It is now glaringly clear that buying a home is a financial risk, not the surefire investment it is often perceived to be. Widespread homeownership may also have a negative impact on the economy, because, among other reasons, displaced workers can't easily relocate to new jobs. And some of the alleged rewards of homeownership, such as greater self-esteem, health, and civic engagement, have been called into question by research. The government, critics argue, should focus on ensuring high-quality, affordable housing rather than promoting homeownership for its own sake.

"There's no reason we should all be homeowners," says Joseph Gyourko, a professor at the Wharton School of Business and coauthor of "Rethinking Federal Housing Policy." "Homeownership has a lot of benefits, but it has costs, too."

5 According to this view, renting offers many advantages, and should be considered a viable long-term option for people of all ages and socioeconomic levels. Renters enjoy flexibility and freedom from the responsibilities of maintenance. Given the often overlooked costs and risks of homeownership, renting is in many cases a wise financial choice. And the experience of a place like Switzerland—a well-functioning country with only about a 35 percent homeownership rate—suggests that rental housing per se does not unmoor society.

Some analysts propose abolishing or limiting the mortgage interest tax deduction, which provides substantial tax breaks for homeowners. Others favor greater security for renters—such as laws making eviction more difficult—or tax deductions for renters, which a few states, such as Massachusetts, already offer. The MacArthur Foundation has launched a major initiative to preserve affordable rental housing in 12 states, including Massachusetts. In the **recent stimulus legislation**, advocates of renting successfully fought additional incentives for homeownership, and they continue to push for a "balanced" housing policy.

Certainly, homeownership still has staunch defenders. Many stand by its psychological and social benefits, and consider a home

COMPLICATIONS

According to the National Association of Realtors, homeownership offers more than obvious financial benefits, such as tax credits for interest of mortgage payments and greater wealth in the form of increasing housing values over time. Homeownership also offers important social benefits. For example, "Home ownership improves neighborhoods. Owners are 28% more likely to improve their home and 10% more likely to participate in solving local problems." In addition, homeowners "are 15% more likely to vote and they volunteer time for political and charitable causes more frequently than renters."

SOURCE: National Association of Realtors.

to be a sound investment. "It's the single most significant source of wealth and most secure source of savings" for Americans, says Jim Carr, chief operating officer for the National Community Reinvestment Coalition. In his view, the real problem has been the dysfunctional market, which we should not conflate with homeownership itself. "In a well-regulated market, homeownership provides a nest egg and an important generational wealth transfer," he says.

Nearly everyone agrees that homeownership is sometimes the right choice: for people with the means, who intend to stay put for a long time and want to customize their houses, it probably makes sense. And the mortgage interest deduction would be difficult to eliminate for political reasons. Yet more and more experts are saying that if we could unsentimentally see the pluses and minuses of each option—and if we had a level playing field in terms of government support—the sensible decision for many Americans would be to refrain from buying a home, perhaps for their whole lives.

Owning a house, we tend to think, is a quasi-magical boon that provides a broad array of goods for individuals and families. There is a logic to the reasoning: If you are financially invested in a neighborhood and expect to stay there for years, you'll be more inclined to tend a garden, bake muffins for your neighbors, and follow developments that affect the community. You have more control

Recent Stimulus Legislation refers to the American Recovery and Reinvestment Act, often called the federal "Stimulus Program," which was passed by Congress in 2009.

over your environment, which seems likely to yield psychological benefits. Studies over the years have suggested that homeowners are healthier and happier, and even that their children perform better in school.

10 But other research has challenged these conclusions. Some studies find no significant relationships between these desirable outcomes and homeownership. And according to several reviews of the literature, many of the studies suffer from methodological flaws: Most importantly, they fail to control adequately for other variables, such as income, age, marital status, and home value. In other words, homeowners tend to do better on a range of measures, but that doesn't mean that the ownership status is the cause; homeowners tend to be older and wealthier, which could account for the differences. And there is little research on the potential negative consequences for low-income families facing the burden of mortgage debt and the possibility (and reality) of foreclosure.

A recent study, which aimed to avoid the problems of previous research, suggests that homeownership confers no real benefits. The study examined self-respect, perceived notions of control, time spent with friends and family, volunteer activities, and enjoyment of the neighborhood, among other things. On all of these measures, after controlling for income, health status, and home value, the study found no significant advantage for homeowners. In fact, homeowners were on average 12 pounds heavier, and they spent less time with friends. They also reported

more "pain"—the term used in the study's survey—deriving from their homes than renters. Grace Wong Bucchianeri, an assistant professor at the Wharton School, conducted the study in 2005, at the top of the market. (All of her subjects occupied single-family homes, so the only difference was ownership status. But her study had limitations too: all of the subjects were women, and it was geographically confined to Ohio.)

"It challenges our notion of engaged, active, healthy homeowners," says Bucchianeri. "We're not looking at a lot of benefit here."

Some of the more concrete financial drawbacks of homeownership should be obvious to any homeowner. There are high transaction costs: 7 to 10 percent of the cost of the house goes to the process of buying and selling. Between "sprucing it up and legal fees, it's not cheap," says Eric Belsky, executive director of the Joint Center for Housing Studies at Harvard. Major repairs, sometimes unexpected, may be needed, and simple upkeep usually costs 2 to 4 percent of the house price per year. These responsibilities can be a hassle as well as an expense. Renting, by contrast, is "inherently efficient," as Matthew Perrenod of the Housing Partnership Network argued at a housing conference at Harvard in mid-March, because the maintenance can be professionalized. Owning also, of course, comes with the risk of losing money if you have to move during a down market, or of being tethered to a house you want to leave.

Renting is often derided, especially by real estate agents, as "throwing money away." But upon close examination, the best financial decision is far from clear, and it's impossible to generalize. Buying entails paying property taxes, as well as the cost of repairs, mortgage payments, and mortgage interest.

15 Some financial analysts say that in terms of dividends, individuals would often be better off renting and using the money saved to invest in stocks. According to the National

CONTEXT

In the midst of the global economic recession that began in 2008, many homeowners lost money as the value of their homes decreased. Many others lost their homes altogether because they could not make their mortgage payments. In many cases, homes were worth less than what the homeowners owed on their mortgages, a situation referred to as being "under water." In 2009, nearly 10 percent of homeowners were delinquent on their mortgage payments, and both the delinquency rate and the rate of foreclosures increased compared to 2008.

Multi-Housing Council's 2008 annual report, a $100 investment in a home in 1985 would have paid off $210 by 2008, but if the same amount had been invested in stocks, it would have grown to $710. (Of course, the recent drop in stock values likely narrowed the gap.)

Some of the advantages of homeownership may be double-edged. Stability has virtues, but the flip side is inflexibility. Especially for low-income homeowners, owning a home can become a trap, preventing them from escaping distressed neighborhoods. For people at all income levels, owning a home may keep them from moving to where jobs are.

In the mid-1990s, Andrew Oswald, a British economist at the University of Warwick, began to notice a correlation between national rates of homeownership and unemployment. Among industrialized nations, Spain had the highest rates of both, while Switzerland had the lowest rates of both. Other variables, such as the generosity of the welfare state, didn't seem to matter nearly as much. He believes a high homeownership rate undercuts the efficiency of the economy: not only does it contribute to joblessness, but workers may take jobs for which they are not ideally suited, based on location rather than skills.

"There's been a presumption that it's really good for a country to have a high rate of homeownership," says Oswald. "But that homeownership equates with inflexibility."

The evidence is mixed on whether homeowners are more civically engaged than renters. But to the extent that they are, their influence in some cases has undesirable societal repercussions. Since houses are the major asset for so many families, homeowners naturally want to protect their property values. This often leads to zoning laws that make it difficult to construct commercial or additional residential buildings. Such laws erect barriers to entrepreneurs and reduce overall housing affordability.

20 Moreover, homeowners are likely to have longer commutes than renters, as *New York Times* columnist Paul Krugman has pointed out. That's because they buy houses on inexpensive land, farther from city centers; this contributes to sprawl and congestion. As awareness has grown about climate change, more and more analysts are citing environmental factors as a reason to prefer renting and the relative density that typically goes along with it.

Given the mixed evidence for the benefits of homeownership for both individuals and society, does it warrant major government promotion?

The **mortgage interest deduction** has aroused widespread criticism. According to many detractors, this tax break does not even foster homeownership; it merely encourages the affluent to buy bigger houses. "When they go to deduct interest, it has a more powerful effect for them," says Belsky. "They're buying more house." For this, the government forgoes large amounts of tax revenue. President Obama's budget proposes reducing the deduction for the top tax bracket, although this provision may be difficult to pass.

Some believe any subsidy for homeownership is misguided, given the uncertain evidence for its benefits, and the indications of downsides. Low-income people may be seen as most deserving of support in buying homes, but in some ways they also stand to lose the most, as has become clear in the recent crisis. People without stable jobs or family situations may find it difficult to meet the responsibilities of homeownership, and efforts to help them buy homes could backfire by ending in foreclosures.

A number of proposals have been advanced by critics of the status quo. Dean Baker, codirector of the Center for Economic and Policy Research, advocates greater protection for renters, so that they are ensured certain standards of quality and "some security," he says, "so that your landlord can't just say 'I want you out.' . . . Renters shouldn't be second-class citizens." (A few cities, such as New York, already offer some strong protections.) The National Multi-Housing Council

Mortgage Interest Deduction

Homeowners are able to deduct from their federal taxes the interest they pay on their home mortgages. This "mortgage interest deduction" has long been a part of federal tax policy and is intended to encourage homeownership.

advocates incentives for rental housing. In the housing stimulus bill passed last July, it successfully lobbied for increased funding for the Low-Income Housing Tax Credit program, which supports the production of affordable rental housing.

25 Some economists, such as Gyourko, don't believe in subsidies for either alternative.

"I think we should have a level playing field," he says. "There's no reason to subsidize homeownership significantly."

The emotional tug of owning a home can't be discounted. But in recent years, as jobs have become less stable, environmental concerns have risen, and the costs of owning a house have become apparent, the case for renting has become more compelling. According to Eric Belsky, "People are saying, 'Hey, it's OK to rent.' " "Instead of starting with a presumption in favor of homeownership," he asks, "Why don't we help people make informed choices?"

Questions for Discussion

1. According to Tuhus-Dubrow, what are the benefits of renting? How does she support the claim that renting "should be considered a viable long-term option for people of all ages and socioeconomic levels"? (par. 5). How persuasive do you find her argument in favor of renting?

2. Tuhus-Dubrow considers both the pros and cons of owning a home. How fairly do you think she represents the opposing sides of this debate? How well does her discussion of the pros and cons of homeownership help support her main argument about the benefits of renting?

3. In paragraph 10 Tuhus-Dubrow states that research has challenged some benefits of homeownership. What kinds of research does she cite to support this claim? What does this research reveal about homeownership? How persuasive do you find Tuhus-Dubrow's discussion of this research? How well does this discussion support her main point?

4. Tuhus-Dubrow quotes several experts to support her various points about the pros and cons of homeownership and renting. Evaluate her use of these experts. How credible do they seem? How effectively does Tuhus-Dubrow use their statements to support her claims?

5. This article was originally published in the *Boston Globe*, and as a journalist Tuhus-Dubrow tries to be objective in her examination of the question of whether homeowning or renting a home is a better choice. Do you think she achieves the goal of objectivity? Why or why not? Cite specific passages from her article to support your answer.

6. In the final paragraph, Tuhus-Dubrow writes that "the case for renting has become more compelling." How effectively has she represented that case in her article?

7. This article might be seen as an argument to inquire (see page 11)—in this case, into an issue (homeownership) that has become more complicated and controversial in recent years. Do you think this article is effective as such an argument? Explain.

③ # Defining an Ownership Society

DAVID BOAZ

The right to own property is fundamental to American culture, but the question of how to balance the rights of private property owners with the common good is a long-standing one in American society. It is also a complicated question. For example, is it more important to share the burden of caring for retired Americans or to allow individuals to decide how best to care for themselves in retirement? The Social Security system, which has been in existence since 1935, is based on the idea that government has some responsibility to take care of all citizens, even if that means limiting some individual choice by taxing everyone to support the Social Security system. Not everyone believes that government should play such a role. In the following essay David Boaz comes down clearly on the side of encouraging and protecting private property. In his view, we are all better off when government policy allows citizens greater ownership of property and protects private property. The roots of his argument extend back to the very founding of the United States, when the American colonists resisted the taxes collected from them by the British government. But as his essay, which was published in 2005, makes clear, those old tensions between individual rights and the common good are still being felt when it comes to ownership and private property. David Boaz is executive vice president of the Cato Institute, a libertarian think-tank, and author of *The Politics of Freedom* (2008). His essay was published by the Cato Institute.

DAVID BOAZ, "Defining an Ownership Society"

1 President Bush says he wants America to be an "ownership society."What does that mean?

People have known for a long time that individuals take better care of things they own. Aristotle wrote, "What belongs in common to the most people is accorded the least care: they take thought for their own things above all, and less about things common, or only so much as falls to each individually." And we all observe that homeowners take better care of their houses than renters do. That's not because renters are bad people; it's just that you're more attentive to details when you stand to profit from your house's rising value or to suffer if it deteriorates.

Just as homeownership creates responsible homeowners, widespread ownership of other assets creates responsible citizens. People who are owners feel more dignity, more pride, and more confidence. They have a stronger stake, not just in their own property, but in their community and their society. Geoff Mulgan, a top aide to British prime minister Tony Blair, explains,

CONTEXT

During the 2004 U.S. presidential campaign, President George W. Bush spoke about his goal of making the United States an "ownership society" characterized by personal responsibility and property ownership. Bush's ideas about an ownership society are based on a belief that individuals should be allowed to achieve economic well-being through their own initiative. From this perspective, the role of government is to promote individual initiative and responsibility and provide for a free market.

COMPLICATION

In the article that begins on page 258, Rebecca Tuhus-Dubrow reviews studies that call into question some of the perceived benefits of homeownership. (See par. 11 on page 260.)

"The left always tended to underestimate the importance of ownership, and how hard it is for a democracy that does not have widespread ownership of assets to be truly democratic.... To escape from poverty you need assets—assets which you can put to work. There is a good deal of historical evidence...as well as abundant contemporary evidence, that ownership tends to encourage self-esteem and healthy habits of behaviour, such as acting more for the long term, or taking education more seriously."

Former prime minister Margaret Thatcher had that goal in mind when she set out to privatize Great Britain's public housing. Her administration sold 1.5 million housing units to their occupants, transforming 1.5 million British families from tenants in public housing to proud homeowners. She thought the housing would be better maintained, but more importantly she thought that homeowners would become more responsible citizens and see themselves as having a real stake in the future and in the quality of life in their communities. And yes, she thought that homeowners would be more likely to vote for lower taxes and less regulation—policies that would tend to improve the country's economic performance—and thus for the Conservative Party, or for Labour Party candidates only when they renounced their traditional socialism.

5 Margaret Thatcher saw that private ownership allows people to profit from improving their property by building on it or otherwise making it more valuable. People can also profit by improving themselves, of course, through education and the development of good habits, as long as they are allowed to reap the profits that come from such improvement. There's not much point in improving your skills, for instance, if regulations will keep you from entering your chosen occupation or high taxes will take most of your higher income.

The United States today has the most widespread property ownership in history.

This year an all-time high of 68.6 percent of American households own their own homes. Even more significantly, increasing numbers of Americans are becoming capitalists—people who own a share of productive businesses through stocks or mutual funds. About half of American households qualify as stockholding in some form. That's up from 32 percent in 1989 and only 19 percent in 1983, a remarkable change in just 20 years. That means almost half of Americans directly benefited from the enormous market appreciation between 1982 and 2000 and are prepared to see their wealth increase again when the current stock market slump ends.

But it also means that about half of Americans are not benefiting as owners from the growth of the American economy (though of course they still benefit as wage-earners and consumers). In general, those are the Americans below the average income. The best thing we could do to create an ownership society in America is to give more Americans an opportunity to invest in stocks, bonds, and mutual funds so that they too can become capitalists. And the way to do that is obvious.

Right now, every working American is required to send the government 12.4 percent of his or her income (up to about $88,000) via payroll taxes. That's $4,960 on a salary of $40,000 a year. But that money is not invested in real assets, and it doesn't belong to the wage-earner who paid it. It goes into the Social Security system, where it's used to pay benefits to current retirees. If we want to make every working American an investor—an owner of real assets, with control of his own retirement funds and a stake in the growth of the American economy—then we should let workers put their Social Security taxes into private retirement accounts, like IRAs or 401(k)s. Then, instead of hoping someday to receive a meager retirement income from a Social Security system that is headed for bankruptcy, American workers would own their own assets in accounts that couldn't be reduced by Congress.

CONTEXT

According to the U.S. Census Bureau, at the end of 2009, the homeownership rate in the United States was 67.2 percent, which was a decrease from 2008. This rate has been declining since 2005, when David Boaz wrote this essay.

President Bush has talked about such a reform since his first campaign, and his President's Commission to Strengthen Social Security proposed three ways to achieve this goal. If he chooses to make Social Security reform part of his reelection campaign, then we may see congressional action in 2005. Sen. John F. Kerry has pledged never to "privatize Social Security." He should be asked why he thinks working-class Americans should not be allowed to invest their savings in stocks and bonds, as his family has done so successfully.

10 Other reforms that could enhance the ownership society include school choice—which would give parents the power to choose the schools their children attend—and wider use of Health Savings Accounts, which transfer control over health care decisions from employers, insurance companies, and HMO gatekeepers to individual patients.

Advancing an ownership society can also improve environmental quality. People take care of things they own, and they're more likely to waste or damage things that are owned by no one in particular. That's why timber companies don't cut all the trees on their land and instead plant new trees to replace the ones they do cut down. They may be moved by a concern for the environment, but the future income from the property is also a powerful incentive. In the socialist countries of Eastern Europe, where the government controlled all property, there was no real owner to worry about the future value of property; consequently, pollution and environmental destruction were far worse than in the West. Vacláv Klaus, prime minister of the Czech Republic, said in 1995, "The worst environmental damage occurs in countries without private property, markets, or prices."

Another benefit of private property ownership, not so clearly economic, is that it diffuses power. When the government owns all property, individuals have little protection from the whims of politicians. The institution of private property gives many individuals a place to call their own, a place where they are safe from depredation by others and by the state. This aspect of private property is captured in the axiom, "A man's home is his castle." Private property is essential for privacy and for freedom of the press. Try to imagine "freedom of the press" in a country where the government owns all the presses and all the paper.

The many benefits of an ownership society are not always intuitively obvious. The famous Harvard economist John Kenneth Galbraith wrote a bestselling book in 1958 called *The Affluent Society*, in which he discussed the phenomenon of "private opulence and public squalor"—that is, a society in which privately owned resources were generally clean, efficient, well-maintained, and improving in quality while public spaces were dirty, overcrowded, and unsafe—and concluded, oddly enough, that we ought to move more resources into the public sector. Thousands of college students were assigned to read *The Affluent Society*, and Galbraith's ideas played a major role in the vast expansion of government during the 1960s and 1970s.

But Galbraith and American politicians missed the real point of his observation. The more logical answer is that if privately owned resources are better maintained, then we should seek to expand private ownership.

15 Widespread ownership of capital assets has many benefits for society: It means that property is better maintained and long-term values are higher, including environmental quality. It means that people have a greater stake in their community and thus become better citizens. It protects people from the arbitrary power of government and gives them more freedom and more confidence as citizens. It produces prosperity because markets can't work without private property. Private retirement accounts and reduced taxes on investment would encourage more ownership for all Americans.

Questions for Discussion

1. What are the primary benefits of promoting what Boaz calls "an ownership society"? What evidence does Boaz offer to support his claims about these benefits? How persuasive do you find his argument in favor of an ownership society? To what extent do you think your reaction to Boaz's argument is a reflection of your own political views?

2. In paragraph 7 Boaz writes, "The best thing we could do to create an ownership society in America is to give more Americans an opportunity to invest in stocks, bonds, and mutual funds so that they too can become capitalists." What support does he offer for this claim? Do you think he is right? Why or why not?

3. Boaz argues that Americans should be allowed to invest the money they now pay in federal taxes to support the Social Security system. What is the advantage of such a policy, according to Boaz? How effectively does he make the case for this policy? To what extent does he support his claim that Social Security is "headed for bankruptcy"? (par. 8)

4. Boaz states that private property ownership "diffuses power" (par. 12). What does he mean by that statement? What support does he offer for that statement?

5. How would you describe Boaz's reasoning in this essay? Does he argue through inductive or deductive reasoning? (See pages 81–83 for a discussion of deductive reasoning and pages 80–81 for a discussion of inductive reasoning.) How convincing do you find his reasoning in favor of an ownership society?

The End of the Ownership Society

MARC GOLDWEIN

Barack Obama was elected president of the United States in 2008 in the midst of the most severe economic crisis since the Great Depression. He immediately began to implement ambitious government policies that were intended to support banks and other businesses as well as private citizens as they tried to weather the crisis. His policies, which reversed many of the economic policies of the previous president, George W. Bush, touched off intense debates about the role government should play in such a crisis—and in the economic lives of its citizens. In the following essay, Marc Goldwein enters those debates. Goldwein, who is a Senior Policy Analyst at the New America Foundation, a nonprofit institute that studies government policy, argues that the policies of President Bush failed to create the kind of "ownership society" that Bush envisioned, and in Goldwein's view, Americans are better off because those policies failed. Whether or not you agree with him, his essay, which was published by the History News Network in February, 2009, raises complicated questions about the role of government in supporting the well-being of its citizens. It also raises questions about whether private ownership is always a good idea.

MARC GOLDWEIN, "The End of the Ownership Society"

1 In his second inaugural address, President Bush offered a vision of an "ownership society."

In America's ideal of freedom, citizens find the dignity and security of economic independence.... To give every American a stake in the promise and future of our country, we will ... build an ownership society. We will widen the ownership of homes and businesses, retirement savings and health insurance—preparing our people for the challenges of life in a free society. By making every citizen an agent of his or her own destiny, we will give our fellow Americans greater freedom from want and fear, and make our society more prosperous and just and equal.

This wasn't a new idea for Bush, who spoke of an ownership society frequently during his presidency. Many critics suggested this concept was used as a rhetorical tool to tie together scantly related policies, or to euphemistically describe a harsh free market ideology. But when studied more deeply, it

becomes clear that the ownership society represents a genuine and coherent set of ideas distinct from **laissez-faire capitalism** with its own historical and intellectual roots. After an eight-year experiment with an ownership agenda, though, it seems the conservative vision of an ownership society will never come to be.

Like their libertarian counterparts, conservative ownership advocates aim to reduce the overall size and scope of the

Laissez-faire capitalism refers to an economic philosophy that advocates individual freedom with minimal government regulation of businesses and markets.

CONTEXT

President George W. Bush delivered his second inaugural address on January 20, 2005. At one point he called for policies to create an "ownership society": "To give every American a stake in the promise and future of our country, we will bring the highest standards to our schools, and build an ownership society. We will widen the ownership of homes and businesses, retirement savings and health insurance—preparing our people for the challenges of life in a free society. By making every citizen an agent of his or her own destiny, we will give our fellow Americans greater freedom from want and fear, and make our society more prosperous and just and equal."

CONTEXT

As prime minister of the United Kingdom from 1979 to 1990, Margaret Thatcher implemented policies to reduce government spending on services such as education and privatize many traditional government services, including public housing. Her conservative economic philosophy was called "popular capitalism" because it was intended to increase private property and enable individual citizens to reap economic benefits.

government and emphasize the importance of individual responsibility. But while free-market supporters address this goal on the supply-side—pushing policies which will either directly reduce government spending or push politicians toward such actions—conservative ownership advocates focus on the demand-side, aiming to reduce the public's need and desire for government assistance. In fact, ownership advocates often support increasing the supply of government upfront, using activist public policies to expand asset-ownership.

5 Supporters of an "ownership society" envision a world in which the vast majority of Americans are able to provide for themselves through the accumulation of appreciating assets—especially real estate and private equities. By owning these assets, the argument goes, individuals will be able to take advantage of the high economic returns to capital and thus be more self-sufficient. Advocates also argue, as President Bush did, that "if you own something, you have a vital stake in the future of our country," and so expanded ownership strengthens citizenship and community involvement. Additionally, supporters of ownership see it as the truest path to freedom, putting individuals in charge of their own social and economic fates. And finally, conservatives believe broad ownership can strengthen their governing coalition by creating a new class of worker-capitalists who are less apt to support redistributive or regulatory government policies—especially those that might hurt asset values.

Ownership has long been a part of the nation's political economy. Such ownership

CONTEXT

For information about the homeownership rate, see Context on page 264.

has been a major component of this nation's private welfare state,[1] and its expansion has been pursued by liberals and conservatives alike (with the former supporting it as a supplement rather than replacement for existing welfare state programs). Bush's particular concept of an ownership society, though, is most closely related to Margaret Thatcher's "popular capitalism." During her time as Prime Minister, Thatcher declared that "*spreading the ownership of property more widely* is central to this Government's philosophy," and passed measures to sell public housing (of which there was a considerable amount) to interested tenants and partially privatize the country's public pension program. This became a source of inspiration for America's conservative ownership agenda.[2]

During his time in office, President Bush pursued a number of policies to increase property ownership—lower capital gains and dividend tax rates, health savings accounts, 529 college savings accounts, expansions of 401(k)s and IRAs, support for small businesses, etc. But in line with Margaret Thatcher's popular capitalism initiatives, the centerpiece of Bush's ownership agenda was housing and Social Security. His goal was to increase homeownership rates and partially privatize Social Security to offer all workers personal retirement accounts. While both initiatives entered the public agenda in the mid-1990s, they were pushed most vigorously during Bush's time in office; and ultimately, both failed under his watch.

The recent push to expand homeownership actually began with President Clinton's "National Homeownership Strategy" in 1995, after which the homeownership rate shot up 5 percentage points in the next decade (having remained stagnant for the three preceding decades). Yet while new initiatives to promote homeownership began under President Clinton, the Bush administration pushed hard for using "the mighty muscle of the federal government…to encourage owning your own home." These measures included tax credits, down payment assistance, vouchers, financial education, regulatory reforms, and pressure on the private sector.

The Social Security privatization movement also became popular in the 1990s, when a number of bipartisan commissions, outside think tanks, and members of Congress began proposing that Social Security have a private accounts component. In running for President, George W. Bush advocated such accounts, and in the first State of the Union address of his second term, he argued that:

> If you're a younger worker, I believe you should be able to set aside part of [your payroll tax] money in your own retirement account, so you can build a nest egg for your own future.... Your money will grow, over time, at a greater rate than anything the current system can deliver...you'll be able to pass along the money that accumulates in your personal account.... And best of all, the money in the account is yours, and the government can never take it away.... It's time to [offer] security, and choice, and ownership to young Americans.

10 President Bush put considerable political capital into both of these ideas. In 2002 he launched *"America's Homeownership Challenge* to homebuilders, realtors, nonprofits, and government-sponsored enterprises that purchase the mortgages made by lenders" in order to "dismantle barriers to homeownership." In particular, the administration established the goal of fostering at least 5.5 million new minority homeowners, lifting the minority homeownership rate above 50%.

In 2005, after winning reelection, President Bush declared that he had "earned capital in the campaign, political capital, and now intend[ed] to spend it...[and] reforming Social Security [would] be a priority of [his] administration." This was followed by the launch of a massive effort to reform Social Security in which he and his surrogates toured the nation advocating for personal accounts.

Ultimately, both of these initiatives failed, although for different reasons.

Social Security privatization represented a political failure, demonstrating the limits of the ownership society's popularity. Despite early favorable polls, a massive publicity campaign, Republican majorities in both houses, considerable outside support, and strong ideological commitment to reform, President Bush was unable to convince the Congress or the people to support the creation of Social Security private accounts. The large benefit reductions or tax increases necessary to restore solvency to Social Security and finance the accounts themselves made reform inherently unpopular. Meanwhile, think tanks and interest groups on the left launched an aggressive counter campaign to stop partial-privatization, which they argued would infuse unnecessary riskiness into workers' retirement security, and ultimately "dismantle Social Security." All this, combined with poor political decisions and bad luck, led supporters of personal accounts to fall flat on their faces. Although some type of Social Security reform remains inevitable, Bush's failed effort has likely destroyed the chance of replacing part of the Social Security system with private accounts.

While Social Security failed politically, homeownership initiatives failed economically, demonstrating the real limits of ownership expansion. Increasing the homeownership rate required either making homes more affordable or raising real incomes for would-be homeowners. Yet with home values rising rapidly (as was desired) and real income stagnant, this meant reducing the price of or barriers to borrowing. Lending standards were therefore relaxed, as Fannie Mae, Freddie Mac, and private investment firms began investing in high-risk Mortgage Backed Securities. This new capital caused a large expansion of questionable loans, such as so-called sub-prime mortgages, many of which offered seemingly cheap loans to high risk borrowers who couldn't afford them over the long run. Ultimately, these mortgages collapsed under their own weight, bringing down global financial markets along with them. Incidents of foreclosure have skyrocketed, home values have plummeted, mortgage availability has disappeared for many Americans, and the prospect of an ever-expanding homeowning class seems to have become a thing of the past.

15 With the administration's two largest ownership initiatives in shambles, conservative ownership advocates appear to have lost. The disastrous political fallout from Bush's attempt at Social Security reform effectively erased private accounts from the debate, and the economic turmoil created from the housing crisis has made expanding home-ownership both unpopular and economically untenable in the near future. Whether or not the idea of the ownership society had value, it has been tainted. And the government's participation in what is arguably the conceptual reverse of the ownership society—the $700 billion public purchase of private capital under the **Troubled Asset Relief Program**—will probably serve as the nail in the coffin.

Meanwhile, despite his support for several asset-promoting initiatives during the campaign, President Obama has been a critic of the ownership society. Alluding to the risk associated with Bush's concept of ownership,

Troubled Asset Relief Program, or TARP, was established as part of the Emergency Economic Stabilization Act, passed by Congress in 2008, in an attempt to support large banks that were in danger of failing as housing market values dropped and mortgage defaults increased.

Obama has rhetorically suggested that an ownership society really means an "on your own society." "If you lose your job," Obama argued, "you're on your own. If you're a child in poverty, pull yourself up by your boot-straps, you're on your own. If you were lured in by deceptive mortgage practices, you're on your own."

Of course, the American concept of ownership is still very much alive, and will continue to play a major role in our lives and policies. But the Thatcherian idea that ownership could supplant much of the welfare state will play a diminished role in American political discourse. For the time being, popular capitalism is dead.

NOTES:

1. For a discussion of the private welfare state, see Jacob Hacker, *The Divided Welfare State: The Battle Over Public and Private Social Benefits in the United States*. New York: Cambridge University Press, 2002.

2. For a more complete discussion of the intellectual roots of the ownership society, see Daniel Béland. *What Ownership Society? Debating Housing and Social Security Reform in the United States*, Hamilton, SEDAP Research Paper 150 (McMaster University), February 2006.

Questions for Discussion

1. In the first five paragraphs of his essay, Goldwein summarizes the position of conservative advocates for an ownership society. How does he characterize their position on ownership and government intervention in private business? What does he emphasize in this summary? How does his summary fit into his larger argument?

2. Goldwein describes two major initiatives that President George W. Bush undertook to pursue his goal of creating an ownership society: increasing home ownership rates and privatizing Social Security (see par. 10 and 11). Goldwein claims that "both of these initiatives failed" (par. 12). What evidence does he offer to support this claim? What conclusions does he draw from his analysis of these initiatives? How does his discussion of these initiatives help him make his main argument about an ownership society?

3. In paragraph 13 Goldwein asserts that President Bush's failure to privatize Social Security demonstrated "the limits of the ownership society's popularity?" What does he mean by that statement? What support does he provide for it? Do you think he's right? Why or why not?

4. According to Goldwein, the concept of ownership is still very much a part of American society (par. 17), yet he criticizes the idea of an "ownership society?" What is Goldwein's vision regarding private property and government policy in the United States? How persuasively do you think he makes a case for his own vision?

5. Much of Goldwein's argument rests on a technical analysis of economic developments and a critique of complex government policies and programs. How effectively do you think his analysis and critique help support his main argument? Do you think his argument is intended for a general audience? Explain, citing specific passages to support your answer.

NEGOTIATING DIFFERENCES

As Al Bellerue notes in "Private Property Ownership" (see Con-Text on page 251), the U.S. Constitution guarantees citizens the right to own private property. This right is among the most cherished by Americans, and it is the basis for much of what is understood to be fundamental to the American way of life, which includes the prospect of owning a home, buying and selling land, and acquiring material goods such as cars that we associate with an American lifestyle. But Bellerue also notes that the Constitution prohibits the government from taking private property "without just compensation" and "without due process of law." In other words, the government *can* take away someone's private property—as long as it does so within the bounds of existing law and as long as it compensates the owner appropriately. What does that mean in practical terms? It means that sometimes the interests of the government to provide for the common good and the rights of individuals as property owners conflict.

A common example of this kind of conflict between individual rights and the common good is the construction of a public highway. In some cases when the need for a new highway is determined, the government might decide that the best route for that highway is through existing private property. In such cases, the government has the right to take possession of that property, which might include private homes, as long as it pays the owners a fair compensation. But often in such cases the property owners don't want to leave their homes and refuse to sell to the government. The question then becomes, Whose interests are more important to protect: the property owners' or the community's?

One famous example of this kind of conflict occurred in New York City in the 1960s. City planners determined that new

highways were needed to allow traffic to move unimpeded through some sections of the city and into New Jersey. The city's plan, which would have required the destruction of many private buildings and historic structures in existing neighborhoods, was extremely controversial. Residents of the neighborhoods that would be eliminated resisted the plan through legal means and through an intense public relations campaign. Although the controversy focused on the potential loss of private homes and businesses in a section of New York City, it raised much larger questions about how to balance the needs of the community against the rights of individuals.

Similar but less-well-known controversies occur regularly throughout the United States whenever a government plan to improve a community requires individual property owners to give up their land. Such conflicts occur in cases involving such projects as flood control, the construction of sewer and water systems, the creation of landfills for trash removal, or the construction of public buildings such as schools.

Imagine that your campus is involved in such a situation. Your college or university has decided it needs to expand its dormitory facilities, but it needs land to do so. After hiring a consulting firm to study the situation, school administrators have identified several private buildings in a neighborhood next to the campus that could be converted into new dormitories. The state has provided special funds for the campus to purchase these buildings. The problem is that several of the property owners refuse to sell, claiming that they do not wish to give up homes that they have occupied for many years. Because the college is an important source of economic growth in your region, it believes that the plan to expand the dormitories is necessary for the continued economic health of the region, especially at a time when the economy is suffering.

You and your classmates have been asked to serve as student representatives on a special committee charged with examining the issue. Your task is to consider the pros and cons of the plan to convert the existing private homes in the neighborhood near campus and to make a recommendation about whether the college should pursue its plan or consider a different plan. In your report, you should discuss your beliefs about private property and individual rights as well as your views about how those rights should be considered when the community's best interests are at stake. In other words, how would you resolve this conflict?

9

Relationships

© Tanya Constantine/Blend Images/Corbis

How Should We Conduct Our Relationships?

Relationships with others are perhaps as important as any other aspect of our lives. Yet most of us probably don't think very often about *how* we conduct those relationships. In fact, the very idea of *conducting* a relationship might seem odd. We *have* relationships; we seek them and value them. But do we *conduct* them? The essays in this cluster suggest that, yes, we do conduct our relationships in many different ways—probably without always realizing that we're doing so. These readings indicate how complex our relationships can be and how difficult it can be to figure out how to conduct them. ■ Take, for example, the matter of dating. There are various expectations and implicit rules for how we should go about dating. But as two of the readings in this cluster indicate, those expectations and rules are always changing and not always obvious. How do we know what is appropriate when dating? That is one question raised by these readings—a question that you may have asked yourself at some point in your life. ■ Such a question becomes even more difficult when applied to situations that may be less familiar or common—like same-sex dating. Do the rules change for same-sex couples? If so, in what ways? And why should they be different in any case? There are no easy answers to such questions, as the readings in this cluster demonstrate. As you read the provocative arguments in this cluster about issues that can be both complex and controversial, consider how your own experience in various relationships might influence your reaction to them. Consider, too, the challenges of constructing effective arguments about such charged topics.

① Why I'm Selling My Virginity

NATALIE DYLAN

Is there a difference between casually "hooking up" with someone and exchanging sex for money? Most people would probably say yes. For one thing, selling sex is illegal in most of the United States—and throughout most of the world. But although many people consider it immoral to have casual sex with someone other than a spouse, it is not illegal, assuming both partners are legal adults, consent to the sex, and exchange no money. Moreover, it is not illegal to lose your virginity to someone who is not your spouse—assuming, again, that the partners consent, are of legal age, and exchange no money. So why not profit from it? That's the question Natalie Dylan poses in this provocative essay. Dylan, a recent college graduate at the time she wrote this essay, argues that if a woman's virginity is so valuable to men, she should be able to profit from it. She justifies her position by pointing out that sex—and specifically virginity—has been valued and controlled by men throughout history. Her essay, which created a sensation when it was first published, will shock many readers, but it poses challenging questions about the complicated matters of gender, sexuality, and capitalism. It also raises questions about whether our moral values are a function of our "own personal belief system," as Dylan claims, or something else. As you read, consider how your own beliefs about sexuality might shape your reaction to her decision—and whether your reaction actually helps make her case about gender and sex. Natalie Dylan (which is a pseudonym) lives in California. Her essay originally appeared in 2009 as a blog post on *The Daily Beast*, an online publication devoted to politics and popular culture.

NATALIE DYLAN, "Why I'm Selling My Virginity"

1 When I put my virginity up for auction in September, it was in part a sociological experiment—I wanted to study the public's response. Now it seems that the tables have turned, and the public is studying me.

I'm a 22-year-old woman who recently earned her Bachelor's Degree in Women's Studies, and soon I'll be entering a Masters Degree program in Marriage and Family Therapy. During the time in between, in addition to my regular 9-to-5, I've been exploring my upcoming thesis project: the value of virginity. To be more specific, I've put my own virginity up for auction on the Moonlite Bunny Ranch website, and

I recently received my highest bid so far: a cool $3.8 million.

In addition to bids, however, I've also received an astonishing, sometimes unnerving, amount of media attention. Many of these reports have portrayed me inaccurately, however, so let me tell you what this is all about.

This all started long before September. In fact, it started in college, where my eyes were opened by my Women's Studies professors and fellow classmates. I came to understand the role of "woman" spanning culture and time. At the university level, I was given permission to think differently and form a moral code of my own design. College opened my eyes.

5 Like most little girls, I was raised to believe that virginity is a sacred gift a woman should reserve for just the right man. But college taught me that this concept is just a tool to keep the status quo intact. Deflowering is historically oppressive—early European marriages began with a dowry, in which a father would sell his virginal daughter to the man whose family could offer the most agricultural wealth. Dads were basically their daughters' pimps.

When I learned this, it became apparent to me that idealized virginity is just a tool to keep women in their place. But then I realized something else: if virginity is considered that valuable, what's to stop me from benefiting from that? It is mine, after all. And the value of my chastity is one level on which men cannot compete with me. I decided to flip the equation, and turn my virginity into something that allows me to gain power and opportunity from men. I took the ancient notion that a woman's virginity is priceless and used it as a vehicle for capitalism.

Are you rolling your eyes? I knew this experiment would bring me condemnation. But I'm not saying every forward-thinking person has to agree with what I'm doing. You should develop your own personal belief system—that's exactly my point! For me, valuing virginity as sacred is simply not a concept I could embrace. But valuing virginity monetarily—now that's a concept I could definitely get behind. I no longer view the selling of sex as wrong or immoral—my time at college showed me that I had too blindly accepted such arbitrary norms. And for what it's worth, the winning bid won't necessarily be the highest—I get to choose.

So, with this value system firmly in place, I contacted the organization I felt could best provide me a safe and legal means through which to execute my idea: The Moonlite Bunny Ranch in Reno, Nevada.

I have been to the Moonlite Bunny Ranch twice to meet with its larger-than-life owner, Dennis Hof. I would describe the environment as a comical hybrid of a sorority house crossed with a laid-back gentlemen's club.

10 The Ranch not only provided me with the publicity to reach bidders through a personal email address on their website, but also as a way to capture a big enough "sample" of the public so I could research their reactions.

Some of these reactions have been surprising. As expected, many people value virginity itself—people who think it's important to save, and men who think it's valuable enough to buy. But I've discovered that others value the lucrative nature of my experiment even more. I've been congratulated for my "entrepreneurial gumption," as one CEO of a Fortune 500 company put it.

I might even be an early adopter of a future trend, if the ads that clutter Craigslist are any indication of the direction we're headed in. These days, more and more women my age are profiting directly from their sex appeal, but I'm not sure other women should follow my lead. One conclusion my experiment has already borne out is that society isn't ready for public auctions like mine—yet.

CONTEXT

In 2007 Craigslist, the popular online listing of classified ads, became the focus of controversy when it became known that many people were using the site to post solicitations for sex. After several widely publicized cases in which women were assaulted or killed after responding to ads on Craigslist, the company implemented a new policy in 2009 to discontinue the "erotic services" section of its online ads.

Questions for Discussion

1. How would you summarize Dylan's main argument in this essay? Do you agree with her? Why or why not? What do you think your reaction to her argument reveals about your own views regarding gender and sexuality?

2. Dylan asserts that "college opened my eyes" (par. 4). What does she mean? How does this assertion relate to her main argument about the role of women in contemporary society?

3. What evidence does Dylan provide to support her claim that virginity is "a tool to keep the status quo intact" (par. 5)? How persuasive do you find her evidence? What evidence do you think might be offered in opposition to her position on virginity?

4. Dylan states that everyone should have his or her own "personal belief system." Why is this statement important to her main argument? Do you think she's right? Why or why not? What are the consequences of everyone having his or her own "personal belief system"? Do you think Dylan adequately takes these consequences into account? Explain.

5. At the beginning of paragraph 7, Dylan asks her readers directly, "Are you rolling your eyes?" Why do you think she poses this question? What does this question assume about her readers and their views regarding sexuality? Do you think she is right in her assumptions about her readers?

6. Dylan claims that her decision to sell her virginity was "a sociological experiment." Do you believe her? Why or why not? Does it matter whether her decision really was such an experiment? Does that make her argument about gender and sex any more or less persuasive?

② Get Your Hand Out of My Pocket

DARRYL JAMES

The founder of Rap Sheet and the author of *Bridging the Black Gender Gap*, Darryl James writes a syndicated column called "The Bridge." The following argument originated as one of his columns, and it is reprinted here as it appeared in the *Los Angeles Sentinel* in March 2005. In this essay, James takes a provocative position—a position signaled by his title. He argues that women should pay their own way on dates and that women who expect men to pick up the tab should make that clear right away. "Perhaps some men will simply offer you a flat fee," he suggests, "to get right to what they want." His argument addresses age-old questions about appropriate behavior when dating; it also raises new questions at a time when the rules for dating are changing.

DARRYL JAMES, "Get Your Hand Out of My Pocket"

1 The lady was smart, pretty and in very good shape. We had been dating for a few weeks and I was enjoying the conversations with her.

We talked about our goals in life and we shared a great deal about ourselves with each other. We both recognized that sharing up front can prevent confusion later on down the line.

We began talking about what we really wanted in relationships when she went there—she said she wanted a man who was "generous." Now, the word itself may seem innocent enough, but let's really take a look at what it means.

When a woman says that she wants a man to be generous, she is typically referring to the dating process—she wants gifts, and she wants to be courted in a lavish manner.

5 We're not talking about some third world nation where women are denied employment and treated as property, we are talking about so-called "independent women" in the good old U.S. of A, who fought and still fight to be treated as equals with all the rights that men have—except in dating.

As an independent woman, you should have no problem picking up the check or at least paying your way. Otherwise, stop saying that you are independent, and stop saying

you want a good man. What you want is a sucker and your honesty will be appreciated.

As far as finances are concerned, anything above wanting someone to carry their own weight is unreasonable.

In addition, there are so many other things to be concerned about that have value, that finances should be last on the list, because at the end of the day, when the conversation turns to finance, most men are turned off.

Being single and dating gets rough enough without all of the confusion of financial expectations. For any rational adult, it makes no sense to expect someone to spend money to entertain your grown behind. That's like saying you want all of the fun but none of the responsibility, and it's a poor way to begin a relationship.

10 A few years back, I was dating a woman who I really believed could have been my soul mate. We communicated beautifully, we were both from Chicago, and we liked the same things. We both had the same method of accepting the things about each other that were divergent from our own individual experiences. However, there was one thing that she presented that I ultimately could not get beyond.

CONTEXT

When James refers here to "beautiful sisters," he signals that he is primarily addressing an African American audience. This essay was first published in the *Los Angeles Sentinel*, a weekly newspaper directed toward African Americans. Founded in 1933, the *Sentinel* is one of the oldest media outlets under black ownership in the western United States. To what extent does James tailor his argument specifically to the readers of this newspaper?

She couldn't stop begging.

Yes, I said begging. It wasn't that I didn't have the money. I was making plenty of cash, but at every turn, she was asking me for money to go out, money to buy new shoes, money to buy birthday gifts for friends and money to spend at the mall.

The thing that was most disturbing was that she didn't even ask for bills or other necessities, she would ask for trinkets and trash just to see what she could get.

It's even difficult sometimes to sit at a bar and exchange conversation without the expectation of drink purchases. Why would any otherwise self-respecting woman want to diminish herself to a common "drink whore"? Be offended, but if you are selling your conversation and/or company for the price of a drink, this is what it amounts to.

15 There is already enough stress involved in trying to merge two individual personalities, which may be divergent based on religion, education, in addition to gender. Add finance to the mix and it's all bad.

It's just sad to watch beautiful sisters who claim to want a real relationship start things off with a focus on avoiding financial responsibility.

Here's another horrible example: One of my close friends in Chicago was scheduled to meet a young lady at a local hangout for drinks. Each time they went out, she created diversions when it was time to pay, or simply stared at the check, leaving him to pay. Once, he asked her to split the check and she claimed to have left her money at home. Outside of her difficulty with paying for her own entertainment, she was actually a nice young lady and my friend liked her very much.

He arranged to meet her again and purposely arrived after she did. She had already ordered a few drinks and food. My friend sat down and ordered water. He declined any food, but otherwise, maintained the same kind of conversation as on previous dates. When the check came at the end of the evening, his date slid it across the table in front of him.

Quick—what would YOU do? Here's what my friend did: He politely slid the check back to her and stated: "I didn't eat or drink anything, so you should go ahead and take care of it." Her reply: "Why would you ask to spend time with me, if you don't want to treat me like a lady?"

20 Ladies, if there is a cost for your time, please make that clear up front. Perhaps some men will simply offer you a flat fee to get right to what they desire. If you are not for sale, you should take the price off of your company.

Now, here's the sad part: When I write pieces like this and give such examples, some sisters say that it's only the circles I run in, but those circles seem to be all across the nation, because not only are my brothers lodging numerous complaints, but many of my honest sisters who pay their own way are aware of the offending behavior as well.

The bottom line is that no matter how you couch it, coming after a man financially is unattractive. Phrase it as "generous," but if you expect to be paid for, then you are practicing a form of prostitution. Don't be surprised or angry if you get some of the same results.

Dating is an expensive venture and difficult to launch properly. In my lectures, my most salient piece of advice to single women is to be unafraid of initiating contact and open to sharing the financial burden of dating.

The dating process should allow two people to get to know each other, ostensibly before making a commitment. A relationship is about partnership and dating should not be any different. In fact, since dating

COMPLICATION

Compare James's perspective on dating to the following advice from Doug Veith, author of *Win Her with Dinner,* as edited by Liesa Goins for publication in a 2004 issue of *Men's Health*:

Recipe for Romance

IMPRESS YOUR DATE. When cooking a romantic dinner, there are so many potential pitfalls—singed eyebrows, scalded crotch. We recommend oven mitts and these tips, . . .

TIME IT WELL. The third date is when the good stuff often happens, says Veith, so it's smart to be close to home. But anniversaries and Fridays are also good times.

AVOID SURPRISES. Always clear the proposed meal with the proposed woman ahead of time, says Veith. Make sure she doesn't have any allergy or diet issues.

IMPROVE THE SETTING. If you have a dining room, great. Otherwise, dress up any flat surface with a tablecloth, cloth napkins, and matching salad and dinner plates. To upgrade the setting, Veigh suggests sunflowers—an innocent and safe flower—and unscented candies.

PLAY MUSIC. Try to pair the song selection with your menu. For a classic American dinner like New York strip steak, try Billie Holiday. For an Italian supper, spin Paolo Conte. Good Charlotte doesn't go with anything. But the book has plenty of other pairing suggestions.

DON'T FORGET DESSERT. At the least, she'll leave with a good taste in her mouth.

may not turn out to be anything permanent, there should be no substantial financial investment. At the end of something that doesn't work out, both people can walk away undiminished.

25 So, ladies, please focus on a man's character, not his wallet, and maybe you will find something to have and to hold. When you approach a man keep your eyes on the prize. And keep your hand out of my pocket.

Questions for Discussion

1. Throughout his essay James uses the term "lady" to refer to single women. How do you interpret his use of this term? How do you respond when he subsequently switches to a phrase like "your grown behind"? What response do you think James hoped to elicit from his readers to such phrases?

2. Early in his essay James asserts, "When a woman says that she wants a man to be generous, she is typically referring to the dating process—she wants gifts, and she wants to be courted in a lavish manner" (par. 4). What support does he offer for this assertion? Do you think this is a valid generalization about women? Is James trying to be provocative with this assertion? If so, what does he gain by doing so?

3. How would you describe the tone of this essay? Do you think the tone makes the argument more or less effective? Explain, citing specific passages in the essay to support your answer.

4. James anticipates the argument that women behave the way he describes only in his own social circle (see par. 21). How well does he respond to this argument with his counterargument?

5. James sometimes addresses his readers directly. For example, in paragraph 14 he writes, "Be offended, but if you are selling your conversation and/or company for the price of a drink, this is what it amounts to." And in paragraph 19 he asks, "Quick—what would YOU do?" Do you think he is primarily addressing men or women in these passages? How effective is this strategy in helping him make his argument?

6. In paragraphs 10–13, James uses his own dating experience to support his assertions about women. How effective do you think this example is? How well does it support James's point? How did you respond to this example? What counterargument might you offer to this example?

③ | # Dorm Brothel

VIGEN GUROIAN

What happens when a college professor grows upset by what he perceives as sexual promiscuity on his campus—the campus of a faith-based college? The following argument by Vigen Guroian is one answer to that question. Guroian, who teaches theology at Loyola College in Baltimore, expresses deep concern about "the sexual attitudes of our youth" and what he sees as widespread casual sex among today's college students. Why, he wonders, is traditional dating "an endangered species"? But the main focus of Guroian's argument is the relationship between a college and its students. Guroian believes that colleges today have abandoned their responsibility for supervising the behavior of their students. He poses the question of whether colleges should honor the tradition of *in loco parentis,* which means that the college or university assumes parental responsibilities for students while they are at college and away from their parents. His essay also prompts us to think about how young people should conduct their relationships. He acknowledges that times have changed since he was in college, and he wonders whether the changes in how young people date signal that something precious in relationships is being lost. Guroian is the author of several books about theology and culture, including *Rallying the Really Human Things: The Moral Imagination in Politics, Literature, and Everyday Life* (2005), from which this essay is excerpted.

VIGEN GUROIAN, "Dorm Brothel"

"The so-called sexual revolution is not, as advertised, a liberation of sexual behavior but rather its reversal. In former days, even under Victoria, sexual intercourse was the natural end and culmination of heterosexual relations. Now one begins with genital overtures instead of handshake, then waits to see what will turn up (e.g., might become friends later). Like dogs greeting each other nose to tail and tail to nose."

The Last Gentleman (1966) Walker Percy

1 Nineteen sixty-six, the year in which Walker Percy's **The Last Gentleman** was published, is also the year I entered as a first-year-man at the University of Virginia. We did not stoop to the State U level of referring to ourselves as freshmen, sophomores, and such—not at "The University." We were all men at

The Last Gentleman by award-winning writer Walker Percy (1916–1990) focuses on the difficulty of a man fitting into the modern world.

U.Va.—"gentlemen," we were told. Young women visited on weekends from Sweet Briar and Randolph-Macon, Mary Washington, and Hollins College. But they did not stay in the dormitory or the fraternity house. They stayed in college-approved housing, more often than not the home of a widow who had a few rooms to let and happily accepted a delegation from the colleges to assume the responsibilities of *in loco parentis.*

Parental rules were enforced even in the fraternity houses—self-enforced by those of us who lived in them. Young women were not permitted in the bedrooms and had to be out of the house by a certain hour. We dated, blind-dated often. We did not know what "hooking up" was. We had never heard of date rape either, though some of us may have committed it. It could happen in the back seat of a car, a cheap motel, a cow pasture, or a Civil War battlefield, but not in a college dormitory or fraternity house bedroom, not yet at least; it was not until the end of the decade that all the rules and prohibitions came tumbling down and the brave new world of the contemporary coeducational college commenced.

Back then, and from the immemorial, so far as I knew, there were the "easy" girls. We had a provocative name or two for them, and they were quickly sorted out from the "other" girls. Word got around fast. These were not young women one seriously considered marrying, and most of us expected and hoped to find a mate in college. If, however, a guy got especially "hungry" or "horny," there was no special stigma attached to taking advantage of what the easy girls had to offer.

The gentlemen of the University of Virginia lived by a double standard, but there were standards. There was little doubt about that. The arrangements the colleges provided for the sexes to meet and mix, strict dorm-visitation hours, approved housing, curfews for female visitors, and the like made that abundantly clear. When we set off on a road trip to a girls school, either by hitchhiking or jamming six or eight into a car, and arrived at the dorm, we did not just mosey on up to our dates' rooms and hang out. We waited, garbed in coat and tie, in the big informal parlor until our dates made their entrance.

5 My college classmates and fraternity brothers at the University of Virginia and I were certainly not Victorians, but we were not post-Christian and postmodern young men either, not quite yet. Maybe we were the last gentlemen, which certainly should not be interpreted to mean that we always behaved like gentlemen, just that we had some appreciation for the meaning of the word and maybe even aspirations to become what it signified. Furthermore, we knew what the opposite of a gentleman was. In fact, in those days "The University" was often called, proudly by some, the Playboy School of the South. So we were gentlemen and playboys both, spirited by our friend Jack Daniels. We knew there was a contradiction in being a gentleman and a Don Juan at the same time. But being a Don Juan or playboy has significance only in a world in which the idea of the gentleman exists, in which fidelity is acknowledged as a virtue, and in which sex is considered most appropriate to the marital union. We had absorbed these notions from a culture that had not yet abandoned them. We knew the game had to end eventually, probably when we met the right girl and got married, and most of us got married by the age of 23 or 24, many to our college sweethearts.

One could say that in 1966, what men and women called dating was a late—and as I look back on it, probably also tenuous—version of courtship. We understood, at least implicitly, that there was an important difference between going whoring and dating. Treating a young woman like a whore was what a Don Juan would do, but not the mark of a gentleman, especially one looking for a future wife. But today is entirely different. My grown children tell me so, as do my students at Loyola College, and much has been written on the subjects of dating, courtship, and the sexual attitudes of our youth that confirms their testimony. But why is dating, as a form of courtship, an endangered practice?

Experts identify a variety of reasons and causes, but I do not pretend to address the subject scientifically or dispassionately. I will not review this literature here. Nor do I have a sentimental attachment to a remembered past. Lest I be misunderstood, I do not call for a return to the "good old days" of dating as it was when I was a youth anymore than I would advocate a return to arranged marriages. As a college professor and father of a college-age daughter, however, I am outraged by the complicity of my college and most other schools in the death of courtship and the emergence of a dangerous and destructive culture of "hooking up."

Doane College in Nebraska recently mailed a recruiting postcard that showed a man

COMPLICATION

Several studies indicate that "hooking up" for casual sex is common among college students and has replaced traditional dating for many students. In one study, for example, conducted in 2000, 87 percent of college students reported having "hooked up." But more recent studies show decreases in the numbers of sexual partners that college students report having, and in 2006 the American College Health Association released a study showing that college students routinely overestimate the numbers of sexual partners their peers have. Scholars describe "hooking up" as more casual and uncommitted compared to traditional dating, but they disagree about what these differences mean.

SOURCE: **American College Health Association; Kathleen Bogle, *Hooking Up* (2008).**

surrounded by women, with a caption that read that students at this college have the opportunity to "play the field." After a public outcry last December, administrators hastily withdrew the marketing campaign, explaining that the postcard was harmless and a metaphor for exploring a variety of education options. But the very fact that the campaign was conceived and approved in the first place speaks volumes. The sexual revolution, if that is an appropriate title, was not won with guns but with genital groping aided and abetted by colleges that forfeited the responsibilities of *in loco parentis* and have gone into the pimping and brothel business.

Sex Carnival

I do not use these words lightly or loosely, and rarely is a college so blatantly suggestive as was Doane, although this attitude about the commendability of sexual experimentation has become an orthodoxy among many who hold positions as deans of student life at our colleges. Of course, some colleges take concrete steps to resist this revolution of morals. Still, in most American college coed dorms, the flesh of our daughters is being served up daily like snack jerky. No longer need young men be wolves or foxes to consume that flesh. There are no fences to jump or chicken coops to break into. The gates are wide open and no guard dogs have been posted. It is easy come and easy go. Nor are our daughters the only ones getting

hurt. The sex carnival that is college life today is also doing great damage to our sons' characters, deforming their attitudes toward the opposite sex. I am witnessing a perceptible dissipation of manly virtue in the young men I teach.

10 Nevertheless, my more compelling concern about this state of affairs is for the young women, our daughters. Since my student years, colleges have abandoned all the arrangements that society had once put in place to protect the "weaker sex" so they could say "no" and have a place to retreat if young men pressed them too far. And although even when these arrangements were in place, one could not always say with confidence that the girl was the victim and the boy the offender, the contemporary climate makes identifying predator and prey even trickier. The lure and availability of sexual adventure that our colleges afford is teaching young women also to pursue sexual pleasures aggressively. Yet, based on my own conversations and observations, there is no doubt that young women today are far more vulnerable to sexual abuse and mistreatment by young men than when I was a college student, simply because the institutional arrangements that protected young women are gone and the new climate says everything goes.

In 1966, my fraternity brothers and I were caught up in a monumental shift in relations between the sexes that Will Barrett, the young protagonist of Walker Percy's tale, struggles to understand and come to terms with. One evening, Will and his love interest, Kitty Vaught, retreat to a cramped camper. They try to dance and then lie together in a bunk with all the expectations ignited by young flesh pressed against young flesh. A conversation ensues that is profoundly emblematic of what my generation went through. Prompted by the intimacy and abandon of the situation, Will tells Kitty a story about how his grandfather took his father to a whorehouse at the age of 16. Kitty asks Will if his father did the same for him. Will answers that he did not.

Then, after some chatter about the meaning of love and the difficulty of it, Kitty says to Will, "Very well, I'll be your whore." Will does not protest, so Kitty injects,

"Then you think I'm a whore?"
"No," that was the trouble. She wasn't. There was a lumpish playfulness, a sort of literary gap in her whorishness.
"Very well, I'll be a lady."

15 "All right."
"No, truthfully. Love me like a lady."
"Very well."

He lay with her, more or less miserably, kissed her lips and eyes and uttered sweet love murmurings into her ear, telling her what a lovely girl she was. But what am I, he wondered: neither Christian nor pagan nor proper lusty gentleman, for I've never really got the straight of this lady-and-whore business. And that is all I want and it does not seem much to ask: for once and all to get the straight of it.

This is what dating was becoming back then, as young men and women without traditional adult oversight started to entrust themselves to one another. A clear sense of the formal stages of courtship had faded and authoritative rules of conduct were dissolving. Percy's scene is not wholly foreign to my students. But neither is it typical. The culture has changed dramatically.

Literary Hook-Ups

20 When, in Tom Wolfe's most recent novel, *I Am Charlotte Simmons*, Charlotte's mother asks her during Christmas break where students go on dates at Dupont University, Charlotte responds: "Nobody goes out on a date. The girls go out in groups and the boys go out in groups, and they hope they find somebody they like." This is Charlotte Simmons's description of "hooking up." "Hooking up" has replaced traditional courtship and dating among today's college students. "Hooking up" is dating sans courtship or expectations of a future relationship or commitment. It is strictly about user sex. I use you and you use me for mutual pleasure. And liquor is more often than not the lubricant that makes things go.

We all are familiar with contemporary sitcoms and so-called reality television shows that bring young men and women together with precisely the intent of getting them to eye each other's genitals like candy at a convenience store, respond to each other's sexual nature in animal fashion, and hop in bed together with no regrets. There are no evident prohibitions or taboos. The comic or dramatic plot is all about sexual adventure and getting as much pleasure from the experience as possible. The rules are strictly instrumental. Often, they are made up along the way merely to facilitate the smooth going of the "game" or "hunt," as it might more appropriately be called. There is no right and wrong.

I cannot say for sure whether these shows influence real life or whether it is the other way around. In the end, it does not much matter. What I do know is that a latter-day Walker Percy could not write the scene I have cited with the belief that it faithfully depicts how contemporary young men and women meet or what is at issue between them.

Take, for another example, the benchmark movies of the '60s about young men and women coming of age, such as *The Graduate* or Francis Ford Coppola's *You're a Big Boy Now*. They are now passé. The sexual innocence depicted and the presence of adult supervision, limited or mocked, against which the young protagonists struggle, are no longer realistic. Frank Capra's classic romantic comedy *It Happened One Night*, released in 1934, contrasts even more strikingly with contemporary sexual mores. In that movie, a newspaper reporter named Peter Warne, played by Clark Gable, heroically and humorously lives up to the standard of a gentleman in his behavior toward a rebellious young heiress named Ellie Andrews, played by Claudette Colbert. Occasions arise that certainly present Peter with opportunities to make sexual

I Am Charlotte Simmons, published in 2004, is a novel by well-known writer Tom Wolfe, in which Wolfe explores college life through the experiences of his main character Charlotte Simmons.

CONTEXT

Film director Frank Capra (1897–1991) won an Oscar for his film *It Happened One Night*, in which a reporter named Peter Warne (played by Clark Gable) tracks down a wealthy heiress, Ellie Andrews (played by Claudette Colbert), who has run away from home rather than marry a stuffy millionaire. Peter and Ellie eventually fall in love, but they are careful not to act upon that love while on the road together. In one famous scene, Peter carefully hangs a blanket to divide the motel room they are forced to share when they are running out of cash. That's the night that gives the movie its title. Consider how Guroian uses this story to help make his point about the changing attitudes of young people regarding success.

advances. But Peter does not take advantage of these occasions, despite his increasing desire for a woman whom at first he disdained. Only after these two spirited combatants of the war between the sexes get wed is it suggested that they are sexually intimate. At the end of the film, a symbolic trumpet sounds, announcing that the "walls of Jericho" are falling.

Over the years, I have asked my students whether they have seen this movie. Only a handful of the students in my course on theology and literature acknowledge even having heard of it. If they were to watch *It Happened One Night*, I do not doubt that some of my students would enjoy it and highly appreciate its artistry and humor. Yet I hardly think many would identify strongly with the characters and their situation. In simple terms, the symbolic curtain that Peter builds from a clothesline and a blanket in order to separate two twin beds in a rented room is hardly the correlative of life in coed college dormitories and apartments.

CONTEXT

Brave New World (1933), by Aldous Huxley, envisions a future world in which procreation is managed at a Hatching and Conditioning Center that produces thousands of nearly identical embryos. Children born and raised in this center are conditioned to dislike books, obey the government, repress personal feelings, and become docile consumers. The book reflected the modern fascination with science and the emergence of totalitarian states in Russia and in Germany.

25 The nature and depth of this cultural disconnect is illustrated by a scene in Aldous Huxley's *Brave New World*, published just two years after *It Happened One Night* premiered. John, the so-called Savage, is brought to London from the Indian reservation. During a conversation with Helmholtz Watson, a young author of radio jingles and touchy-feely movie scripts, John recites lines from *Romeo and Juliet*, a play that has been banned and is unknown to the inhabitants of *Brave New World*. Despite the fact that Helmholtz rebels against the shallowness of life in Brave New World, the plot of Shakespeare's play puzzles him. After listening to the scene of the lovers' first meeting, he wonders what the fuss is all about. He does not understand the nature of the tragedy because he has no knowledge of courtship or the roles of parental and filial love and fidelity in Shakespeare's world.

> Getting into such a state about having a girl—it seemed rather ridiculous... The mother and father (grotesque obscenity) forcing the daughter to have someone she didn't want! And the idiotic girl not saying that she was having someone else whom (for the moment, at any rate) she preferred! In its smutty absurdity the situation was irresistibly comical.

It Happened One Night was filmed more than 300 years after Shakespeare wrote his plays. Nevertheless, its humor and ennobling power rest on standards of propriety and courtship nearer to the 16th century than to Huxley's futuristic London or even today's hook-up culture. The reading public of the first decades of the 20th century might find the abolition of courtship and marriage in *Brave New World* interesting and remote, but my students readily admit the possibility of such a future. I recently gave a lecture at Loyola on *Brave New World*. During the question-and-answer period, there was a brief discussion about the similarities of dormitory life with *Brave New World*. I opined that whatever the resemblances, there is a clear difference between the two: Sexual promiscuity and hooking up among college students is voluntary, I said, whereas in *Brave New World* this behavior is mandatory. A young woman and dormitory resident adviser walked up to me afterwards and chided me: "Dr. Guroian, you are mistaken about that. The peer pressure and the way things are set up make promiscuity practically obligatory. It doesn't matter what the school says officially. The rules are to be broken. This freedom can make girls dizzy and unsure of whatever else they believe about 'saving oneself for marriage.' When it seems like everyone else is 'doing it,' it is hard to say no. It is more like *Brave New World* here than you think. I deal with it or, more frequently, turn my eyes from it, every day as an RA."

During the spring semester, this same young woman, who was enrolled in one of my classes, wrote a brief exposé on what goes on at Loyola College and other colleges. She explains the sundry distinctions today's young men and women make in relationships and sexual liaisons.

> It may not be that dating is at the brink of extinction, but…it has taken a back seat in the modern-day lives of students. Hooking up, going out, going steady, and dating, contrary to what some may think, are not the same thing…If you are "going out" with someone it means that you have a boyfriend or a girlfriend, you are in a "steady" relationship with that person. However, a couple needn't actually go anywhere [go on dates together] to be in this kind of relationship. Hooking up is basically dating without the romance. It has become customary for young adults to simply cut to the chase, the sexual…part of a relationship. A hook-up can be a onetime thing, as it most often is, or it can be a semi-regular thing, but not a

full relationship. Although it may take on the signs of one.

30 One might conclude that modern day youth have simply gotten lazy and careless. Most…are not looking for a romantic relationship; they see the new freedom and plethora of sexual opportunities and simply take what they can get. They get to college, and it's an amusement park with so many different enticing rides, one would be missing out on the whole experience to settle with the first one they tried. And why should they bother with the responsibility and formalities of a date when they have a better chance of getting immediate satisfaction after buying a few drinks at a bar?

I could have foregone quoting this young coed to cite any number of studies that describe these phenomena more "scientifically." These studies try hard to be "objective," but as a result they cannot convey the immediacy and passion of this young woman's narrative or the matter-of-fact manner in which she draws connections between the breakdown of courtship, the rise of a hook-up culture, and what we used to call pimping and prostitution. "Coed dormitories," she continues, "are they an ideal situation or a sad form of prostitution? You go out with your friends on your terms, after a few drinks you're both attracted....Interested and lonely, you go together, no obligations, no responsibilities, and no rules. Then there is that late-night 'booty call.' This has become such a custom of the college lifestyle [that] most have come to accept it, although maybe not respect it. If it were really the ideal situation, the walk home the next day [to one's own room] wouldn't be called 'the walk of shame.'" At Loyola College, the vast majority of students live on campus, and since the college has bought up a number of neighboring high-rise and garden apartments, after the freshman year the "walk of shame" need not even be made. It may be only a few steps from the boy's apartment to one's own, or better yet, from the boy's room to one's own.

The Culpable College

The campaign against alcohol and drugs, which it seems every American college has proudly announced it is waging, is a smokescreen that covers the colleges' great sin. Regulating a substance like alcohol on an urban campus like Loyola's cannot succeed unless there is radical reform of the whole of college life. Nothing that the college does to limit alcohol consumption can make a significant difference until the major incentives to drink are removed, beginning with coed dormitories and apartments. Many of my students have explained to me that drinking, especially binge drinking, serves as the lubricant for the casual sex that living arrangements at Loyola invite and permit. There is no need to find the cheap hotel of yesterday. The college provides a much more expensive and available version of it.

The sexual adventures that follow can take a variety of paths, but what this young Loyola man describes is not atypical.

True story: I woke up at three in the morning one day last year to my roommate having sex in his bed five feet away from me. Taking a moment to actually wake up, I realized what was going on. I got up...heard what was going on, and...recognized the voice of the girl...I had two classes with her the semester before and one that semester...The next morning..., there was no awkward exchange. No childish giggling. I simply told him that I could not believe that she didn't mind having sex with someone for the first time while someone else was in the room sleeping. I also couldn't believe that she hadn't stopped and covered herself up when I had walked out of the room. My roommate looked at me with a casual smile, the same smile I'd seen when talking about the Mets or Red Sox, the same smile I'd seen at our dining-room table over Taco Bell, and he said to me, "Whatever, she's a college girl."

35 This is a disturbing description of the demise of decency and civility between the sexes for which the American colleges are culpable and blameworthy. It is not that what this student describes was unheard of in the late 1960s. Frankly, I can tell similar stories about my college experience. Nevertheless, this was the exception rather than a commonplace occurrence. For colleges made it clear to young men and women that such behavior was unacceptable, and had in place living arrangements with rules and sanctions that discouraged it.

There is nothing new or novel about human depravity or debauchery. Outrage over debauchery is deserved. Nevertheless, as I have suggested already, my outcry is not directed at the debauchery among college students, but rather at the colleges themselves. Today colleges not only turn a blind eye to this behavior, but also set up the conditions that foster and invite it. I am concerned about the young men and women who wish to behave differently, but for whom this is made especially difficult by the living conditions their colleges provide and often insist upon.

In *I Am Charlotte Simmons*, a fictitious counterpart of the young woman and resident advisor whom I cited earlier says to the new freshmen under her supervision, "The university no longer plays the role of parents." She means sex is permitted. The satiric irony is that there are rules against keeping or consuming alcohol in the dorms. Is that not also *in loco parentis*? Charlotte quickly learns, however, that all of these rules are made to be broken and that being "sexiled," which means being expelled from one's room so that the roommate may have sex, is routine and obligatory at Dupont University.

In the new culture that our colleges incubate and maintain, everyone is a "guy." Everyone is "familiar." Young men and women who have never seen anyone of the opposite sex naked or in underwear, other than family members, now must get used to being seen by and seeing others—perfect strangers—in just such a state. Everyone is available to everyone else. It would be antisocial not to be.

Under such conditions, how could dating and courtship possibly survive? How could traditional marriage survive, in the long term? Courtship and dating require an inviolable private space from which each sex can leave at appointed times to meet in public and enjoy the other. In other words, in a courtship culture it ought to be that two people who are "serious" actually do "go out" together and do not merely cohabit in a closeted dormitory or apartment. Yet over the past 40 years, American colleges have created a brave new unisex world in which distinctions between public and private, formal and familiar, have collapsed. The differences between the sexes are now dangerously minimized or else just plain ignored because to recognize them is not progressive or politically correct. This is manifestly the case with coed dorm floors

> **COMPLICATION**
>
> In recent years there has been debate about the extent to which colleges should act as *in loco parentis*. Consider this passage from an essay arguing against the idea of colleges acting *in loco parentis*: "Many college administrators throughout the country are taking great pains to keep their students under tight control....*In loco parentis* has been rejuvenated and returned. Administrators have tapped into the devaluation of personal responsibility illustrated by smoking bans and fast food lawsuits, coupling it with bullish political correctness. The resulting dearth of individual liberties on campuses would have seemed impossible to college students of 25 years ago."
>
> SOURCE: "Welcome to the Fun-Free University" by David Weigel (*Reason* magazine, 2004).

and shared bathrooms and showers. These give the lie to official college rules against cohabitation. They are the wink and nod our colleges give to fornication and dissipation. Even in 1957, when he was chancellor of the University of California at Berkeley, Clark Kerr was almost prophetic when he stated humorously that his job responsibilities were "providing parking for faculty, sex for students, and athletics for the alumni."

40 Loyola College and a great many other colleges and universities simply do not acknowledge, let alone address, the sexualization of the American college. Rather, they do everything possible to put a smiley face on an unhealthy and morally destructive environment, one that—and this is no small matter—also makes serious academic study next to impossible. Most of the rhetoric one hears incessantly from American colleges about caring for young men and women and respecting their so-called freedom and maturity is disingenuous. Should we really count it to their credit that colleges are spending more and more resources on counseling and therapy when the direct cause of many wounds they seek to heal is the brave new world that they have engineered, sold as a consumer product, and supervised?

To serve *in loco parents* involves caring for the whole student not as an employer or client but as parent. In its statement "Vision and Values: A Guide for the Loyola College Community," Loyola says it holds to "an ideal of personal wholeness and integration." The college aims "to honor, care for, and educate the whole person," enjoining the entire college community "to strive after intellectual, physical, psychological, social, and spiritual health and well-being." The statement correctly associates these goals of education with the Roman Catholic faith and the liberal-arts tradition. Many other colleges and universities issue similar statements of aim and purpose on both religious and secular grounds. Yet the climate at Loyola College—and many, many others—produces the antithesis of these aims. It fosters not growth into wholeness but the dissolution of personality, not the integration of learning and everyday living but their radical bifurcation. It most certainly does not support the church's values of marriage and family.

Young men and women are being enticed to think of themselves as two selves, one that is mind and reason in the classroom and another self, active "after hours," that is all body and passion. They begin to imagine—though few entirely believe it—that they can use (that is, abuse) their bodies as they please for pleasure, and that choosing to

do so has nothing to do with their academic studies or future lives. In reality, they are following a formula for self-disintegration and failure.

This is the grisly underbelly of the modern American college; the deep, dark, hidden secret that many parents suspect is there but would rather not face. The long-term damage to our children is difficult to measure. But it is too obvious to deny. I remember once hearing that the British lost the empire when they started sending their children away to boarding schools. I do not know whether anyone has ever seriously proposed that thesis. I am prepared, however, to ask whether America might not be lost because the great middle class was persuaded that they must send their children to college with no questions asked, when in fact this was the near-equivalent of committing their sons and daughters to one of the circles of Dante's *Inferno*.

I have lived long enough to understand and be thankful for the fact that the sins and indiscretions of youth may be forgiven and overcome. Nevertheless, the behavior of our American colleges and universities is inexcusable. Their mendacity is doing great harm to our children, whom we entrust to them with so much love, pride, and hope for the future.

Questions for Discussion

1. What does Guroian achieve by opening with a quotation from Walker Percy's novel *The Last Gentleman*? How does he use this reference in the argument that follows?

2. According to Guroian, what are the main differences between how students conducted their relationships when Guroian was a college student and how college students conduct their relationships today? Why are these differences important, in his view? How persuasive is Guroian in describing these differences? How do they contribute to his larger argument?

3. Guroian acknowledges that he will not address the subject of student dating "scientifically or dispassionately" (par. 7). Do you think such a statement enhances his argument? Why or why not? Is he more or less persuasive by acknowledging early in his essay that he will not try to be objective in making his argument? Explain.

4. Guroian offers a kind of history of dating in the United States in the past fifty years as well as a review of "literary hook-ups." In what ways do these reviews support his main argument? What do you think they reveal about dating? What do they reveal about Guroian?

5. Guroian states that he is drawing upon stories his children have told him, as well as an "exposé" written by one of his students. How credible do these sources seem to you? Do they provide reasonable evidence that his concerns about how college students conduct their relationships are valid? Do you think his concerns are valid, based on your own experience? Explain.

6. Guroian acknowledges that he comes from a very different generation than his students, and his perspective on dating and sexuality has clearly been shaped by his own experience as well as his age. To what extent do you think his age and experience contribute to his argument? Is he more or less credible when it comes to questions about student behavior and sexuality because he writes as an elderly man with long experience? Explain.

7. Guroian believes that colleges should assume greater responsibility for supervising student behavior when it comes to student relationships. Does he make an effective case that colleges should adhere to the tradition of *in loco parentis*? Has college life changed to the extent that such a tradition is no longer necessary or feasible? What rules do you think a college should enforce when it comes to student life on campus?

8. As he concludes his argument, Guroian claims that American parents, when sending children off to college "with no questions asked," are doing "the near-equivalent of committing their sons and daughters to one of the circles of Dante's *Inferno*" (par. 43) and that American colleges and universities are "doing great harm to our children" (par. 44). Do you think his essay effectively leads to these conclusions? Do his evidence and reasoning support such conclusions? How do you respond to these conclusions?

④ | # We're Here! We're Queer! We're Thirteen!

AMY BENFER

Social life in middle school can be difficult for many students. As Amy Benfer explains in this essay, it can be especially challenging for students who are gay or bisexual. The intense controversies over same-sex marriage in recent years indicate that sexual orientation remains a charged issue about which there are deeply felt disagreements shaped by cultural and religious values. But Benfer suggests that times may be changing when it comes to the willingness of gay teens to be public about their identities. Nevertheless, the problem of harassment and bullying is still a significant one for gay teens, and Benfer's argument offers one way to understand—and perhaps solve—that problem. No doubt many readers will reject Benfer's argument on the basis of their own religious or moral views about homosexuality, which is an indication of how challenging it is to make an effective argument about issues such as sexual orientation. Amy Benfer is a freelance writer whose work has appeared in the *New York Times Book Review*, the *San Francisco Chronicle*, and *Salon*, an online magazine of culture and politics, in which this essay appeared in 2009.

AMY BENFER, "We're Here! We're Queer! We're Thirteen!"

Siouxsie Sioux, who was born Susan Janet Ballion in 1957, is an influential British singer-songwriter who was lead singer for the punk rock group Siouxsie and the Banshees. When she performed, she dressed in flamboyant Goth style.

CONTEXT

As Benfer suggests in this passage, the impetus for her essay was an article by writer Benoit Denizet-Lewis titled "Coming Out in Middle School," published in the *New York Times* magazine on September 27, 2009. In the article, Denizet-Lewis explores the often difficult experiences of middle school students who make their gay sexual orientation public. Denizet-Lewis writes, "Though most adolescents who come out do so in high school, sex researchers and counselors say that middle-school students are increasingly coming out to friends or family or to an adult in school. Just how they're faring in a world that wasn't expecting them—and that isn't so sure a 12-year-old can know if he's gay—is a complicated question that defies simple geographical explanations." Notice how Benfer uses a brief summary of Denizet-Lewis's article and several references to specific passages in the article to help make her argument in favor of gay students coming out.

1 When I went to college in the early '90s, freshman and sophomore year was a coming-out fest. I had a few gay friends in high school, but almost none of them dared to come out in our conservative school. So I was pretty shocked—and very proud—when my younger brother's best friend, a punk rock

Czech girl made up like **Siouxsie Sioux,** came out at 14 while attending the same middle school I had five years before. Fifteen years later, this generation of gay and bisexual kids are becoming more comfortable with coming out earlier and earlier, according to a cover story by Benoit Denizet-Lewis in this weekend's *New York Times* magazine.

How early? Most of the kids interviewed by Denizet-Lewis are still in middle school. According to recent studies, most kids don't self-identify as gay or bisexual until 14, 15, or 16, but the mean age at which they become aware of their orientation is 10 (boys tend, on average, to know a year earlier than girls). And some of these kids are coming out to their families and friends and living lives that "would have been nearly incomprehensible to earlier generations of gay youth," according to Ritch Savin-Williams, the author of "The New Gay Teenager."

Many of the scenes in the article are frankly astonishing in their sunny depiction of gay youth: Denizet-Lewis attends a gay dance for middle-schoolers located next to a Baptist church in a small town in Oklahoma, where the place is "practically over run by supportive moms"; he interviews a pair of eighth and ninth grade girls who are dating each other and tell him they met "in church"; and attends a meeting of the Gay Straight Alliance at Daniel Webster Middle School in Los Angeles, where dozens of students and teachers in the mostly Hispanic and African-American school mill around in what seems to be gay-straight heaven. "I feel like I'm in a parallel gay universe," says Denizet-Lewis.

This certainly disrupts the "long-time narrative of gay youth in crisis," and suggests that the higher rates of depression, suicide and substance abuse recorded among gay teens of earlier generations have—no duh—more to do with the difficulties of dealing with homophobia than anything else. And it suggests that gay and straight adults of the previous generation—by pushing for civil rights, gay marriage and the right to parent children—have succeeded in convincing teens and their parents that gay and bisexual teens have just as much a shot at living happy adult lives as their straight peers.

5 Parents who feared for their children's safety were a staple of earlier coming out narratives. "The biggest difference I've seen in the last 10 years isn't with gay kids—it's with their families," says Dan Woog, an openly gay varsity soccer coach in Connecticut. "Many parents just don't assume anymore that their kids will have a sad, difficult life just because they are gay."

But we could still do much better: Only 12 states have laws that explicitly protect students from bullying on the basis of sexual orientation and gender identity or expression, and teens are still being bullied and harassed for their orientation. Denizet-Lewis writes:

> In a 2007 survey of 626 gay, bisexual and transgender middle-schoolers from across the country by the Gay, Lesbian, and Straight Education Network

(GLSEN), 81 percent reported being regularly harassed on campus because of their sexual orientation. Another 39 percent reported physical assaults. Of the students who told teachers or administrators about the bullying, only 29 percent said it resulted in effective intervention.

More visibly gay teens can, unfortunately, translate into more visible homophobia. One parent describes her child's school as a "war zone"; Austin, a 15-year-old living in Michigan was taunted with epithets like "gay freak" and forced off the bleachers by students who told him it wasn't "the queer section." When his mother, Nadia, complained to the principal, she was asked what her son had done to "provoke" the attacks. "So I took a job as the lunch lady at school," she says, "because I felt I had needed to be his bodyguard."

While I want to hug this mother, the solution is obviously not to have every parent of a gay teen physically present to protect their kid. Some administrators worry that just talking about gay and bisexual teens means they have to talk about, well, sex. But knowing one's orientation isn't the same as being sexually active, any more than it is for any other teen: Most of the teens interviewed in this piece had little sexual experience; some hadn't even kissed yet. So how do they know their orientation? Didn't most of us know by middle school who we had crushes on, and with whom we wanted to go steady and slow dance? "My parents said, 'How do you know what your sexuality is if you haven't had any sexual experiences?'", says one 15-year-old boy. "I was like, 'Should I go and have one and then report back?'"

Even some staff members at Daniel Webster, the school with the thriving Gay Straight Alliance that looks like utopia for a gay middle schooler, were "livid" when the principal, Kendra Wallace, first suggested forming the alliance. "They thought it would be about sex, or us endorsing a lifestyle,"

GLBT is an acronym for "gay, lesbian, bisexual, and transgender."

she says. "And the most amazing thing has happened since the GSA started. Bullying of all kinds is way down. The GSA created this pervasive anti-bullying culture on campus that affects everyone."

In other words, protecting **GLBT** students from harassment helped to make middle school safer, kinder and more pleasant for *all* students. Isn't that the kind of change we can all get behind?

Questions for Discussion

1. Benfer describes some of the scenes depicting gay youth in the article by Benoit Denizet-Lewis as "astonishing" (par. 3). What makes these scenes "astonishing," in Benfer's view? How do these scenes set the stage for her main argument?

2. Benfer's essay includes a summary of the *New York Times* article by Benoit Denizet-Lewis as well as extended quotations from it. How does Denizet-Lewis's article fit into Benfer's argument? How effectively do you think Benfer uses the article to make her own argument about gay students coming out?

3. What is the "long-time narrative of gay youth in crisis" that Benfer discusses in paragraph 4? What is Benfer's view of this "narrative"? What evidence does she provide in support of her view? Do you find her position on this issue persuasive? Why or why not?

4. What objections does Benfer acknowledge to the idea of supporting gay teens who wish to come out? How does she answer these objections? How effectively do you think she addresses these objections?

5. If Benfer's essay were characterized as an argument to negotiate differences (see page 14), what problem is she trying to solve? How successfully do you think her argument offers a solution to this problem?

DIFFERENCES

NEGOTIATING

As the authors in this cluster note, conventions about "dating" and sexual behavior are changing, and many of those conventions are relatively new. For example, for many people the idea that couples should never have sex outside of marriage might seem quaint and old-fashioned; social situations depicted on current television sitcoms or dramas seem to suggest that few people believe any longer that sex should be saved for marriage. Yet many people still do believe that couples should refrain from sex until they are married, and they have retained that idea as part of their understanding of how to conduct romantic relationships; moreover, in recent years there have been movements to value virginity and encourage young people to wait until marriage to give up their virginity. The essays in this cluster indicate how charged these issues can be.

In view of the changing nature of the conventions of dating and the conduct of our relationships, how do you know what is appropriate behavior and what isn't? That question is the focus of this assignment.

Working with a group of classmates (or by yourself), use the essays in this cluster as a starting place for an examination of the conventions governing how we conduct relationships today. Look into dating, including same-sex dating, and examine current attitudes about sex and sexuality.

As you conduct your research, consider how factors such as age, gender, geographic location, ethnicity, race, culture, and sexual orientation might influence the way people think about the conventions of dating and the conduct of romantic relationships in general. Consider conducting a survey of students at your school and/or residents of your community as part of your research.

Once you have conducted your research, begin to formulate an answer to the question posed earlier: What is appropriate behavior when we are conducting romantic relationships and what isn't? And how do we know? Working with your classmates (or on your own), identify what you have found to be the main conventions that people today adhere to when conducting such relationships. Be sure to include in your list of conventions any discussion of differences you found that are related to age, gender, ethnicity, etc. And support your list of conventions with evidence you have gathered through your research. In other words, make an argument that these are the conventions people today seem to follow when conducting romantic relationships. Then create a website in which you present your case. If appropriate, design your website for a specific audience.

Alternatively, write a report in which you make your case for the conventions for conducting romantic relationships today.

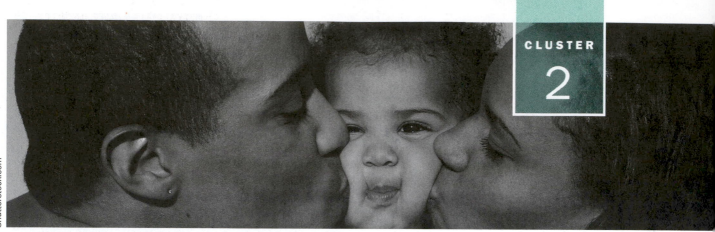

What Does It Mean to Be a Good Parent?

The rules governing the relationship between parents and children seemed relatively simple in the past. For example, there is an old adage that "children should be seen but not heard." And even when children were much loved, they were expected to honor their parents (as the fifth commandment holds and other religious texts convey)—which means not only obeying parents but also respecting them and caring for them in old age. Beginning in the late eighteenth century, however, childhood was reconstructed. The Romantics believed that "the child is father to the man," as the poet William Wordsworth wrote in 1802—in other words, children are born with innate wisdom and imagination and are superior to adults in some respects because they are not yet corrupted by experience in the world. From this concept, increasing deference toward children began to emerge. Rather than take children for granted as "little adults," parents became concerned with what their offspring need besides food, shelter, and authority. To a large extent, this attitude toward parenting seems widespread today.

But how should parents parent? Many parents simply wing it on their own, learning how to parent (or how not to parent) by taking things one day at a time and doing what seems to make sense. Others, however, take parenting classes and consult the growing how-to popular literature on parenting. Of this literature, the various editions of Dr. Benjamin Spock's *Baby and Child Care* have probably had the most influence. First published in 1946, it appeared just in time for the "baby boom" that began after the end of the Second World War and continued until the early 1960s. Thousands of young parents, many of them living far from their own parents, needed up-to-date advice about how to raise a healthy child. Concerned with questions such as "Should babies be picked up whenever they cry?" and "Is it better to breast-feed or to use baby formula?" these parents turned to Dr. Spock—whose work, updated, remains in print.

But the American family has changed dramatically over the last fifty years. Increasing numbers of children are being raised in families in which both parents work outside the home, by a single parent, or in reconfigured families when one of their parents remarries. Moreover, modern science has made conception possible for many couples that would not have been able to have children in the past. It has also made it possible for some potential parents to design the kind of children they wish to have—a topic addressed by the first two arguments in this cluster. The other two essays respond to the increasing complexity of parenting by focusing on the most important things that mothers and fathers can do. Together, these four essays address modern versions of age-old questions about how to be a good parent at a time when these questions seem more challenging than ever.

① # Designer Babies and Other Fairy Tales

MAUREEN FREELY

Because matters of human reproduction are both complex and, to many people, sacred, arguments about reproductive issues can become especially intense. They can encompass medical, economic, ethical, legal, and moral considerations. For example, a couple faced with the prospect of having a baby with a serious genetic disorder must confront the economic question of who will pay the enormous costs of caring for the child once it is born. Physicians may face legal questions if they advise the couple to perform a risky medical procedure on the unborn baby. Others may question the morality of such procedures. Writer Maureen Freely appreciates the complexity of such issues. In fact, she argues that the many different kinds of arguments made about such situations complicate the already difficult decisions facing parents and others who may be involved. Drawing on a reproductive case that caused a sensation in Great Britain in 2002, Freely sorts through the many different voices in debates about reproductive medicine, and she asks you, as a reader, to focus on *how* the issues are being debated. She encourages you to think of these issues as social issues that everyone has a stake in—whether or not you will ever face reproductive decisions yourself. And because these are social rather than private matters, they should properly be debated—and decided—publicly in democratic fashion. As you read, consider how Freely compares the way these issues are addressed in Great Britain to the way they are addressed in the United States. Consider, too, how the complicated questions that can face parents such as the ones she describes in her essay make the old question of what it means to be a good parent even more difficult to answer. Her essay appeared in the British magazine the *New Statesman* in 2002.

MAUREEN FREELY, "Designer Babies and Other Fairy Tales"

Human Fertilisation and Embryology Authority (HFEA)
Established in 1990, the Human Fertilisation and Embryology Authority regulates reproductive research and therapies in Great Britain.

1 Meet Raj and Shahana Hashmi. Their gorgeous three-year-old son, Zain, has a serious blood disorder. He needs a cell transplant, and if they do not find a suitable donor he could die. On 22 February, the **Human Fertilisation and Embryology Authority (HFEA)** gave the Hashmis permission to try to create that donor. Shahana is to have IVF (in vitro fertilization) ... treatment. Any embryos that result will be subjected to genetic diagnosis. The hope is that the couple will find an embryo that could become the child with the bone marrow that will save Zain's life.

The odds are not in their favour. The success rate for a single course of IVF treatment is less than one in three. The likelihood of Shahana Hashmi creating a genetically suitable embryo is one in 16. So she and her husband must have a hard time understanding why so many people think they're playing God. If only, they must be thinking. All they want is to take this one-in-about-50 chance to keep their son alive.

How strange it must be for them to open the paper and read that they are symbols of moral decay. No one is quite ready to condemn them outright. No one who wants to avoid a writ, anyway. No, almost everyone is sure that the Hashmis will love any second child just as much as they love their first. Some have gone on the record to say we can count on this even if something goes amiss and their second born turns out not to be Zain's saviour. But what about the six other couples who have already announced they will be following in the Hashmis' footsteps? What about all the faceless others who are bound to follow them? What if the rules get looser still and this sort of thing becomes standard practice? When we work ourselves up into a moralistic froth about reproductive technology, what exactly are we talking about?

The short answer is that we are talking about too many things at once, and in a very muddled way. The dirge gets played out on the lowest keys on the piano. Many of the fears it evokes are, however, worthy of attention. There is, for example, the entirely legitimate fear of the new—or of the social havoc that can result when new technology makes false claims, or gives people more power than they know how to use, or changes the rules by which we procreate. There is religious fear—about hubris, damnation, sacrilege and playing God. There is the fear of eugenics trying to "get in through the back door." There is the free-floating fear of the wrong people being in control. We are afraid of doctors taking control of our bodies to create a master race, of parents buying into the fantasy of perfection, of babies being turned into consumer products. And what if something goes wrong? What if, instead of creating the perfect baby, the scientists accidentally create a monster?

5 One of the most interesting things about the debate on reproductive medicine is its heavy reliance on the language of fairy tales. There are spectres, monsters and bogeymen, wishes and dreams and magic cures. Babies are not just babies, but potent symbols of our cultural future—what we want to pass on, what we stand to lose if the story goes the wrong way. When people talk about designer babies, they're not just talking about the manipula-

CONTEXT

In vitro fertilization is a process by which eggs are removed from a woman, fertilized with male sperm in a laboratory, and implanted in the woman's uterus, where they can potentially develop into human embryos. The first "test-tube baby" was born as a result of this technique in 1978 in England. The procedure is now common. Although Freely notes in paragraph 2 that typically fewer than one-third of the women who undergo the procedure actually become pregnant, a study published in 2009 in the *New England Journal of Medicine* reported that the chances of a successful live-birth following IVF therapy range between 65 and 86 percent in younger women and between 23 and 42 percent in women aged 40 and older.

tion of genes. They are talking about the next generation and who gets to shape it.

If they sometimes forget that they are talking in symbols and fall too easily into magical thinking, if their ideas about "suitable candidates for treatment" are arch-conservative, and even racist, it is also true that they are asking important questions. A society is not a society unless it can reproduce itself. The social regulation of fertility, the system of controls and supports that decides who gets to have children, and who does not, is what makes a society what it is. Every time a society changes its system, everyone and everything in that society feels the effects. The faster the change, the bigger the disruption.

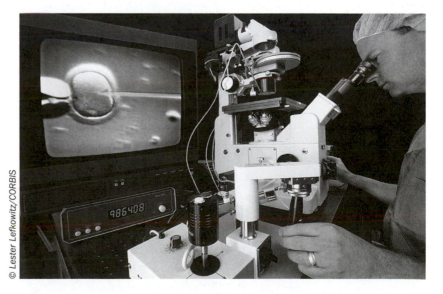

© Lester Lefkowitz/CORBIS

COMPLICATION

In stating that "the regulation of fertility is less and less a private matter" (par. 7), Freely is referring not only to changing laws governing fertility treatments but also to the ongoing controversy about the regulation of fertility. In 1994, the International Conference on Population and Development was held in Cairo, Egypt, amid great controversy. Among the declarations made at that conference was the following statement:

> Women have the individual right and the social responsibility to decide whether, how and when to have children and how many to have; no woman can be compelled to bear a child or be prevented from doing so against her will. All women regardless of age, marital status or other social conditions have a right to information and services necessary to exercise their reproductive rights. (SOURCE: Women Against Fundamentalisms.)

Religious groups have mixed and often conflicting views about these issues, but many religious thinkers see reproduction as a private matter for a woman to decide according to her faith.

In the past generation, we have seen one of the most dramatic changes ever. The regulation of fertility is less and less a private matter: increasingly, it is decided in the public domain. When fertility goes public, the game changes utterly.

Let me give a very obvious example—I cannot live as a free woman, in control of my body, in charge of my choices, unless I live in a society which supports that freedom with affordable, accessible contraception. I depend on the state to make sure that the services I use are regulated and staffed with real doctors. I need to have the right to complain if I find the service poor. I need to know that I can campaign for changes in legislation as and when they seem necessary. I need to bear in mind that other parties are free to do the same, which is why my right to birth control is something I should never take for granted.

As with birth control, so with birth. I need to bear in mind that my right to have a child at all is also subject to political control. If I live in a democratic society, I can fight my corner. If I happen to be in China in the time of the one-child policy, I cannot. If I live in any of the countries that condone the use of sex selection technologies to favour boys and weed out girls, my ability to protest against that policy will depend on the political system within which I am operating.

10 Wherever I am, whatever aspect of reproductive medicine I am talking about, the questions are the same. Who decides? And what ideological agenda are those people serving? Thus, Nazi eugenics was evil because it served Nazi ideals. It was dangerous because it was backed up by a fascist state.

If reproductive medicine is properly regulated and democratically debated, if the use of new technology is overseen by a regulatory agency with a clear ethical framework, it does not lead inexorably to the same place. Our own HFEA is far from perfect, but you have only to look at the chaotic, under-regulated United States to see how lucky we are. In Britain, at least, we have rules and principles. We can harness change, make sure it is not open to abuse, or slow it down so that we have time to think about it.

The HFEA's slow but steady move to a stance in favour of "eugenics for sound

© Arie Skelly/CORBIS

medical reasons" is a case in point. Most experts in the field predict that public attitudes will follow suit. But that is only a tiny part of the picture. The larger, cultural implications of reproductive technology will continue to trouble. Every new technique will challenge power relations within families and kinship networks, and therefore the way we bring up children. Wherever the family loses power over an individual's right to become a parent, the advantage goes not just to the individual but to the medical profession, big business and the state. Is this what we want? If we do not, we are going to have to fight it out politically. But first, we need a more rational debate.

CONTEXT

Established in 1979, the one-child policy of the government of the People's Republic of China (see par. 9) restricts most Chinese couples to having one child. The policy, which was adopted as a measure to control China's rapidly growing population, has been controversial in the decades since it was first implemented. Some human rights observers have charged that the Chinese government has subjected women to forced sterilizations and abortions in carrying out the policy. As a result of the policy, the ratio of males to females in China is 118 to 100 (compared to the average ratio of 105 males to 100 females). In 2003, the Chinese government announced plans to relax the policy.

Questions for Discussion

1. Freely asserts that the public debates about reproductive situations like that of the Hashmis get "muddled" because people "are talking about too many things at once." What does she mean by that statement? How does that point relate to the main argument of her essay?

2. Freely concedes that many of the concerns expressed by people on various sides of the reproductive controversy involving the Hashmis are valid concerns. She even concedes that people who have racist ideas are asking important questions about this controversy. Why do you think Freely makes these concessions? In what ways might these concessions strengthen her main argument?

3. A central point that Freely makes in this essay is that "the regulation of fertility" and reproductive issues in general are increasingly public, rather than private, issues. What counterarguments could you offer to that point?

4. A British writer, Freely writes, "You have only to look at the chaotic, under-regulated United States to see how lucky we are. In Britain, at least, we have rules and principles. We can harness change, make sure it is not open to abuse, or slow it down so that we have time to think about it." She favors deliberate regulation of the technology based on "rules and principles." What purpose does this comparison to the United States serve? Do you think such a comparison is effective, given her audience? (Remember that Freely was writing this essay for a British magazine.) How did you react to this comparison?

5. Freely ends her essay by stating that "we need a more rational debate" about reproductive issues. On the basis of her essay, what do you think she means by a "rational debate"? Do you think her essay is an example of an argument that would be part of such a debate? Explain, citing specific examples from her essay to support your answer.

② | Victims from Birth

WENDY MCELROY

The capability to "engineer" a baby through certain medical reproductive techniques is often described by proponents as a way to avoid serious birth defects and to ensure that a child will be born healthy. But what if a couple wishes their child to be born with what most people consider a disability? Do those parents have the right to "engineer" such a child? Do they "own" that child's physical identity to the extent that they can use medical science to give that child certain characteristics that others find undesirable? In the following essay, feminist activist Wendy McElroy says no. She discusses an unusual case involving two women who used reproductive techniques to make it more likely that the child they would have would be deaf, just like the two of them. As McElroy notes in her essay, these parents believe that deafness is not a disability but a culture, and they wished their child to be part of that culture. But McElroy wonders whether the child would have chosen to be deaf—if allowed such a choice. She argues that the choice should have been the child's. Despite her unequivocal position on this case, McElroy complicates the already difficult questions surrounding genetics and reproductive issues. In a sense, she asks you to consider who owns physical identities in an age when medical science makes it possible to alter and even to determine those identities. Wendy McElroy is the author of numerous articles and books about women's issues, including *XXX: A Woman's Right to Pornography* (1995) and *Liberty for Women: Freedom and Feminism in the 21st Century* (2002). She also blogs, writes a column for FoxNews.com, and edits *iFeminists.com*, a website that supports "individualist feminism" where this essay was published in 2002.

WENDY MCELROY, "Victims from Birth"

Aryan Race Adolf Hitler's infamous ideas about a "master race" were based in part on a belief that a tribe of Indo-Europeans called Aryans invaded and subdued the Indian subcontinent around 1700 BCE. These Aryans were thought to be Nordic in appearance, which contributed to Hitler's belief that Germans were descended from this tribe. Historians and anthropologists generally dismiss the notion that Aryans existed or that any such tribe conquered parts of Eurasia.

1 When Sharon Duchesneau gave birth on Thanksgiving Day to a deaf son, she was delighted.

Duchesneau and her lesbian partner, Candace McCullough, had done everything they could to ensure that Gauvin would be born without hearing. The two deaf women selected their sperm donor on the basis of his family history of deafness in order, as McCullough explained, "to increase our chances of having a baby who is deaf."

So they consciously attempted to create a major sensory defect in their child.

Scientists and philosophers have been debating the morality of new reproductive technologies that may allow us to design "perfect" human beings. Advocates dream of eliminating conditions such as spina bifida; critics invoke images of Nazis creating an **Aryan race**.

5 But what of prospective parents who deliberately engineer a genetic defect into their offspring?

Why? Duchesneau illustrates one motive.

She believes deafness is a culture, not a disability. A deaf lifestyle is a choice she wishes to make for her son and his older sister Jehanne. McCullough said she and her partner are merely expressing the natural tendency to want children "like them."

"You know, black people have harder lives," she said. "Why shouldn't parents be able to go ahead and pick a black donor if that's what they want?"

Passing over the problem of equating race with a genetic defect, McCullough seems to be saying that deafness is a minority birthright to be passed on proudly from parent to child. By implication, those appalled by their choice are compared to bigots.

10 Some in the media have implicitly endorsed their view.

On March 31st, the *Washington Post Magazine* ran a sympathetic cover story entitled "A World of Their Own" with the sub-title, "In the eyes of his parents, if Gauvin Hughes McCullough turns out to be deaf, that will be just perfect." The article features Gauvin's birth and ends with the two women taking him home. There they tell family and friends that, "He is not as profoundly deaf as Jehanne, but he is quite deaf. Deaf enough." The article does not comment critically on the parents' decision not to fit Gauvin with a hearing aid and develop whatever hearing ability exists.

The Duchesneau case is particularly troubling to advocates of parental rights against governmental intrusion. The moral outrage it elicits easily can lead to bad law—laws that may hinder responsible parents from using genetic techniques to remedy conditions such as cystic fibrosis in embryos. Selective breeding, after all, is a form of genetic engineering. The Duchesneau case, then, brings all other forms of genetic engineering into question.

The championing of deafness as a cultural "good" owes much to political correctness or the politics of victimhood, which view group identity as the foundation of all political and cultural analysis.

Disabled people used to announce, "I am not my disability." They demanded that society look beyond the withered arm, a clubbed-foot, or a wheel chair and see the human being, a human who was essentially identical to everyone else.

COMPLICATION

"In the case of Duchesneau and McCullough, there is no ethical issue—the couple have the right to procreate with whomever they want. And many couples with a family history of deafness or disability seek to have a child without that disability. But some deaf couples have expressed the desire to use prenatal genetic testing of their fetus or in vitro fertilisation and preimplantation genetic diagnosis to select a deaf child. These choices are not unique to deafness. Dwarves may wish to have a dwarf child. People with intellectual disability may wish to have a child like them. Couples of mixed race may wish to have a light skinned child (or a dark skinned child, if they are mindful of reducing the risk of skin cancer in countries like Australia)."

SOURCE: Julian Savulescu, "Deaf Babies, 'Designer Disability,' and the Future of Medicine." *British Medical Journal* (October 2002).

---

15 Now, for some, the announcement has become, "I am my deafness. That is what is special about me."

Society is brutal to those who are different. I know. As a result of my grandmother contracting German measles, my mother was born with a severely deformed arm. She concealed her arm beneath sweaters with sleeves that dangled loosely, even in sweltering weather. She hid.

Reuters New Media Inc./CORBIS

Americans with Disabilities Act According to the U.S. Department of Justice, the Americans with Disabilities Act (ADA), passed in 1990, "gives civil rights protections to individuals with disabilities similar to those provided to individuals on the basis of race, color, sex, national origin, age, and religion. It guarantees equal opportunity for individuals with disabilities in public accommodations, employment, transportation, State and local government services, and telecommunications."

Embracing a physical defect, as Duchesneau and McCullough have done, may be a more healthy personal response. Certainly they should be applauded for moving beyond the painful deaf childhoods they describe.

However, I remember my mother telling me that the birth of her children—both healthy and physically unremarkable—were the two happiest moments of her life. I contrast this with Duchesneau who, knowing the pain of growing up deaf, did what she could to impose deafness upon her son.

Deafness is not fundamentally a cultural choice, although a culture has sprung up around it. If it were, deafness would not be included in the **Americans with Disabilities Act**—a source of protection and funding that deaf-culture zealots do not rush to renounce.

20 But if deafness is to be considered a cultural choice, let it be the choice of the child, not the parents. Let a child with all five senses decide to renounce or relinquish one of them in order to embrace what may be a richer life. If a child is rendered incapable of deciding "yes" or "no," then in what manner is it a choice?

> **CONTEXT**
>
> When McElroy's essay was published in 2002 on a website called iFeminists.com, the website defined "independent feminism" as a philosophy that "calls for freedom, choice, and personal responsibility." iFeminists believe that "freedom and diversity benefit women, whether or not the choices that particular women make are politically correct. They respect all sexual choices, from motherhood to porn. As the cost of freedom, iFeminists accept personal responsibility for their own lives. They do not look to government for privileges any more than they would accept government abuse." To what extent does McElroy's argument in this essay reflect an iFeminist philosophy?

Questions for Discussion

1. On what grounds does McElroy criticize Duchesneau and McCullough's efforts to have a deaf child? Do you think her criticisms are valid? Why or why not?

2. Why does McElroy reject the view that deafness is a culture? How convincing is her argument against that view?

3. Why is this case troubling for advocates of parental rights who resist government intrusion on parenting decisions, according to McElroy? In what sense is this point important to McElroy's main argument about this case?

4. In making a point about how difficult it is to be different in a society, McElroy refers to her mother's disability. Evaluate the effectiveness of this use of personal experience. Is McElroy's analogy between her mother's disability and the birth of the deaf child she describes in this essay relevant to her point?

5. McElroy's essay can be described as an argument based on deductive reasoning (see page 81–83). On what fundamental belief or principle does McElroy base her argument? Do you agree with her? Why or why not?

③ | # The Good Enough Mother

ANNA QUINDLEN

Through her column in the *New York Times*—which won her a Pulitzer Prize in 1992—as well as her column in *Newsweek*, Anna Quindlen has become one of the best-known journalists in the country. In addition to publishing collections of her nonfiction, she is the author of five novels and two children's books, *The Tree Came to Stay* and *Happily Ever After.* Much of her writing focuses on family life and parenting. The following argument—which draws upon her experience as a child and as a mother—originally appeared in *Newsweek* in 2005. In her essay, Quindlen makes her case for a more traditional approach to being a mother than most mothers she knows seem to follow today. Her essay asks us to consider what it means to be a "good enough" mother.

ANNA QUINDLEN, "The Good Enough Mother"

1 There was a kind of carelessness to my childhood. I wandered away from time to time, rode my bike too far from home, took the trolley to nowhere in particular and back again. If you had asked my mother at any given time where I was, she would likely have paused from spooning Gerber's peas into a baby's mouth or ironing our school uniforms and replied, "She's around here somewhere."

By the new standards of mothering, my mother was a bust. Given the number of times I got lost when I was young, she might even be termed neglectful. There's only one problem with that conclusion. It's dead wrong. My mother was great at what she did. Don't misunderstand: she didn't sit on the floor and help us build with our Erector sets, didn't haul us from skating rink to piano lessons. She couldn't even drive. But where she was always felt like a safe place.

The idea that that's enough is a tough sell in our current culture, and not simply because if one of my kids had been found wandering far from our home there would have been a caseworker and a cop at the door. We live in a perfection society now, in which it is possible to make our bodies last longer, to manipulate our faces so the lines of laughter and distress are wiped out. We

believe in the illusion of control, and nowhere has that become more powerful—and more pernicious—than in the phenomenon of manic motherhood. What the child-care guru D. W. Winnicott once called "the ordinary devoted mother" is no longer good enough. Instead there is an uber-mom who bounces from soccer field to school fair to play date until she falls into bed at the end of the day, exhausted, her life somewhere between the Stations of the Cross and a decathlon.

A perfect storm of trends and events contributed to this. One was the teeter-totter scientific argument of nature versus nurture. When my mother was raising kids, there was a sub rosa assumption that they were what they were. The smart one. The sweet one. Even the bad one. There was only so much a mother could do to mold the clay she'd been dealt.

CONTEXT

Scientists, psychologists, educators, and others have long debated whether a person's innate characteristics or upbringing plays a greater role in determining that person's identity and capabilities. The debate has important implications for many fields, including education, psychiatry, neuropsychology, linguistics, athletics, and social welfare. Although advances in genetic technologies in recent years have enabled researchers to determine that many important human traits are determined at birth, the debate continues.

5 But as I became a mother, all that was changing. Little minds, we learned from researchers, were infinitely malleable, even before birth. Don't get tense: tense moms make tense infants. (That news'll make you tense!) In a prenatal exercise class, I remember lying on the mat working on what was left of my stomach muscles, listening to the instructor repeating, "Now hug your baby." If I had weak abs, did that mean my baby went unhugged? Keeping up with the Joneses turned into keeping up with the Joneses' kids. Whose mothers, by the way, lied. I now refuse to believe in 9-month-olds who speak in full sentences. But I was more credulous, and more vulnerable, when I had a 9-month-old myself.

This craziness sounds improbable in the face of the feminist revolution that transformed the landscape of America during our lifetime. But at some level it is the fruit of that revolution, a comeuppance cleverly disguised as a calling. Every time we take note of the fact that work is not a choice but an economic necessity—"most women have to work, you know"—it's an apology for freedom. How better to circumvent the power of the new woman than with, the idea of mothering not as care but as creation? Every moment for children was a teachable moment—and every teachable moment missed was a measure of a lousy mom.

My baby-boomer friends and I were part of the first generation of women who took for granted that we would work throughout our lifetime, and like most pioneers we made it up as we went along. In 1976, **Dr. Spock** revised his bible of child care to say that it was all right if we worked and had children as well. There was a slapdash approach to melding these disparate roles, usually reflected in the iconic woman at a business meeting with spit-up on her shoulder. My first sitter was the erstwhile manager of a cult punk band. She was a good sitter, too. We got by.

But quicker than you could say nanny cam, books appeared, seminars were held and modern motherhood was codified as a profession. Professionalized for women who didn't work outside the home: if they were giving up such great opportunities, then the tending of kids needed to be made into an all-encompassing job. Professionalized for women who had paying jobs out in the world: to show that their work was not bad for their kids, they had to take child rearing as seriously as deal making. (Fathers did not have to justify themselves; after all, no man has ever felt moved to say that most guys have to work, you know.)

It's not just that baking for the bake sale, meeting with the teachers, calling the other mothers about the sleepover and looking at the SAT camp made women of both sorts crazy, turning stress from an occasional noun into an omnipresent verb and adverb. A lot of this was not particularly good for kids. If your mother has been micromanaging your homework since you were 6, it's hard to feel any pride of ownership when you do well. You can't learn from mistakes and disappointments if your childhood is engineered so there aren't any.

10 So much has been written about how the young people of America seem to stay young longer now, well into the years when their grandparents owned houses and had families. But their grandparents never had a mother calling the teacher to complain about a bad grade. And hair-trigger attention spans may be less a function of PlayStation and more a function of kids who never have a moment's peace. I passed on the weekend roundelay of kiddie-league sports so our three could hang out with one another. I told people I hoped it would cement a bond among them, and it did. But I really wanted to be reading rather than standing on the sidelines pretending my kids were soccer prodigies. Maybe I had three children in the first place so I wouldn't ever have to play board games. In my religion, martyrs die.

Our oldest child wrestled custody of his life away from me at a fairly early age, perhaps

Dr. Benjamin Spock (1903–1998) was a pediatrician and psychoanalyst whose book *Baby and Child* Care, first published in 1946, Quindlen describes here as "his bible of child care." Spock's ideas on parenting focused on care of the child and common sense of the parents. In *Baby and Child Care* he writes, "You know more than you think you know . . . trust your own instincts."

inspired by an epic bout in which I tried to persuade him to rewrite a perfectly good fourth-grade paper to turn it into an eight-grade paper. Perhaps I'd been addled by the class art projects, some of which looked like the work of a crack graphics design team—and were. I asked the other day about his memories of my mothering. "You sorta freaked out during the college application process," he noted accurately. But then he wrote, "What I remember most: having a good time." You can engrave that on my headstone right this minute.

There's the problem with turning motherhood into martyrdom. There's no way to do it and have a good time. If we create a never-ending spin cycle of have-tos because we're trying to expiate senseless guilt about working or not working, trying to keep up with the woman at school whose kid gets A's because she writes the papers herself, the message we send our children is terrible. By our actions we tell them that being a mom—being their mom—is a drag, powered by fear, self-doubt and conformity, all the things we are supposed to teach them to overcome. It just becomes a gloss on that old joke: Enough about me. What about you? How do you make me feel about myself? The most incandescent memories of my childhood are of making my mother laugh. My kids did the same for me. A good time is what they remember long after toddler programs and art projects are over. The rest is just scheduling.

Questions for Discussion

1. What differences does Quindlen see between being a mother today and being a mother during her own mother's generation? Why are those differences important, in Quindlen's view?

2. What problems does Quindlen see with mothers becoming overly involved in raising their children? Do you think these problems are legitimate ones? Why or why not? What might your answer to that question suggest about your own views regarding parenting?

3. In paragraph 3 Quindlen refers to "the teeter-totter scientific argument of nature versus nurture." What does this "nature versus nurture" debate have to do with being a mother today, in Quindlen's view?

4. How effectively does Quindlen use her own experiences as a mother and as a daughter to support her argument?

5. What does feminism have to do with motherhood, as Quindlen sees it? Do you think her analysis of the role of feminism in influencing attitudes about motherhood is valid? Explain, citing specific passages from her essay to support your answer.

6. Writing as a Catholic, Quindlen concludes paragraph 10 with the line, "In my religion, martyrs die." How does this line apply to being a mother?

7. Quindlen's essay might be seen as an argument based on inductive reasoning (see pages 80–81). What conclusions does she reach about mothering on the basis of her own experience? How effective do you find her reasoning from her experiences?

④ | **What Fathers Do Best**

STEVEN E. RHOADS

In 2009 the U.S. Bureau of Labor Statistics reported that women held 49.8 percent of available jobs in the United States. That was the highest percentage on record. For decades, more and more American women have been entering the workforce, and their numbers reflect significant changes in the traditional roles that men and women have assumed, including primary responsibility for childcare. As Steven E. Rhoads notes in the following essay, stay-at-home dads have become a common figure in contemporary American culture. But that trend doesn't please Rhoads, who argues that the traditional role of a father, which includes many responsibilities that he believes men can fulfill better than women, is good for children. His argument in favor of traditional gender roles for men and women is one answer to the larger question of what makes a good parent. Steven Rhoads teaches public policy at the University of Virginia. He is the author of numerous books, including *Taking Sex Differences Seriously* (2004), as well as articles in publications such as the *New York Times*, *Public Interest*, and the *Weekly Standard,* a magazine known for promoting neoconservative values, in which this essay appeared in 2005.

STEVEN E. RHOADS, "What Fathers Do Best"

1 Father's Day no longer arrives without the national media highlighting Mr. Moms. The year before last, for example, Lisa Belkin of the *New York Times* described the life of one Michael Zorek, whose only job was taking care of his 14-month-old son Jeremy. Zorek, whose wife brought home a good salary as a corporate lawyer, felt he had become "remarkably good" at shopping, at cooking, and at entertaining his energetic toddler. He was angry at a parents' magazine whose essay contest was open only to mothers. "I'm the one who does the shopping, and I'm the one who does the cooking," he reasoned. "Why is it only sexist when women are excluded?"

This year the homemaking fathers even got to horn in on Mother's Day. On May 8, the *Washington Post's* Sunday Outlook section featured William McGee, a single dad who "couldn't help feeling excluded" by all the ads for products that "moms and kids" would both love. He mentioned, for example, the classic peanut butter ad, "Choosy Moms Choose Jif." McGee wanted advertisers to know that he is "one of many caring dads" who are choosy, too.

Brace yourselves for an onslaught of such features this week, even though, in the real world, there are still 58 moms staying home with minor children for every dad who does so. This is not just an accidental social arrangement, to be overcome once the media have sufficiently raised our consciousness about the joys of stay-at-home fatherhood. Mothers are loaded with estrogen and oxytocin, which draw them to young children and help induce them to tend to infants. And the babies themselves make it clear that they prefer their mothers. Even in families where fathers have taken a four-month-long paid parental leave to tend to their newborns, the fathers report that the babies prefer to be comforted by their mothers.

The problem with honoring fathers who do what mothers usually do—what used to be called "mothering"—is this: it suggests that fathers who do what *most* fathers do aren't contributing to their children's well-being. Yet we know this can't be true. Children who grow up in fatherless families are poorer, less healthy, less educated. They die much earlier, commit more crimes, and give birth to more babies out of wedlock.

5 What do most real-world dads do? When the kids get old enough, they teach them how to build and fix things and how to play sports. They are better than moms at teaching children how to deal with novelty and frustration, perhaps because they are more likely than mothers to encourage children to work out problems and address challenges themselves—from putting on their shoes to operating a new toy.

When the kids become older still, Dad is usually better than Mom at controlling unruly boys. **Jennifer Roback Morse** notes that all the surveys of who does what around the house never mention one of her husband's most important functions—he is responsible for glaring. When their son acts up, his glares just seem to have more effect than hers do.

Similarly, a fascinating study in the journal *Criminology* finds that female social ties in a neighborhood—borrowing food, helping with problems, having lunch together—are associated with much lower crime rates. Male social ties in the neighborhood have no effect on crime rates. But the beneficial effect of female ties almost completely disappears in communities dominated by fatherless families! You need husbands and fathers—what the authors call "family rooted men"—if the crime-fighting female ties are really to be effective. Perhaps mothers still say, "Just you wait until your father gets home," or its 21st-century equivalent.

Sometimes moms worry that their rough-housing husbands are making their boys more aggressive. But, in fact, fathers are teaching their sons how to play fight—don't bite, don't kick, stay away from the eyes—a form of play enjoyed by most boys around the world. On the playground, boys without fathers in the home are unpopular because they respond in a truly aggressive manner when other boys try to initiate rough-and-tumble play. A committee brought together by the **Board on Children, Youth, and Families** of the National Research Council has concluded that "fathers, in effect, give children practice in regulating their own emotions and recognizing others' emotional cues."

Of course, dads do a lot for their daughters as well. For example, by providing a model of love for and fidelity to their wives, dads give teenage girls confidence that they can expect men to be interested in them for reasons beyond sex.

10 We could begin to do dads justice if we realized that their nature makes it unlikely that they will like intensive nurturing in the way that most mothers do. Testosterone inhibits nurturing. In both men and women high levels of testosterone are associated with less interest in babies. Low levels of testosterone are associated with a stronger than average interest in nurturing. If you inject a monkey mother with testosterone, she becomes less interested in her baby. And men have much more testosterone than women. Thus, in those two-career families where husband and wife are determined to share domestic and paid work equally, a common argument ensues because dads typically suggest that they get more paid child-care help; moms typically want less paid help and more time with their children.

If dads were as tormented as moms by prolonged absence from their children, we'd have more unhappiness and more fights over who gets to spend time with the children. By faithfully working at often boring jobs to provide for their families, dads make possible moms who can do less paid work and thereby produce less stressed and happier households. Dads deserve a lot of credit for simply making moms' nurturing of children possible. On Father's Day we should more often notice, and then honor, typical fatherly virtues and declare vive la difference.

Board on Children, Youth, and Families According to its website, "The Board on Children, Youth, and Families addresses a variety of policy-relevant issues related to the health and development of children, youth, and families. It does so by convening experts to weigh in on matters from the perspective of the behavioral, social, and health sciences."

Jennifer Roback Morse is a research fellow at the Hoover Institution, a conservative think tank. In her book *Love and Economics: Why the Laissez-Faire Family Doesn't Work* (2001), she argues that the modern substitutes for the family, including the government and single parents, cannot raise children as effectively as a mother and father in a traditional family. She advocates a philosophy of individual autonomy and responsibility rather than an approach based on personal love as a basis for raising families.

Questions for Discussion

1. The original publication of this argument was planned to correspond with Father's Day. To what extent do you think the essay celebrates the idea and practice of being a father? How do you think the timing of the publication of this essay might shape readers' reactions to it?

2. Rhoads makes unsupported claims about how men and women differ in their capacity for nurturing because of estrogen, oxytocin, and testosterone. Could he safely assume that his audience would accept these claims as common knowledge, or should he have provided support for them?

3. Rhoads claims that the children of fatherless families are "poorer, less healthy, less educated" (par. 4). What evidence does he provide to support these claims? Do these claims seem likely to be true?

4. Rhoads describes how fathers teach their sons how to be aggressive and their daughters how to be respected. What assumptions about gender expectations are built into this argument? Do you think he can assume that most readers will share these assumptions? Explain.

5. In his conclusion, Rhoads evokes an image of fathers "faithfully working at often boring jobs to provide for their families." How does this image fit into his main argument about fathers?

DIFFERENCES

NEGOTIATING

Despite the growth of so-called nontraditional families in the past few decades, the U.S. Census Bureau reported in 2008 that seven in ten American children lived with two parents; about six in ten lived with both their biological parents. So most American kids are still growing up in what are called traditional families. But has parenting changed, even if most Americans still live in traditional families?

As the essays by Maureen Freely and Wendy McElroy in this cluster suggest, new medical technologies are among the features of contemporary life that can complicate the challenges of parenting and create new kinds of questions for parents. And the essays by Anna Quindlen and Steven E. Rhoads make it clear that even if male and female roles are changing in American society, many people still advocate traditional gender roles—with men and women assuming different responsibilities for raising children. Quindlen and Rhoads suggest that what makes a good parent today is pretty much the same as it was when they were growing up 30 or 40 years ago.

Are they right? That question is the focus of this assignment, which has two parts.

The first part asks you to examine your own upbringing and consider the kind of parenting you experienced. Whether or not you grew up in a traditional family, you can reflect on the main components of your experience as a child and draw some conclusions about what seemed to work—and what didn't—about the parenting you received. So for this part of the assignment, write an essay describing the kind of parenting you experienced as a child and then a teen. Your essay may be a general description of the main features of the way your parents or guardians raised you. Or you might focus on one or more specific events that illustrate how you were raised. In your essay, try to draw conclusions about what you think was effective—and not so effective—about the way you were raised.

For the second part of this assignment, share your essay with a group of classmates. After you and your classmates have read each other's essays, discuss the similarities and differences in your respective experiences. As a group, identify what seem to be the main features of effective parenting, as they emerge from the experiences you each described in your essays. Then, using the list of features of effective parenting that your group has compiled, collaboratively write an essay in which you describe what it means to be a good parent. In your essay, draw from your individual and collective experiences to make your case for what you believe makes for a good parent today. Consider doing some research into what experts today believe makes a good parent, and consider how the times we live in might affect how parents should raise their children. Assume a general audience that would include people of your own generation as well as of your parents' generation.

What Are Family Values?

If you have paid any attention to recent political campaigns in the United States, then you have encountered the phrase *family values*. Especially in national political campaigns but even in local campaigns, candidates seem to take pains to assure voters that they are in favor of family values. But what exactly does that mean? Answering that question isn't as easy as it might seem.

Start with a search of the Internet. A search for the term "family values" in 2010 would have returned more than 60 million websites. Among the more prominent websites were the following: the American Family Association, which claimed that it "represents and stands for traditional family values and exists to motivate and equip citizens to reform our culture to reflect Biblical truth on which it was founded"; FamilyIQ. com, which defined its mission as teaching parents "how to improve their parenting skills in order to build stronger, more successful families"; Family Values at Work, a labor organization that advocates paid sick days and family leave policies for workers; and an entry in Wikipedia, which at the time defined "family values" as "political and social beliefs that hold the Nuclear family to be the essential ethical and moral unit of society." Just this brief selection suggests that the definitions of "family values" sometimes focus on parenting or public policy, sometimes reflect religious or moral beliefs, and sometimes are based on political views. Apparently, there is no consensus on what "family values" are, despite the fact that politicians and many others routinely use that phrase as if everyone understands exactly what it means.

The essays in this cluster may not provide a definitive answer to the question, What are family values? But they will deepen your understanding of the complexity of this idea. Although these essays focus on marriage, which is so often at the center of debates about family values, they raise broader questions about how we understand the idea of the family and what we value about families. They also suggest that the definition of "family values" is a moving target.

① Fidelity with a Wandering Eye

CHRISTINA NEHRING

The following argument was written in response to a book by Diane Shader Smith called *Undressing Infidelity: Why More Wives Are Unfaithful* (2005). It is, in fact, a review of that book and demonstrates how argument can take the form of a book review. In discussing Smith's book, Nehring argues that the conventional wisdom about the sexual lives of women is misleading; she draws on Smith's research to argue that there are serious problems in the way women are expected to behave in a marriage. In the process, Nehring raises provocative questions about so-called traditional marriages. This review was first published in a 2004 issue of the *Atlantic*, one of the country's oldest and most prestigious magazines. In addition to writing for the *Atlantic*, Christina Nehring writes for *Harper's*, the *Nation*, and *London Review of Books* and is the author of *A Vindication of Love: Reclaiming Romance for the Twenty-First Century* (2009). When you read her argument, you will find that it includes allusions to many writers—so be alert for how those allusions contribute to her case.

CHRISTINA NEHRING, "Fidelity with a Wandering Eye"

1 It's official: the conventional wisdom is false. It's not men who leave their wives for younger, blonder temptresses; it's women who leave their husbands for—well, just about anybody. Or nobody. The fact is, women initiate 66 percent of divorces between partners over forty. That, at least, is what they reported during a major **AARP** study, released last year. That is also the impression one gleans when contemplating a new spate of books and shows, from ABC's already classic Desperate Housewives to hot spring titles including most notably *Undressing Infidelity: Why More Wives Are Unfaithful.*

This is refreshing news—in some senses, at least. It puts a great big dent in sexual stereotypes with which we have been too long saddled: the security-besotted, marriage-angling, nest-squatting female and her counterpart, the freedom-loving, wild-oat-sowing male. Steppenwolf. They made for an insipid image all along, but everybody seemed to conspire in it, from self-help authors (who assumed that their female readers wanted nothing more than tips on how to "catch" and "tame" a husband) to family counselors, magazine pundits, and, of course, evolutionary psychologists (who say it's all biology: girls are made to sit in the straw and warm their eggs; guys are made to fly through the heavens and spread their seed). Women have been told they are helpless and dependent for so long that we have begun to believe it—and to object vociferously when we are not treated as such. If men whose company we enjoy don't assume we want to be their wives and thus propose in short order, we consider it "an insult" (in the approving words of the sexpert-rabbi **Shmuley Boteach**) and declare ourselves aggrieved. The result? Women have grown dull while men have grown smug, offering their hands (when they do) as one might bestow a winning lottery ticket: "There you go, honey, I guess I've made your life." Having given that, they too often feel they have given all; they've done their bit in the kingdom of relationships, and their companions may now live happily ever after.

AARP The American Association of Retired Persons (AARP) is, according to its mission statement, "a nonprofit, nonpartisan membership organization for people age 50 and over [that] is dedicated to enhancing quality of life for all as we age."

Shmuley Boteach (b. 1966) is an American orthodox rabbi, television and radio personality, and author, whose best-known book is *Kosher Sex* (1999).

CONTEXT

Undressing Infidelity: Why More Wives Are Unfaithful (2005), by Diane Shader Smith, which Nehring refers to in paragraph 1, reports on a study of the experiences of fourteen married women who had extramarital affairs. In the introduction to her book, Smith describes her interest in this topic:

I've been married for sixteen years to a man who is loving, intelligent, kind, and handsome—a man who doesn't deserve to be cheated on. But through a series of events, I found myself dangerously attracted to another man.

Because of my own mixed feelings of attraction, guilt, and longing, I became fascinated by the inner workings of extramarital affairs. I began asking questions: Are there circumstances that would justify an affair? Are there men who deserve to be cheated on? What if your husband cheats first? What if your emotional needs aren't being met, or the passion is totally gone? Is having an affair equivalent to marital suicide? I realized that to get the answers I wanted, I didn't need to talk to a shrink or read a self-help book—I needed to talk to the women.

Aristophanes (448 BCE–385 BCE) is considered the greatest of the ancient Greek writers of comedy. In *Lysistrata,* his best-known work, women decide to bring an end to war by refusing to have sex with their husbands until they agree to declare peace.

Ovid Publius Ovidius Naso, usually referred to as Ovid, was a Roman epic poet who lived from 43 BCE to around 18 BCE. He is best known for *Metamorphosis,* a book of poetry about Greek and Roman myths, and *The Art of Love,* an elegiac poem about seduction and love.

Only they generally don't, as the books and studies make all too clear. Women need more than security to thrive, it seems. In fact, they often court the square opposite of security, as Diane Shader Smith learned when she began interviewing women for *Undressing Infidelity.* They court risk; they court intensity, variety, novelty, and disaster—very much like men. It is a peculiarity of our age to portray one sex as nature's safe and law-abiding partner—to cast it as the erotically muted, risk-averse nanny to man. A few hundred years before Jesus Christ, **Aristophanes** presented women as rowdy and ebullient sexual predators, righting uninhibitedly over access to handsome boys. Utopia, as described by Aristophanes' *Congresswomen,* consists of "free fornication," with no grandma left behind. Nubile young girls can legally be seduced "only after the male adolescent has first applied his resources to the full satisfaction of a bona fide senile female." **Ovid** expends many lives in his *Art of Love* warning men against underestimating the ladies' amorous adventurism. In Dante's *Inferno* the circle of hell for sins of the flesh is populated in great part by women. It is the lust of a mother (not, say, an uncle) that so tortures

Shakespeare's Hamlet ("Frailty, thy name is woman"), a girl's sexual fickleness that takes out the hero in *Troilus and Cressida,* a queen's love for an ass that brings down the house in *A Midsummer Night's Dream.* The greatest adulterers in the Western canon—Emma Bovary, Anna Karenina, Molly Bloom, Carmen—have, in fact, been adulteresses. Each had a faithful husband at home.

Why do women leave? "Verbal, physical or emotional abuse" is the first reason cited in the AARP study by wives who initiated divorces. And yet "abuse" played little role in the decisions of Smith's interviewees to risk their unions, most of which sound altogether more docile than violent. So why did they do it? Smith herself is remarkably unhelpful on this score. "The reasons women cheat," she concludes, "are as varied as the women themselves." Fair enough. But surely more-provocative hypotheses might be floated. Mary Wollstonecraft, the author of *A Vindication of the Rights of Woman,* proffered a few as early as the end of the eighteenth century, and her words still resonate today. Women, she declared, are reared for love: the novels they read, the fairy tales they hear, all prepare them for a future of fiery sentiments and gallant attentions. But "a husband cannot long pay those attentions with the passion necessary to excite lively emotions, and the 'female' heart, accustomed to lively emotions, turns to a new lover, or pines in secret."

5 Is this so far wrong today? Don't women even now harbor romantic ideals that are tangibly more central to their lives than to men's, and thus more easily (and disastrously) disappointed? A man may dream of a passionate soulmate, as a woman does, but if he does not find one, he will rechannel that desire into his work, his sports, his substance abuse, his war-making—all things that define a man's identity more commonly than do his emotional efforts. A woman has these occupations open to her as well, but rightly or wrongly (and I think rightly) they are often subordinated to the love plot in her life.

This is something a certain kind of feminist has lamented—and a certain kind of moralist might reasonably find dangerous, since it does indeed make women more sensitive to marital dissatisfaction. But on balance it is a noble hierarchy.

Romantic love has suffered a demotion following the wars of the sexes in recent decades, with the result that we've forgotten it is the source of some of our civilization's greatest acts of heroism and genius. For what else did knights slay dragons in the Middle Ages, did **Petrarch** write poetry, did Dante take on *The Divine Comedy,* Zeus turn himself into a swan, and Penelope weave her gorgeous web? Even evolutionary psychologists say we are never so strong as when we are in love, never so poised for high achievement or fierce battle. (It has to do with dopamine levels, apparently.) Instead of trying to curb the power of this love plot in one of the sexes, as feminists like the late Carolyn Heilbrun have done, might it not be better to re-sanction it in both?

But why re-sanction romantic love if it leads not merely to maladaptive perfectionism but also to a propensity for homewrecking? The easy answer is that it doesn't. If women initiate 66 percent of divorces, they also initiate probably 96 percent of marriage counseling. For every new door they open to love, they have made several attempts to fix the old. That's what you do when you care about eros: you work on all fronts. The hard answer is that sometimes it's okay to wreck a home. Sometimes divorce is the brave and not the cowardly option. We all know couples who shouldn't be together but stay together anyway—excruciatingly, eternally, disastrously. The human animal is no more frivolous and irresponsible than fearful and lethargic. For every person who throws out a sublime relationship, there are two who masochistically cling to a visibly destructive one. (Note the wild success of books like *He's Just Not That Into You* and *How to Break Your Addiction to a Person.*)

Further, women are more frustrated with their marriages than men for myriad reasons—and only one (albeit a big one) is romantic idealism. Another is family culture. If the customer is supposedly king in American stores, the child is incontrovertibly king in American families. Of the women Smith describes in her book, many are overworked soccer moms. She interviews one as she drives—interminably—around town dropping and fetching her kids at after-school enrichment activities. Smith herself mentions in passing that she cooks and serves not three meals a day but three or more dietary regimens.

> Mediterranean for my husband Mark; red meat every two hours for our fourteen-year-old son, Micah; and four hot meals a day for our twelve-year-old daughter, Mallory. And then there are the kids' friends, who show up almost every day with their insatiable, and often picky, teenage appetites.

How can one doubt that these women—all of them attractive, we hear, and not long ago accustomed to lavish attention themselves—fantasize about escape? A place where they can be not just cogs in the domestico-pedagogic machine but colorful individuals, sexual entities, and romantic agents? A woman "cannot contentedly become ... an upper servant after being treated as a goddess," Wollstonecraft observed. And in today's superchild culture the typical wife is not what Wollstonecraft (with her French maid, her cook, and her habit of calling children "animals") would have considered an "upper servant"; she's a lot more like a galley slave.

10 Abjection to children often correlates directly with churlishness to mates. Children are extensions of our egos, so we dote on them, but spouses are often merely co-managers of a home business. As such, they are part of the same unsentimental consumer culture that defines our relationship to, say, submarine sandwiches or coffee drinks. The explosion of Internet dating, in which you

Italian Francesco **Petrarch** (1304–1374) is considered one of the greatest love poets of all time.

announce the traits you want in a lover as you'd announce the ingredients you want in a latte, and remorselessly exchange him if he's not made to specifications, has hastened still further the commodification of romance—and its desanctification.

This, alas, is the worst of the many reasons that modern women trade partners at such a clip: not because they are into ethereal romance but because they are into eternal choice. The mystery and the altruism of love have been subsumed into the ruthless commerce of self-gratification. "I was looking for three things when I married Don," says one woman Smith interviews. "I wanted children, I wanted a house, and I wanted someone I could talk to. Don said he would give me all that.... " We are intended to admire this self-knowledge, because it gets the speaker off compulsive affairs and up to the altar. But it does not do so in a way that could ever be moving—or flattering—to her mate. She might as easily have said, "I wanted a South Seas cruise, a masseur, and someone to keep me in Chanel"—and the person in her arms would have been another man entirely (as, for that matter, the man who fulfilled her domestic and maternal wishes could have been, too). Most of the extramarital relations in Smith's book are, in fact, shallow, opportunistic affairs. What makes them cut so deep is the price at which they come.

Almost all affairs, or all that don't occur in what used to be called an open marriage, are cause for deception. And deception—far more than extracurricular sex alone—is the cardinal relationship killer. If a lover has a single vast advantage over a spouse, it is not that he is newer or more attractive to the woman who takes him; it is that she can be honest with him. He knows about her husband; her husband does not know about him. Result: she feels closer to the person who knows her most fully—her lover. With the man at her hearth she feels the way one feels with all people one tricks: either superior, because of one's imagined cleverness, or inferior, because of

one's ostensible guilt. Or both. But what she rarely feels, either at the moment of deception or afterward, is joined. (All this, of course, is equally true when the sexes are reversed.)

Lightly started, affairs become heavy barriers between partners. If they do not destroy a marriage, as they did for several of Smith's subjects, they take the sap and spark out of it. They turn a soulmate into a dupe, a friend into a jailer, conjugal pleasure into conjugal duty.

At its best, matrimony is a quixotic proposition. The odds that it will go well—or, at least, very well—are slim. The best minds over time (and also the worst) have studied alternatives to it, official and unofficial, public and private. The medieval courtier wed one person and wooed another. Such Romantic writers as Shelley and Byron inaugurated a high-minded promiscuity that took little notice of who was joined to whom. A generation later the long and quietly married Emerson came down hard against formalized vows: "No love can be bound by oath or covenant to secure it against a higher love." Emerson's wilder-eyed contemporary, the Utopian **Charles Fourier**, spent decades formulating theories of democratic sex—as non-possessive as it was non-marital. Even today social scientists who, like Helen Fisher, inform us that amorous loyalty does not naturally exceed twelve to thirty-six months predict a transition to different kinds of unions—for example, marriages contracted for one to five years and, like magazine subscriptions, renewable.

15 And yet for all the rational appeal of such a proposition, no one who has ever been in love, who has ever felt the transformative wand of passion tap his or her shoulder, wants to go to the altar and say "For better or worse, until the next Olympics do us part." The very concept of love brings with it intimations of eternity, even allusions to death. Lovers don't want only to live together; they want to die together. How diminishing it is to let our prudent, miserly reason trump our brave-hearted, generous passion. Perhaps in this case we should let instinct prevail over argument.

François Marie Charles Fourier (1772–1837) was a French philosopher who is credited with coining the term *feminism*. He advocated women's rights as part of his vision for a peaceful utopian society.

A second marriage, as **Samuel Johnson** observed, represents "the triumph of hope over experience." The experience of marriage is one of conflict between ideals: the ideal of loving companionship and that of erotic intensity; the ideal of unflagging devotion to a single person and that of emotional responsiveness to many. And yet some of these ideals are not as irreconcilable—or as irreconcilable with marriage—as they appear. Unshakable loyalty to a central partner does not preclude passionate responses to other people. If it seems that way, it is only because of the puritanism, the pious emotional parsimony, of our American era.

Diane Shader Smith's book provides, ironically, a perfect example of this. Her introduction is an alarmist confession of her attraction to a man other than her husband. She recounts in detail her nervousness around him, her supposedly dangerous fascination with his charm. She criminalizes her feelings. And so, one might add (albeit more understandably, since she has led the way), does her husband. In a different culture her attraction would be viewed by her readers, herself, and her husband as perfectly natural and even commendable. What sort of a creature would you be if, having once found a human being who stirs your heart (and whom you marry, if you follow Rabbi Boteach's example, by age twenty-one), you were never stirred again?

The key is to incorporate chemistry into our marital lives, not to snuff it out. We are erotic and emotional animals, and when we react most fully to people, we react to them erotically and emotionally. We react this way to teachers and to students; to pop stars and to politicians; to interns, novelists, and waiters; to our elders and our juniors. It is a part of what allows us to relate to human beings across the social, political, and cultural spectrums. To demonize this responsiveness is to truncate our sensibility, our humanity. Better to share our passing fancies with our mates, to turn them like colored glass in the light, lest they become blades in our pockets. For this we need magnanimous partners. And we need an 18-karat commitment to those partners, who over the years will inevitably seem less perfect than those glinting shards of novelty in the corner of our sight.

"To fall in love is to create a religion that has a fallible god," said **Jorge Luis Borges**. To love truly is to stay in love after the fall. It is to love more gratefully, more potentially, because our god has come down to earth: the spirit has been made flesh and now walks—and slips, and flounders, and slouches—among us.

20 It's a delicate proposition—counterintuitive, presumptuous, heady, unreasonable. And yet therein lies its nobility and, perhaps, its necessity.

English author **Samuel Johnson** (1709–1784) is best known for having composed the first dictionary of the English language and having inspired one of the most memorable biographies in British literature: James Boswell's *The Life of Samuel Johnson*.

Jorge Luis Borges (1899–1986) was an Argentine writer whose works are considered classics of twentieth-century world literature.

Questions for Discussion

1. Why does Nehring find it "refreshing" to learn that women initiate most divorces? What stereotypes about women are challenged by the fact that women initiate most divorces? What are the implications of these stereotypes, according to Nehring?

2. What social and cultural forces contribute to the frustration many women feel about their marriages? Why are these factors important, in Nehring's view? Do you think she's right? Why or why not?

3. Nehring writes that "sometimes it's okay to wreck a home. Sometimes divorce is the brave and not the cowardly option." Do you agree? What counterargument might be made in response to her position?

4. How would you describe the tone of this essay? To what extent do you think the essay's tone strengthens or weakens Nehring's argument?

5. What are Nehring's complaints about romantic love? How do these complaints fit into her main argument? Do you find her complaints valid? Explain.

6. What kind of marriage does Nehring advocate? How persuasive a case does she make for this kind of marriage?

7. Nehring makes many allusions to classical myths and to eighteenth- and nineteenth-century writers. (See par. 3, for example.) How do these allusions support her argument about women and sex? How effective do you think these allusions are? What might your answer to that question reveal about you as a reader?

② | **A More Perfect Union**

JONATHAN RAUCH

The following argument was first published in the *Atlantic* in 2004, shortly after the Massachusetts Supreme Court declared that the state's marriage laws were unconstitutional because they limited the right to a civil marriage to people of different genders who are assumed to be heterosexual. The state legislature was required to amend the law, and it did so—making Massachusetts the first state to allow same-sex marriage. The Massachusetts law subsequently became an issue in that year's presidential election, in which President George W. Bush defeated Senator John Kerry of Massachusetts. During that election, eleven states passed initiatives to amend their constitutions so that marriage would be confined to a union between a man and a woman. Since then, however, several nations, including Canada and Spain, have legalized gay marriage. And in 2005, the California legislature voted to legalize it in that state, although that law was subsequently challenged in court. So it seems clear that the public debate over gay marriage is likely to continue for some time. The following reading is Jonathan Rauch's contribution to the debate. "A More Perfect Union"—a title that comes from the Preamble of the U.S. Constitution—is an excerpt from Rauch's book, *Gay Marriage: Why It Is Good for Gays, Good for Straights, and Good for America* (2004). In this excerpt, Rauch offers a federalist perspective on the issue of same-sex marriage, arguing that the nation is stronger when states, rather than the federal government, have more control over such issues.

JONATHAN RAUCH, "A More Perfect Union"

1 Last November the Supreme Judicial Court of Massachusetts ruled that excluding gay couples from civil marriage violated the state constitution. The court gave the legislature six months—until May—to do something about it. Some legislators mounted efforts to amend the state constitution to ban same-sex marriage, but as of this writing they have failed (and even if passed, a ban would not take effect until at least 2006). With unexpected urgency the country faces the possibility that marriage licenses might soon be issued to homosexual couples. To hear the opposing sides talk, a national culture war is unavoidable.

But same-sex marriage neither must nor should be treated as an all-or-nothing national decision. Instead individual states should be left to try gay marriage if and when they choose—no national ban, no national mandate. Not only would a decentralized approach be in keeping with the country's most venerable legal traditions; it would also improve, in three ways, the odds of making

COMPLICATION

Opponents of gay marriage argued that it was an issue that should be decided by state governments rather than by the courts. Yet when the California Senate and House of Representatives voted to legalize gay marriage in September 2005, Governor Arnold Schwarzenegger vetoed the legislation on the ground that it was a matter that the people of the state should decide by direct ballot. This raises at least two questions: If neither the courts nor state legislatures can be trusted to act on behalf of the people's good, what is their function? And which issues should be decided directly by the people instead of by the representatives they have chosen?

same-sex marriage work for gay and straight Americans alike.

First, it would give the whole country a chance to learn. Nothing terrible—in fact, nothing even noticeable—seems to have happened to marriage since Vermont began allowing gay civil unions, in 2000. But civil unions are not marriages. The only way to find out what would happen if same-sex couples got marriage certificates is to let some of us do it. Turning marriage into a nationwide experiment might be rash, but trying it in a few states would provide test cases on a smaller scale. Would the divorce rate rise? Would the marriage rate fall? We should get some indications before long. Moreover, states are, as the saying goes, the laboratories of democracy. One state might opt for straightforward legalization. Another might add some special provisions (for instance, regarding child custody or adoption). A third might combine same-sex marriage with counseling or other assistance (not out of line with a growing movement to offer social-service support to so-called fragile families). Variety would help answer some important questions: Where would gay marriage work best? What kind of community support would it need? What would be the avoidable pitfalls? Either to forbid same-sex marriage nationwide or to legalize it nationwide would be to throw away a wealth of potential information.

Just as important is the social benefit of letting the states find their own way. Law is only part of what gives marriage its binding power; community support and social

expectations are just as important. In a community that looked on same-sex marriage with bafflement or hostility, a gay couple's marriage certificate, while providing legal benefits, would confer no social support from the heterosexual majority. Both the couple and the community would be shortchanged. Letting states choose gay marriage wouldn't guarantee that everyone in the state recognized such marriages as legitimate, but it would pretty well ensure that gay married couples could find some communities in their state that did.

5 Finally, the political benefit of a state-by-state approach is not to be underestimated. This is the benefit of avoiding a national culture war.

The United States is not (thank goodness) a culturally homogeneous country. It consists of many distinct moral communities. On certain social issues, such as abortion and homosexuality, people don't agree and probably never will—and the single political advantage of the federalist system is that they don't have to. Individuals and groups who find the values or laws of one state obnoxious have the right to live somewhere else.

The nationalization of abortion policy in the Supreme Court's 1973 *Roe v. Wade* decision created a textbook example of what can happen when this **federalist principle** is ignored. If the Supreme Court had not stepped in, abortion would today be legal in most states but not all; prolifers would have the comfort of knowing they could live in a state whose law was compatible with their views. Instead of endlessly confronting a cultural schism that affects every Supreme Court nomination, we would see occasional local flare-ups in state legislatures or courtrooms.

America is a stronger country for the moral diversity that federalism uniquely allows. Moral law and family law govern the most intimate and, often, the most controversial spheres of life. For the sake of domestic tranquility, domestic law is best left to a level of government that is close to home.

Federalist Principle Federalism is a political philosophy that advocates the sharing of power between a central (or "federal") government and regional governments. In the United States, federalists generally believe that the states, rather than the federal government, should have primary authority for establishing laws governing most aspects of the social and political lives of their citizens.

CONTEXT

In its 1973 *Roe v. Wade* decision, the U.S. Supreme Court ruled that government should not intrude in a woman's relationship with her doctor because that relationship is private. In the decision, which was written by Justice Harry A. Blackmun, the Court argued that the Fourteenth Amendment to the U.S. Constitution guarantees a right to privacy that is "broad enough to encompass a woman's decision whether or not to terminate her pregnancy," thus making the procedure legal in all states.

So well suited is the federalist system to the gay-marriage issue that it might almost have been set up to handle it. In a new land whose citizens followed different religious traditions, it would have made no sense to centralize marriage or family law. And so marriage has been the domain of local law not just since the days of the Founders but since Colonial times, before the states were states. To my knowledge, the federal government has overruled the states on marriage only twice. The first time was when it required Utah to ban polygamy as a condition for joining the union—and note that this ruling was issued before Utah became a state. The second time was in 1967, when the Supreme Court, in *Loving v. Virginia*, struck down sixteen states' bans on interracial marriage. Here the court said not that marriage should be defined by the federal government but only that states could not define marriage in ways that violated core constitutional rights. On the one occasion when Congress directly addressed same-sex marriage, in the 1996 Defense of Marriage Act, it decreed that the federal government would not recognize same-sex marriages but took care not to impose that rule on the states.

10 Marriage laws (and, of course, divorce laws) continue to be established by the states. They differ on many points, from age of consent to who may marry whom. In Arizona, for example, first cousins are allowed to marry only if both are sixty-five or older or the couple can prove to a judge "that one of the cousins is unable to reproduce." (So much for the idea that marriage is about procreation.) Conventional wisdom notwithstanding, the Constitution does not require states to recognize one another's marriages. The Full Faith and Credit clause (Article IV, Section 1) does require states to honor one another's public acts and judgments. But in 1939 and again in 1988 the Supreme Court ruled that the clause does not compel a state "to substitute the statutes of other states for its own statutes dealing with a subject

CONTEXT

In 1996 President Bill Clinton signed into law the Personal Responsibility and Work Opportunity Reconciliation Act. Paired with the Balanced Budget Act of 1997, also signed by President Clinton, this act was intended to reform the federal welfare system by moving people receiving welfare into the workforce. The Welfare-to-Work program officially ended in 2004. In 1996, President Clinton also signed the Defense of Marriage Act, which defines *marriage* under federal law as "a legal union of one man and one woman as husband and wife" and defines a spouse as "a person of the opposite sex who is a husband or a wife." The act allowed each state to recognize or refuse to recognize a marriage performed in another state.

matter concerning which it is competent to legislate." Dale Carpenter, a law professor at the University of Minnesota, notes that the Full Faith and Credit clause "has never been interpreted to mean that every state must recognize every marriage performed in every other state." He writes, "Each state may refuse to recognize a marriage performed in another state if that marriage would violate the state's public policy." If Delaware, for example, decided to lower its age of consent to ten, no other state would be required to regard a ten-year-old as legally married. The public-policy exception, as it is called, is only common sense. If each state could legislate for all the rest, American-style federalism would be at an end.

Why, then, do the states all recognize one another's marriages? Because they choose to. Before the gay-marriage controversy arose, the country enjoyed a general consensus on the terms of marriage. Interstate differences were so small that states saw no need to split hairs, and mutual recognition was a big convenience. The issue of gay marriage, of course, changes the picture, by asking states to reconsider an accepted boundary of marriage. This is just the sort of controversy in which the Founders imagined that individual states could and often should go their separate ways.

Paradoxically, the gay left and the antigay right have found themselves working together against the center. They agree on little else, but where marriage is concerned, they both want the federal government to take over. To many gay people, anything less than nation-wide recognition of same-sex marriage seems both unjust and impractical. "Wait a minute," a gay person might protest. "How is this sup-posed to work? I get married in Maryland (say), but every time I cross the border into Virginia during my morning commute, I'm single? Am I married or not? Portability is one of the things that make marriage differ-ent from civil union. If it isn't portable, it isn't really marriage; it's second-class citizenship. Obviously, as soon as same-sex marriage is approved in any one state, we're going to sue in federal court to have it recognized in all the others."

"Exactly" a conservative might reply. "Gay activists have no intention of settling for mar-riage in just one or two states. They will keep suing until they find some activist federal judge—and there are plenty—who agrees with them. Public-policy exception and Defense of Marriage Act notwithstanding, the courts, not least the Supreme Court, do as they please, and lately they have signed on to the gay cultural agenda. Besides, deciding on a state-by-state basis is impractical; the gay activists are right about that. The sheer inconvenience of dealing with couples who went in and out of matrimony every time they crossed state lines would drive states to the lowest common denominator, and gay marriages would wind up being recognized everywhere."

Neither of the arguments I have just sketched is without merit. But both sides are asking the country to presume that the Founders were wrong and to foreclose the possibility that seems the most likely to suc-ceed. Both sides want something life doesn't usually offer—a guarantee. Gay-marriage sup-porters want a guarantee of full legal equality, and gay-marriage opponents want a guaran-tee that same-sex marriage will never happen at all. I can't offer any guarantees. But I can offer some reassurance.

15 Is a state-by-state approach impractical and unsustainable? Possibly, but the time to deal with any problems is if and when they arise. Going in, there is no reason to expect any great difficulty. There are many prec-edents for state-by-state action. The country currently operates under a tangle of different state banking laws. As any banker will tell you, the lack of uniformity has made inter-state banking more difficult. But we do have interstate banks. Bankers long ago got used to meeting different requirements in different states. Similarly, car manufacturers have had to deal with zero-emission rules in California and a few other states. Contract law, property law, and criminal law all vary significantly from state to state. Variety is the point of federalism. Uniform national policies may be convenient, but they risk sticking us with the same wrong approach everywhere.

My guess is that if one or two states allowed gay marriage, a confusing transitional period, while state courts and legislatures worked out what to do, would quickly lead in all but a few places to routines that everyone would soon take for granted. If New Jersey adopted gay marriage, for instance, New York would have a number of options. It might refuse to recognize the marriages. It might recognize them. It might honor only certain aspects of them—say, medical power of attor-ney, or inheritance and tenancy rights. A state with a civil-union or domestic partner law might automatically confer that law's benefits on any gay couple who got married in New Jersey. My fairly confident expectation is that initially most states would reject out-of-state gay marriages (as, indeed, most states have pre-emptively done), but a handful would fully accept them, and others would choose an intermediate option.

For married gay couples, this variation would be a real nuisance. If my partner and I got married in Maryland, we would need to be aware of differences in marriage laws and make arrangements—medical power of attorney, a will, and so on—for whenever we were out of state. Pesky and, yes, unfair (or at least unequal). And outside Maryland the line between being married and not being married would be blurred. In Virginia, people who saw my wedding band would be unsure whether I was "really married" or just "Maryland married."

Even so, people in Virginia who learned that I was "Maryland married" would know I had made the strongest possible commitment in my home state, and thus in the eyes of my community and its law. They would know I had gone beyond cohabitation or even domestic partnership. As a Jew, I may not recognize the spiritual authority of a Catholic priest, but I do recognize and respect the special commitment he has made to his faith and his community. In much the same way, even out-of-state gay marriages would command a significant degree of respect.

If you are starving, one or two slices of bread may not be as good as a loaf—but it is far better than no bread at all. The damage that exclusion from marriage has done to gay lives and gay culture comes not just from being unable to marry right now and right here but from knowing the law forbids us ever to marry at all. The first time a state adopted same-sex marriage, gay life would change forever. The full benefits would come only when same-sex marriage was legal everywhere. But gay people's lives would improve with the first state's announcement that in this community, marriage is open to everyone.

20 Building consensus takes time. The nationwide imposition of same-sex marriage by a federal court might discredit both gay marriage and the courts, and the public rancor it unleashed might be at least as intense as that surrounding abortion. My confidence in the public's decency and in its unfailing, if sometimes slow-acting, commitment to liberal principles is robust. For me personally, the pace set by a state-by-state approach would be too slow. It would be far from ideal. But it would be something much more important than ideal: it would be right.

The Normality of Gay Marriages

There's nothing like a touch of real-world experience to inject some reason into the inflammatory national debate over gay marriages. Take Massachusetts, where the state's highest court held in late 2003 that under the State Constitution, same-sex couples have a right to marry. The State Legislature moved to undo that decision last year by approving a proposed constitutional amendment to ban gay marriages and create civil unions as an alternative. But this year, when precisely the same measure came up for a required second vote, it was defeated by a thumping margin of 157 to 39.

The main reason for the flip-flop is that some 6,600 same-sex couples have married over the past year with nary a sign of adverse effects. The sanctity of heterosexual marriages has not been destroyed. Public morals have not gone into a tailspin. Legislators who supported gay marriage in last year's vote have been re-elected. Gay couples, many of whom had been living together monogamously for years, have rejoiced at official recognition of their commitment.

As a Republican leader explained in justifying his vote switch: "Gay marriages have begun, and life has not changed for the citizens of the common-wealth, with the exception of those who can now marry who could not before." A Democrat attributed his change of heart to the beneficial effects he says "when I looked in the eyes of the children living with these couples." Gay marriage, it turned out, is good for family values....

Would a state-by-state approach inevitably lead to a nationwide court mandate anyway? Many conservatives fear that the answer is yes, and they want a federal constitutional amendment to head off the courts—an amendment banning gay marriage nationwide. These days it is a fact of life that someone will sue over anything, that some court will hear any lawsuit, and that there is no telling what a court might do. Still, I think that conservatives' fears on this score are unfounded.

Remember, all precedent leaves marriage to the states. All precedent supports the public-policy exception. The Constitution gives Congress a voice in determining which of one another's laws states must recognize, and Congress has spoken clearly: the Defense of Marriage Act explicitly decrees that no state must recognize any other state's same-sex marriages. In order to mandate interstate recognition of gay marriages, a court would thus need to burn through three different firewalls—a tall order, even for an activist court. The current Supreme Court, moreover, has proved particularly fierce in resisting federal incursions into states' rights. We typically reserve constitutional prohibitions for imminent threats to liberty, justice, or popular sovereignty. If we are going to get into the business of constitutionally banning anything that someone imagines the Supreme Court might one day mandate, we will need a Constitution the size of the Manhattan phone book.

Social conservatives have lost one cultural battle after another in the past five decades: over divorce, abortion, pornography, gambling, school prayer, homosexuality. They have seen that every federal takeover of state and local powers comes with strings attached. They have learned all too well the power of centralization to marginalize moral dissenters—including religious ones. And yet they are willing to risk federal intervention in matrimony. Why?

Not, I suspect, because they fear gay marriage would fail. Rather, because they fear it would succeed.

25 One of the conservative arguments against gay marriage is particularly revealing: the contention that even if federal courts don't decide the matter on a national level, convenience will cause gay marriage to spread from state to state. As noted, I don't believe questions of convenience would force the issue either way. But let me make a deeper point here.

States recognized one another's divorce reforms in the 1960s and 1970s without

giving the matter much thought (which was too bad). But the likelihood that they would recognize another state's same-sex marriages without serious debate is just about zero, especially at first: the issue is simply too controversial. As time went on, states without gay marriage might get used to the idea. They might begin to wave through other states' same-sex marriages as a convenience for all concerned. If that happened, however, it could only be because gay marriage had not turned out to be a disaster. It might even be because gay marriage was working pretty well. This would not be contagion. It would be evolution—a sensible response to a successful experiment. Try something here or there. If it works, let it spread. If it fails, let it fade.

The opponents of gay marriage want to prevent the experiment altogether. If you care about finding the best way forward for gay people and for society in a changing world, that posture is hard to justify. One rationale goes something like this: "Gay marriage is so certain to be a calamity that even the smallest trial anywhere should be banned." To me, that line of argument smacks more of hysteria than of rational thought. In the 1980s and early 1990s some liberals were sure that reforming the welfare system to emphasize work would put millions of children out on the street. Even trying welfare reform, they said, was irresponsible. Fortunately, the states don't listen. They experimented—responsibly. The results were positive enough to spark a successful national reform.

Another objection cites not certain catastrophe but insidious decay. A conservative once said to me, "Changes in complicated institutions like marriage take years to work their way through society. They are often subtle. Social scientists will argue until the cows come home about the positive and negative effects of gay marriage. So states might adopt it before they fully understood the harm it did."

Actually, you can usually tell pretty quickly what effects a major policy change is having—at least you can get a general idea. States knew quite soon that welfare reforms were working better than the old program. That's why the idea caught on. If same-sex marriage is going to cause problems, some of them should be apparent within a few years of its legalization.

30 And notice how the terms of the discussion have shifted. Now the anticipated problem is not sudden, catastrophic social harm but subtle, slow damage. Well, there might be subtle and slow social benefits, too. But more important, there would be one large and immediate benefit: the benefit for gay people of being able to get married. If we are going to exclude a segment of the population from arguably the most important of all civic institutions, we need to be certain that the group's participation would cause severe disruptions. If we are going to put the burden on gay people to prove that same-sex marriage would never cause even any minor difficulty, then we are assuming that any cost to heterosexuals, however small, outweighs every benefit to homosexuals, however large. That gay people's welfare counts should, of course, be obvious and inarguable; but to some it is not.

I expect same-sex marriage to have many subtle ramifications—many of them good not just for gay people but for marriage. Same-sex marriage would dramatically reaffirm the country's preference for marriage as the gold standard for committed relationships. Of course there might be harmful and neutral effects as well. I don't expect that social science would be able to sort them all out. But the fact that the world is complicated is the very reason to run the experiment. We can never know for sure what the effects of any policy will be, so we conduct a limited experiment if possible, and then decide how to proceed on the basis of necessarily imperfect information.

If conservatives genuinely oppose same-sex marriage because they fear it would harm straight marriage, they should be willing to let states that want to try gay marriage do so. If, on the other hand, conservatives oppose same-sex marriage because they believe that it is immoral and wrong by definition, fine—but let them have the honesty to acknowledge that they are not fighting for the good of marriage so much as they are using marriage as a weapon in their fight against gays.

Questions for Discussion

1. Why does Rauch believe that the legality of gay marriage is something best determined on a state-by-state level? What advantages does he see to this approach? Do you think he makes a persuasive case for such an approach? Why or why not?

2. According to Rauch, what is the relationship between the law and community standards? Why is this relationship important in the case of same-sex marriage?

3. By writing "some of us" in paragraph 3, Rauch discloses his sexual orientation. How does this disclosure affect his ethos? Do you think it makes his argument more or less effective? Explain.

4. What role does the Supreme Court's 1973 decision in *Roe v. Wade* play in this argument?

5. What objections to his position does Rauch acknowledge? How effectively do you think he answers these objections?

6. This argument might be described as an argument based on deductive reasoning (see pages 81–83). What fundamental principle or belief forms the basis for Rauch's reasoning? Do you think most Americans embrace this principle or belief? Does Rauch need to justify it? How effectively do you think he makes his argument about gay marriage on the basis of that principle or belief?

7. Why do you think people want to amend the U.S. Constitution to prohibit gay marriage? What assumptions are they making about the nature of the Constitution and the role of the federal government in the lives of citizens?

8. Consider Rauch's conclusion. Do you think that the debate over who gets to marry in the United States is truly about marriage law, or could the debate signal larger differences?

③ The Future of Marriage

STEPHANIE COONTZ

Marriage is often considered the bedrock of family values, which may be why issues related to marriage are so hotly debated. Take, for instance, the issue of divorce rates in the United States, which, as Stephanie Coontz notes in the following essay, increased dramatically through the 1970s and 1980s before stabilizing in the 1990s and then declining. It is often reported that about half of all marriages end in divorce, but this figure is misleading, since rates can vary widely depending upon the ages of the couples, the laws of the states where they reside, and whether or not the marriage was the couple's first. But what exactly those figures mean is open to interpretation. Moreover, whatever figures are used, everyone agrees that divorces seem to have been declining, but not everyone agrees about the reasons for the decline. For her part, Stephanie Coontz argues that we need to take a more objective look at historical trends in order to understand what is happening to marriage today. She provides such an examination in her essay, and she argues for policies based on a better understanding of marriage and its implications for both adults and children today. Coontz, who teaches history at Evergreen State College, is Director of Research and Public Education at the Council on Contemporary Families. This essay was published in *Cato Unbound* in 2008.

STEPHANIE COONTZ, "The Future of Marriage"

1 Any serious discussion of the future of marriage requires a clear understanding of how marriage evolved over the ages, along with the causes of its most recent transformations. Many people who hope to "re-institutionalize" marriage misunderstand the reasons that marriage was once more stable and played a stronger role in regulating social life.

For most of history, marriage was more about getting the right in-laws than picking the right partner to love and live with. In the small-scale, band-level societies of our distant ancestors, marriage alliances turned strangers into relatives, creating interdependencies among groups that might otherwise meet as enemies. But as large wealth and status differentials developed in the ancient world, marriage became more exclusionary and coercive. People maneuvered to orchestrate advantageous marriage connections with some families and avoid incurring obligations to others. Marriage became the main way that the upper classes consolidated wealth, forged military coalitions, finalized peace treaties, and bolstered claims to social status or political authority. Getting "well-connected" in-laws was a preoccupation of the middle classes as well, while the dowry a man received at marriage was often the biggest economic stake he would acquire before his parents died. Peasants, farmers, and craftsmen acquired new workers for the family enterprise and forged cooperative bonds with neighbors through their marriages.

Because of marriage's vital economic and political functions, few societies in history believed that individuals should freely choose their own marriage partners, especially on such fragile grounds as love. Indeed, for millennia, marriage was much more about regulating economic, political, and gender hierarchies than nourishing the well-being of adults and their children. Until the late 18th century, parents took for granted their right to arrange their children's marriages and even, in many regions, to dissolve a marriage made without their permission. In Anglo-American law, a child born outside an approved marriage was a "fillius nullius"—a child of no one, entitled to nothing. In fact, through most of history, the precondition for maintaining a strong institution of marriage was the existence of an equally strong institution of illegitimacy, which denied such children any claim on their families.

Even legally-recognized wives and children received few of the protections we now associate with marriage. Until the late 19th century, European and American husbands had the right to physically restrain, imprison, or "punish" their wives and children. Marriage gave husbands sole ownership over all property a wife brought to the marriage and any income she earned afterward. Parents put their children to work to accumulate resources for their own old age, enforcing obedience by periodic beatings.

5 Many people managed to develop loving families over the ages despite these laws and customs, but until very recently, this was not the main point of entering or staying in a union. It was just 250 years ago, when **the Enlightenment** challenged the right of the older generation and the state to dictate to the young, that free choice based on love and compatibility emerged as the social ideal for mate selection. Only in the early 19th century did the success of a marriage begin to be defined by how well it cared for its members, both adults and children.

These new marital ideals appalled many social conservatives of the day. "How will we get the right people to marry each other, if they can refuse on such trivial grounds as lack of love?" they asked. "Just as important, how will we prevent the wrong ones, such as paupers and servants, from marrying?" What would compel people to stay in marriages where love had died? What would prevent wives from challenging their husbands' authority?

They were right to worry. In the late 18th century, new ideas about the "pursuit of happiness" led many countries to make divorce more accessible, and some even repealed the penalties for homosexual love. The French revolutionaries abolished the legal category of illegitimacy, according a "love child" equal rights with a "legal" one. In the mid-19th century, women challenged husbands' sole ownership of wives' property, earnings, and behavior. Moralists predicted that such female economic independence would "destroy domestic tranquility," producing "infidelity in the marriage bed, a high rate of divorce, and increased female criminality." And in some regards, they seemed correct. Divorce rates rose so steadily that in 1891 a Cornell University professor predicted, with stunning accuracy, that if divorce continued rising at its current rate, more marriages would end in divorce than death by the 1980s.

But until the late 1960s, most of the destabilizing aspects of the love revolution were held in check by several forces that prevented people from building successful lives outside marriage: the continued legal subordination of women to men; the ability of local elites to penalize employees and other community members for then-stigmatized behaviors such as remaining single, cohabiting, or getting a divorce; the unreliability of birth control, combined with the harsh treatment of illegitimate children; and above all, the dependence of women upon men's wage earning.

In the 1970s, however, these constraints were swept away or seriously eroded. The result has been to create a paradox with which many Americans have yet to come to terms. Today, when a marriage works, it delivers more benefits to its members—adults and children—than ever before. A good marriage is fairer and more fulfilling for both men and

The Enlightenment is a term used to refer to a series of historical and intellectual developments in Europe in the seventeenth and eighteenth centuries that led to the view that reason rather than tradition or belief is the basis for knowledge or truth. These developments gave rise to modern science and to social and political ideas that challenged traditional authorities such as monarchies and the Church. Enlightenment ideas about individual liberty informed the Declaration of Independence and the founding of the United States.

women than couples of the past could ever have imagined. Domestic violence and sexual coercion have fallen sharply. More couples share decision-making and housework than ever before. Parents devote unprecedented time and resources to their children. And men in stable marriages are far less likely to cheat on their wives than in the past.

10 But the same things that have made so many modern marriages more intimate, fair, and protective have simultaneously made marriage itself more optional and more contingent on successful negotiation. They have also made marriage seem less bearable when it doesn't live up to its potential. The forces that have strengthened marriage as a personal relationship between freely-consenting adults have weakened marriage as a regulatory social institution.

In the 1970s and 1980s, the collapse of the conditions that had forced most people to get and stay married led to dramatic—and often traumatic—upheavals in marriage. This was exacerbated by an economic climate that made the 1950s ideal of the male breadwinner unattainable for many families. Divorce rates soared. Unwed teen motherhood shot up. Since then, some of these destabilizing trends have leveled off or receded. The divorce rate has fallen, especially for college-educated couples, over the past 20 years. When divorce does occur, more couples work to resolve it amicably, and fewer men walk away from contact with their children. Although there was a small uptick in teen births last year, they are still almost 30 percent lower than in 1991.

Still, there is no chance that we can restore marriage to its former supremacy in coordinating social and interpersonal relationships. Even as the divorce rate has dropped, the incidence of cohabitation, delayed marriage and non-marriage has risen steadily. With half of all Americans aged 25–29 unmarried, marriage no longer organizes the transition into regular sexual activity or long-term partnerships the way it used to.

Although teen births are lower than a decade ago, births to unwed mothers aged 25 and older continue to climb. Almost 40 percent of America's children are born to unmarried parents. And gay and lesbian families are permanently out of the closet.

Massive social changes combine to ensure that a substantial percentage of people will continue to explore alternatives to marriage. These include women's economic independence, the abolition of legal penalties for illegitimacy, the expansion of consumer products that make single life easier for both men and women, and the steady decline in the state's coercive power over personal life. Add to this mix the continuing rise in the age of marriage, a trend that increases the stability of marriages once they are contracted but also increases the percentage of unwed adults in the population. Stir in the reproductive revolution, which has made it possible for couples who would once have been condemned to childlessness to have the kids they want, but impossible to prevent single women or gay and lesbian couples from having children. Top it off with changes in gender roles that have increased the payoffs of marriage for educated, financially-secure women but increased its risks for low-income women whose potential partners are less likely to hold egalitarian values, earn good wages, or even count on a regular job. Taken together, this is a recipe for a world where the social weight of marriage has been fundamentally and irreversibly reduced.

The decline in marriage's dominating role in organizing social and personal life is not unique to America. It is occurring across the industrial world, even in countries with less "permissive" values and laws. In predominantly Catholic Ireland, where polls in the 1980s found near-universal disapproval of premarital sex, one child in three today is born outside marriage. China's divorce rate has soared more than 700 percent since 1980. Until 2005, Chile was the only country in the Western Hemisphere that still prohibited

CONTEXT

Several readings in this chapter examine various aspects of what Coontz calls "the reproductive revolution," which refers to the significant advances in medical technology that enable women to become pregnant and to manipulate their pregnancies in various ways. See "Designer Babies and Other Myths," by Maureen Freely (page 298), and "Victims From Birth," by Wendy McElroy (page 302).

divorce. But in today's world, prohibiting divorce has very different consequences than in the past, because people no longer feel compelled to marry in the first place. Between 1990 and 2003, the number of marriages in Chile fell from 100,000 to 60,000 a year, and nearly half of all children born in Chile in the early years of the 21st century were born to unmarried couples.

15 In Italy, Singapore, and Japan, divorce, cohabitation, and out-of wedlock births remain low by American standards, but a much larger percentage of women avoid marriage and childbearing altogether. This suggests that we are experiencing a massive historical current that, if blocked in one area, simply flows over traditional paths of family life at a different spot.

The late 20th-century revolution in the role and function of marriage has been as far-reaching—and as wrenching—as the replacement of local craft production and exchange by wage labor and industrialization. Like the Industrial Revolution, the family diversity revolution has undercut old ways of organizing work, leisure, caregiving, and redistribution to dependents. It has liberated some people from restrictive, socially-imposed statuses, but stripped others of customary support systems and rules for behavior, without putting clearly defined new ones in place. There have been winners and losers in the

marriage revolution, just as there were in the Industrial Revolution. But we will not meet the challenges of this transformation by trying to turn back the clock. Instead we must take two lessons away from these historical changes.

First, marriage is not on the verge of extinction. Most cohabiting couples eventually do get married, either to each other or to someone else. New groups, such as gays and lesbians, are now demanding access to marriage—a demand that many pro-marriage advocates oddly interpret as an attack on the institution. And a well-functioning marriage is still an especially useful and effective method of organizing interpersonal commitments and improving people's well-being. But in today's climate of gender equality and personal choice, we must realize that successful marriages require different traits, skills, and behaviors than in the past.

Marriages used to depend upon a clear division of labor and authority, and couples who rejected those rules had less stable marriages than those who abided by them. In the 1950s, a woman's best bet for a lasting marriage was to marry a man who believed firmly in the male breadwinner ideal. Women who wanted a "MRS degree" were often advised to avoid the "bachelor's" degree, since as late as 1967 men told pollsters they valued a woman's cooking and housekeeping skills above her intelligence or education. Women who hadn't married by age 25 were less likely to ever marry than their more traditional counterparts, and studies in the 1960s suggested that if they did marry at an older age than average they were more likely to divorce. When a wife took a job outside the home, this raised the risk of marital dissolution.

All that has changed today. Today, men rank intelligence and education way above cooking and housekeeping as a desirable trait in a partner. A recent study by Paul Amato *et al.* found that the chance of divorce recedes with each year that a woman postpones marriage, with the least divorce-prone marriages

---

COMPLICATION

In *The Case for Marriage: Why Married People are Happier, Healthier and Better Off Financially* (2001), Linda Waite and Maggie Gallagher write,

Despite the startling rise in divorce, cohabitation, and unwed parenthood, marriage remains a core value and aspiration of many Americans.... We aren't as certain anymore about whether marriage is good for other people, but when it comes to their own life goals, Americans put marriage at the top of the list. Ninety-three percent of Americans rate "having a happy marriage" as either one of the most important, or very important objectives. Asked to select their top two goals, a majority of Americans included a happy marriage as one of the choices, far outpacing such other life goals as "being in good health" (35 percent) or even having "a good family life" (36 percent).

being those where the couples got married at age 35 or higher. Educated and high-earning women are now *less* likely to divorce than other women. When a wife takes a job today, it works to stabilize the marriage. Couples who share housework and productive work have more stable marriages than couples who do not, according to sociologist Lynn Prince Cooke. And the Amato study found that husbands and wives who hold egalitarian views about gender have higher marital quality and fewer marital problems than couples who cling to more traditional views.

20 So there is no reason to give up on building successful marriages—but we won't do it by giving people outdated advice about gender roles. We may be able to bring the divorce rate down a little further—but since one method of doing that is to get more people to delay marriage, this will probably lead to more cohabitation. We may also be able to reverse last year's uptick in teen births and return to the downward course of the late 1990s and first few years of the 21st century—but not by teaching abstinence-only to young people who if they do delay marriage are almost certainly going to have sex beforehand.

The second lesson of history is that the time has passed when we can construct our social policies, work schedules, health insurance systems, sex education programs—or even our moral and ethical beliefs about who owes what to whom—on the assumption that all long-term commitments and caregiving obligations should or can be organized

CONTEXT

The ongoing debates about sex education in schools have occurred in the midst of steady declines in the teen pregnancy rate, which was 41 percent lower in 2006 than it was in 1990. Since 2006, teen pregnancy rates have increased slightly. Advocates for abstinence-only education as well as those who favor comprehensive sex education debate the causes of these changes in teen pregnancy rates. Some research suggests that declines in teen pregnancy rates are attributable primarily to an increase in the use of contraception by teens.

SOURCE: *U.S. Teenage Pregnancies, Births, and Abortions: National and State Trends and Trends by Race and Ethnicity* Guttmacher Institute [2010].

through marriage. Of course we must seek ways to make marriage more possible for couples and to strengthen the marriages they contract. But we must be equally concerned to help couples who don't marry become better co-parents, to help single parents and cohabiting couples meet their obligations, and to teach divorced parents how to minimize their conflicts and improve their parenting.

The right research and policy question today is not "what kind of family do we wish people lived in?" Instead, we must ask "what do we know about how to help every family build on its strengths, minimize its weaknesses, and raise children more successfully?" Much recent hysteria to the contrary, we know a lot about how to do that. We should devote more of our energies to getting that research out and less to fantasizing about a return to a mythical Golden Age of marriage of the past.

Questions for Discussion

1. Coontz devotes much of this essay to an overview of the history of marriage in Europe and the United States. What is the purpose of this overview? How does it fit into her main argument? How well do you think this overview supports that argument?

2. In what ways are modern marriages better for both men and women than marriages in the past, according to Coontz? Why is this important to understand, in her view? Do you think she's right? Why or why not?

3. What factors have weakened marriages today, in Coontz's view? How do these factors explain why marriage cannot be restored "to its former supremacy in coordinating social and interpersonal relationships" (par. 12)?

4. What does Coontz mean when she writes that "the social weight of marriage has been fundamentally and irreversibly reduced" (par. 13)? What does this apparent change in the role of marriage suggest about marriage itself? Do you think Coontz is right that the social weight of marriage has been reduced? Explain.

5. Why is it important that marriage and divorce trends in other nations are similar to trends in the United States, according to Coontz? How effectively do you think she uses this evidence to support her main argument?

6. Coontz draws two main conclusions about marriage on the basis of her historical review and her analysis of current statistics on marriage. How effectively do you think she makes her case for these two conclusions? What counterarguments can you make to these conclusions?

7. This essay might be described as an argument to inquire (see page 11). In a sentence or two, state the question or problem that Coontz seeks to understand through this argument.

④ # The Marriage Gap

KAY HYMOWITZ

The following essay was published in 2008 in *Cato Unbound* as a response to "The Future of Marriage," by Stephanie Coontz (which appears on page 327). As you'll see, Hymowitz takes issue with what she describes as "Coontz's presumption that marriage is not fundamentally linked with reproduction and childrearing." In Hymowitz's analysis, the purpose of marriage cannot be separated from the responsibilities of raising a family; when it is, the consequences are severe—both for individual children who do not grow up in traditional two-parent households and for the rest of society. For Hymowitz, then, "family values" are really everyone's values, since traditional marriage is the foundation of a healthy society. Although her essay was written as a counterargument to Coontz, her argument in favor of a traditional understanding of marriage stands on its own—as does her skepticism about the role of government in supporting such marriages. Hymowitz is the William E. Simon fellow at the Manhattan Institute, a think tank that advocates economic choice and individual responsibility. She has published widely on education and child welfare issues and is the author of *Marriage and Caste in America: Separate and Unequal Families in a Post-Marital Age* (2006).

KAY HYMOWITZ, "The Marriage Gap"

1 Let me begin with a slightly different description than the one given by Stephanie Coontz of where we are marriage-wise in the United States today. She alludes to the fact that almost half of all marriages end in divorce. She also points out that close to 40% of children—38%—are born to unmarried mothers. What she does not mention is that there is a yawning class divide hidden inside these numbers. The large majority of individuals who are divorced or who are never-married parents are low-income and lacking a college, and in many cases a high school, degree. The large majority of middle-class men and women, on the other hand, marry before having children and stay married while raising them. When she assures us that marriage is not on the verge of extinction, she's right—if you're white and went to college.

This marriage gap, as I call it, has profound implications for our political, social and economic prospects for one simple reason: overall, children do better in life if they are raised by their own married parents. Believe me, social scientists didn't want to reach this conclusion and throughout the 1970's and 80's they blithely assured us it couldn't be true. But as research methods have become more sophisticated and as studies have poured in, there has been no escaping it: even controlling for race, income, and maternal education, children raised by single mothers are more prone to school failure, delinquency, emotional problems, alcohol and drug abuse, teen pregnancy, and becoming single parents themselves. Put together these two facts—a breakdown of marriage among low-income men and women and worse outcomes for children of single parents—and what you have is a recipe for entrenched, trans-generational poverty, inequality, racial disparities (the black

Francis Fukuyama (b. 1952) is an American political philosopher best known for his book *The End of History and the Last Man* (1992). *The Great Disruption* (1999) is his analysis of the social and political upheavals of the 1960s and 1970s.

extramarital birth rate is over 70%, almost twice as high as the national average), reduced social and economic mobility, and—libertarians take note!—demands for government taxes to fund programs to correct the mess.

The fact that even in an age that celebrates family diversity kids are better off growing up with their married parents points us to the glaring omission in Coontz's thumbnail history of marriage: children. She states that "marriage has been about picking the right in-laws"; wealthy families sought advantageous connections and the middle class sought respectability. This thesis is like confusing shopping for a car with transportation. It vaults past the obvious fact that unless you had a son and your chosen in-laws had a daughter or vice versa, there was no picking to be done. Evolution has presented societies with three fundamental problems: one, humans' favorite activity, sexual intercourse, leads to babies; two, those babies are helpless for years, leaving their mothers in need of help if both are to survive; three, men have a tenuous tie to those babies. Marriage was the institution designed to solve this predicament; as the anthropologist **Malinowski** best described, it tied a man to a woman and their children.

Polish anthropologist Bronislaw Malinowski (1884-1942) who helped establish ethnography as a method to study human cultures.

Yes, marriage has had other social purposes. Depending on the culture, it provided companionship, it organized kinship groups, it regulated inheritance of property; as reproduction-is-basic-to-marriage skeptics often observe, many cultures have allowed older women, generally widows, to marry if they had enough wealth to attract a suitor. (Less liberal cultures declared them useless and had them burn themselves on their husbands' funeral pyres.) Yet there were many other conceivable ways to regulate property or provide companionship; it was the inevitability of children in a sexual union that made marriage the universal human institution that it became.

5 If this theory is correct, then Coontz's analysis of what happened after "the Sixties"

or what Francis **Fukuyama** calls "The Great Disruption," also misses the big picture. No question about it, Coontz is correct that love—actually I would put it more generally as personal fulfillment—became more central to our understanding of marriage. No question also that after The Disruption people began marrying later than they had in earlier decades, that they starting living together outside of marriage, and that more decided to opt out of wedded bliss altogether. And yes, women's liberation, affluence, and technological advances created the conditions that enabled these choices. But the chasm that separates the post-sixties and the rest of human history is the belief that marriage and childbearing/childrearing could go their separate ways. Working mothers are not new; marrying at later ages is not new. A large population of single mothers and fatherless children? Now, that's new.

This history is worth so many pixels because Coontz's presumption that marriage is not fundamentally linked with reproduction and childrearing has become commonplace in American society. In surveys half of young women say they might consider having a child outside of marriage. Courts are putting the idea into law. Yet here we are almost 40 years after the children-are-one-thing-and-marriage-is-another revolution began and even with mass affluence that relieves us of some of evolution's burden by making single motherhood more economically viable, we find that kids growing up with their married parents are still in a better place in life's sweepstakes. Doesn't that suggest that the revolutionaries were—are—missing something?

Now, as Coontz observes, this is an international revolution. In much of Western Europe, out-of-wedlock childbearing is even more commonplace than in the United States; in 2007 more than half of French babies were born to unmarried women. Growing affluence, women's independence, a global media, the de-stigmatization of sex outside of marriage, and increasing expectations for self-fulfillment are accompanying skyrocketing divorce rates in more unlikely places like Japan, China, and the former countries of the Soviet Union, though out-of-wedlock childbearing remains rare, likely because it constitutes the most radical rejection of human custom.

But I would suggest that the de-linking of marriage and childrearing is a particular dilemma in the United States for reasons that libertarians should find compelling. In America, marriage has been inextricably entwined with national ideals of political and economic freedom. Following the theories of **the Enlightenment and John Locke**, the founders rejected the clannish, patriarchal arrangements of the old country and placed their hopes in what we might call republican marriage. The self-choosing, nuclear couple was to be an economically self-sufficient unit; it was also supposed to socialize the next generation of independent, upstanding republicans, an endeavor that the founders understood to be labor-intensive. Contemporary affluence does not ease the inherent difficulty of raising children in America; in fact, given the intense educational preparation required for success in a knowledge economy, it has made raising kids harder. The founders certainly

wouldn't be surprised to hear that children growing up with their married parents are more likely to graduate from high school and to go to and graduate from college than their single-parented peers. The marriage gap, in other words, produces a human capital gap.

Coontz says we "know a lot ... about how to help every family build on its strengths, minimize its weaknesses, and raise children more successfully ..." Actually, we don't. The United States has spent billions trying to prop up fatherless families through welfare payments, nutrition programs, early childhood education, Title 1, child support, and a teeming, maddening family court system. We don't have much to show for it. I have no idea whether it is possible to restore our understanding of the core meaning of marriage, or to put it in more concrete terms, to increase the percentage of American children growing up with their married parents. This is a cultural problem and it's hard to see that outside warnings from the bully pulpit, government can do very much about it. But I do know that a future that accepts the separation of marriage and childrearing will severely challenge some of America's core ideals, not least of them, limited government.

The Enlightenment and John Locke For information about The Enlightenment, see the box titled "The Enlightenment" on page 328. British philosopher John Locke (1632–1704), one of the most influential thinkers associated with The Enlightenment, developed the "social contract theory" of government and helped establish empiricism, a philosophy of knowledge that helped give rise to the experimental methods of modern science.

Questions for Discussion

1. What is the "marriage gap," as Hymowitz describes it? Why is it important to understand this "gap" in debates about marriage in the United States, in her view? What evidence does she offer to support her argument about this gap? How convincing do you find this evidence?

2. At the end of paragraph 2, Hymowitz warns, "libertarians take note!" that the marriage gap leads to higher government taxes. Why do you think she addresses libertarians directly in this way? What might this brief passage suggest about her own political views?

3. According to Hymowitz, what predicament does traditional marriage solve? Do you agree that marriage should serve this purpose? Explain.

4. What dilemma does the United States face as a result of the purpose of marriage becoming separated from childrearing? Why is this dilemma especially important to the United States? What do you think Hymowitz's position on this dilemma reveals about her political views in general?

5. Why is Hymowitz skeptical about the possibility that the government can solve the problem of the marriage gap? Do you think she's right to be skeptical? Why or why not?

NEGOTIATING DIFFERENCES

As the readings in this cluster indicate, marriage is a powerful social institution. The intensity of the debates about matters like same-sex marriage and the importance of marriage in modern society suggests how seriously many people take these issues. Marriage is also a challenging commitment between two partners to one another. If the readings in this cluster are any guide, that commitment is more difficult than ever to maintain. Perhaps for that reason, many couples now sign prenuptial agreements that set specific financial and legal terms for the marriage. Although such agreements are common when there is a great deal of money at stake in a marriage, less wealthy couples also have reasons to sign such agreements.

Whether or not you plan to marry, consider what kind of marriage you would want to have. If you were preparing to marry, what would be the terms of a prenuptial agreement that you would ask your future spouse to sign? How might those terms reflect your hopes and beliefs about what a marriage should be like? For this assignment, you will try to answer those questions.

Write the first draft of a prenuptial agreement that you would want your future spouse to honor and can promise to honor yourself. Include what you are sure you can contribute to the marriage, as well as what your limits might be. Also include what you expect your spouse to be able to bring to the marriage. Add what forms of behavior would be unacceptable. When you have finished your draft, add as an appendix a draft of the wedding vows you think you can both honor. Remember that your goal in this project is to create a clear understanding about the kind of marriage you hope to build.

©Stefan Zaklin/epa/Corbis

Should There Be Limits on Free Speech?

The First Amendment to the U.S. Constitution, which, along with the rest of the Bill of Rights, was adopted in 1791, states, "Congress shall make no law respecting an establishment of religion, or prohibiting the free exercise thereof; or abridging the freedom of speech, or of the press; or the right of the people peaceably to assemble, and to petition the Government for a redress of grievances." These rights to freedom of religion, assembly, and speech are so basic to American political life that it's safe to say that many Americans take them for granted. But well-publicized cases of those who are persecuted for speaking out can remind Americans that the right to free speech is not universal and that millions of people around the world can place themselves at grave risk by speaking out against their government or writing something that is considered critical of authority.

In 2009, for example, the government of Iran arrested thousands of its citizens for protesting against the presidential elections that were held there. Many citizens were detained simply for posting messages on Twitter that described the massive demonstrations against the government that took place in the streets of Tehran and other large cities in Iran. Accusations were subsequently made that many of those who were arrested were tortured and some even killed—all for criticizing their government.

Or take the case of Aung San Suu Kyi, the Burmese political leader who won the Nobel Peace Prize in 1992. Suu Kyi was arrested by her government in 1990 after winning election as the nation's prime minister. She had become a powerful voice for democratic reform in her country before the election, despite being harassed by her government. But the military government nullified the election and placed Suu Kyi under house arrest. As of 2010 she was still under house arrest, though she continued to speak out against her government through her writing and through her supporters around the world.

Such cases remind us how precious—and fragile—the right to free speech can be. But although the U.S. Constitution guarantees the right of Americans to free expression, it does not tell us exactly what speech should be protected or how to do so. And as the readings in this cluster reveal, deciding when speech should remain free and when it should be restricted is not always easy or straightforward. Should *all* speech be protected, no matter how offensive or potentially damaging it might be? Should *some* kinds of speech—for example, hate speech or speech that incites violence—be restricted? If so, how do we determine what counts as speech that should be restricted as compared to speech that is simply unpopular? And what about something like pornography or obscene music? Should such forms of expression be protected or should they be restricted because they are considered offensive by some members of the community? The readings in this cluster address these and other difficult questions about the complexity of the principle of free speech.

① The Globalization of Censorship

ANNE APPLEBAUM

What are the consequences of censorship? Writer Anne Applebaum addresses that question by considering three controversial decisions by U.S. companies to censor themselves in situations in which they felt at risk. In each of these cases the companies decided to censor information or images that could have created public relations problems or even placed individuals or the companies themselves in danger if that information or the images had been released. In arguing that these companies made the wrong decisions, Applebaum acknowledges these risks, but she maintains that far greater damage was done to the principle of free speech by the actions taken by these companies. Her essay illustrates how difficult it can be to uphold these principles—and how dangerous it can be to put the principles of free expression into practice. Applebaum is the author of *Gulag: A History* (2003) and a columnist for the *Washington Post* and for *Slate*, an online magazine in which this essay appeared in 2009.

ANNE APPLEBAUM, "The Globalization of Censorship"

1 **Item 1:** When it appears in the coming months, look carefully through Yale University Press's new book *The Cartoons That Shook the World*. It is a scholarly account of the controversy that surrounded a Danish newspaper's 2005 publication of 12 cartoons depicting the Prophet Mohammed. The author, Jytte Klausen, argues, among other things, that the controversy was manipulated by Danish imams who showed their followers false, sexually offensive depictions of Mohammed alongside the real ones, which were not inherently offensive. She consulted with several Muslim scholars, who agreed. Nevertheless, you will not find the cartoons themselves printed in the finished book.

Item 2: Pick up a copy of the U.S. edition of September's *GQ*. Buried deep inside, you will find an article titled "Vladimir Putin's Dark Rise to Power," by Scott Anderson. The article, based on extensive reporting, argues that Russian security services helped create a series of bomb explosions in Moscow in 2000—explosions that were blamed on Chechen terrorists at the time. Read it carefully, for you will not find this article in *GQ*'s Russian edition. As of this writing, you will not find this article on *GQ*'s Web site, either: Condé Nast, the media company that owns *GQ*, has ordered all its magazines and affiliates around the world

COMPLICATION

When Yale University Press published *The Cartoons That Shook the World*, by Jytte Klausen, in 2009, the Press's director, John Donatich, released a statement explaining the publisher's decision not to include the cartoons in the book:

> The omission of the cartoons, and of other images of the Prophet Muhammad, has angered many people, who see it as a case of censorship or as a compromise of academic integrity. I believe it is neither of those things....
>
> [T]he cartoons are deliberately grotesque and insulting, gratuitously so. They were designed to pick a fight. They meant to hurt and provoke. At best, they are in bad taste. The Press would never have commissioned or published them as original content. Those alone may be reasons enough not to print them....
>
> In the end, I decided that the press would omit the images, knowing that this was the kind of decision that could not be made without negative consequences. Many people feel that my choice was impolitic or politically incorrect or just plain wrong. Yet I believe it was the responsible, principled, practical, and right thing to do.

SOURCE: Yale University Press.

to refrain from mentioning or promoting this article in any way.

Item 3: If your knowledge of written Chinese characters is up to it, type the word *Tiananmen* into Google.cn. I am reliably informed (not knowing Chinese myself) that your search will retrieve little or no useful information on this subject, nor will it tell you much about Taiwan or Tibet or democracy. This is not an accident: In 2006, Google agreed to a modicum of censorship in China, in exchange for being allowed to operate there at all.

These three incidents are not identical. Yale's press refused to print the cartoons because the university fears retaliatory violence on its campus. Condé Nast refused to promote an article on the Russian secret service because it fears loss of Russian advertisers. Google refuses to let its Chinese users search for *Tiananmen* and other taboo subjects because Google wants to compete against Chinese search engines for a share of the huge Chinese market. All three companies exhibit greatly varying degrees of remorse, from Condé Nast (none) to Yale's press (a lot) to Google (ambivalent: Google founder Sergey Brin initially argued that the company would at least bring *more* information to China, if not *complete* information).

CONTEXT

Google announced in 2006 that it agreed to partially censor its Chinese-language Internet search services in exchange for being allowed to offer those services in China. The company justified its controversial decision by arguing that providing access to some online information to the Chinese population was better than not being able to provide any access at all. In January 2010, just a few months after Applebaum's essay was published, Google announced that it would no longer censor Internet search results in China after a cyber-attack against the company that was believed to be part of an effort by Chinese authorities to gather information on Chinese human rights activists. In its announcement, Google stated, "We have taken the unusual step of sharing information about these attacks with a broad audience not just because of the security and human rights implications of what we have unearthed, but also because this information goes to the heart of a much bigger global debate about freedom of speech."

5 Nevertheless, the three stories lead to one conclusion: In different ways, the Russian government, the Chinese government, and unnamed Islamic terrorists are now capable of placing de facto controls on American companies—something that would have been unthinkable a decade ago. In a world that seems more dangerous and less profitable than it did in the past, greed or fear proved stronger than these companies' commitment to free speech.

By caving in to pressure, they have not made the world a safer place, however, either for themselves or for anyone else. Google's submission to Chinese censorship in 2006 has not prevented the Chinese government from continuing to harass the company, allegedly for distributing pornography. On the contrary, it may have encouraged China to attempt, quite recently, to force companies to place filters on all computers sold in the country. By the same token, Condé Nast's climb-down will only encourage Russian companies—many of which are de facto state-owned—to exert pressure on their Western partners, making it harder for others to publish controversial material about Russia in the future. The fact that Yale's press, one of the most innovative in the country, will not publish the Danish cartoons only makes it harder for others to publish them. (Declaration of interest: I am editing an anthology for YUP and have long admired its commitment to opening Soviet archives.)

In fact, each time an American company caves in to illiberal pressure, the atmosphere is worse for everyone else. Each alteration made in the name of placating an illiberal group or government makes that group or government stronger. What seems a small lapse of integrity now might well loom larger in the future. All these companies are making it much harder for everyone else to continue speaking and publishing freely around the world.

There is no law or edict that can force these companies, or any American companies, to abide by the principles of free speech abroad. But at least it is possible to embarrass them at home. Hence this column.

Questions for Discussion

1. Applebaum begins her essay with three stories about censorship. What conclusion does she draw from these three stories? Do you think this conclusion is a logical one to draw from these situations? Explain. How effectively do you think Applebaum uses these three stories to make her main argument?

2. What evidence does Applebaum present to support her view that the decisions by the three companies she refers to (Yale University Press, Condé Nast, and Google) "have not made the world a safer place" (par. 6)? How persuasive is her reasoning about the consequences of the decisions by these companies?

3. In a parenthetical statement at the end of paragraph 6, Applebaum discloses that she is working on a book to be published by Yale University Press, which is one of the businesses she criticizes in this essay. What impact did this statement have on you as a reader? In what ways did it influence your reaction to Applebaum's main argument, if at all? Should it influence your reaction? Explain.

4. How does Applebaum describe the purpose of her essay? Do you think she has succeeded in achieving this purpose? Why or why not?

5. Is this essay an example of an argument based on inductive or deductive reasoning (see pages 80–83)? Explain, citing specific passages from the essay to support your answer.

② | Them Damn Pictures

DOUG MARLETTE

If you have watched the popular television shows *The Colbert Report* or *The Daily Show* or if you read *The Onion*, you know something about contemporary political satire. Such television shows and publications poke fun at politicians, governments, celebrities, and others, using comedy to criticize decisions or actions that create controversy or make news. Doug Marlette (1949–2007) believed that these shows and publications perform an essential function in an open, democratic society. In the following essay, he argues that satire is a necessary form of free speech that must not be censored, and he criticizes publishers, governments, and others who restrict the publication of controversial satire such as editorial cartoons or support those who censor such speech. But Marlette also acknowledges the great risks that satirists sometimes take when they practice their art. He knew something about those risks, since he himself was the target of threats because of his own cartoons, which some people found insulting to their religion. As you read his pointed argument, consider whether he makes a convincing case that such risks are necessary if we wish to preserve our right to free speech. Marlette was a Pulitzer Prize-winning cartoonist for the *Tulsa World*. This essay appeared in 2006 in *Salon*, an online magazine of politics and culture.

DOUG MARLETTE, "Them Damn Pictures"

Boss Tweed was the nickname of William Tweed (1823-1878), a well-known politician in New York in the late nineteenth century. Known for running a powerful but corrupt political machine in New York, Tweed was eventually convicted of stealing millions of dollars of taxpayer money. Editorial cartoonist **Thomas Nast** (1840-1902) became famous for his satiric cartoons about Tweed's corruption, which helped turn public sentiment against Tweed. Tweed is reported to have said about Nast's cartoons, "Stop them damn pictures!"

1 "Give up the cartoonists; they're in the attic." That is what many of us in the trade feel has been our lot since our brethren in Denmark were forced into hiding after drawing likenesses of the Prophet Mohammed. As art will do, "them damn pictures"—***Boss Tweed's*** term for ***Thomas Nast's*** cartoons from a more innocent time—have exposed not just the internal dynamics of what some have called Islamofascism but the corresponding corruption of our own values and character in the West. Our insides have been illuminated like an electrocuted Daffy Duck in an old Warner Brothers cartoon. And we now see what we're made of: not a lot of guts, or brains either.

Admittedly, there's something about cartoons, which are by definition unruly, tasteless and immature, that brings out, if not the ayatollah, at least the disapproving parent in even the most permissive of adults. And granted, there may be a rights vs. responsibilities debate to be had over the Danish newspaper *Jyllands-Posten's* original decision to commission images of Mohammed. But once these images became a major news story (and given that they easily satisfied Western standards of legitimate commentary and in fact only became internationally controversial after being misrepresented to the larger Muslim world) I can see little reason—other than bodily fear, bottom-line self-preservation, and just poor judgment—that the U.S. media and the public officials entrusted with defending our freedoms wimped out so thoroughly when challenged to live up to their historic obligation under the First Amendment to keep the American public informed. When we withhold information in the name of a misguided sensitivity, by default we allow nihilistic street mobs from London to Jakarta to define the debate in this country.

In effect, we have capitulated to intimidation and threats and negotiated with terrorists. No need for **Zarqawi** to behead us. We do it ourselves.

Defensiveness about caving in to the imams spread across the nation's editorial pages, while the 24-hour cable news talking heads clucked tongues about the irresponsible European press that had reprinted the offending images. Even cartoonist Garry Trudeau assured the *San Francisco Chronicle* that he would never depict the Prophet in his comics in a mocking way; nor would he show improper pictures of Jesus. As "Doonesbury's" Zonker might say, "Dude, this is so not about you!"

The images of Mohammed commissioned by *Jyllands-Posten* do not mock the Prophet any more than I dishonored Jesus Christ when I drew a cartoon of the Last Supper where Welch's grape juice was served. I was exposing the followers of Christ who used the doctrine of inerrancy to promote a crude agenda; the Danish cartoonists were not only exploring issues of self-censorship and intimidation but also depicting the hijacking of Islam by fanatics like the tormentors of **Salman Rushdie** and the murderers of filmmaker **Theo van Gogh.** I would further argue that publishing those cartoons was an act of democratic inclusiveness. In a society of laws, all are treated equally under the law. Law is "insensitive" that way, as is

Marlette © 2005 Tallahassee Democrat

"AT LAST!... THE PERFECT WESTERNER—ALREADY BEHEADED!"

intellectual inquiry, as is satire. By engaging satirically with Islam, these brave artists included Muslims as peers in the tradition of satiric self-examination and irreverence that we have until recently taken for granted in the West. And Denmark's Muslims might have simply expressed their displeasure through the accepted democratic avenues of their adopted country if their unscrupulous imams and the corrupt Arab governments whose tyranny they serve hadn't manipulated the cartoons (by, for example, disseminating some offensive drawings that were not part of the original, rather tame,

Jordanian Abu Masab al-**Zarqawi** (1966–2006) was a leader of an Islamist militant organization called Al Qaeda in Iraq, which opposed the U.S. military presence there. He became notorious for his terrorist activities, especially the beheadings of hostages, including the journalist Daniel Berg in 2004. He was killed in Iraq in 2006.

Prize-winning novelist **Salman Rushdie**, who was born in Bombay, India, in 1947, became internationally famous in 1988 after the publication of his novel *The Satanic Verses* stirred great controversy among many Muslims around the world who considered the book insulting to Islam. In 1989 the spiritual leader of Iran, Ayatollah Ruhollah Khomeini, decreed that Rushdie should be assassinated for blasphemy against Islam. Rushdie went into hiding until 1998, when the Iranian government declared it would no longer actively support any attempt to kill him.

CONTEXT

In September 2005, the Danish daily newspaper *Jyllands-Posten* published satirical cartoons by several cartoonists depicting the prophet Mohammad. Newspapers in other countries also published the cartoons, which were criticized by many Muslims as offensive. Following the publication of the cartoons, large and sometimes violent demonstrations were held in cities around the world to protest the cartoons. In several instances, Danish embassies were attacked as well as embassies of other nations, including Germany, Norway, and Sweden. An attempt was made on the life of one of the cartoonists, and many newspapers and artists were threatened. Some governments became involved. Pakistan's Senate, for example, issued a resolution condemning the Danish newspaper for publishing the cartoons, which were called "blasphemous." The controversy continued for several years, and as late as 2010 Scottish police arrested several persons for conspiring to kill one of the cartoonists.

Danish package) to ignite riots across the Muslim world.

5 As newspapers in Europe and even Muslim editors in Jordan withstood the intimidation of the jihadists by reprinting the cartoons, the continuing timidity of the American media looks increasingly like cowardice, appeasement, or better-you-than-me cynicism. National spokespersons, meanwhile, have seconded the Muslim point of view; the public relations ambassador Karen Hughes compared the drawings to racial slurs, calling them "blasphemous," and former President Clinton described them as "appalling." By denying their audiences the opportunity to decide for themselves by looking at the images, American media outlets, with few exceptions, kept the public in the dark about the roots of one of the year's major news stories. (Though actually, adding to the absurdity of the mainstream media's editorial anguish, the images are only a mouse click away on the Internet.) The press's reticence is not going to make this controversy go away, any more than its ignoring the newly released images out of Abu Ghraib will make them hate us any less in the Arab world.

We expect such bad thinking and Dilbertism from the corporate media culture, but when artists fear for their lives because of something they've drawn, where are the defenders of free expression among their fellow artists in this country? I understand why newspaper cartoonists, who have seen their jobs shrink from more than 200 only 20 years ago to fewer than 80 today, are reluctant to stick their necks out. Hence, no special day sponsored by the American Association of Editorial Cartoonists designated to drawing the Prophet Mohammed or, failing that, turning in blank cartoons in solidarity with our fellow Danish artists in hiding. But what about those artists who enjoy the immunity of celebrity? Earth to Barbra Streisand. Earth to Alec Baldwin.

I first got a whiff of the cosmic ramifications of this story last December when the culture editor of *Jyllands-Posten* contacted me for an interview about the threats I had received after drawing an Arab driving a Ryder Truck loaded with a nuke (this was in 2002, before Iran) under the caption "What Would Mohammed Drive?" Though this cartoon was more inflammatory than any of the ones that have caused riots around the world, I was merely denounced on the front page of the Saudi Arab News by the secretary general of the Muslim World League, and my newspaper, syndicate and home computer were flamed with tens of thousands of e-mails, viruses and death threats aimed at intimidating my publishers and shutting me up.

Still, this was a bit more excitement than I had in mind when I addressed the first East-West journalism conference, held in Prague, in July 1990, about the incendiary role of the cartoonist. I explained to the freshly minted free press there about how the American cartoon was born in revolution. (The very first, designed by Ben Franklin, showed a snake cut into eight segments, each representing one of the colonies. The legend above it read "Join or Die.") The best political cartoons, I told them, are always created in the spirit of the **Prague Spring and the Velvet Revolution**. They question authority, challenge the status

Dutch writer and filmmaker **Theodoor van Gogh** (1957–2004) was murdered by a Dutch-Moroccan Muslim who believed that van Gogh's criticisms of Islam were blasphemous.

Prague Spring refers to a period in 1968 when the government of Czechoslovakia, which was then part of the Warsaw Pact alliance of communist nations in Europe, implemented a series of democratic reforms. The reform effort ended when the army of the Soviet Union and its Warsaw Pact allies invaded Czechoslovakia.

The **Velvet Revolution** occurred in Czechoslovakia in 1989 when the communist government was overthrown in a peaceful revolution that resulted in the formation of a democratic government.

What Would Mohammed Drive?

RYDER MOVING SERVICES

Marlette © 2002 *Tallahassee Democrat*

quo and are inevitably accused of "Disturbing the Peace," borrowing the title of one of Václav Havel's books. If the editorial cartoons are doing their job, efforts will be made to suppress them.

So that week in Prague, hearing the easterners repeatedly admonished to be "responsible in their journalism," I took the opportunity to point out that the Japanese word for cartoon is "irresponsible drawings." Responsibility, of course, like beauty, lies always in the eye of the beholder. The reporting of some of the great journalists present there at that conference—datelined Vietnam, for example—was often labeled "irresponsible." **Václav Havel's** writings were called "irresponsible" by the Soviet thought controllers who not long before had convened in the hotel where we were staying. The list of "irresponsible" expression goes on: from the *Washington Post*'s coverage of Watergate to the *New York Times'* revelations of warrantless wiretapping.

10 Having grown up in the Southern United States during the era of the civil rights movement, I remember how business, civic and religious leaders called Martin Luther King Jr. "irresponsible" as a way of disagreeing with his means without having to actually take a moral stand on his ends. Those cautioning "responsibility" in today's cartoon controversy—in both the West and the Middle East—have much in common with those "good people" of the segregated South, who preferred, as King wrote, "a negative peace which is the absence of tension to a positive peace which is the presence of justice." Their own decent, Christian values were embarrassed by terrorists who burned crosses and bombed churches in the name of Jesus, as Islam has been subverted by the hooded thugs of Muslim extremism. And like the politicians and oligarchs of the segregated South, the corrupt leadership of these Arab countries encourages the anti-cartoonists because their violent passions are a diversion from

the government's own neglect and abuse of its people.

Why haven't the true Muslims, moderate religionists, men and women of good will, risen up to condemn those who so disgrace their faith? We constantly ask this question even though the answer is contained in the reluctance of our own civilization's instruments of free expression to confront the problem. "Fill the jails" was Gandhi's strategy of non-cooperation with a non-democratic system, for making society look at right and wrong in a fresh way, and it was one that Martin Luther King adopted in 1963 when he flooded the jails of Birmingham to defeat segregation. I submit that just as that nonviolent demonstration of solidarity and defiance exposed a corrosive political system and channeled the outrage of helplessness constructively, so would a form of cartoon direct action have advanced the true interests of Islam.

King wrote in his "Letter From a Birmingham Jail," "Actually, we who engage in nonviolent direct action are not the creators of tension. We merely bring to the surface the

Václav Havel (b. 1936) was a Czech writer and dissident who became a leader of the resistance to the communist government of Czechoslovakia and became the first president of the Czech Republic in 1993. Now retired from politics, he continues to campaign for human rights.

Marlette © 2002 Tallahassee Democrat

hidden tension that is already alive. We bring it out in the open, where it can be seen and dealt with."

Here's what the American media might have done and could still do in response to the cartoon riots. In the spiritually expansive style of Gandhi and King, they could summon their aggregate moral authority and humbly dedicate a page of their newspaper or half a minute of their newscasts to showing the cartoons and explaining why they must, not as a taunt but as a restatement of democratic principle, as a prayer for coexistence. If everyone had stood up for Denmark's embattled cartoonists, then the taboo images might have lost their meaning, as going to jail lost its stigma when it was in the service of freedom. Collecting his Nobel Peace Prize on the heels of the Birmingham campaign, King noted that "every crisis has both its dangers and its opportunities." Perhaps one day the *Jyllands-Posten* cartoonists will be recognized for their contributions to democratic health and a peace truer than the one they have disturbed.

Questions for Discussion

1. How does Marlette justify the cartoons that satirized the Prophet Muhammad? Do you find his justification convincing? Why or why not?

2. What is the role of satire in a society, according to Marlette? Do you think he makes a persuasive argument in support of his view of the role of satire? Why or why not? Do you agree with him? Explain.

3. Who is the "we" that Marlette refers to in his opening paragraph? Why do you think Marlette uses the first person in this way? What do you think his use of the first person suggests about who he assumes his readers to be?

4. What responsibilities do editorial cartoonists have, according to Marlette? How does his sense of these responsibilities fit into his main argument?

5. How effectively does Marlette address the objections of those who support the criticism of the cartoons about Muhammad?

6. How would you describe Marlette's tone in this essay? How does he achieve his tone? Do you think his tone is appropriate for his argument? Explain, citing specific passages from his essay to support your answers.

7. Do you think Marlette's argument is more or less effective if his cartoons are published along with? Explain.

8. The controversial cartoons that Marlette describes in this essay (and that Anne Applebaum refers to in her essay on page 341) have not be reprinted in this textbook. Do you think they should have been? Why or why not?

③ # Why We Have Free Speech in America

DON WATKINS

On the surface, the right to free speech in the United States can seem straightforward: The Constitution and Bill of Rights guarantee that Americans are free to express their beliefs, and government cannot suppress speech. But as Don Watkins notes in the following essay, not all forms of free expression are the same; some forms can be threatening and even dangerous. Not surprisingly, many Americans believe that those forms of speech should be suppressed. Watkins argues that any limits on speech amount to government control, from which the Constitution is intended to protect all citizens. He takes issue with the common argument that potentially dangerous forms of speech should be subject to such control, and he examines the ideas of the Founding Fathers to support his position. Watkins, who is a writer and researcher with the Ayn Rand Center for Individual Rights, first published this essay in two separate posts on his blog in June 2009. As you read, consider how the medium for his essay (a blog) might have shaped his argument.

DON WATKINS, "Why We Have Free Speech in America"

1 A few weeks back, I had the pleasure of visiting Montpelier, the former home of James Madison. There were conspicuously few visitors—and none of the others appeared to be under 70 years of age. It was emblematic, I think, of how little awareness there is of the Founding Fathers today. Sure, we still invoke them regularly, but how many Americans actually study their writings?

Contrary to conservatives, the primary value of studying the Founders is not to learn about our "great traditions." It's to discover great minds wrestling with important ideas. And if you think their arguments aren't relevant to today, think again.

In the wake of the recent series of apparently ideologically-motivated shootings, a growing number of voices are warning us that we are seeing the perils of free speech. The most open statement I found was on the **Daily Kos** blog; its author was someone who posts as "citisven." The post was titled, "Why we don't have 'free speech' in Germany."

(You'll have to ask citisven why he put free speech in scare quotes.)

In Germany, where I'm from, we collectively decided after what happened in the 1930's and 40's that there are limits to free speech. Yes, you can have reasonable disagreements, but you cannot incite violence nor can you say things that are blatantly and patently false. Thus it is illegal to display swastikas or say that the holocaust never happened.... In light of the recent murders at the Holocaust Museum and the Wichita church it seems to be a fair question whether freedom of speech is an absolute right or whether it should be limited in certain circumstances.

You can read the entire thing for his defense of Germany's restrictions. But the basic idea is that free speech goes too far. Sure, people should be able to have "reasonable" disagreements—but they shouldn't be

Founded by writer and entrepreneur Markos Moulitsas Zuniga, the **Daily Kos** is a popular political website that describes itself as "the premier online political community with 2.5 million unique visitors per month and 215,000 registered users." It reflects a progressive political perspective.

CONTEXT

In May 2009, Dr. George Tiller, a physician who performed abortions, was murdered in his church in Wichita, Kansas, by an anti-abortion activist. In June 2009, two U.S. Army recruiters were shot in their recruiting office in Little Rock, Arkansas, by a man who claimed to be angry about what he believed to be the Army's inappropriate treatment of Muslims. Also in June 2009, a white supremacist opened fire with a rifle inside the Holocaust Memorial Museum in Washington, D.C., killing a security guard. These are the "ideologically motivated shootings" that Watkins refers to in paragraph 3.

A popular 1801 tract refers to *An Enquiry Concerning the Licentiousness of the Press and the Uncontroulable Nature of the Human Mind* by John Thomson, published in 1801.

able to advocate *any* idea. Ideas that "incite violence" or are "blatantly and patently false" should be taken off the table.

5 Given how crucial the right to free speech is to the maintenance of a free society—and given how many martyrs to that freedom fill the pages of history—you might think that advocates of restricting speech would take great care to understand and grapple with the ideas of the Founding Fathers. But you would be wrong.

Notice, first of all, how citisven blends together two fundamentally different things: "blatant and patently false" speech and "incitement to violence." The Founders recognized that these were two essentially different issues that had to be addressed separately.

First, take the notion that the government should ban speech that is "blatantly and patently false."

According to this view, we gain nothing from "blatant" falsehoods, and we risk much harm by failing to squelch them. We gain nothing by allowing people to deny the Holocaust—and we risk another one if those who hold this position are free to advocate it.

Before the Founders, virtually everyone took it for granted that the government should ban the communication of so-called "false facts." But leading American thinkers identified that such a doctrine threatened all speech.

10 In his dazzling 1799 defense of free speech, George Hay (a member of the Virginia House of Delegates at the time) warned that, should the government start restricting "false" speech:

> The officers of the government would have a right to invade this fortification, and to make prisoners of the garrison, whenever they thought there was a failure in the duty of publishing only the truth, of which failure persons chosen by the government are to judge. This is too absurd even for ridicule.

Hay was saying that allowing the government to suppress falsehoods would make the government the judge of truth—and that *that* would mean the end of free thought. He went on to argue that there is nothing to fear from falsehoods under a regime of free speech, that "truth was always equal to the task of combating falsehood without the aid of government; because in most instances it has defeated falsehood, backed by all the power of government.... [T]ruth cannot be impressed upon the human mind by power, with which therefore, it disdains an alliance, but by reason and evidence only."

And Hay wasn't alone. **A popular 1801 tract** by John Thomson took up the issue of censoring falsehoods and concluded that, "Let not the Government interfere," even in the communication of blatant untruths. "In no case whatever use coercive measures.... Coercion may silence, but it can never convince."

In his Notes on the Virginia Resolutions, a *tour de force* in defense of free speech, James Madison argued that trying to limit censorship to false facts and opinions was hopeless. In order to protect the discovery and communication of true ideas, Madison argued that the Founders had made sure to erect an unqualified, unrestricted principle barring the government from restricting speech: "[I]t would seem scarcely possible to doubt that no power whatever over the press was supposed to be delegated by the Constitution as it originally stood; and that the amendment was intended as a positive and absolute reservation of it."

In my next post, I will discuss the Founders' discussion of the second kind of case: ideas that should supposedly be suppressed on the grounds that they "incite violence."

Why we have free speech in America—Part II

In my last post, I pointed out how today's opponents of free speech would do well to consider the arguments made by the greatest champions of that freedom: America's Founding Fathers. There I discussed their arguments against restricting "blatantly false" ideas. Today I want to look at how the Founders addressed the second restriction on free speech advocated by citisven at the Daily Kos: the suppression of ideas that supposedly "incite violence."

15 The Founders argued that although it's true the government can stop people from "inciting violence," ideas *per se* cannot incite violence. To be charged with inciting violence, one had to commit what they called an *overt act*.

There is a crucial distinction, the Founders held, between ideas and force. There is a difference between goading people into opening fire on Holocaust museum visitors, and claiming that the Jews are evil or the Holocaust is a myth. The former is an overt act the government can rightfully prohibit. The latter, as false and disgusting as it is, is the communication of an idea, which the government must not proscribe. "The Thought," wrote **Montesquieu**, whose writings influenced the Founders on this point, "must be joined with some sort of action."

This was a revolutionary idea. Prior to the distinction between acts and ideas, the common view had been that any communication having a "tendency" to lead to violence could be suppressed. But the Founders saw that this, in the end, enabled the government to suppress *any* idea. Take the murder of abortion doctor George Tiller. There have been tireless references in the media to his killer's "anti-government" ideas. It doesn't take too much imagination to project a left-wing

politician like Barney Frank concluding that "anti-government" ideas have a "tendency" to lead to violence, and calling for the suppression of critics of his tireless efforts to expand government power.

The **Reverend Robert Hall** put it this way in 1793:

> [W]hen the example has been introduced of suppressing opinions on account of their imagined ill tendency, it has seldom been confined within any safe or reasonable bounds.... The law hath amply provided against overt acts of sedition and disorder, and to suppress mere opinions by any other method than reason and argument, is the height of tyranny.

There were people at the time of the Founding who believed the government should suppress views that had a "tendency" to lead to violence: they were the supporters of the Sedition Act of 1798, which put 10 people in jail for speech critical of the government.

I'll remind citisven and anyone else who advocates censoring ideas based on their "tendency" to lead to violence of the words of Thomas Jefferson:

> [T]hat to suffer the civil magistrate to intrude his powers into the field of opinion, and to restrain the profession or propagation of principles on supposition of their ill tendency, is a dangerous fallacy, which at once destroys all religious liberty, because he being of course judge of that tendency will make his opinions the rule of judgment, and approve or condemn the sentiments of others only as they shall square with or differ from his own; that it is time enough for the rightful purposes of civil government, for its officers to interfere when principles break out into overt acts against peace and good order; and finally, that truth is great and will prevail if left to herself, that she is the proper and sufficient antagonist to error, and has nothing to

Charles Louis de Secondat, Baron de **Montesquieu** (1689–1755), was an influential political philosopher whose ideas about the separation of powers in government informed the thinking of the Founding Fathers as they wrote the U.S. Constitution.

The quotation in paragraph 18 is taken from *An Apology for the Freedom of the Press and for General Liberty* by **Reverend Robert Hall** (1764–1831), published in 1793. Hall was an influential Baptist preacher.

fear from the conflict, unless by human interposition disarmed of her natural weapons, free argument and debate, errors ceasing to be dangerous when it is permitted freely to contradict them.

Notice in both issues—both with "blatant falsehoods" and ideas that supposedly "incite violence"—the Founding Fathers defended free speech on principle because they recognized that any exceptions would establish the opposite principle: government control of the mind. This is the basic issue that modern opponents of free speech like citisven are blind to. They casually suggest that America limit free speech, which they justify by invoking arguments demolished by the heroes who established that right centuries ago. We listen to them at our own peril.

Questions for Discussion

1. Watkins's argument was originally published on a blog, and he refers to blogs throughout his essay. What do you think his essay reveals about the nature of political argument that takes place on blogs?

2. "Citisven" asserts that "it seems to be a fair question whether freedom of speech is an absolute right or whether it should be limited in certain circumstances" (par. 3). How does Watkins answer that question? Do you agree with Watkins's position on this question? Why or why not?

3. Watkins asserts that few Americans take the time to understand the ideas of the Founding Fathers, even though Americans routinely invoke those ideas when they argue about free speech rights. Why does Watkins see this as a problem? Why should we pay closer attention to what the Founding Fathers had to say about free speech, in his view?

4. Watkins organizes his argument in response to the blog post by "citisven," which Watkins quotes from and summarizes in paragraphs 3 and 4 and refers to throughout his essay. How effective is this approach to organizing his essay? Do you think it enables Watkins to make a strong case in favor of his position on free speech? Why or why not? Do you think citisven's blog post is an appropriate argument for Watkins to use in this way? Explain.

5. Watkins uses quotations from the Founding Fathers (such as George Hay, James Madison, and Thomas Jefferson) to support his position on free speech today. How effectively do you think these quotations serve as evidence to support Watkins's argument?

6. What is the distinction between "blatant and patently false" speech, and "incitement to violence," according to Watkins? Why is this distinction important? How does Watkins use this distinction to make his main argument about free speech?

7. Why is the distinction between "ideas" and "force" important in understanding the right to free speech, in Watkins's view (see par. 16)? How does Watkins explain this distinction? Do you think this distinction is valid? Does it help clarify the right to free speech in the United States?

④ The Price of Free Speech: Campus Hate Speech Codes

GERALD UELMAN

When Gerald Uelman wrote the following essay in the early 1990s, policies prohibiting hate speech on college campuses in the United States were causing controversy. As Uelman notes, incidents of harassment on campuses had been increasing, and many colleges responded by adopting policies that prohibited racist, homophobic, and other kinds of hate speech. But these policies were widely criticized for limiting free expression, and many colleges found themselves in the uncomfortable position of trying to protect students from harassment by restricting some forms of expression but at the same time advocating academic freedom and free inquiry. In his essay, Uelman examines this dilemma. He reviews the pros and cons of such speech codes and confronts the question of whether they truly do undermine the right to free speech. He recognizes the problems that colleges create when they adopt speech codes, but he also sees value in such codes. Although his essay was written nearly twenty years ago, the questions about free speech that Uelman addresses remain pressing today. His essay reminds us that the struggle to define—and protect—the right to free speech is ongoing. Gerald Uelman is professor of law and director of the Edwin A. Heafey Jr. Center for Trial and Appellate Advocacy at the Santa Clara School of Law. His essay appeared in *Issues in Ethics* in 1992.

GERALD UELMAN, "The Price of Free Speech: Campus Hate Speech Codes"

1 At Emory University, certain conduct that is permissible off campus is not allowed on campus. Specifically, some speech and behaviors are prohibited in Emory's version of what are derogatorily labeled "politically correct" codes but are more commonly known as hate speech codes. Emory's code begins with its definition of banned behavior.

Discriminatory harassment includes conduct (oral, written, graphic or physical) directed against any person or, group of persons because of their race, color, national origin, religion, sex, sexual orientation, age, disability, or veteran's status and that has the purpose or reasonably foreseeable effect of creating an offensive, demeaning, intimidating, or hostile environment for that person or group of persons.

There were approximately 75 hate speech codes in place at U.S. colleges and universities in 1990; by 1991, the number grew to over 300. School administrators institute codes primarily to foster productive learning environments in the face of rising racially motivated and other offensive incidents on many campuses. According to a recent study, reports of campus harassment increased 400 percent between 1985 and 1990. Moreover, 80 percent of campus harassment incidents go unreported.

Hate speech codes follow several formats. Some codes, including Emory's, prohibit speech or conduct that creates an intimidating, hostile, or offensive educational environment. Others ban behavior that intentionally inflicts emotional distress. Still others outlaw general harassment and

CONTEXT

According to the First Amendment Center, "During the 1980s and early 90s many public colleges and universities sought to combat discrimination and harassment on campuses through the use of so-called speech codes. Proponents of the codes often argued the codes were necessary to prevent a rise in discriminatory harassment. Others said the push for the codes was merely part of a general movement of political correctness." Whatever the reason, this time period witnessed an amazing rise in the number of speech codes on college campuses. In 1989 the U.S. Supreme Court struck down the hate speech code at the University of Michigan, but many universities attempted to write policies that discouraged hate speech without violating the constitutional right to free speech. When Uelman wrote this essay in 1992, Emory University was among a number of colleges and universities debating such policies. At Emory, a policy intended to discourage "discriminatory harassment," which Uelman defines in paragraph 2, was criticized by many faculty, students, and others as a speech code that limited free expression. Emory University's current policy, which was revised in 2007, states:

> Discriminatory harassment of any kind is not appropriate at Emory, whether it is sexual harassment or harassment on the basis of race, color, religion, ethnic or national origin, gender, age, disability, sexual orientation, gender identity, gender expression, veteran's status, or any factor that is a prohibited consideration under applicable law. At the same time, Emory recognizes the centrality of academic freedom and the University's determination to protect the full and frank discussion of ideas. Thus, discriminatory harassment does not refer to the use of materials about or discussion of race, color, religion, ethnic or national origin, gender, age, disability, sexual orientation, etc. for scholarly purposes appropriate to the academic context, such as class discussions, academic conferences, or meetings.

SOURCE: Emory University.

Oliver Wendell Holmes (1841–1935) served on the U.S. Supreme Court from 1902 to 1932 and became well known for many of the legal opinions he wrote.

threats, without clarifying what constitutes such conduct. Court rulings have prohibited public (state-run) colleges and universities from enacting codes that restrict the constitutional right to free speech based on content. Private institutions, in contrast, are not subject to these decisions. Emory, for example, as a private university, can ignore public law rulings and draft whatever hate speech policy it chooses.

5 Hate speech codes raise important ethical questions. When civil liberties are pitted against the right to freedom of speech, which does justice favor? Do the costs of hate speech codes outweigh their benefits? Is the harm that results from hate speech so serious that codes to restrict freedom of speech are morally required?

Arguments Against Campus Hate Speech Codes

The most fundamental argument against hate speech codes rests on the idea that they violate a fundamental human right, freedom of speech. Such a fundamental right, it is argued, should not be limited except to prevent serious harm to others.

Libel or shouting "Fire!" in a movie theater, for example, can cause serious harm and, therefore, are legitimately banned. In contrast, what campuses prohibit as "hate speech" is primarily opinion that, while often offensive and unpopular, does not cause serious harm. The fundamental right to free speech should not be restricted merely to prevent hate speech.

Additionally, critics assert that the costs of hate speech codes far outweigh their benefits. Threatened by "politically correct" students who are backed by hate speech codes, students who have reasonable yet nonconforming points of view will be afraid to speak in classes. As a social institution, a university should be open to all opinions, popular and unpopular. As **Oliver Wendell Holmes** commented, "The very aim and end of our institutions is just this: that we may think what we like and say what we think." Hate speech codes thus inflict a major harm on our social institutions.

Censorship is only one example of how hate speech codes undercut the benefits of higher education. If these codes shield students from dissenting opinions, how will they learn to respond to such opinions after they graduate? Hate speech codes encourage an artificial reality on campus that prevents students from learning effectively to tolerate diversity.

Hate speech codes may obstruct the kind of education that promotes tolerance of diversity in other ways. Over time, the same fervor that brought hate speech codes will bring further restrictions by administrators eager to create egalitarian institutions in a nonegalitarian world.

10 The law school at the State University of New York, Buffalo, for example, seeks out and asks state bars to deny admission to former students who violate its hate speech code. And following the 1988 passage of the Civil Rights Restoration Act, which denies federal aid to students of private colleges and universities that violate federal anti-discrimination rules, legislators are considering a law that would force private institutions to require courses on racial sensitivity and ethnic history. From defining what specifically constitutes "hate speech" to choosing the manner in which policies are enforced, codes clearly cause or invite more trouble than they are worth.

In Defense of Campus Hate Speech Codes

Those who advocate hate speech codes believe that the harm codes prevent is more important than the freedom they restrict. When hate speech is directed at a student from a protected group, like those listed in Emory University's code, the effect is much more than hurt feelings. The verbal attack is a symptom of an oppressive history of discrimination and subjugation that plagues the harmed student and hinders his or her ability to compete fairly in the academic arena. The resulting harm is clearly significant and, therefore, justifies limiting speech rights.

In addition to minimizing harm, hate speech codes result in other benefits. The university is ideally a forum where views are debated using rational argumentation; part of a student's education is learning how to derive and rationally defend an opinion. The hate speech that codes target, in contrast, is not presented rationally or used to provoke debate. In fact, hate speech often intends to provoke violence. Hate speech codes emphasize the need to support convictions with facts and reasoning while protecting the rights of potential victims.

As a society we reason that it is in the best interest of the greatest number of citizens to sometimes restrict speech when it conflicts with the primary purpose of an event. A theater owner, for example, has a right to remove a heckler when the heckler's behavior conflicts with the primary purpose of staging a play—to entertain an audience. Therefore, if the primary purpose of an academic institution is to educate students, and hate speech obstructs the educational process by reducing students' abilities to learn, then it is permissible to extend protection from hate speech to students on college or university campuses.

Hate speech codes also solve the conflict between the right to freely speak and the right to an education. A student attending a college or university clearly has such a right. But students exercising their "free speech" right may espouse hateful or intimidating words that impede other students' abilities to learn and thereby destroy their chances to earn an education.

15 Finally, proponents of hate speech codes see them as morally essential to a just resolution of the conflict between civil rights (e.g., freedom from harmful stigma and humiliation) and civil liberties (e.g., freedom of speech). At the heart of the conflict is the fact that underrepresented students cannot claim fair and equal access to freedom of speech and other rights when there is an imbalance of power between them and students in the majority. If a black student, for example, shouts an epithet at a white student, the white student may become upset or feel enraged, but he or she has little reason to feel terror or intimidation.

Yet when a white student directs an epithet toward a black student or a Jewish student, an overt history of subjugation intensifies the verbal attack that humiliates and strikes institutional fear in the victim. History shows that words of hatred are amplified when they come from those in power and abridged when spoken by the powerless.

Questions for Discussion

1. Why do colleges and universities adopt speech codes? Do you think institutions should be concerned about restricting certain kinds of speech? Why or why not?

2. What justification does Uelman provide for the adoption of speech codes by colleges and universities? Do you find his justification convincing? Explain.

3. In paragraph 5, Uelman asks, "Do the costs of hate speech codes outweigh their benefits?" How does he answer that question? How would you answer it?

4. Uelman is a respected professor of law and former law school dean. Does that make any difference when it comes to the effectiveness of his argument? Explain.

5. Why do you think Uelman gave his essay its title? What is the price of free speech, in his view? Is he right? Why or why not?

NEGOTIATING DIFFERENCES

Because universities and colleges promote free inquiry and encourage the free exchange of ideas, they are often the sites of conflict when unpopular or controversial ideas are expressed. In 2009, for example, some students and faculty at Notre Dame University protested the university's decision to invite President Barack Obama to deliver the commencement address; the protesters opposed the decision because they believed that the commencement address at Notre Dame, a Catholic university, should not be delivered by a person who supports abortion rights, as President Obama does. Such protests raise difficult questions about free expression on university campuses. Should universities allow speakers who may promote unpopular positions on controversial issues like abortion to appear on their campuses? How should they decide who gets to speak and who doesn't? Should universities allow *anyone* to speak on the grounds that free speech is a right that must be extended to everyone?

As difficult as these questions can be to answer, they can become even more complicated when they involve speech that is violent, hateful, racist, or intentionally offensive. For example, should a group that promotes overtly racist ideas, such as the Ku Klux Klan, be given the right to speak on a college campus? Should a student have the right to speak on behalf of such a group, even though his or her words would be considered offensive and insulting or even dangerous by most of the other students on campus? Does every student and every faculty member have the right to speak freely, even when they voice openly violent and hateful ideas or promote dangerous behavior? Should colleges and universities protect everyone's right to speak freely, no matter what views they espouse? Or should colleges and universities restrict some kinds of speech on the grounds that they are institutions that promote tolerance and must make their campuses safe for all students? If so, what kinds of speech should be restricted? How will those kinds of speech be defined?

This assignment invites you to confront such questions.

First, determine whether your college or university has a policy regarding certain kinds of speech. If so, examine the policy to see exactly what it states. What kinds of responsibilities does it place on students and faculty? What kinds of expression does it restrict, if any? What is the stated purpose of the policy? What kinds of problems is it intended to solve? On what principles is the policy based? What are the consequences of violating the policy?

Next, decide whether you agree with the policy. Is it a good policy, in your view? Why or why not? What should be changed about it, if anything? How would you change it? Why?

Now write a letter to your college president in which you express your views about the college's speech policy. In your letter, clearly explain your position on the policy and why you do or do not support it. Make an argument in favor of your position, but be sure to acknowledge the college's position and its responsibilities for its students. In making your argument, draw on the readings in this chapter to support your position. You might also consider referring to speech codes on other campuses to support your position. Whatever your position, your argument should be written in a way that tries to solve the problems associated with hate speech and the policies that are intended to protect students from such speech.

If your college or university has no such policy, examine the policies at other institutions, and write a letter to your president to propose a policy for your institution. In your letter, provide a justification for such a policy and explain the principles on which such a policy should be based.

© John Zich/Corbis

What Responsibilities Do Popular Media Have?

The 2004 National Football League Super Bowl became famous—or perhaps notorious—for the "wardrobe malfunction" that occurred during the halftime show. Super Bowl halftime shows have become extravagant events, usually involving well-known pop stars. The show in 2004 was no exception. It featured pop singers Janet Jackson and Justin Timberlake. During their duet, which was a medley of songs by the two singers, Jackson and Timberlake danced what some people considered to be sexually suggestive and inappropriate moves. At one point while they were singing Timberlake's song "Rock Your Body," Timberlake reached across Jackson's chest and pulled away part of her costume, leaving her breast exposed for a split second on live television.

The incident caused immediate controversy. CBS, which broadcast the Super Bowl and put on the halftime show, famously explained the incident as a "wardrobe malfunction." Nevertheless, the Federal Communication Commission, which regulates broadcasters, fined CBS more than a half million dollars for violating FCC rules against indecency in broadcasts—the largest such fine ever issued by the FCC. But the public outcry that followed the Super Bowl went far beyond criticism of CBS for its halftime show. Some critics, including members of Congress and other high-profile public figures, described the incident as a sign of moral decay in popular culture, and many people blamed the media. Popular media, they claimed, including many television shows, movies, music, and video games, promote violence, sex, and irresponsible behavior in a way that is contributing to a widespread decline in moral standards and ethical behavior in contemporary society. Some critics called for greater censorship of popular media.

Whether or not the "wardrobe malfunction" was a sign of social and cultural decline is, of course, open to debate. But the incident caused many people to revisit some long-standing concerns about the role of popular media in our lives and raised questions about the responsibilities that mass media should have in an open society. In the midst of controversies like the 2004 Super Bowl halftime show, we can forget that mass media have always confronted questions about their responsibilities. In the early days of the United States republic, critics complained that newspapers and magazines spread lies and helped corrupt the political process. When radio became an important medium in the early twentieth century, some people worried that it encouraged laziness and immoral behavior. In the 1950s, as television became an increasingly important communication medium, it was famously described as a "wasteland" during a congressional hearing. And today, the Internet and social media such as Facebook and Twitter are sometimes blamed for various social problems, including illiteracy and risky sexual behavior among teens.

There is little question that mass media play a central role in our social, political, and economic lives. But what exactly is that role? What effects do television or the newer digital media have on how we think and what we do? What responsibilities should media companies accept for how individuals use their services? The authors in this cluster take up such questions. They examine some of the ways that various kinds of media influence us, and they explore the implications of those uses of media in our social, political, and professional lives. Together, these readings can illuminate the complicated role of media in our lives—and perhaps make you more aware of how your own life is shaped by the media you use.

Empire of Images in Our World of Bodies

SUSAN BORDO

Susan Bordo is a professor of English and Gender and Women's Studies at the University of Kentucky, where she holds the Otis A. Singletary Chair in the Humanities. She has written about philosophy in books such as *The Flight to Objectivity: Essays on Cartesianism and Culture* (1987), but she is best known as a feminist theorist and author of *Unbearable Weight: Feminism, Western Culture, and the Body* (1993), which she refers to in the following essay. Bordo has been campaigning on behalf of women throughout her distinguished career, and she has written and spoken widely about what she perceives to be the sexism inherent in popular culture. In 2003, as she was preparing for the publication of a special ten-year anniversary edition of her award-winning book *Unbearable Weight*, she wrote the following essay, in which she looks back over her long struggle to oppose what she considers the damaging representations of women in the popular media. In her essay, she proclaims that she continues to criticize popular media to help raise awareness among young women. But she also admits to feeling cynical and sometimes horrified by what she sees in the culture around her. Her argument illuminates the power of popular media and challenges us to consider what responsibility media should have for how we think about ourselves. It was originally published in the *Chronicle Review*.

SUSAN BORDO, "Empire of Images in Our World of Bodies"

1 In our Sunday news. With our morning coffee. On the bus, in the airport, at the checkout line. It may be a 5 a.m. addiction to the glittering promises of the infomercial: the latest in fat-dissolving pills, miracle hair restoration, makeup secrets of the stars. Or a glancing relationship while waiting at the dentist, trying to distract ourselves from the impending root canal. A teen magazine: tips on how to dress, how to wear your hair, how to make him want you. The endless commercials and advertisements that we believe we pay no attention to.

Constant, everywhere, no big deal. Like water in a goldfish bowl, barely noticed by its inhabitants. Or noticed, but dismissed: "eye candy"—a harmless indulgence. They go down so easily, in and out, digested and forgotten.

Just pictures.

Or perhaps, more accurately, perceptual pedagogy: "How To Interpret Your Body 101." It's become a global requirement; eventually, everyone must enroll. Fiji is just one example. Until television was introduced in 1995, the islands had no reported cases of eating disorders. In 1998, three years after programs from the United States and Britain began broadcasting there, 62 percent of the girls surveyed reported dieting. The anthropologist Anne Becker was surprised by the change; she had thought that Fijian aesthetics, which favor voluptuous bodies, would "withstand" the influence of media images. Becker hadn't yet understood that we live in an empire of images and that there are no protective borders.

5 I am not protected either. I was carded until I was 35. Even when I was 45, people

were shocked to learn my age. Young men flirted with me even when I was 50. Having hated my appearance as a child—freckles, Jewish nose, bushy red hair—I was surprised to find myself fairly pleased with it as an adult. Then, suddenly, it all changed. Women at the makeup counter no longer compliment me on my skin. Men don't catch my eye with playful promise in theirs.

I'm 56. The magazines tell me that at this age, a woman can still be beautiful. But they don't mean me. They mean Cher, Goldie, Faye, Candace. Women whose jowls have disappeared as they've aged, whose eyes have become less droopy, lips grown plumper, foreheads smoother with the passing years. They mean Susan Sarandon, who looked older in 1991's *Thelma and Louise* than she does in her movies today. "Aging beautifully" used to mean wearing one's years with style, confidence, and vitality. Today, it means not appearing to age at all. And—like breasts that defy gravity—it's becoming a new bodily norm.

In my 1993 book *Unbearable Weight,* I described the postmodern body, increasingly fed on "fantasies of re-arranging, transforming, and correcting, limitless improvement and change, defying the historicity, the mortality, and, indeed, the very materiality of the body. In place of that materiality, we now have cultural plastic."

When I wrote those words, the most recent statistics, from 1989, listed 681,000 surgical procedures performed. In 2001, 8.5 million procedures were performed. They are cheaper than ever, safer than ever, and increasingly used not for correcting major defects but for "contouring" the face and body. Plastic surgeons seem to have no ethical problem with this. "I'm not here to play philosopher king," said Dr. Randal Haworth in a *Vogue* interview. "I don't have a problem with women who already look good who want to look perfect." Perfect. When did "perfection" become applicable to a human body? The word suggests a Platonic form of timeless beauty—appropriate for marble, perhaps, but not for living flesh.

Greta Van Susteren: former CNN legal analyst, 47 years old. When she had a face-lift, it was a real escalation in the stakes for ordinary women. She had a signature style: no bullshit, a down-to-earth lack of pretense. (During the O.J. trial, she was the only white reporter many black Americans trusted.) Always stylishly dressed and coiffed, she wasn't really pretty. No one could argue that her career was built on her looks. Perhaps quite the opposite. She sent out a subversive message: Brains and personality still count, even on television.

10 When Greta had her face lifted, another source of inspiration and hope bit the dust. The story was on the cover of *People,* and folks tuned in to her new show on Fox just to see the change—which was significant. But at least she was open about it. The beauties rarely admit they've had "work." Or if they do, it's vague, nonspecific, minimizing of the extent. Cher: "If I'd had as much plastic surgery as people say, there'd be another whole person left over!" OK, so how much have you had? The interviewers accept the silences and evasions. They even embellish the lie. How many interviews have you read that began: "She came into the restaurant looking at least 20 years younger than she is, fresh and relaxed, without a speck of makeup."

This collusion, this myth, that Cher or Goldie or Faye Dunaway, unaltered, is what 50-something looks like today has altered my face, however—without benefit of surgery. By comparison with theirs, it has become much older than it is.

My expression now appears more serious, too (just what a feminist needs), thanks to the widespread use of Botox. "It's now rare in certain social circles to see a woman over the age of 35 with the ability to look angry," a *New York Times* reporter observed recently. That has frustrated some film directors, like Baz Luhrmann, who directed *Moulin Rouge.* "Their faces can't really move properly," Luhrmann complained. Last week I saw a sign in the beauty parlor where I get my hair cut. "Botox Party! Sign Up!" So my 56-year-old forehead will now be judged against my neighbor's, not just Goldie's, Cher's, and Faye's. On television, a commercial describes the product (which really is a toxin, a dilution of botulism) as "Botox cosmetic." No different from mascara and blush, it's just stuck in with a needle, and it makes your forehead numb.

To add insult to injury, the rhetoric of feminism has been adopted to help advance and justify the industries in anti-aging and body-alteration. Face-lifts, implants, and liposuction are advertised as empowerment, "taking charge" of one's life. "I'm doing it for me" goes the mantra of the talk shows. "Defy your age!" says Melanie Griffith, for Revlon. We're making a revolution, girls. Step right up and get your injections.

Am I immune? Of course not. My bathroom shelves are cluttered with the ridiculously expensive age-defying lotions and potions that beckon to me at the Lancôme and Dior counters. I want my lines, bags, and sags to disappear, and so do the women who can only afford to buy their alphahydroxies at Kmart. There's a limit, though, to what fruit acids can do. As surgeons develop ever more extensive and fine-tuned procedures to correct gravity and erase history from the faces of their patients, the difference between the cosmetically altered and the rest of us grows more and more dramatic.

15 "The rest of us" includes not only those who resist or are afraid of surgery but the many people who cannot afford basic health care, let alone aesthetic tinkering. As celebrity faces become increasingly more surreal in their wide-eyed, ever-bright agelessness, as *Time* and *Newsweek* (and *Discover* and *Psychology Today*) proclaim that we can now all "stay young forever," the poor continue to sag and wrinkle and lose their teeth. But in the empire of images, where even people in the news for stock scandals or producing septuplets are given instant digital dental work for magazine covers, that is a well-guarded secret. The celebrity testimonials, the advertisements, the beauty columns, all participate in the fiction that the required time, money, and technologies are available to all.

I've been lecturing about media images, eating problems, and our culture of body "enhancement" for nearly 20 years now. Undergraduates frequently make up a large share of my audiences, and they are the ones mostly likely to "get it." My generation (and older) still refers to "air brushing." Many still believe it is possible to "just turn off the television." They are scornful, disdainful, sure of their own immunity to the world I talk about. No one really believes the ads, do they? Don't we all know those are just images, designed to sell products? Scholars in the audience may trot out theory about cultural resistance and "agency." Men may insist that they love fleshy women.

Fifteen years ago, I felt very alone when my own generation said these things; it seemed that they were living in a different world from the one I was tracking and that there was little hope of bridging the gap. Now, I simply catch the eyes of the 20-year-olds in the audience. They know. They understand that you can be as cynical as you want about the ads—and many of them are—and still feel powerless to resist their messages. They are aware that virtually every advertisement, every magazine cover, has been digitally modified and that very little of what they see is "real." That doesn't stop them from hating their own bodies for failing to live up to computer-generated standards. They know, no matter what their parents, teachers, and clergy are telling them, that "inner beauty" is a big laugh in this culture. If they come from communities that traditionally have celebrated voluptuous bodies and within which food represents love, safety, and home, they may feel isolation and guilt over the widening gap between the values they've grown up with and those tugging at them now.

In the world in which our children are growing up, there is a size zero, and it's a status symbol. The chronic dieters have been at it since they were 8 and 9 years old. They know all about eating disorders; being preached to about the dangers turns them right off. Their world is one in which anorexics swap starvation-diet tips on the Internet, participate in group fasts, offer advice on how to hide your "ana" from family members, and share inspirational photos of emaciated models. But full-blown anorexia has never been the norm among teenage girls; the real epidemic is among the girls with seemingly healthy eating habits, seemingly healthy bodies, who vomit or work their butts off as a regular form of anti-fat maintenance. These girls not only look "normal" but consider themselves normal. The new criterion circulating among teenage girls: If you get rid of it through exercise rather than purging or laxatives, you don't have a problem. Theirs is a world in which groups of dorm girls will plow voraciously through pizzas, chewing and then spitting out each mouthful. Do they have a disorder? Of course not—look, they're eating pizza.

Generations raised in the empire of images are both vulnerable and savvy. They snort when magazines periodically proclaim (about once every six months, the same frequency with which they run cover stories about "starving stars") that in the "new" Hollywood one can be "sexy at any size." They are literati, connoisseurs of the images; they pay close attention to the pounds coming and going—on J. Lo, Reese, Thora, Christina Aguilera, Beyoncé. They know that Kate Winslet, whom the director James Cameron called "Kate Weighs-a-lot" on the set of *Titanic,* was described by the tabloids as "packing on," "ballooning to," "swelling to," "shooting up to," "tipping the scales at" a "walloping," "staggering" weight—of 135 pounds. That slender Courtney Thorne-Smith, who played Calista Flockhart's friend and rival on *Ally McBeal,* quit the show because she could no longer keep up with the pressure to remain as thin as the series's creator, David E. Kelley, wanted them to be. That Missy Elliot and Queen Latifah are not on diets just for reasons of health.

CONTEXT

According to the National Association of Anorexia Nervosa and Associated Disorders, in 2010 approximately eight million Americans suffered from an eating disorder; seven million of those were women, and 95 percent were between the ages of 12 and 25. In the past few decades many researchers have studied the apparent increase in dieting as well as eating disorders, such as anorexia nervosa and bulimia, among teens and young adults. Some studies have suggested that the prevalence of idealized media images of the body that emphasize thinness, especially in advertising, may be a factor in eating disorders, but in general these studies have produced complicated results. For example, a study published in 2004 concluded that "advertisements that carry positive images of slimness can exert a strong influence on students.... This study does not, of course, prove that advertising is the sole or even one of the more important contributors to eating disorders. Numerous other influences, such as primary and secondary reference groups, celebrities, and non-advertising messages carried in the mass media could exert a significant impact."

SOURCE: "Eating Disorders and Advertising Effects: An Exploration." Academy of Marketing Studies Journal.

20 I track the culture of young girls today with particular concern, because I'm a mother now. My 4-year-old daughter is a superb athlete with supreme confidence in her body, who prides herself on being able to do anything the boys can do—and better. When I see young girls being diminished and harassed by the culture it feels even more personal to me now. I'm grateful that there's a new generation of female athletes to inspire and support girls like my daughter, Cassie. That our icons are no longer just tiny gymnasts, but powerful soccer, softball, and tennis players, broad-shouldered track stars—Mia Hamm, Sarah Walden, Serena Williams, Marion Jones. During a recent visit to a high school, I saw how the eyes of a 14-year-old athlete shone as she talked about what Marion Jones means to her, and that fills me with hope.

But then, I accidentally tune in to the Maury Povich show, and my heart is torn in two. The topic of the day is "back-to-girl" makeovers. One by one, five beautiful 12-, 13-, and 14-year-old "tomboys" (as Maury called them) are "brought back to their feminine side" (Maury again) through a fashion makeover. We first see them in sweatshirts and caps, insisting that they are as strong as any boy, that they want to dress for comfort, that they're tired of being badgered to look like girls. Why, then, are they submitting to this one-time, on-air transformation? To please their moms. And indeed, as each one is brought back on stage, in full makeup and glamour outfit, hair swinging (and, in the case of the black girls, straightened), striking vampy supermodel "power" poses, their mothers sob as if they had just learned their daughters' cancers were in remission. The moms are so overwhelmed they don't need more, but Maury is clearly bent on complete conversion: "Do you know how pretty you are?" "Look how gorgeous you look!" "Are you going to dress like this more often?" Most of the girls, unsurprisingly, say yes. It's been a frontal assault, there's no room for escape.

As jaded as I am, this Maury show really got to me. I wanted to fold each girl in my arms and get her out of there. Of course, what I really fear is that I won't be able to protect Cassie from the same assault. It's happening already. I watch public-television kids' shows with her and can rarely find fault with the gender-neutral world they portray. We go to Disney movies and see resourceful, spirited heroines. Some of them, like the Hawaiian girls in *Lilo and Stitch,* even have thick legs and solid bodies. But then, on the way home from the movies, we stop at McDonald's for a Happy Meal, and, despite the fact that Cassie insists she's a boy and wants the boy's toy—a hot-wheels car—she is given a box containing a mini-Barbie. Illustrating the box is Barbie's room, and my daughter is given the challenging task of finding all the matching pairs of shoes on the floor.

Later that day, I open a Pottery Barn catalog, browsing for ideas for Cassie's room. The designated boy's room is in primary colors, the bedspread dotted with balls, bats, catching mitts. The caption reads: "I play so many sports that it's hard to pick my favorites." Sounds like my daughter. On the opposite page, the girls' room is pictured, a pastel planetary design. The caption reads: "I like stars because they are shiny." That, too, sounds like my daughter. But Pottery Barn doesn't think a child can inhabit both worlds. If its catalogs were as segregated and stereotyped racially as they are by gender, people would boycott.

I rent a video—*Jimmy Neutron, Boy Genius*—for Cassie. It's marketed as a kids' movie, and the movie is OK for the most part. But then we get to the music video that follows the movie, unaccompanied by any warnings. A group I've never heard of sings a song called "Kids in America." Two of the girls are 13, two are 15, and one is 16—their ages are emblazoned across the screen as each makes her appearance. They are in full vixen attire, with professionally undulating bodies and professionally made-up, come-hither eyes.

25 Why are we told their ages, I wonder? Are we supposed to be amazed at the illusion of womanhood created by their performance? Or is their youth supposed to make it all right to show this to little kids, a way of saying, "It's only make-believe, only a dress-up game"? It wasn't so long ago that people were outraged by news clips of JonBenet Ramsey performing in children's beauty pageants. In 2002, toddler versions of Britney Spears were walking the streets on Halloween night. Can it really be that we now think dressing our daughters up like tiny prostitutes is cute? That's what the psychologist Sharon Lamb, author of *The Secret Lives of Girls,* thinks. She advises mothers to chill out if their 9-year-old girls "play lovely little games in high heels, strip teasing, flouncing, and jutting their chests out," to relax if their 11-year-olds go out with "thick blue eye shadow, spaghetti straps and bra straps intertwined, long and leggy with short black dresses." They are "silly and adorable, sexy and marvelous all at once," she tells us, as they "celebrate their objectification," "playing out male fantasies...but without risk."

Without risk? I have nothing against girls playing dress-up. But flouncing is one thing; strip teasing is another. Thick blue eye shadow in mommy's bathroom is fine; an 11-year-old's night on the town is not. Reading those words "without risk," I want to remind Sharon Lamb that 22 to 29 percent of all rapes against girls occur when they are 11 and younger. We might like to think that those rapes are the work of deranged madmen, so disconnected from reality as to be oblivious to the culture around them. Or that all we need to do to protect our daughters is simply teach them not to take candy from or go into cars with strangers. The reality, however, is that young girls are much more likely to be raped by friends and family members than by strangers and that very few men, whether strangers or acquaintances, are unaffected by a visual culture of nymphets prancing before their eyes, exuding a sexual knowledge and experience that preteens don't really have. Feminists used to call this "rape culture." We never hear that phrase anymore.

Still, progressive forces are not entirely asleep in the empire of images. I think of *YM* teen magazine, for example. After conducting a survey that revealed that 86 percent of its young readers were dissatisfied with the way their bodies looked, *YM* openly declared war on eating disorders and body-image problems, instituting an editorial policy against the publishing of diet pieces and deliberately seeking out full-size models—without identifying them as such—for all its fashion spreads. A colleague suggested that this resistance to the hegemony of the fat-free body may have something to do with the fact that the editors are young enough to have studied feminism and cultural studies while they got their B.A.'s in English and journalism.

Most progressive developments in the media, of course, are driven by market considerations rather than social conscience. So, for example, the fact that 49 million women are size 12 or more is clearly the motive behind new, flesh-normalizing campaigns created by

CONTEXT

The advertising campaigns that Bordo refers to in paragraph 28 were intended to celebrate healthy women whose bodies were not as thin as the models in much advertising. Those campaigns led to similar campaigns by other companies, including the manufacturers of Dove beauty products, which released the ad shown in Figure 10-1. Figure 10-2 shows an ad for a yoga video intended for women with larger body sizes.

"Just My Size" and Lane Bryant. Ad campaigns for these lines of clothing proudly show off zaftig bodies in sexy underwear and, unlike older marketing to "plus size" women, refuse to use that term, insisting (accurately) that what has been called plus size is in fact average. It's a great strategy for making profits, but a species of resistance nonetheless. "I won't allow myself to be invisible anymore," these ads proclaim, on our behalf. "But I won't be made visible as a cultural oddity or a joke, either, because I'm not. I'm the norm."

FIGURE 10-1

Dove Ad

Image courtesy of The Advertising Archives

☐ fat?
☐ fit?

Does true beauty only squeeze into size 8?

campaignforrealbeauty.co.uk ➤ *Dove*

Cheryl Tiegs (b. 1947) was a fashion model who became internationally famous during the 1970s for the photographs of her that appeared in the *Sports Illustrated Swimsuit Issue.*

The amorality of consumer capitalism, in its restless search for new markets and new ways to generate and feed desire, has also created a world of racial representations that are far more diverse now than when I wrote *Unbearable Weight.* This is another issue that has acquired special meaning for me, because my daughter is biracial, and I am acutely aware of the world that she sees and what it is telling her about herself. Leafing through current magazines, noting the variety of skin tones, noses, mouths depicted there, I'm glad, for the moment, that Cassie is growing up today rather than in the '70s, when **Cheryl Tiegs** ruled. It's always possible, of course, to find things that are still "wrong" with these representations; racist codes and aesthetics die hard. The Jezebels and geishas are still with us; and, although black male models and toddlers are allowed to have locks and "naturals," straight hair—straighter nowadays than I ever thought it was possible for anyone's hair to be—seems almost mandatory for young black women.

30 It's easy, too, to be cynical. Today's fashionable diversity is brought to us, after all, by the same people who brought us the hegemony of the blue-eyed blonde and who've made wrinkles and cellulite into diseases. It's easy to dismiss fashion's current love affair with full lips and biracial children as a shameless attempt to exploit ethnic markets while providing ethnic chic for white beauty tourists. Having a child, however, has given me another perspective, as I try to imagine how the models look through her eyes. Cassie knows nothing about the motives of the people who've produced the images. At her age, she can only take them at face value. And at face value, they present a world that includes and celebrates her, as the world that I grew up in did not include and celebrate me. For all my anger, cynicism, and frustration with our empire of images, I cannot help but be grateful for that.

And sometimes, surveying the plastic, digitalized world of bodies that are the norm now, I am convinced that our present state of enchantment is just a moment away from revulsion, or perhaps simply boredom. I see a 20-something woman dancing at a local outdoor swing party, her tummy softly protruding over the thick leather belt of her low-rider jeans. Not taut, not toned, not artfully camouflaged like some unsightly deformity, but proudly, sensuously displayed, reminding me of Madonna in the days before she became the sinewy dominatrix. Is it possible that we are beginning to rebel against the manufactured look of celebrity bodies, beginning to be repelled by their armored perfection?

Such hopeful moments, I have to admit, are fleeting. Usually, I feel horrified. I am sharply aware that expressing my horror openly nowadays invites being thought of as a preachy prude, a relic of an outmoded feminism. At talks to young audiences, I try to lighten my touch, celebrate the positive, make sure that my criticisms of our culture are not confused with being anti-beauty, anti-fitness, or anti-sex. But I also know that when parents and teachers become fully one with the culture, children are abandoned to it. I don't tell them to love their bodies or turn off the television—useless admonitions today, and ones I cannot obey myself—but I do try to disrupt, if only temporarily, their everyday immersion in the culture. For just an hour or so, I won't let it pass itself off simply as "normalcy."

The lights go down, the slides go up. For just a moment, we confront how bizarre, how impossible, how contradictory the images are. We laugh together over Oprah's head digitally grafted to another women's body, at the ad for breast implants in which the breasts stick straight up in the air. We gasp together as the before and after photos of Jennifer Lopez are placed side by side. We cheer for Marion Jones's shoulders, boo the fact that WNBA Barbie is just the same old Barbie, but with a basketball in her hand. For just a moment, we are in charge of the impact the faked images of "perfect" bodies have on us.

We look at them together and share—just for a moment—outrage.

Questions for Discussion

1. What does Bordo mean when she writes that we live in "an empire of images"? How does she support that claim? Do you agree with her? Why or why not?

2. How effectively does Bordo use her own experience as a woman and a mother to help make her case about the impact of media images on women?

3. How does Bordo answer the counterargument that we can resist images by turning off the television or simply ignoring advertisements? Do you find her answer convincing? Why or why not?

4. What are the differences in the reactions of younger and older audiences to Bordo's arguments about advertising? How does she account for these differences? Why are these differences important, according to Bordo?

5. Throughout her essay, Bordo makes many references to film and pop stars, television shows, movies, and other pop culture figures. How effectively does she use these references to support her main argument? Were you familiar with most of these references? Do you think her argument is less effective for readers who may be unfamiliar with many of these references? Explain.

6. Why does Bordo distrust companies that use images of diversity in their advertisements? Do you think her skepticism is justified?

7. In paragraph 32, Bordo tells us that when she is speaking to audiences of young women, her goal is to "try to disrupt, if only temporarily, their everyday immersion in the culture. For just an hour or so, I won't let it pass itself off simply as 'normalcy.'" Do you think she achieves that goal in this essay? Why or why not?

8. Bordo describes herself as a feminist. How does her feminist perspective shape her argument? What does she think about feminism as a way to address the problems she describes in this essay? To what extent does her feminist perspective strengthen or weaken her argument?

9. How would you describe Bordo's voice in this essay? How effectively do you think her voice contributes to her argument? Do you find her voice appropriate for her argument? Explain, citing specific passages from her essay to support your answer.

② | Racism in the Media

IRSHAD MANJI

A common criticism of the press is that it is biased. Newspapers and television news shows are believed to have specific political viewpoints. Fox News, for example, is considered a conservative news outlet, while the *New York Times* is usually thought to have a liberal perspective. Many people, therefore, reject the idea that the press is objective, which raises questions about whether or not journalists have a responsibility to try to be objective and to prevent their own biases from influencing their reporting. Irshad Manji believes that "everyone has an agenda," as she writes in the following essay. In other words, everything is political and ideological, including journalism. In her view, journalists have a responsibility not necessarily to be objective but to identify the politics and ideology inherent in every news story—even to the point of questioning conventional wisdom and challenging the mainstream point of view. She is especially concerned about how racism can find its way into reporting—not overt racism but a subtle racism that results from reporters' unwillingness to pose skeptical questions about matters like multiculturalism and diversity. She challenges her fellow journalists to take on racism when it emerges in the people and events they cover and also to be vigilant of the racism that can infect their own reporting. Irshad Manji is a Canadian journalist and feminist activist who directs the Moral Courage Project at New York University. She is author of *The Trouble With Islam Today: A Muslim's Call for Reform in Her Faith* (2003) and creator of the documentary *Faith Without Fear*, which was nominated for an Emmy Award. The following essay was originally delivered as a speech at a conference on racism in the media in Toronto in 1995. As you read, you will note many references to Canadian culture and journalism, but her argument about responsibility in the media is not limited to Canadian journalists.

IRSHAD MANJI, "Racism in the Media"

1 I'm going to address the responsibility that individuals in the media have to monitor and combat racism.

There are at least two angles from which to explore this issue. The first is the role of journalists to challenge their interview subjects, the non-media people whose "facts" journalists uses to build their story. And the second angle is the role of journalists to challenge each other.

Let me begin with the people whom journalists interview. The bottom line is this:

Everybody has an agenda. To quote the American political scientist, Harold Laswell, "Politics is the process by which it is determined who gets what, when and how." Therefore everything is political. Everything.

Some people enjoy the luxury of not having to identify what they say as "political" or "ideological" because it fits into conventional wisdom.

5 But that's where the sonar of skepticism, the antennae of journalists must go into overdrive. Instead, what we're seeing right now is that the sonar shuts down.

Let me illustrate with a documentary that aired on **CTV's "W5"** on January 31, 1995. The documentary was about multiculturalism, your usual "Has Canada gone too far?" business. And excerpts from the documentary were published later that week in *The Globe and Mail*. So clearly, the documentary caught somebody's eye.

What I find interesting is that this documentary aired in the same week as the controversy erupted in the U.S. over the Smithsonian Institute's historical exhibit on the atomic bomb, the Enola Gay, which was dropped on Japan in WWII. The exhibit consisted of photos of Japanese victims, of burned-out shells of houses and skeletons of children's bicycles, as well as a reproduction of the bomb itself.

Veterans accused the Smithsonian of engaging in "ideology" and "political" commentary, rather than plain historical "facts" by showing pictures of Japanese suffering. Not only did they get the Smithsonian to change the exhibit, they also got a public apology from the Smithsonian that, yes, we've overstepped our bounds as a museum.

To the best of my knowledge, no journalist publicly challenged the veterans on why they don't see their own position as ideological and political. Erasing human suffering from pictures is political. Revealing only the sanitized, American story is ideological. But when you're part of the dominant ideology, your statements are merely common sense. Conventional wisdom.

10 The same assumption applies to racism. When you're part of the "mainstream"—what I call the norm of whiteness—you don't have to take responsibility for racism. You will if you're honest, but you don't have to. It's always what the "other" does that is ideological. It's always what the "other" does that causes "racial division"—never what YOU do. Hey, you're protected by the common sense of whiteness.

And in this "W5" documentary, the journalists bought that assumption.

At one point, the reporter interviewed Karen McNulty, President of the Richmond B.C. Parents' Association, who was lamenting the fact that a Chinese father had left that organization to start the Richmond Chinese Parents' Association. Ms. McNulty said, "I think we're going backwards." She was arguing that racism is eliminated when parents of different cultures can get together in the same room and discuss what's good for the kids.

But the story gave no thought to whose norm would prevail in that room. Indeed, the story zoomed in on editorials warning that the creation of the Chinese Parents' Association would cause "racial division." Again, it's never MY norms that cause racism; it's your resistance to my norms that causes racism, right?

Even the illustrious Eric Malling, host of "W5", exposed this assumption when he introduced part of the story by asking, "Does multiculturalism harm?" But harm what, Eric? Or harm who? With his silence on the issue—not malicious, just matter-of-fact—he meant: Does multiculturalism harm "mainstream" tolerance?

15 But for me, the most transparent part of the story came when the writer **Neil Bissoondath** was being interviewed. He said that multiculturalism has made things so bad that his young daughter is not allowed to identify herself as a Canadian. Not an iota of skepticism from the reporter, here. What I would like to see the reporter ask is: Who is disallowing your daughter from identifying as a Canadian? The opponents of multiculturalism

W5 is an investigative news show on **CTV**, the Canadian television network.

The Globe and Mail is a widely respected national newspaper in Canada. It has the largest circulation of Canada's national newspapers.

Neil Bissoondath (b. 1955) is a Canadian fiction writer known for his criticisms of Canadian policies intended to promote multiculturalism.

CONTEXT

In 1994 the Smithsonian Institution opened an exhibit in its Air and Space Museum to commemorate the 50th anniversary of the dropping of an atomic bomb on Hiroshima, Japan, during World War II. The exhibit, which included the restored *Enola Gay*, the U.S. aircraft from which the atomic bomb was dropped on Hiroshima, was criticized by some groups, including WWII veterans and the American Legion, who charged that it emphasized the suffering of the Japanese and did not sufficiently explain the justification for the bombing; many historians, however, defended the exhibit as an accurate portrayal of the event. As a result of the controversy, the exhibit was closed in 1995.

are encouraging her to identify as simply Canadian. The supporters of multiculturalism would shrug and say, "Okay, if you want to call yourself Canadian and nothing else, fine. Just respect our right to decide how we want to identify ourselves." So in no quarter does it appear that Bissoondath's daughter is forbidden to identify as Canadian. Why didn't the reporter challenge him? Why didn't she ask him for specific incidents? Why didn't she have him explain such a sweeping statement? Because it jived with her own assumptions.

And what do we get the next week? The *Globe* running a transcript from the documentary, but without that particular statement. So nobody is taking Bissoondath on. That's what I mean when I talk about the sonar of skepticism shutting down.

And hence the need for diversity in the media, for different assumptions that will lead to different questions.

Which brings me to the second role of journalists—our responsibility to challenge each other. There was a time when I thought that diversity in the newsroom was enough. But since then I've realized it is not. We need more than different faces and different experiences to combat racism: we need people—people of all backgrounds—with an anti-racist understanding and a commitment to being vocal about it. Being a person of color doesn't guarantee either of those things.

My own experience in a newsroom tells me that when I sat on the editorial board of *The Ottawa Citizen*, there were maybe five people of color in the newsroom. Only one shared my interest in writing an article about racism for the staff newsletter. The rest hesitated for fear of being seen as complainers and making it onto the editor's hitlist at a time of recession.

20 What's interesting is that, at the time, two of the *Citizen's* top journalists were people of color. Each had their stories published regularly on the front page. And both felt uneasy about being vocal on anti-racism— not because they figured that racism does not exist, but because they worried for their professional reputations and job security. So the question arises: When are you ever established enough? When is it ever safe enough? When is there ever enough security for journalists to challenge the driving assumptions of their institution?

The answer is, it's never a 'safe' time. But it's always an 'appropriate' time. I'm not saying that speaking up changes everything. But it does plant the idea that accountability from within is crucial in a craft that purports to be driven by truth, balance and accuracy. And internal accountability is especially important given that, today, the very cornerstones of mainstream journalism stifle challenge.

One cornerstone is the soundbite. When you say something different from the norm, you have to reduce it to 20 seconds or less. And let's face it: it's not easy to debunk conventional wisdom in 20 seconds or less. But it sure is easy to reinforce it!

Another cornerstone is the myth of the two-sided story. Most issues are more than two-sided, they're multi-sided. And by not giving serious attention to the shades of gray, journalists end up by reinforcing the either/or ideology behind discrimination. The final, and most problematic cornerstone, is the "daily" nature of journalism. Often, daily newspapers and current affairs programs are so harried and hurried that there's little time for real thought and internal debate. A challenge is not looked upon well because that's just another "barrier" to getting the product out. So it becomes a vicious cycle: racism is perpetuated and earnest, anti-racist journalists either have to leave or stay and swallow the common sense of whiteness.

As more and more journalists go freelance, my hope is that they won't have to slip into anybody's norms. Until then, the only practical answer I see is two-fold: first, for media outfits not to hire people they're comfortable with, but to make a conscious decision to hire people they're not comfortable with. That is the key to internal accountability and the honest pursuit of balance. Second, for those people hired to be strong enough to stick around (which I wasn't) or be committed enough to run the risk of ruffling a few feathers (which I was). So let me end with a story.

25 The first week I was at the *Citizen*, I questioned a senior editor, not on an issue of racism but on an issue of sexism. Of course, the two are linked. He had written an op-ed article about Sinead O'Connor, the close-cropped, female Irish pop star, and I was asked to proof-read the article for the next day's edition. In it, this editor wrote that Sinead O'Connor "twitches and bitches." I said: Look, I know I'm the new kid on the block, I don't have nearly the kind of experience you do, and please understand that I'm not telling you what to write. But by using the phrase, "she twitches and bitches," you are feeding a myth, a stereotype, that all strong-willed, free-thinking, bald-headed women are aggressive, hysterical and bitchy. So, in the interest of accuracy, if not fairness, I would humbly suggest that you find an alternate, equally imaginative phrase. I was subsequently told by my boss never to challenge a person of his stature again. But in the next day's paper, lo and behold, there was a change. Sinead O'Connor no longer "twitches and bitches." She "twitches and whines." Small steps.

Again, nobody said that being vocal changes everything. But being silent sure won't change anything. Thank you.

Questions for Discussion

1. What does Manji mean when she refers to the "sonar of skepticism"? What concerns her about this "sonar"? Does she sufficiently justify her concern?

2. In Manji's view, how did journalists fail in their coverage of the controversy over the exhibit featuring the Enola Gay at the Smithsonian Institution? What similarities does she see between the news coverage of that controversy and coverage of news related to multicultural and diversity issues? Do you find this comparison effective as a way to support her main argument about racism in the media? Why or why not?

3. What kind of diversity does Manji believe is needed in the media? How would such diversity change news coverage in her view? How effectively does she make the case for this point of view?

4. What responsibilities do journalists have for confronting racism, according to Manji? Do you agree with her that journalists should accept this responsibility? Why or why not?

5. What evidence do you see of racism in the media today? Do you find Manji's criticisms of media coverage of such issues valid? Why or why not? How relevant is her argument about the media's responsibility for combating racism today?

6. Manji is widely known as an outspoken activist who is unafraid to criticize powerful authorities. Do you think her tone in this essay reflects that reputation? Does her tone in this essay strengthen or weaken her argument, in your view? Explain, citing specific passages from her essay to support your answer.

③ Symbolic Gestures

JESSE SMITH

We live in an age of visual media. From magazines to television and film to the Internet with its multimedia capabilities, we are constantly exposed to images of all kinds. We know that much of the power of advertising lies in its effective use of images to persuade us to buy a product or use a service. We know, too, that politicians will orchestrate public appearances so that the images on the television news will convey the politician's intended message to the viewing audience (see Chapter 3). But just how do images convey their messages? That question informs the following essay by writer Jesse Smith. He examines the familiar symbol system that is used at national parks and other public places such as airports to provide important information to visitors. If you have ever visited a national park or an airport, you have seen these symbols, or pictograms, which identify restrooms and picnic areas, indicate where to park your car or buy a meal, and warn about hazards such as a steep trail or an animal crossing on a busy roadway. Smith is interested in understanding how these symbols are able to convey so much important information without words. In doing so, he reminds us of the subtle power of images to influence how we think and what we do. As you follow his inquiry into this symbol system, think about the way other images you encounter might affect your thinking and your behavior—such as television advertisements or public service announcements or even the images on the covers of textbooks like the one you're reading right now. Think, too, about the responsibility we all have to use images appropriately and ethically when we make an argument. Jesse Smith is managing editor of *The Smart Set*, an online magazine devoted to art, culture, politics, and science, in which this essay appeared in 2009.

JESSE SMITH, "Symbolic Gestures"

1 Ken Burns has a new film coming out. In September, the documentarian presents *The National Parks: America's Best Idea* on PBS. If Burns' fans are excited, they can hardly be surprised. The guy's obsessed with America. More specifically, he's obsessed with the things that make America America. His previous films have explored its figures (Mark Twain, Frank Lloyd Wright, Susan B. Anthony, Thomas Jefferson), objects (the Statue of Liberty, Brooklyn Bridge), events (the Civil War, Lewis and Clark's exploration of the West), and cultural products (jazz, baseball). Consider this list and a film on the country's feelings about the land where all this happens begins to feel less like the logical next in line, and more like one that's long overdue. No offense to jazz, but come on.

According to its Web site, *The National Parks* is "a visual feast." It features "some of the most extensive, breathtaking images of the national parks system every [*sic*, PBS!] captured on film." The story of America's treasured parks rolls out "against the most breathtaking backdrops imaginable." In other words, America's national parks are pretty.

FIGURE 10-3
Advertisement for Ken Burns' film *The National Parks*

Newscom

John Brown (1800–1859) was an abolitionist who campaigned to end slavery in the United States, sometimes participating in armed actions. His attack on the U.S. military installation at Harpers Ferry in West Virginia in July 1859, for which he was later executed, is cited by many historians as an important event that helped push the United States toward civil war.

Yes, images of the parks' canyons and caves, glaciers and geysers, waterfalls and wildlife are pleasing visuals. They make great jigsaw puzzles and calendars. But for some of the system's most intriguing visuals, you don't even need to visit a park. Go, instead, to the Web site of the Harpers Ferry Center.

The Center serves as the interpretive design center of the National Park Service—NPS for short. The West Virginia town once produced firearms for the U.S. government (its arsenal famously raided by **John Brown** at the start of the Civil War); today it produces models and museum exhibits and audio tours for NPS sites. "Do you have an exhibit or furnishings project that is stalled because park staff are just too busy to do the research?" the site asks. "Harpers Ferry Center curators have researched projects from forts to stores to saloons at parks from Alaska to the Virgin Islands."

CONTEXT

In 2009, PBS broadcast *The National Parks: America's Best Idea*, a documentary by award-winning filmmaker Ken Burns (b. 1953). Burns, who is perhaps best known for his film *The Civil War*, has developed a distinctive documentary style that relies on archival photographs and film footage. As Smith notes in paragraph 2, Burns' film *The National Parks* was promoted for its stunning photography. Figure 10-3 is one of the many advertisements for his film. Consider how such an image of natural beauty helps Smith make his point about the National Park system's "most stunning visuals" in paragraph 3.

5 As part of its surprising transparency (as a whole, the site makes a fascinating destination for anyone interested in how museums and parks and historic sites work), HFC provides tutorials, tools, and general insight on the process of interpreting America's preserves. This includes the NPS symbols.

Let me explain. You know this man and woman, right?

When they're not in the bathroom or parking in a handicapped space, they're riding elevators and looking for baggage claim and seeking information on hotels and archaically looking for a land line.

They go outside, too. Ever been hiking? Camping? Some of these images are probably familiar to you, even if you've never been to a national park—they're often used on the state and local level, too. The images tell you where you can pitch your tent. Eat. The usual.

Images like these are called pictograms (NPS refers to theirs as pictographs). Their purpose is obvious to most of us: On maps and signs, they indicate where to find or do some thing. Eat *here*, not *there*. Start your hike *here*, and stay out of *there*.

This round-headed man's ubiquitous presence on the visual landscape belies his very particular origin. He was born in the 1920s to Austrian philosopher and social scientist Otto Neurath. A member of the collection of philosophers known as the Vienna Group, Neurath helped develop the theory of logical positivism, a marriage of rationalism and empiricism, of knowledge gained through reason and that gained through experience. For Neurath, the inconsistencies and changing nature of verbal language made it a poor medium for the transmission of knowledge; he sought instead a uniform visual communication system that relied on observation and experience. Working largely with Gernd Arntz—a socialist German artist who depicted the working class in abstract, woodcut figures—Neurath created the International System of Typographic Picture Education, or Isotype, and through it the classic silhouette figure.

Neurath used the Isotypes largely to convey statistical information. Those charts that use, say, eight silhouettes to indicate New York City's population of eight million people, and four for L.A.'s four million residents? Neurath's idea. All kinds of information could be conveyed through isotypes; Arntz himself created over 4,000, including many of natural objects.

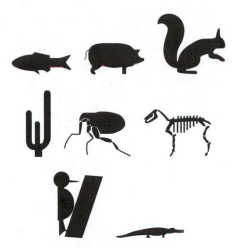

By the late 1960s, variations of "Helvetica Man" (as design critic Ellen Lupton has dubbed him) spanned the globe. Governments and organizers of large events—particularly those that attracted international crowds, like World's Fairs and Olympic games—developed individualized graphic systems to facilitate foot and motorized navigation in their transit systems and on their grounds. Variations were so widespread that in 1974 the U.S. Department of Transportation partnered with the American Institute of Graphic Arts to compare the disparate systems and come up with a single version. The team studied 28 symbol groups from bodies and agencies including the Las Vegas Airport, Swedish park system, Netherlands Railroad, and Olympics of Tokyo, Mexico, Munich, Montreal, and Sapporo. The collection—presented in *Symbol Signs: The System of Passenger/Pedestrian Oriented Symbols Developed for the U.S. Department of Transportation*—is fascinating for both the variety (21 versions of the coffee shop) and subtle differences (the Dallas and Seattle airports included spoons in their restaurant symbols). The project gave us the most common pictograms we see today—those airport icons listed above, as well as the symbols for parking and do not enter and smoking and no smoking.

The pictographs currently used by the National Park Service are a set developed by Meeker and Associates—a New York-based graphic and environmental design firm. Park visitors typically tend to be exposed to only a handful at a time, but see them all at once and the breadth is striking. There are, for instance, several different ways to encounter wildlife:

A few things to do with wood:

More than one way to get from here to there:

Several ways to interact with fish:

The Cooper Union for the Advancement of Science and Art, established in 1859, is a college devoted to the study of art, architecture, and engineering. It awards full scholarships to all of its undergraduate students.

And, of course, many ways to be injured:

But how, exactly, does a simple picture go about telling you, "Be careful here. It's cold, and sometimes ice forms on the roof, and it can fall off, and it can be sharp, and that can hurt you"? Neurath developed his isotypes with two principles in mind: reduction and consistency. In "Reading Isotype"—a *Design Issues* article written by Lupton in conjunction with the 1987 **Cooper Union** exhibition "Global Signage: Semiotics and the Language of International Pictures"—she writes that the silhouette suggests an object's shadow, which is "made without a human intervention, a natural cast rather than a cultural interpretation." This gives the image authority: "The implicit, rhetorical function of reduction is to suggest that the image has a natural, scientific relationship to its object, as if it were a natural, necessary essence rather than a culturally learned sign."

As far as consistency, well, Falling Ice means nothing if it has no relation to Falling Rocks. "[S]tylistic consistency gives the effect of an ordered, self-sufficient 'language,'" Lupton writes. "The repetition of line weights, shapes, boldness, and detail suggests the presence of a logically developed system, a uniform language of visual forms."

Of course some knowledge is ultimately required—you must be aware of ice and gravity before a silhouette and adjacent images can convey the concept. This is where problems can arise. Looking at

you can easily deduce that this indicates a place to view seals. That's the way the average person interacts with seals. See and it's clear you should avoid this place. Rattlesnakes, we know, are dangerous.

But what to make of this?

I assumed this image was a warning, like rattlesnake—you're often warned about bears on camping trips. It actually indicates a place to view the animal, like seals.

These understandings—those both correct and incorrect—are grounded in culture, and are far from objective. The image of a seal on a map made for hunters, for example, might indicate something very different. In that way, a communication system that relies on such cultural knowledge becomes a very logical one for the NPS. We think of the Service as preserving nature. It does. But it preserves a very particular kind of nature. Unlike the Bureau of Land Management (BLM) or U.S. Forest Service (USFS), NPS parks represent more than ecological value. The federal government has carefully chosen these parks in large part for their views, for their natural features, for their beauty— aspects, in other words, not intrinsic to the sites, but imposed on them. NPS holdings, in fact, include many non-natural sites such as Eleanor Roosevelt's New York house, South Carolina's Fort Sumpter, and South Dakota's Mount Rushmore. NPS maps and signs provide the context that helps us get at the pictographs' meaning; their aim is to facilitate enjoyment. Let us help you see a bear, they're saying. And watch out for rattlesnakes!

Indeed, consider the pictographs in aggregate, and a visual language of leisure emerges.

Picture-based communication systems attempt to facilitate understanding across culture and class and all kinds of divisions. But the NPS pictographs create a second layer of egalitarianism. By reducing all the possible things one can do in nature, the pictographs seem to suggest that all these things are possible for one. Scuba diving and spelunking and rock climbing and ski jumping each become as realistic an option as swimming and walking and eating. They require technical know-how, sure, but somehow that seems less a hurdle than it may have before. If Helvetica Man can do it, why can't I?

The pictographs are compelling. But they can not, of course, replace the experience of actually visiting a national park. They instead actually become a celebration of that experience. You can watch *The National Parks* in your living room. You can hang an Ansel Adams calendar in your office. Or you can get outside and

Questions for Discussion

1. How would you summarize Smith's main argument in this essay? How effectively do you think Smith supports his main argument?

2. Smith explains that the origin of Isotype, or "Helvetica Man," was a result of a philosopher's effort to overcome the limitations of verbal language (see paragraphs 8 and 9). How well does Smith explain this history? How effectively does this history contribute to Smith's main argument about the symbol system used in national parks?

3. What role does culture play in the way that symbol systems such as the pictographs described in this essay, communicate information, according to Smith? Why is it important to understand the role of culture in how symbol systems work?

4. Do you think Smith's argument would be as effective if it did not include the pictographs? Why or why not?

5. This essay might be described as an Argument to Inquire (see page 11). How successfully do you think this essay explores its subject? Do you think it is an effective example of an Argument to Inquire? Explain.

① **Why I Love Al Jazeera**

ROBERT KAPLAN

Robert Kaplan is one of the most respected American journalists covering international political issues today. So when he explains why he watches Al Jazeera, the controversial news organization based in Qatar, it's worth paying attention. Many Americans associate Al Jazeera with an anti-American point of view, and critics have complained that Al Jazeera's news coverage is biased. Kaplan doesn't disagree with that criticism, but as he explains in this essay, the matter is more complicated than that. In some ways, according to Kaplan, Al Jazeera covers international news better than major Western news organizations, such as CNN, and that worries Kaplan. He does not argue that Western news organizations should strive to be objective but rather that they should be less provincial and more mindful of the larger world, which does not often share their point of view. In other words, they could be more like Al Jazeera. Kaplan argues that the only way to counteract Al Jazeera's appeal to millions of viewers around the world is for Western news organizations to do what Al Jazeera does better than Al Jazeera. In making his argument, Kaplan not only voices concern about the influence of an organization like Al Jazeera but he also challenges us to think about the responsibilities that journalists have. Kaplan is a national correspondent for *The Atlantic*, in which the following essay was originally published in 2009.

ROBERT KAPLAN, "Why I Love Al Jazeera"

1 Has anyone watched the English-language version of Al Jazeera lately? The Qatar-based Arab TV channel's eclectic internationalism—a feast of vivid, pathbreaking coverage from all continents—is a rebuke to the dire predictions about the end of foreign news as we know it. Indeed, if Al Jazeera were more widely available in the United States—on nationwide cable, for example, instead of only on the Web and several satellite stations and local cable channels—it would eat steadily into the viewership of *The NewsHour With Jim Lehrer*. Al Jazeera—not Lehrer—is what the internationally minded elite class really yearns for: a visually stunning, deeply reported description of developments in dozens upon dozens of countries simultaneously.

Over just a few days in late May, when I actively monitored Al Jazeera (although I watched it almost every evening during a month in Sri Lanka), I was treated to penetrating portraits of Eritrean and Ethiopian involvement in the Somali war, of the struggle of Niger River rebels against the Nigerian government in the oil-rich south of the country, of the floods in Bangladesh, of problems with the South African economy, of the danger that desertification poses to Bedouin life in northern Sudan, of the environmental devastation around the Aral Sea, of Sikh violence in India after an attack on a temple in Austria, of foreign Islamic fighters in the southern Philippines, of microfinancing programs in Kenya, of rigged elections in South Ossetia, of human-rights demonstrations in Guatemala, and of much more. Al Jazeera covered the election campaigns in Lebanon and Iran in more detail than anyone else, as well as the

The NewsHour With Jim Lehrer is a daily television news program broadcast on the Public Broadcasting System (PBS). It began in 1975 as the *MacNeil/Lehrer Report* and has become one of the most trusted news programs in the United States. It was renamed *The PBS NewsHour* in 2009.

The **Swat** Valley is a region of Pakistan that has been a center of operations for the Taliban, the Islamic group that has been fighting against the United States and its allies in Afghanistan since 2002. In the spring of 2009, the Pakistani Army invaded the region to dislodge the Taliban. By June 2009, the Pakistani had gained control of the region, including Mingora, its main town.

Somali war and the Pakistani army offensive in the Swat Valley. There was, too, an unbiased one-hour documentary about the Gemayel family of Christian politicians and warlords in Lebanon, and a half-hour-long investigation of the displacement of the poor from India's new economic zones.

The fact that Doha, Qatar's capital, is not the headquarters of a great power liberates Al Jazeera to focus equally on the four corners of the Earth rather than on just the flash points of any imperial or post-imperial interest. Outlets such as CNN and the BBC don't cover foreign news so much as they cover the foreign extensions of Washington's or London's collective obsessions. And Al Jazeera, rather than spotlighting people who are loaded with credentials but often have little to say, has the knack of getting people on air who have interesting things to say, like the brilliant, no-name Russian analyst I heard explaining why both Russia and China need the current North Korean regime because it provides a buffer state against free and democratic South Korea.

Al Jazeera is also endearing because it exudes *hustle*. It constantly gets scoops. It

has had gritty, hands-on coverage across the greater Middle East, from Gaza to Beirut to Iraq, that other channels haven't matched. Its camera crew, for example, was the first to beam pictures from Mingora, the main town of **Swat**, enabling Al Jazeera to confirm that the Pakistani military had, in fact, prevailed there over the Taliban.

And Al Jazeera also excels at opening your mind. I have spent the past two years reporting from the Indian Ocean region, dealing predominantly with Muslims and indigenous nongovernmental organizations; watching Al Jazeera is the vicarious equivalent of engaging in the kinds of conversations I have been having. One of the multitude of problems I have with Fox News is that even its most analytically brilliant commentators, such as Charles Krauthammer, seem to be scoring points and talking to their own ideological kind rather than engaging in dialogue with others. Watching Fox, you have to wonder whether many of its commentators have ever had a conversation with a real live Muslim abroad.

Of course, Al Jazeera has some overt prejudices. In covering the Israeli-Palestinian dispute, for example, it is clearly on the Palestinian side. Tear-jerking features about the sufferings of the Palestinians are not matched with equal coverage of the Israeli human terrain. What you get from Al Jazeera is the developing-world point of view, or, more specifically, that of the emerging developing-world bourgeoisie; and that outlook is inherently pro-Palestinian, as well as deeply hostile to American military power. You can actually measure President Barack Obama's partial success in already changing America's image abroad by the positive coverage he has been getting lately from Al Jazeera.

Overlying Al Jazeera's pro-Palestinian and anti-Bush sentiment is a breezy, pacifist-trending internationalism. In too many of its reports, the subliminal message appears to be that compromise should be the order of the day. According to Al Jazeera, the politically weak, merely by being so, are automatically in the right. A certain kind of moral equivalency is Al Jazeera's lifeblood. The history of human suffering seemingly begins and ends with that of the Palestinians under Israeli occupation and that of the Iraqis under erstwhile American occupation.

Yet Al Jazeera is forgivable for its biases in a way that the BBC or CNN is not. In the case of Al Jazeera, news isn't so much biased as honestly representative of a middle-of-the-road developing-world viewpoint. Where you stand depends upon where you sit. And if you sit in Doha or Mumbai or Nairobi, the world is going to look starkly different than if you sat in Washington or London, or St. Louis for that matter. By contrast, in the case of the BBC and CNN, you are explicitly aware that rather than presenting the world as they find it, those channels are taking a distinct side—the left-liberal internationalist side—in an honest and fundamental debate over foreign policy.

Halford Mackinder, the turn-of-the-20th-century father of modern geography, stated that provincialism is very useful, since it prevents the tyranny of the wider, geographical majority. What Mackinder feared, writes one of his biographers, W. H. Parker, was the horizontal organization of the world according to class and cultural and ideological tendencies. Instead, Mackinder promoted a vertical organization of the world by regions and localities. And so, just as American states and individual counties curtail the power of the federal government, other news outlets in various parts of the world may pose the only defense there ever will be against Al Jazeera, which, excellent as it is, has its own developing-world perspective.

Unfortunately, the BBC and CNN don't have so much a different viewpoint from Al Jazeera's, as a similar philosophical outlook that is more weakly and dully presented. Then there is Fox, with its jingoistic, meatloaf provincialism straight out of an earlier, black-and-white era. Could Fox cover the world as Al Jazeera does, but from a different, American-nationalist perspective? No, because what makes Fox so provincial is its utter lack of interest in the outside world in the first place, except where that world directly and obviously affects American power. What use does Fox have for Niger River rebels or dispossessed Indian farmers? Thus, we are left with the insidious despotism of Al Jazeera: and it is despotism, because we have really no other serious news channel to turn to.

George Orwell intimated in *1984* that purity can be a form of coercion, and in that respect, I find Al Jazeera's moral rectitude disturbing. Because its cause is that of the weak and the oppressed, it sees itself as always in the right, regardless of the complexity of the issues, and therein lies its power of oppression. But I will continue watching Al Jazeera wherever I can, because I find it so riveting compared with other news channels. And if my politics crawl to the left as a result, that will be yet more evidence of just how insidious Al Jazeera's influence is.

Halford Mackinder (1861–1947) was a British geographer who helped found the prestigious London School of Economics. His theories influenced the modern study of geopolitics.

Questions for Discussion

1. Notice the question with which Kaplan begins his essay. What do you think he accomplishes by beginning his essay in this way? How effective is his question as a way to begin his essay?

2. In the second paragraph of this essay, Kaplan mentions many events that were taking place around the world in the spring of 2009 that were reported by Al Jazeera. Why do you think Kaplan mentions these specific events? How does his description of Al Jazeera's coverage of the events mentioned in this paragraph support his main argument?

3. In Kaplan's view, how does Al Jazeera compare to the main news organizations in Western nations, such as CNN and the BBC? What makes Al Jazeera different from, and sometimes better than, Western news organizations, according to Kaplan? How effectively do you think Kaplan supports his point of view about Al Jazeera?

4. In what sense does watching Al Jazeera "open your mind," according to Kaplan? How does this characteristic of Al Jazeera fit into Kaplan's main argument?

5. What does Kaplan mean when he refers to "the insidious despotism of Al Jazeera"? Why is he concerned about this "despotism"? Do you think he's right? Explain.

6. What kinds of evidence does Kaplan offer to support his claims about Al Jazeera? How credible do you find this evidence?

7. How does Kaplan organize his argument? Does the way he organizes his essay help make his argument clearer? Explain, citing specific passages from his essay to support your answer.

8. If you have access to Al Jazeera online, review some of its news coverage and compare it to news coverage by the major Western news organizations, such as CNN. Based on this comparison, evaluate Kaplan's argument. Does your experience watching Al Jazeera and Western news programs suggest that Kaplan is right about Al Jazeera? Why or why not?

DIFFERENCES

NEGOTIATING

Politicians often criticize the popular media as a way to gain favor with their constituents. How often have you heard conservative politicians complain about the "liberal media," or liberal politicians criticize Fox News for having a right-wing bias? Such criticisms seem to suggest that the news media should be unbiased, and many Americans agree with that viewpoint. For example, in 2009 the Pew Research Center for the People and the Press released a report indicating that Americans' opinions about the press were at their lowest levels since the center began tracking those opinions in 1985. According to the report, only 29 percent of Americans believed that news organizations generally get the facts straight in their reporting and 63 percent believed that news stories are often inaccurate; moreover, 60 percent of Americans believed that news organizations are politically biased. By contrast, in 1985, 45 percent of Americans believed that the press was politically biased.

Whatever the reason for this decline in Americans' opinions of the news media, these surveys suggest that Americans want to have faith in news organizations. They want to be able to believe that what they read in the newspaper or see on a television news program is accurate. But is that a reasonable expectation? Should we expect the news media to be objective? In this assignment you will try to address those questions in three main steps.

Step One is to try to gain a sense of the criticisms of the news media. What are the complaints people are making about the news media today? Who is making these complaints? What are the specific concerns being expressed about the news media? To answer such questions, you can start with the readings in this cluster and search the Internet for examples of the criticisms

being made of the news media. Try to find representative opinions from various political perspectives (liberal, conservative, moderate). As you learn more about what is being said about the news media, try to group the criticisms and concerns into main categories.

Step Two is to try to determine whether these criticisms and concerns are legitimate. Are they fair? Is there validity to what people are saying about the press? To answer those questions you will have to evaluate news coverage in newspapers, on television, and online. Select news outlets based on your research for Step One. For example, if you are seeing many criticisms of a specific newspaper or television news program, select that newspaper or program and review its news coverage. Try to get a better sense of how these news organizations are covering the news. Once you have done that, you can evaluate whether the criticisms of the news media are legitimate.

For Step Three, pull together your research for the first two steps and, based on that research, draw your own conclusions about the news media. To what extent are the media biased? In what ways are they biased? What specific criticisms of the news media do you believe are justified? What does the news media do well? Finally, what *should* the news media do in covering the news? What are their responsibilities? Try to answer such questions as you come to your conclusions about the role and responsibilities of the news media.

Once you have completed these steps, select an appropriate news outlet and write a letter to that news organization in which you express your view about the responsibilities that that news organization has in its reporting. In your letter, explain your own view about the responsibility of the press, and describe how

NEGOTIATING DIFFERENCES

you feel that that news organization does or does not fulfill those responsibilities. Make an argument that they *should* do so. Note that some newspapers have ombudspersons to whom you can write to voice complaints about their news coverage. You might also consider posting your letter to an online site that is maintained by the news organization you select. Whatever forum you choose, write your letter in a way that addresses that specific audience.

How Should We Talk to One Another in the Digital Age?

During the 2008 U.S. presidential election there was much discussion about the perceived lack of civility in American politics as well as in the society in general. Senator Barack Obama, who was the Democratic candidate for president, decried the tone of political debate in the United States and promised to change it. But during the campaign, audience members at several Republican rallies were heard to shout racial epithets and even make death threats toward Obama. Obama's opponent, Republican presidential candidate Senator John McCain, was criticized by some observers for running a campaign based on harsh criticisms of his opponents, but during the campaign he promised to take a more respectful approach. Yet many of his supporters refused to accept his promise. At one rally a few weeks before the election, McCain was booed by his own supporters when he described Barack Obama as a decent family man.

All these events and much more were discussed and debated in every conceivable forum: newspapers and magazines, television news programs, radio talk shows, and online on blogs, discussion boards, and the websites of political advocacy groups. Some people believe that the proliferation of media, especially digital media, in the past decade has made the tone of public debate much worse, because citizens now have many more opportunities than in the past to express their opinions, criticize each other, and spread rumors and misinformation. Moreover, online media can mean that a single incident becomes magnified as it is discussed throughout cyberspace and in what has become known as the "blogosphere." For example, in 2009 during President Obama's State of the Union Address, Republican Congressman Joe Wilson from South Carolina shouted "You lie!" in response to one of Obama's statements about his proposal to reform health care in the United States. Wilson's action was roundly criticized by many as a disrespectful break with decorum, but many others praised Wilson as a hero. For weeks afterwards video clips of Wilson calling the president a liar circulated on the Internet, and intense debates raged on blogs and various websites. The varied reactions to Wilson's act suggested how polarized Americans had become in their public discussions.

Such developments raise many questions about how we interact with one another in discussions about important issues at a time when new technologies are dramatically altering the way we communicate and share information. The essays in this cluster examine some implications of these changes. They explore how digital technologies, including social media such as Twitter and Facebook, and traditional electronic media such as television are reshaping how we talk to one another, and they challenge us to think about how we *should* talk to one another. These selections might also prompt you to consider what your own uses of new media might suggest about how we should talk to one another in this new digital age.

① # The Daily We: Is the Internet Really a Blessing for Democracy?

CASS SUNSTEIN

Democracy is based on the idea that citizens have the right to decide what is in the public interest. Yet studies regularly show that only about half of all eligible Americans vote in national elections and even fewer in local elections. You might put it this way: Citizens have the power to determine what is in their interests as a society, but few exercise that power. Why? One answer might be that people do not have a genuine public forum in which they can debate the issues that affect common interests. That answer might seem surprising in an age characterized by new technologies and social media that seem to keep people informed and connected "24–7." But Cass Sunstein suggests that despite the power of new media—specifically, the Internet—to keep people informed and connected, citizens lack a true public sphere in which, as he writes, "a wide range of speakers have access to a diverse public." The Internet has the potential to be part of that public sphere, a commons for ideas, but according to Sunstein, for most Americans it has become a means for accessing only the information that interests them. As a result, it is not a forum for confronting the diversity of views on which a healthy democracy depends. Sunstein's well-documented argument rests on a particular vision of what a democracy should be and how citizens should participate in it. As you read, ask yourself whether you share his vision—especially in view of your own online experiences and political perspective. Although the Internet has grown and changed dramatically since this article was first published in the *Boston Review* in 2001, the questions Sunstein addresses are still being debated today and his main argument is still relevant. Sunstein is the Karl N. Llewellyn Distinguished Service Professor of Jurisprudence for the law school and department of political science of the University of Chicago. He has written widely on civil rights, technology, and social justice.

CASS SUNSTEIN, "The Daily We: Is the Internet Really a Blessing for Democracy?"

1 Is the Internet a wonderful development for democracy? In many ways it certainly is. As a result of the Internet, people can learn far more than they could before, and they can learn it much faster. If you are interested in issues that bear on public policy—environmental quality, wages over time, motor vehicle safety—you can find what you need to know in a matter of seconds. If you are suspicious of the mass media, and want to discuss issues with like-minded people, you can do that, transcending the limitations of geography in ways that could barely be imagined even a decade ago. And if you want to get information to a wide range of people, you can do that via email and websites; this is another sense in which the Internet is a great boon for democracy.

But in the midst of the celebration, I want to raise a note of caution. I do so by emphasizing one of the most striking powers provided by emerging technologies: the

CONTEXT

Many of the media services and Internet sites that Sunstein describes in this passage have changed or no longer exist. For example, Zatso.net shut down around the time this essay was originally published, and broadcast.com, now owned by Yahoo, no longer provides the services Sunstein describes in item #1 in paragraph 2. These developments suggest not only how much the Internet might have changed since Sunstein wrote this article in 2001 but also how quickly it continues to change. At the same time, the Internet has grown dramatically and now plays an even more important role in contemporary American society than it did when Sunstein wrote his argument.

growing power of consumers to "filter" what they see. As a result of the Internet and other technological developments, many people are increasingly engaged in a process of "personalization" that limits their exposure to topics and points of view of their own choosing. They filter in, and they also filter out, with unprecedented powers of precision. Consider just a few examples:

1. **Broadcast.com** has "compiled hundreds of thousands of programs so you can find the one that suits your fancy.... For example, if you want to see all the latest fashions from France 24 hours of the day you can get them. If you're from Baltimore living in Dallas and you want to listen to WBAL, your hometown station, you can hear it."

2. **Sonicnet.com** allows you to create your own musical universe, consisting of what it calls "Me Music." Me Music is "A place where you can listen to the music you love on the radio station YOU create.... A place where you can watch videos of your favorite artists."

3. **Zatso.net** allows users to produce "a personal newscast." Its intention is to create a place "where you decide what's news." Your task is to tell "what TV news stories you're interested in," and **Zatso.net** turns that information into a specifically designed newscast. From the main "This is the News I Want" menu, you can choose stories with particular words and phrases, or you can select topics, such as sports,

weather, crime, health, government/ politics, and much more.

4. Info Xtra offers "news and entertainment that's important to you," and it allows you to find this "without hunting through newspapers, radio and websites." Personalized news, local weather, and "even your daily horoscope or winning lottery number" will be delivered to you once you specify what you want and when you want it.

5. TiVo, a television recording system, is designed, in the words of its website, to give "you the ultimate control over your TV viewing." It does this by putting "you at the center of your own TV network, so you'll always have access to whatever you want, whenever you want." TiVo "will automatically find and digitally record your favorite programs every time they air" and will help you create "your personal TV line-up." It will also learn your tastes, so that it can "suggest other shows that you may want to record and watch based on your preferences."

6. Intertainer, Inc. provides "home entertainment services on demand," including television, music, movies, and shopping. Intertainer is intended for people who want "total control" and "personalized experiences." It is "a new way to get whatever movies, music, and television you want anytime you want on your PC or TV."

7. George Bell, the chief executive officer of the search engine Excite, exclaims, "We are looking for ways to be able to lift chunks of content off other areas of our service and paste them onto your personal page so you can constantly refresh and update that 'newspaper of me.' About 43 percent of our entire user data base has personalized their experience on Excite."

Of course, these developments make life much more convenient and in some ways much better: we all seek to reduce our exposure to uninvited noise. But from the standpoint of democracy, filtering is a mixed blessing. An understanding of the mix will permit us to obtain a better sense of what makes for a well-functioning system of free expression. In a heterogeneous society, such a system requires something other than free, or publicly unrestricted, individual choices. On the contrary, it imposes two distinctive requirements. First, people should be exposed to materials that they would not have chosen in advance. *Unanticipated encounters*, involving topics and points of view that people have not sought out and perhaps find irritating, are central to democracy and even to freedom itself. Second, many or most citizens should have a range of *common experiences*. Without shared experiences, a heterogeneous society will have a more difficult time addressing social problems and understanding one another.

Individual Design

Consider a thought experiment—an apparently utopian dream, that of complete individuation, in which consumers can entirely personalize (or "customize") their communications universe.

5 Imagine, that is, a system of communications in which each person has unlimited power of individual design. If some people want to watch news all the time, they would be entirely free to do exactly that. If they dislike news, and want to watch football in the morning and situation comedies at night, that would be fine too. If people care only about America, and want to avoid international issues entirely, that would be very simple; so too if they care only about New York or Chicago or California. If people want to restrict themselves to certain points of view, by limiting themselves to conservatives, moderates, liberals, vegetarians, or Nazis, that would be entirely feasible with a simple point-and-click. If people want to isolate themselves, and speak only with like-minded others, that is feasible too.

At least as a matter of technological feasibility, our communications market is moving

---

COMPLICATION

Sunstein suggests in paragraph 3 that filtering out the "uninvited noise" that people hear from various media can have negative consequences for democracy. Some observers have warned about "information overload": There is simply too much information available for us to process adequately. Technology and literacy expert Bertram Bruce wrote,

> In his book *Information Anxiety* (1989), Richard Wurman claimed that the weekday edition of the *New York Times* contains more information than the average person in 17th-century England was likely to come across in a lifetime. This personalizes the oft-cited estimate that more information has been produced in the last 30 years than in the previous 5,000. Statistics like these highlight the phenomenon of an information explosion and its consequence: "information overload" or information anxiety.

SOURCE: "Information Overload: Threat or Opportunity?" (2002).

---

rapidly toward this apparently utopian picture. A number of newspapers' websites allow readers to create filtered versions, containing exactly what they want, and no more. If you are interested in getting help with the design of an entirely individual paper, you can consult a number of sites, including Individual.com and Crayon.net. To be sure, the Internet greatly increases people's ability to expand their horizons, as millions of people are now doing; but many people are using it to produce narrowness, not breadth. Thus MIT professor Nicholas Negroponte refers to the emergence of the "Daily Me"—a communications package that is personally designed, with components fully chosen in advance.

Of course, this is not entirely different from what has come before. People who read newspapers do not read the same newspaper; some people do not read any newspaper at all. People make choices among magazines based on their tastes and their points of view. But in the emerging situation, there is a difference of degree if not of kind. What *is* different is a dramatic increase in individual control over content, and a corresponding decrease in the power of general interest intermediaries, including newspapers, magazines, and broadcasters. For all their problems, and their unmistakable limitations and biases, these intermediaries have performed some important democratic functions.

People who rely on such intermediaries have a range of chance encounters, involving shared experience with diverse others and exposure to material that they did not specifically choose. You might, for example, read the city newspaper and in the process come across a range of stories that you would not have selected if you had the power to control what you see. Your eyes may come across a story about Germany, or crime in Los Angeles, or innovative business practices in Tokyo, and you may read those stories although you would hardly have placed them in your "Daily Me." You might watch a particular television channel—perhaps you prefer Channel 4—and when your favorite program ends, you might see the beginning of another show, one that you would not have chosen in advance. Reading *Time* magazine, you might come across a discussion of endangered species in Madagascar, and this discussion might interest you, even affect your behavior, although you would not have sought it out in the first instance. A system in which you lack control over the particular content that you see has a great deal in common with a public street, where you might encounter not only friends, but a heterogeneous variety of people engaged in a wide array of activities (including, perhaps, political protests and begging).

In fact, a risk with a system of perfect individual control is that it can reduce the importance of the "public sphere" and of common spaces in general. One of the important features of such spaces is that they tend to ensure that people will encounter materials on important issues, whether or not they have specifically chosen the encounter. When people see materials that they have not chosen, their interests and their views might change as a result. At the very least, they will know a bit more about what their fellow citizens are thinking. As it happens, this point is closely connected with an important, and somewhat exotic, constitutional principle.

Public (and Private) Forums

10 In the popular understanding, the free speech principle forbids government from "censoring" speech of which it disapproves. In the standard cases, the government attempts to impose penalties, whether civil or criminal, on political dissent, and on speech that it considers dangerous, libelous, or sexually explicit. The question is whether the government has a legitimate and sufficiently weighty basis for restricting the speech that it seeks to control.

But a central part of free speech law, with large implications for thinking about the Internet, takes a quite different form. The Supreme Court has also held that streets and parks must be kept open to the public for expressive activity.[1] Governments are obliged to allow speech to occur freely on public streets and in public parks—even if many citizens would prefer to have peace and quiet, and even if it seems irritating to come across protesters and dissidents whom one would like to avoid. To be sure, the government is allowed to impose restrictions on the "time, place, and manner" of speech in public places. No one has a right to use fireworks and loudspeakers on the public streets at midnight. But time, place, and manner restrictions must be both reasonable and limited, and government is essentially obliged to allow speakers, whatever their views, to use public property to convey messages of their choosing.

The public forum doctrine serves three important functions.[2] First, it ensures that speakers can have access to a wide array of people. If you want to claim that taxes are too high, or that police brutality against African Americans is common, you can press this argument on many people who might otherwise fail to hear the message. Those who use the streets and parks are likely to learn something about your argument; they might also learn the nature and intensity of views held by one of their fellow citizens. Perhaps their views will be changed; perhaps they will

CONTEXT

The First Amendment to the U.S. Constitution reads, "Congress shall make no law respecting an establishment of religion, or prohibit the free exercise thereof; or abridging the freedom of speech, or of press; or of the right of the people peaceably to assemble, and to petition the government for a redress of grievances."

become curious, enough to investigate the question on their own.

Second, the public forum doctrine allows speakers not only to have general access to heterogeneous people, but also to specific people, and specific institutions, with whom they have a complaint. Suppose, for example, that you believe that the state legislature has behaved irresponsibly with respect to crime or health care for children. The public forum ensures that you can make your views heard by legislators simply by protesting in front of the state legislature building.

Third, the public forum doctrine increases the likelihood that people generally will be exposed to a wide variety of people and views. When you go to work, or visit a park, it is possible that you will have a range of unexpected encounters, however fleeting or seemingly inconsequential. You cannot easily wall yourself off from contentions or conditions that you would not have sought out in advance, or that you would have chosen to avoid if you could. Here, too, the public forum doctrine tends to ensure a range of experiences that are widely shared—streets and parks are public property—and also a set of exposures to diverse circumstances. In a pluralistic democracy, an important shared experience is in fact the very experience of society's diversity. These exposures help promote understanding and perhaps, in that sense, freedom. And all of these points are closely connected to democratic ideals.

15 Of course, there is a limit to how much can be done on streets and in parks. Even in the largest cities, streets and parks are insistently *local*. But many of the social functions of streets and parks as public forums are performed by other institutions, too. In fact, society's general interest intermediaries— newspapers, magazines, television broadcasters—can be understood as public forums of an especially important sort, perhaps above all because they expose people to new, unanticipated topics and points of view.

When you read a city newspaper or a national magazine, your eyes will come across a number of articles that you might not have selected in advance, and if you are like most people, you will read some of those articles. Perhaps you did not know that you might have an interest in minimum wage legislation, or Somalia, or the latest developments in the Middle East. But a story might catch your attention. And what is true for topics of interest is also true for points of view. You might think that you have nothing to learn from someone whose view you abhor; but once you come across the editorial pages, you might read what they have to say, and you might benefit from the experience. Perhaps you will be persuaded on one point or another. At the same time, the front-page headline or the cover story in *Newsweek* is likely to have a high degree of salience for a wide range of people.

Television broadcasters have similar functions. Most important in this regard is what has become an institution: the evening news. If you tune into the evening news, you will learn about a number of topics that you would not have chosen in advance. Because of their speech and immediacy, television broadcasts perform these public forum-type functions more than general interest intermediaries in the print media. The "lead story" on the networks is likely to have a great deal of public salience; it helps to define central issues and creates a kind of shared focus of attention for millions of people. And what happens after the lead story—dealing with a menu of topics both domestically and internationally—creates something like a speakers' corner beyond anything imagined in Hyde Park. As a result, people's interest is sometimes piqued, and they might well become curious and follow up, perhaps changing their perspective in the process.

None of these claims depends on a judgment that general interest intermediaries are unbiased, or always do an excellent job, or deserve a monopoly over the world of communications. The Internet is a boon partly because it breaks that monopoly. So too for the proliferation of television and radio shows, and even channels, that have some specialized identity. (Consider the rise of Fox News, which appeals to a more conservative audience.) All that I am claiming is that general interest intermediaries expose people to a wide range of topics and views and at the same time provide shared experiences for a heterogeneous public. Indeed, intermediaries of this sort have large advantages over streets and parks precisely because they tend to be national, even international. Typically they expose people to questions and problems in other areas, even other countries.

Specialization and Fragmentation

In a system with public forums and general interest intermediaries, people will frequently come across materials that they would not have chosen in advance—and in a diverse society, this provides something like a common framework for social experience. A fragmented communications market will change things significantly.

20 Consider some simple facts. If you take the ten most highly rated television programs for whites, and then take the ten most highly rated programs for African Americans, you will find little overlap between them. Indeed, more than half of the ten most highly rated programs for African Americans rank among the ten least popular programs for whites. With respect to race, similar divisions can be found on the Internet. Not surprisingly, many people tend to choose like-minded sites and like-minded discussion groups. Many of those with committed views on a topic—gun control, abortion, affirmative action—speak mostly with each other. It is exceedingly rare for a site with an identifiable point of view to provide links to sites with opposing views; but it is very common for such a site to provide links to like-minded sites.

With a dramatic increase in options, and a greater power to customize, comes an increase in the range of actual choices.

Those choices are likely, in many cases, to mean that people will try to find material that makes them feel comfortable, or that is created by and for people like themselves. This is what the Daily Me is all about. Of course, many people seek out new topics and ideas. And to the extent that people do, the increase in options is hardly bad on balance; it will, among other things, increase variety, the aggregate amount of information, and the entertainment value of actual choices. But there are serious risks as well. If diverse groups are seeing and hearing different points of view, or focusing on different topics, mutual understanding might be difficult, and it might be hard for people to solve problems that society faces together. If millions of people are mostly listening to Rush Limbaugh and others are listening to Fox News, problems will arise if millions of other people are mostly or only listening to people and stations with an altogether different point of view.

We can sharpen our understanding of this problem if we attend to the phenomenon of *group polarization*. The idea is that after deliberating with one another, people are likely to move toward a more extreme point in the direction to which they were previously inclined, as indicated by the median of their predeliberation judgments. With respect to the Internet, the implication is that groups of people, especially if they are like-minded, will end up thinking the same thing that they thought before—but in more extreme form.

Consider some examples of this basic phenomenon, which has been found in over a dozen nations.[3] (a) After discussion, citizens of France become more critical of the United States and its intentions with respect to economic aid. (b) After discussion, whites predisposed to show racial prejudice offer more negative responses to questions about whether white racism is responsible for conditions faced by African Americans in American cities. (c) After discussion, whites predisposed not to show racial prejudice offer more positive responses to the same question.

(d) A group of moderately profeminist women will become more strongly profeminist after discussion. It follows that, for example, after discussion with one another, those inclined to think that President Clinton was a crook will be quite convinced of this point; that those inclined to favor more aggressive affirmative action programs will become more extreme on the issue if they talk among one another; that those who believe that tax rates are too high will, after talking together, come to think that large, immediate tax reductions are an extremely good idea.

The phenomenon of group polarization has conspicuous importance to the current communications market, where groups with distinctive identities increasingly engage in within-group discussion. If the public is balkanized, and if different groups design their own preferred communications packages, the consequence will be further balkanization, as group members move one another toward more extreme points in line with their initial tendencies. At the same time, different deliberating groups, each consisting of like-minded people, will be driven increasingly far apart, simply because most of their discussions are with one another....

25 Group polarization is a human regularity, but social context can decrease, increase, or even eliminate it. For present purposes, the most important point is that group polarization will significantly increase if people think of themselves, antecedently or otherwise, as part of a group having a shared identity and a degree of solidarity. If, for example, a group of people in an Internet discussion group think of themselves as opponents of high taxes, or advocates of animal rights, their discussions are likely to move toward extreme positions. As this happens to many different groups, polarization is both more likely and more extreme. Hence significant movements should be expected for those who listen to a radio show known to be conservative, or a television program dedicated to traditional religious values or to exposing white racism.

This should not be surprising. If ordinary findings of group polarization are a product of limited argument pools and social influences, it stands to reason that when group members think of one another as similar along a salient dimension, or if some external factor (politics, geography, race, sex) unites them, group polarization will be heightened.

Group polarization is occurring every day on the Internet. Indeed, it is clear that the Internet is serving, for many, as a breeding ground for extremism, precisely because like-minded people are deliberating with one another, without hearing contrary views. Hate groups are the most obvious example. Consider one extremist group, the so-called Unorganized Militia, the armed wing of the Patriot movement, "which believes that the federal government is becoming increasingly dictatorial with its regulatory power over taxes, guns and land use." A crucial factor behind the growth of the Unorganized Militia "has been the use of computer networks," allowing members "to make contact quickly and easily with like-minded individuals to trade information, discuss current conspiracy theories, and organize events."[4] The Unorganized Militia has a large number of websites, and those sites frequently offer links to related sites. It is clear that websites are being used to recruit new members and to allow like-minded people to speak with one another and to reinforce or strengthen existing convictions. It is also clear that the Internet is playing a crucial role in permitting people who would otherwise feel isolated and move on to something else to band together and spread rumors, many of them paranoid and hateful....

Balkanization is a term that is used to describe small-scale independence movements that divide countries into several separate nations. It emerged as a way to describe that process in the Balkan region of Europe. The term has come to be used more widely to describe any process of fragmentation.

CONTEXT

It has been estimated that more than 400 militia groups are active in the United States. Many of them promote violence against specific racial, ethnic, and religious groups. Some are open, with their own websites; others are underground. Some militia groups have been associated with terrorist attacks within the United States. Militia members, many of whom are on the extreme right, tend to see themselves as patriots. The FBI considers them a threat to national security.

Of course we cannot say, from the mere fact of polarization, that there has been a movement in the *wrong* direction. Perhaps the more extreme tendency is better; indeed, group polarization is likely to have fueled many movements of great value, including the movement for civil rights, the antislavery movement, the movement for sex equality. All of these movements were extreme in their time, and within-group discussion bred greater extremism; but extremism need not be a word of opprobrium. If greater communications choices produce greater extremism, society may, in many cases, be better off as a result.

But when group discussion tends to lead people to more strongly held versions of the same view with which they began, and if social influences and limited argument pools are responsible, there is legitimate reason for concern. Consider discussions among hate groups on the Internet and elsewhere. If the underlying views are unreasonable, it makes sense to fear that these discussions may fuel increasing hatred and a socially corrosive form of extremism. This does not mean that the discussions can or should be regulated. But it does raise questions about the idea that "more speech" is necessarily an adequate remedy—especially if people are increasingly able to wall themselves off from competing views.

30 The basic issue here is whether something like a "public sphere," with a wide range of voices, might not have significant advantages over a system in which isolated consumer choices produce a highly fragmented speech market. The most reasonable conclusion is that it is extremely important to ensure that people are exposed to views other than those with which they currently agree, that doing so protects against the harmful effects of group polarization on individual thinking and on social cohesion. This does not mean that the government should jail or fine people who refuse to listen to others. Nor is what I have said inconsistent with approval of deliberating "enclaves," on the Internet or elsewhere,

designed to ensure that positions that would otherwise be silenced or squelched have a chance to develop. Readers will be able to think of their own preferred illustrations. Consider, perhaps, the views of people with disabilities. The great benefit of such enclaves is that positions may emerge that otherwise would not and that deserve to play a large role in the heterogeneous public. Properly understood, the case of "enclaves," or more simply discussion groups of like-minded people, is that they will improve social deliberation, democratic and otherwise. For these improvements to occur, members must not insulate themselves from competing positions, or at least any such attempts at insulation must not be a prolonged affair.

Consider in this light the ideal of "consumer sovereignty," which underlies much of contemporary enthusiasm for the Internet. Consumer sovereignty means that people can choose to purchase, or to obtain, whatever they want. For many purposes this is a worthy ideal. But the adverse effects of group polarization show that, with respect to communications, consumer sovereignty is likely to produce serious problems for individuals and society at large—and these problems will occur by a kind of iron logic of social interactions. . . .

I hope that I have shown enough to demonstrate that for citizens of a heterogeneous democracy, a fragmented communications market creates considerable dangers. There are dangers for each of us as individuals; constant exposure to one set of views is likely to lead to errors and confusions, or to unthinking conformity (emphasized by John Stuart Mill). And to the extent that the process makes people less able to work cooperatively on shared problems, by turning collections of people into non-communicating confessional groups, there are dangers for society as a whole.

Common Experiences

In a heterogeneous society, it is extremely important for diverse people to have a set of common experiences.[5] Many of our practices reflect a judgment to this effect. National holidays, for example, help constitute a nation, by encouraging citizens to think, all at once, about events of shared importance. And they do much more than this. They enable people, in all their diversity, to have certain memories and attitudes in common. At least this is true in nations where national holidays have a vivid and concrete meaning. In the United States, many national holidays have become mere days-off-from-work, and the precipitating occasion—President's Day, Memorial Day, Labor Day—has come to be nearly invisible. This is a serious loss. With the possible exception of the Fourth of July, Martin Luther King Day is probably the closest thing to a genuinely substantive national holiday, largely because that celebration involves something that can be treated as concrete and meaningful—in other words, it is *about something*.

Communications and the media are, of course, exceptionally important here. Sometimes millions of people follow the presidential election, or the Super Bowl, or the coronation of a new monarch; many of them do so because of the simultaneous actions of others. The point very much bears on the historic role of both public forums and general interest intermediaries. Public parks are places where diverse people can congregate and see one another. General interest intermediaries, if they are operating properly, give a simultaneous sense of problems and tasks.

35 Why are these shared experiences so desirable? There are three principal reasons:

1. Simple enjoyment is probably the least of it, but it is far from irrelevant. People like many experiences more simply because they are being shared. Consider a popular movie, the Super Bowl, or a presidential debate. For many of us, these are goods that are worth less, and possibly worthless, if many others are not enjoying or purchasing them too. Hence a presidential debate may be worthy of individual attention, for many people, simply because so many other people consider it worthy of individual attention.

2. Sometimes shared experiences ease social interactions, permitting people to speak with one another, and to congregate around a common issue, task, or concern, whether or not they have much in common with one another. In this sense they provide a form of social glue. They help make it possible for diverse people to believe that they live in the same culture. Indeed they help constitute that shared culture, simply by creating common memories and experiences, and a sense of common tasks.

3. A fortunate consequence of shared experiences—many of them produced by the media—is that people who would otherwise see one another as unfamiliar can come to regard one another as fellow citizens, with shared hopes, goals, and concerns. This is a subjective good for those directly involved. But it can be objectively good as well, especially if it leads to cooperative projects of various kinds. When people learn about a disaster faced by fellow citizens, for example, they may respond with financial and other help. The point applies internationally as well as domestically; massive relief efforts are often made possible by virtue of the fact that millions of people learn, all at once, about the relevant need.

How does this bear on the Internet? An increasingly fragmented communications universe will reduce the level of shared experiences having salience to a diverse group of Americans. This is a simple matter of numbers. When there were three television networks, much of what appeared would have the quality of a genuinely common experience. The lead story on the evening news, for example, would provide a common reference point for many millions of people. To the extent that choices proliferate, it is inevitable that diverse individuals, and diverse groups, will have fewer shared experiences and fewer common reference points. It is possible, for example, that some events that are highly salient to some people will barely register on others' viewscreens. And it is possible that some views and perspectives that seem obvious for many people will, for others, seem barely intelligible.

This is hardly a suggestion that everyone should be required to watch the same thing. A degree of plurality, with respect to both topics and points of view, is highly desirable. Moreover, talk about "requirements" misses the point. My only claim is that a common set of frameworks and experiences is valuable for a heterogeneous society, and that a system with limitless options, making for diverse choices, could compromise the underlying values.

Changing Filters

My goal here has been to understand what makes for a well-functioning system of free expression, and to show how consumer sovereignty, in a world of limitless options, could undermine that system. The point is that a well-functioning system includes a kind of public sphere, one that fosters common experiences, in which people hear messages that challenge their prior convictions, and in which citizens can present their views to a broad audience. I do not intend to offer a comprehensive set of policy reforms or any kind of blueprint for the future. In fact, this may be one domain in which a problem exists for which there is no useful cure: the genie might simply be out of the bottle. But it will be useful to offer a few ideas, if only by way of introduction to questions that are likely to engage public attention in coming years.

In thinking about reforms, it is important to have a sense of the problems we aim to address, and some possible ways of addressing them. If the discussion thus far is correct,

there are three fundamental concerns from the democratic point of view. These include:

(a) the need to promote exposure to materials, topics, and positions that people would not have chosen in advance, or at least enough exposure to produce a degree of understanding and curiosity;

(b) the value of a range of common experiences;

(c) the need for exposure to substantive questions of policy and principle, combined with a range of positions on such questions.

Of course it would be ideal if citizens were demanding, and private information providers were creating, a range of initiatives designed to alleviate the underlying concerns. Perhaps they will; there is some evidence to this effect. New technology can expose people to diverse points of view and creates opportunities for shared experiences. People may, through private choices, take advantage of these possibilities. But, to the extent that they fail to do so, it is worthwhile to consider private and public initiatives designed to pick up the slack.

40 Drawing on recent developments in regulation generally, we can see the potential appeal of five simple alternatives. Of course, different proposals would work better for some communications outlets than others. I will speak here of both private and public responses, but the former should be favored: they are less intrusive, and in general they are likely to be more effective as well.

Disclosure: Producers of communications might disclose important information on their own, about the extent to which they are promoting democratic goals. To the extent that they do not, they might be subject to disclosure requirements (though not to regulation). In the environmental area, this strategy has produced excellent results. The mere fact that polluters have been asked to disclose toxic releases has produced voluntary, low-cost reductions. Apparently fearful of public opprobrium, companies have been spurred to reduce toxic emissions on their own. The same strategy has been used in the context of both movies and television, with ratings systems designed partly to increase parental control over what children see. On the Internet, many sites disclose that their site is inappropriate for children. . . .

Self-Regulation: Producers of communications might engage in *voluntary self-regulation.* Some of the difficulties in the current speech market stem from relentless competition for viewers and listeners, competition that leads to a situation that many broadcast journalists abhor about their profession, and from which society does not benefit. The competition might be reduced via a "code" of appropriate conduct, agreed upon by various companies, and encouraged but not imposed by government. In fact, the National Association of Broadcasters maintained such a code for several decades, and there is growing interest in voluntary self-regulation for both television and the Internet. The case for this approach is that it avoids government regulation while at the same time reducing some of the harmful effects of market pressures. Any such code could, for example, call for an opportunity for opposing views to speak, or for avoiding unnecessary sensationalism, or for offering arguments rather than quick soundbites whenever feasible. On television, as distinct from the Internet, the idea seems quite feasible. But perhaps Internet sites could also enter into informal, voluntary arrangements, agreeing to create links, an idea to which I will shortly turn.

Subsidy: The government might *subsidize speech,* as, for example, through publicly subsidized programming or publicly subsidized websites. This is, of course, the idea that motivates the Public Broadcasting System. But it is reasonable to ask whether the PBS model is not outmoded. Other approaches, similarly designed to promote educational, cultural,

> **CONTEXT**
>
> The Corporation for Public Broadcasting was created by Congress in 1967. According to its mission statement, "The fundamental purpose of public telecommunications is to provide programs and services which inform, enlighten and enrich the public. While these programs and services are provided to enhance the knowledge, and citizenship of all Americans, the Corporation has particular responsibility to encourage the development of programming that involves creative risks and that addresses the needs of unserved or underserved audiences, particularly children and minorities." It has broadcast many popular programs, including *Sesame Street, Nova, Masterpiece Theater,* and the *PBS NewsHour.* It has also been the subject of criticism by conservatives who believe that PBS reflects a liberal bias in its programming. Over the past decade, some members of Congress have tried to eliminate federal funding for PBS.

and democratic goals, might well be ventured. Perhaps government could subsidize a "Public. net" designed to promote debate on public issues among diverse citizens—and to create a right of access to speakers of various sorts.[6]

Links: Websites might use links and hyperlinks to ensure that viewers learn about sites containing opposing views. A liberal magazine's website might, for example, provide a link to a conservative magazine's website, and the conservative magazine might do the same. The idea would be to decrease the likelihood that people will simply hear echoes of their own voices. Of course many people would not click on the icons of sites whose views seem objectionable; but some people would, and in that sense the system would not operate so differently from general interest intermediaries and public forums. Here, too, the ideal situation would be voluntary action. But if this proves impossible, it is worth considering both subsidies and regulatory alternatives.

45 Public Sidewalk: If the problem consists in the failure to attend to public issues, the most popular websites in any given period might offer links and hyperlinks, designed to ensure more exposure to substantive questions. Under such a system, viewers of especially popular sites would see an icon for sites that deal with substantive issues in a serious way. It is well established that whenever there is a link to a particular webpage from a major site, such as MSNBC, the traffic is huge. Nothing here imposes any requirements on viewers. People would not be required to click on links and hyperlinks. But it is reasonable to expect that many viewers would do so, if only to satisfy their curiosity. The result would be to create a kind of Internet "sidewalk" that promotes some of the purposes of the public forum doctrine. Ideally, those who create websites might move in this direction on their own. To those who believe that this step would do no good, it is worth recalling that advertisers are willing to spend a great deal of money to obtain brief access to people's eyeballs. This strategy might be used to create something like a public sphere as well.

These are brief thoughts on some complex subjects. My goal has not been to evaluate any proposal in detail, but to give a flavor of some possibilities for those concerned to promote democratic goals in a dramatically changed media environment.[7] The basic question is whether it might be possible to create spaces that have some of the functions of public forums and general interest intermediaries in the age of the Internet. It seems clear that government's power to regulate effectively is diminished as the number of options expands. I am not sure that any response would be worthwhile, all things considered. But I am sure that if new technologies diminish the number of common spaces, and reduce, for many, the number of unanticipated, unchosen exposures, something important will have been lost. The most important point is to have a sense of what a well-functioning democratic order requires.

Beyond Anticensorship

My principal claim here has been that a well-functioning democracy depends on far more than restraints on official censorship of controversial ideas and opinions. It also depends on some kind of public sphere, in which a wide range of speakers have access to a diverse public—and also to particular institutions, and practices, against which they seek to launch objections.

Emerging technologies, including the Internet, are hardly an enemy here. They hold out far more promise than risk, especially because they allow people to widen their horizons. But to the extent that they weaken the power of general interest intermediaries and increase people's ability to wall themselves off from topics and opinions that they would prefer to avoid, they create serious dangers. And if we believe that a system of free expression calls for unrestricted choices by individual consumers, we will not even understand the dangers as such. Whether such dangers will materialize will ultimately depend on the aspirations, for freedom and democracy alike, by whose light we evaluate our practices. What I have sought to establish here is that in a free republic, citizens aspire to a system that provides a wide range of experiences—with people, topics, and ideas—that would not have been selected in advance.

NOTES

1. *Hague v. CIO*, 307 US 496 (1939).
2. I draw here on the excellent treatment in Noah D. Zatz, "Sidewalks in Cyberspace: Making Space for Public Forums in the Electronic Environment," *Harvard Journal of Law and Technology* 12 (1998): 149.
3. For a general discussion, see Cass R. Sunstein, "Deliberative Trouble? Why Groups Go To Extremes," *Yale Law Journal* (2000).
4. See Matthew Zook, "The Unorganized Militia Network: Conspiracies, Computers, and Community," *Berkeley Planning Journal* 11 (1996), available at http://socrates.berkeley.edu/zook/pubs/Militia_paper.html.
5. I draw here on Cass R. Sunstein and Edna Ullmann-Margalit, "Solidarity Goods," *Journal of Political Philosophy* (forthcoming in 2001).
6. See Andrew Shapiro, *The Control Revolution* (New York: Basic Books, 1999).
7. See Sunstein, Republic.com, for more detail.

Questions for Discussion

1. Early in his essay, Sunstein raises a warning about what he calls the "personalization" of the Internet. What does he mean by that term? Why is that idea of personalizing the Internet important to his main argument? Is his concern valid, in your view? Why or why not? To what extent do you think you "personalize" the Internet?

2. Notice that Sunstein opens his essay with a summary of the benefits of the Internet. How does this opening contribute to his main argument? What advantages and disadvantages do you see to this approach to opening his essay?

3. What is the public forum doctrine? Why is it important, in Sunstein's view? How does it fit into his main argument about the Internet?

4. In paragraphs 24–29, Sunstein discussed the dangers of "group polarization." What does Sunstein mean by this term? In what ways is it important to his main argument? Have you experienced a situation in which group discussion led to reinforcement—or change—of a belief you already had? How might that experience influence your reaction to Sunstein's argument?

5. Sunstein offers five possible solutions to the problems he sees with current trends in media. How effective do you think these measures would be in addressing Sunstein's concerns? What does he achieve by presenting these measures as possibilities rather than certainties?

6. Although Sunstein describes this argument as "brief thoughts on some complex subjects," it nevertheless runs for many pages. Why is this argument so long? What strategies does Sunstein use to organize his argument and to help readers make their way through it? Do you find those strategies effective? Explain.

7. At the end of his argument, Sunstein writes, "My principal claim here has been that a well-functioning democracy depends on far more than restraints on official censorship of controversial ideas and opinions. It also depends on some kind of public sphere, in which a wide range of speakers have access to a diverse public—and also to particular institutions, and practices, against which they seek to launch objections." To what extent does the argument as a whole depend on readers accepting this principle as a premise?

8. Sunstein's essay might be described as an argument based on inductive reasoning. (See pages 80–81 for a discussion of arguments based on inductive reasoning.) How effective do you think his essay is as such an argument? Does he offer sufficient evidence to lead you to his conclusions about the Internet as a public sphere in a democracy? Explain, citing specific passages from his essay in your answer.

② The Revolution Will Not Be Digitized

FARHAD MANJOO

The title of this essay is a reference to the 1971 song by poet and singer-songwriter Gil Scott-Heron, "The Revolution Will Not Be Televised." The song is a critique of television that included references to many TV commercials that would have been familiar to viewers in the late 1960s and early 1970s. It criticizes television as escapist:

> You will not be able to lose yourself on skag and skip,
>
> Skip out for beer during commercials,
>
> Because the revolution will not be televised.

And it ends with the warning, "The revolution will be no re-run, brothers. The revolution will be live." It was a song that reflected the concerns of many Americans of that era about the growing importance of television in American culture, and it captured some of the revolutionary spirit that was associated with the Civil Rights Movement, the protests against the Vietnam War, and the growing counter-culture in American society. Keep that reference in mind as you read the following essay by writer Farhad Manjoo, who updates the term *televised* to *digitized*. Writers like Scott-Heron may have had legitimate worries about the influence of television in the 1970s, but Manjoo argues that we may have more to worry about today when it comes to how new digital technologies can be used to control ideas, information, and people. He focuses on the uses of social media during the violent crackdown on protesters in Iran after that nation's presidential elections in 2009, but his argument is about digital media in general. He raises important questions about how these media are being used today—and how they might be used in the future. Farhad Manjoo is the technology columnist for the online magazine *Slate*, where this essay was first published in June, 2009.

FARHAD MANJOO, "The Revolution Will Not Be Digitized"

Tiananmen is a reference to the pro-democracy protests that occurred in Tiananmen Square in Beijing, China, in 1989, which ended when the Chinese government called in the army to suppress the protests. The government action left several thousand Chinese citizens dead.

1 What happened in Baharestan Square on Wednesday? According to a woman who called in to CNN, Iranian security forces unleashed unimaginable brutality upon a few hundred protesters gathered in central Tehran. "They beat a woman so savagely that she was drenched in blood, and her husband, who was watching the scene, he just fainted," the anonymous caller screamed into the phone. "This was—this was exactly a massacre. You should stop this. You should stop this. You should help the people of Iran who demand freedom. You should help us."

Clips of the phone call ricocheted across the Web and cable TV. The message was corroborated on Twitter, where a post by @persiankiwi brought horrific news from Baharestan Square: "we saw militia with axe choping ppl like meat—blood everywhere—like butcher—Allah Akbar." News organizations around the world told of a brutal crackdown—Iran's **Tiananmen**. But at the same time, other reports suggested the rally was a far tamer encounter. A reader on the *New York Times*' Lede blog wrote in to say that the protest had been cleared by security forces with minimal violence. The blog of the National Iranian American Council, which has been closely following all the news out of Tehran, published a report from a "trusted source" who said that while the rally was "tense," it didn't match the CNN caller's account. "The moment we stood in one place, they would break us up," the source wrote. "I saw many people get blindfolded and arrested, however it wasn't a massacre."

Over the last couple of weeks, those who believe in the transformative powers of technology have pointed to Iran as a test case—one of the first repressive regimes to meet its match in social media, the first revolution powered by Twitter. Even in the early days of the protest, that story line seemed more hopeful than true, as *Slate*'s Jack Shafer, among many others, pointed out. Since last week, though, when the state began to systematically clamp down on journalists and all communications networks leading out of the country, hope has become much harder to sustain. The conflicting accounts about what happened at Baharestan Square are evidence that Iran's media crackdown is working. The big story in Iran is confusion—on a daily basis, there are more questions than answers about what's really happening, about who's winning and losing, about what comes next. The surprise isn't that technology has given protesters a new voice. It's that, despite all the tech, they've been effectively silenced.

The crackdown in Iran shows that, for regimes bent on survival, squashing electronic dissent isn't impossible. In many ways, modern communication tools are easier to suppress than organizing methods of the past. According to the *Wall Street Journal*, Iran has one of the world's most advanced surveillance

networks. Using a system installed last year (and built, in part, by Nokia and Siemens), the government routes all digital traffic in the country through a single choke point. Through "**deep packet inspection**," the regime achieves omniscience—it has the technical capability to monitor every e-mail, tweet, blog post, and possibly even every phone call placed in Iran. Compare that with East Germany, in which the **Stasi** managed to tap, at most, about 100,000 phone lines—a gargantuan task that required 2,000 full-time technicians to monitor the calls. The Stasi's work force comprised 100,000 officers, and estimates put its network of citizen informants at half a million. In the digital age, Iran can monitor its citizens with a far smaller security apparatus. They can listen in on everything anyone says—and shut down anything inconvenient—with the flip of a switch.

5 We've seen the effects of this control over the past couple days. To be sure, a few harrowing pictures and videos have filtered through Iran's closed net. But they're the exceptions; much of what's happened since the start of the week went undocumented. As **the Lede** points out, many of the clips now

CONTEXT

In June 2009, thousands of people in Iran and in other nations protested the results of the Iranian presidential election. After the official Iranian news agency announced on June 13, 2009, that incumbent president Mahmoud Ahmadinejad had won the election, supporters of the other candidates charged that the official election results were fraudulent and began daily protests in many Iranian cities, including Tehran, where they gathered in the city's Baharestan Square. The protests continued for several weeks, during which the Iranian government began to respond with force. In paragraph 1, Manjoo refers to a particularly brutal crackdown on the protests by Iranian police that took place in Baharestan Square on June 25th. Protesters and other eyewitnesses sent information and video clips of the events through their cell phones, and many of them used social media, including Twitter, Facebook, and YouTube, to share information about what was happening. Although the government crackdown, which left dozens of people dead (the exact number is in dispute) and led to the arrests of thousands of Iranian citizens, suppressed the protests, many protesters continued to hold smaller rallies for months after the election and used social media to communicate their concerns to the rest of the world.

Deep packet inspection is a process by which information and communication on the Internet can be examined according to specific criteria set by a computer system administrator. This process allows Internet traffic to be monitored and is used by government agencies and businesses for surveillance, Internet data-mining, and other purposes.

The Stasi was the common term for the Ministry for State Security in East Germany before it was reunified with West Germany in 1990. The Stasi was feared by East German citizens because of its extensive network of surveillance and its brutal repression of protest and dissent.

The Lede is a blog devoted to current news on the *New York Times* website.

being posted to YouTube were first published last week, before Iran shut down its connections with the outside world. In the absence of fresh videos coming out of the country, people have been attaching new dates to old clips in order to stoke new outrage over the security crackdown.

The dearth of new images isn't surprising. The Internet is not anonymous; in places like Iran and China, whatever you do on the Web can be traced back to your computer. Hackers and activists have come up with many clever ways to elude such monitoring, but for most citizens, posting videos and even tweeting eyewitness accounts remains fraught with peril.

There's another problem with expecting digital movements to overthrow repressive governments. Organizing online—using tools like text messaging, Facebook, and Twitter—requires social trust, a commodity in short supply in a police state. Even in America, we've seen movements that look mighty online fizzle when they hit the ground

(see Howard Dean). Imagine how much more difficult this would be if you were sitting in Tehran: You come across a tweet alerting you to a rally this afternoon in Baharestan Square. You'd like to go, but all kinds of fears begin to run through your head. *What if they're watching me? Is this rally for real—or is it disinformation? What if I'm the only one to show up?*

Other than trying to shut down many parts of the Web, we don't know what, precisely, Iranian security forces have done in response to the online protest movement. It's unclear whether they've actually planted disinformation online or tried to trace images and videos back to their original posters. But the uncertainty itself breeds fear. Several times over the last couple weeks, rumors have flooded the Web that the government had already gotten wise to Twitter and was actively seeding the movement with fake news. It was a stark example of how the psychological repression characteristic of authoritarian regimes—the constant fear, the inability to trust anyone—finds particularly fertile ground online.

Here's another one: On Wednesday, a reader alerted the Lede to an Iranian government Website called Gerdab.ir, where authorities had posted pictures of protesters and were asking citizens for help in identifying the activists. That's right—the regime is now using crowd-sourcing, one of the most-hyped aspects of Web 2.0 organizing, against its opponents. If you think about it, that's no surprise. Who said that only the good guys get to use the power of the Web to their advantage?

CONTEXT

During the 2004 U.S. presidential election, Governor Howard Dean of Vermont, a Democratic candidate for president, was praised for using the Internet to organize support and raise funds for his campaign. His use of the Internet was described as revolutionary at the time, but as Manjoo suggests in paragraph 7, his candidacy ended unsuccessfully despite his use of digital media, which led some critics to raise questions about the impact of digital media on political elections. During the 2008 presidential campaign, candidate Barack Obama was credited with using digital media creatively to generate enthusiasm and facilitate communication among his supporters and volunteers, prompting some observers to argue that a new era of political campaigning had arrived.

Questions for Discussion

1. Manjoo wrote this essay while the protests in Iran were still occurring, and he admits that "there are more questions than answers about what's really happening" (par. 3). How does the lack of accurate information about the protests affect his argument?

2. Manjoo rests his argument in large part on the example of the protests that occurred after the presidential election in Iran in June 2009. How appropriate is this example for his argument? How effectively does he use this example to support his main point about digital media?

3. What evidence does Manjoo provide to support his claim that digital technologies can be more easily suppressed by governments than communication techniques used in the past? How convincing is this evidence? What counterarguments can you make to Manjoo's claim?

4. How can governments use digital media for "psychological repression" (par. 8), according to Manjoo? What does this use of digital media suggest to him about the power of these media? Do you think he's right? Why or why not?

5. This essay might be considered an example of an argument based on inductive reasoning (see pages 80–81). How effectively do you think Manjoo reasons from the examples he cites to arrive at his conclusions about digital media? Do you see any weaknesses in his use of this approach to argumentation? Explain, citing specific passages from his essay to support your answer.

③ Why Gen-Y Johnny Can't Read Non-Verbal Cues

MARK BAUERLEIN

If you are a traditional-age college student—that is, between the ages of about 18 and 22—you are a member of Generation Y, a term used to refer to people born between the mid-1970s and the 2000s. That means, according to some social scientists, that you are a multitasker—someone who is comfortable doing several things at once, such as watching a television show while surfing the Internet or sending a text message. You are also someone who grew up with new digital technologies, such as cell phones and social media, that seem to encourage this kind of multitasking, and they are a central part of how you communicate. That worries Mark Bauerlein, a professor of English at Emory University and author of *The Dumbest Generation: How the Digital Age Stupefies Young Americans and Jeopardizes Our Future* (2008). As he explains in the following essay, Bauerlein believes that people who rely on digital technologies for communication, such as text messaging, e-mail, and social media like Facebook, do not develop the full range of communication skills required to function effectively in various social settings. In his view, such people lack the ability to understand and respond appropriately to nonverbal cues and varied social contexts; when it comes to this important kind of communication, he writes, Gen Yers "are all thumbs." If you are a member of Generation Y, you may not share Bauerlein's concerns about the impact of new digital technologies on how we communicate to one another. But his essay, which appeared in the *Wall Street Journal* in September 2009, raises interesting questions about how technology can shape the way we interact and whether we should pay closer attention to its impact.

MARK BAUERLEIN, "Why Gen-Y Johnny Can't Read Non-Verbal Cues"

Nielsen Mobile is part of the Nielsen Company, an international corporation that describes itself as "the world's leading marketing and media information company."

Edward T. Hall (1914–2009) was an influential American anthropologist who studied cross-cultural communication and nonverbal communication, which he explored in his book *The Silent Language* (1973).

1 In September 2008, when **Nielsen Mobile** announced that teenagers with cellphones each sent and received, on average, 1,742 text messages a month, the number sounded high, but just a few months later Nielsen raised the tally to 2,272. A year earlier, the National School Boards Association estimated that middle- and high-school students devoted an average of nine hours to social networking each week. Add email, blogging, IM, tweets and other digital customs and you realize what kind of hurried, 24/7 communications system young people experience today.

Unfortunately, nearly all of their communication tools involve the exchange of written words alone. At least phones, cellular and otherwise, allow the transmission of tone of voice, pauses and the like. But even these clues are absent in the text-dependent world. Users insert smiley-faces into emails, but they don't see each others' actual faces. They read comments on Facebook, but they don't "read" each others' posture, hand gestures, eye movements, shifts in personal space and other nonverbal—and expressive—behaviors.

Back in 1959, anthropologist **Edward T. Hall** labeled these expressive human attributes "the Silent Language." Hall passed away last month in Santa Fe at age 95, but his writings on nonverbal communication deserve continued attention. He argued that body language, facial expressions and stock mannerisms function "in juxtaposition to words," imparting feelings, attitudes, reactions and judgments in a different register.

This is why, Hall explained, U.S. diplomats could enter a foreign country fully competent in the native language and yet still flounder from one miscommunication to another, having failed to decode the manners, gestures and subtle protocols that go along with words. And how could they, for the "silent language" is acquired through acculturation, not schooling. Not only is it unspoken; it is largely unconscious. The meanings that pass through it remain implicit, more felt than understood.

5 They are, however, operative. Much of our social and workplace lives runs on them. For Hall, breakdowns in nonverbal communication took place most damagingly in cross-cultural circumstances—for instance, federal workers dealing with Navajo Indians and misconstruing their basic conceptions of time. Within cultures, Hall assumed, people more or less "spoke" the same silent language.

They may no longer, thanks to the avalanche of all-verbal communication. In Silicon Valley itself, as the *Los Angeles Times* reported last year, some companies have installed the "topless" meeting—in which not only laptops but iPhones and other tools are banned—to combat a new problem: "continuous partial attention." With a device close by, attendees at workplace meetings simply cannot keep their focus on the speaker. It's too easy to check email, stock quotes and Facebook. While a quick log-on may seem, to the user, a harmless break, others in the room receive it as a silent dismissal. It announces: "I'm not interested." So the tools must now remain at the door.

Older employees might well accept such a ban, but younger ones might not understand it. Reading a text message in the middle of a conversation isn't a lapse to them—it's what you do. It has, they assume, no nonverbal meaning to anyone else.

It does, of course, but how would they know it? We live in a culture where young people—outfitted with iPhone and laptop and devoting hours every evening from age 10 onward to messaging of one kind and another—are ever less likely to develop the "silent fluency" that comes from face-to-face interaction. It is a skill that we all must learn, in actual social settings, from people (often older) who are adept in the idiom. As text-centered messaging increases, such occasions diminish. The digital natives improve their adroitness at the keyboard, but when it comes to their capacity to "read" the behavior of others, they are all thumbs.

Nobody knows the extent of the problem. It is too early to assess the effect of digital habits, and the tools change so quickly that research can't keep up with them. By the time investigators design a study, secure funding, collect results and publish them, the technology has changed and the study is outdated.

COMPLICATION

Marc Prensky, an education consultant and self-described futurist, is sometimes credited with coining the term "digital natives" to refer to people who have grown up in an environment rich with digital technologies. Prensky writes,

> Today's students have not just changed *incrementally* from those of the past, nor simply changed their slang, clothes, body adornments, or styles, as has happened between generations previously. A really big *discontinuity* has taken place. One might even call it a "singularity"—an event which changes things so fundamentally that there is absolutely no going back. This so-called "singularity" is the arrival and rapid dissemination of digital technology in the last decades of the 20th century....

> It is now clear that as a result of this ubiquitous environment and the sheer volume of their interaction with it, today's students *think and process information fundamentally differently* from their predecessors. These differences go far further and deeper than most educators suspect or realize.... [I]it is very likely that *our students' brains have physically changed*—and are different from ours—as a result of how they grew up.

SOURCE: "Digital Natives, Digital Immigrants," *On the Horizon*, 2001.

Generation Y refers generally to people born between the mid-1970s and the early 2000s. Also referred to as "Millennials" or "Echo Boomers," people of Generation Y are usually considered to be savvy when it comes to digital technologies, comfortable with multitasking, and culturally more tolerant than previous generations.

10 Still, we might reasonably pose questions about silent-language acquisition in a digital environment. Lots of folks grumble about the diffidence, self-absorption and general uncommunicativeness of **Generation Y**. The next time they face a twenty-something who doesn't look them in the eye, who slouches and sighs for no apparent reason, who seems distracted and unaware of the rising frustration of the other people in the room, and who turns aside to answer a text message with glee and facility, they shouldn't think, "What a rude kid." Instead, they should show a little compassion and, perhaps, seize on a teachable moment. "Ah," they might think instead, "another texter who doesn't realize that he is communicating, right now, with every glance and movement—and that we're reading him all too well."

Questions for Discussion

1. Why is Bauerlein concerned that young people today communicate so extensively through text-based media, such as e-mail, text messages, and social media like Facebook? Do you think his concerns are valid? Why or why not?

2. What is the "silent language" that Bauerlein refers to in paragraphs 3 and 4? Why is this language significant, in his view? What does he mean that this language is "acquired through acculturation, not schooling" (par. 4)? How does that point fit into his main argument?

3. According to Bauerlein, using text-centered communication media, such as e-mail or text messaging, weakens the ability to communicate because it removes the need to learn how to understand nonverbal communication. Based on your own experience, do you think Bauerlein is right? Has your own experience with text-centered communication media weakened your ability to interact socially with others in any way? Explain.

4. Are there advantages to text-based communication that Bauerlein fails to recognize? In what ways might these advantages provide a counterargument to his position?

5. Bauerlein argues that young people who communicate extensively through text-based media lack the social experiences to enable them to "read" nonverbal cues, which he believes is a problem. But in paragraph 9 he writes, "Nobody knows the extent of the problem. It is too early to assess the effect of digital habits, and the tools change so quickly that research can't keep up with them." Do you think this admission weakens his main argument in any way? Explain.

6. This essay was originally published in the *Wall Street Journal*, a respected publication that focuses on business and economic news and is generally thought to reflect a conservative political viewpoint. What assumptions does Bauerlein seem to make about his audience? In what ways do you think Bauerlein's argument is appropriate for readers of the *Wall Street Journal*? How do you think members of "Generation Y" might react to his argument?

④ | The Daily Show and Political Activism

MEGAN BOLER

In 2007, the respected Pew Research Center for the People and the Press released a report indicating that for many "Generation Nexters," who are defined as people born between 1981–1988, *The Daily Show*, a parody of television news programs that is broadcast on the Comedy Central cable channel, is a trusted source of news. According to the report, 13 percent of Gen Nexters regularly view *The Daily Show*, compared to only 6 percent of the general population; moreover, only 10 percent of Gen Nexters regularly watch mainstream news programs on network television (ABC, NBC, and CBS). That means that more people between the ages of 18 and 25 are getting information about major news events from a comedy show than from regular television news programs. But *The Daily Show* isn't just a comedy program. It is a serious satire of contemporary media and American political and cultural life. As a result, mainstream news organizations pay attention to it. And as Megan Boler, a professor of media studies at the University of Toronto, points out in the following essay, there has been a vigorous debate about *The Daily Show* and what its growing influence as a source of information and political views might mean. Boler argues that satire plays an important role in contemporary political life, which may be one reason why satiric shows like *The Daily Show* can sometimes create such controversy; moreover, she sees an important role for online technologies in promoting alternative political viewpoints. Boler is associate chair of the Department of Theory and Policy Studies and coordinator of the History and Philosophy of Education program at the Ontario Institute of Studies in Education at the University of Toronto. This essay was originally published in 2007 in *Counterpunch*, a newsletter devoted to politics that describes itself as "muckraking with a radical attitude."

MEGAN BOLER, "The Daily Show and Political Activism"

1 The popular debate about whether Jon Stewart's *The Daily Show* is "bad for Americans" won't go away. Indeed, worries got so big that now FOX has launched a conservative antidote, "The _ Hour News Show" which premiered this week. Now streaming on YouTube, MSNBC's Joe Scarborough ran a piece featuring Daily Show clips and two pundits debating whether "therapeutic irony is rendering us politically impotent." Similar fears were fanned last year when news media had a fiesta with a questionable study by two academics which claimed that watching *The Daily Show* (TDS) breeds cynicism and lowers young voters' "trust in national leaders." In September, *The New York Times Magazine* ran a savvy piece called "My Satirical Self" about a generation of satire in which Wyatt Mason describes how "ridicule provides a remedy for his rage." In 2003 in an interview with Bill Moyers, Moyers asks Jon Stewart: "I do not know whether you are practicing an old form of parody and satire or a new form of journalism. Stewart replies: "Well then that either speaks to the sad state of comedy or the sad state of news. I can't figure out which one. I think, honestly, we're practicing a new form of desperation (July 2003, PBS).

CONTEXT

In the first two paragraphs Boler reviews the lively discussion in the popular press about the impact of the hit Comedy Central show *The Daily Show*. The debate about *The Daily Show*, which premiered in 1996 and which has been hosted by comedian Jon Stewart since 1999, intensified in 2007, when Boler wrote this essay, as many respected publications and mainstream news programs, which Boler mentions here, began to address the show's growing popularity and its reputation as a trustworthy news source. Various studies suggesting that the show contained as much news as mainstream network news programs fueled the debates about the show. Some critics charged that the show had a liberal bias, and Jon Stewart himself contributed to the debate by criticizing the mainstream media when he appeared on programs such as CNN's *Crossfire* (which Boler mentions in paragraph 13). The debates about *The Daily Show* have continued in the years since Boler's essay was published as the show's popularity continued to grow and Stewart became more vocal in his views of mainstream news media.

The Word is a popular segment on *The Colbert Report*, a satiric show on Comedy Central that parodies right-wing political talk shows such as *The O'Reilly Factor*. In "The Word," the host of the show, comedian Stephen Colbert, uses a word or phrase from the news to poke fun at politicians and others who are being covered in the mainstream press.

Fair-Use Shield of Parody The so-called fair use doctrine, which is part of copyright law in the United States, allows for the limited use of copyrighted material for legitimate purposes of research, scholarship, teaching, and commentary. This doctrine protects comedians and others who use copyrighted materials for the purposes of parody or satire.

But Courtney Martin's January 7 *Baltimore Sun* column touches on the plaguing question of satire's role in politics: "Satire, of course, has a long and proven history as the source of bona fide social change. Aristophanes' *Lysistrata*, Upton Sinclair's *The Jungle*, George Orwell's *Animal Farm*—all of these led to new public awareness that then led to protest, even some pragmatic reforms. Rebels distributed copies of *Animal Farm*, a novella satirizing totalitarianism, to displaced Soviets in Ukraine right after World War II."

However, she laments, TDS viewers are only chatting around the water cooler.

Such claims are not only too simple, but wrong: the court jesters of our dark times translate into far more than chit-chat.

First, the quality political satire of comedians and parodists such as Stewart and Colbert give airtime—and often longer segments of airtime—to topics largely unmentioned by any other media. On February 12, for example, Colbert devoted **The Word** to a story buried or unreported by almost all other news: the latest Defense Department report that evidences Defense Undersecretary **Douglas Feith**'s "pre-war report fabricating a link between Saddam and Al-Qaeda. Putting Al-Qaeda in Iraq may have taken some imagination back then, but thanks to inappropriateness [Feith] made it a reality." Colbert provided three-plus minutes of time to a crucial story of precisely how and who manipulated intelligence. Trust me: go google this report, and you find the briefest of coverage, beginning with a confusing and mealy-mouthed AP version, with most stories headlining Feith's self-defense rather than the critical report.

5 Second, because of the **fair-use shield of parody**, these court jesters can report on politicians' lies and corruption, as well as launch major critiques of media and press failures to hold politicians accountable.

Third, as my research shows, significant counterpublics have formed through web-based communities around such political material as TDS, which do translate into action.

Across our forty interviews with bloggers and online video producers as part of my research project "Rethinking Media and Democracy" funded by the Canadian Social Science and Humanities Research Council, we have discovered that web-based communities sparked by political commentary like *The Daily Show* are vibrant and translating into action. This past week, I interviewed an established blogger who began streaming TDS clips when his Macintosh wouldn't interface

Douglas Feith (b. 1953) served as undersecretary of Defense for Policy during the administration of President George W. Bush from 2001 to 2005. In 2003 he wrote a memo to Congress about apparent links between the Iraqi dictator Saddam Hussein and the terrorist group Al-Qaeda. These links were part of the Bush administration's justification for invading Iraq in 2002. In 2007 the Inspector General of the Pentagon issued a report criticizing Feith's office for its "inappropriate" actions in disseminating information about the possible link between Hussein and Al-Qaeda.

with the Comedy Central site, and decided it would be a service to other Mac users to post clips in Quicktime format. As a result, he unexpectedly began to get voluminous traffic from readers around the globe. I asked him if he thought that his site resulted in any action. It was a surprise to me to hear him report that in fact, as he learns from the ongoing conversations and comments posted on his website, that because of viewing and discussing *The Daily Show* many members of this progressive community have been led to activism. Another blogger was inspired to go join **Cindy Sheehan**'s protest in Crawford because of the conversations engaged through his *Daily Show* postings.

I admit that there are times when I share Martin's worry that we are laughing our way into doomsday. As she writes, "Laughing is inherently healing, and in a time of secret government contracts and State of the Union addresses given in fake Southern accents, we all need a little relief. But like comfort food consumed night after night in place of broccoli, we are gorging ourselves on what feels good instead of processing what feels so bad—and doing something about it. Other than voting, when was the last time you performed a political act more public than sending a link to *The Onion's* funniest new podcast to your old college roommates?"

But the evidence is rolling in to the contrary. Our survey of 160 producers evidences that 52 percent agree that, "My online political activity has caused me to take action in my local community (e.g., protest, boycott, etc.)." A majority, 59.5 percent, say that "My online participation in political forums has led me to join at least one political gathering or protest. Since becoming active online, 29.3% are "more active in 'offline' political activities," and 63.1% "spend about the same amount of time in 'offline' political activities."

10 The question is no longer a simple one of laughter vs. action, or online vs. offline. Similarly misleading is the headline and implication of Jennifer Earl's Washingtonpost.

com commentary (February 4 B01): "Where have all the protests gone? Online". This is simply not true. While the Internet is being used extensively for organizing, as our research shows online activists remain active offline—and more importantly, the protests against U.S. invasion of Iraq on January 27 were attended by hundreds of thousands (despite misrepresentation by hundreds of mainstream newspapers using the inaccurate AP assessment of the crowd as numbering in the "thousands").

It's no longer possible to separate popular perception, mainstream media agenda-setting, Washington electorate decisions, and the critical force of digital dissent including satire. The most sophisticated current scholarship on satire is Paul Lewis's 2006 book *Cracking Up*. Lewis describes, and my studies show as well, that *The Daily Show* writers (as well as most other political comedians, including Stephen Colbert) claim their agenda to be the laugh, and not politics. But Lewis offers the recent instance of the head writer of TDS countering the idea that satire "doesn't make a difference," citing the example of cartoonist **Thomas Nast** "bringing down one of America's first entrenched political rings [William Tweed's Tammany Hall group which ruled New York City from 1866 to 1871]."

We may not be able to trace an easy "cause and effect" (how do we even separate the producers from consumers in this golden age of user-generated content when all of us have been named person of the year by *Time* Magazine?). But there can be little doubt that satirists, bloggers, citizen journalists,

Cindy Sheehan (b. 1957) became well known as an activist against the war in Iraq after her son, Casey, was killed while serving there with the U.S. Army in 2004. Sheehan led several well-publicized and controversial protests, including one near a ranch owned by President George W. Bush in Crawford, Texas, where she and her protesters set up a tent city that they called "Camp Casey."

For information on **Thomas Nast**, see the sidebar on page 344.

and YouTube and other viral video producers around the world are taking action daily and dissenting from mainstream media agendas. Whether one traces the effects of Stewart on *Crossfire*, Colbert at the 2006 White House Press Correspondent's Dinner roasting George W. Bush in front of the President and the world, or blogs that broke the Trent Lott or Rathergate story, the counterpublics created through digital media are far more than water cooler talk.

In 2004, Jon Stewart's appearance on *Crossfire* lambasting corporate media for failing the public good was the top-cited media event in the blogosphere. What matters is that dissenting voices are being aired through increasingly broad and multiformat channels. Corporate-owned news and papers of record are being forced to watch their step by the 24/7 surveillance of a vibrant public demanding accountability.

The comedians may claim to be only interested in the laugh. But those who watch, think critically, and take numerous forms of action do come away each night with renewed political convictions—not least of which is to question a news media that too often fails in its responsibility to speak truth to power.

Questions for Discussion

1. In the opening paragraphs of this essay, Boler reviews the debate about *The Daily Show* and summarizes some of the criticisms of the show. Evaluate her overview of this debate. How clearly does she summarize the main points of this debate? How effectively does her overview of the debate set the stage for her own argument?

2. How does Boler respond to the main criticisms of *The Daily Show*? How effective do you find her response? How does her response to these criticisms help support her main argument about political satire?

3. Boler cites her own academic research as evidence to support her claims about the political importance of satiric programs such as *The Daily Show*. How well do you think her research supports her claims? Does the fact that she is a researcher with expertise in media strengthen or weaken her argument in any way? Explain.

4. What role does satire play in political life, according to Boler? Do you agree with her? Why or why not?

5. Based on this essay, how would you characterize Boler's own political perspective? Does her political perspective, as you understand it from this essay, influence your reaction to her argument? Explain.

6. Boler makes many references to news programs, comedians, writers, journalists, and various events that occurred in the past decade. How important are these references to her argument? Do you think her argument is less effective for readers who may be unfamiliar with these references? Explain, citing specific passages from her essay to support your answer.

DIFFERENCES

As the introduction to this cluster on page 385 indicates, there has been much discussion in recent years about the apparent lack of civility in public discourse and political debate in the United States. Similar concerns have been expressed about the way people talk to one another online—on discussion boards and in chat rooms, on blogs, in e-mails, and on social media such as Twitter and Facebook. In particular, parents and educators have grown increasingly concerned about what has come to be known as "cyberbullying"— that is, harassment that takes place online. In 2007, the Pew Internet and American Life Project, which conducts research on uses of the Internet and related digital media, released a study indicating that nearly a third of all teens who use the Internet reported they have been "targets of a range of annoying and potentially menacing online activities—such as receiving threatening messages; having their private e-mails or text messages forwarded without consent; having an embarrassing picture posted without permission; or having rumors about them spread online." As digital media, and especially social media such as Facebook and Twitter, become more widely used and more fully integrated into our social, political, and professional lives, it is likely that such problems will increase.

Understandably, many schools and parents have begun to take action to protect students not only from cyberbullying but also from other problems that can arise from online activities, such as identity theft. Some schools have implemented policies that stipulate specific penalties for students who harass one another online or who use the Internet inappropriately, and some states have even passed legislation making some kinds of online behavior illegal. But such policies raise difficult questions about whether schools have the authority over student behavior that might occur outside the school day or away from the school grounds. Do schools have the right to monitor student online behavior that has nothing to do with the school itself? Do policies against cyberbullying violate students' right to privacy? How far does a school's authority over students extend? Some court cases have addressed such questions, but because problems like cyberbullying are relatively new, there is a great deal of uncertainty about what schools can legally do when it comes to addressing these problems.

Imagine that officials in the school district in which you live (and perhaps attended school) have grown concerned about some instances of cyberbullying that have occurred among students in that district. As a result of complaints from parents and students, the district officials have decided to create a special committee to investigate the problem and make recommendations about how the district should respond. Officials are aware that the problem is complicated and that there are limits to what the school can do, and they have listened to parents who have expressed concerns about the school district "going too far" in trying to regulate the lives of its students. But officials are also fearful that cyberbullying is putting some of the district's students at serious risk, and they want to try to find a way to protect students.

As a resident of the district, you have been invited to be part of the committee, which has been given the following tasks:

1. Explore the problem of cyberbullying. How widespread is it? What does it involve? Who is likely to be affected by it? What causes it? Is it different from other kinds of bullying? Do online media, such as Facebook, make

DIFFERENCES

NEGOTIATING

the problem worse? Your research should result in a general sense of the nature and extent of the problem of cyberbullying.

2. Examine what other school districts have done. How have schools addressed the issue of cyberbullying? What kinds of policies or measures have been implemented? How have they worked? What questions have arisen about such policies and measures? What have the courts ruled about such policies and measures?

3. Make recommendations to the school district about what kind of policy (if any) it should adopt and justify that policy (or lack of one) on the basis of your research and your own beliefs about the issues involved. Your recommendations should take into account what you have learned about cyberbullying and what the experiences of other schools suggest about how to address

the problem. You should also take into account legal considerations, based on what the courts have ruled about school policies regarding cyberbullying.

On the basis of the work you have done to complete these three tasks, write a report for the school district in which you make recommendations about what your school district should do. In your report, describe the problem of cyberbullying, examine the issues involved, and explain the specific measures or policies that you believe your school district should adopt. Be sure to justify your recommendations. In other words, make an argument in favor of your recommendations. Your report should be addressed to an audience comprising school officials, students, and parents, as well as residents of your school district. Keep in mind that your purpose is to make a case for policies (or lack of policies) in order to try to solve the problem of cyberbullying among students in your district.

11

Education

Louise Gubb/Corbis SABA

Jose Luis Pelaez/Corbis

What Should Students Be Taught?

The question of what should be taught in schools is as old as formal education itself. In the United States the emergence of the public school in the nineteenth century was accompanied by intense debates about the nature and content of the curriculum. Some argued that schools should impart values as well as knowledge; others believed that schools should focus on teaching students the skills needed to be productive workers; still others saw schools as places where immigrants could learn to become Americans. And many believed that public education is central to American democracy; the curriculum, therefore, should foster good citizens. One influential voice who supported this connection between education and democracy was philosopher John Dewey, who argued that the school curriculum should do more than supply students with practical knowledge. For Dewey, schools were places where students learned how to live and work together, where they learned about democracy as a way of life rather than an idea or a set of principles (see Con-Text on page 416). Accordingly, Dewey believed that *how* students are taught is as important as what they are taught. ■ Nearly a century after Dewey formulated his philosophy of education, many Americans share his belief in the connection between education and democracy, even if they do not share his vision for a progressive public school system. This deeply held belief that education is central to democracy explains why education has been such a fierce political battleground in the United States. Conflicts about what students should be taught have been waged in classrooms, town halls, school board meetings, state legislatures, and the U.S. Congress. Sometimes these conflicts focus on a specific idea or theory, such as the long-standing debates about the teaching of evolution as opposed to creationism in science courses. Sometimes, conflicts involve a particular book that students are asked to read; for example, *The Adventures of Huckleberry Finn* by Mark Twain and *The Diary of Anne Frank* are commonly challenged by groups that believe, for various religious or political reasons, that these books should not be required reading in U.S. schools. Other debates focus on how students should be taught—what teaching methods are likely to be most effective. The testing of students has also caused conflict among parents, educators, government officials, and scholars. ■ In one way or another, these battles are about the purpose of education. As the authors of the essays in this section suggest, to make an argument about what to teach students is to make a statement about what you believe education is—or should be—for. There is rarely unanimous agreement among Americans about that question. The writers in this section make arguments about what should be taught in American classrooms, but their arguments all rest on beliefs—implied or explicitly stated—about the kind of society people want schools to help them build. Their views will help you appreciate the always political nature of formal education and perhaps find common ground about the purposes of education.

CON-TEXT

John Dewey on Democracy and Education

Democratic society is peculiarly dependent for its maintenance upon the use in forming a course of study of criteria which are broadly human. Democracy cannot flourish where the chief influences in selecting subject matter of instruction are utilitarian ends narrowly conceived for the masses, and, for the higher education of the few, the traditions of a specialized cultivated class. The notion that the "essentials" of elementary education are the three R's mechanically treated, is based upon ignorance of the essentials needed for realization of democratic ideals. Unconsciously it assumes that these ideals are unrealizable; it assumes that in the future, as in the past, getting a livelihood, "making a living," must signify for most men and women doing things which are not significant, freely chosen, and ennobling to those who do them; doing things which serve ends unrecognized by those engaged in them, carried on under the direction of others for the sake of pecuniary reward. For preparation of large numbers for a life of this sort, and only for this purpose, are mechanical efficiency in reading, writing, spelling and figuring, together with attainment of a certain amount of muscular dexterity, "essentials." Such conditions also infect the education called liberal, with illiberality. They imply a somewhat parasitic cultivation bought at the expense of not having the enlightenment and discipline which come from concern with the deepest problems of common humanity. A curriculum which acknowledges the social responsibilities of education must present situations where problems are relevant to the problems of living together, and where observation and information are calculated to develop social insight and interest.

SOURCE: Chapter 7 of John Dewey, *Democracy and Education* (1916).

① The Humanities for Cocktail Parties and Beyond

RICK LIVINGSTON

The following argument was first published in the *Chronicle of Higher Education* during the winter of 2005. The *Chronicle* reaches a wide audience of professors, administrators, and others in higher education concerned about issues such as academic freedom, teaching practices, and curriculum reform. With this audience in mind, Rick Livingston, the associate director of the Institute for Collaborative Research and Public Humanities and a senior lecturer in comparative studies at Ohio State University, defends the value of the required courses in humanities— that is, courses in disciplines such as English, philosophy, and art history—in an era when many students want courses that relate to career preparation and many professors want to require students to take additional courses in majors that have become increasingly demanding. As Livingston suggests in his essay, the common rationale for studying the humanities—that they provide people with knowledge to use when chatting at cocktail parties— trivializes the humanities instead of seeing them as something that could enrich lives in diverse situations. So the key word in Livingston's title is "beyond." As you read his argument, consider whether his justification for studying the humanities matches your own sense of the purpose of a college education.

RICK LIVINGSTON, "The Humanities for Cocktail Parties and Beyond"

1 In any introductory-humanities course, there is an **elephant-in-the-room** question. I try to wait at least three weeks into the term before asking my students to face it squarely: Why study the humanities?

The students' first response, of course, is because they have to. Most of my courses fulfill one of the general-education requirements at Ohio State University, and I usually have a healthy mix of precocious freshmen and procrastinating seniors.

If I go on to ask why the students think the university has such requirements, they are initially baffled. After trying out a few wiseacre responses ("Because they want our tuition money!"), they almost always say—wait for it— that the humanities help you make small talk at cocktail parties.

With any luck we go on to talk seriously about common knowledge and cultural expectations. But the cocktail-party comment tends to hang in the air like secondhand smoke, clouding the intellectual atmosphere. It suggests that our primary subject is petty snobbery and chitchat. The comment is a cliché, obviously, but one I have to confront every year.

5 Thinking about the cliché sent me back to **T. S. Eliot**'s 1950 play, *The Cocktail*

The expression **"elephant in the room"** is an idiom for describing an important subject that a group of people are aware of but determined to ignore because they think discussing it would be problematic. Successfully ignoring this subject for an extended period is no more likely than being able to ignore for long the presence of an elephant in the room where these people have gathered.

Most widely known as a poet, **T. S. Eliot** (1888–1965) was also a playwright and an influential critic, whose nonfiction includes *Christianity and Culture.* He was born and educated in the United States but became a British subject.

Party. Eliot portrays social life as a series of hypocrisies, deceptions, and embarrassments, redeemable only by religious conversion. Theological insight alone, the play suggests, can help us endure the unending round of mannered niceties that make up an ordinary life.

My students tend to shut down when I start talking about their souls, or they consult the syllabus to see whether I've included a conversion experience among the course requirements. In confronting the cocktail-party cliché, I've had to consider how to convey the value of the humanities without resorting to divine intervention.

Luckily my position as associate director of a humanities institute on my campus has allowed me to experiment with alternative ways of engaging students in humanistic inquiry. One of the institute's missions is to bring students and faculty members together outside traditional classroom settings, as an antidote to the sometimes intimidating experience of attending one of the country's largest universities. Over the years we've learned that it is in such informal settings that students often begin to tie together the different subjects they've been studying. Connecting the dots allows them to get a larger picture of the education they've been receiving. That's why

we've come up with a program we call (only half-jokingly) Big Ideas.

Here's how it works: Each quarter we choose a topic big enough to accommodate a range of approaches and cover more than one discipline. Past examples include evil, passion, war, and cities. We invite both faculty members and outside guests to have dinner with students and to give us their thoughts about the topics. Brief presentations are followed by open conversation, with students taking the lead in raising questions and responding.

Although we do bring in some of the best teachers at the university, the goal of Big Ideas is not really to teach the students specific facts. It is to give them practice in taking ideas seriously and to allow them to experience interesting conversations.

10 You're probably thinking: "Shouldn't they be doing that on their own? When I was in college, we would stay up late talking about ideas. What's wrong with these kids?"

But conversation about ideas seldom happens naturally, and nowadays it is rarer than ever. As historians of talk like Theodore Zeldin and Peter Burke have observed, conversation is not a spontaneous outpouring of well-formed sentences. It is a specific form of social behavior, with its own settings, tacit rules, and strategies. Like any social skill, it improves with practice.

Students today have few chances to practice serious talking. Our most visible examples of conversation come from TV: the political debate that is little more than a shouting match, and the celebrity interview. What students lack is experience with grown-up conversation, in which curiosity and respect can lead to self-discovery and mutual illumination.

At their best, the Big Ideas classes get students involved in such conversations. Our course on evil, for instance, picked up on a President Bush's use of a morally charged vocabulary (the "axis of evil") to orient U.S. foreign policy. We brought in four

---

COMPLICATION

It is not the business of the humanities to save us, no more than it is their business to bring revenue to a state or a university. What then do they do? They don't do anything, if by "do" is meant bring about effects in the world. And if they don't bring about effects in the world they cannot be justified except in relation to the pleasure they give to those who enjoy them.

To the question "of what use are the humanities?", the only honest answer is none whatsoever. And it is an answer that brings honor to its subject. Justification, after all, confers value on an activity from a perspective outside its performance. An activity that cannot be justified is an activity that refuses to regard itself as instrumental to some larger good. The humanities are their own good. There is nothing more to say, and anything that is said…diminishes the object of its supposed praise.

SOURCE: "Will the Humanities Save Us?" by Stanley Fish (2008).

guest speakers: a philosopher, a historian of religion, a theologian, and a judge. Then students talked about personal experiences with evil, ranging from anger to sexual abuse, and about evil in the world—including terrorism and the Holocaust. In the process, students confronted their own beliefs about God and human nature, and tested their intuitions about differences among the illegal, the immoral, and the downright evil. Nothing was resolved, of course, but the students get a clearer sense of the necessity—and the difficulty—of making such distinctions.

In our course on cities, we began by talking about the places where we had grown up, and how they had changed over our lifetimes. We met with an architect to talk about high rises and skylines. Ideas about consumerism and sustainability became the focus of a class with an urban planner, and a sociologist talked with us about the effects of globalization on the shape of cities. Finally, an artist who is designing a waterfront park came to discuss ideas about making public art in and out of neglected urban spaces. Students learned a vocabulary for talking about the changes they can see happening in their neighborhoods as well as in the world at large.

15 Inevitably, there is a certain amount of overlap among the sessions; predictably, discussions sometimes meander and leave the topic altogether. But most of the sessions include a moment when some of the students catch fire and carry the rest of us forward, or when someone gets the idea of dialogical inquiry and asks more, and better, questions. Sometimes students discover that their intuitions don't match their convictions. Most interesting, however, are the times when, as in the discussion of war and peace during the run-up to the invasion of Iraq, we find

CONTEXT

On January 29, 2002, President George W. Bush, in his State of the Union address, said (see par. 13): "North Korea is a regime arming with missiles and weapons of mass destruction, while starving its citizens. Iran aggressively pursues these weapons and exports terror, while an unelected few repress the Iranian people's hope for freedom. Iraq continues to flaunt its hostility toward America and to support terror....States like these, and their terrorist allies, constitute an axis of evil, arming to threaten the peace of the world."

Considering the amount of coverage given to and the tensions surrounding the war in Iraq since it began in 2002, do you think programs like "Big Ideas" are necessary to facilitate discussion of such topics among college students?

ourselves trying hard to make sense of the world together.

I've thought a lot about what makes the courses work. The topics belong to no one field: Different disciplines may contribute perspectives to the issues we cover, but when faced with the problem of evil, for instance, we are all amateurs. We use no set body of material, and students' own experiences and examples often become common points of reference.

Each course is for one academic credit— enough to make the students take the class seriously; but the grade is pass or fail, so students don't need to demonstrate mastery of a subject. To keep the atmosphere informal, we meet in a dining hall rather than a classroom. And mixing up faculty members with outside guests shows that ideas can live off campus, too.

Maybe the most unexpected lesson of Big Ideas, however, is that professors appreciate making conversation, too. It can be tough to step out of the comfort zones of our expertise, to let go of disciplinary jargon. But the opportunity to speak, not as a professional to novices, but as a citizen with other (albeit younger) citizens, can be liberating. It's not just a cocktail party—and that, I think, is the main point.

Questions for Discussion

1. What is the problem with the "cocktail-party cliché," as Livingston sees it? How does that cliché help illuminate problems in the way students understand the value of studying the humanities? How well does it work as a way to set up Livingston's main argument?

2. Livingston suggests that important learning often occurs outside classrooms. How does this point fit into his main argument about the humanities? In your view, how important is the relationship between learning and the place where learning occurs?

3. Do you agree with Livingston's claim that contemporary students "have few chances to practice serious talking"? Does your answer to that question suggest a counterargument to Livingston's position? Explain.

4. Livingston describes his "Big Ideas" program to illustrate the value of studying the humanities. How effectively does that example help him make his argument? What do you think of the "Big Ideas" forums he describes? Would you be interested in participating in one? Why or why not? What might your answer to that question suggest about the effectiveness of Livingston's argument?

5. This article was originally published in the *Chronicle of Higher Education*, which is intended for an audience of college and university educators. How well do you think Livingston's argument works for a more general audience?

② | Liberal Education on the Ropes

STANLEY N. KATZ

A liberal education is generally understood to emphasize traditional areas of study so that students acquire broad knowledge as opposed to mastery of a single academic field. Stanley Katz is concerned about the future of this kind of education. He had the benefit of one, having earned a bachelor's degree in English history and literature as well as a Ph.D. in history from Harvard University. But he sees a worrisome trend at research institutions such as Harvard, which he believes have abandoned the tradition of liberal education, and he devotes much of his essay to tracing the history of this trend. He argues that universities like Harvard must "be clearer about the larger function of general education" if liberal education is to be preserved. In making that argument, he adds his voice to the many thinkers who have addressed the basic question of why we educate students. An accomplished scholar, Katz is director of Princeton University's Center for Arts and Cultural Policy Studies. This essay was first published in the *Chronicle of Higher Education* in April 2005.

STANLEY N. KATZ, "Liberal Education on the Ropes"

1 Surely "liberal education" is the most used and abused phrase in the rhetoric of higher education. Just as surely it has no universal meaning. The Association of American Colleges and Universities recently launched a 10-year campaign to "champion the value of a liberal education"—and to "spark public debate" about just what that is. But the concept may be more alive and well in four-year liberal-arts colleges than it is in our great research universities that are setting the agenda for higher education today. Those institutions are my concern: I fear that undergraduate education in the research university is becoming a project in ruins.

Last year we heard of the renewal of interest in liberal education at those institutions when Harvard University announced that it was reforming its "core curriculum." The obvious question that wasn't asked in all the newsprint devoted to Harvard's statement is whether research universities can purport to offer undergraduates a liberal

> **CONTEXT**
>
> The Association of American Colleges and Universities (AAC&U) describes itself as "the leading national association concerned with the quality, vitality, and public standing of undergraduate liberal education." In 2005 it launched the program that Katz refers to in paragraph 1, called Liberal Education and America's Promise (LEAP). According to AAC&U, LEAP "focuses campus practice on fostering essential learning outcomes for all students, whatever their chosen field of study." The program includes studies of the mission of liberal education and public advocacy efforts in various states to promote a common core curriculum in colleges and universities. LEAP might be seen as part of a broader conversation in the United States about the purpose and future of higher education for the twenty-first century. That conversation included debates about the revision of the famous core curriculum at Harvard University, which Katz mentions in paragraph 2.

education. Furthermore, the questions that were asked indicate just how contested the meaning of liberal education is at research universities. Should the core curriculum offer common knowledge? Or a way of learning? Should it require set courses, or provide student choice? Focus on big questions, or on specialized exploration in a variety of disciplines?

It seems that we have not traveled very far in defining a liberal education at research universities. Not in the last year. Not, perhaps, in the last 100 years.

Reliable truisms are available. The association of colleges and universities currently defines liberal education as: "a philosophy of education that empowers individuals, liberates the mind from ignorance, and cultivates social responsibility. Characterized by challenging encounters with important issues, and more a way of studying than specific content, liberal education can occur at all types of colleges and universities." While the association's new campaign seeks to unite that philosophy with what it calls "practical education," the elements of the definition that have been at the heart of the most important ambitions of liberal education for the last century are likely to remain—empowering students, liberating their minds, preparing them for citizenship. In short, a process rather than a substantive orientation.

5 Through most of the 20th century, liberal education was more or less exclusively identified with the four-year liberal-arts colleges and a handful of elite universities. Both the institutions and its advocates were avowed educational elitists. But times have changed—hence the attempt of the association of colleges and universities to universalize liberal education across all types of institutions. But liberal education is being asked to carry more freight than it did a century ago, and it is not clear that it can succeed.

As it has expanded throughout higher education, it has suffered inevitable losses and unresolved tensions. As it spread from what were once primarily church-related colleges, for example, it lost its focus on moral values. But even the surviving emphasis on an orientation that stresses general values has been an uncomfortable fit in the modern research university, which has increasingly stressed the production of scientific knowledge over the transmission of culture.

Many of the attempts to package liberal education in the modern university have centered on "general education." The idea of general education derives from **Matthew Arnold**, and it was picked up and Americanized in the United States early in the 20th century. Although we seldom recognize the fact, there were actually three streams in American thinking at the time.

The first stream is perhaps one of the oldest, but still continues. It has been the self-conscious rejection of specific courses in favor of a vague notion of enforced diversity of subject matter, to be provided by regular disciplinary departments. Here the pre-eminent example is, alas, my own university, Princeton. Under the leadership of James McCosh in the late 1880s, Princeton developed the "distribution" system that is still all we have to provide structured liberal education at Old Nassau.

At Princeton it was not necessary to offer special courses or designate faculty members to provide the content of liberal education—just to ensure that students did not concentrate too narrowly by requiring a variety of what McCosh called "obligatory and disciplinary" courses. With the exception of a sequence of humanities courses and a large program of freshman seminars, present-day Princeton still has neither nondepartmental general-education courses nor any structured mechanism for thinking about the broader contours of undergraduate liberal education. We review the program periodically, but we seem always to conclude that McCosh had it right. Well, perhaps.

10 The most obvious and most highly publicized example of the next stream began at Columbia University as the United States was entering World War I. This was an attempt to ensure that undergraduates in an increasingly scientific university would be broadly educated across the fields of the liberal arts and to integrate their increasingly fragmented selection of courses into some coherent form. (Admittedly, it was also fueled by a felt need to promote Western civilization in the face of German barbarism.) Combining new synthetic courses outside the disciplinary-obsessed department structure with the inculcation of a notion of democratic citizenship, the curriculum was organized around surveys of "Contemporary Civilization." In essence, the Columbia sequence humanized the now-secular university curriculum by broadly historicizing it. As time passed, most other elite institutions did the same.

In the 1930s Robert Maynard Hutchins and Mortimer J. Adler at the University of Chicago launched an important experiment in this approach. It was complex and somewhat inwardly self-contradictory, but the bottom line was an insistence on the centrality of the Greek classics and other Great Books to undergraduate education, later supplemented by the construction of a "core curriculum" to educate undergraduates across the liberal-arts subjects and to force them to think through and across traditional disciplinary approaches.

In 1945 Harvard, under James Bryant Conant, issued *General Education in a Free Society*, commonly known as the Harvard Red Book. I still have my copy, for it was the basis of my undergraduate education at Harvard beginning in 1951, when as a freshman I took a "Natural Sciences" course in the general-education sequence taught by President Conant, a stunning chemistry professor named Leonard Nash, and an obscure assistant professor of physics named Thomas S. Kuhn. I never had a better undergraduate course. The political rationale for the Red Book was grander than Columbia's or Chicago's, but the basic principles of general education were not that different, based on sweepingly synthetic historical approaches to classically great ideas. The attempt to give all undergraduates at least a taste of different disciplines is now one of the unchallenged principles of general education.

The third stream, which in some ways has had a more profound influence on our actual educational practices, was that championed

COMPLICATION

The idea of basing education upon the study of "great books" assumes that there is wide agreement about which books have had a profound and lasting effect upon civilization. Plato's *Republic* or Chaucer's *The Canterbury Tales* might be considered such works. For many years in the West, numerous scholars and educators believed that such works could be identified and agreed upon. This process of establishing lists of great works is referred to by contemporary scholars as *canon formation*. But most scholars now agree that canon formation is problematic. For example, because "the canon" was formed by men of European descent such as Mortimer J. Adler, it tended to emphasize works by what some contemporary critics call "dead white men." The canon has been widely challenged during the last thirty years by scholars and teachers determined to make it more culturally diverse.

by **John Dewey** and Arthur O. Lovejoy. This effort focused on cognitive development and individual student growth, and its key was the idea of reflective thinking as a goal of liberal education. That concept was institutionalized at Columbia under the leadership of Dewey and at the Johns Hopkins University under Lovejoy. This approach was entirely cognitive, lacking in specific education content. To this day it forms the basis of the stress on process at the heart of approaches to liberal education.

To be sure, there have been many other approaches to liberal education over the years. Until recently, many liberal-arts colleges used both sophisticated distribution systems and a variety of innovative course designs. Many still continue to innovate. As Ernest L. Boyer forcefully noted in *College: The Undergraduate Experience in America*, first published in 1987, some such colleges have become university wannabes or citadels of preprofessional education. In any case, in most of the major four-year institutions that are educating a larger and larger proportion of undergraduates, the challenge has seemed to be modifying the historical principles of general education in order to bring them up to date.

15 Harvard, as usual, got the most publicity, first for the creation of its "core curriculum" in the 1970s—another attempt to problematize

John Dewey (1859–1952) was one of the most influential educators in American history. As a scholar at the University of Chicago, he wrote many books on how education could improve society. He is usually considered the founder of what is sometimes called "progressive education"—that is, education designed to help students reach their full potential as human beings rather than to train them to memorize facts. Dewey believed that progressive education was essential to the successful functioning of a democratic society.

and repackage general-education courses in a manner consistent with the epistemology and intellectual progress of the era. This twist on general education dehistoricized it, organizing the curriculum around abstract concepts like "moral reasoning," "quantitative reasoning," or "social analysis."

Last year Harvard seemed to concede the failure of that approach and has begun to consider what I would call "Core Two." According to the dean of the faculty of arts and sciences, William C. Kirby, reporting to the faculty, the aim is to empower students to "grasp the importance and relevance of fields to which they do not themselves owe personal allegiance and in which they have not developed special expertise" so that they may "understand, criticize, and improve our world constructively."

Harvard is adding to its definition of general education a focus on international studies and one on scientific literacy. New "Harvard College Courses" are proposed to supply the new approaches, along with courses already in the curriculum. Freshman seminars are suggested and other small-group learning engagements for the final three years of college. A parallel aim of the new curriculum is to limit the student's concentration (Harvardese for "major"), by changing when undergraduates begin to major in a particular field from freshman year to the middle of the sophomore year (talk about epicycles!), and to limit the requirements for concentrators. The report also suggests that the university facilitate undergraduate research opportunities. Not one of those seems like either a new or very exciting idea.

The Harvard document, when it is completed and put into effect, will predictably be the most discussed document on liberal education over the next few years. I have no doubt that it will, if put into practice in anything like a full-blooded fashion, significantly improve general education at Harvard. But it is a modest, reformist document.

It defines liberal education in an altogether traditional manner, and each of its proposed reforms is mostly familiar. After all, internationalization has been on everyone's mind for some time, and there has not been a moment in the last century during which some group has not lamented that we are not doing a good job of conveying science to the nonscientist. Similarly, freshman seminars are hardly a new idea (I taught one the first year they were offered at Harvard, in 1961), nor is the call for more small-group instruction or for more undergraduate research. Three years is arguably too long for an undergraduate to major in a discipline. Undergraduates already do research and take courses in professional schools (if, perhaps, that has just been harder at Harvard than at comparable institutions). For those of us at other institutions who are long-term observers of liberal education, there does not seem to be a lot to learn from Harvard.

20 My intention is not to attack any particular definition of liberal education. It is to suggest that we have not traveled far in our definitions over the past 100 years. Until we do, we can do little to fundamentally improve undergraduate education at research universities.

Moreover, whatever the definition, we all face a dilemma. As I've suggested for a number of years, the real problem is that both long-term changes to the social, political, and economic environment for higher education and the recent internal restructuring of the university make it difficult—if not impossible—to achieve a satisfactory liberal education for undergraduates. Even if Dean Kirby can persuade his university significantly to increase the number of faculty members to help teach general-education courses (and President John E. Sexton of New York University is making a similar proposal), what are the odds (a) that Harvard or NYU can afford it, and (b) that they can and will hire the sorts of faculty members competent (and inclined) to be superior undergraduate teachers? Does anyone believe that possible? I do not.

The modern university has been in tension with the liberal-arts college it harbors within its bosom for years. We are at a point in the history of the research university at which, in all likelihood, curriculum reform can no longer plausibly produce what we are looking for, despite the best efforts of admirable administrators like Bill Kirby or John Sexton. That is why I fear that liberal education for undergraduates in the research university, despite the recent hoopla, is in ruins.

There are two ways of thinking about why that is so. The first is the intellectual task of reconceptualizing what the content and curricular mechanisms should be at the beginning of the second century of modern liberal education. The second approach is to consider the structural changes in the modern research university that are relegating undergraduate education to the margins.

I will not attempt more than to gesture at what seem to me the contours of the intellectual problem. The overriding difficulty is the vast expansion of the domains of knowledge from the late 19th century to the early 21st century. After all, the by-now-traditional academic disciplines only took shape from the 1880s to the 1920s. The social sciences, in particular, were very much the original product of that period, and one of the original objectives of general education was to locate the social sciences within the new sociology of knowledge (itself a creation of the first half of the 20th century).

25 As undergraduates increasingly "majored" in a single discipline, the question was how they could relate what they were learning to the larger intellectual cosmology. That was what Columbia and other elite colleges were addressing. But the intellectual panorama was already changing rapidly. By the 1940s, when Harvard introduced its undergraduate curriculum, atomic physics was most obviously where the action was, but the revolution in cell biology was quietly beginning and, with it, the total transformation of the life sciences. New forms and combinations of knowledge

were being institutionalized in the natural sciences along the model that had produced biochemistry in the 1930s. What had begun as a private philanthropic initiative in the 1920s and 1930s was suddenly overwhelmed by the entrance of the federal government following World War II, especially through the mechanisms of the National Science Foundation and the National Institutes of Health. There would soon be no such thing as the generally educated scientist, much less the generally scientifically literate undergraduate student. There was simply too much to know because of the range, depth, and quantity of new scientific scholarship, and of the increasing centrality of complex mathematics to scientific understanding.

Change was afoot in the humanities and social sciences as well. Those were more complicated and subtle stories, but the larger outlines seem clear enough. The social sciences became more complex theoretically, more scientific in their methodology, and more wide-ranging in their ambitions. They became less focused on understanding the problems of building democracy in the United States (as they had begun to do in the 1920s and 1930s), and more interested in fostering both economic and political development abroad, especially in the "underdeveloped" areas of the world. As in every other disciplinary domain, the traditional social-science disciplines splintered, sprouted new lines, and recombined in novel ways.

In the humanities, the focus moved from studies of Europe (especially classical Europe) and America to contemplation of the rest of the world. We discovered world literature, philosophy, history, and music. New subdisciplines developed (the history of everything in the social sciences and humanities, for instance), new languages were studied, new techniques were employed. And the relevance of the humanities to politics became a problem and an opportunity.

For undergraduate education, the center simply could not hold. There were many attempts to identify an essential core of knowledge, and many new attempts will undoubtedly be made. I think them unlikely to succeed given the breadth and complexity of the intellectual content students now confront.

Nor do we seem to have the educational leaders capable of defining new content. Let me say that I do not think the blame should fall on university presidents and deans. It should be assigned to research faculties for whom thoughtful consideration of undergraduate education is simply not on the agenda. They are dominated by scholars committed to disciplinary approaches, who would mostly prefer to teach graduate students and, increasingly, postgrads. The professional schools at least claim to prefer to admit generally educated students, but what about graduate departments? Can we simply presume that the products of American secondary education are already liberally educated? To ask the question is to answer it.

30 And that brings me to my second concern: the extent to which structural changes in the university, especially the research university, tend to marginalize undergraduate education generally and, more important, make it difficult to theorize and put into effect anything like liberal education. Some of those factors also affect colleges and general universities, but the problem is worst in the research universities. Quite apart from

the intellectual transformation I have just described, the most important thing that has changed for higher education is the entirety of the social and political environment in which it is situated.

The most significant shift is from elite to democratic higher education, which began in the 1930s and took off after World War II, heralded by the GI Bill. Since then the numbers of undergraduate students in four-year institutions have expanded exponentially, and student bodies have come to resemble the diversity of the general population of the country. Of course, pluralism requires something less morally prescriptive, less tailored, more diverse, and more practical than the elite higher education of the early-20th century. Notions of democratic higher education originated a century ago, but they took on new urgency and complexity after World War II. That is why Harvard went to such lengths to explore the democratic character of general education in its postwar Red Book.

None of us wants to go back to traditional educational elitism. I assume that the "best" institutions these days aspire to meritocratic elitism, leavened by diversity programs aimed at casting a broad net, and compensating for past deficiencies where necessary. However, in all but the most selective institutions, students have a broad range of motivations for "going to college," and many (if not most of them) cannot choose freely to construct their educations. They are older, part time, and financially hard pressed. That does not mean that they are narrowly preprofessional or unreceptive to the need for a liberal education, but that they are obviously very different sorts of candidates for general education than students of my own or earlier generations.

Over time the social and political pressures that shaped the modern research university have shaped the way that undergraduate education is conceptualized. It is at least arguable that the early research universities genuinely thought of themselves as collegiate institutions—by which I mean a university

CONTEXT

In paragraph 32 Katz writes that students have different motivations for attending college, based on their age, financial situation, and other factors. He is referring to changes in the college student population in the United States that have been occurring for the past few decades. The percentage of students who attend college after completing high school has been growing steadily since the 1980s. Also, college students today are older than in previous generations. For example, according to the U.S. Census Bureau, 15 percent of college students were age 35 or older as of 2007, and in 2009, 38 percent of college students were older than 25. In addition, many students today attend college part time, which may affect their interest in general education programs of the kind that Katz describes in this essay. Consider whether such trends alter the idea of a liberal education as Katz discusses it.

surrounding an undergraduate college. That is still embodied in institutions such as Harvard and Yale University, where the phrase "the college" has some meaning. The term "Harvard graduate" (or "Yale graduate") still means someone who has completed the undergraduate program. But the fuller notion that the liberal arts are the core of the university has eroded badly—mainly, I think, in response to the university's attempt to satisfy concrete and immediate pragmatic social demands.

My contention is that we have gone so far down this road in the major universities that we have reversed our priorities and now give precedence to research and graduate and professional training—in the kind of faculty members we recruit, in the incentives (light or nil teaching loads) we offer them, and even in the teaching we value (graduate over undergraduate students). Our research faculty members have little interest in joining efforts to build core or general-education programs, much less in teaching in them. Moreover, can we be confident that those prized faculty recruits are sufficiently liberally educated to participate in general education? The same is true of our fractionalizing of universities into research centers. Those increasingly become pawns in the faculty recruiting game—we will finance a research center for you, help you recruit postdocs and graduate students to do the research—with little room or thought to undergraduate education.

35 Another problem, though one hard to document and discuss, is the difficulty of financing the humanities and soft social sciences, the fields in which so many undergraduates find their most important liberal-education experiences. We all know that faculty members in those fields teach more, get paid less, and have fewer resources for research than their colleagues in the natural sciences and hard social sciences. They have less leverage in the institution to get what they want, from secretarial services and office space to computers. They are also, on

balance, the faculty members most likely to be concerned with undergraduate education, but they are in a weak position to influence decisions within their universities.

Perhaps most important, those who administer our research universities are less and less likely to be well-known teachers, especially collegiate teachers. Presidents have less and less time to worry about education problems, and even provosts and deans of faculty are incredibly hard pressed to keep the lights on and the laboratories functioning. They themselves seldom teach. Such administrators are often forced to prize efficiency in undergraduate education—the more bodies in a classroom the better, and cheaper. It may well be that in most American universities the economic realities are such that the administrators have few alternatives.

I think I would know what to do about the plight of liberal education in the modern research university if I were offered the magic wand. We all have lovely theories. But none of us, and no university president, has such power. That makes it all the more important that we be conscious of the nature of the task at hand. I asked my friend Charles S. Maler, a professor of history at Harvard who has been working on its curricular review, about the university's recent proposal. "I do think it's a step in the right direction to bury the Core, which essentially said students should understand how scholars do scholarship. The Gen Ed that you and I took was a far more humanist enterprise. But by the early 1970s, faculties no longer had confidence in Values and thus turned toward Expertise," he told me. "At least we now have a sense that Values—aesthetic, civic, moral—are important again, even if we don't have confidence we know which values are important."

I believe he's right. Lest we continue to be mired in incremental reforms, we need to be clearer about the larger function of general education. If we believe that values do have a role in education, then the challenge may be to rehistoricize and rehumanize the underclass curriculum. That does not mean going back to Contemporary Civilization courses or the Red Book. It does mean rethinking the content of knowledge appropriate for our contemporary society, and summoning the intellectual courage to embolden students to make qualitative judgments about the materials they are required to engage with in their underclass years.

Of course, that will not be possible unless we are safely beyond the conflicts of the culture wars of the 1980s and 1990s. That seems to me problematic at the current moment in American history, but perhaps I am too pessimistic.

40 Even if we are able to open a new discussion about reforming the curriculum, however, we will still fall unless we take seriously the structural constraints on higher education today. At best we have been taking those constraints for granted; at worst, enthusiastically embracing them.

The changing structure of the university is the place we may need to start the discussion. A great deal is at stake for undergraduate education, and for the country. If we believe, as so many of the founders of liberal education did, that the vitality of American democracy depends upon the kind of liberal education undergraduates receive, we need to put the reimagination of liberal education near the top of our agenda for education in our research universities.

Questions for Discussion

1. Katz claims that "we have not traveled very far in defining a liberal education at research universities" (par. 3). Why is he concerned about the lack of a widely accepted definition of a liberal education? Do you think his concern is justified? Why or why not?

2. At your school, are you required to take courses outside of your major? Is doing so useful? If there is a core curriculum or set of requirements that all students must fulfill, how long has it been in place? How well does it suit the present climate at your school? How might your answers to these questions shape your response to Katz's argument?

3. What are Katz's complaints about the general education programs at universities like Princeton, where he teaches? How persuasive do you find his discussion of his concerns about these programs? To what extent is your reaction to his argument influenced by your own experience with general education courses?

4. Why do you think Katz provides so much history about the evolution of liberal education during the last century? How does this history contribute to his argument?

5. What two main explanations does Katz provide for his assertion that liberal education in research universities "is in ruins" (par. 22)? How convincing do you find these explanations? How might you respond to Katz's assertion that liberal education is "in ruins"?

6. Katz refers to his own experiences as both a student and a professor. How effectively do you think he uses these experiences to support his argument? Do you think his discussion of his own experiences strengthens or weakens his essay? Explain.

7. Why does Katz devote so much attention to Harvard University's core curriculum? What lessons does he draw from that program and the changes that have been made to it? How do these lessons fit into his main argument?

8. Why does Katz believe that it really isn't possible to identify the basic content of a core curriculum for undergraduates? Do you agree with him? If not, what would you include in such a curriculum? How would you justify your answer to that question?

9. Do you think an undergraduate education should convey values as well as knowledge and expertise? If so, what values? If not, why not? Would your answer to these questions provide the basis for a counter-argument to Katz? Explain.

③ Designing a Signature General Education Program

STEPHEN L. TRAINOR

Colleges and universities invest considerable effort in determining what courses should be required of all students. That's no surprise. For one thing, determining what students should learn is a complex philosophical as well as practical challenge, and it can generate great controversy. In addition, curriculum reform is labor-intensive and sometimes leads to conflict among faculty, which is why schools often leave their core curriculum in place for years. When schools do review the curriculum, disagreements can arise over what courses should be required, how many requirements there should be, and how much choice students should have in selecting courses to fulfill requirements. In the following essay, which first appeared in 2004 in *Peer Review*, a publication of the Association of American Colleges and Universities, Stephen Trainor argues that the key to successful curriculum reform lies in the process a school uses. To illustrate a successful process, he focuses upon what was done at Salve Regina University, where he is a professor of English and also served as dean of undergraduate studies. In making his argument about *how* colleges and universities might change their undergraduate programs, Trainor provides insight into why the question of what students should be taught can be so difficult to answer.

STEPHEN L. TRAINOR, "Designing a Signature General Education Program"

Salve Regina University, located in Newport, Rhode Island, is a private Catholic college founded in 1947. It enrolls 2,500 undergraduate and graduate students.

1 Notoriously contentious and protracted, efforts to reform general education curricula can prove frustrating for the participants, and they often end in failure. In particular, the goal of producing a signature program—a curriculum that captures the distinctive mission and essence of an institution—often remains elusive, sacrificed to the exigencies of political compromise or financial constraints. The source of the problem usually can be traced to the process involved in a given curricular reform. In its effort to develop a new signature general education curriculum, **Salve Regina University** was able to avoid many of the usual pitfalls by adopting a formal problem-solving model that emphasizes creativity and involves the entire faculty in the process.

HOW DOES THE PROCESS AFFECT THE OUTCOME?

The problem is not that colleges and universities do not pay attention to process; rather, difficulties arise from their failure to anticipate the results a given process is likely to produce. In designing a signature program, the typical procedure is to appoint a committee to produce a curricular model and then present it to the entire faculty for consideration, debate, and a vote. Great care is taken to ensure that all viewpoints are represented on this committee, in the hope that the final model will produce consensus among the larger faculty. While it seems plausible on the surface, this process is, for a variety of reasons, unlikely to produce a distinctive signature program.

Precisely because they were chosen as representatives, the committee members are concerned to speak for their constituents' interests—the liberal arts, the professional programs, the humanities or the social sciences, the territory of a single department or discipline. It is the rare faculty member who can transcend his or her own area and speak for the institution as a whole. Thus, this typical process practically guarantees that the committee will be at odds with itself in most of its deliberations.

To produce a model that will achieve consensus among the faculty is a laudable goal; the core curriculum should have widespread support. Yet in striving to reach this elusive goal, the committee may be forced to sacrifice the more distinctive elements of any signature model in favor of domestic harmony. Accordingly, the most likely outcome is a least-common-denominator model designed to offend no one and to garner the necessary votes from the wider faculty.

5 Because they are established up front and the model is developed to satisfy them, the criteria for the new curriculum actually are design elements in disguise. As such, these restrictive criteria can undermine the committee's ability to come up with a distinctive signature program. Finally, since the committee's task is to produce a single model, the voting faculty's only comparative frame of reference is the current core curriculum (aka the devil that you know).

A CREATIVE PROBLEM-SOLVING MODEL

At Salve Regina University, we were able to avoid many of these problems by adopting a problem-solving model outlined by **Vincent Ryan Ruggiero** (2003). Ruggiero's model calls for a progression of four stages: (1) *being aware,* which involves gathering information and defining the problem; (2) *being creative,* which asks the problem-solvers to generate as many creative solutions as possible; (3) *being*

critical, which asks participants to set aside the proposed solutions while they develop the criteria by which the solutions will be judged; and (4) *communicating or acting,* which calls for the selection of a solution based on the criteria and implementing that solution.

This model posits a process that is, in a number of ways, counterintuitive but that nonetheless effectively addresses the process problems discussed above. Rather than a representative committee, the process adopted at Salve Regina calls for multiple design teams brought together by common interests and vision. Every faculty member, either individually or in groups, is invited to propose a model curriculum. Rather than developing a compromise model designed to build consensus, the process calls for choosing whichever model receives a majority of the faculty votes; presumably, that model best represents the university's idea of an integrated signature curriculum.

In order to foster creativity, Ruggiero's model reverses the anticipated order of activities by placing the development of criteria after the brainstorming of solutions. Faculty are thus free to focus on developing a distinctive "dream" curriculum without the usual constraints. The development of a variety of models offers the faculty a broader range of choices than the "take it or leave it" approach implied in the single committee, single curriculum process.

At Salve Regina, we considered a common understanding of the process to be so important that we asked the faculty to endorse it in a formal vote, at which point the stages were linked to a strict timetable designed to get to a decision by the time of the faculty's annual post-commencement meeting in May. A steering committee, composed of eight faculty members and the undergraduate dean, was established to oversee the process and to ensure adherence to the schedule. The process itself suggested a variety of questions along the way,

A recognized leader in promoting an education focused on critical thinking, **Vincent Ryan Ruggiero** has written numerous articles and books, including *The Art of Thinking: A Guide to Critical and Creative Thought* (2003), which Trainor refers to in paragraph 6.

questions worth considering in the development of any signature program.

Stage One: What Is the Problem You Want to Solve?

10 The first task of the steering committee was to define the problem clearly. One aspect of the problem turned on the question of mission. The university community recently had completed a two-year process to develop a new mission statement, and many perceived a cognitive disconnect between the new mission and the set of distribution requirements in place at the time. A second aspect of the problem turned on integrative learning. The distribution requirements had no internal frame of reference or connection; there was no philosophy, no theme, no developmental structure, no interdisciplinary cooperation.

In the end, the steering committee was able to articulate the general dissatisfaction with the current core in a way that gave shape and direction to the problem-solving process. It proposed to the faculty assembly the following clearly defined task; to create a core curriculum of liberal arts and sciences that includes explicit goals and measurable objectives and that is (1) grounded in the university's mission as a Catholic institution founded by the Sisters of Mercy, "to work for a world that is harmonious, just, and merciful," and that is (2) integrated by cooperation.

CONTEXT

According to its website, Salve Regina University seeks to educate "men and women for responsible lives by imparting and expanding knowledge, developing skills, and cultivating enduring values. Through liberal arts and professional programs, students develop their abilities for thinking clearly and creatively, enhance their capacity for sound judgment, and prepare for the challenge of learning throughout their lives." Most colleges and universities have mission statements, which are intended to reflect the fundamental values that inform the school's sense of purpose. Such statements might also be considered each school's answer to the question that is the theme of this cluster of readings: What should students be taught?

Stage Two: How Can You Tap into the Creativity of the Faculty?

Ruggiero's model fosters creativity by reversing the anticipated order of events. Instead of specifying criteria first and then tailoring the solution to fit them, the process asks participants to generate solutions before criteria are established. This is particularly challenging for academics who, usually more critical than creative by training, are apt to want to know the criteria first. But it is Ruggiero's particular insight to see that *a priori* criteria can be thought-stoppers. If one begins with a given set of constraints—e.g., the core will have an upper limit of thirty-nine credit hours; the core will be delivered by the current faculty; the core will not touch the current requirements in English, or history, or modern languages; the core must be completed by the end of sophomore year; the core will not cost any more money than the current curriculum—one can with some accuracy predict the outcome, which is likely to bear a striking resemblance to the status quo. Ruggiero avoids this problem by proscribing the creation of criteria until a number of creative solutions have been generated. Liberated from considerations of staffing and cost (which are administrative problems, anyway) and from the need to achieve consensus on credit allocations (which are turf matters rather than curricular principles), faculty are free to focus on their real task: designing a signature curriculum that reflects the mission and character of the institution.

By the deadline established by Salve Regina's steering committee, five fully developed models and some eighteen focused suggestions had emerged. Two of the models were proposed by individuals, three by teams of two to seven faculty members. The range of approaches and educational philosophies put forth is suggested by the titles of the five models:

- The Seven Frames of Salve Regina University
- The Millennium Core

- Classics Program
- Preparation for Lifelong Learning and World Citizenship
- Searching for a Meaningful Life

The focused suggestions ranged from recommendations about information literacy to competency in the sciences to the inclusion of service learning. The models and the suggestions were collected in a packet and presented, with an opportunity for questions and discussion, at an open session attended by the faculty, the academic administration, and the university's president. The presentation of five fully developed models created a sense of excitement about the process and confidence about the future. The general consensus was that any one of the new models would be much better than the status quo.

Stage Three: How Do You Evaluate the Proposed Models?

15 At this stage of the process, participants set aside the solutions proposed in Stage Two and develop the criteria by which those solutions will be judged. The challenge is to create a set of criteria independent of the existing possible solutions: This is particularly difficult in smaller problem-solving processes where the participants involved in developing Stage Three criteria are the same as those who proposed solutions in Stage Two. At Salve Regina, these difficulties were addressed by a division of labor between the steering committee and the self-generated design teams. Before the solutions were proposed, the steering committee, whose members were not permitted to participate in model design, had set about developing criteria but kept them in strict confidence.

After the five proposed models were presented to the full faculty and academic administration, the steering committee publicly presented its criteria to the faculty assembly. Their original proposal included the following points:

- How is the proposed curriculum based on the concept of the liberal arts and sciences?
- How will the university be able to measure the extent to which the explicit goals and outcomes of the proposal are being achieved?
- How does the proposal implement the university's mission to encourage students to seek wisdom and to "work for a world that is harmonious, just, and merciful"?
- How is the proposed curriculum integrated by cooperation?

In the discussions on the floor of the assembly, various other criteria were proposed and debated; ultimately, two more were added:

- How does the proposed curriculum present all undergraduates with expectations and standards that promote the development of intellect and character?
- How does the proposed curriculum prepare students for a lifetime of learning, service, and career choices?

The faculty involved in developing the five models were asked to explain in writing how their proposals addressed the criteria, and their answers were collected and published to the faculty at large. These faculty also were free to amend their original proposals to address the criteria; however, it was important for the process that they were under no obligation to do so.

Stage Four: Which Model Do You Want? The final stage calls for judging the proposed solutions against the established criteria and selecting a model. Rather than merely using the criteria as a checklist, Stage Four involves choosing the model that is deemed the most effective and attractive in terms of the criteria. Rather than compromising the overall integrity of the model to match the list of criteria perfectly, it may be advisable to overlook weaknesses in satisfying

CONTEXT

As of 2010, the Core Curriculum at Salve Regina University consisted of four "Common Core Courses" and eleven "Complement" courses in seven academic disciplines. The Common Core Courses included "Seeking Wisdom: From Wonder to Justice," "What It Means To Be Human," "Christianity in Dialogue With World Religions," and "Philosophy and Responsibility." Consider how this curriculum suggests a broad answer to the question of what students should be taught in college.

one criterion in view of strengths in satisfying others.

At Salve Regina, the final selection of the model took place over two days at a post-commencement faculty meeting conducted by the officers of the faculty assembly. At this stage in the process, all members of the faculty were vitally engaged in the discussions and debates. For example, the faculty in the professional departments, who had not been extensively involved in proposing possible models, now emerged as important decision makers. They critiqued the various models and argued for or against them. In a straw poll taken at the end of the first day, two models clearly were shown to have widespread support. On the next day, the faculty formally endorsed the model that had garnered the most votes in the straw poll. This model still needed much work; indeed, it required two more years of development before the first courses were offered. Nonetheless, a distinctive, signature curricular model had

been selected over the course of a single academic year.

CONCLUSION

20 Institutions about to embark on a general education curricular revision should give careful attention to process, and particularly to the kind of outcomes a given process is likely to produce. While consensus is a laudable goal in the selection of a model, it can be an impediment at the design level, especially if the goal is to design a distinctive signature program. The Ruggiero problem-solving model used at Salve Regina University had the effect of tapping into faculty creativity by inviting a variety of groups and individuals to propose curricular models and deferring the definition of selection criteria until after the models were published. Thus, faculty members were free to concentrate on mission, content, skills, and pedagogy without worrying about pleasing all possible constituencies and interest groups. When the time came to select a model, the faculty assembly had five distinctive programs to choose from, and the model selected clearly reflected the university mission statement in a high-profile, signature design.

REFERENCE

Ruggiero, Vincent Ryan. 2003. *The Art of Thinking: A Guide to Critical and Creative Thought*. New York: Longman.

Questions for Discussion

1. When Trainor opens his argument by claiming that efforts to reform an undergraduate curriculum are not only "frustrating" but also "notoriously contentious and protracted," what assumptions is he making about his audience? What kind of readers would be likely to accept this as a reasonable claim—the definition of a problem in need of a solution?

2. Why is "process" so important, in Trainor's view? How did the process used at his university differ from those widely used elsewhere? Why are these differences important, according to Trainor?

3. Why would a school's mission statement be essential when evaluating or reforming its curriculum, in Trainor's view?

4. Trainor uses the extended example of the process of curriculum reform at Salve Regina University to make his main argument. How effective do you think Trainor's use of this example is in supporting his argument? Do you think his argument would have been stronger if he had included examples of similar efforts at other universities? Why or why not?

5. Trainor was the dean of undergraduate education at Salve Regina University when the curriculum reform effort he describes in this article was undertaken there. To what extent do you think his position as a dean and his experience as a university educator contributes to the effectiveness of his argument?

6. Trainor goes into great detail to explain the process used at his university to reform the core curriculum there. Is his explanation of this process clear? Does it make his argument more effective, in your view? Why or why not? Do you think readers who are not educators will find this explanation understandable and persuasive? Explain.

7. What do you think Trainor's description of the complicated process of curriculum reform at his university suggests about the nature of colleges and universities as institutions of higher learning? Do you think that the picture Trainor paints of the process of curriculum reform is a positive one? Explain, citing specific passages from his essay to support your answer.

④ | # Life, Liberty, and the Pursuit of Aptitude

WALTER KIRN

If you are reading this textbook for a college class, chances are you took the SAT or the ACT, the two major standardized tests used by colleges in their admissions decisions. In the United States, taking the SAT or ACT is a rite of passage for most high school students who intend to go to college, and not surprisingly, parents, teachers, and students themselves place a great deal of emphasis on these tests, which purportedly reveal a student's readiness for college. Walter Kirn did well on the SAT and believed that his scores proved that he was ready to succeed at Princeton University, the Ivy League institution where he studied. But he found that he wasn't ready for the intellectual challenges of college, despite his good SAT scores. His experience has prompted him to reconsider the idea of "aptitude," which refers to a person's general level of intelligence and ability to perform certain kinds of intellectual tasks. It also led him to question whether it's fair to use a test like the SAT to decide on a student's potential. In the following essay, which was published in the *New York Times* in 2009, he draws on his experience to argue that "certain questions of merit and advancement have no definitive answers and, on occasion, ought to be left blank." Kirn is an accomplished writer and critic whose many publications include a memoir, *Lost in the Meritocracy: The Undereducation of an Overachiever* (2009).

WALTER KIRN, "Life, Liberty, and the Pursuit of Aptitude"

Sonia Sotomayor (b. 1954) was appointed to the U.S. Supreme Court in August 2009, one month after Kirn's essay was published. An accomplished prosecutor and judge, she became the first person of Hispanic descent to serve as a U.S. Supreme Court justice. In the first sentence of this essay Kirn refers to hearings conducted by the Judiciary Committee of the U.S. Senate to confirm or reject any person nominated to the Supreme Court.

1 When **Sonia Sotomayor** sits down next week before the Senate Judiciary Committee to answer questions about her qualifications to serve on the U.S. Supreme Court, thoughtful observers may do well to reflect that, by certain measures, she shouldn't be there. That's because decades ago, in her late teens, Sotomayor faced another important test—the SAT, the traditional route to top-tier placement in our national meritocracy—on which, by her own admission, she didn't do well. What exactly her test scores were she hasn't said, but she has revealed that they "were not comparable to that of my colleagues" at Princeton University, where she was admitted as a self-styled "affirmative-action baby." The fact that she later graduated from Princeton with highest academic honors and went on to reach the upper echelons of her chosen career, the law, speaks well of her intellect, her drive and the discernment of Princeton's admissions office, but it doesn't speak well, necessarily, of the conventional, test-based notions of merit that might well have stopped her, had they been strictly applied, before she even got started.

As a product of the same education system that molded Sotomayor (and as a fellow Princeton graduate who took his degree seven years after she did), I would like to think that I know a tiny something about what she and others experienced while trying to scale, percentile by percentile, the ladder of academic and social distinction. I call this group of contemporary strivers—a group that has largely supplanted the moneyed gentry as our country's governing class—the "Aptocrats," after the primary trait that we were tested for and which we sought to develop in ourselves as a means of passing those tests. As defined by the institutions responsible for spotting and training America's brightest youth, this "aptitude" is a curious quality. It doesn't reflect the knowledge in your head, let alone the wisdom in your soul, but some quotient of promise and raw mental agility thought to be crucial to academic success and, by extension, success in general. All of this makes for a self-fulfilling prophecy. The more aptitude that a young person displays, the more likely it is that she or he will have a chance to win the golden tickets—fine diplomas, elite appointments and so on—that permit you to lead the aptocratic establishment and set the terms by which it operates.

The key aptocratic concept, of course, is fairness. The reason that most thinking Americans consent to our modern procedures for advancement (and the reason some seek to correct their "cultural biases," in the words of Sotomayor, with policies like affirmative action) is that we esteem the ideal on which they're based, namely that of equal opportunity. To America's propertied white male founders, this particular definition of "justice for all" wasn't uppermost in mind, of course, but to me, as a public-school student in the '70s concerned with eventually moving to the head of his generational class, it constituted an entire theology. From the first time I raised my hand in kindergarten, eager to prove that I'd memorized my alphabet, to the day I sat down with three sharpened No. 2 pencils to demonstrate my mastery of analogies on the SAT, I held it as self-evident that being created equal was just Step 1 in the process of proving myself somewhat superior. I eagerly gave myself over to this program, because I believed that its principles were just and that any benefits it conferred on me would be deemed legitimate by all, and especially the students I'd surpassed.

Only when I entered Princeton did I start to have doubts about the system that got me

there. Some took the form of doubts about myself. My impressive performance on the SATs (whose supposed biases I was blind to, perhaps because I was a middle-class Caucasian and they operated in my favor) didn't seem to count for much now that I found myself having to absorb volumes upon volumes of information rather than get the right answers on multiple-choice tests. Yes, I had a large vocabulary, and yes, I knew how to deploy it to good effect in classroom discussions and during professors' office hours, but suddenly my prowess felt slightly fraudulent. Called upon to read whole books, many of them old, obscure and difficult, I discovered that I lacked stamina and insight. The little word puzzles I cut my teeth on were irrelevant to the daunting task of digesting Chaucer and Milton. My solution? I didn't have one. Like countless college students before and since, I relied for my scholastic survival on a combination of verbal bluster, teacher-pleasing good manners and handy study aids.

5   While I dished out the high-level baloney that my aptocratic mind excelled at, I looked around at the students who didn't resemble me in terms of skin color and background and

CONTEXT

The SAT has long been criticized for reflecting a bias in favor of a mainstream white Western cultural tradition (see par. 4). Results from the test show that students from many minority groups, especially blacks and Hispanics, perform less well on the test than white students, and some analyses have shown that the SAT underpredicts the academic success of women in college. In addition, test results show a correlation between family income and achievement on the SAT, and the gap in performance on the test between the lowest and highest income levels has grown in recent years. As a result of these concerns, a number of colleges and universities have reconsidered the use of the SAT and similar standardized tests in their admissions process. As of 2010, approximately 740 colleges and universities had discontinued the use of the SAT and other standardized tests or de-emphasized the importance of such tests in admissions decisions.

wondered how they were staying afloat at all. As a child of the rural Midwest, I felt decidedly out of place at Princeton among the debonair Eastern prep-school graduates who still, in the early 1980s (just a decade or so after the campus went co-ed) seemed to embody its privileged heritage, so I could scarcely imagine the alienation of these other yet more marginalized students. And while I happened to know that some of them gained admission on special terms meant to make up for their social disadvantages, I didn't resent them for this. Not at all. Because I came from a geographic region that Princeton hadn't favored in the past, but which it was now intent on drawing from, I was also a sort of affirmative-action student. What's more, the poorer and browner of my classmates—particularly the women—seemed to study twice as hard as I did, clocking endless hours in the library and forgoing weekend parties for late-night cram sessions. Maybe their SAT scores were lower than mine, but they ranked higher than I did on the effort scale. And on the bravery scale too.

A system of advancement by aptitude, by statistical measurements of mental acuity, doesn't concern itself with determination and courage, but if the world were truly fair, it would. This was one of the things I learned at Princeton, along with the lesson that multiple-choice tests don't predict a student's grasp of

Shakespeare. To judge by her statements about her college days and by her ruling on the use of a vocational examination used to promote firefighters, Sotomayor is also skeptical about one-size-fits-all testing. That's probably natural, given her experience as an aptocrat who needed help, made the most of it when it was offered and may soon succeed to a position that could allow her to see that others receive it. But what does the American public think?

According to a recent New York Times/CBS News poll, 67 percent of Democrats support affirmative action, while 60 percent of Republicans oppose it. These numbers reflect an old philosophical split over the nature of social justice. Does it consist of devising enlightened rules and applying them equally to everyone or does it entail sometimes modifying those rules when it appears that they treat some of us a bit more equally than others? This argument could go on forever (and has), but there's a way out of it, I think, which even my most exacting Princeton professors might not find entirely idiotic. The premise of this solution is that all systems that seek to rank human beings according to "merit"—an inherently complex idea—will inevitably fall short of fully accounting for what merit consists of in the real world. As such, these systems, like our Constitution, should be subject to amendment from time to time, since no definition of merit lasts forever.

The orthodox combination of high-school transcripts and SAT scores that allowed me into Princeton wasn't, I found out after I was admitted, a guarantee of my ability to make the most of its academic offerings. Put simply, I wasted a lot of time there, I engaged in a lot of shoddy, pretentious dodges, and maybe I shouldn't have been there in the first place. Perhaps someone else deserved my spot—someone whose talents weren't so easily indexed but might have been another Sotomayor. How would I know? And that's the point: I can't.

Which is why certain questions of merit and advancement have no definitive answers and, on occasion, ought to be left blank.

Questions for Discussion

1. How does Kirn define "aptitude"? Why is this definition important, in his view? How does it fit into his main argument?

2. Kirn claims that standardized testing and other measures of "aptitude" are tolerated by Americans because these measures seem to be based on the principles of fairness and equal opportunity (see par. 3). How does Kirn support this claim? Do you think he's right? Why or why not?

3. What did Kirn discover about himself once he began his studies at Princeton University? What conclusions does he draw from his experience as a student there? Do you think his conclusions are warranted? Why or why not? How might your own experience as a student influence your answer to that question?

4. Kirn bases his main argument largely on his own experience as a successful student who attended Princeton, a prestigious university. How effectively does Kirn use his experience as a student to support his argument? Do you think his argument would have been more or less effective if he had attended a less prestigious university? Explain.

5. In paragraph 7, Kirn asks whether social justice consists of "devising enlightened rules and applying them equally to everyone or does it entail sometimes modifying those rules when it appears that they treat some of us a bit more equally than others?" How persuasive do you find his answer to that question? How would you answer it?

NEGOTIATING

DIFFERENCES

The writers in this cluster address questions that continue to generate intense discussion and directly affect the lives of students. For example, Rick Livingston and Stanley Katz focus their arguments on what courses students should be required to take and why the idea of a traditional liberal education is frequently challenged. Walter Kirn raises a different question: Should standardized tests be used to determine a student's intellectual ability or promise? Kirn's own experience suggests that he wasn't ready for the kinds of material, such as literature by Shakespeare, that he was required to read in college. All these essays can prompt you to think about what you believe you should be learning in college. That's what you will be asked to do for this assignment.

In his essay in this cluster, Stephen Trainor describes the process used at his school to reform its general education program—the core courses that all students are required to take regardless of the major or minor they choose. Imagine now that your college or university has decided to revise its curriculum. You have been invited to participate in the review process to offer a student perspective on what should be retained from, eliminated from, or added to the current curriculum. As a representative of other students, it is your responsibility to consider whether the curriculum at your school serves the needs of the students who attend your school—not just whether it suits you.

Your task now is to write an essay in which you propose or justify one change in the curriculum or argue on behalf of retaining one of the current requirements. To make your argument, you will need to consider not only your school's curriculum but also its mission statement. You should also consider the kinds of students who attend your school and the reasons they do so. And you should think about what purpose your school serves in the community. Finally, you should imagine that your argument will be read by faculty and administrators who may differ from you in terms of what they consider important. You will need their support if proposing a significant change. So if you are writing, for example, to recommend the elimination of a history requirement, imagine that historians sit on the committee charged with the responsibility for curriculum review.

How Should Students Be Taught?

By this point in your education, you have probably experienced different kinds of teaching methods: lectures, discussions, research with a lab partner, collaborative learning in small groups, and maybe even service learning—a process in which students learn by doing volunteer work in their communities. Different teaching methods—or pedagogies, as educators call them—appeal to different kinds of teachers as well as different kinds of students. Some professors are at their best in a lecture hall, commanding the attention of a large audience; others do their best work by facilitating discussion in which students engage in the open exchange of ideas. Most educators would agree that no single teaching method should be imposed on everyone. How teachers proceed in the classroom must be informed by the nature of the discipline in which they are teaching, their own strengths, and the kinds of students they have.

But underlying the decisions that educators need to make about "how students should be taught" are some fundamental questions: To what extent is the teacher an authority who should be in command within the classroom? To what extent should students have a voice in determining how they learn? Should teaching be designed to pass knowledge on to students who passively receive it, or should teachers encourage active learning in which students question what has been previously believed to be true? And what is the impact of specific kinds of teaching on students? Do some kinds of teaching help students learn better than others? Do some kinds of teaching actually harm students?

Answering such questions raises others: Is it more important for students to leave college with knowledge of facts and figures or with skills such as critical thinking and writing? And if both of these goals are desirable, is it possible for teachers to give equal emphasis to both? As you read the selections in this cluster, you will find diverse views on these issues. One author emphasizes the importance of learning skills that are useful in the workplace, two argue on behalf of giving students power in the classroom, and one emphasizes the importance of engaging the attention of students by focusing on what remains to be discovered rather than on what is already known. As you engage their arguments, consider your own experience as a student and the teaching to which you have been exposed. What kinds of teaching worked for you? What kinds didn't? What might have worked better? Addressing such questions in the context of the four readings in this cluster might lead you to your own conclusions about how students should be taught.

① Lost in the Life of the Mind

BILL COPLIN

Educators traditionally value what can be called "the life of the mind," or the kind of interior life that can be fostered through serious study and reflection. Critics sometimes question whether living such a "life of the mind," which is often associated with professors, can leave a person disconnected from the realities of daily life. Bill Coplin is one such critic. He worries about getting "lost in the life of the mind," as the title of his essay suggests, and he argues that professors sometimes allow the passion they have for their own areas of scholarship to obscure what might be in the best interest of students. In making this argument, he raises challenging questions about the extent to which colleges and universities should focus on helping students to develop skills for the workplace. Coplin teaches public affairs at Syracuse University. His essay was first published in the *Chronicle of Higher Education* in September 2004.

BILL COPLIN, "Lost in the Life of the Mind"

1 "Bait and switch" is usually used to describe the sleazy telephone sales rep who starts, "This is your lucky day. You are the winner of a free vacation in the Bahamas." Schnooks take the bait only to find out the hidden costs.

I felt like a schnook after my second week as an undergraduate in 1956 at Washington College in Chestertown, Md. After a year, I transferred to the Johns Hopkins University, where the switch was even more apparent. My parents, relatives, high-school teachers, and guidance counselor had said, "You are college material," so I thought I'd go to college and live happily ever after.

However, I quickly realized that I had been a victim of a gigantic conspiracy on the part of colleges that was unwittingly supported by the rest of society in the name of the American dream, unfettered social mobility. I took the bait that college would lead to a high-paying and rewarding job. Once there, the switch was on. My role was to please the faculty by showing them I wanted to learn everything they loved to learn. It wasn't until getting my Ph.D. in international relations from American University that I was told by a wise professor, "A college degree and four quarters will get you a dollar."

I thought taking English meant improving my writing skills, that taking Spanish meant that when I went to Mexico I'd be able to converse, that studying history would be an exercise in learning about the past. Wrong on all three counts!

5 English courses at that time were about appreciating literature. (Now many are about deconstructing text and going off on ideological rants.) Spanish taught language that would permit me to read great Spanish novelists and thinkers, not close a deal. History was a study of the study of history—discussion, for instance, of **Charles Beard's** economic interpretation of the Constitution rather than of what the founding fathers actually did.

I was impressed by my English professor's passion and excitement. Wish I could

Charles Beard (1874–1948) was an American historian who argued in his controversial book *An Economic Interpretation of the Constitution of the United States* (1913) that the writers of the Constitution wrote it for the economic interests of landowning white males.

CONTEXT

In recent decades, debates in the United States about whether college should prepare students for the workforce or provide students with a traditional general education have intensified as manufacturing jobs that do not require a college degree have disappeared and other job opportunities for people who do not have college degrees have become more limited (see par. 14). After he took office in 2009, President Barack Obama announced substantial education reforms, including an expansion of support for two-year colleges. In 2010 he said during a weekly radio address,

> Our prosperity in the 20th century was fueled by an education system that helped grow the middle class and unleash the talents of our people more fully and widely than at any time in our history. We built schools and focused on the teaching of math and science. We helped a generation of veterans go to college through the GI Bill. We led the globe in producing college graduates, and in turn we led in producing ground-breaking technologies and scientific discoveries that lifted living standards and set us apart as the world's engine of innovation.

In 2006, the Conference Board, a respected business advocacy organization, released a report on the readiness of American students for the workplace. It concluded that

> basic knowledge and applied skills are perceived to be critical for new entrants' success in the 21st century U.S. workforce, but when basic knowledge and applied skills rankings are combined for each educational level, the top five "most important" are almost always applied skills.

Geoffrey Chaucer (1342–1400) was an English poet and philosopher who is best known for *The Canterbury Tales*, a poem about people who share stories to pass the time while they are on a religious pilgrimage to Canterbury, the site of an important cathedral. Because Chaucer wrote in a version of English that is no longer spoken, professors assigning *The Canterbury Tales* must decide whether to teach it in its original version or to assign an edition that translates Chaucer's language into contemporary English.

have been as excited about **Chaucer**, or even figured out what the hell he was saying. If you haven't had the pleasure, here is a short quote out of Bartlett's Familiar Quotations: "feeld hath eyen, and the wode has eres."

The first thing that strikes you is that if you had this on Microsoft Word, there would be red squiggles under half of it. I had to learn a foreign language called 14th-century English. The professor subjected me to this because he was a professional scholar saying, in essence, "Be like me."

I could not blame him for his missionary zeal because that is why he went into academe in the first place, and what his Ph.D. trained him for. However, I was plenty angry at a system that treated all students as if they were in college to learn for the sake of learning when in fact the vast majority wanted college to prepare them for a successful career. I wanted to learn about life;

they wanted me to lose myself in the life of the mind.

Not much has changed over the past 48 years, and with devastating results, if a recent conversation I had with Joe, let's call him, is any indication. I met Joe in the late 1980s when he was 12 years old in a program in which my undergraduates worked with at-risk youth. Joe adopted me as his mentor because, despite a serious speech impediment, he liked to argue politics. He didn't want to end up, like many of his friends had, in jail or dead, and he didn't want to be on welfare like his parents were.

10 However, Joe could not pass the New York State standardized tests required for graduation. He went into the Job Corps, where he got his GED, became a professional house painter, joined the Army, completed basic training at the top of his class, served overseas, and eventually left the military. He decided he wanted to be a policeman and did OK on the civil-service exam.

He called me in 2003 to tell me that he was in a local community college to study criminal justice and get an associate degree. During the course of the conversation, he said, "Coplin, how come I got to learn the MLA, the APA, and the Chicago style? Can't they make up their minds?"

I told Joe that the college curriculum, even at a community college serving students who don't necessarily want to go on to a four-year liberal-arts degree, was designed to prepare professional scholars. Moreover, the inability to select one citation form was evidence that college faculty members can't reach a consensus on even the most trivial of educational goals. I advised him to play the game. He said, "No problem, I learned to do that in the Army."

Joe would have been far better served if he had spent his time learning to write and speak more clearly and with better grammar. It's tempting to dismiss him as an example because of his socioeconomic background and the faults of the public-school system.

But poor oral and written communication skills are rampant no matter what the educational background of the student or the ranking of the college.

According to employers, college students are not prepared for the work force because they lack the skills and character needed to succeed. Our best and brightest students might take statistics in college and score A's on the tests that measure their ability to solve some abstract problem about white and black Ping-Pong balls, but cannot figure out how to set up a bar graph to display real-world data. They learn calculus, but they can't make budget projections.

15 They learn shortcuts to jump the academic hurdles with a minimum of effort, but not much about honesty and work ethic. A director of sales and marketing for a media company wrote me: "What I found from my hiring—the higher the GPA and the more prestigious the school, the less prepared for the real world the grad was. I was amazed at the basics that these 22- and 23-year-olds lacked. Real basic—like how about we wake up every day and show up for work on time!"

Liberal-arts leaders have no choice but to continue setting the bait. It's a matter of economic survival. Most students and their parents will pay as much as $160,000 only if they believe a college experience will lead to a better economic future.

The important question is to what degree colleges will deliver what they promise. Teaching critical thinking and fostering intellectual well-roundedness are important goals, but too general and self-serving. Faculties need to take more responsibility for helping students acquire the skills employers want. The list needs to be specific enough so that professors can assess skill levels but general enough so that the skills cut across all academic programs.

Those skills include dependability, attention to detail, teamwork, obtaining and analyzing information, problem solving, and writing clearly. Such a list can be found in my recent book 10 Things Employers Want You to Learn in College. Similar lists can be found in a study in 2002 that the National Association of Colleges and Employers based on surveys of 457 employers, or in work from the early 1990s by the Department of Labor's Secretary's Commission on Achieving Necessary Skills, or in the 2003 Business-Higher Education Forum report, "Building a Nation of Learners."

The focus on general professional skills would allow liberal-arts faculties to have their cake and eat it too. On one hand, they would be free to choose whatever curricular content they want. On the other, they would provide students with the opportunity to practice and improve the skills employers expect. Professors just need to keep their eye on the target and to be as rigorous about students' skills as they are about their own research. Whatever content they teach should be applicable beyond the confines of their disciplines. They can do that by incorporating more fieldwork and active learning into their courses.

20 For example, students from a class studying The Canterbury Tales could rewrite one of them in a modern setting (active learning) or present one to a 12th-grade English class in a local high school (fieldwork). Instructors teaching methods in various social sciences could require students, as I have since 1979 in my methods course, to complete a client survey for a community agency serving youth.

Liberal-arts professors will have to accept the implicit social contract with their students. They need to treat undergraduates as clients who learn not only from what is said, assigned, and tested, but also from the professor's own behavior. For their part, students must recognize professors' expertise in their subjects, but also their importance as professional-skills coaches. That means seeking constructive criticism rather than worrying only about grades, and working hard to master the material rather than cramming before tests.

COMPLICATION

Scholars like Coplin will often refer to their own published work to provide additional information about their research or views. Providing a record of publication can also be useful when establishing ethos (see pages 67–73). But are there circumstances in which it might be inappropriate to direct attention to a prior publication? Consider Coplin's reference in paragraph 18 to his book 10 Things Employers Want You to Learn in College. Does it contribute to his argument or distract from it?

Over the past 30 years, service learning, internships, computer-based instruction, team projects, and problem-based interdisciplinary courses have become more widespread. However, they remain the exceptions, helping admissions officers better set the bait. Liberal-arts institutions over all need to embrace a skills perspective to minimize the switch.

Questions for Discussion

1. What is the "gigantic conspiracy" that colleges engage in, according to Coplin? What evidence does he provide that such a "conspiracy" exists? Do you think that Coplin intentionally exaggerates the existence of such a "conspiracy"? What would he gain by doing so?

2. What are Coplin's chief complaints about what colleges teach their students? On what basis does he make his complaints? Do you think his complaints are valid? Why or why not?

3. What harm can be done when a professor conveys, "Be like me"? Could harm be done if professors are not role models to some extent? To what extent might your answers to these questions provide support for Coplin's argument or offer a counterargument to his position?

4. What solutions does Coplin suggest for the problems he sees with the conventional college curriculum? Do you think his solutions are practical? Explain.

5. How does Coplin believe students should be taught? Why do you think he puts more emphasis on the development of professional skills than on the acquisition of specific knowledge? Do you agree with him on this point? Why or why not?

6. What evidence does Coplin offer to support his claims that colleges do not prepare students for the workforce? How valid or convincing do you find his evidence?

7. How would you describe the tone of this argument? What specific characteristics of his writing contribute to his tone? To what extent do you think Coplin's tone strengthens or weakens his essay?

8. This essay might be described as an argument based on deductive reasoning (see pages 81–83). What basic principle or belief about the purpose of a college education does Coplin base his reasoning on? Do you think this principle or belief is widely shared by Americans? Do you share Coplin's basic belief about college? Explain, citing specific passages from his essay to support your answer.

② | # Moving Away from the Authoritarian Classroom

MANO SINGHAM

As the title of the following essay suggests, Mano Singham is interested in working collaboratively with students instead of wielding absolute power in the classroom. In his essay, which was first published in 2005 in *Change* magazine, Singham shares his concern that "trust, respect, and judgment are being squeezed out by an increasingly adversarial relationship between teachers and students." This adversarial relationship is evident in college course syllabi, which Singham believes have become too legalistic and authoritarian. He uses his own experience to argue that when college instructors share authority with their students, everyone benefits. As you read his essay, consider whether your own experience as a student provides support for his argument. Singham is director of the University Center for Innovation in Teaching and Education at Case Western Reserve University, where he also teaches physics. His latest book is *God vs. Darwin: The War Between Evolution and Creationism in the Classroom* (2009). He also maintains a blog at http://blog.case.edu/singham/, where he wrote in 2005 that writing "has the startling effect of revealing gaps in knowledge and weaknesses of logic and reasoning, thus forcing re-evaluation of one's ideas. So writing is not a one-way process from brain to screen/paper. It is a dialectic process. Writing reveals your ideas but also changes the way you think."

MANO SINGHAM, "Moving Away from the Authoritarian Classroom"

1 The professor at the conference handed around a copy of his class syllabus to illustrate how he had implemented his teaching innovation. He seemed a gentle, polite, and concerned teacher, someone who would be well liked by his students. And yet, viewed through the lens of his syllabus, he appeared a tyrant.

The arrogant tone of the document was all too familiar. Instructions to the students read like imperial commands: "You will submit three projects...," "You will make a five-minute report...." His institution's policy on electronic submission of assignments, quoted in the syllabus, was even sterner. "Students bear sole responsibility for ensuring that papers or assignments submitted electronically to a professor are received in a timely manner" and are "obliged to have their e-mail client issue a receipt verifying that the document has been received." Indeed, they should "retain a copy of the dated submission on a separate disk," presumably as proof of having met the deadline.

The school's policy on disabilities was yet more legalistic. "Students with a documented disability must inform the instructor at the close of the first class meeting.... If you do not consult with the instructor and follow up at the Student Support Services office during the first two weeks of classes...you will thereby waive any claim to a disability and the right to any accommodation pertaining thereto."

This harshness is, unfortunately, not uncommon in syllabi. At a subsequent faculty discussion of power in the classroom at my own university, I quoted these sections of the syllabus as examples of an authoritarian faculty mindset. There were embarrassed smiles of recognition all around. One faculty member, also a kindly and concerned teacher, shamefacedly admitted that those phrases could have been lifted directly from her own syllabus. She hadn't realized until that moment how rude they might sound to students.

5 But the sad fact is that students don't seem to be offended by being ordered around in course syllabi. Cynics might argue that this is because no student actually reads them. But even if they do, by the time they come into our college classroom, students have received many similar edicts. They have probably come to think of them as the normal way of doing things.

I find it hard to believe that teachers always treated students so rudely in their syllabi or that syllabi were always so detailed and legalistic, trying to cover almost every eventuality. It is likely that the authoritarian syllabus is just the visible symptom of a deeper underlying problem, the breakdown of trust in the student–teacher relationship. When and why did this state of affairs arise, and how did it become so widespread?

One reason for this breakdown is undoubtedly the lengthening reach of local and national legislatures into the classrooms. For example, a faculty member at my university

was surprised to be told that he had been reported for violating the law by leaving graded homework outside his office for students to pick up at any time. He contacted my office to find out if such an arrangement, convenient for both instructor and students, was indeed illegal. (These issues are dealt with in my own institution's *Undergraduate Instructor's Manual,* but faculty ignore this document the way students ignore syllabi.)

I checked the manual and found that it was: "Graded exams, papers, and homework should never be left outside of office doors or otherwise unattended for students to claim; this is a violation of FERPA and an invitation to theft. Instructors should return graded material to students individually, in class or in office hours, or should arrange to mail final material to students once the semester has ended."

FERPA, as we all come to know sooner or later, stands for Family Educational Rights and Privacy Act, federal legislation that governs the privacy of student educational records.

10 So it has come to this, that the innocuous act of returning homework to students is now overseen by federal statute.

College faculty across the country are probably routinely violating this law one way or another, wittingly or not. For example, in my own 200-student physics course, I had been assigning homework for each class (which met three times a week). The assignments were handed in at the beginning of each class, graded, and returned at the beginning of the subsequent class.

This resulted in a lot of paper moving around: at the beginning of each class, 200 students had to hand in their new homework and pick up their graded assignments. In order to manage this process efficiently, I sorted the graded homework into assigned groups of four and placed the piles in front of the class, so that any one member could pick them up for the entire group before class began. The system worked so well that I did not lose any instructional time at all, despite the seeming complexity of the operation.

But was I breaking the law? Possibly. I was, after all, not returning homework individually, and students were picking up someone else's homework in addition to their own. But after doing this for 10 years for a total of about 4,000 students, I have not heard one student complaint. Maybe the students did not know about FERPA. But even if they knew, they did not care. I think that most students understand when something is done to advance legitimate educational goals, and they will look for rules to invoke only if they feel that the teacher does not have their best interest in mind. It is when that sense of trust is broken that rules and laws become important.

If we were to take the number of rules in a typical syllabus as a measure of that lack of trust, we would have to conclude that at present the college classroom is in a very sorry state indeed. Of course we need some rules and policies at the institutional level. But there should also be room for common sense and judgment about what is and is not appropriate in the classroom, and good learning practices should be the driving force. My concern is that trust, respect, and judgment are being squeezed out by an increasingly adversarial relationship between teachers and students.

15 There is no doubt that in the college classroom, the teacher wields a great deal of institutional power, and students have very little. College ideals about academic freedom are for the benefit of the faculty, and students know this. As long as we are not capricious, abusive, or flagrantly unjust, we can pretty much set the rules of the classroom, and students have to live with them. The problem is that many teachers are not using this flexibility to explore teaching methods that might enhance learning. Instead, we defend ourselves against potential challenges to our authority by wielding the course syllabus, our chief instrument of power, like a club.

My own institution's *Undergraduate Instructor's Manual* is full of useful information on how to prepare course materials, prepare and conduct exams, deal with students with disabilities, respect confidentiality, etc. All these issues are presented with the aim of helping the instructor—especially the novice—avoid the kind of blunders that might generate disputes.

But the tone of the sections that deal with course syllabi are formal and defensive, as if a committee had looked at all the possible things that could go wrong and all the possible laws that might apply, and then had devised rules to prevent disaster. New faculty are also given friendly advice by academic administrators that the syllabus is like a legally binding contract, so they should put in it everything that they expect of students and go over it on the first day of class.

I have before me a legal newsletter from another university in which the author clearly lays out the implied contractual nature of the syllabus:

> The most common of these types of implied agreements, at least from the faculty perspective, is the written syllabus and/or oral recitation of the rules, policies, procedures, and expectations given to students by faculty at the beginning of each academic course. When a dispute arises with a student over course requirements, satisfactory resolution of the dispute frequently rests on the legal enforceability of the terms and conditions of these implied agreements.

20 The author then proceeds to describe what a faculty member needs to put in the syllabus in order to have a solid legal case in the event that a dispute with a student should go to court.

Given this attitude, it should not be surprising that the classroom has become a quasi-courtroom. I have seen course syllabi that extend over 20 pages. A colleague told me the he spent almost all the time of his first three-hour class walking the students carefully through the syllabus, because otherwise he could not be sure that they were aware of all the rules he had established for them to follow. But the result of such an attitude is that we end up viewing all students as potential courtroom adversaries.

I am sure that it is not pleasant for students or teachers or universities to have to go through judicial proceedings because of some classroom disagreement. But why do we assume that this is the worst thing that could happen and must be avoided at all costs? If the price that we pay for our legal protection is the creation of a controlling classroom atmosphere that stifles learning, isn't that a much worse result? Repeated questions by students such as "Will this be on the test?" and "Do we have to know this?" are symptoms of the extent to which following rules has replaced learning as the chief goal in the classroom.

To begin to understand the phenomenon of creeping authoritarianism, I need go no further than my own courses and syllabi and see how they have evolved over the years. When I started teaching my large introductory physics courses, I was convinced that the only way to keep on top of things and maintain clarity, fairness, and uniformity was to be highly organized.

So my syllabi were very detailed, laying out what topics would be covered and when, all the deadlines for homework and dates for exams, detailed penalties for missing anything, and the exact format for writing papers (down to page length, fonts, and font sizes). I even had instructions for how the homework sheets were to be folded before being handed in, and students lost points if they folded them incorrectly or not at all.

25 What is telling is that my monster syllabus came about even though I wasn't trying to prevent legal actions. I had a good educational reasons for all the rules, and for dealing efficiently with large classes I can still justify a few of them. But the list of rules grew year by year, driven by its own internal logic. Initially,

for example, I had no penalties for missing deadlines, since I assumed students would meet them. When a significant number of students did not, my syllabus the following year had penalties that increased each day that the assignment was late.

I also didn't have penalties for papers that had typographical or grammatical errors; I simply assumed that students would proofread anything they handed in. When that didn't happen, I introduced detailed penalties for those infractions too. Each added rule produced requests for exceptions from students who couldn't meet it. So other rules were tacked on to deal with the possible range of exceptions. And so on. Like **Abou Ben Adham**, my name led all the rest when it came to comprehensive, detailed, and authoritarian syllabi.

I confess that my system worked extremely well. The papers came in on time, carefully proofread and edited. Homework was handed in like clockwork, folded correctly. I, like so many teachers before me, had discovered the power of the detailed syllabus to achieve precisely targeted goals. That power went to my head, like power usually does, and I began to think that I could create a rule to achieve whatever I wanted. Some departmental colleagues, marveling at the smoothness with which my course was run, adopted many features of my syllabus for their own courses. Thus are the viruses of complex syllabi spread through academia.

But I discovered that there were important things that I just could not do with my syllabus. I could not make students care about the work, be creative and original, be considerate of others, or write and speak well. All I could do was force them to do very specific things. As I started reading the research literature on good teaching practices, I came to realize that this failure was not due to my technical inability to devise ingenious rubrics to add to my syllabus to achieve those more worthwhile goals. Rather, it was that the very act of creating detailed course requirements and

Abou Ben Adham is the name of a poem by James Henry Leigh Hunt (1784–1859), the last stanza of which reads, "The next night/ [The Angel] came again with a great wakening light,/ And showed the names whom love of God had blessed,/ And lo! Ben Adhem's name led all the rest."

forcing students to obey them actually worked against the higher goal of learning.

The emphasis on tight classroom management, although widespread, goes counter to some of the most compelling research on learning. In *The Learner-Centered Classroom,* Maryellen Weimer argues that learning ensues when instructors relinquish much of their power and cede some decisionmaking power to students. Alfie Kohn, in *Punished by Rewards,* points out that student motivation is enhanced when rewards and punishments are minimized, students are given choices about what and how they learn, and students and teachers collaborate in classroom-policy decisionmaking.

30 In *Power in the Classroom,* Virginia Richmond and James McCroskey emphasize that students have more power than we realize and that the more we try to exercise direct authority, the more likely it is that they will devise ways to thwart us, leading to reduced learning. Robert Boice's work on classroom incivilities in *Advice for the New Faculty Member* shows how student resistance to learning is not necessarily innate but arises from the atmosphere created early on in the classroom.

All this made sense, once I realized what I should have known all along, that learning is an inherently voluntary act that you can no more force than you can force someone to love you. Authoritarianism and fostering a love of learning just do not go together. If they did, the best learning should occur in prison education programs, where the "students" can be coerced to do almost anything.

When I stepped back and looked at my syllabus in the light of this new understanding, it appeared completely foreign to my conception of what an ideal teacher–student relationship should be. Somewhere along the way, I had lost sight of the fact that a learning community has to be a community in the best sense of the word. I had made my classroom into a dictatorship. But it was a dictatorship nonetheless, since I unilaterally made all the decisions that affected the students. My focus on having the trains run on time had prevented me from achieving more fundamental and important learning goals.

I became increasingly uncomfortable with the way my classroom was structured. So when I had the chance to teach a new seminar on the evolution of scientific ideas to a much smaller class of 17 sophomores, I decided that the time had come to make changes. But rather than make incremental changes I decide—like an addict who concludes that the only way to become free of the dependency is to make a clean break—to dispense with a formal written syllabus altogether.

I walked into the first class with only a reading list and a tentative schedule of readings for the first few weeks. We did not talk about rules or grades at all; instead we went straight into a discussion of the course subject matter. While I felt almost naked going into the class with no syllabus in my hand or already posted on the Web, the students did not seem to be at all concerned by its absence. No one mentioned it, lending further support to the thesis that no student ever reads it.

35 It was only after about five weeks into the course, when the students were getting their essays returned with detailed feedback, that one asked whether the essays would be eventually assigned a grade. It was then that we had a class discussion on the topic of course requirements. I told them what my learning goals for the seminar were and said that I was open to discussing how they would be evaluated. However, I also said that I had an ethical obligation to my institution to ensure that the grades were meaningful measures of learning, and also to my discipline to ensure that the course was advancing knowledge in that area.

Within those constraints, we reached a consensus on what the students would need to do to reach the learning goals and to earn their course grades. We selected a fairly traditional mix of short essays, a research paper, a formal presentation, and participation. We also decided on the approximate weights of the assignments, with some flexibility for individual choice.

We reached an agreement about broad criteria for evaluating each item in the mix, with the consensus being that they would leave it up to me to make the final judgment based on my experience and expertise. What was especially interesting to me was that they did not want a reductionist, detailed, itemized scoring of class participation (such as keeping track of how many times each person spoke, the quality of what they said, etc.), which is exactly the kind of thing a legalistic syllabus might spell out. They felt that this led to artificial, points-related behavior and hindered genuine discussion and learning.

They preferred that I make a holistic judgment. I told them that ultimately, assigning a grade has an unavoidably subjective component and that the system would work only if they trusted that I would judge them fairly. The students seemed to treat that statement as if it were obvious, and it went unchallenged. (This is another example of the differences between student and teacher perceptions. While we go to great lengths to persuade students that our grading is objective they, despite our protestations, seem to assume that it is quite subjective.)

We also set up a schedule of deadlines for assignments, again with some flexibility built in to accommodate the students' individual schedules (we sometimes forget that students have other courses and even personal lives outside of our classes) and with respect for mine (I have a life too).

40 In about 30 minutes we thus jointly created a de-facto syllabus. There was no controversy, though the students were extremely surprised that they were being given such leeway in setting up the structure of the course. The course has ended, and so far no one has sued me or even complained about grades or course requirements. A few students missed some of their self-determined deadlines, but only by a few days, and they were profusely apologetic. The students came to class, discussed serious topics in a relaxed way, and wrote excellent papers on topics they chose for themselves and seemed really to care about. In fact, the end of the semester brought with it genuine sadness that we were going our separate ways. It really felt like a community, and the semester was one of the most enjoyable teaching experiences of my life.

Will this idyllic result occur every time? Probably not. When I speak about my experience with colleagues, I am asked what I would do if a student consistently missed deadlines or took advantage in some way of the flexibility and freedom I provided. I say I don't know. I would deal with such situations on an ad hoc, case-by-case basis, because each such case is likely to be caused by factors unique to that individual student. Tolstoy's famous opening line in **Anna Karenina** that "all happy families resemble one another, but each unhappy family is unhappy in its own way" applies to students too.

By devising complex general rules to cope with any and all anticipated behavior, we tend to constrain, alienate, and dehumanize students, and we remove a great deal of the enjoyment from the learning experience. Surely students are like us in flourishing under conditions of freedom. Why is it that given the choice between creating a freer classroom atmosphere that risks the occasional problem and establishing an authoritarian classroom

Anna Karenina, by Leo Tolstoy, published in 1877, is considered a masterpiece of world literature. It tells the story of a beautiful woman who is a member of the social elite in St. Petersburg, Russia, until she leaves her husband to live with a handsome military officer, Count Vronsky. Her husband refuses to give her a divorce and keeps her from seeing their son. Eventually, Vronsky loses interest in Anna. Abandoned by her lover and unwilling to return to a husband she detests, Anna commits suicide by throwing herself under a train.

CONTEXT

Singham's argument in favor of a less authoritarian classroom is part of a long-standing discussion in American education about the kind of classroom environment that best supports student learning. Many education researchers have studied the impact of different teaching styles on student learning and well-being, and much of this research indicates that some of the characteristics of the authoritarian classroom that Singham criticizes here do not facilitate positive student learning outcomes. However, in American popular culture the authoritarian teacher is well established as a fixture in American education and is reflected in such figures as Professor Charles Kingsfield, played by John Houseman in the film *The Paper Chase* (1973), and Jaime Escalante, a high school math teacher played by Edward James Olmos in *Stand and Deliver* (1988)—the kind of tough, demanding teachers that many Americans believe all good teachers must be.

that tries to anticipate and thwart any and all problems, we choose the latter? Surely creating learning conditions that benefit almost all students should be preferred to those aimed at protecting ourselves against the occasional malcontent.

The syllabus has also become a defensive shield against grade complaints. It is rare that students will complain directly to the professor that they did not learn much in the course. They might make this serious charge to their peers, but complaints to teachers are almost always about grades or other sanctions. The formal written syllabus, with all the lists of things that students must and must not do and highly detailed grading schemes that outline how students are to be evaluated, is the teacher's preemptive strike against such complaints.

At some level, we know that grading is an art, not a science. We should come to our judgments with great care and all the expertise, objectivity, and honesty we can muster, but they are judgments nonetheless. Elaborate grading schemes merely create an illusion of objectivity and hide that judgment under a shroud of numbers. If a student complains, the syllabus with its formulas can provide a spurious precision that can mute criticism. We can sigh regretfully and tell the student. "You needed to get an 80 to get a B and unfortunately you scored only 78.6."

45 Complex and precise grading schemes remind me of the highly dramatic ritual that occurs in football games if there is doubt as to whether the ball has been advanced the required 10 yards. A hush falls on the stadium as the game is halted and two officials are called from the sidelines to carefully place the 10-yard chains on the field. The referee then signals that either the effort to advance the ball 10 yards has failed by a few inches or has just barely succeeded. That this is an elaborate farce can be appreciated by noting that where the ball is spotted at the end of the play is only a rough approximation, as are the estimations of the starting point and

of the distances advanced in previous plays. But the players and fans accept the result unquestioningly, cowed by the solemnity of the ritual.

The research of Patricia King and Karen Strohm Kitchener, summarized in their book *Developing Reflective Judgment*, indicates that our incoming college students tend to be largely pre-reflective in their thinking. They view knowledge in black/white, right/wrong terms, and colleges do not do particularly well in nudging them to take a more nuanced view of knowledge or in teaching them how to weigh evidence and arguments in order to arrive at reasoned judgments. When we try to hide the role that judgment makes in our own decisions, we may be inadvertently reinforcing their low-level view of knowledge.

If we dispense with the authoritarian syllabus as a weapon, then the challenge for teachers is to give students confidence that we have the competence to make judgments about their performance, that we have meaningful criteria for doing so, that our assessments are meaningful measures of important learning, and that we have the impartiality to make honest judgments. This is a harder task than creating a watertight syllabus, primarily because it requires a change in mindset on the part of teachers. But in the long run it results in a much more rewarding experience for both teachers and students.

If we are not to be adversaries in the classroom, then what is the appropriate relationship between teachers and students? As I see it, it is that of good neighbors in a small community. The classroom works best when students and teachers perceive it as a place where there is a continuing conversation among interested people, similar to what one might have with neighbors and friends. A sense of community is not created by rules and laws but by a sense of mutual respect and tolerance. Good neighborliness cannot be legislated—it can only be learned by example and experience, and it flourishes in an atmosphere of trust and acceptance of differences.

Can we recover the ideal of the classroom as a collegial conversation among faculty and students where the role of the instructor is to provide the insight that experience and expertise provides, without invoking the institutional power vested in us to coerce students? Or have we gone too far down the path of authoritarian, adversarial classrooms to regain that level of trust, assuming we did have it at some point?

50   When I tell people of my attempts to create a freer classroom atmosphere, I am reminded of those political discussions in which the future of this or that authoritarian country is discussed, and the question is raised as to whether the people of that country are "ready for democracy."

I am asked, are students mature enough to deal with such freedom responsibly? Will they take advantage of the situation to not do any serious work? Might they even sue because the teacher did something that was not in the syllabus? All these things might happen, but this is a chance that I have to take. The possibility that my students may not be ready for democracy worries me a little, but the thought that they should be ready for and accepting of authoritarianism troubles me a great deal more.

I am looking forward to teaching the seminar again. And once more I will start without a syllabus.

Questions for Discussion

1. What concerns Singham about the "arrogant tone" (par. 2) and the detailed nature of college course syllabi? Why is he concerned that "students don't seem to be offended by being ordered around in course syllabi" (par. 5)? Does your own experience as a student support Singham's description of college course syllabi? Are you offended by them? Why or why not?

2. How does Singham explain "the breakdown of trust in the student–teacher relationship" (par. 6)? What evidence does he offer to support this claim? How persuasive is his explanation of this breakdown of trust?

3. What did Singham do in his own classroom to work against what he calls "creeping authoritarianism"? How effectively do you think the changes he made in his own classroom addressed this problem? As a student, would you support the kind of learning environment that Singham tried to create in his own classroom? Why or why not?

4. Singham bases his argument in part on his own experience as a college instructor. How effectively does he use his experience to help make his argument? Do you think his argument is more or less effective because of his experience? Explain.

5. As the note at the beginning of this article indicates, Singham is the director of the University Center for Innovation in Teaching and Education at Case Western Reserve University. Does that fact influence your reaction to his argument in any way? Why or why not?

6. In paragraph 51 Singham poses a series of questions. What do you think these questions are intended to achieve? What assumptions about audience seem to inform Singham's position that it is better to offer democracy prematurely than to become authoritarian?

7. This essay might be considered an example of a Rogerian argument (see pages 126–131). How effectively does Singham's argument resolve the conflict he describes?

③ | # Toward a Radical Feminist Pedagogy

BELL HOOKS

In the late 1970s and early 1980s colleges and universities began to establish new programs in Women's Studies. These programs, which grew out of the feminist movement, encouraged students to examine the role of gender and power relations in society and challenged long-standing ideas about teaching and learning in American education. But like the women's movement itself, Women's Studies faced resistance and often struggled to gain acceptance as a legitimate academic discipline. That sense of struggle is a central part of the vision of feminist teaching presented in the following essay by scholar and writer bell hooks. hooks argues for a kind of education that is both collaborative and confrontational, one that intentionally challenges convention. The very title of hooks's essay is provocative, suggesting that the purpose of her approach to education is radical change. Perhaps it is that sense of purpose that continues to invite controversy, because despite the growth of Women's Studies programs in American higher education and despite the acceptance of feminism as a school of thought, both Women's Studies and feminist theory continue to face criticism inside and outside educational circles. A distinguished professor of English at City College of New York, hooks has been an insistent voice for a progressive view of education based on feminist theory. As you read the following essay, which was published in 1989 in her book *Talking Back*, compare her sense of the purpose of education to your own.

BELL HOOKS, "Toward a Radical Feminist Pedagogy"

1 My favorite teacher in high school was Miss Annie Mae Moore, a short, stout black woman. She had taught my mama and her sisters. She could tell story after story about their fast ways, their wildness. She could tell me ways I was like mama, ways I was most truly my own self. She could catch hold of you and turn you around, set you straight (these were the comments folk made about her teaching)—so that we would know what we were facing when we entered her classroom. Passionate in her teaching, confident that her work in life was a pedagogy of liberation (words she would not have used but lived instinctively), one that would address and confront our realities as black children growing up in the segregated South, black children growing up within a white-supremacist culture.

Miss Moore knew that if we were to be fully self-realized, then her work, and the work of all our progressive teachers, was not to teach us solely the knowledge in books, but to teach us an oppositional world view—different from that of our exploiters and oppressors, a world view that would enable us to see ourselves not through the lens of racism or racist stereotypes but one that would enable us to focus clearly and succinctly, to look at ourselves, at the world around us, critically—analytically—to see ourselves first and foremost as striving for wholeness, for unity of heart, mind, body and spirit.

It was as a student in segregated black schools called Booker T. Washington and Crispus Attucks that I witnessed the transformative power of teaching, of pedagogy. In particular, those teachers who approached their work as though it was indeed a pedagogy, a science of teaching, requiring diverse strategies, approaches, explorations, experimentation, and risks, demonstrated the value—the political power—of teaching. Their work was truly education for critical consciousness. In these segregated schools, the teachers were almost all black women. Many of them had chosen teaching at a historical moment when they were required by custom to remain single and childless, to have no visible erotic or sexual life. Among them were exceptional teachers who gave to their work a passion, a devotion that made it seem a true calling, a true vocation. They were the teachers who conceptualized oppositional world views, who taught us young black women to exult and glory in the power and beauty of our intellect. They offered to us a legacy of liberatory pedagogy that demanded active resistance and rebellion against sexism and racism. They embodied in their work, in their lives (for none of them appeared as tortured spinsters estranged and alienated from the world around them) a feminist spirit. They were active participants in black community, shaping our futures, mapping our intellectual terrains, sharing revolutionary fervor and vision. I write these words, this essay to express the honor and respect I have for them because they have been my pedagogical guardians. Their work has had a profound impact on my consciousness, on my development as a teacher.

During years of graduate schools, I waited for that phase of study when we would focus on the meaning and significance of pedagogy, when we would learn about teaching, about how to teach. That moment never arrived. For years I have relied on those earlier models of excellent teaching to guide me. Most specifically, I understood from the teachers in those segregated schools that the work of any teacher committed to the full self-realization of students was necessarily and fundamentally radical, that ideas were not neutral, that

CONTEXT

Paulo Freire (1921–1997), one of the most influential educational theorists of the twentieth century, advocated a revolutionary theory of education focused on helping students use literacy to gain knowledge and political power. Born in Brazil, Freire developed his ideas about "liberatory education" by working with illiterate Brazilian peasants, for which he was jailed and then exiled in 1964. He returned to Brazil in 1979 and later served as a minister of education. His best-known book is *Pedagogy of the Oppressed* (1970), in which he describes his theory of education as a means of personal and political transformation. Some scholars consider Freire's ideas to be consistent with the kind of feminist education that hooks describes in this essay. hooks often refers to Freire's theories in her writing.

to teach in a way that liberates, that expands consciousness, that awakens is to challenge domination at its very core. It is this pedagogy that Paulo Freire calls "education as the practice of freedom." In his introduction to Freire's *Pedagogy of the Oppressed*, Richard Shaull writes:

> Education either functions as an instrument which is used to facilitate the integration of the younger generation into the logic of the present system and bring about conformity to it, or it becomes "the practice of freedom," the means by which men and women deal critically and creatively with reality and discover how to participate in the transformation of their world.

A liberatory feminist movement aims to transform society by eradicating patriarchy, by ending sexism and sexist oppression, by challenging the politics of domination on all fronts. Feminist pedagogy can only be liberatory if it is truly revolutionary because the mechanisms of appropriation within white-supremacist, capitalist patriarchy are able to co-opt with tremendous ease that which merely appears radical or subversive. Within the United States, contemporary feminist movement is sustained in part by the efforts academic women make to constitute the university setting as a central site for the development and dissemination of feminist

Feminist education refers to an approach to teaching based on feminist theory. Often, programs based on feminist theory are called Women's Studies programs. According to the Center for Women's and Gender Studies at the University of Texas at Austin, there are more than 600 Women's Studies programs in the United States. The center defines the purposes of Women's and Gender Studies as fostering "multi-disciplinary research and teaching that focuses on women, gender, sexuality, and feminist issues [and supporting] the intersections of the above with age, class, race, ethnicity, and nationality."

thought. Women's Studies has been the location of this effort. Given the way universities work to reinforce and perpetuate the status quo, the way knowledge is offered as commodity, Women's Studies can easily become a place where revolutionary feminist thought and feminist activism are submerged or made secondary to the goals of academic careerism. Without diminishing in any way our struggle as academics striving to succeed in institutions, such effort is fully compatible with liberatory feminist struggle only when we consciously, carefully, and strategically link the two. When this connection is made initially but not sustained, or when it is never evident, Women's Studies becomes either an exotic terrain for those politically chic few seeking affirmation or a small settlement within the larger institutional structure where women (and primarily white women) have a power base, which rather than being oppositional simply mirrors the status quo. When feminist struggle is the central foundation for feminist education, Women's Studies and the feminist classroom (which can exist outside the domain of Women's Studies) can be places where education is the practice of freedom, the place for liberatory pedagogy.

5 At this historical moment, there is a crisis of engagement within universities, for when knowledge becomes commoditized, then much authentic learning ceases. Students who want to learn hunger for a space where they can be challenged intellectually. Students also suffer, as many of us who teach do, from a crisis of meaning, unsure about what has value in life, unsure even about whether it is important to stay alive. They long for a context where their subjective needs can be integrated with study, where the primary focus is a broader spectrum of ideas and modes of inquiry, in short a dialectical context where there is serious and rigorous critical exchange. This is an important and exciting time for feminist pedagogy because in theory and practice our work meets these needs.

Feminist education—the feminist classroom—is and should be a place where there is a sense of struggle, where there is visible acknowledgement of the union of theory and practice, where we work together as teachers and students to overcome the estrangement and alienation that have become so much the norm in the contemporary university. Most importantly, feminist pedagogy should engage students in a learning process that makes the world "more rather than less real." In my classrooms, we work to dispel the notion that our experience is not a "real world" experience. This is especially easy since gender is such a pressing issue in contemporary life. Every aspect of popular culture alerts us to the reality that folks are thinking about gender in both reactionary and progressive ways. What is important is that they are thinking critically. And it is this space that allows for the possibility of feminist intervention, whether it be in our classroom or in the life of students outside the classroom. Lately there has been a truly diverse body of students coming to my classes and other feminist classes at universities all around the United States. Many of us have been wondering "what's going on" or "why are all these men, and white men, in the class." This changing student body reflects the concern about gender issues, that it is one of the real important issues in people's private lives that is addressed academically. Freire writes, "Education as the practice of freedom—as opposed to education as the practice of domination—denies that we are abstract, isolated, independent, and unattached to the world; it also denies that the world exists as a reality apart from us."

To make a revolutionary feminist pedagogy, we must relinquish our ties to traditional ways of teaching that reinforce domination. This is very difficult. Women's Studies courses are often viewed as not seriously academic because so much "personal stuff" is discussed. Fear that their courses will be seen as "gut" classes has led many feminist professors to rely more on traditional pedagogical styles. This is unfortunate. Certainly, the radical alternative to the status quo should never have been simply an inversion. That is to say, critical of the absence of any focus on personal experience in traditional classrooms, such focus becomes the central characteristic of the feminist classroom. This model must be viewed critically because a class can still be reinforcing domination, not transforming consciousness about gender, even as the "personal" is the ongoing topic of conversation.

To have a revolutionary feminist pedagogy we must first focus on the teacher–student relationship and the issue of power. How do we as feminist teachers use power in a way that is not coercive, dominating? Many women have had difficulty asserting power in the feminist classroom for fear that to do so would be to exercise domination. Yet we must acknowledge that our role as teacher is a position of power over others. We can use that power in ways that diminish or in ways that enrich and it is this choice that should distinguish feminist pedagogy from ways of teaching that reinforce domination. One simple way to alter the way one's "power" as teacher is experienced in the classroom is to elect not to assume the posture of all-knowing professors. This is also difficult. When we acknowledge that we do not know everything, that we do not have all the answers, we risk students leaving our classrooms and telling others that we are not prepared. It is important to make it clear to students that we are prepared and that the willingness to be open and honest about what we do not know is a gesture of respect for them.

To be oppositional in the feminist classroom one must have a standard of valuation that differs from the norm. Many of us tried new ways of teaching without changing the standards by which we evaluated our work. We often left the classroom feeling uncertain about the learning process or even concerned that we were failing as teachers. Let me share a particular problem I have faced. My classroom style is very confrontational.

It is a model of pedagogy that is based on the assumption that many students will take courses from me who are afraid to assert themselves as critical thinkers, who are afraid to speak (especially students from oppressed and exploited groups). The revolutionary hope that I bring to the classroom is that it will become a space where they can come to voice. Unlike the stereotypical feminist model that suggests women best come to voice in an atmosphere of safety (one in which we are all going to be kind and nurturing), I encourage students to work at coming to voice in an atmosphere where they may be afraid or see themselves at risk. The goal is to enable all students, not just an assertive few, to feel empowered in a rigorous, critical discussion. Many students find this pedagogy difficult, frightening, and very demanding. They do not usually come away from my class talking about how much they enjoyed the experience.

10 One aspect of traditional models of teaching that I had not surrendered was that longing for immediate recognition of my value as a teacher, and immediate affirmation. Often I did not feel liked or affirmed and this was difficult for me to accept. I reflected on my student experiences and the reality that

COMPLICATION

Feminist education and Women's Studies programs have long been the object of intense criticism, which often focuses on the charge that such programs do not have the same kind of intellectual foundation that more traditional disciplines in the sciences and the humanities have. In 1993 writer Karen Lehrman joined the controversy with an article in *Mother Jones* magazine in which she examined the state of Women's Studies programs in the United States. She wrote,

> In many classes discussions alternate between the personal and the political, with mere pit stops at the academic. Sometimes they are filled with unintelligible post-structuralist jargon; sometimes they consist of consciousness-raising psychobabble, with the students' feelings and experiences valued as much as anything the professor or texts have to offer. Regardless, the guiding principle of most of the classes is oppression, and problems are almost inevitably reduced to relationships of power. "Diversity" is the mantra of both students and professors, but it doesn't apply to political opinions.

> Not every women's studies course suffers from these flaws. In fact, the rigor and perspective of individual programs and classes vary widely, and feminist academics have debated nearly every aspect of the field. But it seems that the vast majority of women's studies professors rely, to a greater or lesser extent, on a common set of feminist theories. Put into practice, these theories have the potential to undermine the goals not only of a liberal education, but of feminism itself.

> Lehrman's article provoked much debate about Women's Studies programs. Since her article was published, many critics have continued to charge that Women's Studies programs lack intellectual rigor.

I often learned the most in classes that I did not enjoy and complained about, which helped me to work on the traditional assumption that immediate positive feedback is a signifier of worth. Concurrently, I found that students who often felt that they hated a class with me would return later to say how much they learned, that they understood that it was the different style that made it hard as well as the different demands. I began to see that courses that work to shift paradigms, to change consciousness, cannot necessarily be experienced immediately as fun or positive or safe and this was not a worthwhile criteria to use in an evaluation.

In the feminist classroom, it is important to define a term of engagement, to identify what we mean when we say that a course will be taught from a feminist perspective. Often the initial explanations about pedagogy will have a serious impact on the way students experience a course. It is important to talk about pedagogical strategy. For a time, I assumed that students would just get the hang of it, would see that I was trying to teach in a different way and accept it without explanation. Often, that meant I explained after being criticized. It is important for feminist professors to explain not only what will differ about the classroom experience but to openly acknowledge that students must consider whether they wish to be in such a learning space. On a basic level, students are often turned off by the fact that I take attendance, but because I see the classroom experience as constituting a unique learning experience, to miss class is to really lose a significant aspect of the process. Whether or not a student attends class affects grading and this bothers students who are not accustomed to taking attendance seriously. Another important issue for me has been that each student participate in classroom discussion, that each student have a voice. This is a practice that I think is important not because every student has something valuable to say (this is not always so), but often students who do have meaningful comments to contribute are silent. In my classes, everyone's voice is heard as students read paragraphs which may explore a particular issue. They do not have the opportunity to refuse to read paragraphs. When I hear their voices, I become more aware of information they may not know that I can provide. Whether a class is large or small, I try to talk with all students individually or in small groups so that I have a sense of their needs. How can we transform consciousness if we do not have some sense of where the students are intellectually, psychically?

Concern with how and what students are learning validates and legitimates a focus, however small, on personal confession in classroom discussions. I encourage students to relate the information they are learning to the personal identities they are working to socially construct, to change, to affirm. If the goal of personal confession is not narcisism, it must take place within a critical framework where it is related to material that is being discussed. When, for example, I am teaching Toni Morrison's novel, *The Bluest Eye*, I may have students write personal paragraphs about the relationship between race and physical beauty, which they read in class. Their paragraphs may reveal pain, woundedness as they explore and express ways they are victimized by racism and sexism, or they may express ideas that are racist and sexist. Yet the paragraphs enable them to approach the text in a new way. They may read the novel differently. They may be able to be more critical and analytical. If this does not happen, then the paragraphs fail as a pedagogical tool. To make feminist classrooms the site of transformative learning experiences, we must constantly try new methods, new approaches.

Finally, we cannot have a revolutionary feminist pedagogy if we do not have revolutionary feminists in the classroom. Women's Studies courses must do more than offer a different teaching style; we must really challenge issues of sexism and sexist oppression both by what we teach and how we teach. This is truly a collective effort. We must learn from one another, sharing ideas and pedagogical strategies. Although I have invited feminist colleagues to come and participate in my classes, they do not. Classroom territoriality is another traditional taboo. Yet if we are to learn from one another, if we are to develop a concrete strategy for radicalizing our classrooms, we must be more engaged as a group. We must be willing to deconstruct this power dimension, to challenge, change and create new approaches. If we are to move toward a revolutionary feminist pedagogy, we must challenge ourselves and one another to restore to feminist struggle its radical and subversive dimension. We must be willing to restore the spirit of risk—to be fast, wild, to be able to take hold, turn around, transform.

Questions for Discussion

1. What crisis does hooks see in education? How can Women's Studies programs help address that crisis, in her view?

2. What does hooks mean when she writes that knowledge has become a commodity? What evidence does she offer to support this assertion? Do you agree with her? Why or why not?

3. Why does hooks teach in a way that is confrontational? What is the goal of such an approach to teaching? hooks states that many students find her approach uncomfortable. Why does it not concern her that some of her students do not enjoy her classes? Should it concern her, in your view? Explain.

4. hooks argues that personal experience should be the central focus of the kind of feminist classroom she advocates. Evaluate the way in which hooks uses her experience as a student and a teacher to help her make her argument. How effective is her use of personal experience in this essay?

5. hooks has been both praised and criticized for her unconventional writing style as a scholar. How would you characterize her style? In what ways might her writing style be considered appropriate for the argument she is making about education in this essay?

6. How effectively does hooks address possible objections to her view? What questions would you raise about hooks's approach to education? What might your reaction to her essay reveal about your views regarding the purpose of education?

④ The Art of Teaching Science

LEWIS THOMAS

Lewis Thomas (1913–1993) lived through a period when the practice of medicine underwent dramatic changes as physicians became more specialized, more able to draw upon new procedures and medications, and less likely to visit patients in their homes. A graduate of Harvard Medical School, Thomas was active as both a physician and a researcher; he also taught medicine at Tulane University, New York University, and Yale University, and he later became president of the Sloan-Kettering Institute in New York, helping to make it one of the world's most prominent sites for cancer research. So he knows something about teaching and learning science. In the following essay, he challenges the conventional view of science as a body of well-established facts, and he argues for a different conception of science as a window into human ignorance. The teaching of science, he believes, must be dramatically reformed if science is to become a tool for humans to solve their most pressing problems. This essay was originally published in the *New York Times* in 1982, but Thomas's concerns still seem valid today. It's worth considering whether his vision for the teaching of science has been realized in the nearly 20 years since he wrote this essay. In addition to being an accomplished physician, Thomas was also an acclaimed writer whose award-winning collection of essays, *Lives of a Cell* (1974), attracted a wide audience.

LEWIS THOMAS, "The Art of Teaching Science"

1 Everyone seems to agree that there is something wrong with the way science is being taught these days. But no one is at all clear about when it went wrong or what is to be done about it. The term "scientific illiteracy" has become almost a cliché in educational circles. Graduate schools blame the colleges; colleges blame the secondary schools; the high schools blame the elementary schools, which, in turn, blame the family.

I suggest that the scientific community itself is partly, perhaps largely, to blame. Moreover, if there are disagreements between the world of the humanities and the scientific enterprise as to the place and importance of science in a liberal-arts education and the role of science in 20th-century culture, I believe that the scientists are themselves responsible for a general misunderstanding of what they are really up to.

During the last half-century, we have been teaching the sciences as though they were the same collection of academic subjects as always, and—here is what has really gone wrong—as though they would always be the same. Students learn today's biology, for example, the same way we learned Latin when I was in high school long ago: first, the fundamentals; then, the underlying laws; next, the essential grammar and, finally, the reading of texts. Once mastered, that was that: Latin was Latin and forever after would always be Latin. History, once learned, was history. And biology was precisely-biology, a vast array of hard facts to be learned as fundamentals, followed by a reading of the texts.

Furthermore, we have been teaching science as if its acts were somehow superior to the facts in all other scholarly disciplines—more fundamental, more solid, less subject to subjectivism, immutable. English literature is not just one way of thinking; it is all sorts of ways; poetry is a moving target; the facts that underlie art, architecture and music are not really hard facts, and you can change them any way you like by arguing about them. But science, it appears, is an altogether different kind of learning: an unambiguous, unalterable and endlessly useful display of data that only needs to be packaged and installed somewhere in one's temporal lobe in order to achieve a full understanding of the natural world.

5   And, of course, it is not like this at all. In real life, every field of science is incomplete, and most of them—whatever the record of accomplishment during the last 200 years—are still in their very earliest stages. In the fields I know best, among the life sciences, it is required that the most expert and sophisticated minds be capable of changing course—often with a great lurch—every few years. In some branches of biology the mind-changing is occurring with accelerating velocity. Next week's issue of any scientific journal can turn a whole field upside down, shaking out any number of immutable ideas and installing new bodies of dogma. This is an almost everyday event in physics, in chemistry, in materials research, in neurobiology, in genetics, in immunology.

On any Tuesday morning, if asked, a good working scientist will tell you with some self-satisfaction that the affairs of his field are nicely in order, that things are finally looking clear and making sense, and all is well. But come back again on another Tuesday, and the roof may have just fallen in on his life's work. All the old ideas—last week's ideas in some cases—are no longer good ideas. The hard facts have softened, melted away and vanished under the pressure of new hard facts. Something strange has happened. And it is this very strangeness of nature that makes science engrossing, that keeps bright people at it, and that ought to be at the center of science teaching.

CONTEXT

Concern among American educators and policymakers that American students are not sufficiently educated in science (see par. 1) stretches back at least to 1958, when the U.S. Congress, in reaction to the launching of the Sputnik space satellite by the Soviet Union, passed the National Defense Education Act to provide greater federal support for the teaching of science, math, and related subjects. Since Thomas published this essay in 1982, education reform efforts have focused on reading and math, although science has sometimes become the focus of discussion when controversies arise, such as the controversy surrounding the teaching of evolution in high school science classes. In recent years some studies have revealed that Americans seem to have a limited knowledge of science. In 2009, for example, the California Academy of Sciences released a report indicating that most Americans were unable to pass a basic test of scientific knowledge. Such reports suggest that many of the concerns that Thomas expressed in this essay remain relevant today.

The conclusions reached in science are always, when looked at closely, far more provisional and tentative than are most of the assumptions arrived at by our colleagues in the humanities. But we do not talk much in public about this, nor do we teach this side of science. We tend to say instead: These are the facts of the matter, and this is what the facts signify. Go and learn them, for they will be the same forever.

By doing this, we miss opportunity after opportunity to recruit young people into science, and we turn off a good many others who would never dream of scientific careers but who emerge from their education with the impression that science is fundamentally boring.

Sooner or later, we will have to change this way of presenting science. We might begin by looking more closely at the common ground that science shares with all disciplines, particularly with the humanities and with social and behavioral science. For there is indeed such a common ground. It is called bewilderment. There are more than seven times seven types of ambiguity in science, all awaiting analysis. The poetry of **Wallace Stevens** is crystal clear alongside the genetic code.

10   One of the complaints about science is that it tends to flatten everything. In its deeply reductionist way, it is said, science

Wallace Stevens (1879–1955) was one of the most important American poets of the twentieth century, and his work is still widely studied. But students often find his poetry difficult to understand. Note how Thomas uses the reputation of Stevens's poetry as difficult to make his point about science in this passage.

The Age of Reason is a term used to describe the eighteenth century, a period in which the educated believed in the excellence of the human mind and optimistically thought that intelligence—informed by knowledge and shaped by logic—could solve almost any problem.

F. R. Leavis, John Ruskin, Edmund Wilson F. R. Leavis (1895–1878) and Edmund Wilson (1895–1972) were important literary critics. Leavis was an influential advocate of what is called "New Criticism," which shaped literary studies for much of the twentieth century. During the 1920s, Wilson's reviews of writers such as Ernest Hemingway, F. Scott Fitzgerald, and Eugene O'Neill helped build their reputations. John Ruskin (1819–1900) was considered by many to be the most important art critic in the English-speaking world during much of his lifetime. What all three men have in common is that they eventually turned to what today would be called *cultural criticism*, publishing books that called attention to social injustice and explored the challenges of contemporary life.

removes one mystery after another, leaving nothing in the place of mystery but data. I have even heard this claim as explanation for the drift of things in modern art and modern music: Nothing is left to contemplate except randomness and senselessness; God is nothing but a pair of dice, loaded at that. Science is linked somehow to the despair of the 20th-century mind. There is almost nothing unknown and surely nothing unknowable. Blame science.

I prefer to turn things around in order to make precisely the opposite case. Science, especially 20th-century science, has provided us with a glimpse of something we never really knew before; the revelation of human ignorance. We have been accustomed to the belief, from one century to another, that except for one or two mysteries we more or less comprehend everything on earth. Every age, not just the 18th century, regarded itself as the **Age of Reason**, and we have never lacked for explanations of the world and its ways. Now, we are being brought up short. We do not understand much of anything, from the episode we rather dismissively (and, I think, defensively) choose to call the "big bang," all the way down to the particles in the atoms of a bacterial cell. We have a wilderness of mystery to make our way through in the centuries ahead. We will need science for this but not science alone. In its own time, science will produce the data and some of the meaning in the data, but never the full meaning. For perceiving real significance when significance is at hand, we will need all sorts of brains outside the fields of science.

It is primarily because of this need that I would press for changes in the way science is taught. Although there is a perennial need to teach the young people who will be doing the science themselves, this will always be a small minority. Even more important, we must teach science to those who will be needed for thinking about it, and that means pretty nearly everyone else—most of all, the poets, but also

artists, musicians, philosophers, historians and writers. A few of these people, at least, will be able to imagine new levels of meaning which may be lost on the rest of us.

In addition, it is time to develop a new group of professional thinkers, perhaps a somewhat larger group than the working scientists and the working poets, who can create a discipline of scientific criticism. We have had good luck so far in the emergence of a few people ranking as philosophers of science and historians and journalists of science, and I hope more of these will be coming along. But we have not yet seen specialists in the fields of scientific criticism who are of the caliber of the English literary and social critics **F. R. Leavis and John Ruskin or the American literary critic Edmund Wilson**. Science needs critics of this sort, but the public at large needs them more urgently.

I suggest that the introductory courses in science, at all levels from grade school through college, be radically revised. Leave the fundamentals, the so-called basics, aside for a while, and concentrate the attention of all students on the things that are not known. You cannot possibly teach quantum mechanics without mathematics, to be sure, but you can describe the strangeness of the world opened up by quantum theory. Let it be known, early on, that there are deep mysteries and profound paradoxes revealed in distant outline by modern physics. Explain that these can be approached more closely and puzzled over, once the language of mathematics has been sufficiently mastered.

15 At the outset, before any of the fundamentals, teach the still imponderable puzzles of cosmology. Describe as clearly as possible, for the youngest minds, that there are some things going on in the universe that lie still beyond comprehension, and make it plain how little is known.

Do not teach that biology is a useful and perhaps profitable science; that can come later. Teach instead that there are structures squirming inside each of our cells that provide all the energy for living. Essentially foreign creatures, these lineal descendants of bacteria were brought in for symbiotic living a billion or so years ago. Teach that we do not have the ghost of an idea how they got there, where they came from, or how they evolved to their present structure and function. The details of oxidative phosphorylation and photosynthesis can come later.

Teach ecology early on. Let it be understood that the earth's life is a system of interdependent creatures, and that we do not understand at all how it works. The earth's environment, from the range of atmospheric gases to the chemical constituents of the sea, has been held in an almost unbelievably improbable state of regulated balance since life began, and the regulation of stability and balance is somehow accomplished by the life itself, like the autonomic nervous system of an immense organism. We do not know how such a system works, much less what it means, but there are some nice reductionist details at hand, such as the bizarre proportions of atmospheric constituents, ideal for our sort of planetary life, and the surprising stability of the ocean's salinity, and the fact that the average temperature of the earth has remained quite steady in the face of at least a 25 percent increase in heat coming in from the sun since the earth began. That kind of thing: something to think about.

Go easy, I suggest, on the promises sometimes freely offered by science. Technology relies and depends on science these days, more than ever before, but technology is far from the first justification for doing research, nor is it necessarily an essential product to be expected from science. Public decisions about the future of technology are totally different from decisions about science, and the two enterprises should not be tangled together. The central task of science is to arrive, stage by stage, at a clearer comprehension of nature, but this does not all mean, as it is sometimes claimed to mean, a search for mastery over nature.

Science may someday provide us with a better understanding of ourselves, but never, I hope, with a set of technologies for doing something or other to improve ourselves. I am made nervous by assertions that human consciousness will someday be unraveled by research, laid out for close scrutiny like the workings of a computer, and then—and *then*...! I hope with some fervor that we can learn a lot more than we now know about the human mind, and I see no reason why this strange puzzle should remain forever and entirely beyond us. But I would be deeply disturbed by any prospect that we might use the new knowledge in order to begin doing something about it—to improve it, say. This is a different matter from searching for information to use against schizophrenia or dementia, where we are badly in need of technologies, indeed likely one day to be sunk without them. But the ordinary, everyday, more or less normal human mind is too marvelous an instrument ever to be tampered with by anyone, science or no science.

20 The education of humanists cannot be regarded as complete, or even adequate, without exposure in some depth to where things stand in the various branches of science, particularly, as I have said, in the area of our ignorance. Physics professors, most of them, look with revulsion on assignments to teach their subject to poets. Biologists, caught up by the enchantment of their new power, armed with flawless instruments to tell the nucleotide sequences of the entire human genome, nearly matching the physicists in the precision of their measurements of living processes, will resist the prospect of broad survey courses; each biology professor will demand that any student in his path master every fine detail within that professor's research program.

The liberal-arts faculties, for their part, will continue to view the scientists with suspicion and apprehension. "What do the scientists want?" asked Cambridge professor in **Francis Cornford**'s wonderful "Microcosmographia

Francis Cornford (1874–1943) was an influential literary scholar whose work focused on the literature of ancient Greece. He was a member of a group known as the Cambridge Realists, scholars who drew upon anthropology and philology when interpreting literature because they believed that the key to understanding ancient literature was understanding the cultural rituals and myths to which writers were responding.

Academica." "Everything that's going," was the quick answer. That was back in 1912, and scientists haven't much changed.

But maybe, just maybe, a new set of courses dealing systematically with ignorance in science will take hold. The scientists might discover in it a new and subversive technique for catching the attention of students driven by curiosity, delighted and surprised to learn that science is exactly as the American scientist and educator **Vannevar Bush** described it: an "endless frontier." The humanists, for their part, might take considerable satisfaction in watching their scientific colleagues confess openly to not knowing everything about everything. And the poets, on whose shoulders the future rests, might, late nights, thinking things over, begin to see some meanings that elude the rest of us. It is worth a try.

I believe that the worst thing that has happened to science education is that the fun has gone out of it. A great many good students look at it as slogging work to be got through on the way to medical school. Others are turned off by the premedical students themselves, embattled and bleeding for grades and class standing. Very few recognize science as the high adventure it really is, the wildest of all explorations ever taken by human beings, the chance to glimpse things never seen before, the shrewdest maneuver for discovering how the world works. Instead, baffled early on, they are misled into thinking that bafflement is simply the result of not having learned all the facts. They should be told that everyone else is baffled as well—from the professor in his endowed chair down to the platoons of postdoctoral students in the laboratories all night. Every important scientific

advance that has come in looking like an answer has turned, sooner or later—usually sooner—into a question. And the game is just beginning.

If more students were aware of this, I think many of them would decide to look more closely and to try and learn more about what is known. That is the time when mathematics will become clearly and unavoidably recognizable as an essential, indispensable instrument for engaging in the game, and that is the time for teaching it. The calamitous loss of applied mathematics from what we might otherwise be calling higher education is a loss caused, at least in part, by insufficient incentives for learning the subject. Left by itself, standing there among curriculum offerings, it is not at all clear to the student what it is to be applied to. And there is all of science, next door, looking like an almost-finished field reserved only for chaps who want to invent or apply new technologies. We have had it wrong, and presented it wrong to class after class for several generations.

25 An appreciation of what is happening in science today, and how great a distance lies ahead for exploring, ought to be one of the rewards of a liberal-arts education. It ought to be good in itself, not something to be acquired on the way to a professional career but part of the cast of thought needed for getting into the kind of century that is now just down the road. Part of the intellectual equipment of an educated person, however his or her time is to be spent, ought to be a feel for the queernesses of nature, the inexplicable thing, the side of life for which informed bewilderment will be the best way of getting through the day.

Vannevar Bush (1890–1974) was an influential scientist and inventor best known for his work on what he called the *memex*—a system that would allow individuals to conveniently store all of the information they needed. This concept eventually contributed to the development of the World Wide Web. Bush also recommended the creation of what is now called the National Science Foundation. Although Bush believed that science was an "endless frontier" (as Thomas points out), he had contempt for the humanities.

Questions for Discussion

1. Consider the claim with which Thomas opens this argument. Who would be included in "everyone"—every person alive or every person of a certain kind? To what extent are you included in that "everyone"? Do you agree that science is not taught as well as it could be—especially to students who are unlikely to major in one of the sciences? Explain.

2. Thomas claims that "in real life, every field of science is incomplete" (par. 5). What does he mean by this statement? Why is it important to understand science as "incomplete," in his view? What problems emerge from an understanding of science as hard facts?

3. In what sense does science share common ground with other disciplines, according to Thomas? What are the implications of this common ground when it comes to teaching science, in his view? Do you think he's right? Why or why not?

4. Thomas refers to poets more than once. The last of these references is in paragraph 22: "poets, on whose shoulders the future rests...." What value does Thomas see in poetry? What does poetry have to do with science? How could the future depend upon poets and what they write, in his view?

5. According to Thomas, what is the purpose of studying science? How well does he support his viewpoint about the purpose of studying science? Do you agree with him? Why or why not?

6. What does Thomas mean when he writes that science needs critics but the public needs them more urgently (see par. 13)? What does the public have to do with the study and teaching of science, according to Thomas?

7. How would you describe Thomas's ethos? How does it contribute to this argument? Would his argument be more or less effective if it were composed by a poet rather than by a physician? Explain, citing specific passages from the essay to support your argument.

DIFFERENCES

NEGOTIATING

In most colleges, students are asked to evaluate their courses at the end of the semester. Evaluation forms distributed at the end of the course usually ask students to evaluate both the course itself and the instructor. Typically, the forms include questions about the instructor's preparedness for class, knowledge of the subject matter, ability to communicate effectively with students and to motivate students to learn the course material, and perhaps his or her availability outside of class. In many institutions, these evaluations are reviewed by administrators and used in decisions about hiring, promotion, tenure, and salary increases. Instructors often review them to get a sense of how effective their teaching is and to identify aspects of their teaching that might need improvement. In other words, these evaluations are taken seriously by course instructors and the colleges and universities where they teach.

But it's worth asking what such evaluations really tell us about how well an instructor has taught a course. Some instructors complain that course evaluation forms are little more than a measure of how well the students liked the instructor and the course; these forms, they claim, cannot tell us much about whether an instructor's teaching actually led to student learning. Moreover, students might dislike an instructor or a course yet still benefit from the course. Would the course evaluation reveal such benefit—or would it simply indicate the student's dissatisfaction with the instructor or the course? Such questions indicate how complicated the matter of course evaluations can be, despite their widespread use by colleges and universities. And the difficulties associated with course evaluations reflect the complexity of teaching and learning and the challenge of trying to figure out how best to teach students.

You have probably completed course evaluation forms at your school. Think about whether your answers on those forms really reflected how much you learned in your classes. Furthermore, what kind of course evaluations would best indicate how well an instructor taught a course? For this assignment, you will try to answer that question.

Imagine that you have been given the opportunity by your school to develop or revise the course evaluation forms used there. Your task is to create an evaluation form that will best capture how effectively an instructor has taught a course. Consider what kinds of information you would need to have about the course and the instructor's teaching to accomplish that goal. Then consider what questions the evaluation form should include. As a starting point, you might review the evaluation form currently used at your school as well as the forms used at other colleges and universities. You might also do research to see what is known about how best to evaluate college teaching. And consider interviewing some of the faculty at your school about how best to evaluate teaching. On the basis of your investigation, develop a new course evaluation form.

In addition to creating a course evaluation form, write a brief essay in which you explain your form and justify the specific questions you have included. This essay should in fact be a statement of your beliefs about how students should be taught in college. In other words, in developing your course evaluation form, you are putting into practice some of your beliefs about how college students should be taught. You should discuss those beliefs in your essay.

For this assignment, imagine that your audience includes faculty and administrators at your school.

How Should Learning Be Measured?

In the past decade, standardized tests, which have long been a fixture of American education, have become more widespread and given greater emphasis as states responded to the requirements of President George W. Bush's education reform program, known as No Child Left Behind. That program, which was passed in 2002, required states to set testing standards that all schools had to meet. In effect, the program required schools to prove that their students were learning sufficiently in math and reading so that they weren't "left behind." And the way schools proved that their students were learning was by giving them tests—usually, standardized tests mandated by the state.

This increased emphasis on standardized testing created great controversy. Some states resisted the No Child Left Behind program, arguing that the states, not the federal government, should be responsible for setting policies for educating citizens. Other states, seeking to be in compliance with the federal program, created new standardized tests to measure student achievement. Many teachers and administrators complained that the need to prepare students for these tests forced them to eliminate important material from the school curriculum because there simply wasn't enough time to teach students anything that wasn't on the tests. Some studies showed that this tendency by schools to "teach to the test" resulted in a narrower curriculum and weakened students' education.

In 2009, newly elected President Barack Obama announced his own education reform program, called "Race to the Top." He indicated that the focus on standardized testing that characterized the No Child Left Behind program would change; student learning would still be measured but in more complex ways that included other kinds of assessments along with standardized tests. Although many educators welcomed that change, the new Race to the Top program raised long-standing questions about how we can effectively measure student learning.

The essays in this cluster address those questions from a variety of perspectives. They examine some of the implications of large-scale testing and so-called "high-stakes" tests, which determine whether or not students pass a grade or graduate from high school. One essay looks at "tracking," a process by which students of similar academic ability are grouped together on the basis of test scores and grades. One explores alternatives to testing and grading. And one argues in favor of standardized testing. Together, these essays remind us that measuring student learning is no easy task.

① Tests, Tracking, and Derailment

PATRICIA WILLIAMS

If you have gone to school in the United States, chances are that you have encountered some form of tracking: Advanced Placement or honors classes, special education programs for students with special needs, remedial courses for struggling students, enrichment programs for gifted and talented students. Even if you were not tracked into such a program, it is likely that your school's curriculum offered different options for college-bound students and students who did not intend to go to college. The purpose of all these educational tracks is to match the curriculum to students' needs and abilities. But tracking has always been controversial, in part because it is not clear that special programs or tracks serve their intended purposes. Writer Patricia Williams, for example, believes that tracking students—for whatever purpose—ultimately leads to more problems than it solves. In her essay, which was published in the *Nation* in 2002, she traces what she sees as some of those problems and argues that educational resources can be better spent to ensure that all children benefit from schooling. In one sense her essay suggests that debates about how to measure student learning raise larger questions about the goals of schooling. As you read, consider how Williams's sense of the purpose of education informs her argument against educational tracking.

PATRICIA WILLIAMS, "Tests, Tracking, and Derailment"

1 As state budgets around the country are slashed to accommodate the expense of the war on terror, the pursuit of educational opportunity for all seems ever more elusive. While standardized tests are supposed to be used to diagnose problems and facilitate individual or institutional improvement, too often they have been used to close or penalize precisely the schools that most need help; or, results have been used to track students into separate programs that benefit the few but not the many. The implementation of gifted classes with better student–teacher ratios and more substantial resources often triggers an unhealthy and quite bitter competition for those unnaturally narrowed windows of opportunity. How much better it would be to have more public debate about why the pickings are so slim to begin with. In any event, it is no wonder there is such intense national anxiety just now, a fantastical hunger for children who speak in complete sentences by the age of six months.

A friend compares the tracking of students to the separation of altos from sopranos in a choir. But academic ability and/or intelligence is both spikier and more malleably constructed than such an analogy allows. Tracking students by separating the high notes from the low only works if the endgame is to teach all children the "Hallelujah Chorus." A system that teaches only the sopranos because no parent wants their child to be less than a diva is a system driven by the short-sightedness of narcissism. I think we make a well-rounded society the same way we make the best music: through the harmonic combination of differently pitched, but uniformly well-trained voices.

IQ, or *intelligence quotient*, is a measure of intelligence based partly on the ideas of nineteenth-century French psychologist Alfred Binet. Drawing on his observations of children with and without various disabilities, Binet developed a test to measure a child's "mental age." His test was adapted by several American psychologists and used by the U.S. Army to measure the intelligence levels of its recruits during the First World War. IQ tests have long been criticized as inaccurate and unfair, and criticisms of the tests as racially biased intensified in the 1960s and 1970s.

A parsimony of spirit haunts education policy, exacerbated by fear of the extremes. Under the stress of threatened budget cuts, people worry much more about providing lifeboats for the very top and containment for the "ineducable" rock bottom than they do about properly training the great masses of children, the vibrant, perfectly able middle who are capable of much more than most school systems offer. In addition, discussions of educational equality are skewed by conflation of behavioral problems with **IQ**, and learning disabilities with retardation. Repeatedly one hears complaints that you can't put a gifted child in a class full of unruly, noisy misfits and expect anyone to benefit. Most often it's a plea from a parent who desperately wants his or her child removed from a large oversubscribed

classroom with a single, stressed teacher in an underfunded district and sent to the sanctuary of a nurturing bubble where peace reigns because there are twelve kids in a class with two specialists and everyone's riding the high of great expectations. But all children respond better in ordered, supportive environments; and all other investments being equal, gifted children are just as prone to behavior problems—and to learning disabilities—as any other part of the population. Nor should we confuse exceptional circumstances with behavior problems. The difficulty of engaging a child who's just spent the night in a homeless shelter, for example, is not productively treated as chiefly an issue of IQ.

The narrowing of access has often resulted in peculiar kinds of hairsplitting. When I was growing up, for example, Boston Latin School was divided into two separate schools: one for boys and one for girls. Although the curriculum was identical and the admissions exam the same, there were some disparities: The girls' school was smaller and so could admit fewer students; and the science and sports facilities were inferior to those of the boys.

5 There was a successful lawsuit to integrate the two schools about twenty years ago, but then an odd thing happened. Instead of using the old girls' school for the middle school and the larger boys' school for the new upper school, as was originally suggested, the city decided to sever the two. The old boys' school retained the name Boston Latin, and the old girls' school—smaller, less-equipped—was reborn as Boston Latin Academy. The entrance exam is now administered so that those who score highest go to Boston Latin; the next cut down go to what is now, unnecessarily, known as the "less elite" Latin Academy.

One of the more direct consequences of this is that the new Boston Latin inherited an alumni endowment of $15 million dollars, much of it used to provide college scholarships. Latin Academy, on the other hand, inherited the revenue of the old Girls' Latin alumni association—something under

CONTEXT

In 1972, in response to a state law ending gender-based discrimination in Massachusetts schools, Girls' Latin Academy was changed to Boston Latin Academy and began accepting boys. That same year, girls were accepted into Boston Latin School, which describes itself as the oldest school in America, founded in 1635.

Tom Stewart/Corbis

$200,000. It seems odd: Students at both schools are tremendously talented, the cutoff between them based on fairly insignificant scoring differences. But rather than pool the resources of the combined facilities—thus maximizing educational opportunity, in particular funding for college—the resolution of the pre-existing gender inequality almost purposefully reinscribed that inequality as one driven by wealth and class.

There are good models of what is possible. The International Baccalaureate curriculum, which is considered "advanced" by most American standards, is administered to a far wider range of students in Europe than here, with the result that their norm is considerably higher than ours in a number of areas. The University of Chicago's School Mathematics Project, originally developed for gifted students at the Chicago Lab School, is now recommended for all children—all children, as the foreword to its textbooks says, can "learn more and do more than was thought to be possible ten or twenty years ago." And educator Marva Collins's widely praised curriculum for inner-city elementary schools includes reading Shakespeare.

Imparting higher levels of content requires nothing exceptional but rather normal, more-or-less stable children, taught in small classes by well-trained, well-mentored teachers who have a sophisticated grasp of

Copyright © Eric Fowke/Photo Edit

mathematics and literature themselves. It will pay us, I think, to stop configuring education as a battle of the geniuses against the uncivilized. We are a wealthy nation chock-full of those normal, more-or-less stable children. The military should not be the only institution that teaches them to be all that they can be.

Questions for Discussion

1. Williams compares tracking to separating the singers in a choir. How effectively do you think this comparison helps Williams make her point about the disadvantages of tracking? What does this comparison reveal about her beliefs about the purposes of schooling?

2. Williams refers to "the great masses of children, the vibrant, perfectly able middle who are capable of much more than most school systems offer." What evidence does she offer to support this assertion? Do you think she is right? Why or why not?

3. What point does Williams use the example of the Boston Latin School to illustrate? How effectively does this example help her make her point? How does it contribute to her main argument about tracking?

4. In her final paragraph Williams argues that we should not think of education "as a battle of the geniuses against the uncivilized." To what extent do you think Bertell Ollman and Gregory Cizek, whose essays appear later in this chapter, would agree with Williams? Cite specific passages from their essays to support your answer.

5. Williams's essay might be considered an essay based on inductive reasoning (see pages 80–81). How effectively do you think she uses inductive reasoning to make her argument? How persuasively does she compile evidence to reach her conclusion?

② Unintended Consequences of High-Stakes Testing

GREGORY CIZEK

As author Gregory Cizek notes, the title of the following essay is misleading. We tend to think of "unintended consequences" as negative. But Cizek makes a vigorous case in favor of standardized testing, arguing that high-stakes tests lead to a number of important and beneficial consequences for students, schools, and teachers alike. Like many proponents of such tests, Cizek believes that carefully constructed standardized tests are a crucial element in efforts to improve public education. As you read through his discussion of the benefits of testing, consider what his list of these benefits reveals about his view of the purpose of formal education. Consider, too, the extent to which his fundamental beliefs about education match—or diverge from—the views of the other writers in this section. Gregory Cizek is a professor of educational measurement and evaluation at the University of North Carolina and the author of *Detecting and Preventing Classroom Cheating* (1999). This essay originally appeared in 2002 at **EducationNews.org**, an online news service devoted to educational issues.

GREGORY CIZEK, "Unintended Consequences of High-Stakes Testing"

1 It's **eschatological**. In one tract after another, the zealous proclaim that there is a dire threat posed by the anti-Christ of postmodern education: testing. To be more precise, the Great Satan does not comprise *all* testing, only testing *with consequences*—consequences such as grade retention for students, salaries for educators, or the futures of (in particular) low-performing schools. In this fevered and frenzied battle, what is clear is that any sort of high-stakes test is the beast. On the side of the angels are those who take the path of beast-resistance.

As I reflect on my own writing here, I wondered if I would need to make a confession for the sin of hyperbole. Then I re-read some of the sacred texts. According to Alfie Kohn in a recent issue of the *Kappan*, we must "make the fight against standardized tests our top priority...until we have chased this monster from our schools."[1] A companion article in the same issue discussed high-stakes testing

in an article titled "The Authentic Standards Movement and Its Evil Twin."[2] Still another canonized a list of 22 martyrs and described their sacrifices of resistance to testing.[3] I concluded that there was no need for me to repent.

In addition to the zealotry, there is also heresy. This article is one example. Testifying to the truth of that label, I confess that the very title of this article is somewhat deceptive. Perhaps many readers will, like me, recall having reviewed several articles with titles like the one used here. In those epistles the faithful are regaled with the travails of students who were denied a diploma as a result of a high-stakes test. They illustrate how testing narrows the curriculum, frustrates our best teachers, produces gripping anxiety in our brightest students, and makes young children vomit or cry, or both. This article will not repeat any of those parables, either in substance or perspective. We now turn to the apocrypha.

Eschatology is a branch of theology concerned with the end of the world or of humankind.

COMPLICATION

Alfie Kohn, to whom Cizek refers several times in this essay, is one of the most visible and respected (or vilified) critics of high-stakes tests in the United States. He has argued against such tests on the grounds that their popularity is driven by profits for testing companies and by the desire for votes among political officials who publicly call for "accountability" in education. In one article (which Cizek cites in his essay), Kohn argues that in addition to several other flaws, standardized tests do not accurately measure student achievement:

> The central problem with most standardized tests, however, is simply that they fail to assess the skills and dispositions that matter most. Such tests are generally contrived exercises that measure how much students have managed to cram into short-term memory. Reading comprehension exams usually consist of a concatenation of separate questions about short passages on unrelated topics that call on students to ferret out right answers rather than to engage in thoughtful interpretation. In mathematics, the point is to ascertain that students have memorized a series of procedures, not that they understand what they are doing. Science tests often focus on recall of vocabulary, stressing "excruciatingly boring material," failing to judge the capacity of students to think, and ultimately discouraging many of them from choosing a career in the field, according to Bruce Alberts, president of the National Academy of Science.
>
> In light of all this, it should not be surprising—but it is seldom realized—that the students who perform well on tests are often those who are least interested in learning and least likely to learn deeply. Studies of elementary, middle school, and high school students have found a statistical association between high scores on standardized tests and relatively superficial thinking.

SOURCE: Alfie Kohn, "Burnt at the High Stakes."

REPORTS FROM THE BATTLEFIELD

If nothing else, published commentary concerning high-stakes testing has been remarkable for its uniformity. The conclusion: high-stakes tests are uniformly bad. A recent literature search to locate information about the effects of high-stakes tests turned up 59 entries over the last 10 years. A review of the results revealed that only 2 of the 59 could even remotely be categorized as favorably inclined toward testing. The two entries included a two-page, 1996 publication in a minor source, which bore the straightforward title, "The Case for National Standards and Assessments."[4] The other nominally favorable article simply reviewed surveys of public opinion about high-stakes tests and concluded

that broad support for such tests persists.[5] The other 57 entries reflected the accepted articles of faith concerning high-stakes tests. Examples of the titles of these articles include:

"Excellence in Education versus High-Stakes Testing"[6] (which carries the obvious implication that testing is antithetical to high-quality education)

"The Distortion of Teaching and Testing: High-Stakes Testing and Instruction"[7] (ditto);

"Burnt at the High Stakes"[8] (no explanation required);

"Judge's Ruling Effectively Acquits High-Stakes Test: To the Disadvantage of Poor and Minority Students in Texas"[9] (personally, I thought that the less equivocal title "Analysis Reveals High-quality Test: Everyone Gets the Shaft" could have been used); and

"I Don't Give a Hoot If Somebody Is Going to Pay Me $3600: Local School District Reactions to Kentucky's High-Stakes Accountability Program."[10]

THE ROOTS OF ALL EVIL

5 There have always been high-stakes tests. Testing history buffs have traced high-stakes testing to civil service examinations of 200 B.C., military selection dating to 2000 B.C., and Biblical accounts of the Gilead guards. Mehrens and Cizek relate the story of the minimum competency exam that took place when the Gilead guards challenged the fugitives from the tribe of Ephraim who tried to cross the Jordan river.

"Are you a member of the tribe of Ephraim?" they asked. If the man replied that he was not, then they demanded, "Say Shibboleth." But if he couldn't pronounce the H and said Sibboleth instead of Shibboleth he was dragged away and killed. So forty-two thousand people of Ephraim died there."[11]

In the scriptural account of this assessment, nothing is reported concerning the professional and public debates that may have occurred regarding: what competencies should have been tested; how to measure them; how minimally-proficient performance should be defined; whether paper/pencil testing might have been cheaper and more reliable than performance assessment; whether there was any adverse impact against the people of Ephraim; or what remediation should be provided for those judged to be below the standard. Maybe the Gilead guards should have abandoned their test altogether because it was unclear whether Ephraimites really had the opportunity to learn to pronounce "shibboleth" correctly, because the burden of so many oral examinations was a top-down mandate, or because listening to all those Ephraimites try to say "shibboleth" reduced the valuable instructional time available for teaching young members of the tribe of Gilead the real-life skills of sword fighting and tent making.[12]

While it is certain that high-stakes testing has been around for some time, it is curious that current high-stakes tests in American education face such an inquisition from, primarily, educators. Ironically, for this, too, we should blame those in the field of testing. Those who know and make high-stakes tests have done the least to make known the purposes and benefits of testing. The laws of physics apply: for every action in opposition to tests, there has been and equal and opposite silence.

A REVELATION

One assumption underlying high-stakes testing has received particularly scant attention: the need to make decisions. There is simply no way to escape making decisions about students. These decisions, by definition, create categories. If, for example, some students graduate from high school and others do not, a categorical decision has been made, even if a graduation test was not used. (The

Jose Luis Pelaez, Inc./Corbis

decisions were, presumably, made on *some* basis.) High school music teachers make decisions such as who should be first chair for the clarinets. College faculties make decisions to tenure (or not) their colleagues.

We embrace decision making regarding who should be licensed to practice medicine. All of these kinds of decisions are unavoidable; each should be based on sound information; and the information should be combined in some deliberate, considered fashion.

10 It is currently fashionable to talk as if high-stakes tests are the *single* bit of information used to make categorical decisions that wreak hellacious results on both people and educational systems. But simple-minded slogans like "high stakes are for tomatoes" are, well, simple-minded. One need only examine the context in which high-stakes tests are given to see that they are almost never the single bit of information used to make decisions. In the diploma example, multiple sources of information are used to make decisions, and success on each of them is necessary. For instance: So many days of attendance are required. Just one too few days?: No diploma. (2) There are course requirements. Didn't take American Government?: No diploma. (3) There are credit hour requirements. Missing one credit?: No diploma. (4) And, increasingly, there are high-stakes tests. Miss one too many questions on a test?: No diploma. Categorical decisions are made on each of these four criteria. It makes as much sense to single out a single test as the sole barrier as it does to single out a student's American Government examination as "the single test used to make the graduation decision."

We could, of course, not make success on each of the elements essential. One could get a diploma by making success on, say, three out of the four. But which three? Why three? Why not two? The same two for everyone? That seems unfair, given that some people would be denied a diploma simply on the basis of the arbitrary two that were identified. Even if all other criteria were eliminated, and all that remained was a requirement that students must attend at least 150 out of 180 days in their senior year to get a diploma, then what about the student who attends

149 and is a genius? In the end, as long as any categorical decisions must be made, there is going to be subjectivity involved. If there is going to be subjectivity, most testing specialists—and most of the public—simply favor coming clean about the source and magnitude of the subjectivity, and trying to minimize it.

In the end, it cannot be that high-stakes tests themselves are the cause of all the consternation. It is evident that categorical decisions will be made with or without tests. The real reasons are two-fold. One reason covers resistance to high-stakes testing within the education profession; the second explains why otherwise well-informed people would so easily succumb to simplistic rhetoric centering on testing. On the first count, the fact that high-stakes tests are increasingly used as part of accountability systems provides a sufficient rationale for resistance. Education is one of the few (only?) professions for which advancement, status, compensation, longevity, and so on are not related to personal performance. The entire accountability movement—of which testing has been the major element—has been vigorously resisted by many in the profession. The rationale is rational when there is a choice between being accountable for performance or maintaining a status quo without accountability.

TWO TABLES OF STONE

There is much to be debated about professionalization of teaching and its relationship to accountability. My primary focus here, however, is on the second count—the debate about testing. As mentioned previously, those who know the most about testing have been virtually absent from the public square when any criticism surfaces. In response to 57 bold articles nailed to the cathedral door, 2 limp slips of paper are slid under it. The benefits of high-stakes tests have been assumed, unrecognized, or unarticulated. The following paragraphs present 10 unanticipated consequences of high-stakes testing—consequences that are actually good things that have grown out of the increasing reliance on test data concerning student performance.[13]

I. Professional Development I suspect that most educators painfully recall what passed as professional development in the not-too-distant past. Presentations with titles like the following were all-too-common:

- Vitamins and Vocabulary: Just Coincidence that Both Begin with "V"?
- Cosmetology across the Curriculum
- Horoscopes in the Homeroom
- The Geometry of Rap: 16 Musical Tips for Pushing Pythagoras
- Multiple Intelligences in the Cafeteria

In a word, much professional development was spotty, hit-or-miss, of questionable research base, of dubious effectiveness, and thoroughly avoidable.

15 But professional development is increasingly taking a new face. Much of it is considerably more focussed on what works, curriculum-relevant, and results-oriented. Driven by the demands of high-stakes tests, the press toward professional development that helps educators hone their teaching skills and content area expertise is clear.

II. Accommodation Recent federal legislation enacted to guide the implementation of high-stakes testing has been a catalyst for increased attention to students with special needs. Describing the impact of that legislation, researchers Martha Thurlow and James Ysseldyke observe that, "Both **Goals 2000** and the more forceful IASA indicated that high standards were to apply to all students. In very clear language, these laws defined '*all* students' as including students with disabilities and students with limited English proficiency."[14]

Because of these regulations applied to high-stakes tests, states across the U.S. are scurrying to adapt those tests for all students, report disaggregated results for subgroups, and implement accommodations so that tests more accurately reflect the learning of all students. The result has been a very positive diffusion of awareness. Increasingly, at the classroom level, educators are becoming more sensitive to the needs and barriers faced by special needs students when they take tests—even the ordinary assessments they face in the classroom. If not forced by the context of once-per-year, high-stakes tests, it is doubtful that such progress would have been witnessed in the daily experiences of many special needs learners.

III. Knowledge about Testing For years, testing specialists have documented a lack of knowledge about assessment on the part of many educators. The title of a 1991 *Kappan* article bluntly asserted educators' "Apathy toward Testing and Grading."[15] Other research has chronicled the chronic lack of training in assessment for teachers and principals and has offered plans for remediation.[16] Unfortunately, for the most part, it has been difficult to require assessment training for pre-service teachers or administrators, and even more difficult to wedge such training into graduate programs in education.

Then along came high-stakes tests. What faculty committees could not enact has been accomplished circuitously. Granted, misperceptions about tests persist (for example, in my state there is a lingering myth that "the green test form" is harder than "the red one"), but I am discovering that more educators know more about testing than ever before. Because many tests now have stakes associated with them, it has become *de rigeur* for educators to inform themselves about their content, construction, and consequences. Increasingly, teachers can tell you the difference between a norm-referenced and a criterion-reference test; they can recognize, use, or develop a high-quality rubric; they can tell you how their state's writing test is scored, and so on. In this case, necessity has been the mother of intervention.

20 IV and V. Collection and Use of Information Because pupil performance on high-stakes tests has become of such

Goals 2000 refers to the Educate America Act, passed by the U.S. Congress in 1994 and intended to promote coherent educational standards for K–12 schools by supporting efforts in individual states to set standards for student learning. IASA, or the Improving America's Schools Act, which was also passed in 1994, is broad legislation that provided support for various initiatives, including improving services for students with disabilities, enhancing basic educational programs, upgrading technology, and strengthening substance abuse prevention efforts.

prominent and public interest, there has been an intensity of effort directed toward data collection and quality control that is unparalleled. As many states mandate the collection and reporting of this information (and more), unparalleled access has also resulted. Obtaining information about test performance, graduation rates, per-pupil spending, staffing, finance, and facilities is, in most states, now just a mouse-click away. How would you like your data for secondary analysis: Aggregated or disaggregated? Single year or longitudinal? PDF or Excel? Paper or plastic? Consequently, those who must respond to state mandates for data collection (i.e., school districts) have become increasingly conscientious about providing the most accurate information possible—sometimes at risk of penalties for inaccuracy or incompleteness.

This is an unqualified boon. Not only is more information about student performance available, but it is increasingly used as part of decision making. At a recent teacher recruiting event, I heard a recruiter question a teacher about how she would be able to tell that her students were learning. "I can just see it in their eyes," was the reply. Sorry, you're off the island. Increasingly, from the classroom to the school board room, educators are making use of student performance data to help them refine programs, channel funding, and identify roots of success. If the data weren't so important, it is unlikely that this would be the case.

VI. Educational Options Related to the increase in publicly-available information about student performance and school characteristics is the spawning of greater options for parents and students. Complementing a hunger for information, the public's appetite for alternatives has been whetted. In many cases, schools have responded. Charter schools, magnet schools, home schools, and increased offerings of honors, **IB and AP** courses, have broadened the choices available to parents. And, research is slowly accumulating which suggests that the presence of choices has not spelled doom for

traditional options, but has largely raised all boats.[17] It is almost surely the case that legislators' votes and parents' feet would not be moving in the direction of expanding alternatives if not for the information provided by high-stakes tests—the same tests are being used to gauge the success or failure of these emerging alternatives.

VII. Accountability Systems No one would argue that current accountability systems have reached a mature state of development. On the contrary, nascent systems are for the most part crude, cumbersome, embryonic endeavors. Equally certain, though, is that even rudimentary accountability systems would not likely be around if it weren't for high-stakes tests. For better or worse, high-stakes tests are often the foundation upon which accountability systems have been built. This is not to say that this relationship between high-stakes tests and accountability is right, noble, or appropriate. It simply recognizes the reality that current accountability systems were enabled by an antecedent: mandated, high-stakes tests.

To many policy makers, professionals, and the public, however, the notion of introducing accountability—even just acknowledging that accountability is a *good* innovation—is an important first step. That the camel's nose took the form of high-stakes tests was (perhaps) not recognized or (almost certainly) viewed as acceptable. Debates continue about the role of tests and the form of accountability.

25 A memory that has helped me to understand both sides of accountability debates involves high school sports physicals. I have vivid memories evoked to this day whenever I drive by a marquee outside a high school on which the notice appears: Boys' Sports Physicals Next Tuesday. As an adolescent male trying out for a high-school baseball team, I recall that event as one at which dozens of similarly situated guys would line up mostly naked and be checked over by a hometown physician, who volunteered his

IB refers to International Baccalaureate programs, which are described on page 473. **AP** refers to Advanced Placement programs, which are rigorous high school courses that can lead to college credit. Founded in 1955, the AP program standards are set by the College Board, which also administers the AP exams that students who complete AP courses must usually take to earn college credit.

time to poke, prod, and probe each potential player. The characteristics of the event included that it was: (a) somewhat embarrassing; (b) performed by an external person; (c) somewhat invasive; (d) and had the possibility of denying individuals access to an opportunity. I think that these same four characteristics help explain the reaction of many educators to high-stakes tests.

But the analogy can be extended. At the time—and still—I can see that the physicals were necessary to identify small problems, and to prevent potentially bigger problems. But here's the big difference with high-stakes tests: if one of the players was found to have a heart murmur, it was acknowledged that he had a problem and something was done about it. In education, if a student fails a high-stakes test, we assail the test. Now, we all know that achievement tests aren't perfect, but neither are medical tests. Pregnancy tests are often wrong; blood pressure readings are subjective and variable within an individual; even with DNA tests, experts can only say things like "there is 99.93% chance that the DNA is a match." Yet nobody reports their blood pressure as 120/80 with an associated standard error. Maybe I don't really have high blood pressure. Maybe my pressure is 120/80 plus or minus 17.

People seem inclined to accept medical measurements as virtually error-free because there's no finger pointing, only therapy. Maybe his blood pressure is high because he failed to heed the physician's orders to lay off the salt and lose some weight. Maybe her pregnancy test was positive because she was sexually active. Who should be held accountable for the results of the pregnancy test or blood pressure but the person? We seem resigned to accountability in this context.

Don't get me wrong. When a defective medical measuring device is identified, it gets pulled by the FDA. If there were intolerable error rates in home pregnancy test kits, it would create a stir, and the product would be improved, or fall out of use. In education, however, if a pupil doesn't pass a high-stakes test, there are a lot of possible (and confounded) explanations: lack of persistence, poor teaching, distracting learning environment, inadequate resources, lack of prerequisite skills, poorly-constructed test, dysfunctional home situation, and so on. We know that all of these (and more) exist to greater or lesser extents in the mix. Who should be accountable? The teacher for the quality of instruction? I think so. The student for effort and persistence? Yes, again. Administrators for providing safe learning environment? Yep. Assessment specialists for developing sound tests? Bingo. Communities for providing adequate resources? Sure. Parents for establishing a supportive home environment? Yessirree. The key limitation is that we can only make policies and products to address those factors that are legitimately under governmental control. And, in education, we understand that intervention may or may not prove effective.

Thus, although high-stakes tests have made a path in the wilderness, the controversy clearly hinges on accountability itself. The difficult fits and starts of developing sound accountability systems may actually cause some hearts to murmur. Understanding the importance, complexity, and difficulties as the accountability infant matures will be surely be trying. How—or if—high-stakes tests will fit into the mature version is hard to tell, and the devil will be in the details. But it is evident that the presence of high-stakes tests have at least served as a conversation-starter for a policy dialogue that may not have taken place in their absence.

30 VIII. Educators' Intimacy with Their Disciplines Once a test has been mandated in, say, language arts, the first step in any high-stakes testing program is to circumscribe the boundaries of what will be tested. The almost universal strategy for accomplishing this is to empanel groups of (primarily) educators who are familiar with the ages, grades, and content to be tested. These groups are usually large, selected to be representative, and expert in the subject area. The groups first study relevant documentation (e.g. the authorizing legislation, state curriculum guides, content standards). They then begin the arduous, time-consuming task of discussing among themselves the nature of the content area, the sequence and content of typical instruction, learner characteristics and developmental issues, cross-disciplinary relationships, and relevant assessment techniques.

These extended conversations help shape the resulting high-stakes tests, to be sure. However, they also affect the discussants, and those with whom they interact when they return to their districts, buildings, and classrooms. As persons with special knowledge of the particular high-stakes testing program, the participants are sometimes asked to replicate those disciplinary and logistic discussions locally. The impact of this trickling-down is just beginning to be noticed by researchers—and the effects are beneficial. For example, at one session of the 2000 American Educational Research Association conference, scholars reported on the positive effects of a state testing program in Maine on classroom assessment practices[18] and on how educators in Florida were assimilating their involvement in large-scale testing activities at the local level.[19]

These local discussions mirror the large-scale counterparts in that they provide educators with an opportunity to become more intimate with the nature and structure of their own disciplines, and to contemplate interdisciplinary relationships. As Martha Stewart would say: it's a good thing. And the impulse for this good thing is clearly the presence of a high-stakes test.

IX. Equity There is a flip-side to the common concern that high-stakes tests result in the homogenizing of education. The flip-side is that high-stakes tests promote greater homogeneity of education. Naturally, we should be vigilant about the threat posed by common *low* standards that could be engendered, and it is right to worry about gravitating to the lowest common denominator.[20] On the other hand, there is something to be said for increased equity in expectations and experiences for all students. As a result of schools' aligning their curricula and instructional focus more closely to outcomes embodied in high-stakes tests, the experiences of and aspirations for children in urban, suburban, and rural districts within a state are more comparable than they have been in the recent past.

Surely, inequalities—even savage ones—persist. However, some movement toward greater consistency is perceptible. And, the press toward more uniformity of expectation and experience may be particularly beneficial in an increasingly mobile society. The seamlessness with which a student can move from one district to another—even one school to another within a district—may well translate into incremental gains in achievement sufficient enough to spell the difference between promotion and graduation, or retention and dropping out.

35 X. Quality of Tests The final benevolent consequence is the profoundly positive effect that the introduction of high-stakes consequences has had on the tests themselves. Along with more serious consequences has come heightened scrutiny. The high-stakes tests of today are surely the most meticulously developed, carefully constructed, and rigorously reported. Many criticisms of tests are valid, but a complainant who suggests that today's high-stakes tests are "lower-order" or "biased" or "not relevant" are most likely unfamiliar with that which they purport to critique.

If only for its long history and ever-present watch-dogging, high-stakes tests have evolved to a state of being: highly reliable; free from bias; relevant and age appropriate; higher order; tightly related to important, public goals; time and cost efficient; and yielding remarkably consistent decisions. It is fair to say that one strains the gnat in objecting to the characteristics of high-stakes tests, when the characteristics of those tests is compared to what a child will likely experience in his or her classroom the other 176 days of the school year. It is not an overstatement to say that, at least on the grounds just articulated, the high-stakes, state test that a student takes will, by far, be the best assessment that student will see all year.

A secondary benefit of the quality of typical high-stakes tests is that, because of their perceived importance, they become mimicked at lower levels. It is appropriate to abhor teaching to the test. However, it is also important to recognize the beneficial effects of exposing educators to high-quality writing prompts, document-based questions, constructed-response formats, and even challenging multiple-choice items. It is not cheating, but the highest form of praise when educators then rely on these exemplars to enhance their own assessment practices.

KEEPIN' IT REAL

It would be foolish to ignore the shortcomings and undesirable consequences of high-stakes tests. Current discussions and inquiries are essential, productive, and encouraging. However, amidst the consternation about high-stakes tests, it is equally inappropriate to fail to consider the unanticipated positive consequences, or to fail to incorporate these into any cost-benefit calculus that should characterize sound policy decisions.

Vigorous debates about the nature and role of high-stakes tests and accountability systems are healthy and needed. To these frays, the protestants may bring differing doctrinal starting points and differing conceptions of the source of salvation. It is an exhilarating time of profound questioning. High-stakes tests: we don't know how to live with them; we can't seem to live without them. The oft-quoted first sentence of Charles Dickens' *A Tale of Two Cities* ("It was the best of times,

it was the worst of times") seems especially relevant to the juncture at which we find ourselves. The remainder of Dickens' opening paragraph merely extends the piquant metaphor:

> It was the age of wisdom, it was the age of foolishness, it was the epoch of belief, it was the epoch of incredulity, it was the season of Light, it was the season of Darkness, it was the spring of hope, it was the winter of despair, we had everything before us, we had nothing before us, we were all going direct to Heaven, we were all going direct the other way.[21]

NOTES

1. Alfie Kohn, "Fighting the Tests: A Practical Guide to Rescuing Our Schools," *Phi Delta Kappan,* vol. 82, 2001, p. 349.
2. Scott Thompson, "The Authentic Standards Movement and Its Evil Twin," *Phi Delta Kappan,* vol. 82, 2001, pp. 358–362.
3. Susan Ohanian, "News from the Test Resistance Trail," *Phi Delta Kappan,* vol. 82, 2001, p. 365.
4. Diane Ravitch, "The Case for National Standards and Assessments," *The Clearing House,* vol. 69, 1996, pp. 134–135.
5. Richard Phelps, "The demand for standardized student testing," *Educational Measurement: Issues and Practice,* vol. 17, no. 3, 1998, pp. 5–23.
6. Asa Hilliard, "Excellence in Education versus High-Stakes Testing," *Journal of Teacher Education,* vol. 51, 2000, pp. 293–304.
7. George Madaus, "The Distortion of Teaching and Testing: High-Stakes Testing and Instruction," *Peabody Journal of Education,* vol. 65, 1998, pp. 29–46.
8. Alfie Kohn, "Burnt at the High Stakes," *Journal of Teacher Education,* vol. 51, 2000, pp. 315–327.
9. Karin Chenoweth, "Judge's Ruling Effectively Acquits High-Stakes Test:

To the Disadvantage of Poor and Minority Students in Texas," *Black Issues in Higher Education,* vol. 51, 2000, p. 12.

10. Patricia Kannapel and others, "I Don't Give a Hoot If Somebody Is Going to Pay Me $3600: Local School District Reactions to Kentucky's High-Stakes Accountability Program." Paper presented at the annual meeting of the American Educational Research Association, April 1996, New York (ERIC Document No. 397 135).

11. Judges 12:5-6, *The Living Bible;* cited in William Mehrens and Gregory Cizek, "Standard Setting and the Public Good: Benefits Accrued and Anticipated," in G. J. Cizek (Ed.), *Setting Performance Standards: Concepts, Methods, and Perspectives* (Mahwah, NJ: Lawrence Erlbaum, 2001).

12. Mehrens and Cizek, pp. 477–478.

13. Ordinarily, the 10 items should probably be presented with appropriate recognition of their downsides, disadvantages, etc. However, for the sake of clarity, brevity, and because most readers are probably already all too aware of the counterarguments, I have chosen to avoid any facade of balanced treatment.

14. Martha Thurlow and James Ysseldyke, "Standard Setting Challenges for Special Populations," in G. J. Cizek (Ed.), *Setting Performance Standards: Concepts, Methods, and Perspectives* (Mahwah, NJ: Lawrence Erlbaum, 2001), p. 389.

15. John Hills, "Apathy toward Testing and Grading," *Phi Delta Kappan*, vol. 72, 1991, pp. 540–545.

16. See, for example, Rita O' Sullivan and Marla Chalnick, "Measurement-Related Course Requirements for Teacher Certification and Recertification," *Educational Measurement: Issues and Practice*, vol. 10, 1991, pp. 17–19, 23;

Richard Stiggins, "Assessment Literacy," *Phi Delta Kappan,* vol. 72, 1991, pp. 534–539; and James Impara and Barbara Plake, "Professional Development in Student Assessment for Educational Administrators," *Educational Measurement: Issues and Practice,* vol. 15, 1996, pp. 14–20.

17. Chester Finn, Jr., Bruno V. Manno, and Gregg Vanourek, *Charter Schools in Action: Renewing Public Education* (Princeton, NJ: Princeton University Press, 2000).

18. Jeff Beaudry, "The Positive Effects of Administrators and Teachers on Classroom Assessment Practices and Student Achievement." Paper presented at the annual meeting of the American Educational Research Association, April 2000, New Orleans, LA.

19. Madhabi Banerji, "Designing District-Level Classroom Assessment Systems." Paper presented at the annual meeting of the American Educational Research Association, April 2000, New Orleans, LA.

20. Actually, the concern about low expectations may have passed and, if the experiences of states like Washington, Arizona, and Massachusetts are prescient, the concern may be being replaced by a concern that content or performance expectations (or both) are too high and coming too fast. See http://seattletimes. nwsource. com/news/local/html98/ test_19991010.html; http://www.edweek. org/ew/ewstory.cfm?slug=13ariz.h20; and Donald C. Orlich, "Education Reform and Limits to Student Achievement," *Phi Delta Kappan,* vol. 81, 2000, pp. 468–472.

21. Charles Dickens, *A Tale of Two Cities* (New York: Dodd, Mead, and Company, 1925), p. 3.

Questions for Discussion

1. Examine the way in which Cizek opens this essay, noting especially his use of religious metaphors. How, specifically, does he introduce his subject and establish his own stance toward it? How does he set the tone for his argument? How effective do you think his introduction is in setting up his argument? In your answer, cite specific words and phrases from his introductory paragraphs.

2. Cizek devotes much of his essay to summarizing and responding to the arguments of those who are opposed to testing. Evaluate his use of references to his opponents. How effective are these references in helping him make his own argument in favor of standardized testing? Do you think he represents his opponents fairly? Why or why not?

3. In paragraph 25, Cizek recalls his own experience as a student to introduce an analogy in which he compares high school physical exams to standardized testing. What point does Cizek use this analogy to make? How effectively do you think this analogy helps Cizek make his point? Would the analogy have been less effective if Cizek had not referred to his own experience as a student? Explain.

4. In many ways, Cizek's writing style is unusual for a scholarly essay, especially his use of figurative language. How would you describe Cizek's writing style? In what ways do you think it strengthens or weakens his argument? Cite specific passages from his essay in your answer.

5. Cizek describes the way in which curriculum standards are typically set by panels of experts who determine the appropriate content for specific grade levels in specific subjects. He declares this to be a "good thing." What are some pros and cons that you see in this approach to developing curriculum? Do you think Cizek's discussion of this process enhances his argument?

6. Near the end of his essay, Cizek states that vigorous debates about testing "are healthy and needed" and that it is an "exhilarating time of profound questioning" about testing. Do you agree? Why or why not? To what extent do you think Cizek's essay contributes positively to this ongoing debate?

③ # Why So Many Exams? A Marxist Response

BERTELL OLLMAN

The view that public education in the United States is in crisis is so common that it seems to be almost universal. Rarely does anyone describe the schools as working. Critic Bertell Ollman is someone who does. But he doesn't think that's a good thing. Ollman believes that despite constant criticism of schools and calls for reform, public education in the United States effectively serves the basic economic system on which American society is based: capitalism. In his view, the many problems typically associated with schools reflect of the needs of capitalism rather than the needs of individual students. More specifically, standardized testing is necessary to prepare students for their roles in a capitalist system, and as long as that system remains in place, neither standardized tests nor the problems associated with schooling will go away. Whether or not you agree with Ollman's view of capitalism or his position on testing, his essay is a good example of an argument that reflects a specific theory or political ideology (in this case, Marxism). It suggests as well that educational issues such as testing are related in complex ways to individuals' political and economic lives. Bertell Ollman is a professor of political science at New York University. A well-known Marxist scholar, he has written many books and essays about political and social issues, including *How to Take an Exam…and Remake the World* (2001) and *Ballbuster: True Confessions of a Marxist Businessman* (2002). The following essay was published in 2002 in *Z Magazine*.

BERTELL OLLMAN, "Why So Many Exams? A Marxist Response"

1 Psychologist Bill Livant has remarked, "When a liberal sees a beggar, he says the system isn't working. When a Marxist does, he says it is." The same insight could be applied today to the entire area of education. The learned journals, as well as the popular media, are full of studies documenting how little most students know and how fragile are their basic skills. The cry heard almost everywhere is "The system isn't working."

Responding to this common complaint, conservatives—starting (but not ending) with the Bush administration—have offered a package of reforms in which increased testing occupies the central place. The typical liberal and even radical response to this has been to demonstrate that such measures are not likely to have the "desired" effect. The assumption,

of course, is that we all want more or less the same thing from a system of education and that conservatives have made an error in the means they have chosen to attain our common end. But what if students are already receiving—more or less—the kind of education that conservatives favor? This would cast their proposals for "reform" in another light. What if, as Livant points out in the case of beggars, the system is working?

Before detailing what young people learn from their forced participation in this educational ritual, it may be useful to dispose of a number of myths that surround exams and exam taking in our society.

(1) *Exams are a necessary part of education.* Education, of one kind or another, has existed in all human societies, but exams

have not; and the practice of requiring frequent exams is a very recent innovation and still relatively rare in the world.

5 (2) *Exams are unbiased*. In 1912, Henry Goddard, a distinguished psychologist, administered what he claimed were "culture free" **IQ tests** to new immigrants on Ellis Island and found that 83 percent of Jews, 80 percent of Hungarians, 79 percent of Italians, and 87 percent of Russians were "feebleminded," adding that "all feebleminded are at least potential criminals." IQ tests have gotten better since then, but given the character of the testing process, the attitudes of those who make up any test, and the variety of people—coming from so many different backgrounds—who take it, it is impossible to produce a test that does not have serious biases.

(3) *Exams are objectively graded*. Daniel Stark and Edward Elliot sent two English essays to 200 high school teachers for grading. They got back 142 grades. For one paper, the grades ranged from 50 to 99; for the other, the grades went from 64 to 99. But English is not an "objective" subject, you say. Well, they did the same thing for an essay answer in mathematics and got back grades ranging from 28 to 95. Though most of the grades they received in both cases fell in the middle ground, it was evident that a good part of any grade was the result of who marked the exam and not of who took it.

(4) *Exams are an accurate indication of what students know and of intelligence in general*. But all sorts of things, including luck in getting (or not getting) the questions you hoped for and one's state of mind and emotions the day of the exam, can have an important effect on the result.

(5) *All students have an equal chance to do well on exams*. . . . [E]ven major differences in their conditions of life have a negligible impact on their performance. There is such a strong correlation between students' family income and their test scores, however, that the radical educational theorist, Ira Shor,

has suggested (tongue-in-cheek) that college applications should ignore test scores altogether and just ask students to enter their family income. The results would be the same—with relatively few exceptions, the same people would get admitted into college, but then, of course, the belief that there is equality of opportunity in the classroom would stand forth as the myth that it is.

(6) *Exams are the fairest way to distribute society's scarce resources* to the young, hence the association of exams with the ideas of meritocracy and equality of opportunity. But if some students consistently do better on exams because of the advantages they possess and other students do not outside of school, then directing society's main benefits to these same people compounds the initial inequality.

10 (7) *Exams, and particularly the fear of them, are necessary in order to motivate students to do their assignments*. Who can doubt that years of reacting to such threats have produced in many students a reflex of the kind depicted here? The sad fact is

For an explanation of **IQ tests**, see page 472.

Dennis Brack/IPN/Aurora

The term **capitalism** can be used to refer to an economic system based on a free market in which supply and demand dictate the movement of goods and services. The term can be used more broadly to refer to a social system based on the ideas of individual rights and free choice.

that the natural curiosity of young people and their desire to learn, develop, advance, master, and the pleasure that comes from succeeding—which could and should motivate all studying—has been progressively replaced in their psyches by a pervasive fear of failing. This needn't be. For the rest, if the only reason a student does the assignments is that he/she is worried about the exam, he/she should not be taking that course in the first place.

(8) *Exams are not injurious, socially, intellectually, and psychologically.* Complaining about exams may be most students' first truly informed criticism about society because they are its victims and know from experience how exams work. They know, for example, that exams don't only involve reading questions and writing answers. They also involve forced isolation from other students, prohibition on talking and walking around and going to the bathroom, writing a lot faster than usual, physical discomfort, worry, fear, anxiety, and often guilt.

They are also aware that exams do a poor job of testing what students actually know. But it is here that most of their criticisms run into a brick wall, because most students don't know enough about society to understand the role that exams—especially taking so many exams—play in preparing them to take their place in it.

But if exams are not what most people think they are, then what are they? The short answer is that exams have less to do with testing us for what we are supposed to know than teaching us what the other aspects of instruction cannot get at (or get at as well). To understand what that is we must examine what the **capitalist** class require from a system of education. Here, it is clear that capitalists need a system of education that provides young people with the knowledge and skills necessary for their businesses to function and prosper. But they also want schools to give youth the beliefs, attitudes, emotions, and associated habits of behavior that make it easy for capitalists to tap into this store of knowledge and skills. They need all this not only to maximize their profits, but to help reproduce the social, economic, and even political conditions and accompanying processes that allow them to extract profits. Without workers, consumers and citizens who are well versed in and accepting of their roles in these processes, the entire capitalist system would grind to a halt. It is here—particularly as regards the behavioral and attitudinal prerequisites of capitalist rule—that the culture of exams has become indispensable. So what do exams "teach" students?

(1) The crush of tests gets students to believe that one gets what one works for, that the standards by which this is decided are objective and fair, and therefore that those who do better deserve what they get; and that the same holds for those who do badly. After a while, this attitude is carried over to what students find in the rest of society, including their own failures later in life, where it encourages them to "blame the victim" (themselves or others) and feel guilty for what is not their fault.

15 (2) By fixing a time and a form in which they have to deliver or else, exams prepare students for the more rigorous discipline of the work situation that lies ahead.

(3) In forcing students to think and write faster than they ordinarily do, exams get them ready mentally, emotionally, and also morally for the speed-ups they will face on the job.

(4) The self-discipline students acquire in preparing for exams also helps them put up with the disrespect, personal abuse, and boredom that awaits them on the job.

(5) Exams are orders that are not open to question—"discuss this," "outline that," etc.—and taking so many exams conditions students to accept unthinkingly the orders that will come from their future employers.

(6) By fitting the infinite variety of answers given on exams into the straitjacket of A, B, C, D, and F, students get accustomed to the standardization of people as well as of things and the impersonal job categories that will constitute such an important part of their identity later on.

20 (7) Because passing an exam is mainly good for enabling students to move up a grade so they can take a slightly harder exam, which—if they pass—enables them to repeat the exercise *ad infinitum*, they begin to see life as an endless series of ever more complicated exams, where one never finishes being judged and the need for being prepared and respectful of the judging authorities only grows.

(8) Because their teachers know all the right answers to the exams, students tend to assume that those who are above them in other hierarchies also know much more than they do.

(9) Because their teachers genuinely want them to do well on exams, students also mistakenly assume that those in relation of authority over them in other hierarchies are also rooting for them to succeed, that is, have their best interests at heart.

(10) Because most tests are taken individually, striving to do well on a test is treated as something that concerns students only as individuals. Cooperative solutions are equated with cheating, if considered at all.

(11) Because one is never quite ready for an exam, there is always something more to do, students often feel guilty for reading materials or engaging in activities unrelated to the exam. The whole of life, it would appear, is but preparation for exams or doing what is required in order to succeed (as those in charge define "success").

25 (12) With the **Damocles sword** of a failing (or for some a mediocre) grade hanging over their heads throughout their years in school (including university), the inhibiting fear of swift and dire punishment never leaves students, no matter their later situation.

(13) Coupled with the above, because there is always so much to be known, exams—especially so many of them—tend to undermine students' self-confidence and to raise their levels of anxiety, with the result that most young people remain unsure that they will ever know enough to criticize existing institutions and become even physically uncomfortable at the thought of trying to put something better in their place.

(14) Exams also play a key role in determining course content, leaving little time for material that is not on the exam. Among the first things to be omitted in this "tightening" of the curriculum are students' own reactions to the topics that come up, collective reflection on the main problems of the day, alternative points of view and other possibilities generally, the larger picture (where everything fits), explorations of topics triggered by individual curiosity, and anything else that is likely to promote creative, cooperative, or critical thinking.

(15) Exams also determine the form in which most teaching goes on, since for any given exam there is generally a best way to prepare for it. Repetition and forced memorization, even learning by rote, and frequent quizzes (more exams) leave little time for other more imaginative approaches to

According to Roman myth, **Damocles** was a courtier in Syracuse, Greece, in the fourth century BCE who envied the life of his ruler Dionysius. Given the chance to experience that life, Damocles agreed until he realized that, once seated in the ruler's throne, a large sword was suspended over his head by a single horse hair. The experience prompted him to reevaluate his beliefs about what constitutes a good life.

CONTEXT

The term *globalization* has been used to refer to a complex set of political, social, and economic developments in the last decade or so that have made nations, societies, and regions of the world more interdependent. Commerce, communication, and travel between various regions of the world have increased, and international trade agreements have facilitated economic and social contacts across national borders. According to journalist Thomas Friedman, whose 1999 book *The Lexus and the Olive Tree* examines the effects of globalization, "Globalization is not a phenomenon. It is not just some passing trend. Today it is an overarching international system shaping the domestic politics and foreign relations of virtually every country, and we need to understand it as such." Whether or not globalization is a good thing continues to be intensely debated.

conveying, exchanging and questioning facts and ideas.

(16) Multiple exams become one of the main factors determining the character of the relation between students (with students viewing each other as competitors for the best grades), the relation between students and teachers (with most students viewing their teachers as examiners and graders first, and most teachers viewing their students largely in terms of how well they have done on exams), also the relation between teachers and school administrators (since principals and deans now have an "objective" standard by which to measure teacher performance), and even the relation between school administrations and

CONTEXT

In paragraph 32, Ollman refers to the "current rage for more exams." Since Ollman published this essay in 2002, standardized tests of various kinds have become increasingly common in American schools, largely as a result of the education reform program of President George W. Bush called No Child Left Behind. That program, which was passed into law by Congress in 2002, required all students in certain grades to be tested every year in math and reading. Under the law, states that did not test students would lose some federal funding for education, and schools whose students' tests scores did not improve could face various sanctions, including closure. As a result of these mandates, many states developed new standardized tests or revised existing ones. Some states that did not previously require testing implemented new standardized tests and mandated that they be taken by all students. (The introduction to this cluster of readings on page 469 provides further discussion of these developments.)

various state bodies (since the same standard is used by the state to judge the work of schools and school systems). Exams mediate all social relations in the educational system in a manner similar to the way money mediates relations between people in the larger society with the same dehumanizing results.

30 While exams have been with us for a long time, socializing students in all the ways that I have outlined above, it is only recently that the mania for exams has begun to affect government policies. Why now? Globalization, or whatever it is one chooses to call this new stage, has arrived. But to which of its aspects is the current drive for more exams a carefully fashioned response? The proponents of such educational "reform" point to the intensified competition between industries and workers worldwide and the increasingly rapid pace at which economic changes of all kinds are occurring. To survive in this new order requires people, they say, who are not only efficient, but also have a variety of skills (or can quickly acquire them) and the flexibility to change tasks whenever called upon to do so. Thus, the only way to prepare our youth for the new economic life that awaits them is to raise standards of education, and that entails, among other things, more exams.

A more critical approach to globalization begins by emphasizing that the intensification of economic competition worldwide is driven by capitalists' efforts to maximize their profits. It is this that puts all the other developments associated with globalization into motion. It is well known that, all things being equal, the less capitalists pay their workers and the less money they spend on improving work conditions and reducing pollution, the more profit they make. Recent technological progress in transportation and communication, together with free trade and the abolition of laws restricting the movement of capital, allow capitalists to consider workers all over the world in making their calculations. While the full impact of these developments is yet to be felt, we can already see two of its most important effects in the movement of more and more companies (and parts of companies) out of the U.S. and a rollback of modest gains in wages, benefits, and work conditions that American workers have won over the last 50 years.

The current rage for more exams needs to be viewed as part of a larger strategy that includes stoking patriotic fires and chipping away at traditional civil liberties (both rationalized by the so-called war on terrorism), the promotion of "family values," restrictions on sexual freedom (but not, as we see, on sexual hypocrisy), and the push for more prisons and longer prison sentences for a whole range of minor crimes.

Is there a connection between exams and the privatization of public education? They appear to be separate, but look again. With new investment opportunities failing to keep up with the rapidly escalating surpluses in search of them (a periodic problem for a system that never pays its workers enough to consume all the wealth they produce), the public sector has become the latest "last" frontier for capitalist expansion. Given its size and potential for profit, what are state prisons or utilities or transport or communication systems or other social services next to public education? But how to convince the citizenry that companies whose only concern is with the bottom line can do a better job educating our young than public servants dedicated to the task? What seems impossible could be done if somehow education were redefined to emphasize the qualities associated with business and its achievements. Then—by

definition—business could do the "job" better than any public agency.

Enter exams. Standardization, easily quantifiable results, and the willingness to reshape all intervening processes to obtain them characterize the path to success in both exams and business. When that happens (and to the extent it has already happened), putting education in the hands of businesspeople who know best how to dispense with "inessentials" becomes a perfectly rational thing to do.

35 What should students do about all this? Well, they shouldn't refuse to take exams (unless the whole class gets involved) and they shouldn't drop out of school. Given the relations of power inside education and throughout the rest of society, that would be suicidal and suicide is never good politics. Rather, they should become better students by learning more about the role of education, and exams in particular, in capitalism. Nowhere does the contradiction between the selfish and manipulative interests of our ruling class and the educational and developmental interests of students stand out in such sharp relief as in the current debate over exams. Students of all ages need to get involved in this debate in order to raise the consciousness of young people regarding the source of their special oppression and the possibility of uniting with other oppressed groups to create a truly human society. Everything depends on the youth of today doing better on this crucial test than my generation did, because the price for failure has never been so high. Will they succeed? Can they afford to fail?

CONTEXT

Founded in 1987, *Z Magazine* describes its mission as follows: "Z is a radical print and online periodical dedicated to resisting injustice, eliminating repression, and creating liberty." To what extent does Ollman's essay fit this mission? In what ways do you think Ollman's argument might be effective for a wider audience than the readers of *Z Magazine*?

Questions for Discussion

1. Ollman discusses eight "myths" that he believes surround testing in the United States. Evaluate his discussion of these "myths." How widespread do you think the eight beliefs he calls "myths" really are? How effectively does he dispel each of these beliefs? To what extent does his discussion of these beliefs—and his description of them as "myths"—enhance or weaken his argument?

2. Ollman asserts that "most students don't know enough about society to understand the role that exams...play in preparing them to take their place in it." How does this point contribute to his main argument about testing? How might it reflect his Marxist perspective? Do you agree with him?

3. Ollman claims that a capitalist system requires citizens with certain beliefs, attitudes, and skills who also accept specified roles in American society. He then offers a list of sixteen ways in which testing teaches students what they need to know to serve the capitalist system. How persuasive do you find this list? What responses might you offer to Ollman's lessons? Do you think Ollman expects most Americans to reject his list? Explain.

4. Why does Ollman believe that globalization is an important factor influencing standardized testing? What evidence does he offer in support of this position? Evaluate the effectiveness of that evidence. Do you agree with Ollman about the connection between globalization and testing? Why or why not?

5. Ollman offers advice to students about what they should do about standardized tests. In what ways do you think this advice might enhance the effectiveness of his argument? How realistic do you think his advice is?

6. Ollman's essay can be described as an argument based on deductive reasoning (see pages 81–83). What is the basic premise of his argument? Do you think most Americans would agree with him? Explain.

7. Using the Toulmin model of argumentation (see pages 87–91), identify Ollman's central claim and the warrant (or warrants) on which that claim is based. Do you think most Americans would accept his warrant(s)? Explain.

④ Getting Along Without Grades—and Getting Along with Them, Too

PETER ELBOW

Peter Elbow is one of the most influential and widely respected scholars of writing in the country. He achieved national recognition with the publication of his book *Writing without Teachers* (1973), in which he describes a philosophy of teaching writing that places value on the writer's own sense of purpose and well-being. The following argument is from a more recent book of his, *Everyone Can Write*: *Essays toward a Hopeful Theory of Writing and Teaching Writing* (2000). As the subtitle suggests, much of Elbow's work is about hope. In addition to being hopeful that students have ideas worth communicating and can succeed at expressing these ideas, he is hopeful for teachers, believing that they take their responsibilities seriously and are capable of growth. You will find signs of this hope, as well as references to two of the schools at which Elbow taught (Evergreen State College and the Massachusetts Institute of Technology), in this essay. You will also find that he is aware that some people are inclined to dismiss his ideas as too hopeful or idealistic. You can judge for yourself. As you read, ask yourself what Elbow contributes to the ongoing debates about how we should measure student learning. Elbow is professor emeritus of English at the University of Massachusetts.

PETER ELBOW, "Getting Along without Grades—and Getting Along with Them, Too"

1 In this paper I am driven by the utopian impulse but also the impulse to tinker. On the one hand, I insist on the possibility of large change: grading is neither natural nor inevitable; we can avoid grading; we can step outside the mentality of evaluation; we can even change systems. Yet on the other hand, I insist on the importance of small, pragmatic changes—what some might call mere fiddling. Indeed, most of what I suggest here can be used within a conventional grading system. After all, most of us are obliged to do our evaluating within such systems (for now), and the human tendency to evaluate is inevitable. The utopian and the pragmatic impulses may seem at odds, but the common element is an insistence that things can be better. Change is possible.

My focus is on pedagogy, practice, and by implication, policy. My method is simply to try to think through my own evaluative practices since they are the practices all teachers engage in; this is a report on experience and thinking rather than on research.

When I speak of grades, I'm speaking of the quantitative, official grades that teachers commonly put on papers—and also the course grades we give at the end of the term and the holistic grades we use in large-scale writing assessments. I mean to distinguish between grading (quantitative marks) and the much larger and more various and multidimensional activity evaluation.

This essay is in three parts: first, suggestions for how to step outside of grading; second, suggestions for how to step outside of the very mentality of judging or evaluation;

and third, suggestions for how to use grades more effectively.

1. WAYS TO STEP OUTSIDE OF GRADING

5 If I am suggesting ways to step outside of grading, I suppose I'd better summarize my reasons for wanting to do so. Grades seem to me a problem for these reasons:

- They aren't trustworthy.
- They don't have clear meaning.
- They don't give students feedback about *what* they did well or badly.
- They undermine the teaching-and-learning situation in the following ways:
  - They lead many students to work more for the sake of the grade than for learning.
  - They lead to an adversarial atmosphere; students often resent or even fight us about grades; many students no longer feel the teacher as ally in the learning process and try to hide what they don't understand. (Think of patients hiding symptoms from doctors.)
  - They lead to a competitive atmosphere among students themselves.
- Figuring out grades is difficult, and the task often makes us anxious because fairness is so hard to achieve.

Conventional grading is so ubiquitous that people tend to see it as inevitable and to feel hopeless about making any changes.

Therefore, it's important to realize that grading is not built into the universe; grading is not like gravity—not "natural" or inevitable. If that sounds utopian, I can point to The Evergreen State College. I taught there for nine years. Since it started in 1971, faculty have given narrative evaluations instead of grades. The system works fine on all counts, including success in helping students enter high quality professional and graduate school. Where Evergreen is a nonelite state college in Washington, Hampshire College is an elite private institution here in Amherst, Massachusetts, that also has a solid history of success with no grades. So we mustn't forget that educational institutions can get along just fine without grades. The pressure for grades is probably greatest at the secondary level since grades seem so central to the college admissions process; yet there are secondary schools that prosper without grades.

But discussions of institutions like Evergreen and Hampshire tend to trap people into either/or thinking: whether or not to have grading at all; whether or not to transform the entire curriculum as they've done at Evergreen or Hampshire. Let's wrest the discussion out of this binary rut. Instead of fighting about *Yes* or *No*, let's discuss *When?* and *How much?* I am interested in exploring temporary time-outs from grading, even while operating under a conventional grading system.

And let's jump from the largest scale to the smallest: *freewriting*. To freewrite for ten minutes is to step outside of grading for ten minutes. When I get students to freewrite, I am using my authority to create unusual conditions in order to contradict or interrupt the pervasive feeling in the air that writing is always evaluated. What is essential here are the two central features of freewriting: that it be private (thus I don't collect it or have students share it with anyone else); and that it be nonstop (thus there isn't time for planning, and control is usually diminished). Students quickly catch on and enter into the spirit. It's sad if teachers use freewriting in thoughtless or mechanical ways: just ten minutes now and then for no good reason—and sadder if teachers call it freewriting but collect it and read it. Still, most freewriting is a common instance of a kind of writing that is not really so rare: *nongraded* writing.

Every time teachers get students to do nongraded writing, they are inviting students to notice that the link between writing and grading can be broken: it is possible to write and not worry about how the teacher will grade it; it is possible to write in pursuit of one's own goals and standards and not just someone else's. When teachers assign journal writing and don't grade it, this too is an important time-out from grading.

10 A bigger time-out from grading is the single *nongraded assignment.* These can be "quickwrites" or sketches done in class or for homework; sometimes they are simply "ungraded essays." In either case they are usually unrevised. These writings carry more weight than freewritings if the teacher reads them or asks students to read them to each other, but still they break the link between writing and grading. (It helps to say out loud to the students that this writing is ungraded. Occasionally, students write as *though* it were a graded exercise. And indeed, many students have had the experience of being *told* that something was ungraded and then being surprised.)

These are small time-outs—ten minutes, one or two hours. What if we have *ten days of nongraded writing?* We can do that and still work solidly within a grading system. Many teachers start the semester with this kind of orgy of nongraded writing, and it has a deep effect on students' and teachers' relationship to writing. It improves students' fluency and enlivens their voices on paper; it helps them learn to take risks in writing; and it permits us to assign much more writing than we usually can in two weeks.

Portfolios. Portfolios are a way to refrain from putting grades on individual papers: for a while we can just write comments and students can revise. Grading can wait till we have more pieces of writing in hand—more data to judge. By avoiding frequent ranking or grading, we make it somewhat less likely for students to become addicted to oversimple numerical rankings—to think that evaluation always translates into a simple number. Portfolios permit me to refrain from grading individual papers and limit myself to writerly evaluative comments—and help students see this as a positive rather than a negative thing, a chance to be graded on a body of their best work that can be judged more fairly. Portfolios are particularly helpful as occasions for asking students to write extensive and thoughtful explorations of their own strengths and weaknesses.

Contracts for a Grade. For the last few years, this has been my favorite way to step outside of most grading while still working

CONTEXT

Portfolios became a popular method for assessing writing in the 1980s. They are based on the idea that a writer's ability cannot be judged accurately on the basis of a single paper but on a body of written work. In portfolio assessment, student papers are typically not evaluated separately. Instead, students submit a selection of their work that is usually evaluated as a whole; sometimes, papers that have been individually graded are revised and then resubmitted as part of a portfolio. Often, a portfolio is submitted at the end of the semester and contains final drafts of papers in addition to other material—such as rough drafts, peer comments, and self-assessments. This process encourages students to think critically about their writing and their development as writers over time. Elbow has been a strong advocate for portfolios for most of his career, and he helped develop portfolio assessment systems at the State University of New York at Stony Brook and the University of Massachusetts at Amherst.

within a regular grading system. Contracts provide a way to avoid trying to measure the quality of work or learning and yet still arrive at a grade for the course. A contract says, "If you do x, y, and z, you can count on such and such a grade." For me, the pedagogical principle in using contracts is this: I don't trust my efforts to measure learning or quality of writing, and I hate pretending to do so. I'd rather put my efforts into something I do trust and enjoy: trying to specify activities and behaviors that will lead to learning and good writing.

Most often I have used what might be called a limited or impure or timid contract—a contract that spells out the many, many activities that seem most central to producing learning for the course, and then says, "If you do all these, you are guaranteed a course grade of B." But the contract goes on to say, "If you want an A, I have to judge most of your papers or your portfolio to be excellent." Thus I am not getting rid of all official measurement of quality. But I am vastly reducing it.[1]

---

1. Perhaps I should say that I am still grading, but that my only grades are *excellent, acceptable* and *not acceptable* for the terms of the contract, but the procedure feels more like not grading. Perhaps, in addition, I should not use the word "contract" since I impose this policy unilaterally rather than letting students have a choice about whether to enter into it; and I don't ask students to sign anything. But the word is a convenient shorthand that suggests the general approach.

15 Contracts highlight the distinction between evaluation and grading. My contract minimizes grading (and a full contract eliminates it altogether), but in doing so it *helps evaluation to be more effective*. That is, even though a contract permits me to cut back on evaluation when I find that helpful, I continue to give lots of evaluation, and the contract permits me to make blunter criticisms or pushier suggestions and have students listen to them better. They know that my responses have nothing to do with their grade (up to a B). Students needn't go along with what I say in order to get a good grade. I've set up the contract so that they cannot refrain from making significant revisions, but I emphasize to them that they can revise entirely differently from how I might have suggested or implied—and they don't have to make their revisions necessarily better, just substantively different. In short, by decoupling evaluation from grading, I think we can make it healthier and more productive.

I like the learning situation my contract puts my students into: they have to listen to my reactions, evaluation, and advice, yet they get to make up their own mind about whether to go along with what I say. Their decision will have no effect on their grade (up to a B). This means they have to *think* about my response on its own terms—listen to me as reader and human being—instead of just reacting to me in the thoughtless and habitual ways in which so many students understandably react to teacher feedback. That is, students too often feel, "Of course my teacher is right," or else, "Well that's the kind of junk that *this* teacher wants, so I guess I'll do it for my grade." Either way, these students don't really wrestle in their minds with the crucial question of whether my reactions or comments actually make sense to them. In the end I think my contract gets students to listen to me better. (Of course, students occasionally tell me that they *feel* pressure to go along with my comments—even though they can see that it really won't help their grade. This provides fruitful occasions for me to help students

explore their learning process and how they deal with the role of being a student: how they tend to feel and react to teacher comments and grades.) So whereas some people say that teachers are evading their intellectual responsibility if they don't grade, I would argue that we can create more intellectual engagement by minimizing grades and highlighting evaluation.

I hear an objection:

But we need grades for motivation—to get students to work hard.

But notice how *indirectly* grades motivate students. The casual link between grading and student work is very tenuous. We hope that by awarding fair grades, we will cause students to exert themselves to engage in the learning activities we want them to engage in. But our hope is dashed as often as it is fulfilled. Some students get good grades without much work; some have given up trying to get good grades; a few don't care what grade they get; still others work only to psych out the teacher rather than to learn (and a few of these even cheat or plagiarize*). I prefer the way a contract is more direct and simply requires the activities I think will lead to learning. I'd rather put my time and effort into trying to figure out which activities will in fact help them learn and grow rather than into trying to measure the exact degree of quality of the writing they turn in and hope that my grade leads to effort.

Do I find that using a contract makes everything perfect? No. I think my contract leads to a bit *more* work from the class as a whole, more tasks accomplished by more people. But I think it also leads to a bit less pushing, struggle, or strain from a number of students. This disappoints me, but I have to accept the fact that my real goal is not struggle for its own sake but struggle that comes *from them*— from intrinsic motivation. When students are habituated to struggling mostly or even only

---

*For information about plagiarism, see pages 160–162 and 221–228.

for grades, it's not surprising that they have a hard time coming up with this rarer and more precious kind of struggle. Gradually, pieces of self-motivation begin to kick in, and when that happens it's very exciting for both them and me. But I have to settle for less.

2. WAYS TO STEP OUTSIDE OF THE MENTALITY OF EVALUATION

20 I want to up the ante. If we step outside of grading, we may not be stepping outside the mentality of evaluation or judging. After all, we sometimes read an ungraded assignment and say, "I'm sure glad I don't have to grade this because it really stinks." Is it *possible* to stop judging or seeing writing in terms of quality? Yes. In fact, it's not so unusual. That is, even though it is inevitable that humans often look at things through the lens of judgment or quality, sometimes they don't.

The most obvious example is when we like or love. Sometimes we like or dislike a person, an object, a work of art—and more to the point here, a piece of writing—without any judgment of its quality. We know this can happen because sometimes we are even aware of the two mentalities at once: we like it but we know it is not good—or we dislike it but we know it is good. We often love someone or something because we "value" them, not because we "evaluate" them. The loving or "valuing" is something we do or give or add; we don't necessarily base it on our judgment of the "value" or "quality" of the person or object.

I'm not saying that we always take off the judging lens when we like or love, for sometimes our liking or loving is indeed based on our evaluation of quality. ("It's so great I love it.") I'm simply insisting that liking or loving can operate outside of judging—and often do. When I began to realize this, I found myself liking more often—students and students' writing—without wearing my judging hat. Thus we can get better at liking students and their writing; it's a skill....My main claim, then, is limited, but important: I'm insisting on the empirical observation that it is not unusual for us to spend some time outside the evaluative mentality.

I find it a great relief to do this now and then. It seems to me that these time-outs from the evaluative mentality help my teaching. I think they foster an atmosphere of support and appreciation that helps students flourish, think well, and stretch themselves.

I am not denying that there is a different and more obvious kind of stretching that comes from the opposite atmosphere of judging, evaluating, and criticizing. Many people testify with appreciation to how a tough teacher's evaluative criticism made them stretch. But this stretching-through-evaluative-criticism does not negate the quite different and more delicate kind of stretching that can occur when we reduce or remove the pressure of judgment and evaluation. Sometimes people don't take risks or try out their own values or start to use their own internal motivation until critical thinking is turned off and even nonsense and garbage are welcomed. In such a setting people sometimes think themselves into their best thinking or imagine themselves into being more of who they could be. Nonevaluative support and acceptance are common in the family, especially toward infants and young children, but the evaluative mentality is pervasive in school and college settings. Of course, banishing evaluation does not always lead to this delicate stretching—but then neither does evaluation always lead to that other kind of stretching.

25 This talk of liking and loving tends to sound soft, fuzzy, and unintellectual. I don't want to run away from that most dreaded indictment, *soft*! It's time to insist openly that there's nothing wrong with time-out zones from what is critical, hard, cool, and detached—not just in elementary school but in higher education. We need it, even for good thinking.

Nevertheless, I want to cut through the shallow-minded association between not being evaluative and not being intellectual. That is, we can have time-outs from the evaluative mentality itself and still operate in a fully intellectual, cognitive, academic spirit. We can do so through the use of certain questions about texts—especially about student writing.

Admittedly, the questions we most often ask of student writing are quality questions: "How good or bad is it? What are its strengths and weaknesses? How can it be better?" But these are not the only questions to ask of a text, and indeed they are not the most common questions we ask of important texts in literature, history, biology, or physics—whether in teaching or scholarship. In studying important texts we tend to ask questions like these:

What does the text say? What does it imply or entail? What are its consequences? What does the writer assume? What is the writer's point of view or stance? Who does the text speak to? How does the text ask me to see the world? What would I do if I believed it?

Nothing should stop us from using these questions on student writing. They are simple, obvious, and important questions that have no inherent connection to quality or value. They are all requests to summarize, explicate, or extend the paper (or, carried out step further, to play the "believing game" with it).

Admittedly, when we use these questions on professional writing, we tend to assume value—sometimes even that these are "great works"* and so don't need evaluating. And with student writing, many of these neutral questions have taken on evaluative freight. "What is this paragraph saying?" often means, "I don't think it is saying anything" or "You are confused."

30 But we don't need to use these questions in this way, and it's not hard to answer them without saying anything about a paper's quality. A careful summary of a bad paper need not reveal anything of its badness. Yes, we can summarize a paper by saying, "It says X—which is absurd," or "It says both X and not X—which is self-contradictory." or "It says X and P and there is no relation between them." But we don't need to put a judgmental

spin on summaries. For the fact remains that plenty of excellent papers say things that seem absurd or logically contradictory or seemingly unrelated. Some people can't summarize without praising or criticizing, but that's because they've never practiced.

There is one kind of badness that might seem unavoidable in a summary: if a paper simply doesn't say much at all, a careful summary will contain damningly little. But even this kind of badness will not show up when we answer the other questions: "What does the paper imply or entail, what does the writer assume?" Besides, some *excellent* papers say remarkably little.

So if we learn how to answer these kinds of questions about our students' writing without a habitual edge of evaluation (and it's not so hard) and if we train our students to answer them about each others' writing, we will be doing something perfectly intellectual, academic, cognitive, hard, and detached. We will not be giving in to the dread disease of "softness." Yet we will still be stepping outside of the mentality of judgment. Most of us have done this if only now and again, perhaps inadvertently. As with loving and liking, these questions don't force us out of the mentality of evaluation, but they *invite* us—if we are willing—to take off the lens of judging for a while. We discover it is possible to have long discussions of the meaning and implications of a paper and find we have wholly forgotten about the question of how good it is.

The same goes for other interesting questions we can ask of any text:

How does the paper relate to other events or values in the culture? How does it relate to what other students are writing—or other texts around us? How does this text relate to other things the student has written?

There are related questions that, interestingly, we can't usually answer without the writer's help:

How does the paper relate to events in the writer's life? Why did the writer write these words?

*Because the words "great works" are in quotation marks in this context, they evoke an association with the great works of literature, history, theology, and philosophy that scholars once thought could be identified and listed. See page 423.

Yet these questions are no less intellectual or analytic or interesting. We often ask published writers to answer them. Why not ask our students too?

35 It's a bit harder to strip away our habits of judgment from some of the most interesting and pointed questions about craft and structure in a paper:

> How is the text organized or put together? How does the text function so as to say what it says and do what it does?

But even these questions can be answered in a non-evaluative fashion.

Finally, I would call attention to the most bluntly simple, obvious, and frequently asked questions about a text, and insist that it is also, in fact, entirely irrelevant to quality:

> As reader, what are my thoughts on the topic? Where do I agree or disagree?

For even if I disagree completely with everything the paper says, it does not follow that I consider the paper bad. We often disagree with excellent writing. Even more frequently, we agree with terrible writing. It turns out not to be so very hard simply to talk about our agreement or disagreement and to give our thoughts, and not enter at all into the realm of judgment. If I simply *engage* the issue of the paper and tell my thoughts, I need not be playing the quality game.

Many students have never had a teacher take their message seriously enough to engage with it by saying, "Here are *my* thoughts about your issue." For this reason, students will often *infer* value judgments even if we are not making them. But they can gradually catch on to this more frankly intellectual way of talking about texts—and will be grateful to do so. When teachers talk only about how good or bad a paper is or talk only about its strengths and weaknesses, making suggestions for improvement, this can function as a way to avoid engagement with the topic or the writer.

None of these analytic, academic questions are inherently evaluative, yet they are much more intellectually interesting than questions about quality. In the end, then, I

conclude that the *least* interesting questions we can ask of any text—by students or by published authors—are questions of quality or evaluation. The most intellectually interesting work comes from asking and answering many of our most common analytic and academic questions—questions that invite us (though they do not require us) to step outside the mentality of evaluation.

3. WAYS TO USE GRADES MORE EFFECTIVELY

I turn now to the nitty-gritty: grading itself. The essential fact about grades is that they are one-dimensional. Grades are simply numbers and the essence of numbers is very austere: N is wholly defined as "greater than $N - 1$ and less than $N + 1$." B has no other meaning than "worse than A and better than C." Conventional grades demarcate ten or eleven levels of "pure quality"—wholly undefined and unarticulated. We can visualize the one-dimensional essence of grading quite literally with a simple vertical line. Such a line is pure verticality; it is entirely lacking in the horizontal dimension.

40 This pure, numerical, one dimensional verticality—no words or concepts attached—is the main reason why conventional grades are untrustworthy if they are used as descriptors for *complex* human performances—and thus why grading leads to such difficulty and dispute. We see even more unrelenting verticality when faculty members grade essays on a scale of 1 to 100 (which is, amazingly, not so uncommon, for example, in some law schools).

In this section, I am suggesting two ways to deal with this unrelenting verticality: (A) reduce it somewhat by using fewer grades— what I call "minimal grading"; (B) add a bit of the horizontal dimension by using criteria.

(A) Minimal Grading—Reducing the Vertical

We can reduce the verticality of conventional grades by simply using a scale with fewer levels. Most of us use minimal grades when we make low-stakes assignments and grade them pass/fail or else use $\sqrt{}$ and $\sqrt{} +$ and $\sqrt{} -$. But we tend to assume that if an assignment is important and we want students to take it more seriously and work harder on it, we should use conventional grades with their ten or more levels of quality.

But this assumption is misleading and counterproductive. It rests on a failure to distinguish between *stakes* and *levels*. Every act of grading involves two very different questions: "How much credit is at stake in this performance?" "How many levels of quality shall I use on my evaluation scale?" When students take an assignment more seriously and work harder, it usually has little to do with our having added levels to our grading scale, and much more to do with our having raised the stakes and made the assignment *count* for more of the final grade. Few students will struggle hard for an A that doesn't count much for their final grade. (A few students have become obsessive about any A; a few others will struggle on a low-stakes assignment—not for the grade but because they are particularly interested in the issue.)

Thus the most reliable way to use grades to make students work harder is to raise the stakes—as long as we make the passing level high enough. Even a two-level scale can be very demanding if we put the bar at a high level. At M.I.T. for the last twenty years or so, faculty have given nothing but Pass and Fail as final grades to all first year students in all courses. The stakes are very high indeed and so are the standards, but only two levels are used. We need only increase the number of levels

to three or four if we want to give less-skilled students a goal of "pretty good"—or to spur those students who are hungry to distinguish their work as superior. If we use three levels, we have even more scope for making strategic decisions about where to place the bars.

45 But there is something we reliably achieve by increasing the number of grading levels: we make *our* work harder. Think of the difference between reading a stack of paper in order to give them conventional grades, versus reading them so as only to pick out those that stand out as *notably weak* or *notably strong*.

I'm suggesting, then, that we can get what we need from the grading of important or high-stakes assignments if we use just three (or at most four) levels and make pass hard enough to get. Most of our difficulties with grading come from having too many levels—too much verticality:

- The more levels we use, the more untrustworthy and unfair the results. We know what the history of literary criticism has shown (along with informal research by students turning in the same paper to multiple teachers): good readers do not agree in their rankings of quality: Your A paper is liable to become a B in my hands—or vice versa. Diederich provides the classic research on this matter.
- The more levels we use, the more chances students have to resent or even dispute those fine-grained distinctions we struggled so hard to make in the first place. (Think of the resentment-laden arguments that occur about a plus or a minus!) Thus the more levels we have, the more we slide toward an adversarial student/teacher relationship and consequently the more damage to the teaching/learning climate. Yes, as long as there *are* any distinctions or levels at all, *some* students will be disappointed or resentful at not getting the higher level they were hoping for. But fewer levels means fewer borderline performances.

CONTEXT

Paul Diederich—whose work is cited at the end of this argument—wrote, "As a test of writing ability, no test is as convincing to English teachers, to teachers in other disciplines, and to the public as actual samples of each student's writing, especially if done under test conditions in which one can be sure that each sample is the student's own unaided work." This statement was published in 1974. In the three decades since then, standardized testing of student writing has increased, despite the widespread belief among writing scholars that such testing is inadequate in evaluating students' writing ability. In 2005, the College Board added a timed written essay to the SAT, which is widely used by colleges to decide on admissions. In addition, partly as a result of the federal No Child Left Behind education reform law, passed by Congress in 2002, many states now require students to take standardized writing tests.

■ The more levels we use, the more we establish a competitive atmosphere among students and a pecking order culture.

■ The more levels we use, the more work for us. It's *hard* making all those fine distinctions—say between A and A minus or B plus and B. If we use just three levels all we need to do is pick out papers that *stand out* as notably strong and notably weak.

In short, boundary decisions are always the most untrustworthy and arguable. Fewer boundaries mean fewer boundary decisions (see the highly useful pieces by Haswell and Wyche-Smith).

Let me consider some objections to minimal grading.

But how can we compute a final grade for the semester using eleven levels, if our constituent grades use only three levels?

This is a problem if we only have a couple of constituent grades to work with at the end of the semester, for example, one paper and two exams. But if we have a fair number of papers, exercises, quizzes, or tests on a three-level scale, we can use some mathematical formula to calculate the final grade by simply counting up points (perhaps with different weighings according to how important the assignments are): 3 for a Strong, 2 for Satisfactory, and 1 for Weak. Alternatively, if there are a lot of low-stakes assignments graded Satisfactory/ Unsatisfactory, we can decide that students with Satisfactory on all their low-stakes assignments start off with a foundation of B. Then their final grade is pulled up or down by Strongs or Weaks on their high-stakes assignments. Or vice-versa: we can average the high-stakes pieces, and if the result is some kind of "satisfactory" or "2"—let low-stakes pieces decide the gradations between C and B. A multitude of scoring systems are possible—and I haven't even mentioned other factors that most teachers count in their final

grading, such as attendance, participation, effort, and improvement.

We already use minimal grading: most faculty already give nothing but As and Bs.

Yes, many faculty have fallen into this practice. When some faculty members give a full range of grades and others give mostly As and Bs, we have a situation of semantic chaos. The grade of B has become particularly ambiguous: readers of a transcript have no way of knowing whether it denotes good strong competent work (many college catalogues define it as an "honors grade") or disappointing, second-rate work. C might mean genuinely satisfactory work or virtually failing work. Critics of "grade inflation" charge that even "A" has lost its meaning of genuine excellence (though some research undercuts that charge, see U.S. Department of Education). If instead of using symbols like A, B, and C, teachers used meaningful words like "excellent," "honors," "outstanding," "strong," "satisfactory," "weak," "poor," "unsatisfactory," all parties to grading would have a better understanding of the message.

Some teachers will probably still give mostly Excellent or Strong.

Inevitably so. But the point here is to have teachers take responsibility for signing their names to *words* rather than to completely ambiguous letter grades. And in truth it can happen that most of the performances on an essay or even for the whole course are indeed genuinely excellent or strong, and therefore, we want to sign our name honestly to that assertion. But with conventional grading, when a teacher gives mostly As and B pluses, no one knows whether she is saying, "This was a remarkable outcome" or "I just don't want to make it too hard to get a good grade in my course."

I actually have some hope that we'd see a bit less grade inflation in a three-level scale, where teachers had to use a word like "excellent" or "honors" for the top grade rather than just "A-" or A. If a program or school really wanted to get rid of too many high grades, they could even insist on a term like "top 10%" or "top quarter" for the top grade.

50 And surely the *worst* grade inflation is at the bottom, not the top. Most teachers give passing grades and even Cs to performances that they consider completely unsatisfactory. Grades would be much more meaningful if we had to decide between the categories of "satisfactory" vs. "unsatisfactory" or "unacceptable."

> But minimal grading won't solve the problem of meaninglessness. Grades are just as ambiguous if most students get Satisfactory.

Not really. That is, even though minimal grading will probably give most students the grade of Satisfactory, we will have *clearly communicated* to readers, by the fact of our three-level scale and the use of this word "satisfactory," that this single grade *is* being used for a wide range of performances. This result is not so ambiguous as with conventional grading, where no one knows whether B is being used for a wide range or a restricted range of performances.

> But you're still evading the main problem of all. Sure, sure, it may be technically "unambiguous" to give most of the class a grade like Satisfactory, but the term still remains empty. It doesn't tell us enough. It's too unsatisfying to leave so many students in one undifferentiated lump.

Yes, "unsatisfying" is exactly the right word here. For it's a crucial fact about minimal grade that they carry *less information*: conventional grades records more distinctions. By sorting students into more groups that are thus more finely differentiated, conventional grades give students a sense of seeing themselves as better and worse in relation to more of their peers. Conventional grades feel more precise than minimal grades at the job of telling students exactly how well or how badly they did.

Thus students will tend, at first anyway, to experience minimal grading as *taking something away from them*, and they will be correct—even though what is being taken away from them is bad information. Information itself feels precious; distinctions themselves feel valuable, even spurious precision is missed. When students contemplate moving to minimal grading, they often put out of their minds what most of them actually do know at some level: that this information was bad and this precision was spurious. People are easily seduced into wanting to see themselves sorted into levels—*even* people who have a pretty good idea that they will find the information painful. "Doctor, I need you to tell me if I have cancer."

"Teacher/examiner, I need you to tell me *exactly* how bad my paper is." There may be trustworthy precise knowledge about the cancer, but there can be no trustworthy *precise one-dimensional, numerical* knowledge about how bad a paper is. (Consider further that there often is not trustworthy knowledge even about the cancer. Thus, if we *really* want accuracy and precision in grading, perhaps we should makes grades more analogous to the outcomes of much medical evaluation: "Based on my long training in composition and my extensive experience in teaching writing and my careful examination of your paper, I feel quite confident in saying that there is a 70 percent likelihood that it is a C plus.")

Even if the additional information and precision of conventional grades were entirely trustworthy and accurate, there would still be serious problems. Neither the students nor any other readers of the grades would benefit from the potential information carried by this precision unless they saw all the grades for the whole class. "B minus" means virtually nothing unless we see what grade everyone else got. In addition, that precise, accurate, and trustworthy grade would tell the students nothing at all about what it is they did well or badly.

(B) Using Explicit Criteria in Grading— Adding the Horizontal

I turn now to the second suggestion I am making in this essay. When I argued above for minimal grading, I might have seemed to be pleading for less information. No. I was arguing for less *bad information.* If the only grades we can give are purely one-dimensional or vertical, the only honest recourse is to cut back on information and go for minimal grades. But minimal grading is not our only option. My larger purpose is not to reduce information but to increase it. In this section I want to show that when we take away *bad information* from students by moving to minimal grading, we can give them *better information* in return. We can make minimal grades more full of meaning than conventional grades if we find a way to tell students what they are actually weak, satisfactory, or excellent *at.* To do so, we need to work out the *criteria* for our minimal grades.

That is, up till now I've been arguing only for less verticality. But using criteria, we can add a crucial *horizontal* dimension to grades. By spelling out the various features of writing that we are looking for when we grade, we are saying that "quality in writing" is not a single, monolithic, one-dimensional entity. And, of course, we are giving more information and meaning to our grades and making them less mysterious.

55 How do we name criteria? The simplest criteria are the traditional and commonly used pair, *form* and *content*. The distinction is surely useful in grading. Despite some criticism of the distinction as old fashioned or even theoretically suspect, students obviously benefit from knowing our different judgments about these two general areas: ideas-and-thinking versus clarity-organization-mechanics. Almost as commonly used in evaluating is a more elaborated set of criteria with elements like these: *ideas, organization, syntax/ wording, mechanics.* Furthermore, many teachers like to specify in their evaluation the

intellectual operation that is most central to a particular assignment by using criteria like these: *analysis, details, persuasion, research, documentation.* I have been naming textually oriented criteria. But some teachers use some rhetorically oriented or even process-oriented criteria like these: *connecting with the subject, connecting to an audience, voice, substantive revision.* The important principle here is that we do well to *name and acknowledge and communicate* the features of writing that influence our judgments. Since scholars and critics have failed to agree on what "good writing" really is, we get to decide what we are actually looking for and admit it openly to our students.

If we have a large number of papers to grade and we are assigning lots of papers—or if we are teaching a large class that doesn't center on writing and we have little or no help in grading—we probably need to resort to the simplest, least time-consuming way to use criteria: just give one overall grade (or perhaps form/content grades)—yet nevertheless, spell out explicitly for students the other features or characteristics of writing that we are looking for when we grade. Thus we might

---

CONTEXT

During the past two decades, increasing numbers of English teachers have adopted a "process" model of writing instruction. In this model, sometimes called "the writing process" or "process writing," emphasis is placed on the various activities that writers engage in when completing a writing task. Thus, students are encouraged to engage in prewriting activities (such as brainstorming), share drafts of their writing with peers, and revise after they have had the benefit of learning how their audience has responded to their initial drafts. Teachers using this model often incorporate peer review, usually within small groups, to help students appreciate the complexities of writing for real audiences and give them experience hearing how different readers respond to their writing. The process approach to teaching writing was developed as an alternative to the more traditional "product-centered" approach, in which students complete writing assignments on their own, submit them to be graded, and rarely receive any advice or guidance about *how* to write. Peter Elbow was among the earliest proponents of a process-oriented approach to writing instruction at the college level. Today, the approach is common in K-12 schools as well.

announce, "In grading this set of papers I will try to count these four criteria equally: . . ." Or "I will grade most on the strength of your argument, but I'll also take some account of these other three criteria: . . ." If our criteria are at all complicated, we can explain and describe them in a handout. And in order to help students do the best job of *meeting our criteria*, we need to announce them when we announce the assignment—before they write— and not wait till afterward when we hand back the graded papers.

The point is that even if we give nothing but a single minimal grade, we can make that grade carry much more information and meaning if we spell out our criteria in public. And using criteria even in this minimal way helps us grade more fairly. For the process of figuring out criteria and announcing them publicly renders us less likely to be unduly swayed if one particular feature of the writing is terrible or wonderful. For example, teachers often get annoyed by papers that are full of grammar and spelling mistakes and nonmainstream dialect, and consequently overlook virtues in information, ideas, or reasoning in such papers—and give them unreasonably low grades. We are less likely to slip into this unfairness if we have specifically announced our criteria.

However, we get the most benefit from criteria if we can actually give a grade on each one. We tell each student how well we think he or she did on each of the features of writing we are looking for. In doing this we are making *multiple vertical judgments* of quality.

But this will make grading too much work!

The principle of minimal grading comes to our rescue here. For just as it isn't so hard to read through a set of papers and merely note the ones that stand out as weak or strong, so it isn't so much harder merely to notice if an essay seems notably weak or notably strong on the criteria we have named as important. We hold each criterion in mind for a moment and see if that feature of the paper stands out for being strong or weak. In my efforts not to make it too onerous to use criteria, I even announce to students that Satisfactory is the "default" grade and so I will make a notation *only* if I find something notably strong or weak. If we use criteria in this more complete fashion, we have a kind of grid, and our "grade" on a paper might look something like this:

Weak	Satisfactory	Strong	(Note: No check means "satisfactory.")
			Genuine revision, substantive changes, not just editing
	√		Ideas, insight, thinking
√			Organization, structure, guiding the reader
			Language, sentences, wording
√			Mechanics: spelling, grammar, punctuation, proofreading
√			Overall

This is the form a grid might take when I photocopy a set of blank ones and make check marks. I often write a comment in addition: something more "readerly" and less evaluative—some comment about the responses and reactions I had at various points in reading. I think these discursive comments actually do more good in the long run than quantified evaluations. Indeed, I came to use grids when I gradually realized that my readerly comments were leaving students too dissatisfied, but I didn't want to give a regular grade. Grids were a way to give a bit of quantified evaluation but not on just one dimension.[2]

60 When I write comments on a computer—as I now prefer to do—I put the grid on a tiny file or even a "macro." Then, when I start to write a comment, I bring in the file or macro. This way I can write in little comments about a criterion. If I were using my computer on the same paper as above, my grid response might look like this:

GENUINE REVISION, SUBSTANTIVE CHANGES, NOT JUST EDITING:
IDEAS, INSIGHTS, THINKING: *Strong. I liked the way you complicated things by exploring points that conflict with your main point.*
ORGANIZATION, STRUCTURE, GUIDING THE READER: *Weak. I kept feeling confused about where you were going—though also sensing that my confusion came from your process of complicating your thinking. This confusion would be good if it weren't a final draft.*
LANGUAGE, SENTENCES, WORDING:
MECHANICS: SPELLING, GRAMMAR, PUNCTUATION, PROOFREADING: *Weak. Because of all the mistakes, this paper doesn't fulfill the contract and is not acceptable. I'll call it acceptable this first time IF you give me a fully cleaned up version by next class.*
OVERALL: *Unsatisfactory for now.*

When we use criteria in this fuller way and make *multiple judgments,* we finally make our grades carry explicit meaning—rather than letting them remain mysterious or magical. And we finally give students some valuable feedback on the particular strengths and weaknesses in their writing—feedback that they don't get from conventional grades. Indeed, mere checkmarks on a grid (perhaps with a few short comments) are sometimes clearer and more useful to students than the longer comments we write in our unrevised prose—especially when it's late at night and we are tired.

Grids are particularly useful for responding to a revised final version when we have already given plenty of feedback to a draft. After all, extended commenting makes more sense at the draft stage: we can give encouragement ("Here's what you need to work on to make it better") instead of just giving an

autopsy ("Here's what didn't work"). For the final version, we can read through quickly and then check off criteria on a grid and give no comments at all. We give students better help if we assign papers and give full feedback on drafts and only grid check marks on final versions, than if we assign fewer papers and give full feedback on both drafts and revisions.

Let me explore the interesting issue of figuring out one's criteria. When students ask me, "What are you looking for?" I sometimes feel some annoyance—though I don't think my reaction is quite fair. But I enjoy it when *I* ask the question of myself: "What actually *are* the features in a piece of writing that make me value it?" If I try to answer this question in an insecure, normative way, I tie myself in knots: "What *ought* I to value in student essays?" But we are professionals in our fields and so we get to ask the question in an empirical way: "What *do* I value in writing?" For there is no Platonic correct answer to the question, "What is good writing?"

This process of empirical self-examination can be intellectually fascinating. We learn to

2. Unfortunately, the spatial orientation of my grid works at crosspurposes with my metaphor of vertical and horizontal, but it's easier to represent quality horizontally from left to right if we want to use words to name criteria. And of course I might write an additional discursive comment at the end.

notice more clearly how we read—and this can even lead to some *change* in how we read. For example, some faculty members discover that they are giving more weight than they realized to certain criteria (e.g., to matters of style or correct restatement of textbook and lecture material or correct mechanics)—and this realization leads them to attend more to other criteria. Or they discover that they use different criteria for student writing than for professional writing (e.g., that in student writing they disapprove of the use of first person writing or personal anecdote, but in published professional writing in their field they value it).

65 The use of criteria has a powerful added benefit because it helps students engage in valid and productive *self-evaluation*. When we ask students to give or suggest a conventional grade for themselves, we are putting them in an unhelpfully difficult spot. There are too many unstated criteria to sum up into one number and it's hard for them not to translate the question into characterological and almost moral terms: "Am I an A person or a B person?" It's much easier and more valid for students to grade themselves with a system of minimal grades and multiple criteria. When they rate themselves as strong, satisfactory, or weak on a wide range of skills or abilities, their answers are more likely to be honest and accurate. I ask such questions at the beginning of the semester ("As we start this course, do you rate yourself Strong, OK, or Weak on the following skills or abilities or areas of knowledge?"). This helps them set goals. I ask the questions again at midsemester. Most important, I ask them at the end ("Do you think your performance has been strong, satisfactory, or weak on these criteria this semester?") Also, I find it very productive to ask students themselves to generate the criteria that they think are important—again at the beginning, middle, and end of the semester.

The Institutional Dimension

In the third and final section of this essay, I've suggested two ways to make grades more trustworthy and meaningful—while still working within a conventional grading system: using minimal grades as a way to reduce the bad information in conventional grades; using multiple explicit criteria as a way to make grades more informative and useful as feedback.

But minimal grades and explicit criteria are not just useful *within* a conventional grading system. They could vastly improve institutional grading itself. At present, a transcript consists of countless single letter grades that no reader can trust since faculty members have such different standards. When a student gets a B, it can mean anything from good honors work to disappointing work. Nor can readers translate those grades into meaningful or useful information. Even when a student gets an A, we don't have any idea what skills or kinds of writing the student is good at—and inevitably, not so good at.

Transcripts would be much more useful if they represented a different deployment of energy and ambition. On the one hand, we should be *less* ambitious and stop pretending that we can reliably sort students into eleven vertical levels of quality—or that we can reliably sort students into eleven vertical levels of quality—or that the sortings would mean the same thing in different teachers' hands and in different readers' minds. Transcripts would be more honest, accurate, and trustworthy if we settled for recording only three levels, say, Honors, Satisfactory, Unsatisfactory (or at most four: *Honors, Strong, Fair, Unsatisfactory*).

But on the other hand, it is feasible to be far more ambitious where it counts, and to give grades on *criteria* for each course. Thus, at the end of a course, we would provide the registrar with a small grid of grades for each student. There would be a grade for the student's overall performance—using three or at most four levels. But we would also list the three to six criteria that we think are most important, and for each we would tick off whether we thought this student's work was satisfactory or notably weak or notably strong.

70 Faculty members need not be forced to use the same criteria. There could be a large list of criteria to choose from: textual criteria like *clarity* and *organization;* process criteria like *generating, revising,* and *working collaboratively;* rhetorical criteria like awareness of audience and voice; and genre-related criteria like *analysis* and *argument.* Teachers could even create their own criteria. Indeed, there's no reason why teachers should be obliged to use the same criteria for every student in a course. After all, we might want to bring in certain criteria only for certain students (*creative* or *diligent*—or *unable to meet deadlines*) yet not want to speak about these criteria for all students.

This procedure sounds complicated, but given computers, it would not be hard to manage—both for giving course grades and in producing a transcript. (Elementary school report cards have long used this approach; and many high school teachers now have a list of fifty or more criteria they can add electronically to grades on report cards.) Readers of the transcript would finally get useful information about substance and be spared the untrustworthy information about levels of quality.

I have been suggesting a visual metaphor: Minimal grading asks for less of the vertical; using criteria means more of the horizontal. But my suggestions also imply a move away from the tradition of *norm-based* or measuring assessment toward the tradition of criterion-based or *mastery* assessment. Norm-based or measuring assessment involves making single, complex, all-determining decisions about each student: all are strung out along a single vertical line—each at an exact distance above or below every other student. Criterion-based or mastery assessment, on the other hand, implies multiple simpler decisions about each student: all are placed in a complicated multidimensional space—each student being strong in certain abilities, okay in others, and weak in yet more, with different students having different constellations of strengths

and weaknesses. (See D. C. McClelland for the classic formulating essay in the criterion-based tradition. This tradition is also represented in the "New Standards Project," for which see Myers and Pearson.)

In this paper I am trying to get outside the either/or debates around grading. We can look for ways to step temporarily outside of grading and even of the mentality of evaluations; and we can look for *better ways* to grade and not grade. We can make small pragmatic improvements, but also push for large utopian change. The human impulse to judge or evaluate is inevitable and useful, but we also need to find ways to bypass that impulse. It won't be so hard, really, to have assessments that lead to a healthier climate for teaching and learning, and that give us a more accurate picture of student achievement.

WORKS CITED

Belanoff, Pat, Peter Elbow, and Sheryl Fontaine. *Nothing Begins with N: New Investigations of Freewriting.* Carbondale: Southern Illinois UP, 1991.

Diederich, Paul. *Measuring Growth in English.* Urbana, IL: NCTE, 1974.

Elbow, Peter. "Ranking, Evaluating, Liking: Sorting Out Three Forms of Judgment." *College English* 55.2 (February 1993) 187–206.

Haswell, Richard and Susan Wyche-Smith. "Adventuring into Writing Assessment." CCC 45.2 (May 1994): 220–36.

——. "A Two-Tier Rating Procedure for Placement Essays: Washington State University." *Assessment in Practice: Putting Principles to Work on College Campuses.* San Francisco: Jossey-Bass, 1996. 204–07.

Lakoff, George and Mark Johnson. *Metaphors We Live By.* Chicago: U of Chicago P, 1980.

McClelland, D. C. "Testing for Competence Rather than for Intelligence." *American Psychologist* 28 (1973): 1–14.

Myers, Miles and P. David Pearson. "Performance Assessment and the Literacy Unit of the New Standards Project." *Assessing Writing* 3.1 (1996): 5–29.

U.S. Department of Education. *The New College Course Map and Transcript Files: Changes in Course-Taking and Achievement,* 1972–1992. Washington, DC: Office of Educational Research and Improvement, 1996.

Questions for Discussion

1. Elbow opens his essay by stating that his argument is driven by a "utopian impulse". What does he mean by that phrase? What do you think he accomplishes by admitting that his perspective is "utopian"?

2. In paragraph 5 Elbow identifies several problems with grading. How effectively does he support his claims about these problems with grading? Drawing upon your experience as a student, how do you respond to the claims in his list?

3. Elbow offers a number of alternatives to traditional grading. How practical are these alternatives? How persuasive is his case in support of these alternatives?

4. What objections can you identify to Elbow's suggestions about grading? Do you think he adequately accounts for possible objections to his suggestions? Explain, citing specific passages from his essay to support your answer.

5. What does Elbow mean when he writes that he wants to "step outside the mentality of grading" (par. 20)? Why is doing so necessary, in his view? What are the benefits of doing so? Do you think he makes a convincing case for doing so? Explain.

6. In paragraphs 21–25, Elbow uses words such as "liking" and "loving," which he recognizes could seem "soft, fuzzy, and unintellectual" to his audience. Why does he believe such language is appropriate for the case he is making? How do you respond to it?

7. What assumptions do you think Elbow made about his audience for this argument? Who do you think he expected his audience to be? Are you part of that audience? Is his argument appropriate for a general audience, in your view?

8. How would you describe Elbow's voice in this essay? To what extent do you think his voice strengthens or weakens his essay?

9. This essay might be described as an argument to inquire (see pages 11–14). How effectively do you think Elbow explores the problem of grading student writing? How useful is this argument in addressing this problem?

Few issues in education can generate as much controversy—and anxiety—as testing and grading. As the essays in this cluster indicate, the task of measuring student learning—which is the goal of testing and grading—is extremely complex and challenging. It is also shaped by political and ideological conflict. In the end, however, measuring student learning comes down to individual students taking tests and receiving grades from their teachers.

Think about your own experiences as a student. No matter what kind of schools you have attended, you have likely taken many tests and received grades on many different kinds of assignments. Even students who are home-schooled are subject to evaluation. In large part, to be a student is to be constantly evaluated. And although most students seem to get used to that, testing and grading can nevertheless cause a great deal of anxiety for students, their parents, and teachers as well.

With your own experiences as a student in mind, and taking into account the arguments of the writers in this cluster of readings, consider your views about how students' learning should be measured. For this assignment, you will articulate those views in an open letter to the faculty at your school. Think of your letter as part of the ongoing effort to answer the question, How should we measure student learning? You are trying to answer that question in the context of your college or university and in reference to your own experiences as a student. Your letter should convey to faculty members at your school your specific concerns about testing and grading. Draw on your experiences to explain those concerns. Then offer what you consider to be reasonable, practical solutions to those concerns. If appropriate, draw on the readings in this cluster, and refer to important developments in education if they are relevant to your argument (for example, changes in policies at your school or new education reform efforts, such as President Barack Obama's Race to the Top program). Imagine that your letter will be published in your campus newspaper.

12

American National Identity

Scott Olson/AFP/Getty Images

Scott Olson/AFP/Getty Images

Who Gets to Be an American?

According to the U.S. Census Bureau, more than 13 million legal and illegal immigrants entered the United States between 1990 and 2000. As of 2009, 10.3 million unauthorized immigrants were living in the United States, and an additional 12.6 million immigrants were legally residing in the United States. The Center for Labor Market Studies at Northeastern University determined that immigrants accounted for 50 percent of the 16 million new workers who entered the workforce during the 1990s. Those numbers indicate the significant impact that immigrants can have on the U.S. economy. In fact, Andrew Sum, the director of the Center for Labor Market Studies, speaking in 2002 about his center's study of immigrant labor, declared that "the American economy absolutely needs immigrants." ■ Not everyone would agree. The impact of immigrants on U.S. society has long worried many Americans. As Peter Brimelow, whose essay appears in this section, points out, Americans seem fond of declaring that "we are a nation of immigrants." Indeed, the famous poem inscribed on the Statue of Liberty seems to say unequivocally that America will accept all those who seek a better life here (see *Con-Text* on page 512). Nevertheless, concerns about the effects of immigration on U.S. economic and cultural life have always fueled debates about the extent to which the United States should open its borders to immigrants. Although the patterns of immigration might change from one era to another, the issues surrounding immigration usually do not. In the late nineteenth and early twentieth centuries, when millions of people came to the United States from eastern European and Mediterranean countries, most of them hoping to escape poverty or political conflict, many Americans saw these new arrivals as a threat to economic stability and even to the values that had shaped the U.S. legal and political systems. As you read through the essays in this section, you will encounter some of those same concerns, expressed more than a century later, at a time when increasing numbers of immigrants are arriving from South America and Asia. ■ But arguments about immigration are not just about policy matters or economic worries. They reflect deeper and more complicated concerns about American identity: What exactly does it mean to be an American? Who decides? And *how* should we decide who will become an American? The authors of the essays in this section address these questions, sometimes focusing on policy and sometimes on ethnicity, race, gender, or national origin. These authors represent a range of views on immigration, but perhaps more important is the fact that their essays reveal how complex the questions about immigration and American national identity can be.

CON-TEXT

"The New Colossus"

This is the famous poem that appears on the pedestal of the Statue of Liberty in New York Harbor:

D. Falconer/PhotoLink/Getty Images

The New Colossus

by Emma Lazarus
Not like the brazen giant of Greek fame, With conquering
limbs astride from land to land;

Here at our sea-washed, sunset gates shall stand
A mighty woman with a torch, whose flame
Is the imprisoned lightning, and her name
Mother of Exiles. From her beacon-hand
Glows world-wide welcome; her mild eyes command
The air-bridged harbor that twin cities frame.

"Keep ancient lands, your storied pomp!" cries she
With silent lips.

"Give me your tired, your poor,
Your huddled masses yearning to breathe free,
The wretched refuse of your teeming shore.

Send these, the homeless, tempest-tost to me,
I lift my lamp beside the golden door!"

① # By the Time I Get to Cucaracha

CELIA C. PEREZ-ZEEB

Critics of U.S. immigration policy sometimes charge that the high numbers of illegal immigrants from Mexico and other Central and South American countries place a burden on schools and other social services paid for by U.S. taxpayers; these critics also contend that because many such immigrants are willing to work for low wages, they weaken the job market for legal citizens. These concerns tend to cast the debates about immigration in economic terms. Writer Celia Perez-Zeeb, however, believes that concerns about immigration might have more to do with race and gender than with jobs and taxes. In the following essay, she focuses attention on the laws governing marriages between immigrants and American citizens, and she points out how those complicated laws can place women at a disadvantage. She also examines the role that ethnic stereotypes about Hispanic people play in public debates about immigration. Although she focuses her argument on how Hispanic people are portrayed in these debates and in the popular media, consider whether her argument would apply to other ethnic groups associated with immigration. This essay appeared in *Bad Subjects* in 2002.

CELIA C. PEREZ-ZEEB, "By the Time I Get to Cucaracha"

1 I was watching NBC's *Will and Grace*. It's a show about a woman, Grace, who leaves her fiancé at the chapel on their wedding day and runs off to live with her gay best friend, Will. In this particular episode Karen, Grace's extremely obnoxious socialite assistant, was upset because her housekeeper, Rosario, was going to be deported. In order to keep her in the country they hatched up the old **green card** scam, and picked Will's gay friend, Jack, to be the groom. In one scene Karen and Rosario, who have one of those wacky love-hate relationships, are arguing and Karen says to Rosario, "If it wasn't for this you'd be flying back to Cucaracha on Air Guacamole with live chickens running up and down the aisle!"

I almost fell off the bed. I could not believe my ears.

The people involved in the creation of the show probably justify such blatantly unfunny and racist remarks by making the Karen character super-annoying, self-absorbed and materialistic, thus excusing her ignorance. Maybe they feel they have a little bit of leeway since they have (gasp!) gay characters in the show, and so, of course, they cannot possibly be racist or discriminatory. But, frankly, I think it's messed up that the maid "just happens" to be Latina because, hey, guess what, Latinas are capable of being more than some yuppie's housekeeper! And that said, we should be grateful to all the women, Latina or otherwise, who earn or have earned a living as housekeepers. My mom was a housekeeper when she first came to this country.

Most of the mainstream media seem to believe it's okay to portray Latinos like dirtballs. Not to mention the fact that Latino characters are usually depicted as being in this country illegally. There are plenty of people out there who already view Latinos as hailing from "Cucaracha" without having their beliefs reinforced by the almighty television.

"Green cards" grant noncitizens the right to live permanently in the United States.

CONTEXT

The American Latino Media Arts (ALMA) awards were created in 1995 as part of an effort among advocacy groups to promote fair, accurate, and balanced portrayals of Latinos in television, film, and music. Born as a direct response to negative stereotyping of Latinos in entertainment, these awards honor Latino performers for their outstanding artistic achievement and for enhancing the image of Latinos. The name ALMA, which is Spanish for "spirit" or "soul," is intended to represent the determined spirit of the Latino people as well as the scope of the awards program.

If you think we Latinos have made amazing progress and have many Latino actors on television and in movies that aren't portrayed negatively, how about watching the ALMA awards? It pains me to see the association grasping at straws to have a category in which there are more than two actors and to see how, in most cases, the nominees for awards are supporting actors. Characters not unlike Rosario.

5 But, when I see shows like *Will and Grace*, I wonder where the outrage is? Maybe the right people weren't watching that particular episode and so there was no uproar about it (unlike the whole Taco Bell Chihuahua controversy), but I think there's also something to be said about the fact that people tend to forget that groups other than African-Americans are discriminated against in this country and are often portrayed as racist stereotypes by the media. If the maid had been African-American and "Karen" had made a similarly insulting comment, all hell probably would have broken loose. However, NBC wouldn't have had the balls to even allow such a comment against a black character to air, because it is widely acknowledged that this country has treated black people terribly. And, perhaps more importantly, there are a lot of black activists and groups who would protest. Whatever the reason, it definitely seems to be more acceptable to make fun of certain groups than others.

What's more, pulling this tired and deceptive green card story line is ignorant and misleading. They assume (a) that it's easy to become a legal immigrant in such a manner and (b) that illegal immigrants are gaining residency left and right by marrying for green cards. I think it's fucked up that NBC can get away with letting something so insulting and demeaning to Latinos air, but, frankly, I'm not surprised. I'd seen that story line way too many times already in now-defunct shows like *Jesse* and *Beverly Hills 90210.* It's always portrayed as quick, easy, funny, and oh so romantic. Oh look at this wonderful American marrying this poor wetback just so she can stay in the country. How sweet. Yeah, well it isn't.

The rules governing the attainment of residency by non-citizens married to U.S. citizens are not necessarily clear and not necessarily easy to follow. According to U.S. law, marriages between a citizen and non-citizen must be entered into in "good faith." Then, just before a couple's two-year anniversary, they must undergo an interview with an immigration officer, who attempts to make sure their union isn't a sham. The "investigation" includes weird, personal questions like: what side of the bed does your mate sleep on? Or, What kind of underwear do they wear? During this two-year period the marriage cannot be annulled or terminated unless the spouse dies. And no, permanent resident status isn't automatically granted after two years.

CONTEXT

In 1998 the fast-food company Taco Bell ran a series of advertisements featuring a talking chihuahua that spoke with a pronounced Spanish accent. Despite the ad campaign's apparent commercial success, many people condemned the ads as insulting to Latino people. One critic of the ads was Gabriel Cazares, the mayor of Clearwater, Florida, who was also a former president of the Tampa, Florida, chapter of the League for United Latin American Citizens. Cazares told an interviewer,

I think it was an unfortunate commercial. I think that the use of a dog to depict Mexicans was very demeaning. If Taco Bell wanted to depict someone that would reflect Mexican culture we have many live, two-legged artists, singers, dancers, musicians—some great people in America that could have been selected to give a testimonial for Taco Bell (and) say, 'Yo quiero un taco.' And that wouldn't have been offensive.

A petition has to be entered in order to terminate immigrant status. If it isn't filed then the person can be sent back to their country of origin, unless there's a really good reason for not having filed the petition.

An article in the *Yale Journal of Law and Feminism*, "The Gender Dimensions of U.S. Immigration Policy," argues that female immigrants tend to be at a disadvantage because their entrance into the country often depends more on family ties than other more "legitimate" reasons for entry. For example, employment-based immigration is dominated by men because it tends to favor people who already have advanced degrees in their field, are wealthy, or have much sought after scientific or technological skills. The number of "unskilled" workers who are allowed to enter the country has been lowered; therefore, immigrant women, who tend to come to work as housekeepers or child care providers, have a more difficult time having a "legitimate" reason to enter the United States.

Don't get me wrong, though! The United States does love its immigrants. Of course, on the condition that they can do something for the economy. They don't want to hear about your poverty and persecution, but if you have money or special skills, well, that's a different story. Immigrants are allowed to enter the country legally if they make an outrageous monetary donation. Supermodels are also given special visas as entertainers and as possessors of specialized skills (being skinny and being able to pout on cue, I guess).

10 In 1986 the **Immigration Marriage Fraud amendment** was passed by Congress. This is the amendment that made the two-year minimum marriage period mandatory before a person could be considered for permanent resident status. The *Yale Law* article argues that this piece of legislation gives

Scott Olson/AFP/Getty Images

the spouse who is a citizen, most often the male, excessive power over the immigrant spouse because, believe it or not, after the two-year period is over, if the citizen spouse chooses not to sign the petition for resident status then the immigrant spouse and children, if there are any, can be removed from the United States. So for at least two years an immigrant woman can be at the mercy of whatever her spouse wishes.

You get a whole other story from the senators who spoke at the July 26, 1985, session of Congress for the Subcommittee on Immigration and Refugee Policy. According to Senator Alan K. Simpson (chairman of the subcommittee), "United States citizens legitimately petition for 'mail order brides' advertised in the backs of magazines and tabloids sold at the checkout lines of supermarkets. The alien admitted as a fiancé will go through the appearance of wanting to marry and build a future life until after the actual wedding ceremony. The alien then

The Immigration Marriage Fraud amendment, passed by Congress in 1986 to deter illegal immigration that occurred through fraudulent marriages between American citizens and immigrants, requires the U.S. citizen and his or her foreign spouse to prove two years of valid marriage before the foreign spouse can apply to become a permanent U.S. resident, except under certain special circumstances.

CONTEXT

This essay appeared in 2002 in *Bad Subjects: Political Education for Everyday Life*, a journal published by a nonprofit organization that describes itself as "a collective that...seeks to revitalize progressive politics in retreat." According to its website, *Bad Subjects* believes that "too many people on the left have taken their convictions for granted. So we challenge progressive dogma by encouraging readers to think about the political dimension to all aspects of everyday life. We also seek to broaden the audience for leftist and progressive writing, through a commitment to accessibility and contemporary relevance." In what ways do you think this essay addresses the political viewpoints of people who are likely to read this journal?

promptly abandons his or her spouse." Now, come on. It's okay for these men to order brides through the mail, but god forbid someone try to marry in order to stay in this country and hope for a better life? Does the idea of ORDERING a bride not seem even slightly disturbing to Senator Simpson?

Throughout his speech Alan Simpson made it seem like those who marry immigrants do so either because they "feel sorry" for them or because they are being coerced to do so. The "alien" (what's up with that label?) is portrayed as the scheming good-for-nothing, while the United States citizen is just a poor little lamb who is being manipulated. Simpson states that, "Because the alien and the arranger are well aware of the risks and penalties of disclosure . . . , they feel no compunction in intimidating their United States citizen or resident alien spouses or fiancés." Simpson referred to immigrants who sought marriage for residency as "smooth-talking alien(s)" who made it a practice to convince the citizen that they were going into the marriage out of love and then once they obtained their resident status, they dumped the spouse.

It took Simpson awhile, but he eventually got his main concern off his chest when he argued that most of the illegal immigrants attempting to gain residency through marriage were doing so because they could not obtain residency otherwise. The reasons for their inability to obtain visas, according to Simpson, was because "most aliens" have broken the law in some manner—through illegal entry, or due to the fact that they are terrorists, criminals, narcotics users/dealers, or prostitutes. Note the words "MOST ALIENS."

In the early '80s, before the 1986 amendment was passed, the INS [Immigration and Naturalization Service] estimated that nearly 30% of the cases in which an immigrant had gained resident status through marriage were involved in "suspect marital relationships." When this estimate was revised, the figure was much closer to 8%.

15 Television and movies portray things as if there really are hundreds of thousands of immigrants in the United States getting hitched left and right in order to stay in the country, which is not true. The media makes it seem like a piece of cake to just up and marry and all of a sudden you're an American, which is also not true. Even sadder is that the media completely trivializes the reasons why people come to this country, or why some women might be so desperate not to return to their countries that they would be willing to marry someone they don't know and potentially endure abuse.

The media rarely, if ever, mentions that many of the Central and South American countries these people are fleeing have been historically terrorized by U.S. supported regimes. The media never bothers to mention that the United States quite often turns a blind eye to the terrorism, the disappearances, the tortures, the rapes, and other abuses being suffered by people who come to this country. Apparently, immigrants are most useful to the U.S. when they are performing backbreaking labor or being the brunt of jokes.

Questions for Discussion

1. What is Perez-Zeeb's main point in this essay? Where in the essay does she state that point most directly?

2. Using specific examples of Perez-Zeeb's language to support your answer, describe the tone of this essay. Do you think the tone is appropriate to Perez-Zeeb's argument?

3. Perez-Zeeb objects to the humor involving Latinos on U.S. television shows, and she specifically criticizes an episode of the television show *Will and Grace* in which a marriage is arranged between two characters, one who is a Latina immigrant and one who is an American citizen. What problem involving immigrants does Perez-Zeeb use this episode to introduce? Do you think her criticism of this television show is an effective strategy, given her main argument? Why or why not?

4. Perez-Zeeb refers several times to an article from the *Yale Journal of Law and Feminism.* What do you think she accomplishes by making these references? How might these references enhance (or weaken) her argument?

5. Does the fact that Perez-Zeeb is Latina have any effect on her argument? Explain.

② | A Nation of Immigrants

PETER BRIMELOW

Although born and educated in Great Britain, Peter Brimelow lives and works in the United States, where he has been a strong advocate for restricting immigration. "A Nation of Immigrants" is an editor's title for the following excerpt from a long, controversial article on immigration that Brimelow published in 1992 in *National Review*, a magazine that reflects politically conservative opinions. Although Brimelow addresses the political debate about immigration policy that was occurring in the early 1990s, his argument goes beyond policy issues to the complicated question of what constitutes a nation. Does it have to do with ethnic or racial identity? Or is it a matter of political borders and geographic location? Such questions, Brimelow suggests, must be answered if there is to be any acceptable resolution to the continuing conflicts regarding immigration policy in the United States. Brimelow is the author of a number of books, including *Alien Nation: Common Sense About America's Immigration Disaster* (1995) and *The Worm in the Apple: How Teachers Unions are Destroying American Education* (2003). He edits VDare.com, a website that advocates immigration reform.

PETER BRIMELOW, "A Nation of Immigrants"

1 Everyone has seen a speeded-up film of the cloudscape. What appears to the naked eye to be a panorama of almost immobile grandeur writhes into wild life. Vast patterns of soaring, swooping movement are suddenly discernible. Great towering cumulo-nimbus formations boil up out of nowhere, dominating the sky in a way that would be terrifying if it were not, in real life, so gradual that we are barely aware that anything is going on.

This is a perfect metaphor for the development of the American nation. America, of course, is exceptional. What is exceptional about it, however, is not the way in which it was created, but the speed.

"We are a nation of immigrants." No discussion of U.S. immigration policy gets far without someone making this helpful remark. As an immigrant myself, I always pause respectfully. You never know. Maybe this is what they're taught to chant in schools nowadays, a sort of multicultural Pledge of Allegiance. But it secretly amuses me. Do they really think other nations sprouted up out of the ground? ("Autochthonous" is the classical Greek word.) The truth is that *all* nations are nations of immigrants.

But the process is usually so slow and historic that people overlook it. They mistake for mountains what are merely clouds.

5 This is obvious in the case of the British Isles, from which the largest single proportion of Americans are still derived. You can see it in the place-names. Within a few miles of my parents' home in the north of England, the names are Roman (Chester, derived from the Latin for camp), Saxon (anything ending in *-ton*, town, like Oxton), Viking (*-by*, farm, like Irby), and Norman French (Delamere). At times, these successive waves of peoples were clearly living cheek by jowl. Thus among these place-names is Wallesey, Anglo-Saxon

for "Island of the Welsh"—Welsh being derived from the word used by low-German speakers for foreigners wherever they met them, from Wallonia to Wallachia. This corner of the English coast continued as home to some of the pre-Roman Celtic stock, not all of whom were driven west into Wales proper as was once supposed.

The English language that America speaks today (or at least spoke until the post-1965 fashion for bilingual education) reflects the fact that the peoples of Britain merged, eventually; their separate contributions can still be traced in it. Every nation in Europe went through the same process. Even the famously homogeneous Japanese show the signs of ethnically distinct waves of prehistoric immigration.

But merging takes time. After the Norman Conquest in 1066, it was nearly three hundred years before the invaders were assimilated to the point where court proceedings in London were again heard in English. And it was nearly nine centuries before there was any further large-scale immigration into the British Isles—the Caribbean and Asian influx after World War II. Except in America. Here the process of merging has been uniquely rapid. Thus about 7 million Germans have immigrated to the U.S. since the beginning of the nineteenth century. Their influence has been profound—to my British eye it accounts for the odd American habit of getting up in the morning and starting work. About 50 million Americans told the 1980 Census that they were wholly or partly of German descent. But only 1.6 million spoke German in their homes.

So all nations are made up of immigrants. But what is a nation—the end product of all this merging? This brings us into a territory where words are weapons, exactly as George Orwell pointed out years ago. "Nation"—as suggested by its Latin root *nascere*, to be born—intrinsically implies a link by blood. A nation is an extended family. The merging process through which all nations pass is not merely cultural, but to a considerable extent biological, through intermarriage.

Liberal commentators, for various reasons, find this deeply distressing. They regularly denounce appeals to common ethnicity as "nativism" or "tribalism." Ironically, when I studied African history in college, my politically correct tutor deprecated any reference to "tribes." These small, primitive, and incoherent groupings should, he said, be dignified as "nations." Which suggests a useful definition: tribalism/nativism is nationalism of which liberals disapprove.

10 American political debate on this point is hampered by a peculiar difficulty. American editors are convinced that the term "state" will confuse readers unless reserved exclusively for the component parts of the United States—New York, California, etc. So when talking about sovereign political structures, where the British would use "state," the Germans "*Staat*," and the French "*l'état*," journalists here are compelled to use the word "nation." Thus in the late 1980s it was common to see references to "the nation of Yugoslavia," when Yugoslavia's problem was precisely that it was not a nation at all, but a state that contained several different small but fierce nations—Croats, Serbs, etc. (In my constructive way, I've been trying to introduce, as an alternative to "state," the word "polity"—defined by Webster as "a politically organized unit." But it's quite hopeless. Editors always confuse it with "policy.")

CONTEXT

The concept of *nation-state* is much debated by political scientists, historians, politicians, and others interested in politics and culture. As Brimelow suggests in paragraph 12, *nation-state* is usually defined as a sovereign political entity (a "state") that reflects a specific cultural or ethnic identity (a "nation"). Some theorists argue that the world is becoming increasingly globalized and multicultural, which makes nation-states obsolete. They point to the development of the European Union as an example of this trend. Others, like Brimelow and the influential political scientist Samuel Huntington, argue that nation-states, which most theorists believe evolved in the nineteenth century, remain the source of political power and national identity in the world.

This definitional difficulty explains one of the regular entertainments of U.S. politics: uproar because someone has unguardedly described America as a "Christian nation." Of course, in the sense that the vast majority of Americans are Christians, this is nothing less than the plain truth. It is not in the least incompatible with a secular *state* (polity).

But the difficulty over the N-word has a more serious consequence: it means that American commentators are losing sight of the concept of the "nation-state"—a sovereign structure that is the political expression of a specific ethno-cultural group. Yet the nation-state was one of the crucial inventions of the modern age. Mass literacy, education, and mobility put a premium on the unifying effect of cultural and ethnic homogeneity. None of the great pre-modern multinational empires have survived. (The **Brussels bureaucracy** may be trying to create another, but it has a long way to go.)

This is why **Ben Wattenberg** is able to get away with talking about a "Universal Nation." On its face, this is a contradiction in terms. It's possible, as Wattenberg variously implies, that he means the diverse immigrant groups will eventually intermarry, producing what he calls, quoting the English poet John Masefield, a "wondrous race." Or that they will at least be assimilated by American culture, which, while globally dominant, is hardly "universal." But meanwhile there are hard questions. What language is this "universal nation" going to speak? How is it going to avoid ethnic strife? Dual loyalties? Collapsing like the Tower of Babel? Wattenberg is not asked to reconcile these questions, although he is not unaware of them, because in American political discourse the ideal of an American nation-state is in eclipse.

Ironically, the same weaknesses were apparent in the rather similar concept of "cultural pluralism" invented by Horace M. Kallen at the height of the last great immigration debate, before the **Quota Acts of the 1920s**. Kallen, like many of today's pro-immigration

enthusiasts, reacted unconditionally against the cause for "Americanization" that the 1880-to-1920 immigrant wave provoked. He argued that any unitary American nationality had already been dissipated by immigration (sound familiar?). Instead, he said the U.S. had become merely a political state (polity) containing a number of different nationalities.

15 Kallen left the practical implications of this vision "woefully undeveloped" (in the words of the *Harvard Encyclopedia of American Ethnic Groups*). It eventually evolved into a vague approval of tolerance, which was basically how Americans had always treated immigrant groups anyway—an extension, not coincidentally, of how the English built the British nation.

But in one respect, Kallenism is very much alive: he argued that authentic Americanism was what he called "the American Idea." This amounted to an almost religious idealization of "democracy," which again was left undeveloped but which appeared to have as much to do with non-discrimination and equal protection under the law as with elections. Today, a messianic concern for global "democracy" is being suggested to conservatives as an appropriate objective for U.S. foreign policy.

And Kallenism underlies the second helpful remark that someone always makes in any discussion of U.S. immigration policy: "America isn't a nation like the other nations—it's an idea."

Once more, this American exceptionalism is really more a matter of degree than of kind. Many other nations have some sort of ideational reinforcement. Quite often it is religious, such as Poland's Roman Catholicism; sometimes cultural, such as France's ineffable Frenchness. And occasionally it is political. Thus—again not coincidentally—the English used to talk about what might be described as the "English Idea": English liberties, their rights as Englishmen, and so on. Americans used to know immediately what this meant. As Jesse Chickering wrote in 1848 of his diverse fellow Americans: "English laws and institutions, adapted to the circumstances of the country, have been adopted here....The tendency of things is to mold the whole into one people, whose leading characteristics are English, formed on American soil."

What is unusual in the present debate, however, is that Americans are now being urged to abandon the bonds of a common ethnicity and instead to trust entirely to ideology to hold together their state (polity). This is an extraordinary experiment, like suddenly replacing all the blood in a patient's body. History suggests little reason to suppose it will succeed. Christendom and Islam have long ago been sundered by national quarrels. More recently, the much-touted "Soviet Man," the creation of much tougher ideologists using much rougher methods than anything yet seen in the U.S., has turned out to be a Russian, Ukrainian, or Kazakh after all.

20 Which is why Shakespeare has King Henry V say, before the **battle of Agincourt**, not "we defenders of international law and the dynastic principle as it applies to my right to inherit the throne of France," but

We few, we happy few, we band of brothers.

However, although intellectuals may have decided that America is not a nation but an idea, the news has not reached the American people—especially that significant minority who sternly tell the Census Bureau their ethnicity is "American." (They seem mostly to be of British origin, many generations back.) And it would have been considered absurd throughout most of American history.

John Jay in *The Federalist Papers* wrote that Americans were "one united people, a people descended from the same ancestors, speaking the same language, professing the same religion, attached to the same principles of government, very similar in their manners and customs." Some hundred years later, Theodore Roosevelt in his *Winning*

of the West traced the "perfectly continuous history" of the Anglo-Saxons from King Alfred to George Washington. He presented the settling of the lands beyond the Alleghenies as "the crowning and greatest achievement" of "the spread of the English-speaking peoples," which—though personally a liberal on racial matters—he saw in explicit terms: "it is of incalculable importance that America, Australia, and Siberia should pass out of the hands of their red, black, and yellow aboriginal owners, and become the heritage of the dominant world races."

Roosevelt himself was an example of ethnicities merging to produce this new nation. He thanked God—he teased his friend Rudyard Kipling—that there was "not a drop of British blood" in him. But that did not stop him from identifying with Anglo-Saxons or from becoming a passionate advocate of an assimilationist Americanism, which crossed ethnic lines and was ultimately to cross racial lines.

The Battle of Agincourt, fought in 1415, was one of the key battles in what has come to be known as the Hundred Years War between France and England. King Henry V of England led an invading army into France over a land dispute and defeated an apparently stronger French force near a fortified town named Agincourt. His exploits were immortalized in Shakespeare's *Henry V.*

© Robert Essel NYC/CORBIS

David Barber / PhotoEdit

And it is important to note that, at the height of the last great immigration wave, Kallen and his allies totally failed to persuade Americans that they were no longer a nation. Quite the contrary: once convinced that their nationhood was threatened by continued massive immigration, Americans changed the public policies that made it possible. While the national origins quotas were being legislated, President Calvin Coolidge put it unflinchingly: "America must be kept American."

Everyone knew what he meant.

CONTEXT

Often, debates about immigration policy in the United States focus on the issue of *assimilation*, which refers to the process by which immigrants become part of American culture by adopting the values, traditions, ideals, and even the language of the United States. Sometimes, the metaphor of the "melting pot" is used to describe this process: People of many different backgrounds and identities are mixed together to form a single American nation. When Brimelow describes Theodore Roosevelt as an "advocate of an assimilationist Americanism" in paragraph 23, he is also referring to a belief in the importance of assimilation in maintaining American identity. When he states in paragraph 11 that "the vast majority of Americans are Christians," he is partly defining that American identity. When he refers in paragraph 19 to "a common ethnicity," he is referring to the same Anglo-Saxons that he tells us Roosevelt aligned himself with—an ethnic group that, for Brimelow, constitutes the American identity. However, in the last few decades, many Americans, especially those from minority groups, have questioned this idea of one nation in which one's ethnic, racial, and religious identities become subsumed by his or her identity as an "American." Instead, arguing that diversity rather than assimilation is what makes America unique and strong, these critics have proposed the metaphor of a mosaic, in which each person retains his or her racial or ethnic identity while becoming a piece of the larger American cultural "mosaic."

Questions for Discussion

1. In his essay, Brimelow describes words as weapons. What does he mean? In what way is his concern about language—and about the definitions of specific terms—central to his argument?

2. Brimelow distinguishes between nation and state. Why does he believe that the distinction is important? How does he use that distinction in building his argument?

3. According to Brimelow, how has the debate over immigration changed? Why is he concerned about this change? Do you think his concern is justified? Why or why not?

4. In paragraphs 21 and 22, Brimelow appeals to American figures of historical importance, such as John Jay and Theodore Roosevelt. Has he strengthened his case by making these references? Explain. In what ways might he have left himself open to counterargument on this point?

5. Brimelow asserts that Americans do not agree with the statement that America is an idea, not a nation. Why is this point important to Brimelow? Do you think he is right? Why or why not?

6. Brimelow concludes by stating that "everyone" knew what it meant to be American in the 1920s. What is Brimelow implying here? How effective is that statement as a conclusion to his argument?

7. Does the fact that Brimelow was born in England influence the way you read his argument? Does it give him more or less credibility, in your view? Explain.

③ | **Keep the Borders Open**

JACOB G. HORNBERGER

Arguments about immigration in the United States often focus on concerns about jobs and money. Many Americans worry that immigrants will take jobs away from them; some fear that immigrants will strain city and state budgets, resulting in higher taxes. These are valid and serious concerns, and Jacob Hornberger acknowledges them in the following essay. But unlike many critics of U.S. immigration policy, Hornberger is concerned about a more basic issue: individual freedom. He makes his argument in favor of an open immigration policy from his perspective as a libertarian (see the Context box on page 525). Hornberger is founder of the Future of Freedom Foundation, an organization that advocates in favor of libertarian positions on issues such as immigration. As you read his essay, which was published in 2002, notice how he builds his argument on his fundamental libertarian views about individual citizens and the role of the state. Consider how those views might make his argument more or less effective among readers who have allegiances to other political perspectives.

JACOB G. HORNBERGER, "Keep the Borders Open"

1 In times of crisis, it is sometimes wise and constructive for people to return to first principles and to reexamine and reflect on where we started as a nation, the road we've traveled, where we are today, and the direction in which we're headed. Such a reevaluation can help determine whether a nation has deviated from its original principles and, if so, whether a restoration of those principles would be in order.

It is impossible to overstate the unusual nature of American society from the time of its founding to the early part of the 20th century. Imagine: no Social Security, Medicare, Medicaid, income taxation, welfare, systems of public (i.e., government) schooling, occupational licensure, standing armies, foreign aid, foreign interventions, or foreign wars. Perhaps most unusual of all, there were virtually no federal controls on immigration into the United States.

With the tragic and costly exception of slavery, the bedrock principle underlying American society was that people should be free to live their lives any way they chose, as long as their conduct was peaceful. That is what it once meant to be free. That is what it once meant to be an American. That was the freedom that our ancestors celebrated each Fourth of July.

Let's examine the issue of immigration because it provides a good model for comparing the vision of freedom of our ancestors with that which guides the American people today.

In economic terms, the concept of freedom to which our Founders subscribed entailed the right to sustain one's life through labor by pursuing any occupation or business without government permission or interference, by freely entering into mutually beneficial exchanges with others anywhere in the world, accumulating unlimited amounts of wealth arising from those endeavors, and freely deciding the disposition of that wealth.

The moral question is: Why shouldn't a person be free to cross a border in search of work to sustain his life, to open a business, to tour, or simply because he wants to? Or to put it another way, under what moral authority does any government interfere with the exercise of these rights?

Most Americans like the concept of open borders within the United States, but what distinguished our ancestors is that they believed that the principles of freedom were applicable not just domestically but universally. That implied open borders not only for people traveling inside the United States but also for people traveling or moving to the United States.

One important result of this highly unusual philosophy of freedom was that throughout the 19th century, people all over the world, especially those who were suffering political tyranny or economic privation, always knew that there was a place they could go if they could succeed in escaping their circ[...]

[...]donment of open immigra[...] tury has had negative con[...] rally and economical[...] ne examples.

10[...] World War II, U.S. gov[...] entionally used immigra[...] nt German Jews from es[...] Nazi Germany by coming[...] us are familiar with the [...] f the damned," where U. [...] permit a German ship to [...] because it carried Je[...] many people know th[...] mmigration controls to[...] d Eastern European Je[...] United States even af[...] concentration camps became well known?

Indeed, how many Americans know about the one million anti-communist Russians whom U.S. and British officials forcibly repatriated to the Soviet Union at the end of World War II, knowing that death or the gulag awaited them?

Ancient history, you say? Well, consider one of the most morally reprehensible policies in the history of our nation: the forcible repatriation of Cuban refugees into communist tyranny, a practice that has been going on for many years and that continues to this day.

Let me restate this for emphasis: Under the pretext of enforcing immigration laws, our government—the U.S. government—the same government that sent tens of thousands of American GIs to their deaths in foreign wars supposedly to resist communism, is now forcibly returning people into communism.

We have seen the establishment of Border Patrol passport checkpoints on highways and airports inside the United States (north of the border), which inevitably discriminate

CONTEXT

Hornberger's statement that "the bedrock principle underlying American society was that people should be free to live their lives any way they chose, as long as their conduct was peaceful" (par. 3) reflects his libertarian beliefs. According to the website of the Libertarian party, "Libertarians believe in the American heritage of liberty, enterprise, and personal responsibility"; they believe in "a free-market economy and the abundance and prosperity it brings; a dedication to civil liberties and personal freedom that marks this country above all others; and a foreign policy of non-intervention, peace, and free trade as prescribed by America's founders" (see **www.lp.org**). In short, libertarians believe in maximizing individual freedom and minimizing the power of the state. This political philosophy has a long history in American society. Although the Libertarian Party itself does not have sufficient membership to challenge the Democrats and Republicans in national elections, it plays an important political role in some states, and many Americans share its views on issues such as immigration and foreign policy.

In 1939 the S.S. *St. Louis* sailed for Cuba from Germany carrying 900 Jewish passengers who were fleeing Nazi persecution and who hoped eventually to enter the United States. The passengers were refused entry into Cuba, and after several weeks the ship was forced to return to Germany. The incident came to be known as the "**voyage of the damned**."

CONTEXT

U.S. immigration policy regarding Cuba has long been a source of controversy. Because Cuba's communist government has been considered a threat to U.S. national security, immigrants from Cuba have sometimes been granted special status. Before 1995 thousands of Cuban citizens who fled their country and entered the United States illegally were allowed to stay. However, because of episodes in the 1980s and 1990s during which many thousands of Cubans attempted to enter the United States, the United States changed its policies in 1995. Under the new policies, many Cubans who tried to enter the United States have been returned to Cuba if they did not meet the new criteria for political asylum. This policy change provoked controversy, as Hornberger's statements in paragraph 12 suggest. The controversy continues today. Some critics argue that the United States should have the same immigration policies toward Cuba that it has toward other Central American nations. Other critics advocate stricter policies that limit immigration from most nations, including Cuba.

David McNew/Getty Images

against people on the basis of skin color. We have seen the criminalization of such things as transporting, housing, and hiring undocumented workers, followed by arbitrary detentions on highways as well as raids on American farms and restaurants.

15 We have seen the construction of a fortified wall in California. This wall, built soon after the fall of the ugliest wall in history, has resulted in the deaths of immigrants entering the country on the harsh Arizona desert. Would Washington, Jefferson, or Madison have constructed such a wall?

We have come a long way from the vision of freedom set forth by our Founding Fathers.

Let's consider some of the common objections to open immigration:

1. *Open immigration will pollute America's culture.* Oh? Which culture is that? Boston? New York? Savannah? New Orleans? Denver? Los Angeles? I grew up on the Mexican border (on the Texas side). My culture was eating enchiladas and tacos, listening to both Mexican and American music, and speaking Tex-Mex (a combination of English and Spanish). If you're talking about the danger that my culture might get polluted, that danger comes from the north, not from the south. America's culture has always been one of liberty—one in which people are free to pursue any culture they want.

2. *Immigrants will take jobs away from Americans.* Immigrants displace workers in certain sectors but the displaced workers benefit through the acquisition of higher-paying jobs in other sectors that expand because of the influx of immigrants. It is not a coincidence that historically people's standard of living has soared when borders have been open. Keep in mind also that traditionally immigrants are among the hardest-working and most energetic people in a society, which brings a positive vitality and energy to it.

3. *Immigrants will go on welfare.* Well maybe we ought to reexamine whether it was a good idea to abandon the principles of our ancestors in that respect as well. What would be wrong with abolishing welfare for everyone, including Americans, along with the enormous taxation required to fund it? But if Americans are in fact hopelessly addicted to the government dole, there is absolutely no reason that the same has to happen to immigrants. Therefore, the answer to the welfare issue is not to control immigration but rather to deny immigrants the right to go on the government dole. In such a case, however, wouldn't it be fair to exempt them from the taxes used to fund the U.S. welfare state?

4. *Immigrants will bring in drugs.* Lots of people bring in drugs, including Americans returning from overseas trips. Not even the harshest police state would ever alter that fact. More important, why not legalize drugs and make the state leave drug users alone? Is there any better example

A Ramey/PhotoEdit

of an immoral, failed, and destructive government program than the war on drugs? Why should one government intervention, especially an immoral, failed one, be used to justify another?

5. *There will be too many people.* Oh? Who decides the ideal number? A government board of central planners, just like in China? Wouldn't reliance on the free market to make such a determination be more consistent with our founding principles? Immigrants go where the opportunities abound and they avoid areas where they don't, just as Americans do.

6. *Open immigration will permit terrorists to enter our country.* The only permanent solution to terrorism against the United States, in both the short term and long term, is to abandon the U.S. government's interventionist foreign policy, which is the breeding ground for terrorism against our country.

No immigration controls in the world, not even a rebuilt Berlin Wall around the United States, will succeed in preventing the entry of people who are bound and determined to kill Americans.

More than 200 years ago, ordinary people brought into existence the most unusual society in the history of man. It was a society based on the fundamental moral principle that people everywhere are endowed with certain inherent rights that no government can legitimately take away.

Somewhere along the way, Americans abandoned that concept of freedom, especially in their attachment to such programs and policies as Social Security, Medicare, Medicaid, income taxation, economic regulation, public (i.e., government) schooling, the war on drugs, the war on poverty, the war on wealth, immigration controls, foreign aid, foreign intervention, and foreign wars—none of which our founders had dreamed of.

20 The current crisis provides us with an opportunity to reexamine our founding principles, why succeeding generations of Americans abandoned them, the consequences of that abandonment, and whether it would be wise to restore the moral and philosophical principles of freedom of our Founders. A good place to start such a reexamination would be immigration.

Questions for Discussion

1. What main reasons does Hornberger cite in support of his position on immigration? Do you find his reasons persuasive? Why or why not?

2. Hornberger identifies six main arguments against immigration and offers a rebuttal to each one. Do you think this way of addressing the position of those who oppose immigration is an effective one? Why or why not?

3. Hornberger is a libertarian (see the box on page 525). Identify specific points in his article that reveal his libertarian views. To what extent do you think most Americans would agree with his views?

4. How would you describe the tone of this essay? To what extent do you think Hornberger's tone strengthens or weakens his argument?

5. Hornberger's essay is an example of an argument based on deductive reasoning (see pages 81–83 in Chapter 4). What is the fundamental belief or principle on which he bases his argument? Do you share his belief in this principle? Do you think most Americans do? Do you think this strategy for argumentation is an effective one when it comes to the issue of immigration? Why or why not?

④ | ## Too Many: Looking Today's Immigration in the Face

STEVEN CAMAROTA

Steven Camarota is the director of research at the Center for Immigration Studies (CIS), a nonprofit organization devoted to analyzing the effects of immigration on the United States and generally favoring greater restrictions on immigration to the United States (see www.cis.org/). He is a well-known voice in public discussions about immigration. The following essay, which first appeared in 2002 in *National Review*, a respected politically conservative magazine, lays out his position on immigration in detail. In his essay Camarota addresses the main issues that often emerge in debates about immigration: concerns about jobs, schools, taxes, and poverty. But in addressing those issues and providing extensive factual evidence to support his points about each, Camarota is also presenting a view of what he believes America should be.

STEVEN CAMAROTA, "Too Many: Looking Today's Immigration in the Face"

1 When the history of the 1990s is written, the most important story may not be the GOP takeover of Congress, the boom economy, or the Clinton impeachment. The big story may be the decade's unprecedented level of immigration: a social phenomenon of enormous significance, affecting everything from the nation's schools to the political balance between the two parties.

Newly released census figures show that the foreign-born population reached 31.1 million in 2000 (including some 7 to 8 million here illegally). This is by far the largest immigrant population in U.S. history, and represents a 57 percent increase from 1990. The rate of increase is itself unprecedented: Even during the great wave of immigration from 1900 to 1910, the foreign-born population grew by only about 31 percent (from roughly 10 million to 13.5 million). Over the past 30 years, the number of immigrants in the U.S. has tripled. If current trends are allowed to continue, the foreign-born share of the population will in fact pass the all-time high by the end of this decade. Many defenders of high immigration argue that the current immigration is not really unusual, because

although the numbers and growth are without precedent, the total U.S. population was smaller 100 years ago and immigrants constituted a larger share of the total. It is true that the 11.1 percent of the nation's population that is foreign-born today is lower than the all-time high of nearly 15 percent reached in 1910. But one may ask why 1910 should be the benchmark by which to judge today's immigration. In evaluating its effect

COMPLICATION

From *Immigration Policy Reports* (March 2002), a project of the American Immigration Council:

> With 56 million, or 20 percent of the current U.S. population estimated as foreign-born, the Census Bureau's report claims these numbers are the highest in history. However, past demographic data shows otherwise. For example, at the turn of the century when the total foreign-born percentage was 13, the first and second generation accounted for nearly 35 percent of the U.S. population—much higher than today's 20 percent. In fact, from 1870 through 1930, the combination of these two generations was even larger, totaling $\frac{1}{3}$ of the total population.

> In 2008, according to data from the U.S. Census Bureau, nearly one in four Americans was an immigrant or the child of an immigrant. Twenty percent of immigrants came to the United States before 1990.

on modern society, it seems more reasonable to compare today's immigration with that of the more recent past. And in that context, today's figures represent a fundamental break with prior decades: From 1940 to 1990 the foreign-born population averaged less than 7 percent, and as recently as 1970 it was less than 5 percent.

The implications for American society are enormous. For example, a good deal of attention has been given to the fact that the number of people who live in poverty did not decline in the 1990s, despite a strong economy. What has generally not been reported is that new immigrants and their U.S.-born children accounted for the nation's stubborn poverty rate. The primary reason so many immigrant families live in poverty is that a large percentage have very little education. Newly arrived adult immigrants, for example, are more than three times as likely as natives to lack a high-school education.

Immigrants and their children also account for nearly two-thirds of the increase in the population lacking health insurance over the last decade. By dramatically increasing the uninsured population, immigration creates significant costs for taxpayers, and it drives up costs for insured Americans as providers pass along the costs of treating the uninsured to paying customers. The central role immigration has played in creating the nation's health-insurance quandary has largely gone unreported.

5 The impact on public schools is even more significant. In the last 20 years the school-age population has grown by roughly 8 million. Most observers agree that this increase has strained resources in districts across the country. What most media accounts of this growth leave out is that census data indicate that there are about 8 million school-age children from immigrant families—and, because they are much poorer on average than natives, this increase in enrollment has not been accompanied by a corresponding increase in local tax revenue. Moreover, because of language barriers, the children of immigrants often cost significantly more to educate than those of natives. Most news coverage of the issue discusses how to meet the needs of these children, but fails to point out that federal immigration policy created the problem in the first place.

Despite the clear implications mass immigration has for the future of American society, many boosters still argue that today's immigration is very much like that of 1910. No doubt, there are similarities, but the differences are profound and striking to even the casual observer. America is a fundamentally different place than it was 100 years ago, and today's immigration is also very different.

As far as assimilation is concerned, numbers matter at least as much as

Bettmann/Corbis

percentages. For example, a quarter of a million immigrants in a metropolitan area are enough to create linguistic isolation: neighborhoods where immigrants can live and work without ever learning much English. Large numbers also create politically influential ethnic organizations whose leaders often adhere to an anti-assimilation multicultural ideology. Whether the immigrants in question represent 10 percent or 30 percent of a city's population is not so important; it's the raw numbers that count, and the numbers are already well over twice what they were in 1910.

In one sense, today's immigrants are more diverse than ever before, in that significant numbers arrive from all continents and races. But in a more important sense, today's immigration wave is considerably less diverse than those of the past, because Spanish speakers dominate in a way no other group ever did before. While German speakers accounted for a little over a quarter of all immigrants in the late 1800s and Italians for about one-fifth in the first decades of the 1900s, such concentrations were transitory. In contrast, the domination of immigrants from Latin America has grown steadily. In 1970, 19 percent of the foreign-born were from Latin America; by 2000, it was more than half. One ethno-linguistic group can now predominate in schools, neighborhoods, entire metropolitan areas, and even whole states.

One institution that helped immigrants and their children acquire an American identity in the past was public education. Schools brought children from different immigrant backgrounds into contact with natives and helped to forge a common American culture. But today, basic demographics makes this much more difficult. Unlike in the past, immigrants now have many more children on average than natives, which means kids from immigrant families very quickly predominate in public schools. For example, although about a quarter of California's total population is foreign-born, half of the school-age population is from immigrant families. In many districts in high-immigration states, immigrant families now account for more than 80 percent of school kids.

10 Of course, neighborhood schools in 1910 saw heavy immigrant concentrations. But because of the large differences in fertility rates, immigration today creates many more districts in which the cultural norms are set by children from immigrant families, who have

Will Hart/Photo Edit

relatively little contact with their counterparts from native families.

There is, of course, another problem with expecting public schools to play the role they did in the past of assimilating immigrants: Schools don't want to. A very significant share of the U.S. elite has embraced the anti-assimilation ethos, which regards America as a collection of peoples, each with its own distinct culture, which vie for political power as groups. America's educational establishment has embraced this multicultural vision. This is why history textbooks look as they do, and why bilingual education remains widely popular among educators. This trend shows no signs of abating; in fact, the growing number of immigrants only feeds the multiculturalist perspective. Immigration provides further justification for it by creating an ever larger aggrieved class, whose cultures must be preserved in the face of an oppressive majority culture.

Of course, some form of assimilation does take place, even in the modern public school. While language acquisition almost certainly has slowed in recent years, most immigrants learn to speak at least some English. But assimilation is much more than learning to speak English, or driving on the right side of the road. It involves what John Fonte of the Hudson Institute calls "patriotic assimilation," the belief that American history is one's own history. A century ago it meant that immigrants and their children came to see America's past as something "we" did, not something "they"—white people of European ancestry—did. To the extent that immigrants are assimilating they are doing so, in many cases, as "multicultural" Americans.

Some conservatives, and even some liberals, have a different conception of assimilation, but it is not at all clear that those who wish to see a more robust love of country inculcated in our children (immigrant or native) are winning the debate. It simply makes no sense, therefore, for a society that cannot agree on its own history or even what it means to be an American to welcome over a million newcomers each year from outside.

Technology is another obstacle to assimilation. It is now possible to call—or even to visit—one's home country with a frequency that was inconceivable even 50 years ago. One can listen to a hometown radio station or read the local newspapers on the Internet. The costs of travel and communication are now so low that many wealthier immigrants can live in two countries at the same time, traveling back and forth with ease. In such a world, it is less likely that immigrants will develop a deep attachment to the U.S.

15 The American economy is also fundamentally different, with serious consequences for the assimilation process. A century ago, manufacturing, mining, and agriculture employed the vast majority of the workforce, creating plentiful work for unskilled immigrants. These jobs eventually led to solid working-class incomes for immigrants and their children. (In fact, most native-born Americans a century ago worked in the same kinds of jobs.) Though most people were poor by today's standards, most historians agree that there was not a very large economic gap between the standard of living of natives and that of immigrants; this was because, on average, immigrants were not that much less skilled than natives. Data are limited, but in terms of years of schooling or literacy, immigrants 100 years ago were roughly equal to natives.

This is no longer the case. While a number of today's immigrants are quite skilled, immigrants overall are significantly less educated than natives. As a result, when it comes to average income, poverty rates, welfare use, and other measures of economic well-being,

CONTEXT

In 1995 education scholar Mike Rose reported on the increasing diversity of American public schools. At Pasadena High School in California, for example, more than thirty-eight different languages were spoken by students enrolled there.

SOURCE: *Possible Lives* (1995).

today's immigrants are much worse off than natives. Unlike that of 1910, today's U.S. economy offers very limited opportunity for those with little education, and this creates a very sizable gap between the two groups.

Another important change since 1910 is the profound expansion in the size and scope of government. Spending on everything from education to infrastructure maintenance is many times greater than it was back then. With federal, state, and local government now eating up roughly one-third of GDP, the average individual must be able to pay a good deal in taxes to cover his use of public services. In practice, the middle and upper classes pay most of the taxes; the poor, immigrant or native, generally consume significantly more in public services than they pay in taxes.

This means that the arrival of large numbers of relatively poor immigrants has a significant negative effect on public coffers in a way that was not the case in the past. In 1997 the National Academy of Sciences estimated that immigrant households consumed between $11 and $20 billion more in public services than they were paying in taxes each year. (Other estimates have found this deficit to be even higher.) A smaller government may well be desirable, but it is politically inconceivable that we would ever return to the situation of 100 years ago, when government accounted for a tiny fraction of the economy. Thus, continually allowing in large numbers of unskilled immigrants has very negative implications for taxpayers.

The situation of today's immigrants is, then, dramatically different from what it was at the turn of the last century. But even if one ignores all these differences, one undeniable fact remains: The last great wave of immigration was stopped, as an act of government policy. World War I, followed by restrictive legislation in the early 1920s, dramatically reduced immigration to about a quarter of what it had been in previous decades. This immigration pause played a critically important role in turning yesterday's immigrants into

Americans. So if the past is to be our guide, then we should significantly reduce immigration numbers.

20 If we don't, the assimilation problem will only get worse. We know from experience that it is often the children of immigrants who have the greatest difficulty identifying with America. While their parents at least know how good they have it, the children tend to compare their situation to that of other Americans, instead of that in their parents' homeland. Unless the gap between themselves and other Americans has been closed in just one generation, something few groups have been able to accomplish, this can be a source of real discontent. Moreover, it is children born in the U.S. to immigrant parents who often feel caught between two worlds and struggle with their identity.

What we should do is call a halt to the current heedless increase in annual immigration, and reduce the numbers to something like their historical average of 300,000 a year. In the mid 1990s, the bipartisan immigration-reform panel headed by the late Barbara Jordan suggested limiting family immigration to the spouses and minor children of U.S. citizens and legal non-citizens, and to the parents of citizens. However, we should probably eliminate the preferences for the spouses and minor children of non-citizens, since these provisions apply to family members acquired after the alien has received a green card but before he has become a citizen. If we also eliminated the parents of U.S. citizens as a category, family immigration would fall to less than half what it is today. The Jordan panel also wisely suggested eliminating the visa lottery and tightening up the requirements for employment- and humanitarian-based immigration.

These changes would, taken together, reduce legal immigration to roughly 300,000 annually. Only if we get the numbers down to this reasonable level can we begin the long process of assimilating the huge number of immigrants and their children who are already here.

Questions for Discussion

1. Examine Camarota's use of statistical information as evidence to support his argument, especially in paragraph 2. What specific point do these statistics help him make? How effectively do you think he uses these statistics to support his claims?

2. Camarota asserts that "America is a fundamentally different place than it was 100 years ago, and today's immigration is also very different." What does he mean? What evidence does he offer to support this assertion? Do you think he is right? Why or why not?

3. What is Camarota's view of the assimilation of immigrants into U.S. society? What does he mean when he refers to "the assimilation problem"? How does his view of assimilation fit into his overall argument? Do you agree with him about this issue? Why or why not? How might your views about immigration affect your reaction to Camarota's point about assimilation?

4. Camarota writes that "in terms of years of schooling or literacy, immigrants 100 years ago were roughly equal to natives." How does he arrive at this conclusion? What evidence does he present? Do you think he makes a persuasive case that this point is valid? Explain.

5. Evaluate the way in which Camarota uses history to make his argument about immigration policy today. What historical events or developments does he cite? How does he use these historical references to build his argument? What do you think is his general view of America's past? How does that view influence his use of historical references in his argument? Identify specific passages in his essay to illustrate your answer.

6. Several times in his essay Camarota refers to "liberals" and to "boosters"—that is, people who favor immigration. Who exactly are these boosters? Where in the essay are they described or identified? Does Camarota see any common ground between him and boosters of immigration? If so, how does this common ground influence his argument?

NEGOTIATING DIFFERENCES

Each of the authors in this section presents an argument about immigration policy in the United States. But each author also presents a vision of what America is—and what it should be. Part of the challenge in sorting through debates about immigration policy is understanding how these visions of America inform the views of participants in these debates. Ultimately, decisions about immigration policy reflect some general agreement about what America is and who Americans are. In other words, when laws governing immigration are passed by the U.S. Congress, or when policies regarding immigrants are adopted by schools or state agencies, these laws are implicitly saying, "This is the kind of nation or society we believe we want to have."

With that in mind, imagine that you are part of a committee created by your state government to examine the impact of immigration on your state. Your committee's task is to draft a report to the governor in which you present and justify a general immigration policy in your state. That task requires you to investigate immigration in your state: who the immigrants in your state are; where they have come from and why; how many there are; and what impact they have on schools, jobs, and social life. It also requires you to consider your own views about what kind of society you believe America should be and who should be allowed to become an American.

Working by yourself or with a group of your classmates, write a report to your governor in which you make an argument for a general immigration policy for your state. In your report, you might draw on the perspectives presented in the four essays in this section and on any other relevant material.

© Bo Zaunders/Corbis

What Does It Mean to Be a Good American Citizen?

In a famous line from his inaugural address, President John F. Kennedy challenged Americans: "Ask not what your country can do for you. Ask what you can do for your country." (See Con-Text on page 537.) His challenge implied a sense of duty that he hoped all Americans would feel. To be a good citizen, Kennedy seemed to be saying, means placing the nation's good before your own. ■ Many Americans have shared Kennedy's belief in this sense of duty, especially in times of war and crisis. But the question of what it means to be an American citizen has never been simple and at times has created great conflict. During the Vietnam War, for example, some Americans believed fervently that it was their patriotic duty to serve their country by fighting with the U.S. armed forces in southeast Asia. Others believed just as fervently that the demands of citizenship required them to oppose their country's involvement in Vietnam through protest and resistance to the draft. Still others supported the American war effort in Vietnam despite genuine misgivings about it. The deep divisions among Americans caused open conflict as well as soul-searching about what it meant to be a good citizen. ■ Such debate and conflict about citizenship and patriotism date back to the beginnings of the United States. During the Revolutionary War many Americans remained loyal to the British Crown as their rightful government. The Civil War highlighted the conflicting loyalties that many Americans felt to their states and to their national government. In our own time a different kind of war—what many call the "war on terror"—and the related wars in Iraq and Afghanistan have again provoked debate about citizenship, patriotism, and duty. As several of the writers in this section demonstrate, these conflicts have prompted Americans to examine not just their opinions about their government's response to terrorism but also their most fundamental beliefs about citizenship, patriotism, and American identity. Once again, the great sacrifice of citizens who risk their lives for their country inevitably causes many Americans to think hard about what they must do—and what they *should* do—as citizens. ■ Even in peacetime Americans wrestle with the idea of citizenship, which sometimes seems to conflict with beliefs about individual freedom and self-determination that run deep in U.S. culture. As the following essays suggest, the problem of defining what it means to be a good citizen can emerge in such seemingly common activities as voting or expressing political opinions. It might be that these more mundane acts of citizenship can give Americans cause to wonder about the relationship between their duties as citizens and their religious or ethnic loyalties. ■ In the end, the question of what it means to be a good citizen is a complicated and difficult one in part because it can be answered in so many different ways. As you engage the various arguments about citizenship in this section, ask yourself how your own view of what it means to be an American shapes your sense of duty as a citizen—and how you would respond to President John F. Kennedy's challenge.

CON-TEXT

President John F. Kennedy's 1961 Inaugural Address

1 ...In your hands, my fellow citizens, more than mine, will rest the final success or failure of our course. Since this country was founded, each generation of Americans has been summoned to give testimony to its national loyalty. The graves of young Americans who answered the call to service surround the globe.

Now the trumpet summons us again—not as a call to bear arms, though arms we need—not as a call to battle, though embattled we are—but a call to bear the burden of a long twilight struggle, year in and year out, "rejoicing in hope, patient in tribulation"—a struggle against the common enemies of man: tyranny, poverty, disease and war itself.

Can we forge against these enemies a grand and global alliance, North and South, East and West, that can assure a more fruitful life for all mankind? Will you join in that historic effort?

In the long history of the world, only a few generations have been granted the role of defending freedom in its hour of maximum danger. I do not shrink from this responsibility—I welcome it. I do not believe that any of us would exchange places with any other people or any other generation. The energy, the faith, the devotion which we bring to this endeavor will light our country and all who serve it—and the glow from that fire can truly light the world.

5 And so, my fellow Americans: ask not what your country can do for you. Ask what you can do for your country.

My fellow citizens of the world: ask not what America will do for you, but what together we can do for the freedom of man.

Finally, whether you are citizens of America or citizens of the world, ask of us here the same high standards of strength and sacrifice which we ask of you. With a good conscience our only sure reward, with history the final judge of our deeds, let us go forth to lead the land we love, asking His blessing and His help, but knowing that here on earth God's work must truly be our own.

① **Needed: Informed Voters**

JOHN BALZAR

The right to vote is a fundamental right guaranteed to Americans by the U.S. Constitution. It is a hallmark of the political system, central to the workings of democracy. But it is a right that has not always been enjoyed by all Americans. Women were not allowed to vote in the United States until 1920, and African Americans were often prevented from voting by local and state restrictions even after Congress passed the Voting Rights Act in 1963. Perhaps Americans take this hard-won right for granted, because only about half of eligible voters usually turn out for presidential elections and often fewer than half vote in local and state elections. As reporter John Balzar notes in the following essay, which was first published in 2002, political commentators routinely lament these low voter turnouts, suggesting that low participation in American political campaigns weakens democracy. Balzar has a some- what different view. He believes not only that voting is a right but also that it entails responsibility. In his view, it is not enough simply to show up at the polling place to vote. Citizenship requires more than that. As you engage his argument, consider your views about voting. How important is the right to vote? What responsibilities come with that right? Does being an American *require* you to vote? Or does it mean that you can choose not to exercise that right? Balzar has covered politics and served as a foreign correspondent for the *Los Angeles Times*. The author of *Yukon Alone* (1999), Balzar has won the Scripps-Howard Foundation Prize for his human interest and adven- ture stories.

JOHN BALZAR, "Needed: Informed Voters"

James Fenimore Cooper (1789– 1851) was an American writer best known for his novel *The Last of the Mohicans* (1826). Like Mark Twain, author of *The Adventures of Huckleberry Finn* (1884), Cooper was also widely known in his day as a social and political critic whose writings about American democracy were often controversial.

1 More than 150 years ago, the writer **James Fenimore Cooper** put it this way: "The man who can right himself by a vote will seldom resort to a musket."

Cooper found agreement on the point even with his old nemesis, Mark Twain, who set aside humor to observe: "Where every man in a state has a vote, brutal laws are impossible."

Ah, voting. When you read through American civics, you find that almost every- body who presumed to comment on our nation had something celebratory to say about the franchise.

The United States, no one should forget, pioneered the idea of self-governance on a grand scale by way of popular elections.

5 Only elections aren't so popular anymore. In the 2002 primaries, 83 percent of eligible Americans exercised their rights as free citi- zens and chose not to vote. Far more people stake their hopes on playing the Lotto than on participating in democracy. We now bemoan the results: With the onset of autumn, the public begins to lay eyes on the matchups of candidates chosen by tiny fractions of their neighbors.

Yikes.

Our normal suspicions about those who seek political office turn into outright alarm. Consequently, fewer people muster the enthu- siasm to drive down the block and cast a vote in the election.

Two truths: I've never met anyone who would forfeit his or her right to vote. Likewise, everyone knows that the United States would be a much different country if everyone availed himself of the opportunity and actually cast an informed vote.

So, do we have a crisis on our hands? Instinctively, we are conditioned to say yes. But I don't think it's quite as simple as that.

10 The hand-wringers have been telling us for decades now that something must be way wrong in the land for participation to be so low. Yet many nonvoters I know are not distraught, but content.

We live in an age of decidedly centrist politics, driven in large measure by personality. Most candidates are foursquare in favor of a full-employment economy, equal opportunity, a healthy environment, good schools and health care. Thus, political differences boil down to the tactics and philosophy of governance, and for a good number of people, it's enough to leave that choice to others.

There's another matter, usually too delicate to be discussed directly. That's the distinction between voting and voting wisely.

For as long as I've covered politics, I've listened to experts say that we need to make registration and voting simpler, easier. In truth, registration has never been simpler in most places, and it's getting more so all the time.

The real difficulty in voting is the preparation involved. To cast an intelligent ballot requires more than casual exposure to TV commercials.

15 Many Americans have lost faith in those who offer considered election guidance, whether political parties, newspaper editorials or interest groups. Thus the rise of the vaunted "independent voter."

Sounds lofty. But in truth, the homework necessary to inform oneself about the issues and candidates in most elections is no less than that faced in an upper-division college class.

CONTEXT

When he refers to the "independent voter" in paragraph 15, Balzar is invoking the belief that Americans tend to vote for their favored candidates regardless of party affiliation. In other words, especially in presidential elections, voters will vote for the candidate they like best, whether or not that candidate represents their own party. According to the Pew Research Center for the People & the Press, in 2008, a presidential election year, 36 percent of registered voters in the United States identified themselves as Democrats and 27 percent as Republicans; 37 percent claimed no party affiliation. The percentage of American voters who consider themselves independents has increased steadily since 2001, one year before Balzac wrote this article.

From what I can tell, many Americans aren't up to the task. Reading through opinion surveys is always as amusing as it is sobering. Almost half the nation believes that the communist creed "from each according to

CONTEXT

In paragraph 16, Balzar asserts that being an informed voter requires "homework" equivalent to the work required in "an upper-division college class." Is he right? According to political commentator Thomas Sowell,

Ideally, each citizen should both become informed about issues and candidates and go to the polls on Election Day. But the real question is what to do in a world that is seldom ideal. Even informed voters sometimes have trouble understanding that they can only choose among alternatives actually available. Some voters vote—or don't vote—according to whether their elected officials have lived up to all their hopes. Seldom can any officials in a democracy do that ("High Stakes Elections," 2002).

According to Martin Wattenberg, Americans who choose not to vote tend to have less education than those who do vote. In 1998, for example, U.S. college graduates voted at 36 percent above the national average; those with "some high school" voted at 43 percent below it.

In 1849 Henry David Thoreau wrote in his famous essay "Civil Disobedience,"

All voting is a sort of gaming, like checkers or backgammon, with a slight moral tinge to it, a playing with right and wrong, with moral questions; and betting naturally accompanies it....Even voting *for the right is doing nothing* for it. It is only expressing to men feebly your desire that it should prevail. A wise man will not leave the right to the mercy of chance, nor wish it to prevail to the power of the majority.

SOURCE: *Where Have All the Voters Gone?* 2002.

Dennis Hastert (b. 1942) was elected to the U.S. House of Representatives as a Republican from Illinois in 1987 and served as Speaker of the House from 1999 to 2007, when he resigned the post amid a political scandal.

his abilities, to each according to his needs" is spelled out in the U.S. Constitution. And although 66 percent of adults can identify Regis Philbin as host of a TV game show, only 6 percent can name **Dennis Hastert**,

R-Ill., as speaker of the U.S. House of Representatives.

So, would our democracy be better served if more people voted? As I said, it's not as simple as answering yes.

Questions for Discussion

1. What do you think Balzar accomplishes with his references in paragraphs 1 and 2 to two well-known American writers from the nineteenth century, James Fenimore Cooper and Mark Twain? How do those references relate to his main argument?

2. Why does Balzar disagree with political commentators who believe there is a crisis among U.S. voters because of low turnout rates for elections? What support does he offer for his position on voter turnout rates in the United States?

3. Balzar states that "we live in an age of decidedly centrist politics." What does he mean? Do you agree with him that politics today are "driven in large measure by personality"? Explain.

4. What evidence does Balzar offer for his assertion that "many Americans aren't up to the task" of informing themselves on the issues and candidates in most elections? Do you find his evidence convincing? Why or why not?

5. Balzar argues that voters have an obligation to be informed before casting their votes. What reasoning does he offer to support that assertion? Do you think most Americans would agree with him on this point? Do you? Why or why not?

6. What do you think are the implications of Balzar's argument? What might his view of U.S. voters say about democracy? What might it suggest about how elections should be run? What response would you offer to his argument?

② America: Idea or Nation?

WILFRED M. MCCLAY

The question that Wilfred McClay poses in the title of the following essay suggests that the answer must be that the United States is *either* an idea *or* a nation. But in his carefully reasoned essay, McClay makes it clear that the issue is more complicated than that. He makes it clear, too, that because understanding America as an idea and a nation can be challenging, patriotism is also a challenging concept. McClay explores what it means to be a patriot in a nation that is a powerful symbol of democracy both for its own citizens and for citizens of other nations. In exploring the symbolic importance of America, McClay refuses to simplify the issue of patriotism. The complexity of his argument might be appropriate, because McClay believes that many Americans have not thought carefully enough about what it means to be a patriotic citizen. His essay challenges you to reflect on your own patriotism and how it relates to your sense of identity. McClay is the SunTrust Bank Chair of Excellence in Humanities and a professor of history at the University of Tennessee at Chattanooga; he is also the author of a number of books, including *Religion Returns to the Public Square: Faith and Policy in America* (2003). The following essay was published in the *Public Interest* in 2001.

WILFRED M. MCCLAY, "America: Idea or Nation?"

1 At first glance, American patriotism seems a simple matter. But it is simple only until one actually starts to think about it, inquire after its sources, and investigate its manifestations. Consider a small but significant case in point, an observation recently made by a distinguished rabbi who serves a large and prosperous Reform congregation in the New York suburbs. This man takes the business of premarital counseling very seriously, and therefore gets to know many of his congregation's younger members in a fairly intimate way. In the course of interviewing and counseling them over the years, he has discovered an interesting pattern: a high correlation between the level of these young people's patriotic sentiments and the extent of their opposition to intermarriage, meaning marriage to non-Jews. In other words, those with the strongest love of country were also those most firmly committed to marrying only within the Jewish faith. Conversely, those most indifferent or hostile to patriotism were also most likely to have no reservations about intermarriage—and most likely to find fault with those who do.

LOYALTIES LARGE AND SMALL

The rabbi's observation rings true to me. And yet if it is true, it would seem to throw much of our conventional wisdom about patriotism into a cocked hat. Don't we generally assume that loyalty to the nation is a form of belonging that tends, as it intensifies, to divert, diminish, or even swallow up lesser loyalties and more particular affiliations? Doesn't the study of European history indicate precisely this, that the modern **nation-state** grew in power and prestige at the expense of local and regional identities and affinities, including those of religion? Wouldn't it

The Merriam-Webster dictionary defines **nation-state** as "a form of political organization under which a relatively homogeneous people inhabits a sovereign state; especially: a state containing one as opposed to several nationalities." (For more information about the idea of nation-state, see the box on page 519.)

French political writer **Alexis de Tocqueville** (1805-1859) examined the characteristics of the American political system and the American people in his classic book *Democracy in America* (1835). He argued that a crucial component of democracy is "self-interest rightly understood," which refers to a citizen's understanding that acting in ways that society deems good is actually in one's own self-interest. **Edmund Burke** (1729-1797) was an influential British politician of Irish birth whose political theories are regarded by many scholars to have shaped modern political conservatism.

therefore be more reasonable to predict that observant American Jews would value their nation less, because they value their faith more—particularly when theirs is a faith that sets them apart from the vast majority of Americans? And by the same token, wouldn't it stand to reason that intensely patriotic American Jews would see an act of such primal loyalty to the Jewish community, particularly on a matter as personal and intimate as the question of a marriage partner, as an atavism and a betrayal of the American promise of universal liberty and equality?

Reasonable guesses all, except that they happen not to be borne out by this rabbi's experiences. To be sure, this seeming paradox may have a lot to do with the history and current state of the factions within American Jewry. But it also is wonderfully illustrative of a more general truth, which is this: A considerable part of the genius of American patriotism resides in the fact that being a proud and loyal American does not require one to yield up all of one's identity to the nation. On the contrary, American patriotism has generally affirmed and drawn upon the vibrancy and integrity of other, smaller-scale, and relatively independent loyalties. Far from weakening American national sentiment, or causing it to be half-hearted or anemically "thin," these other traditions have strengthened it immeasurably. Nor is this ideal a recent innovation, brought on by the nation's growing ethnic diversity and the vogue of multiculturalism. Instead, it is an ideal as old as the nation itself, going back to the fundamental concept of a federated republic, which consisted of free and self-governing states, counties, and townships, and which loomed so large in the minds of the nation's Founders.

Needless to say, it has not been an easy ideal to realize or sustain, as recurrent crises in American history from the Whiskey Rebellion to the Civil War to the post–World War II conflicts over school desegregation and voting rights have shown. America's national government has grown steadily in power and influence, and the political, economic, legal, technological, and social forces tending to impose homogeneity upon the national culture are stronger than ever. Yet there is an enduring power in this more diffuse patriotic ideal, which seats the general in the local, and asserts that one does not become more of an American by becoming less of something else—less Southern, less Virginian, less small-town, less black, less Jewish, less whatever.

5 Of course, there will always be instances in which certain profound loyalties come into conflict, in ways that cannot be reconciled. Such is the human condition, and such is the stuff of civil wars, religious martyrdoms, and Sophoclean tragedies. But the American patriotic ideal has generally been wise and generous about granting the widest possible berth to our disparate loyalties and in assuming a certain respect for the multiplicity of the person. Loyalty, like love, is not necessarily a zero-sum game, in which any loyalty accorded to X is thought to take away from what Y might have received. A husband does not love his wife less because he also loves his children; if anything, the opposite is the case. And, as **Burke and Tocqueville** both well understood, something of the same is true of political and social life. By giving as free a hand as possible to the "little platoons," local institutions, and independent associations in a free society, the nation not only makes it possible for many citizens to be meaningfully involved in the work of public life but also elicits from them a deep, unfeigned, and uncoerced patriotism. In a word, the health of local and particular freedoms strengthens the nation....

THE PROBLEMS OF COMMERCE

So where will the next generation of American patriots come from? The particulars of the situation are not terribly encouraging. There is no iron-clad guarantee that there will even be such a generation. The heart of the problem is the well-known fact that the cultivation of patriotic virtue does not come naturally to a commercial society such as the United States. When the self-interested pursuit of material well-being, rather than the inculcation of public-spiritedness, has become the glue of social cohesion and the chief engine of social progress, where can such a society catch a glimpse of broader and longer horizons, or find compelling rationales for sacrificial acts devoted to the common good? Tocqueville showed persuasively how far the principle of "self-interest rightly understood" could go in reproducing many of the salutary effects of virtue. Rather than appealing to an obsolete standard of noble thoughts and character, the principle of "self-interest rightly understood" succeeded by persuading citizens that it was both prudent and useful for them to behave in outwardly virtuous ways. But even that principle has its limits, and it reaches those limits at precisely the moment when the utilitarian payoff for virtuous behavior is no longer so plainly evident.

The martial virtues fall first. How can the principle of self-interest serve to persuade a soldier to lay down his life for his country or to risk life and limb by withholding confidential information when he is held prisoner? Or, on a less heroic level, how does this principle command sufficient loyalty from the general populace to fight an extended, costly war, or form affective bonds that will take precedence over self-interest in moments of national crisis? Even the self-restraints entailed by more commonplace virtues such as thrift, modesty, and marital fidelity are likely to weaken when there is no obvious utility in respecting them, and no obvious risk in disdaining them. In any event, the broad spirit of patriotism, which blends the martial virtues with the commonplace ones, cannot thrive without being nourished by moral sources, ones that the principle of self-interest cannot provide. Finding and sustaining those alternative sources turns out to be one of the perennial problems of American society. It is a problem very much facing us in the prosperous present.

Happily complicating the matter, however, is the undeniable fact that the United States has managed to produce more than its share of genuine patriots—warriors and heroes great and small, gallant and unprepossessing, romantic and gritty, aristocratic and plebeian, all united by a willingness to put their lives on the line for their country. How then, in light of the formidable obstacles mentioned above, has the United States managed to bring forth such patriots? And how can it find the means to honor them properly in the present, and—most important of all—produce more of them in the future? The answers to these questions have never been obvious, either to the generation of the Founders or to our own, but a great deal hangs upon the way they are answered, or not answered. Hence it is a fortunate event that Walter Berns, one of our most thoughtful political philosophers, has come forward with a lucid new book, Making Patriots, the fruit of his many years of reflection on the American polity and society, to address precisely these questions. "Designing a public-spirit curriculum for such a people" is, Berns writes, "no easy task." But few are better qualified to help initiate the process.

CONTEXT

"The Founders...knew, and accepted as a fact, that the nation was formed by self-interested men, men, as John Locke puts it, naturally in a 'state of perfect freedom to order their actions and dispose of their possessions and persons as they think fit...without asking leave or depending on the will of any other man.' But they also knew, as Locke knew, that these men ceased to be autonomous, or simply self-interested men, when they entered civil society and agreed to be governed. That agreement made them citizens, and a citizen is obliged to think of his fellows and of the whole of which he is a part. This requires that he possess certain qualities of character, or virtues, and, as Madison says in Federalist 55, 'republican government presupposes the existence of these qualities in a higher degree than any other form [of government].' Because these qualities cannot be taken for granted, they must somehow be cultivated."

SOURCE: Walter Berns, Making Patriots (2001).

AMERICAN EXCEPTIONALISM

To begin with, Berns argues, we need to recognize that patriotism in America is an entirely different animal from patriotism in other times and places. The ancient Greek city-state of Sparta, for example, which Berns takes to represent the apex of the classical world's understanding of patriotism, was legendary for its public-spirited citizenry. But it achieved that distinction at far too high a cost, at least according to our standards, by imposing a comprehensive regime of severe, near-totalitarian control upon its people. Every aspect of life, from education to marriage to childrearing to eating, fell under the state's purview. Ruthlessly obliterating any elements of privacy or individuality in its citizen's lives, or any of the institutions that mediated between the state and the individual, Sparta sought to achieve a homogeneous, mobilized, martially virtuous populace, imbued with an overwhelming sense of duty to the collective whole, and rendered invulnerable to the siren songs of self-interest and self-gratification. All private sentiments became displaced onto the state itself, so that self-love was sublimated and absorbed entirely into the love of Sparta. Such discipline made for a mighty and disciplined war machine. But it neglected nearly every other aspect of human potentiality and would be entirely inappropriate as a model of patriotism or patriot-formation for the American republic.

10 This is true in part because the American polity would emphasize commerce over warmaking, and protection of men's natural rights over enforcement of their social obligations. But it also is true, Berns points out, because the classical model had long before been shattered by the advent of Christianity, which separated the spiritual duties of men from their political ones and the things of God from the things of Caesar. This decisively changed the nature of patriotism, driving a wedge between the private and public virtues, and demoting the latter to a decisively subordinate role. If Sparta had made the cultivation of public

virtue and patriotic sentiment the be-all and end-all of social existence, then Christianity did something like the opposite, downgrading the sentiment of patriotism and presenting it with an enduring dilemma. Would patriotism become conflated with religious sentiment, and thereby absorbed into the vision of a crusading worldly theocracy? Or would it remain aloof from religious sentiment, and thereby run the risk of becoming the distant junior partner of agnostic, otherworldly faith?

The American solution, which could not have been arrived at without the clarifying help of centuries of European religious wars, managed to split the difference, with a decisive move in the direction of separation, though also with a healthy expression of generalized Protestant civil religion undergirding and enlivening the whole. It is a settlement that defies easy formulation and is more fragile than many Americans appreciate. Berns overstates matters a bit in asserting baldly that the Founders "consigned [religion] to the private sphere." In fact, that prospect didn't come fully into view until the century just past, and its effects have always been highly controversial. But Berns is right, in the end, to say that the Constitution the Framers devised did not envision the United States government as the custodian of men's souls. That was to be the task of other entities. Instead, the Constitution was designed to free men to engage in the self-interested pursuits of a bourgeois society.

Which brings us back to the central problem: How does a republic that is based upon cupidity and self-seeking make public-spirited patriots? Thomas Jefferson, like [Jean-Jaques] Rousseau before him, was himself dubious about the possibility, which was one reason why he preferred the agrarian ideal of a virtuous landowning yeomanry over the Hamiltonian vision of a restless and inventive commercial class of continental-minded men. A farmer, after all, lived a settled life and had a citizen's substantial stake in the land he inhabited and cultivated. But what about the holder of stocks, bonds, and bank notes? He was a man ever on the move, a citizen of no place, a man whose only home was the market.

Yet Jefferson was also principal author of the document that, for Berns, provides the one sure basis for American patriotism: the Declaration of Independence. The key to American patriotism, in Berns's view, is that it is twofold, entailing not only devotion to one's country but also devotion to the principles upon which that country had been founded and to which it was consecrated. These principles are not peculiar to Americans, but are thought to be universal in scope, grounded self-evidently in human nature. First among these principles are the famous assertions that all men are created equal, that they are endowed by their Creator with certain inalienable rights, including life, liberty, and the pursuit of happiness, and that governments derive their legitimacy from the consent of the governed and are instituted for the purpose of securing these rights. From these principles may be derived a more generalized commitment to democratic self-government, which Lincoln called government "of the people, by the people and for the people." This is the creed to which Americans assent, Berns argues, and it is out of admiration for these ideals, and not merely out of filial loyalty to "their" country, that American patriots derive their animating sentiments.

The figure of Abraham Lincoln looms especially large for Berns. He is "patriotism's poet," the uncommon common man whose words and personal example offer eloquent testimony to the possibilities of American democracy. Hence Berns twice cites words from Lincoln's 1852 eulogy to **Henry Clay** as a definitive statement on the shape of American patriotism. Clay, Lincoln said, "loved his country partly because it was his own country, but mostly because it was a free country; and he burned with a zeal for its advancement, because he saw in such, the advancement, prosperity, and glory of human liberty, human right, and human nature."

CONTEXT

Thomas Jefferson and Alexander Hamilton were central figures in the founding of the United States as a nation, but they held different ideals for American democracy. Jefferson believed that democracy could be fostered through a society of landowning farmers whose stake in preserving their land and their way of life would ensure good citizenship; this vision is what McClay means by "the agrarian ideal" in paragraph 12. Hamilton envisioned a nation built on commerce driven by American entrepreneurship that is regulated by a strong central government.

It was this sense of America's mission, as the carrier and leading advocate for universal ideals, and not merely as another nation seeking to preserve its territory or expand its place in the sun, that animated Clay and Lincoln. And, Berns argues, it has animated the generations of American patriots who fought to preserve the Union and to defeat the totalitarian powers of the twentieth century.

15 Berns does not deny the stains on the national record, particularly the institution of slavery and its aftermath. But he is determined that those failures be estimated properly, as the ex-slave Frederick Douglass himself did, as remediable defects in an otherwise admirable and promising structure, rather than be exaggerated and used to denigrate the whole. Berns endorses Lincoln's contention that America represents "the last, best hope of earth," with all the enormous responsibilities that that entails. And he concludes by insisting that it is all-important to defend the legitimacy of America's liberal democracy and the ideal it embodies against the armies of its postmodernist, relativist, and multiculturalist detractors. For once this legitimacy is damaged, and once the foundational truths are no longer regarded as self-evident by the citizenry, then the American nation will be uprooted and fatally undermined to the detriment not only of America but of all humanity.

DANGEROUS ABSTRACTIONS

Berns is himself a member of the generation of patriots, now gradually disappearing from our midst, that fought in the war against

Henry Clay (1777–1852) was a politician from Kentucky who served for many years in the U.S. Senate and as Speaker of the U.S. House of Representatives. A skillful legislator, he worked hard to mediate political differences before the Civil War.

Hitler. That poignant fact echoes through his pages, subtly but unmistakably, giving an added measure of authority to his words. He has written a deeply moving book, personal without being the least bit mawkish or confessional and vibrant with the full range of human emotions—pride, reverence, tenderness, and occasional flashes of anger. This is, after all, his country that he is writing about. He manages to convey a keen sense of connection to the American past, a sense that is much more than merely historical. There is a feeling of urgency, too, a concern that the rising generations have not been taught about what they have inherited, about what their inheritance cost—and about those who were willing to pay the price for it. "Ours is not a parochial patriotism," Berns insists, because "it comprises an attachment to principles that are universal." Anything less would be "un-American."

One hopes there will be young readers of Berns's book who will find themselves stirred by such a full-throated and unabashed endorsement of America's sense of heroic mission. But there will be other readers, even ones as admiring as this reviewer, who may want to pause at such words and the argument they embody. For there is a danger in coming to regard America too exclusively as an idea, the carrier of an idea, or the custodian of a set of principles, rather than as a real nation that exists in a world of other nations, with all the features and limitations of a nation, including its particular history, institutions, and distinctive national character.

To be sure, Berns is right to stress the twofold character of American patriotism: The patriot loves America partly because it is his own country and partly because of his love for the ideals for which the country stands. The two motives are in tension, but they also are inseparable and mutually indispensable. America is not a class-ridden traditional society or a homogeneous blood-and-soil nation-state, but neither is it a universalistic ideological crusade. What is worrisome and lopsided in Berns's account of American patriotism is the near-exclusive weight he gives to the abstract and ideological dimensions of American patriotism, to the virtual exclusion of all other elements.

Indeed, at one point in his book he unfairly ridicules (and misquotes) a famous toast delivered in 1815 by the heroic American naval officer Stephen Decatur, declaring the words to be unpatriotic, even "un-American," because of their failure to endorse abstract universal principles of political right. The toast goes like this: "Our country! In her intercourse with foreign nations may she always be in the right; but our country, right or wrong!" In his rendering, Berns omits the words "In her intercourse with foreign nations," which changes the meaning of the quote rather dramatically. But even in its truncated form, the quote does not deserve the scorn Berns heaps upon it. For patriotism, like any love, withers and dies if it is not accorded some degree of instinctive assent. Berns's position could be interpreted to be that our country deserves our support only when its motives are demonstrably pure and its course of action demonstrably unassailable, that our loyalty to it is always revocable, that the nation stands every day freshly before the bar of judgment, to be assessed solely on the basis of its consonance that day with the universal principles of political right. This is much too brittle and unstable a foundation for any durable patriotism—particularly, one might add, in a nation's intercourse with foreign nations.

20 Berns, of course, is not advocating any such thing. But his words inadvertently point to the problem with interpreting America exclusively as an idea. Obviously, no decent patriotism can ever be completely unconditional, blindly loyal on all occasions, deaf to the claims of morality. That way lies tyranny and human degradation. But compelling reasons of state do not always translate into readily apprehended principles of universal morality, and there are times when being a patriot means being like a soldier, following leaders who have had to make complex judgments beyond the soldier's ken. Even Berns's beloved Lincoln is vulnerable to the charge that the human rights of slaves and such fundamental rights as habeas corpus were less important to him than the preservation of the Union, that the Emancipation Proclamation was primarily a cynical and calculated war measure, and that only the relentless pressure of events and other men led Lincoln to end slavery. If those charges sound familiar, it is because they are the same charges that two generations of morally indignant historians have hurled at Lincoln, convicting him by reference to a universalistic (and unrealistic and ungenerous) standard very much like the one Berns advocates.

WE ARE FAMILY?

So how might one arrive at a more complex understanding of the mixed nature of American patriotism? One might find some insight in an analogy to marriage, an institution in which something very much like Berns's twofold division of motives obtains. The parallels are suggestive. A man is devoted to his wife partly because she is admirable—and partly because she is his. And it is easy to see how, in a marriage, one cannot separate these two things in practice. A man may perhaps initially fall in love with a woman because she is admirable and lovely. But it is an entirely different matter to explain why he stays married and faithful to her, even when he knows full well that she is not always admirable and lovely. Should a man continue to love and honor his wife only if she is always admirable? Of course not. We all recognize that only a very shallow and insubstantial love would express itself in this way. Are there not occasions when a good husband honors and defends his wife, even when she may be in the wrong, simply because she is his and he is hers? Is there not a mutual obligation subsisting between them, far more deep-seated than any transient wrong?

Obviously. Are there times when the strict pursuit of justice in a marriage takes a back seat to the preservation of the union? Yes. Can a happy and healthy marriage endure when justice is always subordinated to the preservation of the union? No.

In other words, the nature of the commitment made in a good marriage is a complex blend of motives, ideal and primal, extrinsic and intrinsic, practical and impractical. It would be unthinkable, and in fact somewhat ludicrous, to imagine that one set of motives could exist without the counterbalance of the other. There is merit in a love that is directed toward a person who possesses abundant admirable qualities. But there is even more merit in a love that is able, over time, and within the enclosure of a mutual commitment, to acknowledge and accept—up to a point—what is less than fully admirable, what is all-too-human, about the otherwise admirable other. Where that point is located and when it is reached are questions almost impossible to answer in any general way. [Leo] **Tolstoy**, wrong in so many other things, was also wrong in proposing that happy families are always the same. General principles may be helpful, but they always have to be weighed against other considerations.

One might also extend the analogy to encompass other relationships within the family. If a country is like a spouse, it is also like a parent, since it constitutes one of the irreducible sources of one's being. One's gratitude to one's forebears is very much like the gratitude a patriot should feel toward those, like Walter Berns, who fought to preserve their nation. So then: Is it a good thing to admire one's father (and to be an admirable father)? Of course. Should one's love for one's father be conditional upon his always having been an admirable person and having always done admirable things? Of course not. Should one love one's father even when he has behaved shamefully, as a criminal or a traitor? That is more difficult. Perhaps even then, though only

Anna Karenina (1877), by **Leo Tolstoy** (1828–1910) one of the great novels of the nineteenth century, begins: "Happy families are all alike; every unhappy family is unhappy in its own way."

up to a point. But then, who is to say? The truth of the matter is buried in the particulars.

Like all analogies, these marital and familial ones break down at some point. Mario Cuomo's famous words notwithstanding, a nation is not a family. Indeed, the analogy becomes problematic when overtaxed precisely because (as Berns points out) Americans have never spoken of their country as a "fatherland," in the way so many Europeans spoke of their own nations in the pre-European Union era. In fact, it might be said that America was the country one came to in order to escape from one's father, both literally and figuratively. It was the country where one put aside the heavy lumber of inherited identity and tradition, and was freed to begin again. Hence Berns much prefers **G. K. Chesterton**'s notion that America, far from being a fatherland, is "the only nation in the world that is founded on a creed," and is therefore "a nation with the soul of a church." To be an American, in this view, is not a matter of whose child you are but of what principles you accept. It is a nation of the twice-born, politically and culturally, a nation founded not upon descent but consent.

A CREEDAL NATION?

25 There is profound truth in this, but it is not the whole of the matter. The Chestertonian analogy breaks down too—or more precisely, it tells us more than was intended. Indeed, it goes directly to the heart of what is so troubling about Berns's view of American patriotism. For a church is much more than its creed. The creed is indispensable, as an intellectual guidepost, a check upon heresy, a means of instructing the young, and a handy distillation of church doctrine. Documents like the Westminster Confession are masterpieces of theological clarity and concision. But a church that had only a creed would be no church at all. One need only visit an old churchyard and see the gravestones of several generations of a family clustered together to understand how this is so. All churches, even the most nouveau-Protestant ones, possess a rich storehouse of conscious and unconscious traditions, liturgies, songs, rituals, and customs. Over time these become inseparable in the minds and hearts of the worshipers from the content of their faith. Creeds are useful, but the Biblical and liturgical texts and the sacraments and rituals are not finally reducible to propositional statements; they are not reducible to anything less than themselves. There is a seamless web that unites every piece of church life with every other, for better or worse. This is why any changes in the pattern of church life become fraught with peril: Such changes may seem to disturb the bones of the dead and tamper with the very structure of the cosmos.

So a creed can be useful to shake up the musty complacency and cultural stasis that can creep into such a hidebound environment. It may also have defensive uses, as a means of keeping the train from going off the tracks. But it is not the soul of a church or a nation. Or, to put it another way, a living creed is a distillation and codification of beliefs that are grounded elsewhere—embodied in the habits and mores and institutions of the people. The words have to be made flesh and dwell among us. Without such quickening, a creed soon becomes a dead letter.

And for the same reasons, indoctrination into the principles of the Declaration of Independence alone will not make our young Americans into patriots. It is a beginning, but only a beginning. As both Thomas Jefferson and John Adams made clear, the Americans of the Revolutionary generation did not

Poet, novelist, playwright, and journalist **G. K. Chesterton** (1874–1936) was also a Catholic who argued for a moral political philosophy based on Christian values.

CONTEXT

In his keynote address to the delegates at the **1984 Democratic Convention**, where **Walter Mondale** was chosen as the Democratic candidate for president, **Mario Cuomo**, who was then the governor of New York, said, "We believe we must be the family of America, recognizing that at the heart of the matter we are bound to one another." Throughout his speech he invoked the idea of the nation as a family.

need instruction in what their Declaration declared. Their Declaration was mainly a press release to the world which attempted to put into words what most Americans already believed and embodied in their way of life. For our young people to know about it is, in the end, indispensable. But what is just as needful—perhaps even more so—is a recognition that there can be no meaningful patriotism in a society whose most privileged young people know nothing, remember nothing, respect nothing, cherish nothing, feel responsible for nothing, and are grateful for nothing.

This litany is not meant as a disparagement of the young but of those adults who have abdicated their responsibility for the young's formation, setting them free to be shaped by cable television, shopping malls, Internet chat rooms, and all the other flotsam of our feckless commercial culture. That irresponsibility, I think, is what has produced the conditions that sadden, anger, and worry Walter Berns, as they should all of us. But if no grand national program of ideological revitalization can rebuild what has been eroded, there is still hope for America in the patriotism of those young Jews mentioned earlier who have chosen to swim against the tide by paying homage to their birthright. A second birth does not have to renounce the first, and faithfulness in large things begins with faithfulness in smaller ones. The genius of American patriotism resides here just as much as it does in the Declaration of Independence. And if taken seriously, it will do far more to change the way Americans live.

A final image. When Lincoln wondrously invoked the "mystic chords of memory" in his first inaugural address, he envisioned them as the emanations of musical strings, "stretching from every battlefield and patriot grave to every living heart and hearthstone all over this broad land." It is an amazingly rich and well-considered image. We should not miss the fact that the strings are held in place not only by the deeds of warriors at one end but also by the domestic world, the world of family and home, at the other. Gratitude to one's country, however principled, must also draw upon forms of gratitude that are more primary—upon the things that are personal, particular, and singular. The things, in short, that are one's own. Without them, there can be no music, no memory, and no chorus of the Union.

Questions for Discussion

1. What is the central problem that McClay believes the United States faces when it comes to encouraging a patriotic citizenry? Why, in McClay's view, does the United States face this problem?

2. McClay devotes much of his essay to discussing the ideas of Walter Berns in the book *Making Patriots* (see the box on page 543). Why does McClay discuss Berns's book at such length? What main points does he use Berns's ideas to make? Do you think this is an effective strategy on McClay's part? What other strategies might be used to make these points?

3. What is the danger that McClay sees in thinking of the United States as an idea and a set of principles rather than as a real nation that exists in the world? Do you share his concern? Why or why not?

4. McClay has divided his essay into six main sections. What point does he make in each of these sections? How does each of these main points fit together to help McClay make his main argument about patriotism? Do you think his way of organizing his argument is effective? Why or why not?

5. How would you describe the tone and style of this essay? Compare McClay's tone and style to those of the other writers in this section. In what ways do his tone and style contribute to the main argument of this essay?

6. In his essay McClay makes many references to young Americans as well as to older Americans. How does he characterize young Americans? Do you think his characterization is accurate and fair? Given these references to young Americans, whom do you think McClay imagined as his primary audience for this essay? To whom is his argument primarily addressed? Do you think his argument is effective for that audience? Why or why not? Cite specific passages from his essay to support your answer.

7. McClay uses several analogies in his essay. For example, he compares patriotism to the loyalty two married people feel toward each other. Evaluate McClay's use of these analogies. What do they contribute to his main argument? How effectively do they help him make his points?

8. This essay makes a complicated argument. Using the Toulmin model of argument (see pages 87–91), identify and evaluate McClay's major claims and warrants. On the basis of your analysis, would you describe McClay's essay as an effective argument? Explain.

A Patriotic Left

MICHAEL KAZIN

It is an old practice in American politics for a candidate to question an opponent's patriotism during an election. It is also common for those who question U.S. policies or actions to be called unpatriotic. As Michael Kazin suggests in the following essay, Americans with leftist political views seem to regularly endure the accusation of being unpatriotic. Whether it is true or not that left-leaning Americans are more commonly charged with being unpatriotic than are their fellow citizens with more moderate or conservative views, Kazin believes that patriotism is an important element in political debate. As an avowed leftist, he refuses to accept the criticism that leftists are unpatriotic because of their willingness to question their government. For Kazin, patriotism is more complicated than loyalty or love of country. It involves a deep sense of duty founded on the moral and ethical principles implicit in the U.S. Constitution. That duty might sometimes require the true patriot to question or criticize the government, as many important political figures in America's history have done. In making his argument, Kazin looks to those figures in America's past—people such as Frederick Douglass, Mother Jones, and Eugene Debs—to highlight the long tradition in American politics of patriots criticizing the U.S. government in their efforts to create a more just America. You might disagree with Kazin's politics, but consider how his argument can help you clarify your sense of what it means to be a patriot. Kazin serves on the editorial board of *Dissent* magazine, in which this essay was published in 2002.

MICHAEL KAZIN, "A Patriotic Left"

1 I love my country. I love its passionate and endlessly inventive culture, its remarkably diverse landscape, its agonizing and wonderful history. I particularly cherish its civic ideals—social equality, individual liberty, a populist democracy—and the unending struggle to put their laudable, if often contradictory, claims into practice. I realize that patriotism, like any powerful ideology, is a "construction" with multiple uses, some of which I abhor. But I persist in drawing stimulation and pride from my American identity.

Regrettably, this is not a popular sentiment on the contemporary left. Antiwar activists view patriotism as a smokescreen for U.S. hegemony, while radical academics mock the notion of "American exceptionalism" as a relic of the cold war, a triumphal myth we should quickly outgrow. All the rallying around the flag after September 11 increased the disdain many leftists feel for the sentiment that lies behind it. "The globe, not the flag, is the symbol that's wanted now," scolded Katha Pollitt in the *Nation*. Noam Chomsky described patriotic blather as simply the governing elite's way of telling its subjects, "You shut up and be obedient, and I'll relentlessly advance my own interests."

Both views betray an ignorance of American history, as well as a quixotic desire to leap from a distasteful present to a gauzy future liberated from the fetters of nationalism. Love of country

CONTEXT

The term "American exceptionalism" (see paragraph 2) refers to the idea that the United States is unique among nations because of the special circumstances of its beginnings as a democracy built on principles of individual liberty and self-determination, which were radical ideas when the United States was founded. The idea of American exceptionalism can be traced to Alexis de Tocqueville, who described what he considered to be the special character of American political life in his book *Democracy in America* (1835). But this idea has long been controversial. Some critics, for example, charge that it serves as a justification for arrogant and misguided foreign policy. In recent years the debate about whether the United States is exceptional among nations has been rekindled in the disagreements about whether or not the United States was justified in invading Iraq in 2003 and pursuing a foreign policy that promotes American-style democracy in all regions of the world.

was a demotic faith long before September 11, a fact that previous lefts understood and attempted to turn to their advantage. In the United States, Karl Marx's dictum that the workers have no country has been refuted time and again. It has been not wage earners but the upper classes—from New England gentry on the Grand Tour a century ago to globe-trotting executives and cybertech professionals today—who view America with an ambivalent shrug, reminiscent of Gertrude Stein's line, "America is my country, Paris is my hometown."

One can, like [authors Katha] Pollitt and [Noam] Chomsky, curse as jingoistic all those "United We Stand" and "God Bless America" signs and hope somehow to transcend patriotism in the name of global harmony. Or one can empathize with the communal spirit that animates them, embracing the ideals of the nation and learning from past efforts to put them into practice in the service of far-reaching reform.

5 An earlier version of American patriotism was a forerunner of the modern genre: pride in the first nation organized around a set of social beliefs rather than a shared geography and history. In its novelty, Americanism gave citizens of the new republic both a way to understand and to stand for purposes that transcended their self-interest. Of course,

these purposes were not always noble ones. As historian Gary Gerstle points out in his recent book *American Crucible*, "racial nationalism" dominated much of American life through the nineteenth century and into the early decades of the twentieth. It led some white Americans to justify exterminating Indians, others to hold slaves, and still others to bar immigrants who did not possess "Anglo-Saxon" genes. But the tolerant alternative, which Gerstle calls "civic nationalism," also inspired many Americans in the modern era to help liberate Europe from fascism and Stalinism and to organize at home for social and economic justice.

For American leftists, patriotism was indispensable. It made their dissent and rebellion intelligible to their fellow citizens—and located them within the national narrative, fighting to shape a common future. Tom Paine praised his adopted homeland as an "asylum for mankind"—which gave him a forum to denounce regressive taxes and propose free public education. Elizabeth Cady Stanton issued a "Woman's Declaration of Rights" on the centennial of the Declaration of Independence and argued that denying the vote to women was a violation of the Fourteenth Amendment. Union activists in the Gilded Age such as Eugene Debs and Mother Jones accused employers of crushing the individuality and self-respect of workers. When Debs became a socialist, he described his new vision in the American idiom, as "the equal rights of all to manage and control" society. Half a century later, Martin Luther King, Jr., told his fellow bus boycotters, "If we are wrong, the Supreme Court of this nation is wrong" and proclaimed that "the great glory of American democracy is the right to protest for right."

One could easily list analogous statements from such pioneering reformers as Jane Addams and Betty Friedan, unionists Sidney Hillman and Cesar Chavez, and the gay liberationist Harvey Milk. Without patriotic appeals, the great social movements that attacked inequalities of class, gender, and race in the United States—and spread their messianic rhetoric around the world—would never have gotten off the ground.

Even slavery couldn't extinguish the promise radicals found in the American creed. On Independence Day, 1852, Frederick Douglass gave an angry, eloquent address that asked, "What to the slave is the Fourth of July?" Every account quotes the fugitive-turned-abolitionist speaking truth to white power: "Your celebration is a sham; your boasted liberty, an unholy license; your national greatness, swelling vanity; your sounds of rejoicing are empty and heartless; your denunciations of tyrants, brass fronted impudence; your shouts of liberty and equality, hollow mockery." But fewer commentators note that when, at the end of his speech, Douglass predicted slavery's demise, he drew his "encouragement from the Declaration of Independence, the great principles it contains, and the genius of American Institutions," as well as from a spirit of enlightenment that he believed was growing on both sides of the Atlantic. After emancipation, Douglass never stopped condemning the hypocrisy of white Americans—or continuing to base his hopes for equality on traditions he and they held in common.

A self-critical conception of patriotism also led Americans on the left to oppose their leaders' aggressive policies abroad. Anti-imperialists opposed the conquest of the Philippines after the war of 1898 by comparing President William McKinley to King George III. Foes of U.S. intervention in World War I demanded to know why Americans should die to defend European monarchs and their colonies in Africa and Asia. In 1917, a mass movement led by socialists and pacifists called for a popular referendum on the question of going to war. Neither group of

Amy Etra/Photo Edit

resisters succeeded at the time, but each gained a mass hearing and saw its arguments incorporated into future policies. Congress promised independence to the Philippines sooner than colonial officials favored. And, challenged by such antiwar voices as Debs, Robert LaFollette, and William Jennings Bryan, Woodrow Wilson proclaimed national self-determination to be the core principle of a new world order.

CONTEXT

Adopted in 1868, the Fourteenth Amendment to the U.S. Constitution addresses issues related to voting, such as the number of congressional representatives each state should have. When Elizabeth Cady Stanton, a nineteenth-century activist who campaigned for women's right to vote, invoked this amendment in her famous "Women's Declaration of Rights" (see paragraph 6), she was referring to Section 1, which states,

All persons born or naturalized in the United States, and subject to the jurisdiction thereof, are citizens of the United States and of the state wherein they reside. No state shall make or enforce any law which shall abridge the privileges or immunities of citizens of the United States; nor shall any state deprive any person of life, liberty, or property, without due process of law; nor deny to any person within its jurisdiction the equal protection of the laws.

10 A good deal that we cherish about contemporary America was thus accomplished by social movements of the left, speaking out for national ideals. It may be, as the idiosyncratic Trotskyist Leon Samson argued in 1935, that Americanism served as a substitute for socialism, an ideology of self-emancipation through equal opportunity that inoculated most citizens against the class-conscious alternative. But leftists made what progress they did by demanding that the nation live up to its stated principles, rather than dismissing them as fatally compromised by the racism of the founders or the abusiveness of flag-waving vigilantes. After all, hope is always more attractive than cynicism, and the gap between promise and fulfillment is narrower for Americanism than it is for other universalist creeds such as communism, Christianity, and Islam.

It's difficult to think of any radical or reformer who repudiated the national belief system and still had a major impact on U.S. politics and policy. The movement against the Vietnam War did include activists who preferred the Vietcong's flag to the American one. But the antiwar insurgency grew powerful only toward the end of the 1960s, when it drew in people who looked for leadership to liberal patriots such as King, Walter Reuther, and Eugene McCarthy rather than to Abbie Hoffman and the Weathermen.

Perhaps one exception to this rule was Malcolm X, who stated, in 1964, that he was a "victim of Americanism" who could see no "American dream," only "an American nightmare." But Malcolm was primarily a spokesman for black anger and pride, not a builder of movements or a catalyst of reforms to benefit his people.

He was, however, a prophetic figure. Soon after Malcolm's death, many on the left, of all races, began to scorn patriotic talk and, instead, to celebrate ethnic and sexual differences. In 1970, writer Julius Lester observed, "American radicals are perhaps the first radicals anywhere who have sought to make a revolution in a country which they hate." At the time, there were certainly ample reasons to consider Americanism a brutal sham. After World War II, the word itself became the property of the American Legion, the House Un-American Activities Committee, and the FBI. In the 1960s, liberal presidents bullied their way into Indochina in the name of what Lyndon Johnson called "the principle for which our ancestors fought in the valleys of Pennsylvania." Fierce love for one's identity group—whether black, Latino, Asian, Native American, or gay or lesbian—seemed morally superior to the master narrative that had justified war abroad and racial exclusion at home.

Yet the history of the last thirty years has also exposed the outsized flaw in such thinking. Having abandoned patriotism, the left lost the ability to pose convincing alternatives for the nation as a whole. It could take credit for spearheading a multicultural, gender-aware revision of the humanities curriculum, but the right set the political agenda, and it did so in part because its partisans spoke forcefully in the name of American principles that knit together disparate groups—anti-union businesspeople, white evangelicals, Jewish neoconservatives—for mutual ends.

15 In the face of such evidence, many leftists would respond that civic idealism should not be confined within national borders. In a provocative 1994 essay, philosopher Martha Nussbaum argued that patriotism is "morally dangerous" because it encourages Americans to focus on their own concerns and minimize or disregard those of people in other lands. "We should regard our deliberations," she wrote, "as, first and foremost, deliberations about human problems of people in particular concrete situations, not problems growing out of a national identity that is altogether unlike that of others." Echoing her words, activists and intellectuals talk of challenging global exploitation with some form of global citizenship.

As an ethicist, Nussbaum is certainly on solid ground. Americans ought to take a massacre in Africa as seriously as one that takes place in lower Manhattan and demand that their government move rapidly to halt it. But she offers no guidance for how global leftists can get the power to achieve their laudable objectives. A planetary government is hardly on the horizon, and rich nations would no doubt hog its agenda if it were.

In the meantime, Americans who want to transform the world have to learn how to persuade the nation. At minimum, this means putting pressure on the national government, organizing coalitions of people from different regions and backgrounds, and debating citizens who think their tax money ought to be spent only at home. Disconnected as they are from any national or local constituency, global leftists now live at risk of being thrust to the margins—abstract sages of equity, operatives of nongovernmental organizations engaged in heroic but Sisyphean tasks, or demonstrators roving from continent to continent in search of bankers to heckle.

In the wake of September 11, the stakes have been raised for the American left. Even if the "war against terrorism" doesn't continue to overshadow all other issues, it will inevitably force activists of every stripe to make clear how they would achieve security

for individual citizens and for the nation. How can one seriously engage in this conversation about protecting America if America holds no privileged place in one's heart? Most ordinary citizens understandably distrust a left that condemns military intervention abroad or a crackdown at home but expresses only a pro forma concern for the actual and potential victims of terrorism. Without empathy for one's neighbors, politics becomes a cold, censorious enterprise indeed.

There's no need to mouth the Pledge of Allegiance or affix a flag pin to your lapel or handbag. But to rail against patriotic symbols is to wage a losing battle—and one that demeans us and sets us against the

CONTEXT

In making his argument, Kazin refers to a well-known essay by legal scholar Martha Nussbaum. Kazin asserts that Nussbaum sees patriotism as "morally dangerous." However, in her essay Nussbaum does not say that all patriotism is morally dangerous; rather, she argues that only some types of patriotism are morally dangerous, and only insofar as patriotism is incompatible with a decent concern for the rights of people everywhere. She writes,

"I believe...that this emphasis on patriotic pride is both morally dangerous and, ultimately, subversive of some of the worthy goals patriotism sets out to serve—for example, the goal of national unity in devotion to worthy moral ideals of justice and equality. These goals, I shall argue, would be better served by an ideal that is in any case more adequate to our situation in the contemporary world, namely the very old ideal of the cosmopolitan, the person whose primary allegiance is to the community of human beings in the entire world....

As students here grow up, is it sufficient for them to learn that they are above all citizens of the United States, but that they ought to respect the basic human rights of citizens of India, Bolivia, Nigeria, and Norway? Or should they, as I think—in addition to giving special attention to the history and current situation of their own nation—learn a good deal more than is frequently the case about the rest of the world in which they live, about India and Bolivia and Nigeria and Norway and their histories, problems, and comparative successes?...Most important, should they be taught that they are above all citizens of the United States, or should they instead be taught that they are above all citizens of a world of human beings, and that, while they themselves happen to be situated in the United States, they have to share this world of human beings with the citizens of other countries?

SOURCE: from Martha Nussbaum, "Patriotism and Cosmopolitanism," 1994.

© Reuters/CORBIS

"The protesters object to what they see as unfair IMF policies that benefit wealthier nations at the expense of developing nations. The IMF disagrees, saying it is the poor of the world who are benefited by its policies." (From **CNN.com**, September 27, 2002.)

overwhelming majority of Americans for no worthwhile moral or political purpose.

20 Instead, leftists should again claim, without pretense or apology, an honorable place in the long narrative of those who demanded that American ideals apply to all and opposed the efforts of those who tried to reserve them

for favored groups. When John Ashcroft denies the right of counsel to a citizen accused of terrorism or a CEO cooks the books to impress Wall Street, they are soiling the flag and ought to be put on the patriotic defensive. Liberals and radicals are the only people in politics who can insist on closing the gap between America as the apotheosis of democratic strivings and the sordid realities of greed and arrogance that often betray it.

There is really no alternative. In daily life, cultural cosmopolitanism is mostly reserved to the rich and famous. Radical environmentalists and anti-IMF [International Monetary Fund] crusaders seek to revive the old dream of internationalism in a version indebted more to John Lennon's "Imagine" than to V. I. Lenin's *Comintern*. But three years after bursting into the headlines from the streets of Seattle, that project seems stalled indefinitely in the Sargasso Sea that lies between rhetorical desire and political exigency.

In hope of a revival, left patriots might draw inspiration from . . . the white, conservative skeptic George Santayana, [who] observed that "America is the greatest of opportunities and the worst of influences. Our effort must be to resist the influence and improve the opportunity." . . .

Throughout our history, and still today, the most effective way to love the country is to fight like hell to change it.

Questions for Discussion

1. In the opening paragraphs of his essay, Kazin summarizes some of the criticisms of leftists who dismiss American patriotism. On what grounds does Kazin disagree with these leftists? What benefit might there be to debating this issue with others who share your political views?

2. Evaluate Kazin's introduction to this essay. What does he accomplish by beginning his argument with the statement that he loves his country? What audience do you think Kazin was primarily addressing with this introduction?

3. Kazin makes many references in this essay to historical events and people, tracing the history of several important political developments in the United States in the eighteenth, nineteenth, and twentieth centuries. What role does history play in Kazin's argument? How effectively do you think he uses history to help him make his main argument? (You might compare the way Kazin uses history to Steven Camarota's use of history in his essay on pages 529–534.)

4. How does Kazin define patriotism in this essay? Does his understanding of patriotism differ from the ideas of Wilfred McClay, whose essay appears earlier in this section? Explain. Do you think most Americans would agree with Kazin about what it means to be patriotic? Do you agree with him? Why or why not?

5. Evaluate the evidence that Kazin uses to support his claims in this essay. What kinds of evidence does he cite? How persuasive is this evidence in supporting his claims?

6. Kazin is a leftist, but he expresses concern about the views of other leftists about patriotism. He is concerned as well about the way those on the political right understand patriotism. Do you think he offers a compelling alternative to the views of the leftists and rightists he criticizes? On the basis of your answer to that question, how effectively do you think his essay works as an example of a Rogerian argument? (See pages 126–131 for a discussion of Rogerian argument.)

④ | # Class Warfare

JOSIAH BUNTING, III

When Josiah Bunting III wrote the following argument in 2005, the United States was engaged in wars in Iraq and Afghanistan, and the long-standing debate about whether or not the United States should reinstate the military draft was being renewed. Those wars were stretching the capabilities of the U.S. military, and some politicians and military professionals believed a draft was necessary to keep the military strong. Some critics noted that the all-volunteer armed forces had become a kind of employment service for many of the nation's poorer, less educated men and women, and they pointed out that the wars were changing enlistment trends so that fewer educated and financially well-heeled Americans were enlisting. Others who opposed the war in Iraq believed that a draft would make it less likely that the United States would end the war soon. In the midst of these debates, Bunting, a lieutenant general who has served as superintendent of Virginia Military Institute, argued in favor of a return to compulsory military service, pointing to the benefits of a draft for both individual citizens and their country. As someone who was awarded a Bronze Star for his service in Vietnam and who has taught at the U.S. Military Academy at West Point, Bunting understands the challenges of military service, and his essay prompts us to reconsider the question of whether military service is one of a citizen's responsibilities. And his argument is timely, given that the United States was still engaged in 2010 in the same two wars that were being fought when this essay was published in 2005 in the *American Scholar*, the journal of the Phi Beta Kappa Society.

JOSIAH BUNTING, III, "Class Warfare"

> **It may be laid down as a primary position, and the basis of our system, that every Citizen who enjoys the protection of a free Government, owes not only a proportion of his property, but even of his personal services to the defence of it.**
>
> —George Washington, "Sentiments on a Peace Establishment"

1 For some years I worked as headmaster of a large boarding school. By that time, the late 1980s and early '90s, "chapel" had become a weekly, not a daily, ritual—although the usages of custom and of a certain civic religion sometimes brought the school together in chapel on other days. Sunday chapel rites were mainly Anglican in tone, despite the school's Presbyterian heritage: lordly preludes and processionals, antique calls to worship, lessons that concluded with "endeths," hymns from a confident epoch in British history. The ambience remained very much that of the nineteenth-century school, redolent with the communicated sense of duty to the less fortunate and less privileged—the nave hung with banners and heraldic flags, its walls studded with bronze plaques offering the Loyola Prayer for Generosity and tributes to deceased masters and alumni. Among them there was a testimonial to a master who had given his life to the school and who had lived "a life of Christian self-forgetfuness." I remember phrases and verses from certain favored hymns: "Noble mirth." What was that? "Who follows in his train?" "Faint not, nor fear!"—the exclamation mark communicating to the congregant it's all right, you'll be fine! "By the light of burning martyrs, Christ, Thy bleeding feet I track." And from Scripture: "Where moths and rust doth corrupt, and where thieves break through and steal." Most particularly I remember four flags of scarlet, white, and gold, rectangular in shape, that hung before us, on either side of the altar. These were memorial flags that commemorated graduates of the school who had died in four wars: 1917–1918; 1941–1945; 1950–1953; 1965–1973. They framed a great gold altar cross on which was inscribed: I WILL LIFT UP MY EYES UNTO THE HILLS.

Lifting my eyes up to the flags and their rows of stars, one star for each child of the school who had been killed Fighting For Our Country, I used to consider not only what the stars signified but also what they meant: what the young men thought they might have to die for what they gave up in losing their lives, and what the shattered families learning of their deaths felt. These were boys (all in the school then were boys) who had sat where my wife and I were sitting now, who had sung the same hymns and recited the same comforting creeds, who had dispersed out onto the virid **Frederick Olmsted Circle** and come to our house for coffee and singing—songs from Gilbert and Sullivan, Cole Porter, Rodgers and Hammerstein. Chapel itself always ended with a brisk, triumphant postlude, a Handel or a Widor anthem. Once, I remember, it ended with "Stout-Hearted Men." The intention and the consequence were to uplift us.

The business of war was fully remote from these proceedings, and remote increasingly from a particular segment of the American people. For the memorial flags told another story, a kind of second lead. In World War I,

some forty sons of the school, which then enrolled about four hundred students, had been killed. Pershing's army had fought only one really large campaign, the Meuse-Argonne offensive, and that was late in the war. Its butcher's bill, combined with our losses earlier in places with such names as Cantigny, Belleau Wood, St. Mihiel, exceeded 350,000 killed and wounded.

For World War II there were approximately sixty stars on the flag. United States forces were engaged for about forty-five months, not counting the service of those who had volunteered and gone off to fight for Canada or Britain. For Korea, ten stars: three years' fighting, but a much smaller American force serving in a much smaller theater. Finally, Vietnam: only five stars for eight years of war; at its height the American force "in country" was about 550,000. I do not know how many graduates of the school died in Desert Storm, or have died to date in the present fighting in Iraq and Afghanistan. None, I hope; very few, I imagine—even as I ponder the ageless fact of war: that overwhelmingly those we send off to die are but a year or two, perhaps five, from the ages of the children who sat with my wife and me in the Lawrenceville Chapel singing "I sing a song of the saints of God."

5 The flags commemorate terrible but noble deaths. **Dulce et decorum est pro patria mori**. That is some recompense, I suppose. But there is, as I say, a second story here. The diminishing numbers of war dead disclose another phenomenon: the withdrawal of the American clerisy (I will call it, after **Coleridge**), the privileged intellectual and professional and commercial classes, and their novitiates and children, from the active military service of our country. It is dangerous, it is unworthy, it is wrong. When I hear U.S. Representative Charles Rangel, his voice passionate and cracking, demand that the country begin drafting young people for the armed forces, I know exactly what he means.

"Dulce et decorum est pro patria mori" are the first lines in an ode by Horace, a great poet in ancient Rome. Translated from the Latin, the words mean "It is sweet and right to die for one's country." But Bunting's reference in paragraph 6 to the English poet Wilfred Owen (1893–1918) suggests that he is aware that this statement can be a "lie." Owen's poem was written at the end of World War I, which was then called the Great War—a war that had produced unprecedented slaughter.

Frederick Olmsted Circle refers to part of the landscaping design for the Lawrenceville School in Lawrenceville, New Jersey. The design was created by Frederick Law Olmsted (1822–1903), one of the most influential landscape architects in American history. Olmsted's most famous creation is Central Park in New York City.

English poet **Samuel Taylor Coleridge** (1772–1834) was a major figure in Romanticism and author of the famous poems "Kubla Khan" and "The Rhime of the Ancient Mariner." He coined the term clerisy to refer to class of educated state bureaucrats.

A close associate of Vladimir Ilyich Lenin, **Leon Trotsky** (1879–1940) was a leader of the Communist revolution in Russia. After Lenin's death in 1924, Trotsky lost political control of what was by then the Soviet Union to Joseph Stalin and was later exiled and assassinated in Mexico City.

"I no longer take the cigarette out of my mouth when I write 'deceased' over their names," wrote the English poet and lieutenant Wilfred Owen near the end of World War I. Owen was himself killed a few days afterward. He had become, almost, inured to such deaths, just as we are inured to, and so terribly removed from, the deaths of our soldiers in Iraq. But few, very few indeed, of these are the deaths of children of those who lead our country, who control its resources and institutions, direct and inflect its tastes and opinions, batten most avidly upon its treasures and most lavishly upon its expensive entertainments. No one wants any American to die in a war. But if there is harm's way to tread, should not all who are our national bounty's beneficiaries tread it together or, at least, be liable to be asked by their country to do so?

Representative Rangel's message might be communicated in a twenty-first-century adaptation of the peppery, flag-snapping Victorian jingle:

1895 We don't want to fight by Jingo
But by Jingo if we do
We've got the men, and we've got the ships
And we've got the money too!
2005 We don't want to fight by Jingo,
But by Jingo if we do
The smart and privileged people,
They'd better join us, too!

I mean "smart" not in the sense of the social éclat of places like San Francisco or New York, but as the easy synonym Americans use for academic success: intelligence as it is measured in rankings and grades, acceptances and advancement to, and within, these nurseries for the most privileged young people, the great boarding schools and revered public high schools (say, New Trier or Bronx Science) and the famous private universities and colleges of the coasts. For it is in these places, and the culture that nourishes them, that ignorance of military service is so deep-seated as to be, almost, unconscious. He went where? Into the marines? These places, once the veriest source of eager and idealistic young military leaders and volunteers in 1898, 1917, and 1941, are fully settled in 2004 in their contempt or condescension for the profession of arms. And it has been so since the mid-1960s for reasons that are perfectly obvious.

You may not be interested in war, observed **Trotsky**, but war is interested in you. The issue of military conscription is deeply controversial, of course; and it is one of a family of public policy questions, recurrent and vexed, upon whose difficulties people advance, make nervous reconnaissances, and then withdraw, unwilling to engage them fully. It is also an issue that excites a multiplicity of opinions that seem unhinged from regular political affiliations, parties, and philosophies. I have never met anyone able to consider the question with anything approaching

CONTEXT

In January 2003, as the U.S. military fought in Afghanistan and prepared to invade Iraq, U.S. Representative Charles Rangel, a Democrat from New York, introduced a bill in Congress to reinstate the military draft (see para.5). His bill would have required men and women in the United States between the ages of 18 and 26 to serve in the military. In proposing such a bill, Rangel reignited an old controversy in the United States about compulsory military service which stretches back to the Revolutionary War. The United States had a formal draft from 1948 until 1973, when President Richard Nixon abolished it amid controversy arising from inequalities in the military during the Vietnam War. During that war, many critics observed that the war was being fought disproportionately by Americans who were poor, from minority backgrounds, and of limited political influence. Deferments from service were available to college and graduate students, and many wealthy, well-connected young men were able to avoid serving in Vietnam. But the creation of an all-volunteer army in 1973 did not eliminate these social inequities. The all-volunteer army drew many of its members from segments of the American population that had fewer educational and economic choices than those of more privileged backgrounds. To highlight these problems, some critics noted that neither of President George W. Bush's daughters volunteered for military service after the president ordered the invasion of Iraq in 2003.

disinterestedness. There are, of course, many approaches to it, not the least of them, in 2005, the fact that the armed force is far too small to do what is being asked of it. And it is not certain, in a world of competing sovereignties—many of them hostile to us, some close to being able to deploy nuclear weapons—what may be asked, or required, of it in the future.

What is certain is how distant all things military, all the appurtenances and actions and needs of war and warriors, have become from the informed and thoughtful consideration of those to whom our commerce and culture have given the most. When a successful National Football League athlete, having left his sport and its gigantic emoluments to enlist in the army and serve in the active theater of operations, is killed in combat, his death is not only mourned. That he went off to serve at all strikes people as flat-out astounding. How could a young American abandon the pursuit of those two things Americans most deeply venerate, money and celebrity, to join the army? Not very long ago, the Northwestern University sociologist Charles Moskos reminds us, a Princeton graduating class, his own, sent 400 of its number (of 900) into the military, some volunteers, some drafted, within a year or two of graduation. That was in 1956. Thus far in 2004 the same university has sent, of a class of 1,110, nine.

10 The continuing allure of the generations that led and served in the Second World War testifies to our national uneasiness about the profoundly unequal sharing of the military burden in the early years of the twenty-first century. A veteran of the landings on Normandy or Tarawa is about eighty years old today. His generation, modest and reticent about its time in uniform, refers to that period of their lives simply as the service. "I was in the service." The consequent phrase is omitted: " . . . of my country."

Of the enduring cultural testimonials to that service—novels, plays, movies, most of them celebratory—the universal expression of the American experience is the polyglot infantry squad: by honest happenstance, eight or ten Americans, eighteen or twenty years old, are thrown together in basic training. The tired melting-pot metaphor is for once apt. Birth, creed, color, and wealth are no longer the criteria of judgment, acceptance, or advancement. The student of architecture and the Navajo, the college boy and the Italian American from Oakland are wonderfully commingled in a transcending mission. The survivors—most survive—are immensely the better for their service together. All have won through to a new quality—moral, intellectual, temperamental all at once—which is judgment, a kind of canny wisdom, that will make them better citizens for the rest of their lives. (Of that sense of national commonality, we in our turn experienced a frission in the week or so after 9/11. It has not lasted.)

COMPLICATION

In 2007, a U.S. marine who served in the war in Iraq, published an article in *Newsweek* magazine titled "Why We Need a Draft," in which he argued that the United States could not win the war in Iraq unless it reinstated a military draft. In response, Michael Boldin, a libertarian writer, published an essay titled "The Military Draft: A Moral Abomination." In that essay, Boldin wrote,

> The most important argument against the draft is moral. Whatever the excuse given for its implementation, the draft is a form of slavery. Period.

> Forcing someone to work for the state; forcing someone to kill or be killed; forcing someone to do anything at the point of a gun—under threat of prison or even death—*is* involuntary servitude. Of all the forms of slavery that have existed throughout history, forcing someone to fight and die in war is among the most disgusting and is a form of murder against all who don't survive.

SOURCE: *Freedom Daily*, January 2008.

The point is that many went into the military and learned from the experience. Today when we watch a dusty squad of nineteen-year-old marines moving along a street in Fallujah, windswept and sere, and we hear a chirping MSNBC voice-over use language like "The artillery has already softened up" the area, we know we are listening to someone mouthing words whose meaning he cannot possibly guess. He doesn't really know, nor can he really communicate to us, what is happening, but he feels obliged to try. The young marines are of the same métier as their World War II grandfathers—but now the college boy and the senator's kid are missing.

World War II is called a good war. No war is a good war, though some, patently, are more necessary than others. The war in Iraq, terribly controversial like the police action in Korea and the war in Vietnam, has splintered away from the conscious concern of most of those in whose behalf it is said to be prosecuted; and since such wars, not to say the "war on terror," are the template for future conflict, it seems unlikely that this will change. "The abuse of greatness is when it disjoins remorse from power"; the line from *Julius Caesar* makes the predicament plain. Those for whom the war is being waged are disjoined from its costs.

In another Shakespeare play, *Henry V*, the physical and moral devastation of France has led, a speaker remarks, to a terrible coarsening of its life and landscape. Things now grow "as soldiers will, that nothing do but mediate on blood." My sense of the generation that led the soldiers of World War II, particularly of that generation's professional soldiers, is very different. Its most senior officers, most born between 1875 and 1890, nowadays subsist in the common memory as awkward clusters of attendant lords, gathered about the seated icons of Allied leadership, Churchill, Stalin, Roosevelt, and later Atlee and Truman. They appear preternaturally calm and self-possessed, anything but war-like in appearance; dutiful, forbearing, wise and weary. These leaders are models of a certain kind of disinterestedness, their counsel offered (as U.S. Grant's was provided Lincoln) without reference to themselves or their advancement. With a couple of famous exceptions, they were uneasy in a celebrity they had certainly not sought. They embodied a kind of mature civic wisdom, not measurable in the ways our age defines "leadership ability" or cleverness, and they were far from the caricature of militarism and its punctilios the clerisy imputes to today's soldiers.

15 We see men like George Marshall, Hap Arnold, Dwight D. Eisenhower, and Admirals Ernest King and William Leahy as heirs to the tradition of U.S. Grant and Robert E. Lee: functional soldiers, noble and dutiful, devoted only to the mission, leaders to whom citizens might safely entrust the services of their children, men for whom the attractions of money and fame were nonexistent. (It was not proper, Marshall believed, for him to write his memoirs; these would invariably give pain to those he would be obliged to mention. Nor indeed was it proper for him to allow himself to receive any American decoration during the course of the war, because the soldiers he led were having a far harder, more dangerous time of it than he.)

Such leaders in their day defined civil society's expectations of wartime military commanders. They were themselves distant cousins of our clerisy. Most were products of the American heartland, of villages and farms. But their families did venerate learning, strong exemplary tutelage, and advancement to secure professional careers. No brassy

CONTEXT

Fallujah, a major city in central Iraq and the site of several important Muslim holy shrines, was the scene of a significant battle between Iraqi insurgents and U.S. forces and their allies in April 2004. The battle was part of an effort to regain control of the city from insurgents. It was sparked in part by the murder and mutilation of several American civilian contractors who were working as security guards in Iraq. Although more than two dozen Americans and hundreds of Iraqis were killed during the battle, it was considered a turning point in the war and a major defeat for insurgents opposed to the U.S. presence in Iraq.

vocation to soldier had called them to West Point. They went to the academies because the academies were free and provided a good education. These leaders seemed the best expressions of a moral democracy; they weren't commanders coarsened and insensitive to the value of what they had been called upon to destroy. They were fatherly in their concern, in their love, for their soldiers. Their commitment to their profession, too, their allegiance to the principle embodied in such commitment, had kept them in uniform through the long, bleak winter of the 1920s and 1930s: unpromoted, ill paid, often in assignments that seemed far beneath their talents.

That generation is gone, tone and tint, and those who served in the ranks, 1941–1945, are leaving us each month by the tens of thousands. But a citizen who sees and acknowledges the deepening chasm that is separating those who serve from those whom they serve (which no number of eyewitness news teams and Veterans Day editorials can usefully bridge) can only deplore a civic culture that removes the burdens of military service from those it has blessed most abundantly. We may be grateful, we may even rejoice, when we see fewer and fewer stars on the memorial flags that hang from the walls of the chapels and halls of the nurseries of the American clerisy, of the schools of privilege earned and unearned. But our own education in these places, moral, liberal, civic, has failed us terribly if we do not also remember that such stars are accumulating somewhere: only somewhere else. Fifty-one Americans died in Fallujah in eleven days. More than four hundred were wounded. Those are mounting numbers, and each number, each star, is a devastation—but each is a devastation out there, just not where we are.

Twenty years ago a young woman named Wendy Kopp graduated from Princeton. By passionate and focused effort she founded and has led a remarkable program called Teach for America. Idealistic and bright graduates of universities like Princeton and Stanford and Brown are recruited to teach, for two years and for a small stipend, in public schools that badly need teachers: most of them in difficult places, hardscrabble, sometimes in violent neighborhoods. At a meeting, a questioner wondered whether Kopp expected her young volunteers to make careers of teaching in such places. No, she said, probably not. But someday they will be forty or fifty years old. They will serve on school boards. They will be appointed or elected to offices. They will carry the inestimable benefit of having themselves done what they will be asking another young generation to do; they will know the costs and difficulties and sometimes dangers of such duties. So it should be with—to use a word that has gone utterly out of fashion—soldiering in behalf of the American republic. It is not idle of us to remind a new generation of undergraduates and those educating them, not to say their own families, that this generation in its turn will ask young men and women to wear the uniform of our country, to serve in harm's way, and that it is—there is no other word for it— better that they themselves have something to remember about what it is that a private or a second lieutenant does in a war. In the service.

Questions for Discussion

1. Evaluate Bunting's opening paragraphs as an introduction to his essay. What does Bunting achieve by opening with a description of an elite boarding school? In what ways does this description set up his main argument? How effective do you find his introduction?

2. Consider the numbers Bunting provides in paragraphs 3, 4, and 9. What do these numbers signify? How do they help support his main argument?

3. Throughout this essay, Bunting makes many references to literature, historical events, scholars, and important historical figures. What do these many references suggest about Bunting as an author? What do they indicate about the assumptions he made about his audience? To what extent do these references contribute to the effectiveness of his argument?

4. Bunting declares that in 2005 "the armed force is far too small to do what is being asked of it." Do you think that events that have occurred since 2005 have justified this claim? Explain.

5. Without calling for a return of the draft, an issue that he describes as "deeply controversial," Bunting clearly believes that military service has value. What is the nature of that value? Why, in his view, is it important for men and women of diverse backgrounds—including diverse social classes—to serve in the military? How persuasively do you think he makes his case for the value of military service? What counterarguments to his sense of this value might you make?

6. In paragraph 16, Bunting raises the idea of "moral democracy." What does that phrase mean? How would a moral democracy be different from a political democracy? How would it be similar? How does this idea fit into Bunting's main argument about military service?

7. What does the story of Wendy Kopp in the final paragraph contribute to this argument? Why do you think Bunting chose to use it for his conclusion? How well does it work as a conclusion?

DIFFERENCES

NEGOTIATING

In his essay in this section, Michael Kazin refers explicitly to the events of September 11, 2001, and suggests that those events underscore the importance of examining the question of what it means to be patriotic. He argues that being a patriot requires more than loyalty to America, more than even a willingness to go to war. Wilfred McClay reinforces this idea by asking how people justify the decision to fight and perhaps even to die for their country. John Balzar shows that even the act of voting, which Americans may take for granted, places a responsibility on citizens that goes beyond simply expressing an opinion. And Josiah Bunting argues that America's elite should share the responsibility for military service that is carried mostly by citizens who are less privileged. In short, these essays suggest that citizenship is more than a matter of which country you happen to live in; they challenge you to think about what citizenship requires of each citizen, including yourself.

After September 11, 2001, these questions about citizenship and patriotism understandably preoccupied many Americans. On many college campuses, controversies arose when professors or students have openly criticized the U.S. government's actions in its efforts to fight terrorism. In a few cases, faculty members have been sanctioned by their schools for such criticisms. In other cases, some courses have been criticized because they seem to be sympathetic to the views of America's enemies.

Imagine that such a controversy has emerged at your college or university. A professor has been publicly criticized for teaching a course that seems to be sympathetic to the point of view of groups that openly espouse violence against Americans. In response to the controversy, your school's administration has decided to address the issue by reexamining the school's curriculum. One proposal that is under consideration would require all students to take a newly designed course in citizenship. In effect, the course would teach students how to be good citizens. Not surprisingly, this proposal has generated further controversy as students, faculty, and community members debate what such a course should include and even whether such a course should be required. In the wake of this controversy, students have been invited to express their views about the proposal in writing.

Write an essay in which you present your position on the question of whether students should be required to take a course in citizenship. In your essay, define what you believe a good citizen is, and discuss what responsibilities citizens have. Using the essays in this section and any other relevant sources you find, make a case for or against the proposed course in citizenship, or suggest some alternative way of addressing the school's concerns about encouraging students to become good citizens. Keep your audience in mind as you construct your argument: the administrators and faculty of your school as well as students who attend the school. Try to construct your argument in a way that might address their concerns and help your school community find a solution to the controversy about the proposed course. Also take into account recent events that might have relevance to the question of what makes a good citizen.

Bettmann/Corbis

How Should Americans Govern Themselves?

Americans consider the Declaration of Independence to be a sacred document (see Con-Text on page 567). American children learn in school that the Declaration, written mostly by Thomas Jefferson, was a catalyst for the American Revolutionary War. Its presentation to King George III of England made it clear that the American colonists were rejecting the British government that had ruled them. What students often overlook is how radical a step the colonists had taken. In the eighteenth century the idea that citizens, rather than governments, ultimately hold political power was almost unheard of—an idea that flew in the face of the established order, under which people were viewed as the subjects of their rulers. But in the Declaration of Independence, Jefferson and his cosigners stated unequivocally that it should be the other way around: Leaders served at the behest of citizens; if those leaders should compromise the inherent rights of the citizens, then citizens were legally and morally justified in removing those leaders. Power to the people. ■ In this sense the founding of the United States ushered in a new era in which the whole idea of government was redefined, but it also created a new set of questions about the relationship between a government and its citizens. If political power ultimately resides in the people, then what is the role of government? How is that role determined? And how much power should a government have over citizens? These questions are not answered in the Declaration of Independence except in the abstract. Jefferson and his cosigners famously declared that government exists to secure the rights of citizens to "Life, Liberty, and the pursuit of Happiness," but they left it up to later generations to define exactly what the phrase "life, liberty, and the pursuit of happiness" means. And each generation has wrestled with the question of how much power government should have to fulfill that purpose—in other words, how Americans should govern themselves. ■ The essays in this section reveal some of the ways in which Americans have confronted this question. As a group, these essays provide various perspectives on the relationship between a government and its citizens. They also suggest that Americans are still trying to answer the same questions Thomas Jefferson and others raised when they signed the Declaration of Independence more than 225 years ago.

CON-TEXT

"The Declaration of Independence"

1 When in the Course of human events, it becomes necessary for one people to dissolve the political bands which have connected them with another, and to assume among the powers of the earth, the separate and equal station to which the Laws of Nature and of Nature's God entitle them, a decent respect to the opinions of mankind requires that they should declare the causes which impel them to the separation.

We hold these truths to be self-evident, that all men are created equal, that they are endowed by their Creator with certain unalienable Rights, that among these are Life, Liberty and the pursuit of Happiness. That to secure these rights, Governments are instituted among Men, deriving their just powers from the consent of the governed. That whenever any Form of Government becomes destructive of these ends it is the Right of the People to alter or to abolish it, and to institute new Government, laying its foundation on such principles and organizing its powers in such form, as to them shall seem most likely to effect their Safety and Happiness. Prudence, indeed, will dictate that Governments long established should not be changed for light and transient causes; and accordingly all experience has shown, that mankind are more disposed to suffer, while evils are sufferable, than to right themselves by abolishing the forms to which they are accustomed. But when a long train of abuses and usurpations, pursuing invariably the same Object evinces a design to reduce them under absolute Despotism, it is their right, it is their duty, to throw off such Government, and to provide new Guards for their future security. Such has been the patient sufferance of these Colonies; and such is now the necessity which constrains them to alter their former Systems of Government....

① First Inaugural Address

THOMAS JEFFERSON

Most Americans probably think of Thomas Jefferson as the primary author of the Declaration of Independence (see page 567), but he was also a philosopher, political theorist, architect, inventor, and scientist whose many accomplishments include the founding of the University of Virginia. And he served as president for eight years during a time of unprecedented growth and change for the young nation. When he took the oath of office on March 4th, 1801, Jefferson gave the following speech. He had been elected in the midst of deep divisions among Americans about the power and role of the federal government. A few years earlier President Washington ordered federal troops to suppress an insurrection in Pennsylvania that came to be known as the Whiskey Rebellion (because the rebels opposed a federal tax on whiskey). It was the first time the federal government used its power in this way, and it caused intense controversy that continued through the election of 1800. That presidential campaign was especially bitter, characterized by vicious rumors and slanderous personal smears. The political parties accused each other of such outrageous acts as burning churches. Although Jefferson won by a wide margin over incumbent John Adams, the controversy over the power of the federal government continued through Jefferson's presidency. In this inaugural address, you will encounter references to the bitter divisions among Americans that characterized his era. But you will also hear an argument for Jefferson's vision of what role the U.S. government should play in the lives of American citizens. If much of what Jefferson said on that day in 1801 sounds familiar, it may be because Americans are still arguing about these important questions.

THOMAS JEFFERSON, First Inaugural Address

1 Friends and fellow-citizens, called upon to undertake the duties of the first executive office of our country, I avail myself of the presence of that portion of my fellow-citizens which is here assembled to express my grateful thanks for the favor with which they have been pleased to look toward me, to declare a sincere consciousness that the task is above my talents, and that I approach it with those anxious and awful presentiments which the greatness of the charge and the weakness of my powers so justly inspire. A rising nation, spread over a wide and fruitful land, traversing all the seas with the rich productions of their industry, engaged in commerce with nations who feel power and forget right, advancing rapidly to destinies beyond the reach of mortal eye—when I contemplate these transcendent objects, and see the honor, the happiness, and the hopes of this beloved country committed to the issue and the auspices of this day, I shrink from the contemplation, and humble myself before the magnitude of the undertaking. Utterly, indeed, should I despair did not the presence of many whom I here see remind me that in the other high authorities provided by our Constitution I shall find resources of wisdom, of virtue, and

of zeal on which to rely under all difficulties. To you, then, gentlemen, who are charged with the sovereign functions of legislation, and to those associated with you, I look with encouragement for that guidance and support which may enable us to steer with safety the vessel in which we are all embarked amidst the conflicting elements of a troubled world.

During the contest of opinion through which we have passed the animation of discussions and of exertions has sometimes worn an aspect which might impose on strangers unused to think freely and to speak and to write what they think; but this being now decided by the voice of the nation, announced according to the rules of the Constitution, all will, of course, arrange themselves under the will of the law, and unite in common efforts for the common good. All, too, will bear in mind this sacred principle, that though the will of the majority is in all cases to prevail, that will to be rightful must be reasonable; that the minority possess their equal rights, which equal law must protect, and to violate would be oppression. Let us, then, fellow-citizens, unite with one heart and one mind. Let us restore to social intercourse that harmony and affection without which liberty and even life itself are but dreary things. And let us reflect that, having banished from our land that religious intolerance under which mankind so long bled and suffered, we have yet gained little if we countenance a political intolerance as despotic, as wicked, and capable of as bitter and bloody persecutions. During the throes and convulsions of the ancient world, during the agonizing spasms of infuriated man, seeking through blood and slaughter his long-lost liberty, it was not wonderful that the agitation of the billows should reach even this distant and peaceful shore; that this should be more felt and feared by some and less by others, and should divide opinions as to measures of safety. But every difference of opinion is not a difference of principle. We have called by different names brethren of the same principle.

We are all Republicans, we are all Federalists. If there be any among us who would wish to dissolve this Union or to change its republican form, let them stand undisturbed as monuments of the safety with which error of opinion may be tolerated where reason is left free to combat it. I know, indeed, that some honest men fear that a republican government can not be strong, that this Government is not strong enough; but would the honest patriot, in the full tide of successful experiment, abandon a government which has so far kept us free and firm on the theoretic and visionary fear that this Government, the world's best hope, may by possibility want energy to preserve itself? I trust not. I believe this, on the contrary, the strongest Government on earth. I believe it the only one where every man, at the call of

© Corbis

CONTEXT

In this passage Jefferson refers to the bitter political campaign of 1800 in which he was elected president (see the introduction to this reading on page 568). In our own time, politicians and voters routinely complain that political campaigns have become meaner and uglier and the political disagreements deeper. But many Americans continue to embrace the principle that Jefferson articulates here. In his own inaugural address, delivered on January 27, 2009, President Barack Obama referred to the bitter political campaign in which he was involved. Compare his words to Jefferson's, which were spoken more than 200 years apart:

On this day, we gather because we have chosen hope over fear, unity of purpose over conflict and discord. On this day, we come to proclaim an end to the petty grievances and false promises, the recriminations and worn out dogmas, that for far too long have strangled our politics. We remain a young nation, but in the words of Scripture, the time has come to set aside childish things. The time has come to reaffirm our enduring spirit; to choose our better history; to carry forward that precious gift, that noble idea, passed on from generation to generation: the God-given promise that all are equal, all are free, and all deserve a chance to pursue their full measure of happiness.

CONTEXT

The question of how much political power should be wielded by the central government and how much should be retained by the individual states dates back to the very beginnings of the United States as a sovereign nation. In Jefferson's day, this question, which he refers to in this passage in paragraph 4, was still relatively new, because no other democratic government existed in the Western world. Americans were trying to figure out how to balance power in this new political experiment. Jefferson himself was wary of giving the federal government too much power, as he indicates at several points in this speech. But the question has not been resolved. The so-called Tea Party Movement that emerged in the United States in 2009 to oppose federal reform of the nation's health care system was founded on a basic belief that the federal government has limited power over states and individual citizens. In opposing the federal government Tea Party activists made some of the same arguments in favor of state's rights that were being made while Jefferson was president.

the law, would fly to the standard of the law, and would meet invasions of the public order as his own personal concern. Sometimes it is said that man can not be trusted with the government of himself. Can he, then, be trusted with the government of others? Or have we found angels in the forms of Kings to govern him? Let history answer this question.

Let us, then, with courage and confidence pursue our own Federal and Republican principles, our attachment to union and representative government. Kindly separated by nature and a wide ocean from the exterminating havoc of one quarter of the globe; too high-minded to endure the degradations of the others; possessing a chosen country, with room enough for our descendants to the thousandth and thousandth generation; entertaining a due sense of our equal right to the use of our own faculties, to the acquisitions of our own industry, to honor and confidence from our fellow-citizens, resulting not from birth, but from our actions and their sense of them; enlightened by a benign religion, professed, indeed, and practiced in various forms, yet all of them inculcating honesty, truth, temperance, gratitude, and the love of man; acknowledging and adoring an overruling Providence, which by all its dispensations proves that it delights in the happiness of man here and his greater happiness

hereafter—with all these blessings, what more is necessary to make us a happy and a prosperous people? Still one thing more, fellow-citizens—a wise and frugal Government, which shall restrain men from injuring one another, shall leave them otherwise free to regulate their own pursuits of industry and improvement, and shall not take from the mouth of labor the bread it has earned. This is the sum of good government, and this is necessary to close the circle of our felicities.

About to enter, fellow-citizens, on the exercise of duties which comprehend everything dear and valuable to you, it is proper you should understand what I deem the essential principles of our Government, and consequently those which ought to shape its Administration. I will compress them within the narrowest compass they will bear, stating the general principle, but not all its limitations. Equal and exact justice to all men, of whatever state or persuasion, religious or political; peace, commerce, and honest friendship with all nations, entangling alliances with none; the support of the State governments in all their rights, as the most competent administrations for our domestic concerns and the surest bulwarks against antirepublican tendencies; the preservation of the General Government in its whole constitutional vigor, as the sheet anchor of our peace at home and safety abroad; a jealous care of the right of election by the people—a mild and safe corrective of abuses which are lopped by the sword of revolution where peaceable remedies are unprovided; absolute acquiescence in the decisions of the majority, the vital principle of republics, from which is no appeal but to force, the vital principle and immediate parent of despotism; a well disciplined militia, our best reliance in peace and for the first moments of war till regulars may relieve them; the supremacy of the civil over the military authority; economy in the public expense, that labor may be lightly burthened; the honest payment of our debts and sacred preservation of the public faith; encouragement of agriculture, and of commerce as its handmaid; the diffusion of information and arraignment of all abuses at the bar of the public reason; freedom of religion; freedom of the press, and freedom of person under the protection of the habeas corpus, and trial by juries impartially selected. These principles form the bright constellation which has gone before us and guided our steps through an age of revolution and reformation. The wisdom of our sages and blood of our heroes have been devoted to their attainment. They should be the creed of our political faith, the text of civic instruction, the touchstone by which to try the services of those we trust; and should we wander from them in moments of error or of alarm, let us hasten to retrace our steps and to regain the road which alone leads to peace, liberty, and safety.

5 I repair, then, fellow-citizens, to the post you have assigned me. With experience enough in subordinate offices to have seen the difficulties of this the greatest of all, I have learnt to expect that it will rarely fall to the lot of imperfect man to retire from this station with the reputation and the favor which bring him into it. Without pretensions to that high confidence you reposed in **our first and greatest revolutionary character**, whose preeminent services had entitled him to the first place in his country's love and destined for him the fairest page in the volume of faithful history, I ask so much confidence only as may give firmness and effect to the legal administration of your affairs. I shall often go wrong through defect of judgment. When right, I shall often be thought wrong by those whose positions will not command a view of the whole ground. I ask your indulgence for my own errors, which will never be intentional, and your support against the errors of others, who may condemn what they would not if seen in all its parts. The approbation implied by your suffrage is a great consolation to me for the past, and my future solicitude will be to retain the good opinion of those who have bestowed it in advance, to conciliate that of others by doing them all the good in my power, and to be instrumental to the happiness and freedom of all.

Relying, then, on the patronage of your good will, I advance with obedience to the work, ready to retire from it whenever you become sensible how much better choice it is in your power to make. And may that Infinite Power which rules the destinies of the universe lead our councils to what is best, and give them a favorable issue for your peace and prosperity.

Our first and greatest revolutionary character is a reference to George Washington (1732–1799), the first president of the United States.

Questions for Discussion

1. Jefferson devotes the first lines of his address to describing the magnitude of his task as president and the "weakness" of his own powers to accomplish that task. Why do you think he begins his speech in this way? What might he gain by doing so?

2. What vision of government does Jefferson offer in this speech? How does he justify this vision? To what extent do you think Americans today share this vision? Explain, citing specific passages from his speech to support your answer.

3. In paragraph 4, Jefferson lists what he calls "the essential principles of our Government." How effectively does this list help him make his main argument? How relevant is this list today?

4. At several points in this essay, Jefferson refers to himself as weak, humbled, and imperfect. How would you describe the ethos that Jefferson creates in this speech? What impact did his ethos have on you as a reader? What impact do you think it might have had on citizens of his day? Does his ethos strengthen or weaken his argument about government power? Explain.

5. What assumptions do you think Jefferson makes about Americans? Do you think his assumptions would be relevant today? Why or why not?

6. This speech might be characterized as an argument to reconcile differences (see pages 14–17). How effective do you think Jefferson's argument is? How well does it resolve the differences he refers to early in the speech?

② Where Did 'We' Go?

THOMAS FRIEDMAN

Thomas L. Friedman is one of the nation's most respected journalists. He shares his ideas about politics, culture, and economics in his popular column in the *New York Times* as well as in his best-selling books, including *Hot, Flat, and Crowded: Why We Need a Green Revolution and How It Can Renew America* (2009). Political leaders seek his council, and millions of readers pay attention to his opinions. It is safe to say that Friedman's voice is an influential one in the ongoing discussions about important issues facing the nation. But as he reveals in the following essay, which appeared in his column in the *New York Times* in 2009, Friedman is both worried and angry about the nature of political discussions in the United States today. The title of his essay suggests that he believes Americans have lost a sense of community, and he blames that loss on many factors. More important, he is worried about what this loss of "we" means for the nation's future. In sharing these concerns, Friedman raises difficult questions about how we should conduct our political affairs in a nation founded on the idea of liberty and free expression. He reminds us that political power can be as much a matter of what we say as of what we do, and he argues that Americans need to talk differently to one another about political matters if they are to retain a sense of their national identity.

THOMAS FRIEDMAN, "Where Did 'We' Go?"

1 I hate to write about this, but I have actually been to this play before and it is really disturbing.

I was in Israel interviewing Prime Minister **Yitzhak Rabin** just before he was assassinated in 1995. We had a beer in his office. He needed one. I remember the ugly mood in Israel then—a mood in which extreme right-wing settlers and politicians were doing all they could to delegitimize Rabin, who was committed to trading land for peace as part of the Oslo accords. They questioned his authority. They accused him of treason. They created pictures depicting him as a Nazi SS officer, and they shouted death threats at rallies. His political opponents winked at it all.

And in so doing they created a poisonous political environment that was interpreted by one right-wing Jewish nationalist as a license to kill Rabin—he must have heard, "God will be on your side"—and so he did.

Others have already remarked on this analogy, but I want to add my voice because the parallels to Israel then and America today turn my stomach: I have no problem with any of the substantive criticism of President Obama from the right or left. But something very dangerous is happening. Criticism from the far right has begun tipping over into delegitimation and creating the same kind of climate here that existed in Israel on the eve of the Rabin assassination.

5 What kind of madness is it that someone would create a poll on Facebook asking respondents, "Should Obama be killed?" The choices were: "No, Maybe, Yes, and Yes if he cuts my health care." The Secret Service is now investigating. I hope they put the jerk in

Yitzhak Rabin (1922–1995) served as the Prime Minister of Israel from 1974 to 1977 and again from 1992 to 1995, when he was assassinated by a right-wing Israeli activist who opposed Rabin's support for a peace agreement between Israel and the Palestine Liberation Organization.

CONTEXT

In this passage (see paragraph 9) Friedman refers to several incidents in 2009 that he believes reflect the intensely divided and increasingly harsh political climate in the United States. In January 2009, Republican Congressman Joe Wilson from South Carolina shouted "You lie!" during President Obama's State of the Union Address in response to one of Obama's statements about his proposal to reform health care in the United States. Although Wilson later apologized and was roundly criticized for being so disrespectful to a president, many critics of Obama praised Wilson as a hero. During the 2008 presidential campaign, some people began to question whether Obama was a legitimate U.S. citizen; some of these so-called "birthers" charged that Obama was born in Kenya (his father's birthplace) rather than Hawaii, and others claimed he was born in Indonesia, where he attended school for a short time. As Friedman notes, such unfounded charges were treated as legitimate by some mainstream conservative politicians and media figures, including Lou Dobbs, the host of a popular business television program on CNN, whom Friedman mentions in this paragraph.

jail and throw away the key because this is exactly what was being done to Rabin.

Even if you are not worried that someone might draw from these vitriolic attacks a

COMPLICATION

In recent years many politicians, critics, and scholars have complained that the dramatic growth of mass media, including cable television news shows, blogs, political talk radio, and social media such as Twitter and Facebook to report news events, have influenced the political process in the United States in detrimental ways (see paragraph 12). Ken Auletta, a respected journalist who reports on the news media, wrote in 2010,

> Between 2006 and 2008, daily online news use jumped by a third, which meant that one-quarter of Americans were getting the news online. As media outlets multiply and it becomes easier to disseminate information on the Web and on cable, the news cycle is getting shorter—to the point that there is no pause, only the constancy of the Web and the endless argument of cable. This creates pressure to entertain or perish, which has fed the press's dominant bias: not pro-liberal or pro-conservative but pro-conflict. The historian Michael Beschloss recalls that after President John F. Kennedy spoke to the nation about the Cuban missile crisis, in October, 1962, "the networks immediately went back to their normal programming." Today, he says, "pundits comment immediately on Presidential speeches, and cable news dissects the speech for hours. A President doesn't have the unchallenged voice he once had." The transformation of media has not only undermined the imperial institutions of the mainstream media; it has undermined the imperial Presidency.

SOURCE: "Non-Stop News." *New Yorker* Magazine (2010).

license to try to hurt the president, you have to be worried about what is happening to American politics more broadly.

Our leaders, even the president, can no longer utter the word "we" with a straight face. There is no more "we" in American politics at a time when "we" have these huge problems— the deficit, the recession, health care, climate change and wars in Iraq and Afghanistan— that "we" can only manage, let alone fix, if there is a collective "we" at work.

Sometimes I wonder whether George H.W. Bush, president "41," will be remembered as our last "legitimate" president. The right impeached Bill Clinton and hounded him from Day 1 with the bogus Whitewater "scandal." George W. Bush was elected under a cloud because of the Florida voting mess, and his critics on the left never let him forget it.

And Mr. Obama is now having his legitimacy attacked by a concerted campaign from the right fringe. They are using everything from smears that he is a closet "socialist" to calling him a "liar" in the middle of a joint session of Congress to fabricating doubts about his birth in America and whether he is even a citizen. And these attacks are not just coming from the fringe. Now they come from Lou Dobbs on CNN and from members of the House of Representatives.

10 Again, hack away at the man's policies and even his character all you want. I know politics is a tough business. But if we destroy the legitimacy of another president to lead or to pull the country together for what most Americans want most right now—nation-building at home—we are in serious trouble. We can't go 24 years without a legitimate president—not without being swamped by the problems that we will end up postponing because we can't address them rationally.

The American political system was, as the saying goes, "designed by geniuses so it could be run by idiots." But a cocktail of political and technological trends have converged in the last decade that are making it possible for the idiots of all political stripes to overwhelm and paralyze the genius of our system.

Those factors are: the wild excess of money in politics; the **gerrymandering** of political districts, making them permanently Republican or Democratic and erasing the political middle; a 24/7 cable news cycle that makes all politics a daily battle of tactics that overwhelm strategic thinking; and a blogosphere that at its best enriches our debates, adding new checks on the establishment, and at its worst coarsens our debates to a whole new level, giving a new power to anonymous slanderers to send lies around the world. Finally, on top of it all, we now have a permanent presidential campaign that encourages all partisanship, all the time among our leading politicians.

I would argue that together these changes add up to a difference of degree that is a difference in kind—a different kind of American political scene that makes me wonder whether we can seriously discuss serious issues any longer and make decisions on the basis of the national interest.

We can't change this overnight, but what we can change, and must change, is people crossing the line between criticizing the president and tacitly encouraging the unthinkable and the unforgivable.

Gerrymandering refers to the process by which political parties who are in power redraw the boundaries of congressional districts to give them an advantage in upcoming elections.

Questions for Discussion

1. In the beginning of this essay, Friedman compares the political climate in the United States in 2009 to the tense situation in Israel in 1995, when Israel was negotiating a controversial peace settlement with the Palestine Liberation Organization. Do you think Friedman makes a valid comparison? Why or why not? How effective is this comparison in setting up Friedman's argument?

2. Friedman claims that there is no longer any "we" in American politics. What does he mean? How does he support such a claim? Do you think he is right? Why or why not? What evidence could you present to counter Friedman's claim?

3. How does Friedman explain the lack of political decorum and tolerance in the United States today? Do you find his explanation persuasive? Why or why not?

4. Friedman's language and tone are frequently passionate in this essay. In paragraph 5, for example, he mentions a person who created a Facebook poll that asked for responses to the question, "Should Obama be killed?"; he writes of that person, "I hope they put the jerk in jail and throw away the key." What impact do you think Friedman expected such language to have on his readers? What effect did it have on you? Do you find such language appropriate in this context? Is it effective in helping Friedman make his argument? Explain.

5. What solution does Friedman offer to the problems he describes with the current political climate in the United States? Do you think his solution can work? Explain.

6. What do you think Friedman's essay suggests about the nature of American democracy? What does it suggest about the challenges of American democracy? Are these challenges different today than in the early years of the United States? Explain.

③ | Letter from a Birmingham Jail

MARTIN LUTHER KING, JR.

Martin Luther King, Jr. (1929–1968) was the most important leader of the movement to secure civil rights for black Americans during the mid-twentieth century. Ordained a Baptist minister in his father's church in Atlanta, Georgia, King became the founder and director of the Southern Christian Leadership Conference, an organization he continued to lead until his assassination in 1968. He first came to national attention by organizing a boycott of the buses in Montgomery, Alabama (1955–1956). An advocate of nonviolence who was jailed fourteen times in the course of his work for civil rights, King was instrumental in helping secure the passage of the Civil Rights Bill in 1963. His efforts on behalf of civil rights led to many awards, most notably the Nobel Peace Prize in 1964. "Letter From a Birmingham Jail" was written in 1963, when King was jailed for eight days as the result of his campaign against segregation in Birmingham, Alabama. In the letter, King responds to white clergymen who had criticized him for breaking the law. But "Letter From a Birmingham Jail" is more than a rebuttal of criticism; it is a well-reasoned and carefully argued defense of civil disobedience as a means of securing civil liberties. In justifying his refusal to obey what he believed were unjust laws, King invokes a high moral standard by which to judge a government's actions. His famous essay thus should prompt you to consider the limits of governmental power and the responsibilities of citizens in supporting or opposing that power.

MARTIN LUTHER KING, JR., "Letter from a Birmingham Jail"

April 16, 1963

My Dear Fellow Clergymen:

1 While confined here in the Birmingham city jail, I came across your recent statement calling my present activities "unwise and untimely." Seldom do I pause to answer criticism of my work and ideas. If I sought to answer all the criticisms that cross my desk, my secretaries would have little time for anything other than such correspondence in the course of the day, and I would have no time for constructive work. But since I feel that you are men of genuine good will and that your criticisms are sincerely put forth, I want to try to answer your statement in what I hope will be patient and reasonable terms.

I think I should indicate why I am here in Birmingham, since you have been influenced by the view which argues against "outsiders coming in." I have the honor of serving as president of the Southern Christian Leadership Conference, an organization operating in every southern state, with headquarters in Atlanta, Georgia. We have some eighty-five affiliated organizations across the South, and one of them is the Alabama Christian Movement for Human Rights. Frequently we share staff, educational, and financial resources with our affiliates. Several months ago the affiliate here in Birmingham asked us to be on call to engage in a nonviolent direct-action program if such were deemed necessary. We readily consented, and when the hour came we lived up to our promise. So I, along with several members of my staff, am here because I was invited here. I am here because I have organizational ties here.

But more basically, I am in Birmingham because injustice is here. Just as the prophets of the eighth century B.C. left their villages and carried their "thus saith the Lord" far beyond the boundaries of their home towns, and just as the Apostle Paul left his village of Tarsus and carried the gospel of Jesus Christ to the far corners of the Greco-Roman world, so am I compelled to carry the gospel of freedom beyond my own home town. Like Paul, I must constantly respond to the Macedonian call for aid.

Moreover, I am cognizant of the interrelatedness of all communities and states. I cannot sit idly by in Atlanta and not be concerned about what happens in Birmingham. Injustice anywhere is a threat to justice everywhere. We are caught in an inescapable network of mutuality, tied in a single garment of destiny. Whatever affects one directly, affects all indirectly. Never again can we afford to live with the narrow, provincial, "outside agitator" idea. Anyone who lives inside the United States can never be considered an outsider anywhere within its bounds.

5 You deplore the demonstrations taking place in Birmingham. But your statement, I am sorry to say, fails to express a similar concern for the conditions that brought about the demonstrations. I am sure that none of you would want to rest content with the superficial kind of social analysis that deals merely with effects and does not grapple with underlying causes. It is unfortunate that demonstrations are taking place in Birmingham, but it is even more unfortunate that the city's white power structure left the Negro community with no alternative.

In any nonviolent campaign, there are four basic steps: collection of the facts to

Bettmann/Corbis

determine whether injustices exist; negotiation; self-purification; and direct action. We have gone through all these steps in Birmingham. There can be no gainsaying the fact that racial injustice engulfs this community. Birmingham is probably the most thoroughly segregated city in the United States. Its ugly record of brutality is widely

CONTEXT

Inspired by the ideas of Mahatma Gandhi, whose nonviolent movement helped end the British rule of India, King developed a philosophy of nonviolent resistance based on the Christian ideal of brotherly love. In an essay published in 1960, King wrote that "the Christian doctrine of love operating through the Gandhian method of nonviolence was one of the most potent weapons available to oppressed people in their struggle for freedom." In a related essay, King responded to a critique of pacifism by Christian philosopher Reinhard Neibuhr by arguing that "pacifism is not unrealistic submission to evil power, as Niebuhr contends. It is rather a courageous confrontation of evil by the power of love." King's philosophy was put to the test in 1956 during the bus boycott in Montgomery, Alabama, during which blacks and civil rights activists were harassed and sometimes physically attacked. In the end, King's nonviolent protest movement resulted in a Supreme Court decision that declared segregation on public buses unconstitutional.

known. Negroes have experienced grossly unjust treatment in courts. There have been more unsolved bombings of Negro homes and churches in Birmingham than in any other city in the nation. These are the hard, brutal facts of the case. On the basis of these conditions, Negro leaders sought to negotiate with the city fathers. But the latter consistently refused to engage in good-faith negotiation.

Then, last September, came the opportunity to talk with leaders of Birmingham's economic community. In the course of the negotiations, certain promises were made by the merchants—for example, to remove the stores' humiliating racial signs. On the basis of these promises, the Reverend Fred Shuttlesworth and the leaders of the Alabama Christian Movement for Human Rights agreed to a moratorium on all demonstrations. As the weeks and months went by, we realized that we were the victims of a broken promise. A few signs, briefly removed, returned; the others remained.

As in so many past experiences, our hopes had been blasted, and the shadow of deep disappointment settled upon us. We had no alternative except to prepare for direct action, whereby we would present our very bodies as means of laying our case before the conscience of the local and the national community. Mindful of the difficulties involved, we decided to undertake a process of self-purification. We began a series of workshops on nonviolence, and we repeatedly asked ourselves: "Are you able to accept blows without retaliating?" "Are you able to endure the ordeal of jail?" We decided to schedule our direct-action program for the Easter season, realizing that except for Christmas, this is the main shopping period of the year. Knowing that a strong economic-withdrawal program would be the byproduct of direct action, we felt that this would be the best time to bring pressure to bear on the merchants for the needed change.

Then it occurred to us that Birmingham's mayoral election was coming up in March, and we speedily decided to postpone action until after election day. When we discovered that the Commissioner of Public Safety, Eugene "Bull" Connor, had piled up enough votes to be in the run-off, we decided again to postpone action until the day after the run-off so that the demonstrations could not be used to cloud the issues. Like many others, we waited to see Mr. Connor defeated, and to this end we endured postponement after postponement. Having aided in this community need, we felt that our direct-action program could be delayed no longer.

10 You may well ask, "Why direct action? Why sit-ins, marches, and so forth? Isn't negotiation a better path?" You are quite right in calling for negotiation. Indeed, this is the very purpose of direct action. Nonviolent direct action seeks to create such a crisis and foster such a tension that a community which has constantly refused to negotiate is forced to confront the issue. It seeks so to dramatize the issue that it can no longer be ignored. My citing the creation of tension as part of the work of the nonviolent resister may sound rather shocking. But I must confess that I am not afraid of the word "tension." I have earnestly opposed violent tension, but there is a type of constructive, nonviolent tension which is necessary for growth. Just as Socrates felt that it was necessary to create a tension in the mind so that individuals could rise from the bondage of myths and half-truths to the unfettered realm of creative analysis and objective appraisal, so must we see the need for nonviolent gadflies to create the kind of tension in society that will help men rise from the dark depths of prejudice and racism to the majestic heights of understanding and brotherhood.

The purpose of our direct-action program is to create a situation so crisis-packed that it will inevitably open the door to negotiation. I therefore concur with you in your call for negotiation. Too long has our beloved Southland been bogged down in a tragic effort to live in monologue rather than dialogue.

One of the basic points in your statement is that the action that I and my associates have taken in Birmingham is untimely. Some have asked: "Why didn't you give the new city administration time to act?" The only answer that I can give to this query is that the new Birmingham administration must be prodded about as much as the outgoing one, before it will act. We are sadly mistaken if we feel that the election of Albert Boutwell as mayor will bring the millennium to Birmingham. While Mr. Boutwell is a much more gentle person than Mr. Connor, they are both segregationists, dedicated to maintenance of the status quo. I have hoped that Mr. Boutwell will be reasonable enough to see the futility of massive resistance to desegregation. But he will not see this without pressure from devotees of civil rights. My friends, I must say to you that we have not made a single gain in civil rights without determined legal and nonviolent pressure. Lamentably, it is an historical fact that privileged groups seldom give up their privileges voluntarily. Individuals may see the moral light and voluntarily give up their unjust posture; but, as **Reinhold Niebuhr** has reminded us, groups tend to be more immoral than individuals.

We know through painful experience that freedom is never voluntarily given by the oppressor; it must be demanded by the oppressed. Frankly, I have yet to engage in a direct-action campaign that was "well timed" in the view of those who have not suffered unduly from the disease of segregation. For years now I have heard the word "Wait!" It rings in the ear of every Negro with piercing familiarity. This "Wait" has almost always meant "Never." We must come to see, with one of our distinguished jurists, that "justice too long delayed is justice denied."

We have waited for more than 340 years for our constitutional and God-given rights. The nations of Asia and Africa are moving with jetlike speed toward gaining political independence, but we still creep at horse-and-buggy pace toward gaining a cup of coffee at a lunch counter. Perhaps it is easy for those who have never felt the stinging darts of segregation to say, "Wait." But when you have seen vicious mobs lynch your mothers and fathers at will and drown your sisters and brothers at whim; when you have seen hate-filled policemen curse, kick, and even kill your black brothers and sisters; when you see the vast majority of your twenty million Negro brothers smothering in an airtight cage of poverty in the midst of an affluent society; when you suddenly find your tongue twisted and your speech stammering as you seek to explain to your six-year-old daughter why she can't go to the public amusement park that has just been advertised on television, and see tears welling up in her eyes when she is told that Funtown is closed to colored children, and see ominous clouds of inferiority beginning to form in her little mental sky, and see her beginning to distort her personality by developing an unconscious bitterness toward white people; when you have to concoct an answer for a five-year-old son who is asking, "Daddy, why do white people treat colored people so mean?"; when you take a cross-country drive and find it necessary to sleep night after night in the uncomfortable corners of your automobile because no motel will accept you; when you are humiliated day in and day out by nagging signs reading "white" and "colored"; when your first name becomes "nigger," your middle name becomes "boy" (however old you are) and your last name becomes "John," and your wife and mother are never given the respected title "Mrs."; when you are harried by day and haunted by night by the fact that you are a Negro, living constantly at tiptoe stance, never quite knowing what to expect next, and are plagued with inner fears and outer resentments; when you are forever fighting a degenerating sense of "nobodiness"—then you will understand why we find it difficult to wait. There comes a time when the cup of endurance runs over, and men are no longer willing to be plunged into the abyss of despair. I hope, sirs, you can

Reinhold Niebuhr was a Protestant theologian who explored how Christianity related to modern politics.

Bettmann/Corbis

understand our legitimate and unavoidable impatience.

15 You express a great deal of anxiety over our willingness to break laws. This is certainly a legitimate concern. Since we so diligently urge people to obey the Supreme Court's decision of 1954 outlawing segregation in

the public schools, at first glance it may seem rather paradoxical for us consciously to break laws. One may well ask: "How can you advocate breaking some laws and obeying others?" The answer lies in the fact that there are two types of laws; just and unjust. I would be the first to advocate obeying just laws. One has not only a legal but a moral responsibility to obey just laws. Conversely, one has a moral responsibility to disobey unjust laws. I would agree with St. Augustine that "an unjust law is no law at all."

Now, what is the difference between the two? How does one determine whether a law is just or unjust? A just law is a man-made code that squares with the moral law or the law of God. An unjust law is a code that is out of harmony with the moral law. To put it in the terms of St. Thomas Aquinas: An unjust law is a human law that is not rooted in eternal law and natural law. Any law that uplifts human personality is just. Any law that degrades human personality is unjust. All segregation statutes are unjust because segregation distorts the soul and damages the personality. It gives the segregator a false sense of superiority and the segregated a false sense of inferiority. Segregation, to use the terminology of the Jewish philosopher Martin Buber, substitutes an "I–it" relationship for an "I–thou" relationship and ends up relegating persons to the status of things. Hence segregation is not only politically, economically, and sociologically unsound, it is morally wrong and sinful. Paul Tillich has said that sin is segregation. Is not segregation an existential expression of man's tragic separation, his awful estrangement, his terrible sinfulness? Thus it is that I can urge men to obey the 1954 decision of the Supreme Court, for it is morally right; and I can urge them to disobey segregation ordinances, for they are morally wrong.

CONTEXT

On May 17, 1954, Chief Justice Earl Warren read the decision of the unanimous U.S. Supreme Court in the case of *Brown v. Board of Education of Topeka, Kansas,* which overturned the previous policy of providing "separate but equal" education for black children:

> We come then to the question presented: Does segregation of children in public schools solely on the basis of race, even though the physical facilities and other "tangible" factors may be equal, deprive the children of the minority group of equal educational opportunities? We believe that it does....We conclude that in the field of public education the doctrine of "separate but equal" has no place. Separate educational facilities are inherently unequal. Therefore, we hold that the plaintiffs and others similarly situated for whom the actions have been brought are, by reason of the segregation complained of, deprived of the equal protection of the laws guaranteed by the Fourteenth Amendment.

(For information about the Fourteenth Amendment, see the box on page 554.)

Let us consider a more concrete example of just and unjust laws. An unjust law is a code that a numerical or power majority group compels a minority group to obey but does not make binding on itself. This is *difference* made legal. By the same token, a just law is a code that a majority compels a minority to follow and that it is willing to follow itself. This is *sameness* made legal.

Let me give another explanation. A law is unjust if it is inflicted on a minority that, as a result of being denied the right to vote, had no part in enacting or devising the law. Who can say that the legislature of Alabama which set up that state's segregation laws was democratically elected? Throughout Alabama all sorts of devious methods are used to prevent Negroes from becoming registered voters, and there are some counties in which, even though Negroes constitute a majority of the population, not a single Negro is registered. Can any law enacted under such circumstances be considered democratically structured?

Sometimes a law is just on its face and unjust in its application. For instance, I have been arrested on a charge of parading without a permit. Now, there is nothing wrong in having an ordinance which requires a permit for a parade. But such an ordinance becomes unjust when it is used to maintain segregation and to deny citizens the First-Amendment privilege of peaceful assembly and protest.

20 I hope you are able to see the distinction I am trying to point out. In no sense do I advocate evading or defying the law, as would the rabid segregationist. That would lead to anarchy. One who breaks an unjust law must do so openly, lovingly, and with a willingness to accept the penalty. I submit that an individual who breaks a law that conscience tells him is unjust, and who willingly accepts the penalty of imprisonment in order to arouse the conscience of the community over its injustice, is in reality expressing the highest respect for law.

Of course, there is nothing new about this kind of civil disobedience. It was evidenced sublimely in the refusal of Shadrach, Meshach, and Abednego to obey the laws of **Nebuchadnezzar**, on the ground that a higher moral law was at stake. It was practiced superbly by the early Christians, who were willing to face hungry lions and the excruciating pain of chopping blocks rather than submit to certain unjust laws of the Roman Empire. To a degree, academic freedom is a reality today because Socrates practiced civil disobedience. In our own nation, the Boston Tea Party represented a massive act of civil disobedience.

We should never forget that everything Adolf Hitler did in Germany was "legal" and everything the **Hungarian freedom fighters** did in Hungary was "illegal." It was "illegal" to aid and comfort a Jew in Hitler's Germany. Even so, I am sure that, had I lived in Germany at the time, I would have aided and comforted my Jewish brothers. If today I lived in a Communist country where certain principles dear to the Christian faith are suppressed, I would openly advocate disobeying that country's anti-religious laws.

I must make two honest confessions to you, my Christian and Jewish brothers. First, I must confess that over the past few years I have been gravely disappointed with the white moderate. I have almost reached the regrettable conclusion that the Negro's great stumbling block in his stride toward freedom is not the White Citizen's Counciler or the Ku Klux Klanner, but the white moderate, who is more devoted to "order" than to justice; who prefers a negative peace which is the absence of tension to a positive peace which is the presence of justice; who constantly says, "I agree with you in the goal you seek, but I cannot agree with your methods of direct action"; who paternalistically believes he can set the timetable for another man's freedom; who lives by a mythical concept of time and who constantly advises the Negro to wait for a "more convenient season."

Nebuchadnezzar, King of Babylon, destroyed the temple at Jerusalem and brought the Jewish people into captivity. He set up a huge image in gold and commanded all to worship it. Shadrach, Meshach, and Abednego refused and were thrown into a fiery furnace from which they emerged unscathed. (See *Daniel* 3.)

In 1956 **Hungarian** citizens temporarily overthrew the communist dictatorship in their country. Unwilling to confront the Soviet Union, Western democracies stood by when the Red Army suppressed the revolt by force.

Shallow understanding from people of good will is more frustrating than absolute misunderstanding from people of ill will. Lukewarm acceptance is much more bewildering than outright rejection.

I had hoped that the white moderate would understand that law and order exist for the purpose of establishing justice and that when they fail in this purpose they become the dangerously structured dams that block the flow of social progress. I had hoped that the white moderate would understand that the present tension in the South is a necessary phase of the transition from an obnoxious negative peace, in which the Negro passively accepted his unjust plight, to a substantive and positive peace, in which all men will respect the dignity and worth of human personality. Actually, we who engage in nonviolent direct action are not the creators of tension. We merely bring to the surface the hidden tension that is already alive. We bring it out in the open, where it can be seen and dealt with. Like a boil that can never be cured so long as it is covered up but must be opened with all its ugliness to the natural medicines of air and light, injustice must be exposed, with all the tension its exposure creates, to the light of human conscience and the air of national opinion, before it can be cured.

25 In your statement you assert that our actions, even though peaceful, must be condemned because they precipitate violence. But is this a logical assertion? Isn't this like condemning a robbed man because his possession of money precipitated the evil act of robbery? Isn't this like condemning Socrates because his unswerving commitment to truth and his philosophical inquiries precipitated the act by the misguided populace in which they made him drink hemlock? Isn't this like condemning Jesus because his unique God-consciousness and never-ceasing devotion to God's will precipitated the evil act of crucifixion? We must come to see that, as the federal courts have consistently affirmed,

it is wrong to urge an individual to cease his efforts to gain his basic constitutional rights because the quest may precipitate violence. Society must protect the robbed and punish the robber.

I had also hoped that the white moderate would reject the myth concerning time in relation to the struggle for freedom. I have just received a letter from a white brother in Texas. He writes: "All Christians know that the colored people will receive equal rights eventually, but it is possible that you are in too great a religious hurry. It has taken Christianity almost two thousand years to accomplish what it has. The teachings of Christ take time to come to earth." Such an attitude stems from a tragic misconception of time, from the strangely irrational notion that there is something in the very flow of time that will inevitably cure all ills. Actually, time itself is neutral; it can be used either destructively or constructively. More and more I feel that the people of ill will have used time much more effectively than have the people of good will. We will have to repent in this generation not merely for the hateful words and actions of the bad people, but for the appalling silence of the good people. Human progress never rolls in on wheels of inevitability; it comes through the tireless efforts of men willing to be coworkers with God, and without this hard work, time itself becomes an ally of the forces of social stagnation. We must use time creatively, in the knowledge that the time is always ripe to do right. Now is the time to make real the promise of democracy and transform our pending national elegy into a creative psalm of brotherhood. Now is the time to lift our national policy from the quicksand of racial injustice to the solid rock of human dignity.

You speak of our activity in Birmingham as extreme. At first I was rather disappointed that fellow clergymen would see my nonviolent efforts as those of an extremist. I began thinking about the fact that I stand in the middle of two opposing forces in the Negro community. One is a force of complacency, made up in part of Negroes who, as a result of long years of oppression, are so drained of self-respect and a sense of "somebodiness" that they have adjusted to segregation; and in part of a few middle-class Negroes who, because of a degree of academic and economic security and because in some ways they profit by segregation, have become insensitive to the problems of the masses. The other force is one of bitterness and hatred, and it comes perilously close to advocating violence. It is expressed in the various black nationalist groups that are springing up across the nation, the largest and best-known being Elijah Muhammad's Muslim movement. Nourished by the Negro's frustration over the continued existence of racial discrimination, this movement is made up of people who have lost faith in America, who have absolutely repudiated Christianity, and who have concluded that the white man is an incorrigible "devil."

I have tried to stand between these two forces, saying that we need emulate neither the "do-nothingism" of the complacent nor the hatred and despair of the black nationalist. For there is the more excellent way of love and nonviolent protest. I am grateful to God that, through the influence of the Negro church, the way of nonviolence became an integral part of our struggle.

If this philosophy had not emerged, by now many streets of the South would, I am convinced, be flowing with blood. And I am further convinced that if our white brothers dismiss as "rabble-rousers" and "outside agitators" those of us who employ nonviolent direct action, and if they refuse to support our nonviolent efforts, millions of Negroes will, out of frustration and despair, seek solace and security in black-nationalist ideologies—a development that would inevitably lead to a frightening racial nightmare.

30 Oppressed people cannot remain oppressed forever. The yearning for freedom eventually manifests itself, and that is what has happened to the American Negro. Something within has reminded him of his birthright of freedom, and something without has reminded him that it can be gained. Consciously or unconsciously, he has been caught up by the *Zeitgeist*, and with his black brothers of Africa and his brown and yellow brothers of Asia, South America, and the Caribbean, the United States Negro is moving with a sense of great urgency toward the promised land of racial justice. If one recognizes this vital urge that has engulfed the Negro community, one should readily understand why public demonstrations are taking place. The Negro has many pent-up resentments and latent frustrations, and he must release them. So let him march; let him make prayer pilgrimages to the city hall; let him go on freedom rides—and try to understand why he must do so. If his repressed emotions are not released in nonviolent ways, they will seek expression through violence; this is not a threat but a fact of history. So I have not said to my people, "Get rid of your discontent." Rather, I have tried to say that this normal and healthy discontent can be channeled into the creative outlet of nonviolent direct action. And now this approach is being termed extremist.

But though I was initially disappointed at being categorized as an extremist, as I continued to think about the matter I gradually gained a measure of satisfaction from the label. Was not Jesus an extremist for love: "Love your enemies, bless them that curse you, do good to them that hate you, and

---

CONTEXT

Elijah Muhammad was a charismatic leader of the Nation of Islam who advocated an ideology of black superiority and urged blacks to reject Christianity, which he described as a tool for the enslavement of blacks by whites. Muhammad and his followers criticized King for his nonviolent philosophy, arguing that violent resistance is necessary to defeat white racism and achieve freedom for blacks. King's letter was addressed to white ministers who criticized his Birmingham campaign, but he surely knew that members of the Nation of Islam would read it, too.

pray for them which despitefully use you, and persecute you." Was not Amos an extremist for justice: "Let justice roll down like waters and righteousness like an everflowing stream." Was not Paul an extremist for the Christian gospel: "I bear in my body the marks of the Lord Jesus." Was not Martin Luther an extremist: "Here I stand; I cannot do otherwise, so help me God." And John Bunyan: "I will stay in jail to the end of my days before I make a butchery of my conscience." And Abraham Lincoln: "This nation cannot survive half slave and half free." And Thomas Jefferson: "We hold these truths to be self-evident, that all men are created equal...." So the question is not whether we will be extremists, but what kind of extremists we will be. Will we be extremists for hate or for love? Will we be extremists for the preservation of injustice or for the extension of justice? In that dramatic scene on Calvary's hill three men were crucified. We must never forget that all three were crucified for the same crime—the crime of extremism. Two were extremists for immorality, and thus fell below their environment. The other, Jesus Christ, was an extremist for love, truth, and goodness, and thereby rose above his environment. Perhaps the South, the nation, and the world are in dire need of creative extremists.

I had hoped that the white moderate would see this need. Perhaps I was too optimistic; perhaps I expected too much. I suppose I should have realized that few members of the oppressor race can understand the deep groans and passionate yearnings of the oppressed race, and still fewer have the vision to see that injustice must be rooted out by strong, persistent, and determined action. I am thankful, however, that some of our white brothers in the South have grasped the meaning of this social revolution and committed themselves to it. They are still all too few in quantity, but they are big in quality. Some—such as Ralph McGill, Lillian Smith, Harry Golden, James McBride Dabbs, Ann Braden, and Sarah Patton Boyle—have written about our struggle in eloquent and prophetic terms. Others have marched with us down nameless streets of the South. They have languished in filthy, roach-infested jails, suffering the abuse and brutality of policemen who view them as "dirty nigger-lovers." Unlike so many of their moderate brothers and sisters, they have recognized the urgency of the moment and sensed the need for powerful "action" antidotes to combat the disease of segregation.

Let me take note of my other major disappointment. I have been so greatly disappointed with the white church and its leadership. Of course, there are some notable exceptions. I am not unmindful of the fact that each of you has taken some significant stands on this issue. I commend you, Reverend Stallings, for your Christian stand on this past Sunday, in welcoming Negroes to your worship service on a nonsegregated basis. I commend the Catholic leaders of this state for integrating Spring Hill College several years ago.

But despite these notable exceptions, I must honestly reiterate that I have been disappointed with the church. I do not say this as one of those negative critics who can always find something wrong with the church. I say this as a minister of the gospel, who loves the church; who was nurtured in its bosom; who has been sustained by its

COMPLICATION

King describes a number of revered historical figures, including Thomas Jefferson, Abraham Lincoln, and even Jesus, as "extremists" for love and justice. In 1964, a year after King wrote this letter, Arizona Senator Barry Goldwater, then running for nomination as the Republican Party's candidate for president, said in a speech at the Republican Party's national convention, "Extremism in the defense of liberty is no vice"—a statement for which he was severely criticized by many. In 2001 the men who carried out the attacks on the United States on September 11 were routinely described in the press and by U.S. government officials as "extremists." To what extent are all of these uses of the term extremist similar? To what extent are they different? To what extent is the effectiveness of King's use of this term dependent on the time in which he wrote his essay?

spiritual blessings and who will remain true to it as long as the cord of life shall lengthen.

35 When I was suddenly catapulted into the leadership of the bus protest in Montgomery, Alabama, a few years ago, I felt we would be supported by the white church. I felt that the white ministers, priests, and rabbis of the South would be among our strongest allies. Instead, some have been outright opponents, refusing to understand the freedom movement and misrepresenting its leaders; all too many others have been more cautious than courageous and have remained silent behind the anesthetizing security of stained-glass windows.

In spite of my shattered dreams, I came to Birmingham with the hope that the white religious leadership of this community would see the justice of our cause and, with deep moral concern, would serve as the channel through which our just grievances could reach the power structure. I had hoped that each of you would understand. But again I have been disappointed....

There was a time when the church was very powerful—in the time when the early Christians rejoiced at being deemed worthy to suffer for what they believed. In those days the church was not merely a thermometer that recorded the ideas and principles of popular opinion; it was a thermostat that transformed the mores of society. Whenever the early Christians entered a town, the people in power became disturbed and immediately sought to convict the Christians for being "disturbers of the peace" and "outside agitators." But the Christians pressed on, in the conviction that they were "a colony of heaven," called to obey God rather than man. Small in number, they were big in commitment. They were too God-intoxicated to be "astronomically intimidated." By their effort and example they brought an end to such ancient evils as infanticide and gladiatorial contests.

Things are different now. So often the contemporary church is a weak, ineffectual voice with an uncertain sound. So often it is an archdefender of the status quo. Far from being disturbed by the presence of the church, the power structure of the average community is consoled by the church's silent—and often even vocal—sanction of things as they are.

But the judgment of God is upon the church as never before. If today's church does not recapture the sacrificial spirit of the early church, it will lose its authenticity, forfeit the loyalty of millions, and be dismissed as an irrelevant social club with no meaning for the twentieth century. Every day I meet young people whose disappointment with the church has turned into outright disgust.

40 Perhaps I have once again been too optimistic. Is organized religion too inextricably bound to the status quo to save our nation and the world? Perhaps I must turn my faith to the inner spiritual church, the church within the church, as the true *ekklesia* and the hope of the world. But again I am thankful to God that some noble souls from the ranks of organized religion have broken loose from the paralyzing chains of conformity and joined us as active partners in the struggle for freedom. They have left their secure congregations and walked the streets of Albany, Georgia, with us. They have gone down the highways of the South on torturous rides for freedom. Yes, they have gone to jail with us. Some have been dismissed from their churches, have lost the support of their bishops and fellow ministers. But they have acted in the faith that right defeated is stronger than evil triumphant. Their witness has been the spiritual salt that has preserved the true meaning of the gospel in these troubled times. They have carved a tunnel of hope through the dark mountain of disappointment.

I hope the church as a whole will meet the challenge of this decisive hour. But even if the church does not come to the aid of justice, I have no despair about the future. I have no fear about the outcome of our struggle in Birmingham, even if our motives are at present misunderstood. We will reach the goal

The word *ekklesia* is a Greek word meaning assembly, congregation, or church.

of freedom in Birmingham and all over the nation, because the goal of America is freedom. Abused and scorned though we may be, our destiny is tied up with America's destiny. Before the pilgrims landed at Plymouth, we were here. Before the pen of Jefferson etched the majestic words of the Declaration of Independence across the pages of history, we were here. For more than two centuries our forebears labored in this country without wages; they made cotton king; they built the homes of their masters while suffering gross injustice and shameful humiliation—and yet out of a bottomless vitality they continued to thrive and develop. If the inexpressible cruelties of slavery could not stop us, the opposition we now face will surely fail. We will win our freedom because the sacred heritage of our nation and the eternal will of God are embodied in our echoing demands.

Before closing I feel impelled to mention one other point in your statement that has troubled me profoundly. You warmly commended the Birmingham police force for keeping "order" and "preventing violence." I doubt that you would have so warmly commended the police force if you had seen its dogs sinking their teeth into unarmed, nonviolent Negroes. I doubt that you would so quickly commend the policemen if you were to observe their ugly and inhumane treatment of Negroes here in the city jail; if you were to watch them push and curse old Negro women and young Negro girls; if you were to see them slap and kick old Negro men and young boys; if you were to observe them, as they did on two occasions, refuse to give us food because we wanted to sing our grace together. I cannot join you in your praise of the Birmingham police department.

It is true that the police have exercised a degree of discipline in handling the demonstrators. In this sense they have conducted themselves rather "nonviolently" in public. But for what purpose? To preserve the evil system of segregation. Over the past few years I have consistently preached that nonviolence

demands that the means we use must be as pure as the ends we seek. I have tried to make clear that it is wrong to use immoral means to attain moral ends. But now I must affirm that it is just as wrong, or perhaps even more so, to use moral means to preserve immoral ends. Perhaps Mr. Connor and his policemen have been rather nonviolent in public, as was Chief Pritchett in Albany, Georgia, but they have used the moral means of nonviolence to maintain the immoral end of racial injustice. As T. S. Eliot has said, "The last temptation is the greatest treason: To do the right deed for the wrong reason."

I wish you had commended the Negro sit-inners and demonstrators of Birmingham for their sublime courage, their willingness to suffer, and their amazing discipline in the midst of great provocation. One day the South will recognize its real heroes. They will be the **James Merediths,** with the noble sense of purpose that enables them to face jeering and hostile mobs, and with the agonizing loneliness that characterizes the life of the pioneer. They will be old, oppressed, battered Negro women, symbolized in a seventy-two-year-old woman in Montgomery, Alabama, who rose up with a sense of dignity and with her people decided not to ride segregated buses, and who responded with ungrammatical profundity to one who inquired about her weariness: "My feets is tired, but my soul is at rest." They will be the young high school and college students, the young ministers of the gospel and a host of their elders, courageously and nonviolently sitting in at lunch counters and willingly going to jail for conscience's sake. One day the South will know that when these disinherited children of God sat down at lunch counters, they were in reality standing up for what is best in the American dream and for the most sacred values in our Judeo-Christian heritage, thereby bringing our nation back to those great wells of democracy which were dug deep by the founding fathers in their formulation of the Constitution and the Declaration of Independence.

In the fall of 1962 **James Meredith** became the first black student to enroll at the University of Mississippi. His act, which sparked riots on the university's campus that resulted in two deaths, is widely considered an important event in the civil rights movement.

45 Never before have I written so long a letter. I'm afraid it is much too long to take your precious time. I can assure you that it would have been much shorter if I had been writing from a comfortable desk, but what else can one do when he is alone in a narrow jail cell, other than write long letters, think long thoughts, and pray long prayers?

If I have said anything in this letter that overstates the truth and indicates an unreasonable impatience, I beg you to forgive me. If I have said anything that understates the truth and indicates my having a patience that allows me to settle for anything less than brotherhood, I beg God to forgive me.

I hope this letter finds you strong in the faith. I also hope that circumstances will soon make it possible for me to meet each of you, not as an integrationist or a civil-rights leader but as a fellow clergyman and a Christian brother. Let us all hope that the dark clouds of racial prejudice will soon pass away and the deep fog of misunderstanding will be lifted from our fear-drenched communities, and in some not too distant tomorrow the radiant stars of love and brotherhood will shine over our great nation with all their scintillating beauty.

Yours for the cause of Peace and Brotherhood,

Martin Luther King, Jr.

Questions for Discussion

1. What reason does King give for writing this letter? What justification does he provide for its length? In what ways might these explanations strengthen his argument?

2. One of the many charges brought against King at the time of his arrest was that he was an "outsider" who had no business in Birmingham. How does he justify his presence in Birmingham? How convincing do you think his justification is?

3. What does King mean by nonviolent "direct action"? Why did he believe that such action was necessary in Birmingham? How does he build his case for the nonviolent campaign in Birmingham? Do you think he does so convincingly? Why or why not?

4. Examine the images that King invokes in paragraph 14. What does he accomplish with these images? How do they contribute to his overall argument? Do you think he is intentionally making an emotional appeal here? What does he achieve by including an unusually long sentence in this paragraph?

5. How does King distinguish between a just and an unjust law? Why is this distinction important for his main argument? What evidence does King provide to support his contention that unjust laws must be broken? Do you think King's original audience of white ministers would have found his argument on this issue convincing?

6. What specific features of King's letter reveal that it was written originally for an audience of white Christian ministers? What strategies does King employ that might be effective for such an audience? Do you think King intended his letter only for that audience? Explain.

7. At one point in his essay King explains that one purpose of the campaign in Birmingham was "to create a situation so crisis-packed that it will inevitably open the door to negotiation." Do you think King's letter itself is intended to lead to negotiation? Explain, citing specific passages in his letter to support your answer.

8. King had much experience as a preacher when he wrote this famous letter. Is there anything about its style that reminds you of oratory? How effective would this letter be if delivered as a speech?

④ | # Americans, Common Law, and Freedom: What You Need To Know

MELINDA PILLSBURY-FOSTER

Serving on a jury is a civic responsibility of all Americans. It is one of the few ways in which citizens participate directly in the legal system that is an integral part of American democracy. It is also one of the few contexts within which individual citizens make decisions that can have serious consequences on other citizens and for the society in general. Melinda Pillsbury-Foster, a well-known libertarian activist, takes the idea of serving on a jury very seriously. As she writes in the following essay, serving on a jury is not only a citizen's civic duty but also a means for citizens to claim their political authority and govern themselves. Pillsbury-Foster argues that the common law tradition in the United States, by which courts set precedents that determine the laws we live by, is the primary tool for Americans to wield political power. Her argument emphasizes the idea that despite the enormous size and complexity of the United States, power can still reside with the people. The question she addresses is how we should use that power. Melinda Pillsbury-Foster is director of the Heritage Association and has been active in the Libertarian Party. This essay appeared on Nolan Chart, a libertarian website, in 2008.

MELINDA PILLSBURY-FOSTER, "Americans, Common Law, and Freedom: What You Need To Know"

We hold these truths to be self-evident, that all men are created equal, that they are endowed by their Creator with certain unalienable Rights, that among these are Life, Liberty and the pursuit of Happiness. That to secure these rights, Governments are instituted among Men, deriving their just powers from the consent of the governed...

1 When you read the preamble to the Declaration of Independence, remember what the world looked like to the men who wrote it. Then look at our world through their eyes; understanding their world and the institutions they used routinely brings understanding of what has gone so wrong with our world today.

Their world was the same and different. The agreement to go to war came after a long process of discourse over the issues,

not by leaders, but by ordinary people. The Committees of Correspondence drove a dialogue on why the people should govern themselves, enacting formally what they had been doing for two centuries. They were a people who expected to cooperate, looking across into each other's eyes, never up to anyone in government.

Over that time they had built a vibrant and robust society that was stretching out in all directions. The people governed themselves, using a system of organizing tools, proven over time. Those tools were town government operating with transparency, ensuring that real control remained directly in the hands of the people. For justice, they used the Common Law, brought with them from England.

Control of the functions of government through the town ensured that government would never eat up the seed corn. Direct scrutiny by the people on what was spent, the authority always with them to approve or deny, kept government small and honest. Delving back in time you see these people assumed that no one went into government to make money or secure their retirement because the pay was terrible and there were no benefits. Those serving in government were assumed to have enough money to be able to donate their time. That model still persists in some parts of New England. The same principles were in use for the justice system through the Common Law Courts. Judges performed a service to the community, drawing from their own time to do so.

5 In use by the people for centuries, the common law was not something apart from the people but like the air they breathed. School children saw it operating and were prepared to use it themselves when they became adults. Going to court was serious, a process treated with respect, but instead of dividing them they entered into that process knowing that, ultimately, there would be justice. Contrast that to how the system of courts looks to us today.

The Common Law is a system for justice that is handled directly by the people. That is the system our Founders assumed would continue; it was one of those tools, used sparingly, that allowed a free people to govern themselves directly. Town government, with its absolute transparency and resulting low costs, along with the Common Law, were the foundation for freedom that the Founders assumed would continue.

Elections handled directly by the people; the votes totaled openly and transparently.

Spending by government overseen directly by the people.

Common law courts that possessed the right to judge both the facts and the law.

10 The system worked. It remains the system intended by our Founders. It can still work today.

How do we become, again, a people who govern themselves? That we can do so is inherent in our mission statement. The Declaration of Independence says,

CONTEXT

Common law is a legal system based on precedent, tradition, and common practice. Under this system, which is sometimes called "case law," courts hand down opinions on the basis of previous court decisions, thereby establishing precedent. In making decisions, courts consult previous cases and interpret precedent as it applies to current cases. Adapted from England when the United States was founded, common law in the United States functions at the state and local levels; however, in the federal court system, courts make decisions on the basis of statutes (laws passed by Congress) but must consult state court decisions for precedent when deciding matters that have been ruled upon in state courts.

That whenever any Form of Government becomes destructive of these ends, it is the Right of the People to alter or to abolish it, and to institute new Government, laying its foundation on such principles and organizing its powers in such form, as to them shall seem most likely to effect their Safety and Happiness.

Prudence, indeed, will dictate that Governments long established should not be changed for light and transient causes; and accordingly all experience hath shewn that mankind are more disposed to suffer, while evils are sufferable than to right themselves by abolishing the forms to which they are accustomed. But when a long train of abuses and usurpations, pursuing invariably the same Object evinces a design to reduce them under absolute Despotism, it is their right, it is their duty, to throw off such Government, and to provide new Guards for their future security.

The first Amendment of the Bill of Rights owes its existence to a common law case heard in New York in 1735. In 1735 the Royal Governor of New York attempted to suborn the right of jury to decide fact and law. It had begun with the publication of the *New-York Weekly Journal* in 1633 with Zenger as the editor. The paper began because Crosby, the

John Peter Zenger (1697–1746) was the editor of the *New York Weekly Journal* who was tried in 1735 for publishing false and seditious statements in his newspaper. In defiance of the judge's instructions, the jury acquitted Zenger of the charges. The case is considered an important one in establishing the principles of freedom of the press in the United States.

Royal Governor, was corrupt and the people needed the truth. Zenger was arrested and incarcerated for telling the truth on November 17, 1734. The bail set made his release impossible.

The **Zenger Case** was heard on August 4th of that year and saw a jury of twelve men render the verdict of not guilty, thus overthrowing the law and setting a course that lead to the principle that the truth is its own defense. It was this case that remained in the minds of our Founders when they wrote the Bill of Rights, addendum to the Constitution, which was intended to limit government, never us.

The verdict of Not Guilty affirmed the right of anyone to break a law that violated the conscience of the community and the right of an individual to speak the truth.

15 The Zenger Case is with you any time you serve on a jury.

The Common Law is the muscle behind our rights.

Many today think of the Common Law as antiquated and impractical; nothing could be further from the truth. The disused understanding of these tools are waiting for us to pick up. They are easy to use and bring with them amazing benefits, also forgotten, that created the American people as different from any nation on the face of the Earth.

When you are empaneled as a juror on a Common Law Court, you already understand that this is a grave responsibility. You take up the charge to become, with those others serving, the conscience of your community. You leave behind you any prejudices. Those who serve understand they must see the matter at hand dispassionately, demand the facts, scrutinize the evidence, see beyond evasion to the root of the issues. Then, the juror must reflect on each other point, listening as if the life of their community depended on it.

America itself owes its existence, in part, to another case where the jury refused to

violate the conscience of the community and the right of the individual. That jury heard its case in England in 1670. King Charles II demanded the prosecution of William Penn for the crime of preaching his Quaker faith. The jury foreman, Edward Bushel, along with the rest of the jury, found the law unjust, in violation of the people's right to worship. The case was heard at the Old-Bailey from the 1st to the and 5th of Sept.

20 Afterwards, the jury was incarcerated for returning a verdict that outraged the judge. He directed that the jury reconsider their verdict. They retired and returned with the same verdict, Not Guilty. The judge then confined the jury in Newgate Prison to remain without food or water until the desired verdict was rendered. They continued to hold that William Penn was not guilty. Eventually they were fined and released.

William Penn, then 26, immigrated to Pennsylvania. The lesson of the right of the jury to decide is the birth right of all Americans and the midwife of our freedom.

The Common Law and its principles remain in use, though those now in power try to disguise their existence. A pivotal example of the same kind of courage shown in the Zenger and Penn cases took place in the township of Credit River, Minnesota on 12th December 1968. The issue was the fraud being perpetrated by banks across the world. It is known as the Credit River Case.

Jerome Daly faced eviction from his home. Daly had sued the bank, his house in foreclosure; while reviewing the papers and practices he had noticed that the mortgage was issued with no legal consideration. The verdict rendered hinged on the admission by the president of the First National Bank of Montgomery that there was no legal consideration with the loan written for Jerome Daly's mortgage. The bank president testified, "this was standard banking practice exercised by their bank in combination with the Federal Reserve Bank of Minneapolis, another private bank, further that he knew of no United States Statute or law that gave the plaintiff the authority to do this."

Daly kept his home. Two weeks later the judge in the case, Mahoney, was murdered. No one ever said that freedom and justice would come without costs.

25 Courts that follow the common law accept the tenet that the jury decides on all issues, both fact and law; they can demand more information. Nothing is hidden from them. The judge is only there to be called on by the jury. They must understand that the rights of individuals trump statute, and, most importantly, they are acting as the incarnation of the conscience of the community.

Arguably, the most important check and balance to power in government is the power of the informed jury to decide on the issues of both law and fact. Today, we as Americans face the need to restore to use the tools that connect us to our own power, granted not by government, but by God.

Start with your local county, establish your own **Heritage Association** on the common law and the Constitution.

Let your local law enforcement know what their obligations are under the Constitution.

Celebrate Jury Rights Day, September 5th. Get to know the Fully Informed Jury Association.

30 A free people will govern themselves; a people who will be free do it themselves.

According to its website, the **Heritage Association** "is a community based effort founded to renew an appreciation for the legacy of the Constitution and Common Law."

Questions for Discussion

1. Pillsbury-Foster devotes the first few paragraphs of this essay to a review of the history of self-government in the early United States. What purpose does this historical review serve in this essay? How does it relate to Pillsbury-Foster's main argument?

2. What benefits does Pillsbury-Foster see to common law? Do you find her discussion of common law persuasive? Why or why not?

3. What evidence does Pillsbury-Foster provide for her claim that Americans no longer govern themselves as intended by the Founding Fathers? Do you find her support for this claim persuasive? Explain.

4. Pillsbury-Foster quotes from the Declaration of Independence at the beginning of her essay and then again in paragraph 11. Why do you think she does so? What purpose do these quotations serve in her essay? How effective are they in supporting her argument?

5. Pillsbury-Foster cites several landmark court cases in her discussion of common law in the United States. What conclusions does she draw from these cases? Are her conclusions justified? Explain. How effectively does she use these cases to support her main argument?

6. What steps does Pillsbury-Foster believe Americans can take to reclaim their right to self-government? Do these steps seem practical to you? Why or why not? Do you share her concerns about the loss of self-government in the United States? Why or why not?

DIFFERENCES

NEGOTIATING

In his famous "Letter from a Birmingham Jail," Martin Luther King, Jr. argues on moral grounds that citizens are justified and even obligated to resist their government if that government imposes unjust laws on them. Many people who resisted the military draft during the Vietnam War made the same argument, asserting that their government was forcing them to fight in an unjust war, so they were justified in defying the laws that required them to submit to the military draft. In a sense, arguments about U.S. government actions in response to the terrorist attacks on September 11, 2001, focus on the same basic questions of the civic and moral responsibility of citizens. For most Americans these arguments about government power and individual responsibility can seem abstract. But they can become real when the government takes action that directly affects the lives of citizens, as the military draft did during the Vietnam War. Americans who have never faced such a situation might wonder, "What would *I* do?"

Since 2003 the possibility that some Americans would have to answer that question has existed in the form of wars in Iraq and Afghanistan. Because of the many demands placed on Armed Services, some politicians have called for the reinstatement of a military draft, which would require young men and women to serve in the military. These men and women would, in effect, be asked to sacrifice their own safety and liberty for the sake of their government and other citizens.

What would you do in such a case? In an essay in which you draw on the readings in this chapter (and any other appropriate sources), put forth your position on the question of the government's authority to ask you to sacrifice your life for your country. Under what circumstances do you think the government is justified in compelling young men and women to serve in the military and possibly go to war? When is it acceptable for a government to ask you to sacrifice your health and maybe your life? When is it not acceptable? To what extent are you justified in blatantly disobeying the laws that would require you to serve in the military? On what moral or legal or philosophical grounds would you do so? And do Americans have any special obligations to serve their country because of its history? In other words, how does your idea of America figure into your answer to these questions?

These are some of the questions you should try to address in your essay. In effect, you are writing a position paper on the military draft in which you make an argument about the extent and the limits of your government's power over you and other citizens.

13

Environment

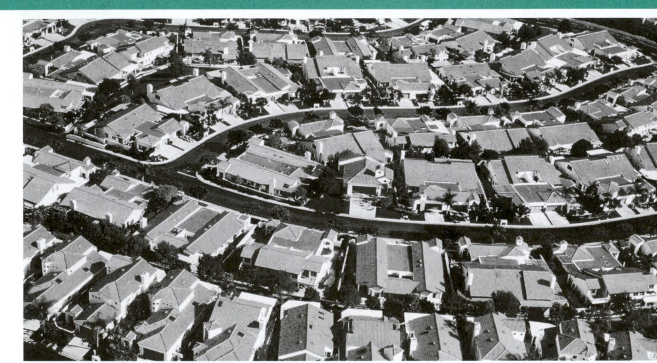

Courtesy of Gerard Fritz

How Should We Design Communities?

Visitors to Washington, D.C., sometimes complain about how difficult it can be to drive in that city. The streets seem to be laid out in a confusing pattern, with several main thoroughfares cutting across otherwise parallel streets at odd angles. It might surprise those visitors to learn that Washington, D.C., was originally designed from scratch by French architect Pierre L'Enfant, who was commissioned by President Washington in 1791. If you look at a street map of the city, you can make out the main features of that original design. For instance, those angled thoroughfares radiate from the central location of the Capitol Building; the famous Mall in front of the Capitol reflects L'Enfant's vision for a wide, central avenue. L'Enfant's original design was changed in several ways even as the city was being built, and in the years since it was constructed, the city, like many American cities, has grown dramatically. The confusing street patterns partially reflect the lack of planning and regulation as the city has grown; other oddities have occurred as builders and city leaders have tried to accommodate the original design. For example, some buildings, such as the FBI Building and the East Building of the National Gallery of Art, are not square or rectangular but have unusual angles (such as a trapezoid) to fit into the odd-shaped city blocks created by those radiating thoroughfares. ■ The growth of cities and towns tends to be seen as a good thing. But as the example of Washington, D.C., indicates, growth can create problems, too. As cities and towns expand, new residents and businesses require more services, which can lead to even more growth. There is an increasing need for more energy and more space. Not surprisingly, such growth often occurs at the edges of cities, where farmland and rural communities once existed. Despite the economic benefits, residents sometimes resist growth because it inevitably changes the quality of life in their communities. Famous architect Frank Lloyd Wright, whose building designs reflected his belief that structures should be part of the natural environment where they are located, once scolded the people of Miami about the unnatural way in which their city developed (see Con-Text on page 596). Wright's argument was really a call to create livable communities that foster a certain quality of life. But "quality of life" might not be the same for all people, and that is where conflicts can arise. Ultimately, growth raises questions about the kinds of communities people want: how should we design our communities? ■ All the essays in this section address that question. On the surface, these essays are about the problems associated with the growth of communities: A few of the writers discuss "sprawl," which is the rapid and seemingly unchecked growth of cities and towns into surrounding rural areas; others describe the "smart growth" movement that emerged in the 1990s, partly as a reaction to sprawl, and the more recent "green growth" movement that emerged as a response to daunting environmental challenges, such as global climate change. But in making their arguments, these writers offer their respective visions for the kinds of communities people should have. Their essays are reminders that when you argue about practical problems such as sprawl, you are really addressing deeper—and often more difficult—questions about how people should live together.

CON-TEXT

"A Beautiful Place Made Ugly"

1 We were coming in on the plane looking over this great, marvelous and very beautiful plateau and what do we see? Little tiny subdivisions of squares, little pigeonholes, little lots, everything divided up into little lots, little boxes on little lots, little tacky things.

And you come downtown and what's happening? Plenty of skyscrapers. You call them hotels. You can't tell whether they're hotels or office buildings or something in a cemetery. They have no feelings, no richness, no sense of this region.

And that, I think is happening to the country. It's not alone your misfortune.

You want to live in a way becoming to human beings with your spirit and a devotion to the beautiful, don't you? Well, why don't you? Why would you accept this sort of thing? Why would you let them put it over on you? You say because of economic reasons.

5 Well, if that's what this country talks about as the highest standard of living in the world, then I think it isn't at

all the highest, it's only biggest—and quite ignorant.

Nature must be ashamed of these hotels that you're building down here. Nature must be ashamed of the way this place has been laid out and patterned after a checkerboard and parceled out in little parcels where you stand on each other's toes, face the sidewalk, your elbows in the next neighbor's ribs.

SOURCE: Frank Lloyd Wright, public address, Miami, Florida (1955).

① # The Lived-In City: A Place in Time

JANE HOLTZ KAY

Why would anyone want to live in a city, when the suburbs offer affordable housing, private yards, and convenient shopping—not to mention the reassuringly familiar flavors of chain restaurants such as TGIF and the Olive Garden? The city, on the other hand, can so easily be considered a place where it is hard to find a parking space, crime is common, and everything costs too much. But cities can also be sites for diversity, privacy, and excitement—as Jane Holtz Kay argues in the following essay, first published in a 2004 collection of essays about the urban experience. The challenge, Kay argues, is how to design cities so that they remain vital and livable. The author of several books on urban planning, including *Lost Boston* (1980) and *Asphalt Nation* (1997), Kay writes regularly about art, architecture, and natural environments for well-respected newspapers and magazines.

JANE HOLTZ KAY, "The Lived-In City: A Place in Time"

1 Robert, or rather Robairrrrrr, as even our monolingual lunch-goers managed to say, rolling his French forename with the same care he devoted to our sandwiches, was the host of our lunch hour. Endowed with the memory to recall three preferences while slicing and dicing a fourth, he was the maître d' of our neighborhood. ("So are you turkey rollup today or..." he would prompt one customer as he minced onions for a second while joshing along yet a third.) Time after time, he would jive us geographic provincials with a really bad joke about a trip he had just taken to his native Haiti...to play hockey, enlisting the assembled flock in his riff as the lines grew longer.

Now, our spirited chef, our slicer-dicer, our Haitian-born master of ceremonies has left, was let go: axed with the speed of his dancing sandwich knife, it seemed. In a day, the deli counter at the 24-store where he worked was swiftly sanitized, all signs of unwrapped food-stuffs swept away. The gleaming silver counter was gone, the food trays vanished. Just a shelf of neon-toned bottles, snappleracklepop drinks parading behind the vacant cook 'n' serve space. And the Oasis 24-store was on to slicker things.

In his stead, the next day, strangers handed out free sandwiches with every drink purchase, plastic-wrapped fare, thin and meager next to Robert's oozing composite sandwiches, customized for our daytime neighborhood. And the neighborhood he created missed more than the food. More than the eating, the absence was in the serving, the rock 'n' rolling repartee—the power to unite us odd-lot Bostonians: more folks of color, more mix in income than any other eatery around this downtown edge, from stiff-jawed suits to slackers jiving with idle chatter. More nodding and smiling customers than I had found before, or would again in its sanitized reincarnation. And the absence went beyond the loss and lack within our strange but powerful semi-demi neighborhood of city life. For what was lacking in the aftermath was what defines cities: the everyday urbanity that exists nowhere else.

So it ended, one day in late June, and, by now, the bustling "before" has become a sterile "after," as empty of life as the lost memory

Cheers was a popular television sitcom in the 1980s in which a regular cast of characters met in a bar by that name. In the show's theme song, the bar, which was supposed to exist in Boston, was described as a place "where everybody knows your name."

A **pastiche** in this context refers to an architectural imitation; the term also suggests a somewhat haphazard collection of things "pasted" together.

Perhaps the most famous landscape architect in American history, Frederick Law Olmsted (1822–1903) is best known for designing Central Park in New York City. He also designed a series of parks for Boston.

Back Bay is a section of Boston that was created in the nineteenth century when a swamp was drained and developed as part of a carefully drawn plan for expanding the city. It is now a large and elegant neighborhood.

Laissez-faire, a French term meaning "to allow to choose," refers to economic and social policies that promote free enterprise with minimal interference by government.

of our casual comrades in line those many months. Well, not quite comrades. For the urbanity that this corner collage boasted was based on the anonymity that defines a city. Oasis, unlike **Cheers**, was actually the place where *nobody* knows your name. And that was just fine, thank you. We knew one another's faces, the banter, the menu, of course, but not much beyond. And as a city lover, delighting in the absentminded but congenial anonymity that is downtown's hallmark, I say thank God for that: sing a hymn for the hammering, clambering hammering of the city's impersonal connections. Casual discourse, casual multiracial, mixed-income elbowing of our neighbors is at a zero in most suburbs (and, admittedly, in parts of this town). So is walking, even talking. Here, we mingled and moved, rubbed elbows casually, not nervous in anonymous urbanity. And that was fine, too. For the strange pertinence of the city's everyday, predictable flux was the very definition the serious city: mixing ephemeral ease in everlasting surrounding the lived-in city shares space as it does the centuries.

5   Need I stress, then, that lived-in cities like Boston are not the place "where everybody knows your name"? That, in fact, they can be proud fortresses of *not* knowing your name? Only real cities can teach us the meaning of place and time that is the opposite of television's "have a-good-day" nonplaces like Cheers, which is now a tourist stop of T-shirts and trinkets tucked into the ground floor of an otherwise elegant Beacon Hill row house—a faux tourist place more faux than even television.

Is this the comment of a tourist xenophobe? Yes, I confess, but also of a partisan of the city, a visceral and intellectual city lover possessed of the conviction that cities, eternal cities, are, indeed—well—too grown up, too historically genuine to turn a blind eye to Disney-style **pastiche** inflated along the street.

Not all American cities are the inheritors of four centuries of comings and goings as

Boston is, of course, but they have time on their side. Serious time. And it is that sense of permanence and flux growth and instability, tolerance and suspicion visible on their worm streets and sidewalks that lends character.

Diversity in place and time is just one of many partnerships it the city, of course. City life is the sharing of space with absent-minded courtesy—the chance encounters of strangers and neighbors. (Check the subways to see how we suffer crowds politely, if not happily. Check the city, but not the suburbs, for acceptance of the Other, cheek to jowl, backpack to briefcase.) Urbanity is about mingling and hanging back, about civility and bellicosity, quirkiness and constancy. Above all, serious cities actively decline uniformity despite the Gaps—in both senses—that mar our streets: their flanks and facades offer an eclectic mingling that stands in contrast to the uniformity of the malls and supermalls that bloat the landscape in our new suburbs and outburbs.

Suburbanity, so to speak, is about another kind of civility, I concede: the civility of good schools and good roads, of manicured lawns and well-groomed street trees. It is, alas, about how the lopsided subsidies of our federal government have fed urban flight, promoting the pattern of settlement that breeds suburban wealth and urban poverty as Washington subsidized the highway exodus from downtown and dug our nation's Great Divide—urban versus suburban—and maintained it for a half century or more. Doubt it? Think, then: no one has yet to strive "toward a livable *suburb*."

10   Strangely, even those who struggle for a livable planet, intermingling the built and natural environments in these days of global malaise and environmental activism, have yet to turn to the lived-in city to ally the green and the grid—the country and the city—as did our ancestors. Few follow the 150-year-old tradition of **Frederick Law Olmsted's masterworks** of naturalizing the city and urbanizing the planet's biological systems;

fewer peruse the more recent classics *Design with Nature* and *Granite Garden,* invoking the need for whole earth systems in our urban zones. Is the city cacophonous? Irritating? Disrupted? Yes. Is the glass half full? Half empty? Yes, of course, but, and at the same time. Name it what you will, but add one thing: it is also this fragile planet's last, best hope—the only alternative to settling on the ever-contracting fringes, consuming the last chance landscape, extinguishing resources and species. If we are ever to become ecofluent, as the green warriors put it, the strengthening of our lived-in cities is where it must take place.

To be sure, our livable cities tally wins along with losses; some big-box blanders along with a legion of local activists battle the most invasive attack of the chains in our nation's history. Meanwhile, an ethnic flavor continues to spice the eateries, and even the chains, in our quasi-cosmopolitan downtown and urban neighborhoods. Muslim women, their heads swathed in scarves, serve at Dunkin' Donuts. Newcomers from Afghanistan, El Salvador, and Algeria chat up customers at Bean and Leaf Café, as do two generations of Greeks under the Grecian blue letters of the Odysseus restaurant, inscribing their diversity in the architecture as it always has been: five centuries worth—from the Union Oyster House, solid as its colonial bricks, to the upscale anyplaces of contemporary cuisine, the new-comer Irish bars and after-work scenes.

And yet, the Anyplace USA establishments proliferate more rapidly than ever before: in the Franco-fake Bon Pain, the Starbucks and Wendy's, undercutting diversity, destroying vivacity, while neighborhood by neighborhood we fight the good fight. Since Staples super-store came downtown, stationery stores have dwindled. A month-at-a-glance pocket calen-dar is nowhere to be found, nor the chance to buy *one* pen, *one* pad of paper, *one* anything, it sometimes seems. In the **Back Bay** row house world where I live, empty storefronts have succumbed to soap and cell phone

shops as rents rise and the economy slides. An eyeglass shop papered over with neon images stares like empty eyes. Chain stores sit in the old Prince School while the nearby Exeter Theatre, once the Spiritualist Temple, has fallen from grace over the years: a Friday's sits on one of its corners, an Internet company in the space above. And every site seems tentative.

Perhaps they always have. In the time line of the historic city, change is the constant. Yet the loss of flavor and the larger-scaled anonymity seem more rampant these days…the pace faster, bigger…the city planners more **laissez-faire**, the renters greedier here now, as across the country. A Shakespeare and Company bookstore bowing to a New York Barnes & Noble has its counterparts, and, across the ocean, cities in "Old" Europe and old everyplace fail to ward off the monopolies in our sprawling, ever-globalizing world.

Change, as history teaches us, can be good and bad alike. The grand design of Paris by its great builder, **Baron Von Haussmann**, caused the ferocious leveling of its medi-eval, quirky, charming streets for the grand boulevards, which we also love. So, too, the filling of Boston's murky Back Bay following

Baron Georges-Eugene Haussmann (1809–1891), one of the most influential city planners in history, was commissioned in 1853 by French Emperor Napoleon III to transform Paris into a modern city. To ease congestion and improve traffic flow, Haussmann destroyed much of the city's medieval architecture and created broad, tree-lined boulevards radiating from and toward major monuments such as the Arc de Triomphe; his plan also included a new water supply, a huge network of underground sewers, new bridges and railroad stations, and new buildings such as the Paris Opera House. His costly plan was highly controversial because the extensive demolition and construction over decades was socially disruptive. He thus represents the kind of planner willing to destroy historic architecture and cause people enormous inconvenience to achieve a magnificent master plan.

CONTEXT

In paragraph 10 Kay refers to two classic books about urban and architectural design. In *Design with Nature* (1969), Ian L. McHarg (1920–2001) advocates an approach to urban planning and landscape architecture that emphasizes harmony with the natural environment. *The Granite Garden* (1985), by Anne Whiston Spirn, also emphasizes incorporating natural habitats into buildings and other structures as a way to make urban areas more livable. Both books influenced a generation of landscape architects, city planners, and policymakers and helped create a new movement, sometimes referred to as "Smart Growth," that promotes the design and construction of more livable, sustainable com-munities. In recent years, concerns about global climate change and other seri-ous environmental problems have prompted a renewed interest in the ideas of thinkers like McHarg and Spirn. Many planners, architects, policymakers, and environmentalists now support the view that Kay expresses in this essay: That carefully planned cities are the best way to address environmental problems like climate change.

Von Haussmann's lead in splendid avenues would never pass an environmental impact statement. Yet the planners who filled the bay with pilings to create the mile-long stretch of streets shaped splendid structures on the French model, as they had created English housing modes atop Beacon Hill. Again, is the cup of city change half full or half empty? One must always ask.

15 Today, truth be told, the cup seems overflowing. The pace has quickened, and change—rightfully—alarms us. The props for greedy growth are strong, the planning weak, the scale of building grandiose. For all the landmark legislation and historic cache that make these surroundings livable, neither neighbors nor activists can ward off the construction booms that turn land to unminted gold and money to "serious money" for serious building—building too serious to fret about architecture's ease and accommodation with its surroundings. As pernicious as any suburban subdivider, today's city builders focus on the bottom line, caring little for proper fit and public process in a city where planning is a lost art and politicians pay back the piper. And so a new generation builds. Chunky, pricey postmodern buildings rise, stage sets of history for architectural appeasement flourish, and the tall towers for the rich rise above the church steeples where the homeless take an icy night's winter sleep beneath timeless porticoes.

In the lived-in, not always livable city, such issues become visible. That is the joy, and trial, of their heft and density. The city, as always, reflects **"the times that try men's souls,"** and in these times of terror and increasing economic inequality, social malaise is manifest on its streets. The newly refurbished Bulfinch State House, with its 1789 golden dome and rolling front lawn, partakes of troubled times as they hide the security cameras that pry into passing sound and sights. The fear of terrorist attack combines with privatism to virtually bar access to the landmark Custom House tower whose once-public balcony offered a splendid view of the city's wraparound world of water.

Downtown, the alliance of politics and money dictates, and the city skyline soars. Towers break through barriers to appropriate the sky. Human scale is lost while the winds they churn affront walkers. Blank-walled facades squeeze out shops below and rising property values threaten old ethnic neighborhoods like Chinatown with high-rise holdouts for the rich. The hot spot seaport sites in South Boston are being sliced and diced to serve the upper income, not the long-time artists.

And yet, the paradox of urban life defies its shortcomings as restored buildings enliven main streets and bustling neighborhoods thrive with new ethnic vitality. The city survives with a novelty and energy that baffle expectations. For all our days deploring slapdash change, a visit to the area once dubbed the Combat Zone offers a new/old downtown in a new after-hours world. Plunging through the streets of the newly named Ladder Blocks, we seek a meal in Restaurant Land's new digs and find one: FELT (so-called) dazzles our eyes. Across from old Washington Street's decay, we enter a black, cavernous space, dazzled by designer lights and silver mirrors. Lofty ceilings rise high, offering images of James Bond to the Great God of Retro Chic... and good food. On the second and third floors above, billiard tables explain the "felt" nomenclature and more glitz offers the decor du jour. Soon, the floor above will echo to dancing bands. The crowd's average age is not much beyond the twenties. A minimiracle. How did this hip factor return again to the tired streets of the moribund picture palace world that headlined "Banned in Boston"? The endless city will survive a new generation, and surprise an old one.

Robert will survive, as well. His Oasis stand-ins say he has found work. In fact, from time to time, I have seen him in the Back Bay, driving by the Clarendon Street Baptist Church with his family, one of many immigrant

"These are the times that try men's souls" is the first line of Thomas Paine's *The American Crisis* (1776), in which Paine, writing on the eve of the American Revolution, advocated secession from England and the formation of an independent American nation.

and ethnic parishioners who have rescued this old Yankee edifice. In the shifting, lived-in city, the Back Bay's volume of nineteenth-century churches is a loose-leaf scrapbook of change. Its "proper Bostonian" members drifted off to the suburbs long ago, leaving fraying carpets, crumbling brownstone facades, and shrinking budgets. Today's urban influx brings a fascinating miscellany of new members—secular condo dwellers, social do-gooders, and a colorful congregation of immigrants. Five earlier incarnations of the Baptist assemblage and more than 300 years stand between the first Clarendon Street Church and its ethnic rainbow of newcomers who fill the chambers on Sundays and celebrate their weddings in spring and summer as the celebratory stretch limos line the block and flower-strewn brides in white gowns reflect the world's outposts, from Haiti to Vietnam.

20 To me, a sometime historian of this evanescent city, the city is a tale to be twice or thrice told, depending on willing audiences, and this peripatetic church that finally lit here in 1872 is one of my favorites. The very early work of two geniuses, **Henry Hobbs Richardson and Frédéric Auguste Bartholdi**, its design is decidedly the best of neither. Richardson, the great architect of nineteenth-century America, launched his career here, and the marginal and not altogether pleasing proportions of the church show his unsure hand. Ah, that lumbering campanile. Bartholdi, too, better known (and better accomplished elsewhere) at the Statute of Liberty, arrived in 1871 and created the sculpture adorning its peak with dubious success. Alike, the Richardson building and the Bartholdi figure tooting its horn in an ungainly pose caused the locals to dub the structure the Church of the Holy Beanblower. The name stuck.

The New Land above the Back Bay pilings was a city of churches reflecting the flux of population from downtown to the burgeoning new town, and, though their congregations have fallen off, the new members reflect

history's ever-constant vigor and diversity as the new gallery of worshippers offer music events and instill art galleries to pay the bills in myriad ways, adding new life to the old neighborhood. And more. The Unitarian-Universalist Arlington Street Church a few blocks from the Clarendon Street congregation continues the open-minded political policies demonstrated by its basement horde of Sandista papers exploded by counter-radicals a few decades ago. On a cold winter day, the front stairs are packed with singers bundled against the chill, and "If I Had a Hammer," the song of sixties activism, wafts from the front steps of the church—a countercry to the president's State of the Union call to invade Iraq. The spiritual and the political ally visibly here. Internet activism has an alternative in the city's public streets. "Life is not about speed," said the church signboard, quoting Gandhi as its members prayed for peace and paid for restoring its Tiffany windows.

Still, God loses out to Mammon, that Syrian deity, in the embattled city, and even ecclesiastical masterpieces are not safe from his claims. In fact, a soaring twentieth-century version dedicated to the monetary deity—the one-hundred-story-high glass John Hancock tower—famously just about undid that bastion of the former, Trinity Church. Designed by Richardson, who, by a mathematical irony, began creating his masterpiece there in 1872, exactly a century before the insurance company did, the tower suffered assaults from the new building from the start. The glass rhomboid cresting upward seemed hellbound from the beginning, despite (because of ?) its proud and prestigious architect, I. M. Pei. As a young architecture critic for the *Boston Globe*, I deplored (still do) the overweening height of the sixty-two-story structure looming over Copley Square, whiplashing its famous public space, creating hostile wind tunnels for pedestrians, and diminishing surrounding architectural marvels including **the magnificent Boston Public Library by McKim, Mead and White**.

Henry Hobbs Richardson (1838–1886) was one of the most important American architects in the nineteenth century; he designed the famous church that Kay refers to in paragraph 20. **Frédéric Auguste Bartholdi** (1834–1904), a prominent sculptor in the nineteenth century, is best known for designing the Statue of Liberty in New York Harbor.

McKim, Mead and White was one of the country's most prestigious architectural firms in the late nineteenth and early twentieth centuries, responsible for designing such famous buildings as Pennsylvania Station in New York City (which was torn down in the 1960s) and the Boston Public Library, which is still much admired today. (See Figure 13-2.)

What ego! What arrogance, I thought, to break the barrier of this low-rise landscape, to create this antisocial climate change. And more, for suddenly it seemed that the sky-breaking building had caused yet another phenomenon: the sun reflected in its mirror-glass walls was glaring at Mass. Turnpike drivers from miles away, blinding them. A hue. A stew. A cry. An article. But first, of course, a call to the public relations staff about what the new "sunset" was doing to the accident rate. Did a building have the right? I asked.

FIGURE 13-1

The John Hancock Tower in Boston

Image copyright Chee-Onn Leong 2010. Used under license from Shutterstock.com

"Would you ask God to stop the sunsets?" came the reply. Not even the *Fountainhead* school of ego architecture had prepared me for the conceit of someone equating an act of the Almighty with an insurance company's phallic gesture. It was a first but not a last.

Worse luck, the glass windows began to pop, and wooden panels replaced them. A strange patchwork indeed. "The U.S. Plywood Building," they called it, as lawyers scrapped and engineers hemmed and hawed and failed for a long time, a very long time, to fix it. Worse still, the wooden foundations that secured the adjacent Trinity Church's foundations in solid soil below its watery bed began to quiver from the insurance company's construction work while the elegant Copley Plaza Hotel, on the other side, next door, was wobbling...and...

25 To cut to the chase: they did it with dollars. You can say that a city is where everything has a price and nothing has a value, where everything is negotiated, not planned, but this was remarkable even in the annals of urban myths. After suits and a newspaper splash nationally, the Hancock's wealthy insurance folks bought the Copley to salve the suit and forked out the funds to fix up the church. But not quickly. Only now, decades later, has the church opened its basement to reveal the repaired foundations and take tourists through the site...just in time, it seems, for the flagging insurance folks to put their falling business up for sale in—ahhh, the indignity of it!—a package with other relatively dwarfed buildings they owned totaling perhaps a billion dollars.

Ego rises, ego falls...likewise architecture in the lived-in city. Is it that nothing is sacred in the striving city? Or, more positively, that the city is—happily and by definition—a striving city: the place of all places where we try...and try...to get it right? Incredibly, too, the square where these structures sit has also gone through three lives in the same time span. The square's nineteenth-century shape, an erratic and triangular landscape in early postcards, became a subterranean plaza in the 1970s, which, in turn, became the local

FIGURE 13-2
The Boston Public Library

subterranean "needle park," which was, then, more positively, raised and fountained and tree-filled and paved with a potpourri of brick patterns, statuary, and grass. And, yet again in the restless, lived-in city, as summer nears, the square is being enlarged. A portion of a road that straddles its western side will expand the space. With any luck, we could live through still more evolutions by folks who think they've really, finally, definitely, absolutely got it right this time, in the endlessly striving, endlessly lived-in city.

And why not? Belief in striving for the New New Thing could be the city's most important product. Not just here, though, but everywhere. Our oldest, best, and brightest cities—San Francisco, Chicago, New York, you know them—grew because they were built by some folks with nothing left to lose and some folks with a lot to gain. (They are also best, of course, because they are oldest and bound by preindustrial, "natural" laws of craftsmanship and gravity and kinship to that nature.) Without the will to do better, and, of course, to do well in the most brazen financial manner, cities would not grow. Without cities we would not have the coming together, the sense of history,

the outrage that keeps us on edge. Only cities can teach us both the permanence and the impermanence of human handiwork. There is stability and its opposite, beauty and its lack, but always history in the midst of assault, creativity in the midst of destruction, and, for me, always stories to see and tell in the life and death, the liveliness and torpor, the wealth and poverty of their ever-shifting landscapes.

In the early morning hours, I hear a tinny rattle in the alley five flights below my bedroom window. A man with very white sneakers beneath a ragtag outfit and a silver shopping bag dangling from his hand has hit the heap of trash in the parking space beneath the alianthus. It is very, very cold and as I watch him make his way through our rejects, I calculate the rentals for such alley parking lots. The premium to rent this paved plot is three hundred dollars a month, about the same sum to bed and board this trash picker shuffling below the weed tree; the price to buy it is an astounding $129,000— offensive: "profane," as the sixties had it.

The city throws such inequities before public eyes, but not the suburbs. Is that why the deepest inhumanity, the inhumanity of indifference, lies in the isolated homes behind the greenest laws in those affluent outposts? You can run but you can't hide in the lived-in city. There is color as well as sorrow here, I think as I survey the sad scene amid the beauty and the affluence. For even the weed trees shade the brick buildings in the summer and blush their alleys with bounteous red berries in the fall.

30 Yet cities themselves rise and fall in time, on the small scale—the loss of Robert to the neighborhood, I think—and on the large as well, I muse, contemplating the rising sea levels that could wash over my neighborhood on its watery pilings. The city's sunrise is over in a minute in the long span of planetary life. Still, ephemeral or not, I cling to the belief that cities are the finest record of human will and human creativity. In flux, yes, and flawed, but lived-in, they link their living neighbors and long-gone ancestors in a way that confirms our sense of community and the genius of humanity to create art from habitat.

Questions for Discussion

1. Why do you think Kay begins this essay with the story of Robert, the deli owner in her neighborhood? What does Kay accomplish by beginning her essay with this story, to which she returns near the end of her argument?

2. What does Kay mean when she celebrates the city's "impersonal connections"? In what sense is the city "impersonal" and thus private? In what sense does it still offer daily opportunities for "connections"?

3. What are the benefits of urban life as Kay sees them? How does she make her case that urban life is desirable? How persuasive is her case, in your view?

4. Kay claims that the federal government has "fed urban flight" by encouraging suburban growth through subsidies for highway construction (see par. 9). What evidence does Kay provide to support this claim? What are the negative effects of the federal policies that she refers to in this passage? Do you see any advantages to policies that encourage the construction of highways? To what extent might your answer to that question provide a counter-argument to Kay's claim?

5. Why does Kay criticize suburbs? What does her criticism of suburbs suggest about her views about how we should design our communities? Do you think she's right? Why or why not?

6. In paragraph 18, Kay provides a description of "urban life." What ideas about urban life does this description convey? How does this description help support Kay's main point in this essay?

7. Why does Kay devote so much of her essay to criticizing specific buildings (for example, see paragraphs 22–25)? How do these criticisms figure into her main argument about cities?

8. How would you describe Kay's voice and tone in this essay? Do you think her voice and tone strengthen or weaken her essay? Explain, citing specific passages from her essay to support your answer.

9. This essay might be seen as an argument based on deductive reasoning (see pages 81–83). On what is the basic principle regarding communities does Kay base her argument? How effectively does she make her case on the basis of this principle?

② So What Can We Do—Really Do—about Sprawl?

DONELLA MEADOWS

Debates about sprawl—a term that refers to the spread of housing developments, strip malls, and office buildings into rural areas—often focus on concerns about quality of life, economic growth, and environmental damage. But Donella Meadows demonstrates that sprawl is also a public policy issue. She is clearly an opponent of unchecked development, but she refuses simply to criticize developers. "We can't blame those who make the money," she writes. "They're playing the game according to the rules." For Meadows, combating sprawl means understanding—and changing—those rules, which include tax laws and zoning ordinances. Meadows refuses to reduce the problem of sprawl to a pro-versus-con debate. Everyone, she suggests, benefits from municipal services and economic development, no matter how fervently some might support environmental protection. So people cannot simply say that they are for or against development. Her argument encourages you to think about protecting the environment and enhancing quality of life in terms of such mundane (and perhaps dull) matters as taxes and zoning. In doing so, you might also think about your responsibilities—as a consumer and as a citizen of a town or city—for the problems caused by sprawl. In this sense her essay is an effort to address a complex problem by understanding it rather than by opposing those who might disagree with her. Meadows, who died in 2001, was the director of the Sustainability Institute and the author or coauthor of nine books, including the best-selling *Limits to Growth* (1972). This essay appeared in her weekly "Global Citizen" column in 1999.

DONELLA MEADOWS, "So What Can We Do—Really Do—about Sprawl?"

1 In my mind St. Louis is the poster city for sprawl [see photo on page 606]. It has a glittering, high-rise center where fashionable people work, shop and party. Surrounding the center are blocks and blocks of empty lots, abandoned buildings, dying stores, a sad wasteland through which the fashionable people speed on wide highways to the suburbs. In the suburbs the subdivisions and shopping centers expand rapidly outward onto the world's best farmland.

When I imagine the opposite of sprawl, I think of Oslo, Norway [see photo on page 607]. Oslo rises halfway up the hills at the end of a fjord and then abruptly stops. What stops it is a huge public park, in which no private entity is allowed to build anything. The park is full of trails, lakes, playgrounds, picnic tables, and scattered huts where you can stop for a hot drink in winter or cold drink in summer. Tram lines radiate from the city to the park edges, so you can ride to the end of a line, ski or hike in a loop to the end of another line and ride home.

That is a no-nonsense urban growth boundary. It forces development inward. There are no derelict blocks in Oslo. Space no longer useful for one purpose is snapped up for another. Urban renewal goes on constantly everywhere. There are few cars, because there's hardly any place to park and anyway most streets in the shopping district

St. Louis Sprawl

©Corbis

are pedestrian zones. Trams are cheap and frequent and go everywhere. The city is quiet, clean, friendly, attractive and economically thriving.

How could we make our cities more like Oslo and less like land-gulping, energy-intensive, half-empty St. Louis? There is a long list of things we could do. Eben Fodor, in his new book *Better Not Bigger*, (the most useful piece of writing on sprawl control I've seen) organizes them under two categories: taking the foot off the accelerator and applying the brake.

5 The accelerator part comes from widespread public subsidies to sprawl. Fodor lists ten of them, which include:

- Free or subsidized roads, sewer systems, water systems, schools, etc. (Instead charge development impact fees high enough to be sure the taxes of present residents don't go up to provide public services for new residents.)
- Tax breaks, grants, free consulting services, and other handouts to attract new businesses. (There's almost never a good reason for the public to subsidize a private business, especially not in a way that allows it to undercut existing businesses.)
- Waiving environmental or land-use regulations. (Make the standards strong enough to protect everyone's air, water, views and safety and enforce those standards firmly and evenly.)
- Federally funded road projects. (The Feds pay the money, but the community puts up with the sprawl. And where do you think the Feds get the money?)

Urban growth accelerators make current residents pay (in higher taxes, lower services, more noise and pollution and traffic jams) for new development. There is no legal or moral reason why they should do that. Easing up on the accelerator should at least guarantee that growth pays its own way.

Applying the brake means setting absolute limits. There are some illegal reasons for wanting to do this: to protect special privilege, to keep out particular kinds of persons; to take private property for public purpose without fair compensation. There are also legal reasons: to protect watersheds or aquifers or farmland or open space, to force growth into places where public services can be efficiently

CONTEXT

"Our cities and towns keep growing and growing. 'To what end?' you might ask. Are big cities so much better than small cities that we should strive to convert every small city into a bigger one? It seems clear from looking at many of the world's largest cities that we have little reason to envy them. Maybe there is some ideal size where all the best qualities of a community come together to reach an optimal state of urban harmony? If there is such a size, would we know when we've reached it? Would we be less able to stop growing once we were there? The reality is that we just grow and grow, regardless of our community's size or whether further growth is good or bad for us. Endless growth is the only plan on the table."

SOURCE: Eben Fodor, *Better Not Bigger* (1999).

delivered, to slow growth to a rate at which the community can absorb it, to stop growth before land, water, or other resources fail.

Fodor tells the stories of several communities that have limited their growth and lists many techniques they have used to do so. They include:

- Growth boundaries and green belts like the one around Oslo.
- Agricultural zoning. Given the world food situation, not another square inch of prime soil should be built upon anywhere.
- Infrastructure spending restrictions. Why should a Wal-Mart that sucks in traffic force the public to widen the road? Let Wal-Mart do it, or let the narrow road limit the traffic.
- Downzoning. Usually met with screams of protest from people whose land values are reduced, though we never hear objections when upzoning increases land values.
- Comprehensive public review of all aspects of a new development, such as required by Vermont's Act 250.
- Public purchase of development rights.
- Growth moratoria, growth rate limits, or absolute caps on municipal size, set by real resource limitations.

Boulder, Colorado, may be the American town that has most applied growth controls, prompted by a sober look at the "build-out" implications of the city's zoning plan. Boulder voters approved a local sales tax used to acquire greenways around the city. A building height limitation protects mountain views. Building permits are limited in number, many can be used only in the city center, and 75 percent of new housing permits must be allocated to affordable housing. Commercial and industrial land was downzoned with the realization that if jobs grow faster than housing, commuters from other towns will overload roads and parking facilities.

©Corbis

Oslo waterfront

10 All that and more is possible in any city. But controlling growth means more than fiddling at the margins, "accommodating" growth, "managing" growth. It means questioning myths about growth, realizing that growth can bring more costs than benefits. That kind of growth makes us poorer, not richer. It shouldn't be celebrated or welcomed or subsidized or managed or accommodated; it should be stopped.

We have planning boards. We have zoning regulations. We have urban growth boundaries and "smart growth" and sprawl conferences. And we still have sprawl. Between 1970 and 1990 the population of Chicago grew by four percent; its developed land area grew by 46 percent. Over the same period Los Angeles swelled 45 percent in population, 300 percent in settled area.

COMPLICATION

Boulder, Colorado, is sometimes listed among America's most desirable cities, but it has also developed a reputation for being an expensive place to live. In 1998 (a year before Meadows wrote this essay), a study of the cost of living in Colorado found that Boulder County had an above-average cost-of-living index, which measures the cost of household expenditures for various common items. Boulder remains among the most popular cities in the United States but also routinely ranks well above the national average for cost of living.

Sprawl costs us more than lost farmland and daily commutes through landscapes of stunning ugliness. It costs us dollars, bucks straight out of our pockets, in the form of higher local taxes. That's because our pattern of municipal growth, especially land-intensive city-edge growth, consistently costs more in public services than it pays in taxes.

In his new book *Better Not Bigger*, Eben Fodor cites study after study showing how growth raises taxes. In Loudon County, Virginia, each new house on a quarter-acre lot adds $705 per year to a town budget (in increased garbage collection, road mainte- nance, etc. minus increased property tax). On a five-acre lot a new house costs the community $2232 per year. In Redmond, Washington, single-family houses pay 21 percent of property tax but account for 29 percent of the city budget. A study in California's Central Valley calculated that more compact development could save municipalities 500,000 acres of farmland and $1.2 billion in taxes.

There are dozens of these studies. They all come to the same conclusion. New subdivi- sions reach into the pockets of established residents to finance additional schools and services. Commercial and industrial develop- ments sometimes pay more in taxes than they demand in services, but the traffic and pollution they generate reduces nearby prop- erty value. New employees don't want to live near the plant or strip, so they build houses and raise taxes in the NEXT town. Large, well- organized companies, such as sports teams and Wal-Mart, push city governments to widen roads, provide free water or sewage lines, offer property tax breaks, even build the stadium.

15 Given all the evidence to the contrary, it's amazing how many of us still believe the myth that growth reduces taxes. But then, every myth springs from a seed of truth. Municipal growth does benefit some people. Real estate agents get sales, construction companies get jobs, banks get more depositors and borrow- ers, newspapers get higher circulations, stores

get more business (though they also get more and tougher competition). Landowners who sell to developers can make big money; developers can make even bigger money.

Those folks are every town's growth pro- moters. Eben Fodor calls them the "urban growth machine" and cites an example of how the machine is fueled. Imagine a proposed development that will cost a com- munity $1,000,000 and bring in $500,000 in benefits. The $500,000 goes to ten people, $50,000 apiece. The $1,000,000 is charged to 100,000 people as a $10 tax increase. Who is going to focus full attention on this project, be at all the hearings, bring in lawyers, chat up city officials? Who is going to believe sincerely and claim loudly that growth is a good thing?

Fodor quotes Oregon environmentalist Andy Kerr, who calls urban growth, "a **pyramid scheme** in which a relatively few make a kill- ing, some others make a living, but most [of us] pay for it." As long as there is a killing to be made, no tepid "smart-growth" measures are going to stop sprawl. We will go on having strips and malls and cookie-cutter subdivi- sions and traffic jams and rising taxes as long as someone makes money from them.

We can't blame those who make the money. They're playing the game according to the rules, which are set mainly by the market, which rewards whomever is clever enough to put any cost of doing business onto some- one else. They get the store profits, we build the roads. They hire the workers (paying as little as they can get away with, because the market requires them to cut costs), we sit in traffic jams and breathe the exhaust. They get jobs building the subdivision, we lose open lands, clean water, and wildlife. Then we subsidize them with our taxes. That, the tax subsidy, is not the market, it's local politics. Collectively we set out pots of subsidized honey at which they dip. We can't expect them not to dip; we can only expect them to howl if the subsidy is taken away.

The "we-they" language in the previous paragraph isn't quite right. They may profit more

A **pyramid scheme** is a fraudulent way of making money through which someone creates an illusion of a profitable business by attracting new investment through false claims. "Profits" are made by attracting new investors, not because the company is succeeding in producing or selling anything. When new investment dries up, the pyramid collapses.

than we do, but we flock to the stores with the low prices. We buy dream homes in the ever-expanding suburbs. We use the services of the growth machine. (With some equally amateur friends I'm trying to create a 22-unit eco-development, and I'm learning to appreciate the skills needed and the risks borne by developers.) We want our local builders and banks and stores and newspapers to thrive.

20 So what can we do about this spreading mess, which handsomely rewards a few, which turns our surroundings into blight, which most of us hate but in which most of us are complicit—and which we subsidize with our tax dollars?

Concrete answers to that question take a long chapter in Fodor's book and will take another column here. The general answer is clear. Don't believe the myth that all growth is good. Ask hard questions. Who will benefit from the next development scheme and who will pay? Are there better options, including undeveloped, protected land? How much growth can our roads, our land, our waters and air, our neighborhoods, schools and community support? Since we can't grow forever, where should we stop?

Questions for Discussion

1. In her opening paragraphs, Meadows contrasts St. Louis and Oslo. How effective is this contrast? To what extent does her argument as a whole depend on comparison or contrast?

2. Meadows devotes much of her essay to summarizing the work of Eben Fodor. Evaluate her use of Fodor's ideas. Does she tell you enough about his work for you to understand the principles he advocates? In what ways do you think her argument about sprawl is strengthened or weakened by her use of Fodor's ideas?

3. Drawing on Fodor's work, Meadows uses the metaphors of growth accelerators and brakes to explain her concerns about sprawl. How effectively does this metaphor enable her to explain her concerns? Do you think the metaphors of accelerators and brakes are appropriate in this case? Explain.

4. Meadows asserts that there is "no legal or moral reason" that current residents of an area should be compelled to pay for new development of that area. What does this assertion reveal about Meadows's fundamental beliefs and assumptions about communities and development? Do you agree with her? Why or why not?

5. Meadows cites various statistics related to development and growth, and she also cites several studies. How persuasive is her use of such evidence to support her claims?

6. According to Meadows, who is responsible for urban sprawl? Do you agree? Why or why not?

7. Meadows ends her argument with a series of questions. How effectively do you think her questions conclude her argument? In what sense might they be appropriate, given her main argument about sprawl?

8. Meadows asserts that the problem of sprawl is not really a "we-they" problem. In other words, it is not possible to reduce the issue to two sides: one in favor and one against. She encourages you to consider how everyone involved has some responsibility for the problem. In this regard, her argument might be considered a Rogerian argument (see pages 126–131). Evaluate Meadows's essay as a Rogerian argument. Do you think it can justifiably be described as a Rogerian argument? Explain. How effective do you think it is as such an argument?

③ # Enough Snickering. Suburbia Is More Complicated and Varied Than We Think

ROBERT WILSON

When people debate about sprawl, they usually talk about suburbs, since the growth that creates sprawl tends to occur there. But just what do they mean by the term suburb? Robert Wilson seeks to answer that question. He argues that we need to understand suburbs in part because they reflect our values and visions for the lives we wish to have. In the following essay, Wilson explores not only what suburbs are but also what they mean to our sense of ourselves as Americans. Although he is not a big fan of the way suburbs have evolved since the early twentieth century, he sees suburbs as an important part of American culture. Furthermore, he points out, many people love them. Notice that Wilson approaches his subject from the perspective of a journalist and citizen deeply interested in preserving American culture. At the time this essay was published in the *Architectural Record* in 2000, he was the editor of *Preservation*, the magazine of the National Trust for Historical Preservation, which is devoted to preserving historically and culturally significant buildings and places.

ROBERT WILSON, "Enough Snickering. Suburbia Is More Complicated and Varied Than We Think"

Award-winning novelist **John Updike** is especially known for a series of novels focused on a character named Harry "Rabbit" Angstrom, who responds with mixed results to the opportunities and challenges of suburban, middle-class life.

1 As the editor of *Preservation* magazine, a publication that sees itself as being about place, I've realized recently that we have been overlooking a pretty significant subject: suburbia, the place where half of Americans live. We have run stories about sprawl and the New Urbanism and made the usual condescending references to cookie-cutter houses and placeless places. But we have failed to look at the suburbs with the same curiosity and courtesy that we've shown to Dubrovnik, say, or Sioux Falls or Paducah. "Why is that?" I now wonder. Snobbery is part of the answer. Nothing can be less hip than suburbia. At a time when our cities are showing new signs of life and our open space is still being chewed up at an exponential rate, whose imagination is going to catch fire over the problems of the suburbs? Part of the answer is also linguistic. The s-word itself has become so ubiquitous and so baggage-laden that it barely means anything anymore. There is a paradox lurking here. The word suburbia has been used to describe the increasingly varied places where more and more of us live—gritty inner suburbs that share many of the problems of their urban neighbors, immigrant neighborhoods at every economic level, and new greenfield developments sporting one McMansion bigger than the next. Yet our definition of the word remains fixed in a former time, decades ago, when women worked at home and men commuted to work. The biggest problem with suburbia is that we are all so certain that we know what it means. We watched *Father Knows Best* and read our **Updike**, and even a recent film like the Oscar-laden *American Beauty* confirms what we think we know: suburbia is a dull, sterile, unhappy place.

A PERSISTENT BIAS

As this suggests, the problem is also cultural. For the most part, American culture and opinion are still created, even in the Internet age, in cities at either edge of the continent. City dwellers, whether native born or the still more unforgiving recent converts, think of the suburbs as a mediocre place for mediocre people, a place where they will never venture or from which they have happily escaped. Even those who work in cities and live in suburbs (many of which now offer more urban amenities than nine-to-five cities) share this antisuburban frame of mind. If intellectuals do deign to look at the suburbs—whether cleverly in a film like *American Beauty* or clumsily, as in another recent film, the ugly paranoid fantasy *Arlington Road*—they assume that so much banality must be hiding something deeply evil.

BEYOND THE MOVIES

I'm really not here to defend suburbia, only to suggest that it is a more complicated, more various, and more quickly evolving place than we think. Two writers I admire, Witold Rybczynski and Joel Garreau, have helped me reach this state of cautious curiosity. The former, in his recent biography of **Frederick Law Olmsted** and elsewhere, has reminded me that the suburb was a noble idea that was often, in the first decades of its existence, nobly executed. Many of these places, such as Chevy Chase near Washington, D.C., continue to function admirably well. Garreau's insight is that Venice didn't become Venice the instant it was built, but developed over a period of centuries. If we remember that the suburbs, especially the postwar suburbs over which we do most of our hand-wringing, are still relatively new places, the question becomes not "Why are they so bad?" but, "What is the next step to making them better?"

WHO'S TO BLAME?

As a journalist, I am naturally filled with righteous indignation about the subject. My instincts are first to find someone to blame and second to flatter myself that I know the solution. So, here goes: One reason that the suburbs are not better is that the best minds

CONTEXT

Many critics saw the Academy Award–winning film *American Beauty* (see par.1), released in 1999, as a critique of life in white suburbia. In contrast to the seemingly healthy and happy suburban families portrayed in *Father Knows Best* or *Ozzie and Harriet*, which were popular television shows in the 1950s and 1960s, the dysfunctional family in *American Beauty* displays deep dissatisfaction with their apparently normal lives.

in architecture abandoned them. Once, not just Olmsted but **Frank Lloyd Wright, Le Corbusier, Clarence Stein**, and others considered, in an urgent and serious way, the questions of where and how people might live if they didn't live in cities or on farms. Am I wrong in believing that between the Garden City movement of the 1910s and 1920s and the New Towns of the 1960s there was a wasteland of ideas beyond the city limits—just as the suburbs began to lay waste to vast portions of the American landscape? And that there was precious little between the New Towns and the New Urbanists? Isn't this why the design and execution of suburbs have been so disappointing, because the field was abandoned to the merely avaricious? For anyone who is irritated by how much attention the New Urbanists get, here is the simple answer to their popularity with the media: However retrograde their ideas, however short their accomplishments to date might fall, at least they have an idea and at least they have acted upon it.

Frank Lloyd Wright (1869–1959), **Le Corbusier** (1887–1967), and **Clarence Stein** (1882–1975) were influential architects in the early twentieth century. Stein, in particular, is associated with the Garden City movement, which sought to create beautifully landscaped communities within easy access of major cities.

Frederick Law Olmsted (1822–1903) is considered one of our country's most important landscape architects. With his partner Calvert Vaux, he created the winning design for the creation of Central Park in New York City. He also designed the grounds for the U.S. Capitol, among many other projects of national significance.

CONTEXT

The New Towns movement in regional planning gained popularity in the United States in the 1920s. It focused on carefully designed and largely residential communities located away from urban centers. These New Towns, also called "Garden Cities," sometimes developed into large suburban areas. New Urbanism, which emerged in the 1990s, is a reaction to the New Town idea of community planning. As an alternative to sprawl, New Urbanism emphasizes the integration of housing, workplaces, businesses, and recreation into small neighborhoods connected by public transportation. The New Urbanism has influenced more recent movements in regional planning that emphasize "green" building and sustainable communities.

5 The New Urbanists spent a certain amount of time reacting to Vincent Scully's suggestion that they should really be thought of as the New Suburbanists, but in their new book, *Suburban Nation: The Rise of Sprawl and the Decline of the American Dream*, Andres Duany, Elizabeth Plater-Zyberk, and Jeff Speck frankly admit and defend their suburban focus. Whether they helped create the slow-growth, sustainable-growth, antisprawl movements that have captured the imagination of so many voters in recent elections at all levels of government, or whether they merely capitalized on these movements, their book seems timely. In a recent front-page article, the *New York Times* reported that academics have suddenly taken an urgent interest in suburbia. Other major newspapers across the country have latched on to the subject, perhaps as an outgrowth of the widening interest in sprawl.

Recent stories in *Preservation*, beginning with a cover story on the new suburban immigrants, have not thrilled hardcore preservationists, for whom suburbia has always been a particular bete noire. For me, this resistance is only a speed bump on the road to the movement's democratization.

Do I foresee the wholesale preservation of postwar suburbs? Probably not. Rapid evolution would be far more desirable. Still, alarms were sounded recently in Houston, where a whole neighborhood of brick ranch houses was under siege. The truth is that most people love their suburban homes and neighborhoods and will fight to save them. And if preservationists have learned anything in the last century or so, it is that the notion of what is worth preserving changes. Just recall how Victorian buildings were despised as recently as a few decades ago. Perhaps the split-level will be the retro rage in 2050.

Topical Press Agency/Getty Images

Wes Thompson/Corbis

DESIGN CREEPS IN

As money and newly sophisticated consumers pour into the suburbs, good design and architecture are beginning to follow. In my neck of suburbia, northern Virginia, where even a determined electorate has had trouble slowing sprawl, there are nonetheless hopeful signs that good ideas are arriving—from town-center schemes for shopping and living to interesting and appealing buildings for churches, college campuses, and office complexes.

Most welcome of all, perhaps, is the improved architecture for public buildings, including schools, which were the most bereft places we allowed to be built in the bad old days just ending. May all of you who read these words enthusiastically enter the fray, enriching yourselves even as you enrich a vast part of our landscape that urgently needs you.

Questions for Discussion

1. Wilson opens his argument by establishing that he is editor of *Preservation* magazine. To what extent does this information make him a credible source? Does his position as editor of an important magazine about architecture and design influence your reaction to his argument in any way? Explain.

2. On what grounds might preservationists try to protect suburban neighborhoods that some critics find ugly? Do you think Wilson does justice to a more positive view of suburban communities? Explain.

3. Wilson suggests in this essay that suburbs can be better. What does he mean? What does his position reveal about his beliefs regarding the ideal community? Do you agree with him? Why or why not?

4. Notice the many references Wilson makes in his essay to films, literature, historical developments, and social movements. What do these references suggest about the audience Wilson is addressing in this essay? Does that audience include you? Explain.

5. Wilson's essay raises questions about how people think about the communities they live in. How does his argument affect the way you think communities should be designed? Do you think he wishes to challenge conventional views about community design? Explain, citing specific passages from his essay to support your answer.

④ | # The Green Case for Cities

WITOLD RYBCZYNSKI

Most of us probably do not think of cities—with their crowds, traffic, and pollution—as "green." Scholar and architect Witold Rybczynski does, and in this brief essay he explains why. Rybczynski, who has devoted his life to understanding urban design, argues that cities are inherently green because they concentrate population, structures, and services in relatively small areas, thus using the land much more efficiently than suburbs. His perspective on this subject is being embraced by a growing number of people who are concerned about how to address potentially catastrophic environmental problems such as global climate change. Solving such problems, many people believe, will require significant changes in the way we live, including the kinds of communities we create and inhabit. In Rybczynski's view, cities are a big part of the solution; they are an important answer to the question, How should we design our communities? Witold Rybczynski is the Martin & Margy Meyerson Professor of Urbanism in the Wharton School of Business at the University of Pennsylvania. He has written many articles and books on housing and urban design, including *City Life: Urban Expectations in a New World* (1995). This essay appeared in the *Atlantic Monthly* in 2009.

WITOLD RYBCZYNSKI, "The Green Case for Cities"

1 Nowhere has the greening message had a bigger impact than in the building industry. Green or sustainable architecture is all the rage—as well it should be, because buildings use a lot of energy. The construction and operation of residential and commercial buildings consume as much as 40 percent of the energy used in the United States today.

The calculation of a building's total environmental impact must factor in everything from annual energy consumption to how and where building materials are manufactured and the handling of storm water. This requires some sort of rating system, and there are currently more than 40 of them in use around the world. Most, like LEED (Leadership in Energy and Environmental Design), which has become the standard in the United States, award points based on a checklist—daylighting, water recycling, solar panels, bicycle racks, and so on.

Although it is estimated that fewer than 6,000 projects have been certified in the United States in the 10 years since LEED was established, the program has significantly

CONTEXT

According to the U.S. Green Building Council, Leadership in Energy and Environmental Design (LEED) is "is an internationally recognized green building certification system, providing third-party verification that a building or community was designed and built using strategies aimed at improving performance across all the metrics that matter most: energy savings, water efficiency, CO_2 emissions reduction, improved indoor environmental quality, and stewardship of resources and sensitivity to their impacts." Developed in the 1990s as a method of certifying that a building is "green," LEED has become recognized as one of the most important standards for environmentally friendly construction practices. As Rybczynski suggests in this passage, however, establishing and enforcing green building standards is a complicated task, and there is disagreement among builders, environmentalists, and planners about which criteria should be used to judge whether a building is truly "green." As a result, no single standard for green building has yet been accepted among the many rating systems that are being used around the world.

raised public and professional awareness. Yet a checklist approach has drawbacks. It tends to focus attention on unusual features, such as green roofs. Growing grass on a roof is definitely photogenic, but it is not as energy- and cost-efficient as simply painting the roof white. And checklists—even weighted checklists—may produce misleading results. Both a suburban office campus and an urban high-rise office building, for example, can receive a high rating. As David Owen points out in his forthcoming *Green Metropolis: Why Living Smaller, Living Closer, and Driving Less Are the Keys to Sustainability*, in the office campus, people work in sprawling buildings and drive between them; in the high-rise, people work in a compact building, use elevators (which are inherently energy-efficient, since they are counterweighted), and walk to lunch.

Putting solar panels on the roofs doesn't change the essential fact that by any sensible measure, spread-out, low-rise buildings, with more foundations, walls, and roofs, have a larger carbon footprint than a high-rise office tower—even when the high-rise has no green features at all.

5 The problem in the sustainability campaign is that a basic truth has been lost, or at least concealed. Rather than trying to change behavior to actually reduce carbon emissions, politicians and entrepreneurs have sold greening to the public as a kind of accessorizing. Keep doing what you're doing, goes the message. Just add a solar panel, a wind turbine, a hybrid engine, whatever. But a solar-heated house in the burbs is still a house in the burbs, and if you have to drive to it, even in a Prius, it's hardly green.

Architectural journals and the Sunday supplements tout newfangled houses tricked out with rainwater-collection systems, solar arrays, and bamboo flooring. Yet any detached single-family house has more external walls and roof—and hence more heating loads in winter and cooling loads in summer—than a comparable attached townhouse, and each consumes more energy than an apartment in a multifamily building. Again, it doesn't really matter how many green features are present. A reasonably well-built and well-insulated multifamily building is inherently more sustainable than a detached house. Similarly, an old building on an urban site, adapted and reused, is greener than any new building on a newly developed site.

A **Thoreau-like existence** in the great outdoors isn't green. Density is green. Does this mean that we all have to live in Manhattan? Not necessarily. Cities such as Stockholm and Copenhagen are dense without being vertical. And closer to home is Montreal, where the predominant housing form is a three- or four-story walk-up. Walk-ups, which don't require elevators, can create a sufficient density—about 50 people per acre—to support public transit, walkability, and other urban amenities. Increasing an area's density requires changing zoning to allow smaller lots and compact buildings such as walk-ups and townhouses.

In other words, being truly green means returning to the kinds of dense cities and garden suburbs Americans built in the first half of the 20th century. A tall order—but after the binge of the last housing boom, many Americans might be ready to consider a little downsizing.

Henry David **Thoreau** (1817–1862) was an influential American writer and philosopher. His famous book *Walden* (1854), in which he describes his experiences living alone in a small cabin in the forest outside Concord, Massachusetts, influenced the environmental movement in the 1970s and remains an inspirational statement for many people about the relationship between humans and their environment. (An essay by Thoreau appears in Chapter 8 of this book.)

Questions for Discussion

1. What criticisms of so-called green, or sustainable, building practices does Rybczynski make in this essay? On what grounds does he make these criticisms? How do these criticisms fit into his main argument about cities?

2. Examine Rybczynski's use of statistics as evidence to support his points about green building and cities. What kinds of statistics does he use? How credible do you find these statistics? How effectively do these statistics serve as evidence to support his argument?

3. What is the main problem with the arguments of those who advocate green building, according to Rybczynski? Why is this problem significant, in his view? Do you think he's right? Why or why not?

4. What does Rybczynski mean when he writes that "density is green" (par. 7)? How does this point fit into his main argument? To what extent do you think this idea of density as green is a challenge to the way most people think about cities? Do you think Rybczynski intended this point to be provocative? Explain.

5. Rybczynski ends his essay by suggesting that "Americans might be ready to consider a little downsizing." What does he mean by that statement? What does it suggest about his view of the kinds of communities Americans should create? Do you think most Americans would agree with him? Why or why not?

NEGOTIATING DIFFERENCES

The authors included in this section all offer a vision for the kinds of communities we should create. Jane Holtz Kay and Witold Rybczynski advocate urban communities. Donella Meadows raises concerns about the impact of "sprawl"—that is, the expansion of suburbs on previously undeveloped land—while Robert Wilson argues in favor of suburbs as livable communities. As a group, these essays suggest some of the complexities to be confronted when we think about the kinds of communities we want to live in, especially in view of the daunting environmental problems facing humanity at the beginning of this new millennium. This assignment gives you the opportunity to confront these complexities and answer the question posed in this section: How should we design our communities? It focuses on your campus community: How can your college or university campus become the kind of community that you believe we should create today?

Imagine that you have been invited to be part of a committee of students, faculty members, administrators, and local residents, politicians, and business leaders who have been asked to answer that question for your school. Your committee's task is to submit a report in which you propose a plan for making your campus a *livable community*, as you define that term. In your report, be sure to define what you mean by "livable community" and identify the principles by which you will design your campus community. You should also discuss the characteristics of your campus that you believe should be preserved, and you should identify the problems you see with the campus as it currently exists. Most important, your report should include a proposal for updating, changing, or redesigning your campus so that it fits the principles of a livable community as you define them. Include as part of your proposal a rationale that makes a persuasive case for your proposed changes.

For this assignment, you might consider speaking to members of your campus community to get their perspective on what a livable community should be and to identify some of the challenges to creating such a community on your campus. Also consider other college campuses that you think might provide good models for the kind of livable community you imagine for your school. If your instructor allows it, consider doing this assignment in collaboration with several of your classmates.

© Maximilian Stock Ltd/photocuisine/Corbis

What (and How) Should We Eat?

The question of what to eat might seem a matter of personal preference. People can choose to eat what they like, and different people like—and dislike—different foods. But not everyone has choice when it comes to deciding what they should eat. The United Nations estimates that more than one billion people worldwide, which is approximately 15 percent of the world's population, do not have enough to eat. By some estimates, more than 10 percent of households in the United States, the world's richest nation, experience hunger at some point during the year because they don't have enough money to buy food. For these people, the question of what to eat is a question of survival; they simply don't have enough food, and just about any food will do. ■ For those who are fortunate enough to be able to afford the food they need to survive, the question of what to eat becomes more complicated. For one thing, it is matter of health. What you eat plays a central role in almost every aspect of your physical well-being, and eating too much or eating the wrong foods can create many different health problems. If you eat healthier foods, then you should be a healthier person. But how does your choice of what to eat affect others—in your family, in your community, and around the world? The coffee you drank for breakfast might have been made from coffee beans picked by a worker in South America who is being paid unfairly for his labor. The grapes from Chile that you buy in your local supermarket in January might help put a farmer in Georgia out of business. Conversely, your decision not to buy lettuce in January because it has to be trucked a great distance to your community might help put a migrant farm worker out of work. So what you choose to eat, no matter how healthy, can affect many other people, not always in good ways. ■ Moreover, your choice of foods can affect the earth itself. Many gallons of gasoline or diesel fuel have to be burned to get lettuce from a farm in California to a market in Massachusetts, which contributes to pollution and possibly to climate change. That fuel was very likely made from crude oil pumped from the ground in the Middle East and transported halfway around the world in a tanker ship (which pollutes the oceans) to an oil refinery in the southern United States, where it is made into fuel, a process that causes further pollution and environmental damage (not to mention health problems for workers and local residents).

The fertilizer used to grow the lettuce was probably also made from petroleum and thus contributed to environmental degradation. And the trucks and tankers used to haul the fuel and the lettuce were all manufactured in ways that cause significant damage to the land, water, and air. And so on. So the customer who buys lettuce in Massachusetts—or New York or Wisconsin or Missouri—is part of a complicated network that may be damaging the earth. ■ So what should we eat? Obviously, it isn't a simple question. The essays in this section present arguments that may help you answer it for yourself.

① | Eat This Now!

SUSAN BRINK AND ELIZABETH QUERNA

In 2005, *U.S. News & World Report* published the following article by reporters Susan Brink and Elizabeth Querna. It provides a useful introduction to contemporary concerns about the increase in obesity in the United States. Experts disagree about how serious the problem is, but there seems to be widespread agreement that U.S. citizens are overeating and underexercising. As Brink and Querna report, temptations to snack abound, portion sizes are growing, and too much of what is eaten consists of food with little nutritional value. Their title suggests that many Americans may be more interested in eating quickly than in eating wisely. In reviewing the medical evidence about obesity, Brink and Querna remind us that our choices of what to eat are influenced by many factors, and those choices can have serious health consequences. The authors also help us see that *how* we eat can be as important as *what* we eat when it comes to our health.

SUSAN BRINK AND ELIZABETH QUERNA, "Eat This Now!"

1 It's everywhere. Tank up your car, and you walk past soft pretzels with cheese sauce. Grab a cup of coffee, and you see doughnuts, danishes, and cookies the size of hubcaps. Stop at Staples for an ink cartridge, and you confront candy bars at the register.

Stroll past the receptionist's desk at the office, and find somebody's leftover Christmas cookies, Valentine's Day candy, Easter Peeps, birthday cake, or vacation saltwater taffy. "We're just surrounded. Food is available every time you turn around," says Marilyn Tanner, dietitian at Washington University School of Medicine in St. Louis.

Overeating and its lethal companion underexercising are the recognized culprits in this country's rise in obesity rates. Today, two thirds of American adults are obese or overweight. A national team of researchers reported in last week's *New England Journal of Medicine* that obesity already reduces the current life expectancy in the United States by four to nine months.

What's worse, they project that the rise in obesity rates among children and teens could knock off as many as five years from today's average of 77 years as overweight people in that generation grow up and die prematurely. Diseases associated with obesity, such as diabetes, heart disease, kidney disease, and some cancers, are likely to strike at younger ages. It would be the first time in 200 years that children would be statistically likely to live shorter lives than their grandparents.

5 It's a controversial prediction, called speculative and "excessively gloomy" by Samuel Preston, a demographer at the University of Pennsylvania.

And the outcome is far from inevitable. All it would take to change that dire prediction is

CONTEXT

In paragraph 3 Brink and Querna quote statistics from 2005, when they wrote this article. According to a study published in the *Journal of the American Medical Association* in 2010, 68 percent of Americans were either obese or overweight (which the researchers defined as a Body Mass Index of 25 or greater). As Brink and Querna indicate in this article, however, there is disagreement about how to measure obesity and about healthy weights for adults. Several studies published in 2009, for example, suggested that being slightly overweight (that is, having a Body Mass Index of 25 or 26) might not increase one's risk of mortality.

to have millions of people change their habits. That means diet, exercise, and a strong will within every individual to pass up high-calorie temptations. Right?

It's not that easy, as every failed and yo-yo dieter knows. The playing field is heavily tilted—by advertising, fast-paced lives, convenience foods, and treats every time you turn around—away from healthful eating choices. Many experts in nutrition, public health, and law believe that the national obesity problem doesn't simply come down to millions of failures of individual will.

ATTITUDE SHIFT

A generation ago, it was considered rude to eat in front of others. Now, Americans eat everywhere, all day long—an average of five meals a day, counting snacks. Cars have cupholders, but they arguably need trays, too. Americans eat 30 meals a year in their vehicles. "That's the average. I'm sure it's higher when it comes to people driving to work," said Harry Balzer, vice president of the NPD Group, a consumer marketing research firm that tracks how Americans eat. "Look at our cars. They look like restaurants."

Riddled with anxiety, we take our meals with equal parts pleasure and guilt. We might say an internal no a dozen times a day, then give in to the Krispy Kreme near the bus stop on the way home. Or if we pass up the doughnut shop, we get home only to find that the latest issue of *Cooking Light* has arrived in the mail—with a cover photo of pecan pie. We have few common rituals around dining but a common hurried pace through eating. All of these triggers and gustatory seductions play into an obesity epidemic—even as the messages manipulate the national obsession with health.

10 Food is more than a way of staying alive, more than an edible commodity. "Food is never just the physical product itself," says Stephanie Hartman, who teaches a course at Catholic University of America in Washington, D.C., called "Food and Media." "It's invested with national meanings, associated with comfort and nostalgia. There are class associations. Food can be elegant or cultured." Or it can carry a reverse snobbery. Where once the elite sampled truffles, today they might seek the best barbecued ribs or the richest macaroni and cheese.

Certainly, the descendants of immigrants may still prepare pasta or pirogi recipes handed down from the old country, but Americans as a whole don't have shared food values. We don't all cook with the same oil, have an attachment to a certain variety of plum, or dine with predictable ceremony. Such culinary eclecticism may make us uniquely vulnerable to fads. "We don't have a culture of eating, a national cuisine, a traditional way of eating that guides us," says Tanner. "So we fall prey to the latest fad or scientific pronouncement. The fact that we're more responsive to medical trends makes us more responsive to marketing." As soon as science tells us that oat bran is good for preventing heart disease, people start buying potato chips sprinkled with oat bran. "This is who we are. We're always looking for the newest way to attack this problem. We're going to try to figure out this health issue by eating," says Balzer.

Why, even when we know better, do we succumb to the lure of rich desserts and nutritionally empty snacks? Why is the look—even stronger, the smell—of the forbidden so

CONTEXT

According to some estimates, more than $10 billion is spent every year on fast-food advertising aimed primarily at children and teens, who see approximately 40,000 commercials for food and related items annually. Such advertising is ubiquitous, extending well beyond television and print publications such as magazines. Food advertising is now common online and even in video games as well as in movies through so-called "product placement," in which recognizable brands of foods are visible in various scenes. In one study, researchers analyzed 200 popular films released between 1996 and 2005 and found that 69 percent featured at least one food, beverage, or retail establishment. Figure 13-3 shows a scene from the popular film *Talladega Nights* (2006) in which the main characters are eating a leading brand of fast food.

compelling? "I've seen evidence that bakeries and supermarkets pipe faked aromas out in the store," says Doug Kysar, a professor at Cornell Law School who teaches consumer law and studies deceptive advertising. "Things like taste and smell and sight can overcome one's awareness. The classic example is the candy gantlet at the supermarket. We have a long-term desire to maintain a healthful life, but the short-term desire can trump the long-term."

Marketers know what works. They tell us we're worth it, that we deserve it. "Magnify that by 45,000 different products, add in the fake bakery smell, the mood music in supermarkets calculated to lower blink rates to a somnolent state, the way the aisles are set up to keep people in the store for a longer time—that's an enormous amount of situational forces to weaken the will," says Kysar.

FOOD TO SELL

America is truly a horn of plenty. In the early 1980s, food production came to an average of 3,300 calories a day available to every person. Then farm policy changed, and farmers no longer plowed food under or slaughtered animals to be entitled to subsidies. Today, America produces enough food to allow every man, woman, and child 3,900 calories a day. "That additional food production had to be sold," says Marion Nestle, professor in the department of nutrition at New York University and author of *Food Politics*. "One of the first things that happened was portion sizes started getting bigger."

15 Many Americans feel entitled to big servings on a top-of-the-line chocolate bar as a way to get some short-term happiness. "You walk past a doughnut shop, and you say, 'Yum. Doughnuts.' Part of you says, 'No, I'll get fat.' But another part is like Scarlett O'Hara saying, 'Tomorrow is another day.' This feels good now," says Gail Saltz of the New York Psychoanalytic Institute.

Almost all of us are prone to comfort ourselves with food when we feel deprived in other ways. Many families have forsaken the shared meal and the long time of food preparation, dining, and cleanup as a communal effort. Along with it, they've lost an important psychological support. "If we take a good hour

FIGURE 13-3

Scene from *Talladega Nights*

©Sony Pictures/Courtesy Everett Collection

and a half to talk about our day, go slowly through the meal, maybe have a glass of wine—we're much more psychologically filled at the end of that meal than if I decide to eat alone. Then, I'm going to grab a hamburger and some chips," says psychoanalyst Kathryn Zerbe, vice chair for psychotherapy at Oregon Health and Science University.

Of course, we can just say no. But it's a David and Goliath fight. We're battling an entire environment, massive societal change, government policy, and billions of dollars in advertising.

THE EXPERTS' TIPS

- Don't walk into a bakery or chocolate shop without a buddy who might sober you up enough to keep your order from getting out of hand.
- Know that what you buy at the grocery store will get eaten. Some 37 percent of dinner menus are planned spontaneously with what's available in the house, says Harry Balzer, vice president of the NPD Group. So don't bring fattening or unhealthful foods home.
- If you eat out a lot, it's no longer a special occasion. Don't order as if it's a party.
- Be aware of how advertising is trying to manipulate your need for comfort, quick gratification, or self-indulgence. "The only way to outsmart them is to know what they're tapping into and not have it go directly to your unconscious," says Gail Saltz, a psychoanalyst with the New York Psychoanalytic Institute.
- Cleaning your plate will not help starving children in the Third World. If you've been served too hefty a portion, it's better to scrape it into the garbage than shovel it into your stomach.

Questions for Discussion

1. Brink and Querna present a great deal of statistical and factual information to support their points about eating and obesity. How credible is this information? How effectively do they use it to help make their main argument?

2. Why is there reason to believe that children may eventually suffer more serious consequences from obesity than those currently experienced by adults? What evidence do the authors present to support this belief? How persuasive is this evidence, in your view?

3. According to the authors, it used to be considered rude to eat in front of others, but today Americans routinely eat in front of one another. Why do the authors emphasize this point? What conclusions do they draw from it? How does it fit into their main argument?

4. What cultural factors could make Americans especially vulnerable to overeating, according to Brink and Querna? Why are these factors important when it comes to addressing the problem of obesity?

5. This article originally appeared in *Newsweek*, a widely circulated newsmagazine that reaches a general audience. What assumptions do you think the authors make about their audience? Do you think readers of different ages will react differently to the authors' argument? Explain, citing specific passages from the text to support your answer.

6. The authors end this article by describing the struggle to overcome obesity as "a David and Goliath fight". What do you think they intend to suggest by using that metaphor? Do you think they are right? Why or why not?

② | Voting With Your Fork

MICHAEL POLLAN

Michael Pollan has become one of the nation's preeminent voices on the subject of food. He has been writing about gardening, food production, and eating for two decades and is the author of many award-winning articles and books, including *Second Nature: A Gardener's Education* (1991) and *The Botany of Desire: A Plant's Eye View of the World* (2001), which was the basis for a PBS television special. But it was his book *The Omnivore's Dilemma: A Natural History of Four Meals*, published in 2006, that ignited a national debate about how Americans produce and consume their food. As the following essay indicates, Pollan isn't interested only in eating a diet that makes us healthy; he is also interested in promoting a diet that is healthy for the planet. His examination of our current system of food production and distribution leads to a pointed critique of what and how we eat, and he makes a vigorous argument that we have to change not only our eating habits but also the way we think about food. As you'll see, Pollan's writing is provocative and his voice is earnest. His arguments about what and how we should eat may change the way you think about food. The following essay was published in the *New York Times* in 2006.

MICHAEL POLLAN, "Voting with Your Fork"

1 To someone who's spent the last few years thinking about the American food chain, a visit to Manhattan's Union Square in the spring of 2006 feels a little like a visit to **Paris in the spring of 1968** must have felt, or perhaps closer to the mark, **Peoples Park in Berkeley in the summer of 1969**. Not that I was in either of those places at the appointed historical hour, or that the stakes are quite as high. (Isn't hyperbole an earmark of Internet literary style? O.K. then.) But today in these few square blocks of lower Manhattan, change is in the air, and the future—at least the future of food—is up for grabs.

When Whole Foods planted its flag on 14th Street last year, setting up shop an heirloom tomato's throw from one of the nation's liveliest farmer's markets, two crucial visions of an alternative American food chain—what I call, somewhat oxymoronically, Industrial Organic and Local—faced off. And then this spring Trader Joe's opened in Union Square, further complicating the picture (for both the farmer's market and Whole Foods) with its discount take on both organic and artisanal food.

The shopping choices laid out so succinctly for New Yorkers in Union Square today neatly encapsulate the kinds of question we will all be grappling with over the next few years as we navigate an increasingly complex, politicized and ethically challenging food landscape. The organic strawberry or the conventional? The grass-fed or the organic beef? And, if the grass-fed, the Whole Foods steak from New Zealand or the Hudson Valley steak across the street? The organic tomato or the New Jersey beefsteak? The omega-3 fortified eggs or the cage-free eggs? (That last phrase is one of my favorite snatches of recent supermarket prose: I mean, does an

In May 1968, millions of French workers and students went on strike to protest what they believed was the corruption of modern industrial society. In April 1969, thousands of people occupied a section of the campus of the University of California at Berkeley that was to be used for a parking lot; they planted flowers and grass and converted the land into a "People's Park" until they were removed by California National Guard troops. Both events were associated with a sense of change, or even revolution, as Pollan suggests in paragraph 1.

Monsanto, a multinational agricultural company based in the United States, is one of the world's largest producers of herbicides, pesticides, and genetically modified seeds for crops such as corn.

egg really care whether it's caged or not?) The ultra-pasteurized milk or the raw? The farmed fish or the wild? In January, the jet-setting winter asparagus from Argentina or the rutabaga from Upstate? And how do you cook a rutabaga, anyway?

I've been doing a lot of food reporting over the past couple years and have discovered there are no simple, one-size-fits-all answers to these questions (several of which I hope to take up in future columns). But it seems to me the crucial thing is that such questions about how we should eat, and how what we eat affects both our health and the health of the world, confront us today in a way they never before have. My explorations of the American food chain—or now, food chains—have convinced me that these questions (except perhaps the one about rutabaga) are actually political questions, and much depends on how we choose to answer them. The market for alternative foods of all kinds—organic, local, pasture-based, humanely raised—represents the stirrings of a movement, or rather a novel hybrid: a market-as-movement. Over the next month I plan to use this column as a place to conduct a conversation with readers (or "r-eaters," as someone at a lecture proposed the other night) about the politics of food.

5 Union Square, which 75 years ago served as the red-hot center of the labor movement, is now, at least symbolically, ground zero of the food movement. And while much

separates the various choices and philosophies on offer here, it's important to recognize what unifies the Whole Foods and Trader Joe's and the farmer's market, and what has brought so many of us 21st century food foragers to Union Square and all places like it: the gathering sense that there is something very wrong with our conventional food system—what I call the industrial food chain, by which I mean typical supermarket and fast food.

It has become a commonplace to say that the industrial food system is not "sustainable"—indeed, even **Monsanto** now acknowledges that American agriculture is not sustainable. (Which is why it supposedly needs the company's genetically modified organisms in place of pesticides.) But it's worth taking a moment to think through exactly what it means to say that a system is unsustainable, lest the word lose its force. What it means, very simply, is that a practice or activity cannot go on as it has much longer—that, because of various internal contradictions, it will sooner or later break down.

This is the case with our industrial food chain: evidence of failure is all around us. While it is true that this system produces vast quantities of cheap food (indeed, the vastness and cheapness is part of the problem), it is not doing what any nation's food system foremost needs to do: that is, maintain its population in good health. Historians of the future will marvel at the existence of a civilization whose population was at once so well-fed and so unhealthy. This is unprecedented. For most of history, the "food problem" has been a problem of quantity. Our shocking rates of obesity, diabetes, cardiovascular disease, foodborne illness and nutrient deficiency suggest that quantity is not the problem—or the solution.

To say a system is unsustainable also means it cannot endure indefinitely for the simple reason that it is using up the very resources it depends on: it is eating its seed corn. Certainly this is the case in industrial agriculture, which is literally consuming the soil and the genetic diversity on which it depends: there's half as much topsoil in Iowa today as there was a century ago, and our single-minded focus on a tiny number of crops (and within those crops a tiny number of varieties) is driving untold numbers of plant and animal varieties to extinction. These are genes whose disappearance we will rue when our monocultures fail, as all monocultures sooner or later do.

"Unsustainable" also means a system can't go on indefinitely paying the costs of doing business as it has been doing. In the case of the industrial food chain, that includes the cost to the treasury ($88 billion in agricultural subsidies over the last five years); to the environment (water and air pollution, especially from our factory animal farms); and to the public health. Cheap food, it turns out, is unbelievably expensive. Many of the costs of cheap food are invisible to us, but they will soon force themselves onto our attention. Take energy, for example. The industrial food system is at bottom a system founded on cheap fossil fuel, which we depend on to grow the crops (the fertilizers and pesticides are made from petroleum), process the food, and then ship it hither and yon. Fully a fifth of the fossil fuel we consume in America goes to feeding ourselves, more than we devote to personal transportation. (Unfortunately the industrial organic food chain guzzles nearly as much fossil fuel as the nonorganic.) If the era of cheap energy is really drawing to a close, as it appears, so will the era of cheap industrial food.

10 The last sense in which the industrial food chain is unsustainable is that it depends on our ignorance of how it works for its continued survival. Indeed, our ignorance of its methods is as important to its workings as cheap energy. If I've learned anything over the past several years, as I've followed the industrial food chain from the supermarkets and fast food outlets back through the meatpacking plants and C.A.F.O.'s (Confined Animal Feeding

© David R. Frazier Photolibrary, Inc./Alamy

CONTEXT

Pollan suggests in this passage (see par. 10) that if Americans knew more about how their food was produced, they would change their eating habits. He goes on to mention Confined Animal Feeding Operations, or CAFOs, which have been criticized by animal rights activists and critics concerned about the safety of the American food supply. Figure 13-4 shows hogs in such a facility. Consider whether such images support Pollan's argument.

Operations) and food science laboratories and farm fields, it is that the more you know about this food, the less appetizing it becomes to eat. If people could peer over the increasingly high walls of our industrial agriculture they would surely change the way they eat.

FIGURE 13-4

A Confined Animal Feeding Operation

CONTEXT

In May 2006, producers of soft drinks announced that they would voluntarily remove sodas from vending machines in schools throughout the United States and would also limit other high-calorie soft drinks such as fruit drinks. The announcement was part of an agreement involving the beverage industry, the American Heart Association, former president Bill Clinton, and Arkansas governor Bill Huckabee that was aimed at reducing childhood obesity. Some critics claimed that the agreement was too weak and was intended only to avoid additional government regulation of the food industry. In paragraph 12, however, Pollan suggests that the agreement was part of a larger national debate about how and what Americans eat.

Increasing numbers of Americans aren't waiting: they're changing now. This desire for something better—something safer, something more sustainable, something more humane and something tastier—is what's bringing people to the Whole Foods and the farmer's market, as well as to C.S.A.'s (community-supported agriculture programs, about which more in a subsequent post) and directly to farmers over the Internet. Taken together the fastest growing segment of the American food system are these alternatives to it. Change is indeed in the air.

And this change is not limited to the marketplace. A vibrant grass-roots movement to change food (and beverages) in the schools is rapidly spreading across the country—witness last week's tactical retreat of the soda makers from school cafeterias. A debate is just getting underway about food policy at the federal level, as Congress starts work on the next farm bill; it will have to decide whether the government should continue to subsidize high-fructose corn syrup at a time when we have an epidemic of Type 2 diabetes. Animal rights groups are forcing the fast food industry to change the miserable condition in which billions of food animals now live.

I write from the road, where I'm on tour promoting my book, and I'm hearing a lot of anxiety around the subject food but also a lot of hope. Indeed, of all the issues before us today, the food issue is one of the most hopeful. As the tableaux in Union Square demonstrates, we have choices. We no longer have to take the food on offer, which makes this issue unique.

A couple of weeks ago we all paid our taxes. Whenever I write that check, I can't help but think of the various uses to which that money is put. Whatever your politics, there are activities your tax money supports that I'm sure you find troublesome, if not deplorable. But you can't do anything about those activities—you can't withdraw your support—unless you're prepared to go the jail. Food is different. You can simply stop participating in a system that abuses animals or poisons the water or squanders jet fuel flying asparagus around the world. You can vote with your fork, in other words, and you can do it three times a day.

15 So this column will take the form of a discussion about how to cast those sorts of votes. I take seriously this idea of conversation. I've found that publishing a book in the Internet era (my last one came out in 2001, before the word blog had even been coined) is a completely new and bracing experience, far more reciprocal than writing has ever been. I get e-mail from people reporting they're on page six and have a question they'd like answered before they go on. (This seems a bit much!) When I go on the radio and say something dubious or sloppy, inevitably someone will straighten me out within the hour. Daily, readers and listeners force me to rethink my positions or consider questions I'd never known to ask. Make no mistake: not all of these questions are so provocative. The other day a reader emailed to ask, "So what do you think about dried fruit?"

I take all these questions (well, almost all of them) as a sign of a healthy ferment rising around the politics of food, and have undertaken this blog to air the best of them in a more public way than my e-mail correspondence. So come gather around this table to talk. About anything—except, unless you absolutely insist, dried fruit.

Questions for Discussion

1. What does Pollan mean when he writes that the future of food is "up for grabs"? What support does he provide for such a claim? Do you think he's right? Why or why not?

2. In paragraph 3 Pollan poses a series of questions about possible food choices that a consumer might face. What do his questions suggest about our food choices? How effective is this strategy in helping him make his point?

3. How does Pollan define "sustainable" in reference to food habits? Why is it important to define this term, in his view? How does his definition of "sustainable" figure into his main argument in this essay?

4. In what sense are our food choices political and ethical, according to Pollan? Why is it important to understand our food choices in these terms, in his view? How effectively do you think he supports this point of view about our food choices?

5. In building his main argument, Pollan makes several key claims about the current system of food production in the United States and the changes he sees happening today. Using the Toulmin approach to claims and warrants (see pages 87–91), identify and evaluate Pollan's main claims and their warrants in this essay. On the basis of your evaluation, determine how sound Pollan's argument is.

6. As a solution to the problems he sees with the way Americans eat, Pollan proposes that consumers should "vote with their forks." What exactly does he mean? How effective is this solution in addressing the problems Pollan identifies in this essay?

7. At the end of paragraph 4 and again in paragraph 15, Pollan indicates that this essay was part of a special guest column that he wrote for the *New York Times* in 2006. His column was published online, where readers could post comments in response to Pollan's essays. In fact, Pollan indicates in paragraph 15 that he considers his column a conversation with his readers. To what extent do you think Pollan might have adjusted his argument in this essay for such an online medium, in which he knew his readers could comment and share their responses with him and with each other? Do you think his strategies for making his argument are effective for such a forum? Explain, citing specific passages from his essay to support your answer. Do you think his strategies would have been different if his essay were published only in print form without an easy way for readers to respond? Why or why not?

③ | The Omnivore's Delusion

BLAKE HURST

In recent years the question of what (and how) we should eat has focused new attention on how foods are produced in the United States. Many critics, such as Michael Pollan (whose essay appears on page 625), have argued that so-called "industrial farming" practices in the United States are a big part of the reason why the foods Americans eat aren't as healthy as they could be; moreover, these critics charge that conventional farming creates a host of environment problems, including water pollution, erosion of good farmland, and the spread of harmful chemicals throughout ecosystems and the food chain. Such criticisms have become common in the increasingly heated national debates about food, health, and the environment. But as you'll see in the following essay, Blake Hurst, who is himself a farmer, has had enough of such criticisms. He takes on critics like Pollan and defends modern farming practices against their charges. As a farmer, Hurst speaks from experience that few policymakers or writers have, and he adds a voice that is often missing from important discussions about food and farming policy. His essay appeared in 2009 in *The American*, a journal published by the American Enterprise Institute, an influential conservative think tank.

BLAKE HURST, "The Omnivore's Delusion"

1 I'm dozing, as I often do on airplanes, but the guy behind me has been broadcasting nonstop for nearly three hours. I finally admit defeat and start some serious eavesdropping. He's talking about food, damning farming, particularly livestock farming, compensating for his lack of knowledge with volume.

I'm so tired of people who wouldn't visit a doctor who used a stethoscope instead of an MRI demanding that farmers like me use 1930s technology to raise food. Farming has always been messy and painful, and bloody and dirty. It still is.

But now we have to listen to self-appointed experts on airplanes frightening their seatmates about the profession I have practiced for more than 30 years. I'd had enough. I turned around and politely told the lecturer that he ought not believe everything he reads. He quieted and asked me what

kind of farming I do. I told him, and when he asked if I used organic farming, I said no, and left it at that. I didn't answer with the first thought that came to mind, which is simply this: I deal in the real world, not superstitions, and unless the consumer absolutely forces my hand, I am about as likely to adopt organic methods as the *Wall Street Journal* is to publish their next edition by setting the type by hand.

He was a businessman, and I'm sure spends his days with spreadsheets, projections, and marketing studies. He hasn't used a slide rule in his career and wouldn't make projections with tea leaves or soothsayers. He does not blame witchcraft for a bad quarter, or expect the factory that makes his product to use steam power instead of electricity, or horses and wagons to deliver his products instead of trucks and trains. But he expects me to farm like my grandfather, and not incidentally, I suppose, to live like him as well. He thinks farmers are too stupid to farm sustainably, too cruel to treat their animals well, and too careless to worry about their communities, their health, and their families. I would not presume to criticize his car, or the size of his house, or the way he runs his business. But he is an expert about me, on the strength of one book [*Omnivore's Dilemma*], and is sharing that expertise with captive audiences every time he gets the chance. Enough, enough, enough.

INDUSTRIAL FARMING AND ITS CRITICS

5 Critics of "industrial farming" spend most of their time concerned with the processes by which food is raised. This is because the results of organic production are so, well, troublesome. With the subtraction of every "unnatural" additive, molds, fungus, and bugs increase. Since it is difficult to sell a religion with so many readily quantifiable bad results, the trusty family farmer has to be thrown into the breach, saving the whole organic movement by his saintly presence, chewing on his straw, plodding along, at one with his environment, his community, his neighborhood. Except that some of the largest farms in the country are organic—and are giant organizations dependent upon lots of hired stoop labor doing the most backbreaking of tasks in order to save the sensitive conscience of my fellow passenger the merest whiff of pesticide contamination. They do not spend much time talking about that at the **Whole Foods** store.

The most delicious irony is this: the parts of farming that are the most "industrial" are the most likely to be owned by the kind of family farmers that elicit such a positive response from the consumer. Corn farms are almost all owned and managed by small family farmers. But corn farmers salivate at the thought of one more biotech breakthrough, use vast amounts of energy to increase production, and raise large quantities of an indistinguishable commodity to sell to huge corporations that turn that corn into thousands of industrial products.

Most livestock is produced by family farms, and even the poultry industry, with its contracts and vertical integration, relies on family farms to contract for the production of the birds. Despite the obvious change in scale over time, family farms, like ours, still meet around the kitchen table, send their kids to the same small schools, sit in the same church pew, and belong to the same civic organizations our parents and grandparents did. We may be industrial by some definition, but not our own. Reality is messier than it appears in the book my tormentor was reading, and farming more complicated than a simple morality play.

On the desk in front of me are a dozen books, all hugely critical of present-day farming. Farmers are often given a pass in these books, painted as either naïve tools of corporate greed, or economic nullities forced into their present circumstances by the unrelenting forces of the twin grindstones of corporate greed and unfeeling markets. To the farmer

Whole Foods is a national chain of supermarkets known for selling organic foods.

CONTEXT

Bioengineered foods, which Hurst calls "biotech crops" and which are also known as genetically modified foods, are plants that have been developed through genetic engineering to have specific characteristics that are considered desirable. For example, corn can be genetically modified to resist certain herbicides that will kill most other plants, allowing farmers to use strong herbicides on their cornfields without harming the corn crop itself. As Hurst indicates in this essay, such crops have been a boon to farmers in the past fifty years, resulting in greater yields per acre. In part because of these crops, American farmers are the most productive in the world. But these crops have also been controversial. Some critics cite possible health hazards for humans as well as animals who consume genetically modified foods. Other critics point to unintended consequences of genetic engineering. For example, some genetically modified crops can harm desirable insects and plants, as in the case of a special kind of corn called Bt maize, which can kill Monarch Butterflies; in addition, there is concern that undesirable weeds could develop resistance to herbicides by coming into contact with genetically modified crops. Such concerns have led some nations, including Hungary and Venezuela, to ban some genetically modified crops.

on the ground, though, a farmer blessed with free choice and hard won experience, the moral choices aren't quite so easy. Biotech crops actually cut the use of chemicals, and increase food safety. Are people who refuse to use them my moral superiors? Herbicides cut the need for tillage, which decreases soil erosion by millions of tons. The biggest environmental harm I have done as a farmer is the topsoil (and nutrients) I used to send down the Missouri River to the Gulf of Mexico before we began to practice no-till farming, made possible only by the use of herbicides. The combination of herbicides and genetically modified seed has made my farm more sustainable, not less, and actually reduces the pollution I send down the river.

Finally, consumers benefit from cheap food. If you think they don't, just remember the headlines after food prices began increasing in 2007 and 2008, including the study by the Food and Agriculture Organization of the United Nations announcing that 50 million additional people are now hungry because of increasing food prices. Only "industrial farming" can possibly meet the demands of an increasing population and increased demand for food as a result of growing incomes.

10   So the stakes in this argument are even higher. Farmers can raise food in different ways if that is what the market wants. It is important, though, that even people riding in airplanes know that there are environmental and food safety costs to whatever kind of farming we choose.

PIGS IN A PEN

In his book *Dominion*, author Mathew Scully calls "factory farming" an "obvious moral evil so sickening and horrendous it would leave us ashen." Scully, a speechwriter for the second President Bush, can hardly be called a man of the left. Just to make sure the point is not lost, he quotes the conservative historian Paul Johnson a page later:

The rise of factory farming, whereby food producers cannot remain competitive

except by subjecting animals to unspeakable deprivation, has hastened this process. The human spirit revolts at what we have been doing.

Arizona and Florida have outlawed pig gestation crates, and California recently passed, overwhelmingly, a ballot initiative doing the same. There is no doubt that Scully and Johnson have the wind at their backs, and confinement raising of livestock may well be outlawed everywhere. And only a person so callous as to have a spirit that cannot be revolted, or so hardened to any kind of morality that he could countenance an obvious moral evil, could say a word in defense of caging animals during their production. In the quote above, Paul Johnson is forecasting a move toward vegetarianism. But if we assume, at least for the present, that most of us will continue to eat meat, let me dive in where most fear to tread.

Lynn Niemann was a neighbor of my family's, a farmer with a vision. He began raising turkeys on a field near his house around 1956. They were, I suppose, what we would now call "free range" turkeys. Turkeys raised in a natural manner, with no roof over their heads, just gamboling around in the pasture, as God surely intended. Free to eat grasshoppers, and grass, and scratch for grubs and worms. And also free to serve as prey for weasels, who kill turkeys by slitting their necks and practicing exsanguination. Weasels were a problem, but not as much a threat as one of our typically violent early summer thunderstorms. It seems that turkeys, at least young ones, are not smart enough to come in out of the rain, and will stand outside in a downpour, with beaks open and eyes skyward, until they drown. One night Niemann lost 4,000 turkeys to drowning, along with his dream, and his farm.

Now, turkeys are raised in large open sheds. Chickens and turkeys raised for meat are not grown in cages. As the critics of "industrial farming" like to point out, the sheds get quite crowded by the time Thanksgiving rolls around and the turkeys are fully grown. And yes, the birds are bedded in sawdust, so the turkeys do walk around in their own waste. Although the turkeys don't seem to mind, this quite clearly disgusts the various authors I've read who have actually visited a turkey farm. But none of those authors, whose descriptions of the horrors of modern poultry production have a certain sameness, were there when Niemann picked up those 4,000 dead turkeys. Sheds are expensive, and it was easier to raise turkeys in open, inexpensive pastures. But that type of production really was hard on the turkeys. Protected from the weather and predators, today's turkeys may not be aware that they are a part of a morally reprehensible system.

15 Like most young people in my part of the world, I was a 4-H member. Raising cattle and hogs, showing them at the county fair, and then sending to slaughter those animals that we had spent the summer feeding, washing, and training. We would then tour the packing house, where our friend was hung on a rail, with his loin eye measured and his carcass evaluated. We farm kids got an early start on dulling our moral sensibilities. I'm still proud of my win in the Atchison County Carcass competition of 1969, as it is the only trophy I have ever received. We raised the hogs in a shed, or farrowing (birthing) house. On one side were eight crates of the kind that the good citizens of California have outlawed. On the other were the kind of wooden pens that our critics would have us use, where the sow could turn around, lie down, and presumably act in a natural way. Which included lying down on my 4-H project, killing several piglets, and forcing me to clean up the mess when I did my chores before school. The crates protect the piglets from their mothers. Farmers do not cage their hogs because of sadism, but because dead pigs are a drag on the profit margin, and because being crushed by your mother really is an awful way to go. As is

being eaten by your mother, which I've seen sows do to newborn pigs as well.

I warned you that farming is still dirty and bloody, and I wasn't kidding. So let's talk about manure. It is an article of faith amongst the agri-intellectuals that we no longer use manure as fertilizer. To quote Dr. Michael Fox in his book *Eating with a Conscience*, "The animal waste is not going back to the land from which the animal feed originated." Or Bill McKibben, in his book *Deep Economy*, writing about modern livestock production: "But this concentrates the waste in one place, where instead of being useful fertilizer to spread on crop fields it becomes a toxic threat."

In my inbox is an email from our farm's neighbor, who raises thousands of hogs in close proximity to our farm, and several of my family member's houses as well. The email outlines the amount and chemical analysis of the manure that will be spread on our fields this fall, manure that will replace dozens of tons of commercial fertilizer. The manure is captured underneath the hog houses in cement pits, and is knifed into the soil after the crops are harvested. At no time is it exposed to erosion, and it is an extremely valuable resource, one which farmers use to its fullest extent, just as they have since agriculture began.

In the southern part of Missouri, there is an extensive poultry industry in areas of the state where the soil is poor. The farmers there spread the poultry litter on pasture, and the advent of poultry barns made cattle production possible in areas that used to be waste ground. The "industrial" poultry houses are owned by family farmers, who have then used the byproducts to produce beef in areas where cattle couldn't survive before. McKibben is certain that the contracts these farmers sign with companies like Tyson are unfair, and the farmers might agree. But they like those cows, so there is a waiting list for new chicken barns. In some areas, there is indeed more manure than available cropland. But the trend in the industry, thankfully, is toward a dispersion of animals and manure, as the value of the manure increases, and the cost of transporting the manure becomes prohibitive.

WE CAN'T CHANGE NATURE

The largest producer of pigs in the United States has promised to gradually end the use of hog crates. The Humane Society promises to take their initiative drive to outlaw farrowing crates and poultry cages to more states. Many of the counties in my own state of Missouri have chosen to outlaw the building of confinement facilities. Barack Obama has been harshly critical of animal agriculture. We are clearly in the process of deciding that we will not continue to raise animals the way we do now. Because other countries may not share our sensibilities, we'll have to withdraw or amend free trade agreements to keep any semblance of a livestock industry.

20 We can do that, and we may be a better society for it, but we can't change nature. Pigs will be allowed to "return to their mire," as

Kipling had it, but they'll also be crushed and eaten by their mothers. Chickens will provide lunch to any number of predators, and some number of chickens will die as flocks establish their pecking order.

In recent years, the cost of producing pork dropped as farmers increased feed efficiency (the amount of feed needed to produce a pound of pork) by 20 percent. Free-range chickens and pigs will increase the price of food, using more energy and water to produce the extra grain required for the same amount of meat, and some people will go hungry. It is also instructive that the first company to move away from farrowing crates is the largest producer of pigs. Changing the way we raise animals will not necessarily change the scale of the companies involved in the industry. If we are about to require more expensive ways of producing food, the largest and most well-capitalized farms will have the least trouble adapting.

THE OMNIVORES' DELUSIONS

Michael Pollan, in an 8,000-word essay in the *New York Times Magazine*, took the expected swipes at animal agriculture. But his truly radical prescriptions had to do with raising of crops. Pollan, who seemed to be aware of the nitrogen problem in his book *The Omnivore's Dilemma*, left nuance behind, as well as the laws of chemistry, in his recommendations. The nitrogen problem is this: without nitrogen, we do not have life. Until we learned to produce nitrogen from natural gas early in the last century, the only way to get nitrogen was through nitrogen produced by plants called legumes, or from small amounts of nitrogen that are produced by lightning strikes. The amount of life the earth could support was limited by the amount of nitrogen available for crop production.

In his book, Pollan quotes geographer Vaclav Smil to the effect that 40 percent of the people alive today would not be alive without the ability to artificially synthesize nitrogen. But in his directive on food policy, Pollan damns agriculture's dependence

---

COMPLICATION

In paragraph 22, Hurst criticizes Pollan for "leaving nuance behind" in a 2008 *New York Times* article. In a previous *New York Times* article, published a year earlier, Michael Pollan included the following passage about the use of nitrogen fertilizers:

If there is one word that covers nearly all the changes industrialization has made to the food chain, it would be simplification. Chemical fertilizers simplify the chemistry of the soil, which in turn appears to simplify the chemistry of the food grown in that soil. Since the widespread adoption of synthetic nitrogen fertilizers in the 1950s, the nutritional quality of produce in America has, according to U.S.D.A. figures, declined significantly. Some researchers blame the quality of the soil for the decline; others cite the tendency of modern plant breeding to select for industrial qualities like yield rather than nutritional quality. Whichever it is, the trend toward simplification of our food continues on up the chain. Processing foods depletes them of many nutrients, a few of which are then added back in through "fortification": folic acid in refined flour, vitamins and minerals in breakfast cereal. But food scientists can add back only the nutrients food scientists recognize as important. What are they overlooking?

SOURCE: Michael Pollan, "Unhappy Meals," *New York Times Magazine*, 2007.

on fossil fuels, and urges the president to encourage agriculture to move away from expensive and declining supplies of natural gas toward the unlimited sunshine that supported life, and agriculture, as recently as the 1940s. Now, why didn't I think of that?

Well, I did. I've raised clover and alfalfa for the nitrogen they produce, and half the time my land is planted to soybeans, another nitrogen producing legume. Pollan writes as if all of his ideas are new, but my father tells of agriculture extension meetings in the late 1950s entitled "Clover and Corn, the Road to Profitability." Farmers know that organic farming was the default position of agriculture for thousands of years, years when hunger was just around the corner for even advanced societies. I use all the animal manure available to me, and do everything I can to reduce the amount of commercial fertilizers I use. When corn genetically modified to use nitrogen more efficiently enters the market, as it soon will, I will use it as well. But none of those things will completely replace commercial fertilizer.

25 Norman Borlaug, founder of the **Green Revolution**, estimates that the amount of nitrogen available naturally would only support a worldwide population of 4 billion souls or so. He further remarks that we would need another 5 billion cows to produce enough manure to fertilize our present crops with "natural" fertilizer. That would play havoc with global warming. And cows do not produce nitrogen from the air, but only from the forages they eat, so to produce more manure we will have to plant more forages. Most of the critics of industrial farming maintain the contradictory positions that we should increase the use of manure as a fertilizer, and decrease our consumption of meat. Pollan would solve the problem with cover crops, planted after the corn crop is harvested, and with mandatory composting. Pollan should talk to some actual farmers before he presumes to advise a president.

Pollan tells of flying over the upper Midwest in the winter, and seeing the black,

CONTEXT

In the 2008 article to which Hurst refers in paragraph 23, Michael Pollan wrote an open letter to President Barack Obama about U.S. food policy. Here is the passage to which Hurst refers:

> There are many moving parts to the new food agenda I'm urging you to adopt, but the core idea could not be simpler: we need to wean the American food system off its heavy 20th-century diet of fossil fuel and put it back on a diet of contemporary sunshine. True, this is easier said than done—fossil fuel is deeply implicated in everything about the way we currently grow food and feed ourselves. To put the food system back on sunlight will require policies to change how things work at every link in the food chain: in the farm field, in the way food is processed and sold and even in the American kitchen and at the American dinner table. Yet the sun still shines down on our land every day, and photosynthesis can still work its wonders wherever it does. If any part of the modern economy can be freed from its dependence on oil and successfully resolarized, surely it is food.

SOURCE: Michael Pollan, "Farmer in Chief," *New York Times*, 2008.

fallow soil. I suppose one sees what one wants to see, but we have not had the kind of tillage implement on our farm that would produce black soil in nearly 20 years. Pollan would provide our nitrogen by planting those black fields to nitrogen-producing cover crops after the cash crops are harvested. This is a fine plan, one that farmers have known about for generations. And sometimes it would even work. But not last year, as we finished harvest in November in a freezing rain. It is hard to think of a legume that would have done its thing between then and corn planting time. Plants do not grow very well in freezing weather, a fact that would evidently surprise Pollan.

And even if we could have gotten a legume established last fall, it would not have fixed any nitrogen before planting time. We used to plant corn in late May, plowing down our green manure and killing the first flush of weeds. But that meant the corn would enter its crucial growing period during the hottest, driest parts of the summer, and that soil erosion would be increased because the land was bare during drenching spring rains. Now we plant in early April, best utilizing our spring

The Green Revolution refers to a series of political initiatives and developments in agricultural technologies that were intended to increase crop production in developing nations after World War II and through the 1970s. Although the Green Revolution is often credited with dramatically improving farming in poor developing nations during that time, it has also been criticized for promoting an industrial model of agriculture and destroying local farming cultures.

rains, and ensuring that pollination occurs before the dog days of August.

A few other problems come to mind. The last time I planted a cover crop, the clover provided a perfect habitat in early spring for bugs, bugs that I had to kill with an insecticide. We do not normally apply insecticides, but we did that year. Of course, you can provide nitrogen with legumes by using a longer crop rotation, growing clover one year and corn the next. But that uses twice as much water to produce a corn crop, and takes twice as much land to produce the same number of bushels. We are producing twice the food we did in 1960 on less land, and commercial nitrogen is one of the main reasons why. It may be that we decide we would rather spend land and water than energy, but Pollan never mentions that we are faced with that choice.

His other grand idea is mandatory household composting, with the compost delivered to farmers free of charge. Why not? Compost is a valuable soil amendment, and if somebody else is paying to deliver it to my farm, then bring it on. But it will not do much to solve the nitrogen problem. Household compost has somewhere between 1 and 5 percent nitrogen, and not all that nitrogen is available to crops the first year. Presently, we are applying about 150 pounds of nitrogen per acre to corn, and crediting about 40 pounds per acre from the preceding years soybean crop. Let's assume a 5 percent nitrogen rate, or about 100 pounds of nitrogen per ton of compost. That would require 3,000 pounds of compost per acre. Or about 150,000 tons for the corn raised in our county. The average truck carries about 20 tons. Picture 7,500 trucks traveling from New York City to our small county here in the Midwest, delivering compost. Five million truckloads to fertilize the country's corn crop. Now, that would be a carbon footprint!

30 Pollan thinks farmers use commercial fertilizer because it is easier, and because it is cheap. Pollan is right. But those are perfectly defensible reasons. Nitrogen quadrupled in price over the last several years, and farmers are still using it, albeit more cautiously. We are using GPS monitors on all of our equipment to ensure that we do not use too much, and our production of corn per pound of nitrogen is rapidly increasing. On our farm, we have increased yields about 50 percent during my career, while applying about the same amount of nitrogen we did when I began farming. That fortunate trend will increase even faster with the advent of new GMO hybrids. But as much as Pollan might desire it, even President Obama cannot reshuffle the chemical deck that nature has dealt. Energy may well get much more expensive, and peak oil production may have been reached. But food production will have a claim on fossil fuels long after we have learned how to use renewables and nuclear power to handle many of our other energy needs.

FARMING AND CONNECTEDNESS

Much of farming is more "industrial," more technical, and more complex than it used to be. Farmers farm more acres, and are less close to the ground and their animals than they were in the past. Almost all critics of industrial agriculture bemoan this loss of closeness, this "connectedness," to use author Rod Dreher's term. It is a given in most of the writing about agriculture that the knowledge and experience of the organic farmer is what makes him so unique and so important. The "industrial farmer," on the other hand, is a mere pawn of Cargill, backed into his ignorant way of life by forces too large, too far from the farm, and too powerful to resist. Concern about this alienation, both between farmers and the land, and between consumers and their food supply, is what drives much of the literature about agriculture.

The distance between the farmer and what he grows has certainly increased, but, believe me, if we weren't closely connected, we wouldn't still be farming. It's important to our critics that they emphasize this alienation, because they have to ignore the "industrial" farmer's experience and knowledge to say the things they do about farming.

But farmers have reasons for their actions, and society should listen to them as we embark upon this reappraisal of our agricultural system. I use chemicals and diesel fuel to accomplish the tasks my grandfather used to do with sweat, and I use a computer instead of a lined notebook and a pencil, but I'm still farming the same land he did 80 years ago, and the fund of knowledge that our family has accumulated about our small part of Missouri is valuable. And everything I know and I have learned tells me this: we have to farm "industrially" to feed the world, and by using those "industrial" tools sensibly, we can accomplish that task and leave my grandchildren a prosperous and productive farm, while protecting the land, water, and air around us.

Questions for Discussion

1. Hurst begins this essay with an anecdote about encountering a passenger on an airplane who was "talking about food, damning farming, particularly livestock farming." He describes this passenger as a self-appointed "expert about me, on the strength of one book" and he goes on to indicate that he's had enough of such "experts." Why do you think Hurst begins his essay in this way? What does this introduction convey about Hurst? How effectively do you think it sets up his main argument?

2. What is Hurst's complaint about the way farmers are portrayed in books like *The Omnivore's Dilemma* by Michael Pollan? How does this complaint fit into his main argument about farming and food production? What alternative to this view of the farmer does Hurst present? How does his view of farmers figure into his main argument?

3. Hurst is a farmer and at several points in his essay refers to his own farming experience as well as to the experiences of other farmers. To what extent does his experience as a farmer contribute to the effectiveness of his argument? Is his argument more credible because of his experience? Explain.

4. In paragraph 20 Hurst writes that "we can't change nature." Why does he make that statement? How does it fit into his main argument about modern farming?

5. What is the "nitrogen problem," according to Hurst? Why is it important? How does he use this "problem" to refute arguments against modern farming methods made by Michael Pollan? How effectively do you think Hurst makes his case on this point?

6. How would you describe Hurst's tone in this essay? How appropriate is his tone for the purposes of his argument? Do you think his tone strengthens or weakens his argument? Explain, citing specific passages from his essay to support your answer.

7. In a sense, Hurst's entire essay is a response to *The Omnivore's Dilemma* by Michael Pollan, and Hurst devotes much of the essay to refuting specific points that Pollan makes about farming in his book. How persuasive do you find Hurst's refutation of Pollan's criticisms of farming? How effective do you think this strategy is as a way for Hurst to make his main argument? Do you think this strategy would be more effective with readers who have read Pollan's book? Why or why not? (For more information about Pollan, see the introduction to Pollan's essay on page 625; Pollan's essay, which was published two years before his book *The Omnivore's Dilemma*, also provides some information about Pollan.)

8. Do you think this essay might fairly be described as an argument to prevail (see page 10)? Why or why not? If so, do you think the essay accomplishes the author's goal? Explain.

In Defense of Michael Pollan

(4)

CAPITAL TIMES

Like many colleges and universities, the University of Wisconsin at Madison has a common reading program for its students. Under this program, which is called *Go Big Read* (a play on the cheer commonly heard at the university's athletic events: "Go Big Red!"), all students are invited to read a book selected by a committee. The purpose of the program is to promote a campus-wide conversation about important issues and, according to its website, "to engage students, faculty, staff and the entire community in a vibrant, academically driven experience." In 2009, the university selected for its *Go Big Read* program a book by well-known food writer Michael Pollan, *In Defense of Food: An Eater's Manifesto* (2009). That decision didn't sit well with many farmers in Wisconsin who see Pollan as an enemy of modern farming. But the *Capital Times,* a newspaper published in Madison, the capital of the state of Wisconsin, defended the university's decision on the grounds that it would help spark a much-needed conversation about what and how Americans eat. In this editorial, which was published in 2009, shortly after the university announced its selection of Pollan's book for the *Go Big Read* program, the newspaper also defends Pollan as someone who is raising important questions about food and farm policy in the United States. In this regard, this editorial is a good example of how argumentation can contribute to important conversations that can affect people's lives.

CAPITAL TIMES, "In Defense of Michael Pollan"

1 These are tough times for Wisconsin farmers.

Dairy prices are down. And big dairies are making moves to buy from factory farms rather than those operated by Wisconsin families.

Big agri-business is taking advantage of weak enforcement of antitrust laws to consolidate its grip on production.

Trade policies are stacked against Wisconsin farmers and local food processors.

5 Last week, members of the Wisconsin Farmers Union traveled to Washington to stand with Vermont Sen. Bernie Sanders as he and a bipartisan coalition of senators called for legislation to support dairy farmers. Specifically, Sanders is proposing an amendment to the agriculture appropriations bill that would provide $350 million for milk price supports and increased government purchases of surplus dairy products.

The WFU members also lobbied for the Milk Import Tariff Equity Act, which would close a loophole that allows milk protein concentrates to be imported by American dairies in a move that undermines prices for U.S. farmers.

The Farmers Union activists worked with the office of Wisconsin Sen. Herb Kohl, who agreed to pressure the U.S. Department of Agriculture and the Department of Justice to examine antitrust abuses by the conglomerates that dominate the dairy products market. They secured the support of Wisconsin Sen.

Russ Feingold, who like Kohl is a member of the Senate Judiciary Committee, for the antitrust investigation. And they huddled with Feingold to discuss trade and energy policy issues that concern Wisconsin farmers.

Not bad work.

So what was the **Wisconsin Farm Bureau Federation** doing?

10 Griping about a book that is being read by University of Wisconsin students.

The Farm Bureau bureaucracy is all hot and bothered because the UW's Go Big Read program—which seeks to promote a campus-wide discussion about a particular book—selected Michael Pollan's "In Defense of Food" as the text students and faculty will be discussing.

"Pollan has narrow and elitist ideas about how you should eat and how farmers should (or shouldn't) feed a hungry and growing world," argues the federation's president.

Actually, Pollan, whose work has revolutionized the discussion about food and food production in the United States, argues that Americans should eat locally grown foods—especially plants—and should be wary of the claims of "a 32 billion-dollar food-marketing machine" that keeps telling us the best way to eat just happens to be the way that yields the highest profits for multinational corporations.

Pollan—who will deliver the Go Big Read lecture at 7 p.m. Thursday at the Kohl Center and then speak at 10 a.m. Saturday at the Food for Thought Festival off the Capitol Square—also argues that we should "return food to its proper context" by eating breakfast, lunch and dinner at a table with our families and friends rather than wolfing down processed foods in our cars.

15 The Farm Bureau, with its close ties to big agri-business and that "food-marketing machine," may think this is a narrow and elitist approach.

But it is also an approach that reconnects working farmers with consumers, and that has the potential to both increase income for farm families and create a constituency for farm policies that favor farmers as opposed to multinational agri-business conglomerates.

This is not to say that Pollan is right about everything. It happens that, as one of the few newspapers in the country that consistently take the side of working farmers, we have some differences with Pollan. Much of what he proposes, while appealing in a philosophical sense, is unlikely to be achieved in the short term—or maybe even the long term, since some of us lack the green thumbs to grow the gardens he suggests.

Pollan understands this. He identifies his books as "manifestos." They propose ideas and new ways to think about old issues. His purpose, as he freely admits, is to get people thinking about food and food production.

Pollan recognizes that this is where better policies begin. And he remains remarkably flexible with regard to those policies and the direction of the debate.

20 Yet the Farm Bureau spin would have us believe that "Pollan's plan would starve much of the world and require the rest to spend more time and money in pursuit of food. In a book littered with unsupportable claims, its conclusion is downright disturbing and immoral."

In fact, the opposite is true.

The **Wisconsin Farm Bureau Federation** is an advocacy group founded in 1920 that describes itself as "the state's largest general farm organization representing the needs and interests of all farmers for all commodities."

CONTEXT

In an essay published in September 2009 in the *Capital Times* (the same newspaper in which this editorial was published), Wisconsin Farm Bureau Federation president Bill Bruins wrote,

> The farm organization I lead, the Wisconsin Farm Bureau Federation, works hard to teach youths that milk comes from cows on farms like mine. We inform consumers about the realities of what it takes to bring America's safe, nutritious and abundant food supply from our farm gates to your food plates. Pollan has narrow and elitist ideas about how you should eat and how farmers should (or shouldn't) feed a hungry and growing world. To make these claims you would think he's a food scientist instead of a creative writer with an agenda.
>
> I hope readers will realize that Wisconsin's diverse farms look nothing like the picture Pollan paints of modern agriculture.

SOURCE: Bill Bruins, *Capital Times*, 2009.

According to its website, the **Wisconsin Farmers Union** is a member-driven organization that is "committed to enhancing the quality of life for family farmers, rural communities and all people through educational opportunities, cooperative endeavors and civic engagement."

Bad trade and development policies, which have emphasized enriching multinational import-export firms and speculators rather than working farmers, are currently causing much of the world to starve. Pollan's proposals would restore local production and encourage approaches that provide farmers with better returns for the essential service they provide to their communities and society in general.

Too often, the Farm Bureau leadership in Washington has been on the wrong side of debates about those policies, arguing the free-trade brief of multinational corporations rather than Wisconsin farmers.

Reasonable people can disagree about food and agriculture policy. And there certainly are times when the Farm Bureau gets things right. But the consistency with which it aligns itself with agri-business giants is unsettling.

25 It is even more unsettling to think that the Farm Bureau bureaucracy's misread of Pollan's book may have less to do with any threat his ideas pose to working farmers than to the "32 billion-dollar food-marketing machine" that the author questions.

No matter what the motivations, no matter whether the misread of "In Defense of Food" is malignant or misguided, the bottom line is that Pollan is not the problem for working farmers. He may, in fact, be a part of the solution. So it is good that his book is being read by UW students and it is great that he is coming to Madison to further the discussion.

It is also great that, while other groups are griping about reading lists, the **Wisconsin Farmers Union** is keeping its eye on the prize and working to ensure that the interests of working farmers from this state are raised and advanced in Washington.

Questions for Discussion

1. Why do you think the authors begin this essay with a description of why "these are tough times for Wisconsin farmers"? How does this description help set up their main argument?

2. How do the authors of this editorial answer the criticisms of Michael Pollan made by the Wisconsin Farm Bureau Federation? What evidence do they use to refute those criticisms? How persuasive do you find that evidence?

3. What criticism do the authors make of the Wisconsin Farm Bureau Federation itself? To what extent do you think this criticism of the Farm Bureau Federation weakens the Federation's criticisms of Pollan? How effective do you find this strategy for refuting an opponent's argument?

4. In the latter part of this essay, the authors acknowledge that Pollan, whom they defend, makes some mistakes in his arguments about farming. What effect does this discussion have on the main argument in this essay? Do you think it weakens or strengthens the authors' main argument? Explain.

5. How would you summarize the main point of this essay? To what extent do you think this essay is about Michael Pollan? To what extent is it about the Wisconsin Farm Bureau Federation?

NEGOTIATING DIFFERENCES

As the essays in this section indicate, questions about what and how we should eat have become more complicated in recent years as many people have begun to appreciate some of the environmental, economic, social, and health implications of our food choices. In view of these developments, many college campuses have taken on the challenge of deciding what we should eat. On some campuses, farmers markets are held to promote the purchase of locally grown foods. Some campus dining halls have begun adjusting their menus to emphasize healthier, sustainable foods, and many colleges have implemented programs to help students make wiser food choices. The challenge facing you for this assignment is to confront the question of deciding what students should eat on *your* campus.

First, look into the food and dining situation on your campus. What kinds of foods are available to students? What choices do they have? Does your campus host fast-food chain restaurants, hold farmers markets, or offer local foods in its dining halls? Also, where does the campus get its foods? Are foods purchased from local producers or do most of the foods on your campus come from large national

suppliers? To answer these questions you may need to talk to someone in your campus dining services or residential life office.

Now look into how students on your campus make their choices about what to eat. Talk to some classmates or your roommates to find out where they eat and what foods they choose. Try to find out how they decide what to eat, and ask them what kinds of food choices they'd like to see on your campus. You might consider conducting a survey to find out how students choose their foods.

Finally, consider the arguments of the authors in this section as well as other arguments you have encountered about food, and try to identify your own basic views about what to eat and why.

Having looked into these issues, you can now write a letter to the editor of your school newspaper in which you make a case for what and how you believe the members of your campus community should eat. In your letter, identify problems you see with the food choices currently available on your campus and propose changes you'd like to see. Be sure to support your proposals with reasoning and evidence to make a persuasive case to your campus community.

What Is Our Responsibility to the Earth?

In his famous essay, "Walking" (see Con-Text on page 643), nineteenth-century American writer Henry David Thoreau announces, "Life consists with wildness. The most alive is the wildest. Not yet subdued to man, its presence refreshes him." Perhaps this idea that people require "the wild" to be truly alive helped make Thoreau a favorite writer of the environmental movement that emerged in the United States in the 1960s and 1970s. Certainly, many people who support wilderness preservation and who venture into wilderness areas find solace and revitalization there. They argue that wilderness helps us understand who we are. ■ But in "Walking," Thoreau argues that wilderness doesn't help us understand who we are; for Thoreau wilderness *is* who we are. Indeed, Thoreau criticized the cultivation of farmland and the construction of cities and towns not because they destroyed wilderness areas but because they destroyed human life as he believed it should be lived: "Hope and the future for me are not in lawns and cultivated fields," he wrote, "not in cities and towns, but in the impervious and quaking swamps." For Thoreau wilderness and humans are not distinct but the same. And that relationship means that humans have a special responsibility to Nature, for to take care of Nature is to take care of ourselves. ■ The essays in this section explore this connection between humans and the natural world, and in one way or another they take up the challenge of defining our responsibility to the earth. It seems to be an especially important challenge at the beginning of the twenty-first century, because not only is wilderness under great pressure from development and population growth, but the earth itself is threatened by unprecedented environmental problems such as global climate change. Individuals, communities, and nations are now facing hard choices about altering lifestyles that are damaging the earth. The essays in this section explore these choices and may help you think about your own responsibility to the earth.

CON-TEXT

Thoreau's Wildness

1 Life consists with wildness. The most alive is the wildest. Not yet subdued to man, its presence refreshes him. One who pressed forward incessantly and never rested from his labors, who grew fast and made infinite demands on life, would always find himself in a new country or wilderness, and surrounded by the raw material of life. He would be climbing over the prostrate stems of primitive forest trees.

Hope and the future for me are not in lawns and cultivated fields, not in towns and cities, but in the impervious and quaking swamps....

In short, all good things are wild and free. There is something in a strain of music, whether produced by an instrument or by the human voice—take the sound of a bugle in a summer night, for instance—which by its wildness, to speak without satire, reminds me of the cries emitted by wild beasts in their native forests. It is so much of their wildness as I can understand. Give me for my friends and neighbors wild men, not tame ones. The wildness of the savage is but a faint symbol of the awful ferity with which good men and lovers meet....

SOURCE: Henry David Thoreau, "Walking," 1862.

① | # The Obligation to Endure

RACHEL CARSON

If the environmental movement in the latter part of the twentieth century can be traced to any single work, it is probably *Silent Spring* (1962), Rachel Carson's widely read analysis of how pesticides and other chemicals were polluting the earth and endangering both wildlife and human life. An aquatic biologist with the U.S. Bureau of Fisheries, Carson (1907–1966) became the editor-in-chief of the publications of the U.S. Fish and Wildlife Service. The values that Carson espouses regarding the natural world—values that deeply influenced a generation of environmental advocates—emerge subtly but powerfully in her discussion of the physical and biological effects of chemicals in the environment. She writes as a scientist, but as you read, consider whether science is the primary perspective from which she examines the problem of pesticides. More important, perhaps, is Carson's perspective on our responsibility to the earth. She argues for a gentler way of living on the earth, which might account for the enduring popularity of her book. "The Obligation to Endure" is the second chapter of *Silent Spring.*

RACHEL CARSON, "The Obligation to Endure"

1 The history of life on earth has been a history of interaction between living things and their surroundings. To a large extent, the physical form and the habits of the earth's vegetation and its animal life have been molded by the environment. Considering the whole span of earthly time, the opposite effect, in which life actually modifies its surroundings, has been relatively slight. Only within the moment of time represented by the present century has one species—man—acquired significant power to alter the nature of his world.

During the past quarter century this power has not only increased to one of disturbing magnitude but it has changed in character. The most alarming of all man's assaults upon the environment is the contamination of air, earth, rivers, and sea with dangerous and even lethal materials. This pollution is for the most part irrecoverable; the chain of evil it initiates not only in the world that must support life but in living tissues is for the most part irreversible. In this now universal contamination of the environment, chemicals are the sinister and little-recognized partners of radiation in changing the very nature of the world—the very nature of its life. Strontium 90, released through nuclear explosions into the air, comes to earth in rain or drifts down as fallout, lodges in soil, enters into the grass or corn or wheat grown there, and in time takes up its abode in the bones of a human being, there to remain until his death. Similarly,

CONTEXT

More than 2,000 nuclear tests have been conducted since 1945, and more than 700 of them were conducted in the earth's atmosphere or under its oceans. When Carson wrote her argument in 1962, above-ground nuclear testing was routine. Since 1980 most nations have agreed to avoid above-ground nuclear testing, but tests are still conducted underground, under the ocean, and in space. In 1996 Greenpeace estimated that the tests that had been conducted by then had left 3,830 kilograms of plutonium in the ground and 4,200 kilograms of plutonium in the air.

chemicals sprayed on croplands or forests or gardens lie long in soil, entering into living organisms, passing from one to another in a chain of poisoning and death. Or they pass mysteriously by underground streams until they emerge and, through the alchemy of air and sunlight, combine into new forms that kill vegetation, sicken cattle, and work unknown harm on those who drink from once pure wells. As Albert Schweitzer has said, "Man can hardly even recognize the devils of his own creation."

It took hundreds of millions of years to produce the life that now inhabits the earth—eons of time in which that developing and evolving and diversifying life reached a state of adjustment and balance with its surroundings. The environment, rigorously shaping and directing the life it supported, contained elements that were hostile as well as supporting. Certain rocks gave out dangerous radiation; even within the light of the sun, from which all life draws its energy, there were shortwave radiations with power to injure. Given time—time not in years but in millennia—life adjusts, and a balance has been reached. For time is the essential ingredient; but in the modern world there is no time.

The rapidity of change and the speed with which new situations are created follow the impetuous and heedless pace of man rather than the deliberate pace of nature. Radiation is no longer merely the background radiation of rocks, the bombardment of cosmic rays, the ultraviolet of the sun that have existed before there was any life on earth; radiation is now the unnatural creation of man's tampering with the atom. The chemicals to which life is asked to make its adjustment are no longer merely the calcium and silica and copper and all the rest of the minerals washed out of the rocks and carried in rivers to the sea; they are the synthetic creations of man's inventive mind, brewed in his laboratories, and having no counterparts in nature.

5 To adjust to these chemicals would require time on the scale that is nature's; it would require not merely the years of a man's life but the life of generations. And even this, were it by some miracle possible, would be futile, for the new chemicals come from our laboratories in an endless stream; almost five hundred annually find their way into actual use in the United States alone. The figure is staggering and its implications are not easily grasped—500 new chemicals to which the bodies of men and animals are required somehow to adapt each year, chemicals totally outside the limits of biologic experience.

Among them are many that are used in man's war against nature. Since the mid-1940s over 200 basic chemicals have been created for use in killing insects, weeds, rodents, and other organisms described in the modern vernacular as "pests"; and they are sold under several thousand different brand names.

These sprays, dusts, and aerosols are now applied almost universally to farms, gardens, forests, and homes—nonselective chemicals that have the power to kill every insect, the "good" and the "bad," to still the song of birds and the leaping of fish in the streams, to coat the leaves with a deadly film, and to linger on in soil—all this though the intended

Justin Sullivan/Getty Images

target may be only a few weeds or insects. Can anyone believe it is possible to lay down such a barrage of poisons on the surface of the earth without making it unfit for all life? They should not be called "insecticides," but "biocides."

The whole process of spraying seems caught up in an endless spiral. Since DDT was released for civilian use, a process of escalation has been going on in which ever more toxic materials must be found. This has happened because insects, in a triumphant vindication of Darwin's principle of the survival of the fittest, have evolved super races immune to the particular insecticide used, hence a deadlier one has always to be developed—and then a deadlier one than that. It has happened also because, for reasons to be described later, destructive insects often undergo a "flareback," or resurgence, after spraying, in numbers greater than before. Thus the chemical war is never won, and all life is caught in its violent crossfire.

Along with the possibility of the extinction of mankind by nuclear war, the central problem of our age has therefore become the contamination of man's total environment with such substances of incredible potential for harm—substances that accumulate in the tissues of plants and animals and even penetrate the germ cells to shatter or alter the very material of heredity upon which the shape of the future depends.

10 Some would-be architects of our future look toward a time when it will be possible to alter the human germ plasm by design.

For more information about **DDT** see the Complication box on page 652.

But we may easily be doing so now by inadvertence, for many chemicals, like radiation, bring about gene mutations. It is ironic to think that man might determine his own future by something so seemingly trivial as the choice of an insect spray.

All this has been risked—for what? Future historians may well be amazed by our distorted sense of proportion. How could intelligent beings seek to control a few unwanted species by a method that contaminated the entire environment and brought the threat of disease and death even to their own kind? Yet this is precisely what we have done. We have done it, moreover, for reasons that collapse the moment we examine them. We are told that the enormous and expanding use of pesticides is necessary to maintain farm production. Yet is our real problem not one of *overproduction*? Our farms, despite measures to remove acreages from production and to pay farmers not to produce, have yielded such a staggering excess of crops that the American taxpayer in 1962 is paying out more than one billion dollars a year as the total carrying cost of the surplus-food storage program. And is the situation helped when one branch of the Agriculture Department tries to reduce production while another states, as it did in 1958, "It is believed generally that reduction of crop acreages under provisions of the Soil Bank will stimulate interest in use of chemicals to obtain maximum production on the land retained in crops."

All this is not to say there is no insect problem and no need of control. I am saying, rather, that control must be geared to realities, not to mythical situations, and that the methods employed must be such that they do not destroy us along with the insects.

The problem whose attempted solution has brought such a train of disaster in its wake is an accompaniment of our modern way of life. Long before the age of man, insects inhabited the earth—a group of extraordinarily varied and adaptable beings. Over the course

CONTEXT

The Agricultural Act of 1956, usually called the Soil Bank Act, provided federal funds to farmers to keep certain lands out of agricultural production, sometimes as a way to control the prices of some agricultural products. The act was repealed in 1965, three years after Carson's *Silent Spring* was published. But the policy of using federal funds to keep agricultural lands out of production continued under subsequent legislation.

of time since man's advent, a small percentage of the more than half a million species of insects have come into conflict with human welfare in two principal ways: as competitors for the food supply and as carriers of human disease.

Disease-carrying insects become important where human beings are crowded together, especially under conditions where sanitation is poor, as in time of natural disaster or war or in situations of extreme poverty and deprivation. Then control of some sort becomes necessary. It is a sobering fact, however, as we shall presently see, that the method of massive chemical control has had only limited success, and also threatens to worsen the very conditions it is intended to curb.

15 Under primitive agricultural conditions the farmer had few insect problems. These arose with the intensification of agriculture—the devotion of immense acreages to a single crop. Such a system set the stage for explosive increases in specific insect populations. Single-crop farming does not take advantage of the principles by which nature works; it is agriculture as an engineer might conceive it to be. Nature has introduced great variety into the landscape, but man has displayed a passion for simplifying it. Thus he undoes the built-in checks and balances by which nature holds the species within bounds. One important natural check is a limit on the amount of suitable habitat for each species. Obviously then, an insect that lives on wheat can build up its population to much higher levels on a farm devoted to wheat than on one in which wheat is intermingled with other crops to which the insect is not adapted.

The same thing happens in other situations. A generation or more ago, the towns of large areas of the United States lined their streets with the noble elm tree. Now the beauty they hopefully created is threatened with complete destruction as disease sweeps through the elms, carried by a beetle that would have only limited chance to build up large populations and to spread from tree to

James Shaffer/PhotoEdit

tree if the elms were only occasional trees in a richly diversified planting.

Another factor in the modern insect problem is one that must be viewed against a background of geologic and human history: the spreading of thousands of different kinds of organisms from their native homes to invade new territories. This worldwide migration has been studied and graphically

CONTEXT

U.S. agricultural production more than doubled between the late 1940s and the 1980s, in part because of the increased use of pesticides to control insects that damaged some agricultural products and lowered agricultural yields. However, concerns about the health risks associated with pesticides grew in the years after *Silent Spring* was published. In addition, some insects have demonstrated resistance to pesticides. Despite increased use of pesticides, some studies show a slight rise in crop losses because of insects among major crops (such as corn) over the past century. These developments, along with the growing influence of the environmental movement in the 1970s and 1980s, have prompted some farmers to consider alternatives to conventional farming methods that rely on pesticides to control insects. "Organic" or "natural" farming uses a variety of methods to control insects, including crop rotation and biological controls (for example, introducing one kind of insect to control other insects that damage crops).

described by the British ecologist Charles Elton in his recent book *The Ecology of Invasions*. During the Cretaceous Period, some hundred million years ago, flooding

Bettmann/Corbis

seas cut many land bridges between continents and living things found themselves confined in what Elton calls "colossal separate nature reserves." There, isolated from others of their kind, they developed many new species. When some of the land masses were joined again, about 15 million years ago, these species began to move out into new territories—a movement that is not only still in progress but is now receiving considerable assistance from man.

The importation of plants is the primary agent in the modern spread of species, for animals have almost invariably gone along with the plants, quarantine being a comparatively recent and not completely effective innovation. [See "Context" on this page.] The United States Office of Plant Introduction alone has introduced almost 200,000 species and varieties of plants from all over the world. Nearly half of the 180 or so major insect enemies of plants in the United States are accidental imports from abroad, and most of them have come as hitchhikers on plants.

In new territory, out of reach of the restraining hand of the natural enemies that kept down its numbers in its native land, an invading plant or animal is able to become enormously abundant. Thus it is no accident that our most troublesome insects are introduced species.

20 These invasions, both the naturally occurring and those dependent on human assistance, are likely to continue indefinitely. Quarantine and massive chemical campaigns are only extremely expensive ways of buying time. We are faced, according to Dr. Elton, "with a life-and-death need not just to find new technological means of suppressing this plant or that animal"; instead we need the basic knowledge of animal populations and their relations to their surroundings that will "promote an even balance and damp down the explosive power of outbreaks and new invasions."

Much of the necessary knowledge is now available but we do not use it. We train ecologists in our universities and even employ them in our governmental agencies but we seldom take their advice. We allow the chemical death rain to fall as though there were no alternative, whereas in fact there are many, and our ingenuity could soon discover many more if given opportunity.

Have we fallen into a mesmerized state that makes us accept as inevitable that which is inferior or detrimental, as though having lost the will or the vision to demand that which is good? Such thinking, in the words of the ecologist Paul Shepard, "idealizes life with only its head out of water, inches above the limits of toleration of the corruption of its own environment.... Why should we tolerate a diet of weak poisons, a home in insipid surroundings, a circle of acquaintances who are not quite our enemies, the noise of motors with just enough relief to prevent insanity? Who would want to live in a world which is just not quite fatal?" Yet such a world is pressed upon us. The crusade to create a chemically sterile, insect-free world seems to have engendered a fanatic zeal on the part of many specialists and most of the so-called control agencies. On every hand there is evidence that those engaged in spraying operations exercise a ruthless power. "The regulatory entomologists... function as prosecutor, judge and jury, tax assessor and collector and sheriff to enforce their own orders," said Connecticut entomologist Neely Turner. The most flagrant abuses go unchecked in both state and federal agencies.

It is not my contention that chemical insecticides must never be used. I do contend that we have put poisonous and biologically potent chemicals indiscriminately into the hands of persons largely or wholly ignorant of their potentials for harm. We have subjected enormous numbers of people to contact with these poisons, without their consent and often without their knowledge. If the Bill of Rights contains no guarantee that a citizen shall be secure against lethal poisons distributed either by private individuals or by public officials, it is surely only because our forefathers, despite their considerable wisdom and foresight, could conceive of no such problem.

I contend, furthermore, that we have allowed these chemicals to be used with little or no advance investigation of their effect on soil, water, wildlife, and man himself. Future generations are unlikely to condone our lack of prudent concern for the integrity of the natural world that supports all life.

There is still very limited awareness of the nature of the threat. This is an era of specialists, each of whom sees his own problem and is unaware of or intolerant of the larger frame into which it fits. It is also an era dominated by industry, in which the right to make a dollar at whatever cost is seldom challenged. When the public protests, confronted with some obvious evidence of damaging results of pesticide applications, it is fed little tranquilizing pills of half truth. We urgently need an end to these false assurances, to the sugar coating of unpalatable facts. It is the public that is being asked to assume the risks that the insect controllers calculate. The public must decide whether it wishes to continue on the present road, and it can do so only when in full possession of the facts. In the words of Jean Rostand, "The obligation to endure gives us the right to know."

Questions for Discussion

1. What kinds of evidence does Carson present to support her claim that the environment is at risk? How persuasive do you find her evidence?

2. Carson asks, "How could intelligent beings seek to control a few unwanted species by a method that contaminated the entire environment and brought the threat of disease and death even to their own kind?" How would you answer her?

3. Ronald Bailey, whose essay begins on page 651, asserts that the effectiveness of Carson's book was largely because of her language rather than the strength of her evidence. Evaluate Carson's writing style and tone in this essay. How effective do you find them? In what ways do you think they contribute to her argument? Do you think Bailey is right?

4. On the basis of the essay, what fundamental values do you think Carson holds about humans and their relationship to the environment? Do you think most Americans share these values today? Explain.

5. As the box on page 647 indicates, crop losses because of insect damage can be significant for farmers, and many agricultural experts believe that the appropriate use of pesticides remains the best way to control insects. In what ways does Carson address this concern in her essay? Does her effort to address this concern strengthen or weaken her argument in any way? Explain.

6. *Silent Spring* was published in 1962. What elements of Carson's argument do you think are still relevant? Do you think that any of the concerns raised by Carson have been resolved? Explain.

7. Carson's essay might be described as an argument to negotiate differences (see page 14). If so, what problem is she trying to solve? How effectively do you think her argument solves this problem?

② | Silent Spring at 40

RONALD BAILEY

Rachel Carson's best-selling and widely influential book *Silent Spring* (see pages 644–650) is usually thought of as a scientific work—a careful analysis of the effects of pesticides. In the following essay, Ronald Bailey suggests that it is something else. Its influence, he argues, lies in its persuasiveness as an argument more than in the quality of its scientific analysis. In fact, Bailey argues that Carson played fast and loose with scientific facts in making her argument against pesticide use, and he offers an extensive examination of those facts in an effort to call Carson's argument into question. In doing so, Bailey provides a reminder that any text can be understood as an argument and that even science relies on argument and rhetoric. Whether or not you agree with Bailey's critique of Carson, the real value of his essay might be in the way it reveals the rhetorical and argumentative character of scientific texts. He helps us see, too, that this is as it should be, because issues such as pesticide use are not just scientific issues but social and political issues that can directly affect lives. Argument, in other words, is one of the means by which people try to address these issues together—including crucial questions about our responsibility to our environment. Bailey is the science correspondent for *Reason* magazine, in which the following essay appeared in 2002, and the author of many articles and books on current issues in science, including *Liberation Biology: The Moral and Scientific Case for the Biotech Revolution* (2005).

RONALD BAILEY, "Silent Spring at 40"

1 The modern environmentalist movement was launched at the beginning of June 1962, when excerpts from what would become Rachel Carson's anti-chemical landmark *Silent Spring* were published in *The New Yorker.* "Without this book, the environmental movement might have been long delayed or never have developed at all," declared then-Vice President Albert Gore in his introduction to the 1994 edition. The foreword to the 25th anniversary edition accurately declared, "It led to environmental legislation at every level of government."

In 1999 *Time* named Carson one of the "100 People of the Century." Seven years earlier, a panel of distinguished Americans had selected *Silent Spring* as the most influential book of the previous 50 years. When

I went in search of a copy recently, several bookstore owners told me they didn't have any in stock because local high schools still assign the book and students had cleaned them out.

Carson worked for years at the U.S. Fish and Wildlife Service, eventually becoming the chief editor of that agency's publications. Carson achieved financial independence in the 1950s with the publication of her popular celebrations of marine ecosystems, *The Sea Around Us and The Edge of the Sea.* Rereading *Silent Spring* reminds one that the book's effectiveness was due mainly to Carson's passionate, poetic language describing the alleged horrors that modern synthetic chemicals visit upon defenseless nature and hapless humanity. Carson was moved to write

Silent Spring by her increasing concern about the effects of pesticides on wildlife. Her chief villain was the pesticide DDT.

The 1950s saw the advent of an array of synthetic pesticides that were hailed as modern miracles in the war against pests and weeds. First and foremost of these chemicals was DDT. DDT's insecticidal properties were discovered in the late 1930s by Paul Muller, a chemist at the Swiss chemical firm J.R. Geigy. The American military started testing it in 1942, and soon the insecticide was being sprayed in war zones to protect American troops against insect-borne diseases such as typhus and malaria. In 1943 DDT famously stopped a typhus epidemic in Naples in its tracks shortly after the Allies invaded. DDT was hailed as the "wonder insecticide of World War II."

5   As soon as the war ended, American consumers and farmers quickly adopted the wonder insecticide, replacing the old-fashioned arsenic-based pesticides, which were truly nasty. Testing by the U.S. Public Health Service and the Food and Drug Administration's Division of Pharmacology found no serious human toxicity problems with DDT. Muller, DDT's inventor, was awarded the Nobel Prize in 1948.

DDT was soon widely deployed by public health officials, who banished malaria from the southern United States with its help. The World Health Organization credits DDT with saving 50 million to 100 million lives by preventing malaria. In 1943 Venezuela had 8,171,115 cases of malaria; by 1958, after the use of DDT, the number was down to 800. India, which had over 10 million cases of malaria in 1935, had 285,962 in 1969. In Italy the number of malaria cases dropped from 411,602 in 1945 to only 37 in 1968.

The tone of a *Scientific American* article by Francis Joseph Weiss celebrating the advent of "Chemical Agriculture" was typical of much of the reporting in the early 1950s. "In 1820 about 72 per cent of the population worked in agriculture, the proportion in 1950 was only about 15 per cent," reported Weiss. "Chemical agriculture, still in its infancy, should eventually advance our agricultural efficiency at least as much as machines have in the past 150 years." This improvement in agricultural efficiency would happen because "farming is being revolutionized by new fertilizers, insecticides, fungicides, weed killers, leaf removers, soil conditioners, plant hormones, trace minerals, antibiotics and synthetic milk for pigs."

In 1952 insects, weeds, and disease cost farmers $13 billion in crops annually. Since gross annual agricultural output at that time totaled $31 billion, it was estimated that preventing this damage by using pesticides would boost food and fiber production by 42 percent. Agricultural productivity in the

COMPLICATION

From a public health statement by the Agency for Toxic Substances and Disease Registry (1989):

Short-term exposure to high doses of DDT affects primarily the nervous system. People who either voluntarily or accidentally swallowed very high amounts of DDT experienced excitability, tremors, and seizures. These effects on the nervous system appeared to be reversible once exposure stopped. Some people who came in contact with DDT complained of rashes or irritation of the eyes, nose, and throat. People exposed for a long-term at low doses, such as people who made DDT, had some changes in the levels of liver enzymes, but there was no indication that DDT caused irreversible harmful (noncancer) effects. Tests in laboratory animals confirm the effect of DDT on the nervous system. However, tests in animals suggest that exposure to DDT may have a harmful effect on reproduction, and long-term exposure may affect the liver. Studies in animals have shown that oral exposure to DDT can result in an increased occurrence of liver tumors. In the five studies of DDT-exposed workers, results did not indicate increases in the number of deaths or cancers. However, these studies had limitations so that possible increases in cancer may not have been detected. Because DDT caused cancer in laboratory animals, it is assumed that DDT could have this effect in humans.

United States, spurred by improvements in farming practices and technologies, has continued its exponential increase. As a result, the percentage of Americans living and working on farms has dropped from 15 percent in 1950 to under 1.8 percent today.

But DDT and other pesticides had a dark side. They not only killed the pests at which they were aimed but often killed beneficial organisms as well. Carson, the passionate defender of wildlife, was determined to spotlight these harms. Memorably, she painted a scenario in which birds had all been poisoned by insecticides, resulting in a "silent spring" in which "no birds sing."

10 The scientific controversy over the effects of DDT on wildlife, especially birds, still vexes researchers. In the late 1960s, some researchers concluded that exposure to DDT caused eggshell thinning in some bird species, especially raptors such as eagles and peregrine falcons. Thinner shells meant fewer hatchlings and declining numbers. But researchers also found that other bird species, such as quail, pheasants, and chickens, were unaffected even by large doses DDT.

On June 14, 1972, 30 years ago this week, the EPA banned DDT despite considerable evidence of its safety offered in seven months of agency hearings. After listening to that testimony, the EPA's own administrative law judge declared, "DDT is not a carcinogenic hazard to man.... DDT is not a mutagenic or teratogenic hazard to man.... The use of DDT under the regulations involved here [does] not have a deleterious effect on freshwater fish, estuarine organisms, wild birds or other wildlife." Today environmental activists celebrate the EPA's DDT ban as their first great victory.

Carson argued that DDT and other pesticides were not only harming wildlife but killing people too. The 1958 passage by Congress of the Delaney Clause, which forbade the addition of any amount of chemicals suspected of causing cancer to food, likely focused Carson's attention on that disease.

For the previous half-century some researchers had been trying to prove that cancer was caused by chemical contaminants in the environment. Wilhelm Hueper, chief of environmental cancer research at the National Cancer Institute and one of the leading researchers in this area, became a major source for Carson. Hueper was so convinced that trace exposures to synthetic chemicals were a major cause of cancer in humans that he totally dismissed the notion that smoking cigarettes caused cancer. The assertion that pesticides were dangerous human carcinogens was a stroke of public relations genius. Even people who do not care much about wildlife care a lot about their own health and the health of their children.

In 1955 the American Cancer Society predicted that "cancer will strike one in every four Americans rather than the present estimate of one in five." The ACS attributed the increase to "the growing number of older persons in the population." The ACS did note that the incidence of lung cancer was increasing very

---

CONTEXT

Part of the Federal Food, Drug and Cosmetic Act, the Delaney Clause sets a standard of "zero cancer risk" for residues of pesticides in food additives. This standard means, in effect, that any residues of any substance considered a carcinogen are prohibited from food products. According to the National Council for Science and the Environment,

Such a risk standard does not allow an assessment of any possible agricultural benefits from the use of pesticides. Several groups, including the pesticide and food industries, want Congress to replace the Delaney Clause with a "negligible risk" standard. The pesticide industry claims that a single "negligible risk" standard would set one risk standard for all foods and would allow newer, safer pesticides to be marketed even with some evidence of carcinogenicity. However, Delaney Clause supporters argue that Delaney reduces risks associated with carcinogenic pesticide chemicals and no carcinogenic substances should be added voluntarily to food; there are enough natural carcinogenic toxins already in the food supply.

rapidly, rising in the previous two decades by more than 200 percent for women and by 600 percent for men. But the ACS also noted that lung cancer "is the only form of cancer which shows so definite a tendency." Seven years later, Rachel Carson would call her chapter on cancer "One in Four."

15 To bolster her case for the dangers of DDT, Carson improperly cited cases of acute exposures to the chemical as proof of its cancer-causing ability. For example, she told the story of a woman who sprayed DDT for spiders in her basement and died a month later of leukemia. In another case, a man sprayed his office for cockroaches and a few days later was diagnosed with aplastic anemia. Today cancer specialists would dismiss out of hand the implied claims that these patients' cancers could be traced to such specific pesticide exposures. The plain fact is that DDT has never been shown to be a human carcinogen even after four decades of intense scientific scrutiny.

Carson was also an effective popularizer of the idea that children were especially vulnerable to the carcinogenic effects of synthetic chemicals. "The situation with respect to children is even more deeply disturbing," she wrote. "A quarter century ago, cancer in children was considered a medical rarity. Today, more American school children die of cancer than from any other disease." In support of this claim, Carson reported that "twelve per cent of all deaths in children between the ages of one and fourteen are caused by cancer."

Although it sounds alarming, Carson's statistic is essentially meaningless unless it's given some context, which she failed to supply. It turns out that the percentage of children dying of cancer was rising because other causes of death, such as infectious diseases, were drastically declining.

In fact, cancer rates in children have not increased, as they would have if Carson had been right that children were especially susceptible to the alleged health effects of modern chemicals. Just one rough comparison illustrates this point: In 1938 cancer killed 939 children under 14 years old out of a U.S. population of 130 million. In 1998, according to the National Cancer Institute, about 1,700 children died of cancer, out of a population of more than 280 million. In 1999 the NCI noted that "over the past 20 years, there has been relatively little change in the incidence of children diagnosed with all forms of cancer; from 13 cases per 100,000 children in 1974 to 13.2 per 100,000 children in 1995."

Clearly, if cancer incidence isn't going up, modern chemicals can't be a big factor in cancer. But this simple point is lost on Carson's heirs in the environmental movement, who base their careers on pursuing phantom risks. The truth is that both cancer mortality and incidence rates have been declining for about a decade, mostly because of a decrease in the number of cigarette smokers.

20 The Great Cancer Scare launched by Carson, and perpetuated by her environmentalist disciples ever since, should have been put to rest by a definitive 1996 report from the National Academy of Sciences, *Carcinogens and Anticarcinogens in the Human Diet*. The NAS concluded that

Cary Anderson/Aurora

levels of both synthetic and natural car-cinogens are "so low that they are unlikely to pose an appreciable cancer risk." Worse yet from the point of view of anti-chemical crusaders, the NAS added that Mother Nature's own chemicals probably cause more cancer than anything mankind has dreamed up: "Natural components of the diet may prove to be of greater concern than synthetic components with respect to cancer risk."

Meanwhile, Carson's disciples have man-aged to persuade many poor countries to stop using DDT against mosquitoes. The result has been an enormous increase in the number of people dying of malaria each year. Today malaria infects between 300 million and 500 million people annually, killing as many as 2.7 million of them. Anti-DDT activists who tried to have the new U.N. treaty on persis-tent organic pollutants totally ban DDT have stepped back recently from their ideological campaign, conceding that poor countries should be able to use DDT to control malaria-carrying mosquitoes.

So 40 years after the publication of *Silent Spring*, the legacy of Rachel Carson is more troubling than her admirers will acknowledge. The book did point to problems that had not been adequately addressed, such as the effects of DDT on some wildlife. And given the state of the science at the time she wrote, one might even make the case that Carson's concerns about the effects of synthetic chemi-cals on human health were not completely unwarranted. Along with other researchers, she was simply ignorant of the facts. But after four decades in which tens of billions of dollars have been wasted chasing imaginary risks without measurably improving American health, her intellectual descendants don't have the same excuse.

Questions for Discussion

1. Bailey begins this essay with a description of the impact that *Silent Spring* had—and continues to have—after its publication in 1962. He also discusses the praise Rachel Carson received for that book. Why do you think Bailey begins his essay, which is critical of Carson's *Silent Spring*, in this way? How well does this beginning help set up his main argument?

2. Bailey claims that the effectiveness of *Silent Spring* "was due mainly to Carson's passionate, poetic language describing the alleged horrors that modern synthetic chemicals visit upon defenseless nature and hapless humanity." What evidence does he provide to support that claim? Why, in Bailey's view, should people be concerned that *Silent Spring* was persuasive largely because of Carson's "passionate, poetic language"? Evaluate Bailey's own use of language in this essay. To what extent does he employ some of the same argumentative strategies that he claims Carson used in her book? Cite specific passages from his essay to support your answer.

3. Bailey essentially accuses Carson either of ignoring important facts about the dangers or safety of DDT or of not telling the whole story. What kinds of evidence does he present to support this accusation? How persuasive is this evidence, in your view? Do you think Bailey's argument is influenced by his views about the environment, as he believes Carson's argument was influenced by her views about the environment? Explain, citing specific passages from the essay to support your answer.

4. In Bailey's view, what are the consequences of the problems that he describes with Carson's *Silent Spring*? Why is it important to understand these consequences? What should be done about this situation, in his opinion? Do you agree? Why or why not?

5. Bailey's essay was published in *Reason* magazine, which is considered libertarian in its viewpoint and which advocates individual choice and minimal government involvement in citizens' lives. To what extent do you think Bailey's essay reflects the perspective of *Reason*? How effective do you think his argument would be for an audience that advocates environmental protection—for example, members of the Sierra Club? Do you think Bailey would be concerned if such readers were to dismiss his argument? Explain.

6. Given the intensity of arguments about environmental issues—and given the potential health and economic consequences of environmental damage—evaluate Bailey's contributions to the ongoing debates about protecting the environment. What value do you think Bailey's essay has in these debates? To what extent does Bailey's essay help people better address the challenge of finding fair and reasonable ways to protect the environment?

③ # Human Nature

MARK DOWIE

When you think of *wilderness*, what image comes into your mind? According to Mark Dowie, if you're like most Americans, you think of a stunning but empty natural landscape, one that includes beautiful natural formations, such as mountains or streams, as well as plants and animals, but no humans. For Dowie, that image of wilderness is a problem, and in the following essay he explains why. Dowie examines what he sees as a conflict between this common view of wilderness, which he associates with the field of biology, and an anthropological view, which understands humans as an integral part of wilderness. He argues that if we hope to preserve the earth, we need to abandon the biological view and begin to accept the idea that humans are a part of—not apart from—the environment. His argument has significant consequences for the way we understand our responsibility to the earth. Mark Dowie is an award-winning journalist and historian who has written widely about environmental issues. The following essay, which appeared in *Guernica*, an environmental journal, in 2009, is excerpted from *Conservation Refugees: The Hundred-Year Conflict between Global Conservation and Native Peoples* (2009).

MARK DOWIE, "Human Nature"

One way to guarantee a conversation without a conclusion is to ask a group of people what nature is.

—Rebecca Solnit, University of California

1 In the course of "preserving the commons for all of the people," a frequently stated mission of national parks and protected areas, one class or culture of people, one philosophy of nature, one worldview, and one creation myth has almost always been preferred over all others. These favored ideas and impressions are at some point expressed in art. And it is through art that our earliest preconceptions and fantasies about nature are formed. The mystique of Yosemite, for example, was largely created by photographers like Charles Leander Weed, Carleton Watkins, Ansel Adams, and Edward Weston, all of whose magnificent images of the place are completely bereft of humanity or any sign of it having been there. Here, they said (and

they all knew better) is an untrammeled landscape, virgin and pristine, not a bootprint to be seen, not a hogan or teepee in sight.

Here in this wild place one may seek and find complete peace. They and their friends who sought to preserve an idealized version of nature called it "wilderness," a place that humans had explored but never altered, exalted but never touched. It was the beginning of a myth, a fiction that would gradually spread around the world, and for a century or more drive the conservation agenda of mankind.

> **CONTEXT**
>
> In paragraph 2 Dowie argues that the idealized view of nature that he believes most Americans embrace was created largely through the work of photographers like Ansel Adams, who took many famous photographs of Yosemite Valley in California, including the photograph in Figure 13-5. What is the image of wilderness and nature that such photographs promote?

FIGURE 13-5

"Thunderstorm, Yosemite Valley," by Ansel Adams

George Perkins Marsh (1801–1882) was an American diplomat who is sometimes considered the nation's first environmentalist. Among his many books was **Man and Nature** (1864), which, as Dowie suggests in this passage, influenced the attitudes of many prominent Americans about wilderness.

They all knew better, the portrayers of wilderness; in fact, Adams assiduously avoided photographing any of the local Miwok who were rarely out of his sight as he worked Yosemite Valley. He filled thousands of human-free negatives with land he knew the Miwok had tended for at least four thousand years. And he knew that the Miwok had been forcibly evicted from Yosemite Valley, as other natives would later be from national parks yet to be created, all in the putative interest of protecting nature from human disturbance.

5 One can be fairly certain that Weed, Watkins, Adams, and Weston had all at one time in their lives read **George Perkins Marsh**'s 1864 classic *Man and Nature* and recalled Marsh arguing passionately for the preservation of wild virgin nature, which he said was justified as much for artistic reasons as for any other. Marsh also believed that the destruction of the natural world threatened the very existence of humanity. We know that naturalist John Muir read Marsh and so did Teddy Roosevelt. They both say

so in their journals and memoirs. So when the topic of a park in Yosemite came up, Muir and Roosevelt were, so to speak, on the same page.

DUELING SCIENCES

Natural science is just one way of understanding nature.

—Bill Adams, Cambridge University

The Yosemite model of conservation, which still expresses itself in a fairly consistent form, has sparked a worldwide conflict between two powerful scientific disciplines: anthropology and conservation biology.

These two august sciences remain at odds with one another over how best to conserve and protect biological and cultural diversity, and perhaps more perplexing, how best to define two of the most semantically tortured terms in both their fields—nature and wilderness.

Cultural anthropologists spend years living in what many of us would call "the wild," studying the languages, mores, and traditions of what many of us would call "primitive peoples." Eventually the anthropologists come to understand the complex native cultures that keep remote communities thriving without importing much from outside their immediate homeland.

"We do not ask if indigenous peoples are allies of conservation or what sort of nature they protect," write Paige West and Dan Brockington, two anthropologists who have spent most of their careers researching the impact of protected areas on indigenous cultures; "instead we draw attention to the ways in which protected areas become instrumental in shaping battles over identity, residence and resource use."[1] Their experience has convinced them that the best way to protect a thriving natural ecosystem is to leave those communities pretty much alone, where and as they are, doing what they've done so well for so many generations—culturing a healthy landscape, or what development experts would call "living sustainably."

10 Wildlife biologists also spend much of their careers in remote natural settings, but tend to prefer landscapes void of human hunters, gatherers, pastoral nomadics, or rotational farmers. They find anthropologists somewhat "romantic" about indigenous cultures, particularly tribes that have become partly assimilated and modernized; which generally means the tribes are in possession of environmentally destructive technologies such as shotguns, chainsaws, and motorized vehicles, conveniences that Western naturalists know from their own civilization's experience can wreak havoc on healthy ecosystems.

These two disciplines are also at odds over what they mean by nature and the degree to which humanity is part of it. And they have a different sense of wildness and wilderness. It is in this regard that one is more likely to hear anthropologists calling naturalists "romantic." Listening to this exchange of insults one might conclude one is witnessing a clash of romantic tendencies.

William Cronon, an environmental historian at the University of Wisconsin, has spent much of his intellectual career grappling with these conflicts. His thinking on the subject eventually came together in 1995 with publication of a widely read and controversial essay titled "The Trouble with Wilderness, Getting Back to the Wrong Nature."

"The time has come to rethink wilderness," Cronon begins his essay. He goes on to challenge the widely held and decidedly romantic notion of environmentalists that "wilderness stands as the last remaining place where civilization, that all too human disease, has not fully infected the earth." That concept, Cronon believes, gives credence to "the illusion that we can somehow wipe clean the slate of our past and return to the tabula rasa that supposedly existed before we began to leave our marks on the world." That fiction, which Cronon believes is based on a profound misunderstanding of nature, and our place in it, creates a force that is antagonistic to conservation. "The myth of wilderness," he writes, "is that we can somehow leave nature untouched by our passage." He goes on to challenge the shopworn and often misunderstood shibboleth of **Henry David Thoreau** that "in wildness is the preservation of the world."

American philosopher **Henry David Thoreau** (1817–1862) wrote the famous line—"In wildness is the preservation of the world"—in his essay, "Walking" (1862).

CONTEXT

William Cronon, a respected professor of History, Geography, and Environmental Studies at the University of Wisconsin–Madison and an influential voice on environmental issues, begins his controversial essay "The Trouble With Wilderness" in this way:

The time has come to rethink wilderness.

This will seem a heretical claim to many environmentalists, since the idea of wilderness has for decades been a fundamental tenet—indeed, a passion—of the environmental movement, especially in the United States. For many Americans wilderness stands as the last remaining place where civilization, that all too human disease, has not fully infected the earth. It is an island in the polluted sea of urban-industrial modernity, the one place we can turn for escape from our own too-muchness. Seen in this way, wilderness presents itself as the best antidote to our human selves, a refuge we must somehow recover if we hope to save the planet. As Henry David Thoreau once famously declared, "In Wildness is the preservation of the World." (1)

But is it? The more one knows of its peculiar history, the more one realizes that wilderness is not quite what it seems. Far from being the one place on earth that stands apart from humanity, it is quite profoundly a human creation—indeed, the creation of very particular human cultures at very particular moments in human history. It is not a pristine sanctuary where the last remnant of an untouched, endangered, but still transcendent nature can for at least a little while longer be encountered without the contaminating taint of civilization. Instead, it's a product of that civilization, and could hardly be contaminated by the very stuff of which it is made. Wilderness hides its unnaturalness behind a mask that is all the more beguiling because it seems so natural.

SOURCE: William Cronon, "The Trouble With Wilderness," *Environmental History*, 1996.

The removal of aboriginal human beings from their homeland to create a commodified wilderness is a deliberate charade.

15 Cronon concludes: "The more one knows of its peculiar history, the more one realizes that wilderness is not quite what it seems. Far from being one place on earth that stands apart from humanity, it is quite profoundly a human creation—indeed, the creation of very particular human cultures at very particular moments in human history. It is not a pristine sanctuary where the last remnant of an untouched, endangered, but still transcendent nature can for at least a little while longer be encountered without the contaminating taint of civilization. Instead, it is a product of that civilization."

These are fighting words to a "civilization" that has set millions of square miles of valuable land aside as "wilderness," passed a national law—the 1964 Wilderness Act—to both define and protect wilderness, and still supports a dozen or so well-heeled national organizations to lobby for more wilderness set-asides and convince the public that figuratively walling off large expanses of unoccupied land is the only way to preserve nature and biological diversity. But how natural is wilderness? To Cronon, not as natural as it seems.

"Wilderness hides its unnaturalness behind a mask that is all the more beguiling because it seems so natural," he says. By glorifying pristine landscapes, which exist only in the imagination of romantics, Western conservationists divert attention from the places where people live and the choices they make every day that do true damage to the natural world of which they are part.

So the removal of aboriginal human beings from their homeland to create a commodified wilderness is a deliberate charade, a culturally constructed neo-Edenic narrative played out for the enchantment of weary human urbanites yearning for the open frontier that their ancestors "discovered," then tamed, a place to absorb the sounds and images of virgin nature and forget for a moment the thoroughly unnatural lives they lead.

SO WHAT IS WILD?

What counts as wilderness is not determined by the absence of people, but by the relationship between people and place.

—Jack Turner, philosopher

On several occasions during my research, an interview would be brought to a dead stop after I included the word wild or wilderness in a question. The word simply didn't exist in the dialect of the person I was interviewing. My interpreter would stare at me and wait for a better question.

20 When I tried to explain what I meant by wild to Bertha Petiquan, an Ojibway woman in northern Canada whose daughter was interpreting, she burst out laughing and said the only place she had ever seen what she thought I was describing as wild was a street corner outside the bus station in Winnipeg, Manitoba.

In Alaska, Patricia Cochran, a Yupik native scientist, told me "we have no word for 'wilderness.' What you call 'wilderness' we call our back yard. To us none of Alaska is wilderness as defined by the 1964 Wilderness Act—a place without people. We are deeply insulted by that concept, as we are by the whole idea of 'wilderness designation' that too often excludes native Alaskans from ancestral lands." Yupiks also have no word for biodiversity. Its closest approximation means *food*. And the O'odham (Pima) word for *wilderness* is etymologically related to their terms for *health, wholeness*, and *liveliness*.[2]

Jakob Malas, a Khomani hunter from a section of the Kalahari that is now Gemsbok National Park, shares Cochran's perspective on wilderness. "The Kalahari is like a big farmyard," he says, "It is not wilderness to us.

We know every plant, animal, and insect, and know how to use them. No other people could ever know and love this farm like us."

"I never thought of the Stein Valley as a wilderness," remarks Ruby Dunstan, a Nl'aka'pamux from Alberta. "My Dad used to say 'That's our pantry.' Then some environmentalists declared it a wilderness and said no one was allowed inside because it was so fragile. So they put a fence around it, or maybe around themselves."[3]

25 The Tarahumara of Mexico also have no word or concept meaning *wilderness*. Land is granted the same love and affection as family. Ethnoecologist Enrique Salmon, himself a Tarahumara, calls it "kincentric ecology." "We are immersed in an environment where we are at equal standing with the rest of the world," he says. "They are all kindred relations—the trees and rocks and bugs and everything is in equal standing with the rest."[4]

When wildness is conflated with wilderness, and wilderness with nature, and nature is seen as something separate and uninfluenced by human activity, perhaps it's time to examine real situations and test them against the semantics of modern conservation. Are Maasai cattle part of nature? Perhaps not today, but when they wandered through the open range by the thousands, tended by a few human herdsman whose primary interest was to keep the biota healthy for their livestock and other wildlife, one might say they were "wild," certainly as wild as the springbok, eland, elephant, and buffalo that daily leave the open pasture to ravage Maasai farms for fodder.

AND WHO IS NATURE?

We forget the reciprocity between the wild in nature and the wild in us.

—Jack Turner, philosopher

In one of the many conversations about nature I have been part of over the past three years, I said to a man—an educated, erudite, and generous supporter of international conservation, whose view of nature differed considerably from my own—"You are nature." He looked at me and laughed nervously. I had not insulted him, he assured me. He just didn't appreciate the notion that he was part or product of a system that also created "snails, kudzu, mules, earthquakes, grizzly bears, viruses, wildfires, and poison oak." It turned out also that his younger sister had, years before, been badly mauled by a mountain lion.

Well, how do you convince someone with that experience that he is kin with the lion? Perhaps you can't, I thought, but he seemed interested in continuing the conversation. Others joined in, and by the end of the evening he had accepted himself as an equal in the same creation with the lion that mauled his sister, a creation he was willing to call "nature," a creation of which he was not apart, but a part.

When one perceives humanity to be something separate from nature, it becomes easier to regard landscapes in their "natural state" as landscapes without human inhabitants and aspire to preserve wilderness by encouraging the existence and survival in landscape of as many species as possible, minus one—humans.

30 The valuable contribution anthropology has made to conservation is perhaps best expressed by Paige West and Dan Brockington, who advise conservationists to be more aware of "local ways of seeing," and that the practice of conservation will be more successful "if practitioners learn local idioms for understanding people's surroundings before they begin to think about things in terms of nature and culture." There is a need, they say, for conservationists "to grasp the complicated ways that people interact with what they rely on for food, shelter, as well as spiritual, social and economic needs."[5]

Enrique Salmon believes that "language and thought works together. So when a people's language includes a word like

CONTEXT

In the past few decades many scientists and environmentalists have become alarmed about the disappearance or extinction of many species of insects, plants, and animals throughout the world (see par. 35). Their concerns arise from the view that such extinctions reduce the diversity of life, which can make various species, including humans, more vulnerable to disease, natural disasters, and changes in ecosystems. The Millennium Ecosystem Assessment estimates that the world's biodiversity declined by 40 percent between 1970 and 2000.

'wilderness,' that shapes their thoughts about their relationship to the natural world. The notion of wilderness then carries the notion that humans are bad for the environment."[6]

Certainly someone who regards the forest as his "pantry" is going to see the flora, fauna, soil, and water in a somewhat different light than the tourist, biologist, miner, or logger. But is there not something that can be seen by all of them, some common ground on which the forest's intrinsic value can be considered and agreed upon?

One example of a very different local idiom that Western naturalists have difficulty understanding is that of the Gimi, one of the hundreds of remote, Stone Age cultures in central Papua New Guinea. The Gimi "have no notion of nature or culture," say West and Brockington. "They see themselves in an ongoing set of exchanges with their ancestors [who they believe are] animating and residing in their forests, infusing animals, plants, rivers, and the land itself with life. When people die their spirits go back to the forest and infuse themselves into plants, animals and rivers. When the living use these natural resources they do not see it as a depletion but rather as an ongoing exchange" of energy and spirit.

The final arbiters in this scientific conflict should be indigenous peoples themselves.

35 When the Gimi kill and eat an animal, "they understand it to be generated by their ancestors' life forces and it will work to make their life force during this lifetime. When they die that force will go back to the forest and replenish it."[7] This is an admittedly difficult cosmology for the Western mind to contemplate or accept. But the fact that every atom in every living thing has existed since the beginning of time gives some scientific grounding to the Gimis' belief that spirit is simply reorganized force and matter. That said, their understanding "of the relationship between humans and their surroundings [remains] extremely difficult to reconcile with arguments about the decline and loss of biological diversity."[8]

However, if Western conservationists in central Papua New Guinea know that the Gimi believe all matter is here for eternity, that it simply changes form over time, they will be better equipped to work with local communities in the preservation of biodiversity. But if they dismiss that cosmology as primitive animism and seek to impose Western science and religion on the Gimi people, their conservation initiative will almost certainly fail.

Of course, the final arbiters in this scientific conflict should be indigenous peoples themselves, the very people that early advocates for Yellowstone Park said had no interest in raw nature or the park area.

They were alleged to be afraid of the geysers and fumaroles. (Not true. They cooked over them.) The truth is that much of what the rest of us know about nature and have incorporated into the various sciences we use to protect it—ecology, zoology, botany, ethnobotany—we learned from the very people we have expelled from the areas we have sought to protect.

NOTES

[1] P. West and D. Brockington, "An Anthropological Perspective on Some Unexpected Consequences of Protected Areas," *Conservation Biology* 20, no. 3 (2006): 609-616.

[2] Gary Nabhan, *Cultures of Habit* (Counterpoint Press, 1997).

[3] World Rainforest Movement, *Protected Areas, Protected Against Whom?*, p. 14.

[4] John Roach, "Indigenous Group Keeps Ecology All in the Family," *National Geographic*, June 29, 2006.

[5] Ibid.

[6] World Rainforest Movement, *Protected Areas, Protected Against Whom?*, p. 14.

[7] Ibid.

[8] Ibid.

Questions for Discussion

1. Why does Dowie criticize the common view of wilderness as unspoiled by humans? What are the implications of such a view, in his opinion? Do you think he's right? Why or why not?

2. Dowie claims that the fields of anthropology and conservation biology disagree about the definitions of *nature* and *wilderness*. What exactly is the disagreement between these two fields? Why is this disagreement important, in Dowie's view? What does it tell us about *nature* and *wilderness*? What might this disagreement suggest about the relationship between humans and the natural environment? How does this disagreement fit into Dowie's main argument?

3. Why does Dowie devote so much of his essay to a summary of the ideas of William Cronon (see paragraphs 12–18)? What purpose does this summary serve in Dowie's main argument? Do you find this summary effective in the context of Dowie's argument? Explain.

4. Dowie, who has conducted research on native peoples, writes that native communities such as the Ojibway and Yupik have no word in their languages for *wilderness*. What conclusions does he draw from that fact? How does he use that fact to support his main argument?

5. At one point in his essay, Dowie includes a quotation suggesting that language and thought work together (see par. 31). What does he mean by that statement? What are the implications of the idea that language and thought work together when it comes to the environment?

6. In paragraph 34 Dowie writes, "The final arbiters in this scientific conflict should be indigenous peoples themselves." What is the scientific conflict to which he is referring? Why does he believe that indigenous peoples will resolve this conflict? Do you think he has made a persuasive case to support that claim? Explain, citing specific passages from his essay to support your answer.

7. In the final paragraph of this essay, Dowie writes that "much of what the rest of us know about nature and have incorporated into the various sciences we use to protect it—ecology, zoology, botany, ethnobotany—we learned from the very people we have expelled from the areas we have sought to protect." Who is the "we" he refers to in this passage? What do you think this statement indicates about his intended audience for this essay?

8. This essay might be considered an argument to reconcile differences. To what extent do you think Dowie's argument successfully addresses the scientific conflict he describes?

(4) # Forget Short Showers

DERRICK JENSEN

For many people, serious environmental problems such as global climate change can seem overwhelming. It seems reasonable to ask, What can one person do in the face of such gigantic, complicated challenges? In recent years many people have answered that question by changing their lifestyles. They have consciously tried to reduce their own environmental impact by driving their cars less, making their homes more energy-efficient, eating organic and locally grown foods, and refusing to buy products from companies known to damage the earth. People who take such steps are motivated by the idea that anyone can make a difference by making the right choices in their daily lives. Making the right choices might make people feel better about problems like climate change, but according to environmental activist Derrick Jensen, it won't make a difference. In the following essay, which was published in *Orion* magazine in 2009, Jensen argues that the scale of the environmental problems facing humans today calls for much more than individual acts like using less energy or buying local foods. He makes the case that such acts, no matter how well intentioned, are ultimately misguided and ineffective when it comes to solving problems like climate change. Instead, he says, a wholesale change in the way our society is structured and managed is needed. It is not a comforting argument, but it may provoke you into rethinking your own responsibilities as an inhabitant of the earth. Jensen is the author of many articles and books about environmental issues, including *How Shall I Live My Life* (2008) and the award-winning *Thought to Exist in the Wild: Awakening From the Nightmare of Zoos* (2007).

DERRICK JENSEN, "Forget Short Showers"

1 Would any sane person think dumpster diving would have stopped Hitler, or that composting would have ended slavery or brought about the eight-hour workday, or that chopping wood and carrying water would have gotten people out of Tsarist prisons, or that dancing naked around a fire would have helped put in place the Voting Rights Act of 1957 or the Civil Rights Act of 1964? Then why now, with all the world at stake, do so many people retreat into these entirely personal "solutions"?

Part of the problem is that we've been victims of a campaign of systematic misdirection. Consumer culture and the capitalist mindset have taught us to substitute acts of personal consumption (or enlightenment) for organized political resistance. *An Inconvenient Truth* helped raise consciousness about global warming. But did you notice that all of the solutions presented had to do with personal consumption—changing light bulbs, inflating tires, driving half as much—and had nothing to do with shifting power away from corporations, or stopping the growth economy that is destroying the planet? Even if every person in the United States did everything the movie suggested, U.S. carbon emissions would fall by only 22 percent. Scientific consensus is that emissions must be reduced by at least 75 percent worldwide.

Or let's talk water. We so often hear that the world is running out of water. People are dying from lack of water. Rivers are dewatered from lack of water. Because of this we need to take shorter showers. See the disconnect? *Because I take showers, I'm responsible for drawing down aquifers?* Well, no. More than 90 percent of the water used by humans is used by agriculture and industry. The remaining 10 percent is split between municipalities and actual living breathing individual humans. Collectively, municipal golf courses use as much water as municipal human beings. People (both human people and fish people) aren't dying because the world is running out of water. They're dying because the water is being stolen.

Or let's talk energy. Kirkpatrick Sale summarized it well: "For the past 15 years the story has been the same every year: individual consumption—residential, by private car, and so on—is never more than about a quarter of all consumption; the vast majority is commercial, industrial, corporate, by agribusiness and government [he forgot military]. So, even if we all took up cycling and wood stoves it would have a negligible impact on energy use, global warming and atmospheric pollution."

5 Or let's talk waste. In 2005, per-capita municipal waste production (basically everything that's put out at the curb) in the U.S. was about 1,660 pounds. Let's say you're a die-hard simple-living activist, and you reduce this to zero. You recycle everything. You bring cloth bags shopping. You fix your toaster. Your toes poke out of old tennis shoes. You're not done yet, though. Since municipal waste includes not just residential waste, but also waste from government offices and businesses, you march to those offices, waste reduction pamphlets in hand, and convince them to cut down on their waste enough to eliminate your share of it. Uh, I've got some bad news. Municipal waste accounts for only 3 percent of total waste production in the United States.

CONTEXT

Former U.S. vice president Al Gore's 2006 Academy Award–winning documentary film *An Inconvenient Truth* is credited with raising public awareness about global climate change and prompting many people to join his efforts to begin living a more sustainable, carbon-neutral lifestyle. As Jensen indicates in paragraph 2, these efforts focused on changing individual habits. However, many activists and policymakers used the publicity surrounding *An Inconvenient Truth* (see Figure 13–6) to advocate for larger changes in U.S. energy policies and related measures that would affect important aspects of American life such as transportation, housing, and the food supply.

FIGURE 13-6

Promotional Poster from *An Inconvenient Truth*

©Paramount Classics/Courtesy Everett Collection

I want to be clear. I'm not saying we shouldn't live simply. I live reasonably simply myself, but I don't pretend that not buying much (or not driving much, or not having kids) is a powerful political act, or that it's deeply revolutionary. It's not. Personal change doesn't equal social change.

So how, then, and especially with all the world at stake, have we come to accept these utterly insufficient responses? I think part of it is that we're in a double bind. A double bind is where you're given multiple options, but no matter what option you choose, you lose, and withdrawal is not an option. At this point, it should be pretty easy to recognize that every action involving the industrial economy is destructive (and we shouldn't pretend that solar photovoltaics, for example, exempt us from this: they still require mining and trans- portation infrastructures at every point in the production processes; the same can be said for every other so-called green technology). So if we choose option one—if we avidly par- ticipate in the industrial economy—we may in the short term think we win because we may accumulate wealth, the marker of "success" in this culture. But we lose, because in doing so we give up our empathy, our animal human- ity. And we really lose because industrial civilization is killing the planet, which means everyone loses. If we choose the "alternative" option of living more simply, thus causing less harm, but still not stopping the industrial economy from killing the planet, we may in the short term think we win because we get to feel pure, and we didn't even have to give up all of our empathy (just enough to justify not stopping the horrors), but once again we really lose because industrial civilization is still killing the planet, which means everyone still loses. The third option, acting decisively to stop the industrial economy, is very scary for a number of reasons, including but not restricted to the fact that we'd lose some of the luxuries (like electricity) to which we've grown accustomed, and the fact that those in power might try to kill us if we seriously

impede their ability to exploit the world—none of which alters the fact that it's a better option than a dead planet. Any option is a better option than a dead planet.

Besides being ineffective at causing the sorts of changes necessary to stop this culture from killing the planet, there are at least four other problems with perceiving simple living as a political act (as opposed to living simply because that's what you want to do). The first is that it's predicated on the flawed notion that humans inevitably harm their landbase. Simple living as a political act consists solely of harm reduction, ignoring the fact that humans can help the Earth as well as harm it. We can rehabilitate streams, we can get rid of noxious invasives, we can remove dams, we can disrupt a political system tilted toward the rich as well as an extractive economic system, we can destroy the industrial economy that is destroying the real, physical world.

The second problem—and this is another big one—is that it incorrectly assigns blame to the individual (and most especially to individ- uals who are particularly powerless) instead of to those who actually wield power in this system and to the system itself. Kirkpatrick Sale again: "The whole individualist what-you- can-do-to-save-the-earth guilt trip is a myth. We, as individuals, are not creating the crises, and we can't solve them."

10 The third problem is that it accepts capitalism's redefinition of us from citizens to consumers. By accepting this redefinition, we reduce our potential forms of resistance to consuming and not consuming. Citizens have a much wider range of available resistance tactics, including voting, not voting, running for office, pamphleting, boycotting, organizing, lobbying, protesting, and, when a government becomes destructive of life, liberty, and the pursuit of happiness, we have the right to alter or abolish it.

The fourth problem is that the endpoint of the logic behind simple living as a political act is suicide. If every act within an industrial economy is destructive, and if we want to stop this destruction, and if we are unwilling (or unable) to question (much less destroy) the intellectual, moral, economic, and physical infrastructures that cause every act within an industrial economy to be destructive, then we can easily come to believe that we will cause the least destruction possible if we are dead.

The good news is that there are other options. We can follow the examples of brave activists who lived through the difficult times I mentioned—Nazi Germany, Tsarist Russia, antebellum United States—who did far more than manifest a form of moral purity; they actively opposed the injustices that surrounded them. We can follow the example of those who remembered that the role of an activist is not to navigate systems of oppressive power with as much integrity as possible, but rather to confront and take down those systems.

Questions for Discussion

1. Jensen begins his essay with a list of historical events that involved great struggle or conflict, including the Holocaust, slavery, and the Voting Rights and Civil Rights Acts. Why do you think he chooses these specific events? What do these choices convey about Jensen's views regarding the environmental problems he refers to in the rest of this essay? Do you think the comparison between these environmental problems and the historical events listed in the first paragraph is justified? Why or why not?

2. Why does Jensen believe that individual people should not take primary responsibility for the problems associated with climate change? Who should assume that responsibility, in his view? Do you think he's right? Why or why not?

3. What evidence does Jensen provide for his claims about who should assume responsibility for climate change and related environmental problems, such as diminished world water supplies or increasing waste production? How effective is this evidence in supporting his case? What counterarguments might you offer to his claims?

4. How would you describe Jensen's tone in this essay? What do you think his tone suggests about his assumptions about his readers? Do you find his tone effective in helping him make his main argument? Explain, citing specific passages from his essay to support your answer.

5. How does Jensen explain the widespread view that personal change equals social change? What does his explanation suggest about his political views? Do you find his explanation persuasive? Why or why not?

6. Jensen discusses four problems with the idea that a simple lifestyle is a political act that can make a difference in saving the planet from environmental destruction. How persuasive do you find his discussion of these four problems? On what fundamental principles is his reasoning based? Do you think most Americans would share these principles? Why or why not?

668 CHAPTER 13 | ENVIRONMENT

DIFFERENCES

NEGOTIATING

As the essays in this section indicate, environmental concerns have not disappeared since Rachel Carson's *Silent Spring* was published in 1962; rather, they have in many ways intensified, despite increasing awareness of some of the risks that Carson highlighted in her famous book. One of the challenges people now face is how to set environmental priorities and then use them to identify specific actions that can be undertaken to benefit the environment, especially in view of the growing realization that global climate change will likely lead to even greater environmental problems than even Carson warned about in 1962. Part of that challenge is deciding where to place responsibility for some of the environmental problems ahead. For example, whose responsibility is the increased air pollution and greater use of oil that result from the popularity of SUVs? The drivers who purchase such vehicles? The companies that manufacture and sell them? The U.S. government, whose policies allow SUVs to avoid the stricter emissions controls placed on cars? How should we determine that responsibility when so many different people seem to have a hand in environmental degradation?

With these points in mind, identify an environmental problem in your geographic region (or identify a national environmental issue that affects your region), and determine who you believe bears responsibility for this problem. Using whatever sources seem appropriate, including the essays in this section, try to learn about the problem to identify the factors that seem to have helped create it. Look also for potential solutions to it. Then write an essay to a local audience (for example, the readers of your local newspaper or residents of an area affected by the problem) in which you argue for what you think is the most feasible solution to the problem. For example, if you were to write your essay about the problem of SUVs mentioned in the previous paragraph, you would want to learn about the environmental damage SUVs might cause, as well as related problems. And you would want to learn about the extent of those problems in your region. Whatever your topic, try to write an argument that would persuade environmentalists and others affected by the problem that your approach would be a reasonable one.

Credits

Chapter 2: p. 29: Old People Need "Friends," Too: Using Social Media By Shari Lifland

Chapter 3: p. 36: Al Neuharth Is Back to School Starting too early? from USA TODAY, August 2, 2002, p 9A

Chapter 3: p. 55: "The Degrading Effects of Terrorism Fears" by David Brooks. This article first appeared in Salon.com at http://www.salon.com/opinion/greenwald/2010/01/02/fear/print.html. An online version remains in the Salon archives. Reprinted by permission.

Chapter 3: p. 71: Letter to Editor by Pamela Bailey from CLEVELAND PLAIN DEALER.

Chapter 3: p. 72: Keith Sollenberger, "Myers' Success Rests on Bad Humor" letter to editor, USA TODAY, 8/2/02, p. 8A. Used by permission of the author.

Chapter 4: p. 69: It Takes a School, Not Missles by Nicholas Kristof from THE NEW YORK TIMES, July 13, 2008. http://www.nytimes.com/2008/07/13/opinion/13kristof.html. Copyright (c) 2008 The New York Times Co. Reprinted by permission.

Chapter 4: p. 71: "Why You Can Hate Drugs and Still Want to Legalize Them" by Joshua Wolf Shenk from THE WASHINGTON MONTHLY, October 1995. Reprinted with permission from The Washington Monthly. Copyright by Washington Monthly Publishing, LLC, 733 15th St., NW, Suite 520, Washington, DC 20005. (202) 393–5155. Website: www.washingtonmonthly.com.

Chapter 4: p. 74: Excerpt from "Why Nick" by Jeanne Shields from NEWSWEEK, May 8, 1978, p. 23.

Chapter 4: p. 77: "Ronaldo Earns his Glory" by Filip Bondy, July 1, 2002. Reprinted by permission of TMSReprints.

Chapter 4: p. 82: THE NEW YORK TIMES, June 24, 2002, p. A22.

Chapter 4: p. 95: "Letter from Birmingham Jail" by Dr. Martin Luther King, Jr. Reprinted by arrangement with the Estate of Martin Luther King Jr., c/o Writers House as agent for the proprietor New York, NY. Copyright 1963 Martin Luther King Jr., copyright renewed 1991 Coretta Scott King.

Chapter 5: p. 146: From "Is the Trend of Trashing Textbooks in Texas Going National?" by John F. Borowski from COMMONDREAMS.org, August 27, 2002.

Chapter 8: p. 209: "Standing Up for the Power of Learning" by Jay Mathews from THE WASHINGTON POST, June 4, 2002. Copyright c 2002, The Washington Post, reprinted with permission.

Chapter 9: p. 308: "What Fathers Do Best" by Steven E. Rhoads as appeared in THE WEEKLY STANDARD, June 20, 2005, Vol. 10, No. 38. Reprinted by permission of the author. Steven Rhoads has taught public policy at the University of Virginia for over 30 years. His book TAKING SEX DIFFERENCES SERIOUSLY is newly available in paperback.

Chapter 9: p. 313: "Fidelity with a Wandering Eye" by Christina Nehring from THE ATLANTIC MONTHLY, July/ August 2005. Reprinted by permission of the author.

Chapter 9: p. 319: "A More Perfect Union" by Jonathan Rauch from THE ATLANTIC MONTHLY, April 2004, p. 88. Copyright c Jonathan Rauch 2004. Reprinted by permission.

Chapter 9: p. 327: "The Future of Marriage" by Stephanie Coontz from Cato Unbound, Jan. 14, 2008; http:// www.cato-unbound.org/2008/01/14/stephanie-coontz/the-future-of-marriage/. Reprinted by permission.

Chapter 9: p. 333: "The Marriage Gap" by Kay Hymowitz from Cato Unbound, Jan. 16, 2008; http://www. cato-unbound.org/2008/01/16/kay-s-hymowitz/the-marriage-gap/. Reprinted by permission.

Chapter 10: p. 341: "The Globalization of Censorship" by Anne Applebaum from Slate.com, Sept. 14, 2009; http://www.slate.com/id/2228263/T. Reprinted by permission.

Chapter 10: p. 344: "Them Damn Pictures" by Doug Marlette, February 24, 2006. This artlce first appeared in Salon.com, at http://www.salon.com. An online version remains in the Salon archives. Reprinted with permission.

Chapter 10: p. 349: Ayn Rand Center, June 17, 2009; http://blog.aynrandcenter.org/ why-we-have-free-speech-in-america-part-i/

Chapter 10: p. 353: "The Price of Free Speech: Campus Hate Speech Codes" by Gerald Uelman. Reprinted by permission of the author.

Chapter 10: p. 360: The Chronicle Review. From the issue dated December 19, 2003 http://chronicle.com/ weekly/v50/i17/17b00601.htm

Chapter 10: p. 368: "Racism in the Media" by Irshad Manji from http://www.media-awareness.ca/english/ resources/articles/diversity/racism_media.cfm. Reprinted by permission of the author.

Chapter 10: p. 372: "The Naturalist: Symbolic Gestures" by Jesse Smith from THE SMART SET, Drexel University, July 24, 2009 (http://www.thesmartset.com/print/article/article07140901.aspx). Reprinted by permission of the author.

Chapter 10: p. 379: "Why I Love Al-Jazeera" by Robert Kaplan as appeared in THE ATLANTIC MONTHLY, October 2009; http://www.theatlantic.com/doc/200910/al-jazeera. Reprinted by permission of the author.

Chapter 10: p. 387: "The Daily We: Is the Internet Really a Blessing for Democracy" by Cass Sunstein from BOSTON REVIEW, Vol. 26, Summer 2001

Chapter 10: p. 400: "The revolution will not be digitzed" by Farhad Manjoo from Slate, June 25, 2009. Copyright (c) 2009. Reprinted by permission of The Slate Group.

Chapter 10: p.404: "Why Gen-Y Johnny Can't Read Non-Verbal Cues" by Mark Bauerlein from WALL STREET JOURNAL Sept. 4, 2009. Copyright (c) 2009 Dow Jones & Co. Reprinted by permission.

Chapter 11: p. 407: Counterpunch, Feb. 20, 2007; http://www.counterpunch.org/boler02202007.html

Chapter 11. p. 417: "The Humanities for Cocktail Parties and More" by Rick Livingston as appeared in THE CHRONICLE REVIEW, January 7, 2005. Reprinted by permission of Robert Eric Livingston.

Chapter 11: p. 421: "Liberal Education on the Ropes" by Stanley N. Katz from THE CHRONICLE REVIEW, April 1, 2005. Reprinted by permission of the author

Index